COMPUTERS AND DATA PROCESSING
Concepts and Applications
Second Edition

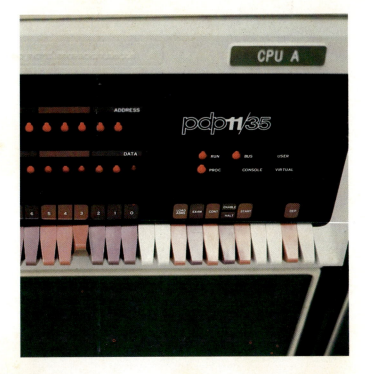

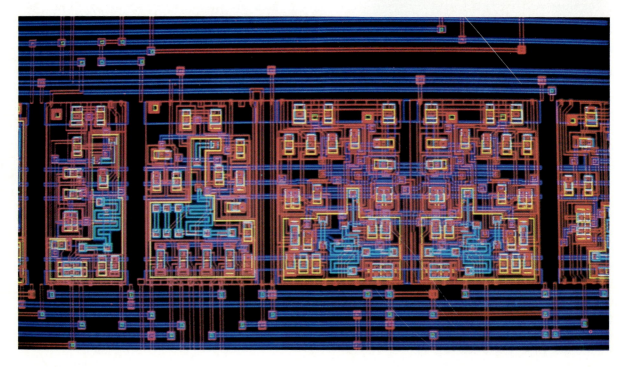

COMPUTERS AND DATA PROCESSING
Concepts
and Applications
Second Edition

with BASIC

STEVEN L. MANDELL
Bowling Green State University

WEST PUBLISHING COMPANY
Saint Paul   New York   Los Angeles   San Francisco

Library of Congress Cataloging in Publication Data

Mandell, Steven L.
    Computers and data processing.

    Includes index.
    1. Electronic data processing.   2. Electronic
digital computers.   3. Basic (Computer program
language)   I. Title.
QA76.M27472   1982   001.64   81-21870
ISBN 0-314-63263-8   AACR2
3rd Reprint—1983

INTL. ED. ISBN 0-314-68191-4
2nd Reprint—1983

COPY EDITOR   Beverly Peavler
ARTWORK   Barbara Hack
COMPOSITION   The Clarinda Company
CHAPTER OPENING ART   Courtesy of Laser
                      Fantasy, Division of
                      Innovation Inc.,
                      Floyd Rollefstad,
                      Photographer.

A study guide has been developed to assist you in mastering concepts presented in this text. The study guide reinforces concepts by presenting them in condensed, concise form. Additional illustrations and examples are also included. The study guide is available from your local bookstore under the title, *Study Guide to Accompany Computers and Data Processing: Concepts and Applications Second Edition,* prepared by Steven L. Mandell.

To an inspiration
GRACE MURRAY HOPPER

CONTENTS

CHAPTER 9   Software Development 210

CHAPTER 10   Programming Languages 234

PREFACE

The development work associated with a second edition is far more productive than the efforts involved with the original book. Feedback from instructors using the text provides an excellent road map for implementing necessary changes, and nothing can replace the actual classroom testing of material when attempting to improve the content. After a first edition has proven highly successful, critical time can be spent updating and refining the book rather than creating an entirely new version. The final result is an updated edition of a textbook vastly improved in structure and substance.

It is appropriate at this point to thank the following people who reviewed the book and provided invaluable comments based on their experience using the first edition of *Computers and Data Processing*.

Ray Bunch
Chemeketa Community College, Oregon

William R. Cornette
Texas Tech

E. Reed Doke
Southwest Missouri State

Richard R. Dye
Air Force Academy, Colorado

Peter G. Kauber
Bowling Green State University, Ohio

Robert T. Keim
Arizona State

Jean Longhurst
William Rainey Harper C.C., Illinois

John F. Schank
George Mason University, Virginia

Seshagiri Rao Vemuri
California State University, Fresno

Peter L. Irwin
Richland College, Dallas

Ronald S. Lemos
California State University, Los Angeles

Peter Simis
California State University, Fresno

R. Fedrick
El Camino College, Torrance

NEW FEATURES

Readers familiar with the first edition of the text will notice several changes incorporated into the second edition:

- Current technology
- Increased coverage of minicomputers and microcomputers
- Rewritten communications and programming language chapters
- Improved presentation of programming logic
- Redesigned systems section
- New chapter on computer security, privacy, and the law
- New articles and updated applications
- Reduced punched card coverage
- Major new section covering office of the future
- In the language version, a greatly expanded coverage of BASIC including microcomputer implementation.
- Introduction of a new feature, called Highlights, which present interesting or controversial computer applications.
- New full-color sections that illustrate a "Tour of a Computer Facility" and "The World of Computers."

The most inspiring lectures on computers that I have had the fortune to attend were presented by Captain Grace Hopper, a legend in her own time. In analyzing her material, which always seemed so interesting, it became apparent to me that no new concept was permitted to remain abstract. Rather, actual examples were described, encouraging the listener to visualize its application. In a like manner, each chapter in this book is followed by an application that shows how a corporation or government agency implements the concepts presented.

Several other important features are included within each chapter. A meaningful outline of the subject matter to be covered begins the chapter. The introductory section serves a dual purpose: transition between chapters and preview of material. An article that invokes attention and acts as a motivator follows. Highlights containing interesting computer applications or controversial topics are a new feature included to maintain reader interest. A chapter summary and review questions are also provided. At the end of the text is a comprehensive glossary and a separate index.

I have had one paramount objective throughout the development of this book. The material is designed to be student oriented, and all incorporated approaches are designed to assist students in the learning process. Important concepts are never avoided, regardless of their complexity. Many books on data processing emphasize one of two aspects of data processing—informational relationships or computer capabilities. This text attempts to balance and blend both subjects.

The material is structured according to an approach used successfully by several thousand business and computer science students in a course entitled "Introduction to Information Systems" at Bowling Green State University. The book is divided into five parts: Information Processing, Technology, Programming, Systems, and Computers in Society. The Information Processing section presents an introduction to the basic concepts of data processing and a historical perspective. The Technology section concentrates on computer hardware, including internal storage and input/output devices. System and applications software, program development, languages, and structural approaches constitute the Programming section. The Systems section provides a discussion of the methods and approaches to designing information systems. Finally, the Computers in Society section includes material concerning security and privacy while presenting a view of the future.

SUPPLEMENTARY EDUCATIONAL MATERIALS

The study guide for this text includes numerous materials for student reinforcement. The instructor material is designed to reduce administrative efforts. Transparency masters are provided to adopters of the text as well as color slides (with a written script) of a tour of a modern computer facility. WESTEST is a computerized testing service available from West Publishing Company with over one thousand questions.

ACKNOWLEDGMENTS

Many individuals and companies have been involved in the development of the material for this book. The corporations and government agencies whose applications appear in this book have provided invaluable assistance. Many professionals provided the assistance required for completion of a text of this magnitude: Patricia Cooke, Kris Eridon, Rod Harris, Patricia Ostrowski, Rebecca Parks, Patricia Parrish, Lynn Probst, and Kathy Voss on student material; Terrye Gregory and Stephen Gregory with BASIC; and Norma Morris and Donna Pulschen in manuscript development. The design of the book is a tribute to the many talents of William Stryker. One final acknowledgment goes to my publisher and valued friend, Clyde Perlee, Jr., for his unfaltering support.

Steven L. Mandell

SECTION I
Information Processing

CHAPTER 1

Introduction to Data Processing

Introduction

The computer has become a dominant force in society. Business corporations, government agencies, and other organizations depend on it to process data and make information available for use in decision making. Computers are responsible, to a large extent, for the standard of living typical in the United States today. As the costs for computer equipment continue to decrease, computers will become an even more integral part of daily life. It is therefore essential that people gain a basic understanding of computers—their capabilities, limitations, and applications.

This chapter gives a basic description of the computer and its uses and distinguishes between data and information. A computerized example of payroll processing is used to demonstrate how computers can be programmed to provide meaningful information. Finally, some of the major advances and problems that have resulted from using computers are presented as evidence of the computer's growing impact on all parts of society.

"It's Stupid, But Faster"

Art Buchwald

I finally got sucked in by all the ads and bought a home computer. The day it arrived and I unpacked it, my wife said, "What did you buy that for?"

"Because it will solve all our household economic problems. All I have to do is feed the computer how much money we have coming in and how much money we have going out, and it will tell us if we're spending too much."

"I can tell you that," she said.

"Ah, yes, but this computer can tell it to us 100 times faster. Let me show you. We have to buy a new furnace for $3,500 or we can have the old furnace repaired for $2,000. How much will we save by having it repaired?"

"Nothing," my wife said.

"You're wrong. The computer says we'll save $1,500."

"Did the computer tell you even if we have the old furnace repaired, there is no guarantee that it will work, and then it will cost us $5,500?"

"How does the computer know it won't work?"

"It doesn't, but the furnace man said he couldn't guarantee it."

"Well, then, we'll have to feed that in. A computer is only as

good as the information it receives.

"Tell it the furnace man said if the old one fails on us after it is repaired, the house will fill up with carbon monoxide, which we won't be able to smell."

"All right."

"What did it say?"

"We're all going to die."

"I could have told you that," my wife said.

"But not as fast as the computer," I pointed out. "There are always people putting down computers because they don't understand them. Now I will type in how much I make and how much I will save under Ronald Reagan's tax cuts. In the first year we will be ahead by $1,780,"

"The computer is wrong. We will be behind by $2,560."

"How can you say that?"

"Our real-estate taxes came today. The city has raised them by 25 percent to make up for the tax cuts Reagan gave the people.

"Why didn't you tell me that before I fed the computer?"

"Why didn't Reagan tell us that before he gave out a tax cut?"

"I know what your problem is: You're afraid of my computer, and you are showing your hostility by pretending to know more than it does. But we programmers are used to skeptics. I shall now prove to you that this electronic marvel is worth every dollar I paid for it. Let's say we are spending

roughly $30 a week for groceries."

"You couldn't get a roast beef for $30."

"You mean we're spending more than $30 a week for groceries?"

"Would you believe $150 a week?"

"Nobody spends $150 a week for groceries."

"Put it in the computer, buster. Now ask it where we can cut down on our food budget? . . . What does it say?"

"It keeps repeating the words, FOOD STAMPS."

"I could have told you that."

"I will not be deterred. This home computer is programmed to tell you how you can make enormous cuts in your electricity bills. I will put in this disc and type in the question, 'How can I save on electricity?'"

"What does it say"

"Turn off all the lights in the house when you aren't using them."

"Do you know how we could have really saved money this year? By not buying that stupid computer."

"Maybe you're right. I'll call the man who sold it to me and tell him we really don't need it."

I returned a few moments later.

"What did he say?" my wife asked.

"He said he wouldn't take it back."

"I could have told you that."

Buchwald's satirical article is both humorous and instructive. The importance of data and its transformation into information useful for decision-making is the computer's reason for being. The first chapter explains this basic computer process.

BACKGROUND

Many individuals envision an electronic marvel with mystical powers when they think of the word *computer*. In reality, the computer's capabilities are quite limited. Its success can be directly attributed to the imagination of people. A computer has no independent intelligence. It cannot perform any tasks that a person has not predetermined. Therefore, the computer's IQ is zero!

Computers can perform only three basic functions:.

1. Add, subtract, multiply, and divide.
2. Compare (test the relationship of two values to see if they are equal, if the first is greater than the second, or vice versa; these values can be either numeric or alphabetic).
3. Store and retrieve information.

The number of unique instructions required to direct a computer to perform these three functions is quite limited, often fewer than one hundred. These instructions control the basic logical and arithmetical procedures such as addition, subtraction, and comparison. Together, they constitute the *instruction set* of the computer. Engineers design the instruction set into the electronic circuitry of the machine. By manipulating this small instruction set, people can create computer programs that harness the computer's power to help them achieve desired results.

Most computers can be used for many purposes. They are referred to as general-purpose machines. Special-purpose, or dedicated, machines are similar to general-purpose computers but have been specifically adapted to perform specialized tasks. In all cases, a human determines the combination of instructions that a machine will perform.

Computers derive most of their amazing power from three features: speed, accuracy, and memory. Two factors control the speed of a computer: the switching speed of the electronic circuits that make up the computer and the distances that electric currents have to travel. Recent advances in technology have made it possible to increase the switching speed of electronic circuits; other advances have made it possible to reduce the lengths of interconnections by packing circuits closer together. And technological breakthroughs continue with each passing year. Modern computers are capable of performing millions of calculations in one second. Their speed is fast reaching the physical limitation of the speed of light, which is about 186,000 miles per second. Generally, computer speed is expressed as the time required to perform one operation. The following units of time apply:

UNIT	SYMBOL	FRACTIONS OF A SECOND	
Millisecond	ms	one-thousandth	(1/1,000)
Microsecond	μs	one-millionth	(1/1,000,000)
Nanosecond	ns	one-billionth	(1/1,000,000,000)
Picosecond	ps	one-trillionth	(1/1,000,000,000,000)

The time required to perform one addition ranges from 4 microseconds to 200 nanoseconds. This means that some machines can do more than one million additions in one second. Obviously, such speed of processing far exceeds human capabilities.

The accuracy of computers is due in part to the inherent reliability of the electronic circuits that make up a computer. In our daily lives, we take advantage of this aspect of circuitry every time we switch on an electric device and assume it will come on. Our assumption is based upon our past experience; we expect the same activity to yield the same result. Similarly, in a computer, passing the same type of current through the same electrical circuits yields the same result. This constancy of computer-generated results is referred to as *accuracy*.

However, the accuracy of a computer relates to its internal operations. To say that a computer is accurate does not imply that what comes out of the computer is correct—that depends on what was put into it. If the *input* collected and fed into the computer is incorrect or is not relevant to the problem being solved, then it is impossible for the computer to manipulate that input and produce meaningful *output*. Bad processing instructions will also produce bad output; so the correctness of programs used to manipulate the data is also important. This concept, called *garbage in–garbage out*, is fundamental to understanding computer "mistakes."

The part of the computer that stores data is the computer's *memory*, or storage. Computers can store a virtually unlimited amount of data and retrieve it at incredible speeds. We could store similarly vast quantities of data in paper files, but the files would become extremely bulky and require a good deal of storage space. Further, the job of manually extracting data from such a file would become increasingly tedious and time consuming as the size of the file increased. The computer's memory can store the same data in considerably less space and retrieve it in a fraction of the time.

The amount of storage available in today's computers can be increased or decreased according to user requirements. Users can purchase the amount of memory they need; and continuing advances in technology have led to steady reductions in its cost. Once data has been placed in the computer's memory, efficient and accurate processing and retrieval operations can be performed.

DATA PROCESSING

In the past, manual techniques of collecting, manipulating, and distributing data to achieve certain objectives were known as *data processing*. As technology advanced, electromechanical machines were developed to perform these functions. The term *automatic data processing (ADP)* was introduced to describe the use of such machines. Today, the electronic computer is used to achieve results formerly accomplished by humans and machines. This is known as *electronic data processing (EDP)*. (The term *data processing* is sometimes used as a shorthand reference to EDP.)

The objective of all data processing, whether manual, electromechanical, or electronic, is to convert raw data into information that can be used in decision making. *Data* refers to raw facts that have been collected from various sources but not organized. Data cannot be used to make meaningful decisions. For example, a daily list of all checks and deposit slips of all branch offices may mean very little to a bank manager. But through manipulation of the data in one fashion or another, useful information may be provided—perhaps in the form of a summary report giving the number and amount of deposits and withdrawals at each branch. *Information*, then, is data that has been organized and processed. Information increases understanding and helps people make intelligent decisions.

To be useful to decision makers, information must meet several requirements. It must be accurate, timely, complete, concise, and relevant. That is, information should be delivered to the right person, at the right time, in the right place. If information fails to meet these requirements, it fails to meet the needs of those who must use it and is thus of little value.

To derive information from data, all data processing follows the same basic flow pattern: input, processing, and output (see Figure 1–1).

Input involves three steps: data must be *collected*, *verified*, and *coded*.

● Collect: Collection involves gathering data from various sources and assembling it at one location.
● Verify: After data has been gathered, its accuracy and completeness must be checked.

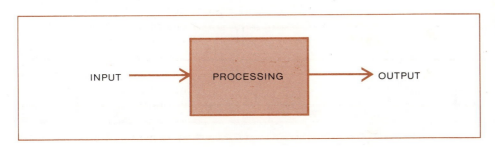

FIGURE 1–1
Data Flow

● Code: Data must be converted into machine-readable form so that it can be entered into the data processing system. Keying data onto cards or tape is one example of coding.

The terms *classify*, *sort*, *calculate*, *summarize*, and *store* are used to refer to the steps in processing data.

● Classify: Classification involves categorizing data according to certain characteristics so that it is meaningful to the user. For example, sales data can be grouped according to salesperson, product type, customer, or any other classification useful to management.

● Sort: After it is classified, data must be sorted. That involves arranging the grouped data elements into a predetermined sequence to facilitate processing. For example, an employee file may be sorted by social security number or by last name. Sorting can be done on numbers, letters, special characters ($+$, $-$, ¢, and the like), or a combination of these.

● Calculate: The arithmetical or logical manipulation of data is referred to as calculation. Examples include computation of students' grade-point averages, customers' bank balances, and employees' wages.

● Summarize: Reducing large amounts of data to a concise, usable form is called summarizing. This logical reduction of data is necessary to provide information that is useful, while eliminating everything else. An example of reduced data is a top-management report that summarizes a company's accounting data to determine its profit performance.

● Store: The data can be placed on a storage medium such as paper, magnetic tape, or microfilm for retrieval when needed. The cost of storage should not exceed the benefit of having the facts available for future use. Obviously, only facts that may be needed later should be stored.

Once data has been processed according to some or all of the steps above, information is available for distribution to the user. The three steps involved in the output phase of data flow are to *retrieve*, *convert*, and *communicate*.

● Retrieve: The computer can retrieve stored information so that it can be referenced by the user.

● Convert: Often people cannot use information in the form in which the computer stores it. Conversion involves translating such information into a

FIGURE 1–2
Organization of a Data Base

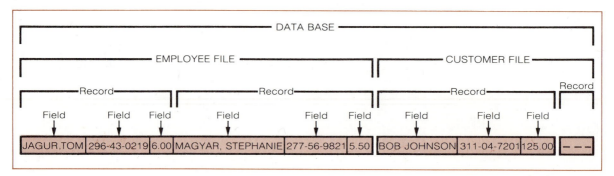

form that humans can understand and use, such as a CRT display or a printed output. If several users require the same output, the information must also be duplicated.

● Communicate: Information must be in the right place at the right time. Communication occurs when information reaches the proper users at the proper time in an intelligible form.

To achieve effective data processing, data should be organized in an integrated way so that all anticipated needs of users for information can be met. For example, a business firm may want to maintain specific data about all employees—home address, social security number, wage per hour, withholding tax, gross income, and so on. Each of these categories is called a *field*. A collection of fields that relate to a single unit (in this case a single employee) is a *record*. A grouping of all related records (in this case all employee records) is a *file*. The structuring of data to satisfy a wider variety of information needs than can be supported by a single file is a *data base*. We shall consistently use the terms *field*, *record*, *file*, and *data base* in this manner (see Figure 1–2).

A DATA-PROCESSING APPLICATION

One common application of data processing is payroll preparation. The inputs to this application are employee time cards and a personnel file. This data is processed to provide paychecks for all employees and a payroll report containing summary information for management (see Figure 1–3).

FIGURE 1–3
Payroll Processing

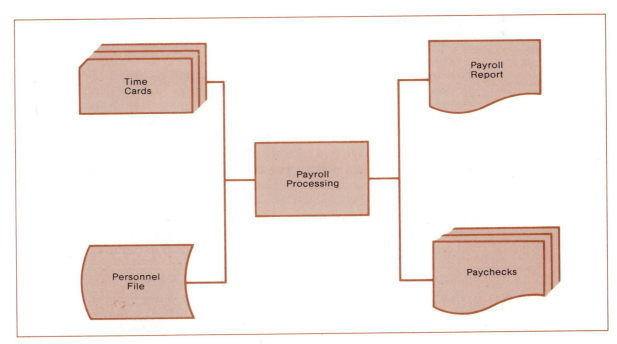

Payroll preparation is suitable for electronic data processing because it involves a well-defined, repetitive procedure and a large number of records. The computer must take the following steps in preparing a paycheck:

1. Read total hours worked from time card.
2. Compute gross pay by multiplying total hours worked by employee hourly wage rate.
3. Calculate withholding tax and social security tax.
4. Deduct withholding tax and social security tax from gross pay to get net pay.
5. Write paycheck.

In most payroll applications, the computer must also check for other conditions, such as overtime, maximum or mininum allowable work hours, other deductions, and special wage rates for overtime work.

The payroll report includes summary information such as number of employees paid, total dollar value of payroll for the period, total withholding, and breakdowns of payments for all departments of the company. This report helps management to make decisions about labor costs, cash flow planning, and the like.

IMPACT OF COMPUTERS

We are in the midst of the computer revolution. The computer's ability to store, retrieve, and analyze data at tremendous speeds and at low cost has made possible such advances as space travel, electronic banking, and body scanners. The potential of computers seems unlimited—new applications appear every day. And as the costs of computers continue to decrease while human labor costs increase, more applications are inevitable.

Perhaps the greatest impact of computers has been on business. Today, most businesses are involved in electronic data processing. The power to process data rapidly and disseminate the results of processing to users is critical to technological progress. Further, business organizations are concerned with using scarce resources in an optimal manner to achieve their objectives of profit and growth. Often, in their attempts to achieve these goals, managers have had to make decisions in the face of uncertainty and with inadequate information. The computer, by providing information that is timely, concise, and relevant, has improved the decision-making process. The computer is also beginning to change the organization of the office itself. Information can be transmitted from one office to another next door or across a continent by electronic mail. *Word processors* are facilitating many tedious jobs performed by secretaries, freeing them to perform other tasks.

The computer is much like any other tool used by humans. It has not replaced people, but it is displacing them into new and different jobs. The computer has enhanced their problem-solving capabilities and increased their capacity to handle complex relationships. Thus, computers are being used for straighforward clerical tasks (payroll processing, inventory control,

and billing) and for complex applications (budgeting, facilities planning, market research, and corporate planning).

Government's use of computers parallels business's as far as conventional data processing is concerned. But the government also uses computers extensively in development of military weapons and defense systems. Examples of the latter include computerized radar systems and automatically guided missiles. The government also uses computers for land resource planning, health service planning, transportation planning, and police telecommunication systems.

Computers have had a significant impact on education—one of society's largest industries. Like business, it needs computers to store and process large amounts of data. Recently, computers have begun to be used in teaching as well. *Computer-assisted instruction (CAI)* involves direct interaction between a computer and a student. This method of teaching holds promise, since the computer can deal with a large number of students on an individual basis.

In the health-care field, computers are being used for making medical diagnoses, maintaining medical histories, and monitoring patients. The advantage of computer monitoring of intensive-care patients is that critical factors like pulse rate, breathing, and body temperature can be checked several times a second. This type of monitoring could not be provided by individuals. Moreover, the computer does not suffer fatigue, and it makes no mistakes once it has been correctly set up.

The use of personal computers is also increasing. Decreasing costs have made computer use in the home possible and attractive. Home computers are being used to balance checkbooks, regulate fuel consumption, plan menus, and even turn lights and appliances on and off at prescribed times.

While many people are excited about all these uses of computers, many others are concerned about the problems they may create—problems like

11

worker displacement, invasion of privacy, and depersonalization in business operations. The advantages of a new technology are often obvious, but the problems that may arise are much more difficult to assess. This was so with automobiles. It may very well be the case with computers. However, computers are here to stay. We could not maintain our present life styles without them. Indeed, it is essential that we be familiar with their capabilities, limitations, and real and potential social impact. This text introduces the basic workings of the computer, discusses recent computer innovations, and points to some of the issues that face the computer generations.

SUMMARY

- A computer possesses no intelligence. It can only perform tasks predetermined by humans.
- All computer processing involves the basic machine functions of performing simple arithmetic (addition, subtraction, and so on), comparing values (either numeric or alphabetic), and storing and retrieving information.
- The computer derives its power from three features: speed, accuracy, and memory.
- The speed of computer processing is limited by the switching speed of its electronic circuits and the distances that electric currents must travel through these circuits. Advances in technology have resulted in computers that can perform operations in nanoseconds (billionths of a second).
- Computers' accuracy is enhanced by the internal, self-checking features of electronic circuits. Although the internal operations of the computer are essentially error-free, its output will not be valid unless valid input was used. Understanding this "garbage in–garbage out" concept is fundamental to understanding computer "mistakes."

● The collection, manipulation, and dissemination of data is known as data processing. The use of machines to perform these functions is called automatic data processing. When an electronic computer is used, electronic data processing (EDP) is performed.

● Data refers to unorganized, raw facts. Information is data that has been organized and processed so that it can be used to make intelligent decisions. In order for information to be useful, it must be accurate, timely, complete, concise, and relevant.

● The conversion of data to information follows the pattern: Input through processing to output. Input involves collecting, verifying, and coding data. Processing involves classifying, sorting, calculating, summarizing, and storing it. Information retrieved and converted so that it can be communicated to the user in an intelligible form is output.

● Data must be organized to be processed effectively. A data item is called a field; a collection of fields relating to a single unit, a record; and grouping of related records, a file. The structuring of data to support the information needs of a wide variety of users creates a data base.

● The capability of the computer to store, retrieve, and analyze data at tremendous speeds has made possible new advances such as space travel and electronic banking. Computers' impact on society is growing; we are becoming increasingly dependent on them in our daily lives.

REVIEW QUESTIONS

1. Although computer processing is essentially error-free, mistakes can and do occur. Explain how. What is meant by the phrase "garbage in–garbage out."

2. Distinguish between data and information. What are some of the functions performed in converting data into information? Give an example of how a computer can be used to perform these functions.

3. List five ways in which the computer has had some impact on you.

4. What are some problems created by computers? Can these problems be solved? Discuss.

APPLICATION

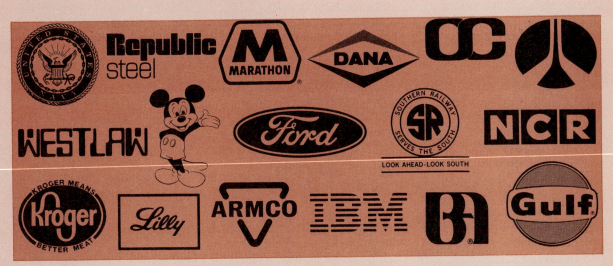

© Walt Disney Productions

Walt Disney Productions

Leisure time is an integral part of society today. People everywhere find time for amusement and recreation. Among the most unique entertainment experiences of the past two decades is the "theme park," a concept created by Walt Disney in his imaginative reworking of the old-time amusement park. These parks enchant visitors by surrounding them with a whole new world, shutting out reality and allowing them to "leave today and enter the world of yesterday, tomorrow, and fantasy."

There are now nearly fifty major theme parks across the nation. But the grandfather of these parks, and still the leader of the industry, is Disneyland. Opened at Anaheim, California, in 1955, Disneyland is visited by more people each year than all professional football and basketball games of the year combined. It draws more than twice the combined annual attendance at Yosemite, Yellowstone, and the Great Smokies national parks.

From Anaheim, the Disney imagination spread across the United States to Lake Buena Vista, Florida, where Walt Disney World opened in 1971. An investment of more than $700,000,000, Walt Disney World is the number-one destination resort in the world. Disneyland and Disney World's combined annual revenues of $640,436,000 (1980 Annual Report) account for about 40 percent of the theme park industry's total.

COMPUTERS IN THEME PARKS

Computers play an integral part in the operation of the Disney theme parks. They are used for entertainment-facility control as well as for monitoring and controlling the parks' operating conditions. One use of the computer for entertainment-facility control is to animate lifelike figures for the numerous show attractions. (This use will be discussed later.) A distributed system involving seven computers controls the WEDway Peoplemover transportation system at Walt Disney World.

The RCA Space Mountain double roller coaster is also computer-controlled. The roller coasters run next to each other on two almost identical courses inside a huge six-story concrete planetarium. For safety, the cars on each roller coaster must stay at least eighteen seconds apart. This safety feature is controlled by a computer. If a car begins to gain on the one ahead of it, the tailgating car is slowed down. Computers also release the blast-off roar in the final tunnel of the ride and control the forty projectors that create the Milky Way, meteors, and stars.

In the major hotels, or theme resorts, in the Florida park, computer terminals are used for guest reservations, registrations, and checkouts. For example, as guests prepare to leave, they check out at any of the terminals in the hotel lobby, where the clerks punch their room numbers into terminal keyboards. The terminals print itemized statements for payment at the cashier's window.

At Walt Disney World, a computerized monitoring and control system checks the operating conditions of everything from fire alarms to golf-course sprinklers. If an equipment malfunction or an alarm condition such as a fire occurs, the system identifies the problem by flashing coded messages on computer terminals located at two fire stations and two security locations and on the maintenance console in the main service area.

DIGITAL ANIMATION CONTROL (DAC) SYSTEM

"Audio-Animatronics,"® a patented Disney invention, is one of Disney's most important and popular contributions to the entertainment world. The system is known as the Digital Animation Control (DAC) System or the Disney Audio-Animatronic Control System. It enables voices, music, and sound effects to be electronically combined and synchronized with lifelike movements of three-dimensional objects ranging from birds and flowers to humans. Eight major attractions at Walt Disney World use Audio-Animatronics—the forty presidents in Liberty Square's Hall of Presidents, the Country Bear Jamboree, the Haunted Mansion, the Enchanted Tiki Birds, the Mission to Mars, the Pirates of the Caribbean, the Jungle River Ride, and the Carousel of Progress.

A highly simplified configuration of the DAC System is shown in Figure 1–4. As the figure shows, the system is divided into two areas: a central area and a show area. The equipment in the central area is used only to support the animator's task; the equipment in the show area is used both to move the Audio-Animatronics (AA) figures and to allow the animator to communicate with the figures via the computer.

To compose a show, the animator sits at a desk-sized programming console, which contains several dozen switches and indicator lights. By manipulating these switches, the animator sends data in the form of electronic signals to a general-purpose computer that processes the data to make the figures move. So quickly does the data travel from the console to the computer and from the computer to the figure that the animator appears to have direct and instantaneous control. The action is actually generated in a "frame-by-frame" sense, like film animation. The computer stores the data for each "frame of figure motion." Once the animator decides that a show, or session of a show, is ready, all the data for that show or

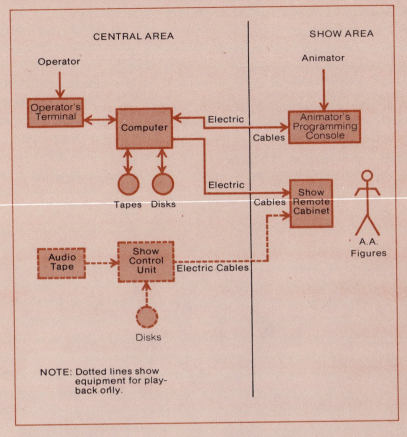

CENTRAL AREA

Operator

Operator's Terminal

Computer

Electric Cables

Tapes Disks

Electric Cables

SHOW AREA

Animator

Animator's Programming Console

Show Remote Cabinet

A.A. Figures

Audio Tape

Show Control Unit

Electric Cables

Disks

NOTE: Dotted lines show equipment for play-back only.

FIGURE 1–4
Simplified DAC System
Configuration for
Animation only

glorified record player. The "record" is the show control disk. Its signals can activate slight movements, such as the fluttering of an eyelash, or large movements, such as Lincoln standing to deliver a speech. Devices used in conjunction with the show control unit allow a show to be played in perfect synchronism with a sound track. A typical thirty-minute show can involve up to a thousand different computer-controlled functions, including character movements, stage effects, and sound effects.

Computers are indispensable in theme parks. They aid not only the operation of the parks but also the generation, animation, and monitoring of animated shows and park rides.

DISCUSSION POINTS

1. A computerized automatic monitoring and control system is used at Walt Disney World to monitor the operation of fire alarms and golf-course sprinklers. How might a similar system be used in the park's hotels?
2. In what way is the method of generating in Audio-Animatronic figures similar to film animation?

session is stored as electronic signals on a magnetic tape.

When the show has finally been edited and fully satisfies the animators and art directors, it is prepared for repetitive automatic playback; the

electronic signals are transferred from the magnetic tape to a storage medium called the show control disk. In the central area mentioned earlier is a computer called the show control unit—a sort of

CHAPTER 2

Evolution of Computers

Introduction

Although the computer is a relatively recent innovation, its development rests on centuries of research, thought, and discovery. Advances in information-processing technology are responses to the growing need to find better, faster, cheaper, and more reliable methods of handling data. The search for better ways to store and process data is not recent—data-processing equipment has gone through generations of change and improvement. An understanding of the evolution of data processing is especially helpful in understanding the capabilities and limitations of modern computers.

This chapter presents significant events that lead to the development of the computer. A brief history of data processing is given, beginning with the earliest calculating machines and ending with the state of the art today. Since developments in computer programs *(software)* are as important as developments in computer equipment *(hardware)*, major advances in both areas are presented.

""First Large-Scale Computer, Eniac, Turns 35 Years Old""

Lois Paul, *Computerworld* Staff

Although there was no ice cream and cake, a birthday was celebrated here [in Philadelphia] this week as Enaic (Electronic Numerical Integrator and Computer), the world's first large-scale computer, turned 35.

Eniac was built for the Army during World War II at the Moore School of the University of Pennsylvania School of Engineering and Applied Science. It weighed 30 tons, took up 15,000 sq ft of space and cost $400,000 to build in 1945. Its 18,000 vacuum tubes consumed 150 kilowatts and it

could do 5,000 calculations per second.

One of the two men credited with its creation, J. Presper Eckert, Jr., described Eniac in a recent interview as "the equivalent to a simple Radio Shack computer of the type that sells for $500."

However, during the celebration of Eniac's anniversary this week, University of Pennsylvania students proved that even a Radio Shack Corp. TRS-80 can beat the old veteran. Using sections of the original Eniac and a TRS-80, the students ran a program to square all integers from one to 10,000. Eniac suffered a crushing defeat, completing the task in six seconds to the TRS-80's one-third of a second.

Eckert, who at 61 is a vice-president of Sperry Univac in suburban Montgomery County, built Eniac with Dr. John Mauchly, who was a physicist at Ursinus College when they met.

With the nation at war, Mauchly suggested in 1942 that research be conducted on an electronic computer.

Needing a device to speed calculations required to improve the accuracy of artillery, the Army Ballistics Research Laboratory in Aberdeen, Md., approved the project in 1943. Three years later, Eckert and Mauchly completed Eniac and it was moved to Aberdeen and used there for about two years.

Eckert and Mauchly formed Eckert-Mauchly Computer Corp., which was bought in 1950 by Remington Rand. This later became the Sperry Univac division of Sperry Corp. Eckert said that he and Mauchly each made about $250,000 in selling their company to Remington Rand. Mauchly died in 1980.

As for Eniac, which was once an electronic marvel and remains a historic landmark, most of it has been stored in the Smithsonian Institution, out of sight, for more than a quarter of a century.

By human standards, thirty-five years old is the prime of life. However, by machine standards, thirty-five is a venerable old age, as evidence by this article. Chapter 2 recounts the evolution of computers from simple calculating tools to the marvelous electronic devices available today.

EARLY DEVELOPMENT

Trying to piece together the separate inventions, discoveries, and events that culminated in the creation of the modern-day computer requires some guesswork, an open mind, and a little creative imagination. For one thing, at what point in history should such a search start? People always have had difficulty calculating answers to problems and keeping track of the answers. Ancient sheepherders tied knots in pieces of string in order to keep accurate counts of their herd. Could that have been a forerunner of today's computer?

Perhaps a more realistic start would be with the development of the abacus. It is one of the earliest known computational devices; its use dates back to antiquity. Although its creation is attributed to the Chinese, it emerged independently in several cultures. The abacus is composed of several wires each strung with ten beads. Additions or subtractions are performed by manipulating the beads on the wires, and the computed result is read from the final positions of the beads (see Figure 2–1). It is very useful for addition and subtraction, but multiplication and division are more complex and time consuming. The abacus represents a tool that aided the user in calculating answers to information problems and in storing the results. However, computing "instructions" were little more than carefully planned manipulations of the beads by someone well versed in its operation.

Viewed imaginatively, the invention of the mechanical clock in the Middle Ages can be seen to foreshadow the development of the computer. Through a closed system, the mechanical parts of the clock continuously calculated the time of day, displaying the results through the positions of two hands on its face. Loosely speaking, its "instructions" were pre-programmed by the inventor in the way the mechanism translated the pull of weights and the swing of a pendulum into the movement of gears and the position of the hands.

Mathematical discoveries played their part in the history of the computer. John Napier, a Scotsman, discovered in the mid–1600s that he could multiply and divide numbers by simply adding and subtracting their representations in geometrical series called logarithms. Although the mathematical concepts behind logarithms are complex, it was the practical use to which he put this discovery that is noteworthy here. Napier placed the logarithms of numbers on a set of ivory rods (nicknamed "Napier's bones"). By sliding

FIGURE 2–1
The Abacus

FIGURE 2–2

Napier's "Bones"

the "bones" up and down, in effect adding or subtracting the numbers' geometrical series, he performed multiplications and divisions (see Figure 2–2). His invention was translated into the slide rule around 1650 by Robert Bissaker, who placed those numbers on sliding pieces of wood instead of ivory rods. For the computer historian, these inventions represent the development of crude but effective manual calculators.

The development of the first real mechanical calculator is attributed to Blaise Pascal, around 1642. It added and subtracted numbers by using a series of eight rotating gears, or wheels. As the first wheel counted out ten digits (one complete revolution), a pin on its edge would rotate the wheel next to it. This second wheel, in turn, would rotate the next, and so on (see Figure 2–3). (The same principle is used today in many odometers to keep

FIGURE 2–3

Pascal's Adding
Machine

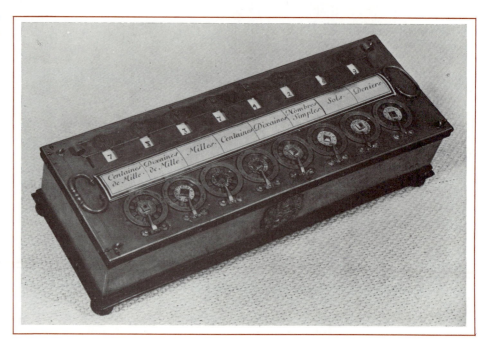

track of a car's mileage.) Later in that century—around 1690—a German mathematician named Gottfried van Leibnitz developed a machine that could not only add and subtract but multiply, divide, and calculate square roots as well. In both inventions, the "instructions" on how to do the calculations were programed into the machines mechanically by the way the gears turned one another as they moved. Naturally, the instructions could not be changed without changing the operation of the machines.

One of the first developments in programmable instructions for machines came from the weaving industry in the early 1800s. In an attempt to automate the weaving process, a weaver named Joseph Jacquard developed a loom controlled by a series of punched cards. These cards, made of card-

FIGURE 2–4
Jacquard's Loom

board, were actual instructions "read" by the machine as they passed over a series of rods; the machine translated the holes in the cards into colors in the weave. Since each card represented one loop operation, a whole collection of cards was necessary to operate the loom (see Figure 2–4). This concept was a forerunner of what nearly everyone recognizes today as the classic IBM punched card.

One of the tragedies in the history of the computer lies with Charles Babbage, a man truly ahead of his time. Babbage set out to develop a machine that could perform calculations without human intervention. The machine he envisioned would calculate logarithm tables and print the results, avoiding the printing errors so common in his day. His idea relied on the "method of differences," and in 1812 he managed to build a small model of what he called the *difference engine* (see Figure 2–5). The tragedy was that

FIGURE 2–5
Babbage's Difference
Engine

when he strove to make a larger version of the model, parts could not be manufactured to the tolerances required by his machine. The current-day technology was not sophisticated enough!

Undaunted, Babbage conceived of the idea of building a device which could perform any calculation—adding, subtracting, multiplying, or dividing—according to instructions coded on cards. Even intermediate results could be stored in a memory unit. This device, called the *analytical engine*, contained many features similar to those found in today's computers—in the early 1800s! An arithmetic unit called the "mill" performed the calculations; and the memory unit, the "store," kept intermediate and final results as well as the instructions for each stage of the calculations. Instructions and data were fed into the device by means of punched cards, and output was automatically printed. All of this, of course, was to be done mechanically, not electronically.

Although the analytical engine was originally conceived in 1833, Babbage died before it could be constructed. Nevertheless, a model based on his drawings and notes was put together in 1871 by his son. To his tribute, it worked. Although Babbage was never able to see his inventions become reality, they nevertheless earned him the reputation of being the "father of computers."

Babbage's vision of using punched cards for inputting data and instruction went relatively unnoticed until the late 1880s. At that time, Dr. Herman Hollerith, a statistician, put it to good use. It seems the United States Government was encountering problems in trying to process data gathered in the census. The last census, taken in 1880, had required some seven and a half years of manual calculations to tabulate. Significant population increases since then would make manual processing of the next census almost unthinkable. Hollerith was commissioned by the government to reduce the time required to process the census data.

To do this, he developed a series of machines that stored census data on cards. Each card had twelve rows and eighty columns, the same as the modern-day punched card. The coding scheme he developed for use in punching the cards is still used today. The *Hollerith code* permitted the machines to sort the census data according to the United States Government's information needs. His machines reduced the time required to process the census data to two and a half years, despite a population increase of three million (see Figure 2–6). Not only had Hollerith developed the first computer card, his project comprised the first large-scale data processing environment.

His successful experience with the government led Hollerith to set up the Tabulating Machine Company to manufacture and market punched card equipment for commercial use. His machines were first sold to railroads to be used to compute freight schedules. In 1911, his Tabulating Machine Company merged with several other corporations to form the International Business Machines Corporation (IBM). If Hollerith could only have known the future success of that merger!

In a different vein, William S. Burroughs was making advances with mechanical adding machines around the same time Hollerith's census machines

FIGURE 2–6
Hollerith's Census
Machine

FIGURE 2–6
Hollerith's Census
Machine

were being put to use on the 1890 Census. He developed a key-driven calculating-printing machine operated by a crank. The machine, which could record, summarize, and calculate, was patented and sold by the Burroughs Adding Machine Company, which also became a giant in the computer industry.

From the 1900s on, it becomes more difficult to sort out the different inventions, discoveries, and events that affected the development of the computer, so fast were they all occurring. In the late 1920s and early 1930s, significant advances in punched card equipment resulted in machines' not only adding and subtracting, but multiplying as well. As these machines were further enhanced with the ability to interpret alphabetic data, full-scale record keeping and accounting functions could be supported. These enhanced machines were called *accounting machines,* or tabulators (see Figure 2–7).

The first real step toward the development of the modern-day computer, however, was made in 1944, by Howard Aiken of Harvard University. Harvard, IBM, and the U.S. War Department embarked on a joint project precipitated by the need to handle the high volume of number crunching (complex equation solving) required in logistic calculation. The efforts of this team produced the first automatic calculator, which was called the *Mark I* (see Figure 2–8). It was not an electronic computer, but rather utilized electromagnetic relays and mechanical counters. When it ran, the clicking noise

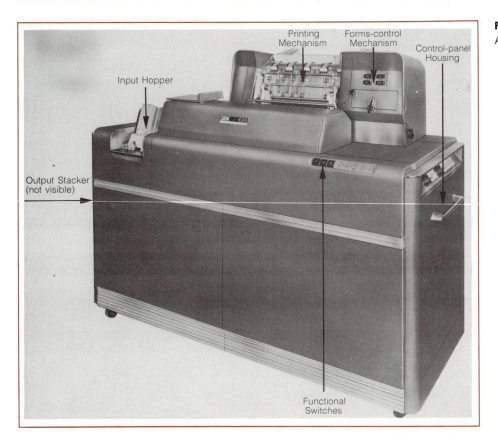

FIGURE 2–7
Accounting Machine

FIGURE 2–8
The Mark I Computer

from the relays was deafening! Babbage's vision of automatic computation was realized in this machine. Instructions were fed into the Mark I by means of holes punched in paper tape and results were obtained in the form of holes punched in cards.

An electronic computer was developed some two years later by J. Presper Eckert and John W. Mauchly at the University of Pennsylvania. The project, sponsored by the War Department and considered classified, resulted in a machine called the *ENIAC*, short for Electronic Numerical Integrator and Calculator. It could perform a multiplication in three-thousandths of a second, compared with the about three seconds required by the Mark I. The ENIAC was a huge machine; its 18,000 vacuum tubes took up a space ten feet high, ten feet wide, and some hundred feet long (see Figure 2–9). Since the ENIAC had no internal memory, instructions had to be fed into it by use of combinations of switches.

Not until Jon Von Neumann proposed a method of encoding instructions in the same language used for data did it become possible to store instructions within the computer. Von Neumann's principles, developed in the late 1940s, spurred the development of the first *stored-program computer*. As it turned out, two groups of people were working simultaneously to create such a machine. In the United States, the University of Pennsylvania was developing the EDVAC (Electronic Discrete Variable Automatic Computer),

FIGURE 2–9
The ENIAC

while in England, Cambridge University was creating the *EDSAC* (Electronic Delay Storage Automatic Computer). History awarded the EDSAC the title of first stored-program computer, although it was completed only a few months before the EDVAC.

The EDSAC was the first computer to perform arithmetic and logical operations without human intervention, depending solely on stored instructions. It could perform a computation in three milliseconds. The EDSAC marked the end of the quest to develop a stored-program, self-sufficient calculating machine and marked the beginning of the computer age and the information-rich society it made possible. Refinements of the computer concept have focused on speed, size, and cost. The rest of the chapter is devoted to these developments, which can be usefully divided into four categories: first-generation, second-generation, third-generation, and fourth-generation computers.

FIRST GENERATION: 1951–1958

In 1951, the first commercial electronic computer was sold to the U.S. Census Bureau. It was the *UNIVAC I* (Universal Automatic Computer), built by John W. Mauchly and J. Presper Eckert, who had also been responsible for the development of the ENIAC. This event marked the beginning of *first-generation computers* (see Figure 2–10).

Before the UNIVAC I, computers had been one-of-a-kind machines developed specifically for scientific and military purposes. However, the UNIVAC I was dedicated to business data processing applications. For the first time, business firms were exposed to the possibilities of computer data process-

FIGURE 2–10
The UNIVAC I
Computer

ing. (Most first-generation computers, however, were still oriented toward *scientific applications* rather than *business data processing*.)

The characteristic that distinguished first-generation computers from subsequent machines was the use of vacuum tubes to control internal operations. The vacuum tubes were fairly large, and they generated considerable heat, much as light bulbs do. Thus, first-generation computers were huge, requiring a lot of space and special air-conditioning equipment to dissipate the tube-generated heat. Even with the considerable maintenance they required, their reliability was poor. Although first-generation computers were much faster than earlier mechanical or electromechanical devices, they were slow compared with today's computers, and their internal storage capacity was limited.

Many used *magnetic drums* as a storage medium. These cylinders, coated with magnetizable material, stored data as tiny magnetized spots on their outer surface. The drum was rotated at high speeds, and read/write heads above the drum surface could write or read data as required. Other types of storage media were also used. Operators performed input and output operations by using punched cards.

The computer, a binary machine, can distinguish between only two states—say, "on" or "off," or spots magnetized in one direction or the opposite. These early first-generation computers were programmed using "on" and "off" states called *machine language*. Machine language consists of strings of zeroes and ones that act as instructions to the computer, specifying the desired electrical states of its internal circuits and memory banks. Obviously, writing a machine-language program was extremely cumbersome, tedious, and time consuming.

To make programming easier, *symbolic languages* were developed. Such languages enabled instructions to be written with symbolic codes (called *mnemonics,* or memory aids) rather than strings of ones and zeroes. One word or mnemonic, was used to represent a series of zeroes and ones that stood for a particular machine language instruction (see Figure 2–11). These symbolic instructions were then translated into corresponding binary codes (machine-language instructions). The first set of programs, or instructions, to tell the computer how to do this translation was developed by Dr. Grace Hopper in 1952 at the University of Pennsylvania. After this breakthrough, most first-generation computers were programmed in symbolic language. Of those first-generation computers used in business, most processed payroll and billing, since they were easy to program and to cost justify.

FIGURE 2–11
Machine Language
versus Symbolic
Language

MACHINE CODE TO ADD TWO FIELDS

11111010010000111000001000010100100000010101100

SYMBOLIC CODE TO ADD TWO FIELDS

AP   TOTAL,AMOUNT

SECOND GENERATION: 1959–1964

In the late 1950s, tiny, solid-state *transistors* replaced vacuum tubes in computers. The elimination of vacuum tubes greatly reduced generated heat and made possible the development of computers significantly smaller and more reliable than their predecessors. These new computers were faster, had increased storage capacity, and required less power to operate. They were *second-generation computers*.

Magnetic cores replaced magnetic drums as the primary internal storage medium. Cores are very small doughnut-shaped rings of ferromagnetic (magnet-like) material strung on thin wires. The passage of an electric current through wires on which a core is strung magnetizes the core to represent either an ''on'' or an ''off'' state and thus enables it to store data. Data stored in magnetic cores can be located and retrieved for processing in a few millionths of a second—faster than with magnetic-drum storage.

In many second-generation computer systems, the *internal*, or *main, storage* capacity of the computer was supplemented by the use of *magnetic tapes* for *external*, or *auxiliary, storage*. Substituting magnetic tapes for punched cards or punched paper tape increased input/output processing speeds by a factor of at least fifty (see Figure 2–12).

Other significant changes that occurred during this period were the development of magnetic disk storage, modular hardware, and improved input/output devices. *Magnetic disks* can be compared to phonograph records. Data is stored in circular tracks on the flat outer surfaces of the platter, or disk, which are coated with ferromagnetic material. The main advantage of disk storage is that it enables the user to locate a particular record on a set of disks rotating at high speeds in a fraction of a second. Unlike magnetic tape, records on disks do not have to be processed sequentially. The computer can go directly to the record it needs without having to read everything that comes before it. Thus, disks provide *direct*, or *random, access* to records in a file.

The modular-hardware concept involved using a building-block approach to the design of electronic circuits. With this approach, complete modules

FIGURE 2–12
A Second-Generation
Computer System

(sometimes called "breadboards") could be replaced in case of malfunctions, greatly reducing downtime, the processing time lost because of malfunctions. It also added flexibility, since new modules could be added to the system to increase its capabilities.

The improvement in input/output (I/O) devices could be seen in faster printing speeds and automatic detection and correction of input/output errors. These advances allowed the devices to be connected directly to the computer (to be *online*) without significantly lowering the overall efficiency of the computer system.

Second-generation computers were programmed in *high-level languages*, which resembled English a lot more than their predecessors had. These languages were application- and problem-oriented rather than machine-oriented. The first high-level language to achieve widespread acceptance was called *FORTRAN* (for *FOR*mula *TRAN*slator), developed during the period from 1954 through 1957 by IBM. The version of the language known as FORTRAN IV was standardized in 1963 and is still used extensively for scientific applications.

Because FORTRAN lacked many features desirable for business data processing, another language, called *COBOL* (*CO*mmon *B*usiness-*O*riented *L*anguage), was developed in 1961. Among COBOL's significant features are its file-processing, editing, and input/output capabilities.

Second-generation computers, like their predecessors, were designed either for business data processing or for scientific applications. The most popular business-oriented computer was the IBM 1401. Typical applications included payroll processing, invoicing, and maintaining personnel records. All of these applications involved *batch processing*—the collection of data over a certain period of time and its subsequent processing in one computer run. Magnetic tape was the principal storage medium associated with batch processing.

THIRD GENERATION: 1965–1970

Continued technological advances in electronics and solid-state physics brought further reductions in computer size, even greater reliability and speed, and lower costs. *Integrated circuits (ICs)* replaced the transistors of second-generation equipment in machines referred to as *third-generation computers*. Through techniques like etching and printing, hundreds of electronic components could be included on silicon circuit chips less than one-eighth-inch square. (see Figure 2–13).

The transition from the second to the third generation occurred when IBM introduced the System/360 computers. This "family," or series, consisted of six different computers, each offering a different main storage capacity. The series was designed to provide all types of processing; its computers were capable of supporting forty different input/output and auxiliary storage devices. Within a short time after the introduction of the System/360, other manufacturers announced their versions of third-generation computers. RCA, Honeywell, Univac, Burroughs, and others began competing with

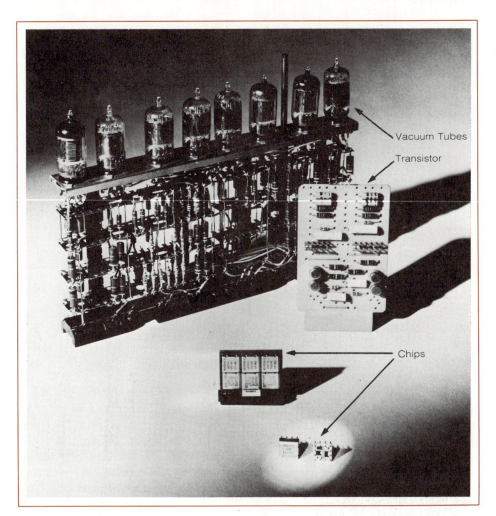

FIGURE 2–13
First-, Second-, and
Third-Generation
Components

Vacuum Tubes

Transistor

Chips

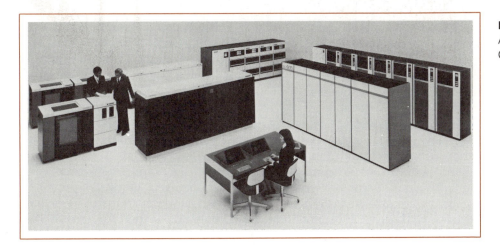

FIGURE 2–14
A Third-Generation
Computer System

IBM, and before long over 25,000 third-generation computer systems were installed across the United States (see Figure 2–14).

Between 1965 and 1970, manufacturers invested millions of dollars in research into and development of hardware and software technologies. Competition was intense, and the cost to remain in the industry was high. As a result, some manufacturers did not survive. RCA left the computer business in 1972, followed by Xerox Corporation in 1975.

Although third-generation computers were smaller, faster, and less expensive than their predecessors, using them was not without problems. Many of the programs written for second-generation computers were based on an *architecture*, or internal design, significantly different from that of third-generation computers. Thus, these programs had to be rewritten. In addition, the skills of thousands of programmers became outdated with the introduction of this new architecture, resulting in a major need for re-education of programmers and operators.

Users also faced a problem—that of acquiring software and operating systems. An operating system is a series of programs designed to control the computer's operations, to communicate with the computer operator, and to provide continuous operation with limited manual intervention. When IBM announced the System/360 in 1965, an operating system was scheduled to accompany the installation of the hardware. However, the development of the operating system fell behind schedule, and it took several years to perfect the system. Over the next several years, extensive progress was made in operating system development.

Because of the overwhelming need for reliable software, a new industry—the software industry—emerged. Firms specializing in the development of software were able to cash in on the growing computer industry by selling software packages, series of standardized programs written for applications such as payroll and billing. Software packages gained widespread acceptance, since many users found it more profitable to purchase the prewritten packages than to write the programs themselves.

The advances in solid-state technology that led to third-generation computers also led to the emergence of *minicomputers* (see Figure 2–15). A small computer manufacturer called Digital Equipment Corporation (DEC) introduced the first commercially accepted minicomputer in 1965 and has since grown into the largest manufacturer of minicomputers in the United States. Minicomputers offer many of the same features as full-scale computer systems (such as an IBM System/360 computer), but on a smaller scale. These machines are physically smaller with smaller main storage capacities and slower processing speed than full-scale machines. However, they provide a powerful computer system and a cost-efficient alternative for small businesses.

Other important improvements in third-generation equipment included:

- Greater storage capacity.
- Versatile programs that automated many tasks previously handled by human operators.
- Greater compatibility of components, allowing easier expansion of computer systems.
- Ability to perform several operations simultaneously.

FIGURE 2–15
A Minicomputer That Uses Third-Generation Miniaturization Techniques

● Ability to perform processing more sophisticated than simple batch processing.

● Capability to handle both business and scientific applications in the same machine.

Another third-generation innovation involved *remote terminals*, terminals placed at various geographic locations and used to communicate directly with a central computer. Using such terminals, many users could interact with the central computer at the same time and receive almost instantaneous results in what was called a *time-sharing* environment.

Third-generation computers, like those of the present, were used for such diverse applications as inventory control, scheduling labor and materials, and bank credit-card billing.

FOURTH GENERATION: 1971–?

State of the Art: The Present

In 1971, IBM began delivering its System/370 computers. This family of computers, and those developed by other large computer manufacturers in the 1970s, incorporated further refinements, among them monolithic semiconductor memories, self-diagnostic operating systems, wide-spread use of virtual storage techniques, and further miniaturization through *large-scale integrated (LSI) circuits* (LSI is a technological process that allows circuits containing thousands of transistors to be densely packed on a single silicon chip).

Computers of this period are referred to as *fourth-generation computers*, because they offer significant performance and price improvements over third-generation computers. In addition, fourth-generation computers are gradually getting smaller, as evidenced by the emergence of microcomputers. As time progresses LSI may be replaced by *VLSI (very-large-scale integration)*, which is now being perfected by scientists and engineers. This could mean that computers could become smaller still.

Performance improvements in present-day computer systems include increased speeds, greater reliability, and storage capacities approaching billions of characters, all made possible by large-scale integrated circuitry. The emphasis is on ease of use and application, often called being "user friendly." Most systems have communication capabilities; they permit remote input and output via communication channels such as ordinary telephone lines. The use of TV-like display screens has become increasingly common.

Data-recording equipment to capture data at its point of origin in a form directly suitable for computer processing has been developed; common examples are magnetic-ink character readers (MICRs) and optical-character recognition (OCR) devices. The former are especially suited for applications like check processing for banks; the latter include point-of-sale (POS) terminals that record data about sales transactions as they occur. These devices

do away with the need for a special data-entry step that uses other input devices. Thus, more accurate and faster entry of data for computer processing is achieved.

As computer technology progresses, computer hardware prices will continue to drop. A greater proportion of the cost of installing and maintaining a computer system is invested in personnel and software support costs (see Figure 2–16). Larger and larger portions of the costs go for personnel sala-

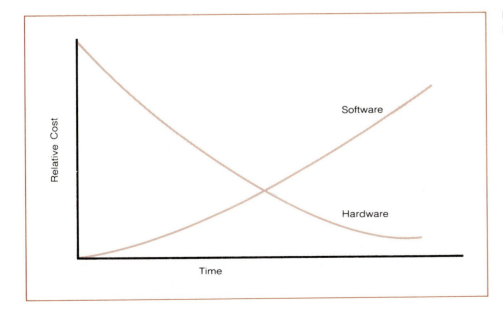

FIGURE 2–16
Historical Cost Pattern

TABLE 2–1 Computer Advancements	PERIOD	COMPUTER SYSTEM CHARACTERISTICS
	First Generation 1951–1958	Use of vacuum tubes in electronic circuits Magnetic drum as primary internal-storage medium Limited main-storage capacity Slow input/output; punched-card-oriented Low-level symbolic-language programming Heat and maintenance problems Applications: payroll processing and record keeping Examples: IBM 650 UNIVAC I
	Second Generation 1959–1964	Use of transistors for internal operations Magnetic core as primary internal-storage medium Increased main-storage capacity Faster input/output; tape orientation High-level programming languages (COBOL, FORTRAN) Great reduction in size and heat generation Increased speed and reliability Batch-oriented applications: billing, payroll processing, updating inventory files Examples: IBM 1401 Honeywell 200 CDC 1604
	Third Generation 1965–1970	Use of integrated circuits Magnetic core and solid-state main storage More flexibility with input/output; disk-oriented Smaller size and better performance and reliability Extensive use of high-level programming languages Emergence of minicomputers Remote processing and time-sharing through communication Availability of operating-system programs (software) to control I/O and do many tasks previously handled by human operators Applications: airline reservation systems, market forecasting, credit-card billing Examples: IBM System/360 NCR 395 Burroughs B6500
	Fourth Generation 1971–??	Use of large-scale integrated circuits Increased storage capacity and speed Modular design and compatibility between equipment (hardware) provided by different manufacturers (customer no longer tied to one vendor) Availability of sophisticated programs for special applications Greater versatility of input/output devices Increased use of minicomputers Introduction of microprocessors and microcomputers Applications: mathematical modeling and simulation, electronic funds transfer, computer-aided instruction, and home computers Examples: IBM 3033 Burroughs B7700 HP 3000 (minicomputer)

ries. Even with the trend toward pre-written software packages, programmers are needed to tailor the package to fit the organization's needs and to provide ongoing maintenance to keep the programs up-to-date. This phenomenon has prompted greater research into software products to increase computer personnel productivity.

The fourth generation has also been marked by the growth of the home computer market. By using LSI technology, manufacturers are able to produce densely packed chips called *microprocessors*. Microprocessors are beginning to appear in many of the devices people use every day, such as microwave ovens, sewing machines, thermostats, and even automobiles. A microprocessor in combination with other densely packed chips for storage and input/output operations form a *microcomputer*. Microcomputers are now being used in the home for such things as recording Christmas card lists, balancing checkbooks, keeping track of recipes, and amusing people with games. As we move into the future, computers will play an even larger part in our everyday lives.

SUMMARY

- Machines to perform arithmetic calculations were developed as early as the 1600s by Pascal and Leibnitz. The first machine employing concepts similar to those of a computer was the analytical engine designed by Charles Babbage in 1833. This machine was doomed to failure because its production was beyond the technology of its time.
- The use of electromechanical calculating machines was first implemented by Herman Hollerith in the 1890 census. These machines used punched-card input, and performed simple arithmetic calculations and card-sorting operations. Electromechanical punched-card machines such as accounting machines were used extensively in the early and mid-1900s. They were controlled by hand-wired control panels.
- The Mark I was the first automatic calculator. Introduced in the late 1930s, the Mark I used electromagnetic relays and counters for performing calculations. It was an electromechanical, rather than an electronic computer.
- In the mid-1940s, the ENIAC (Electronic Numerical Integrator and Calculator) was developed. The ENIAC was the first electronic digital computer. Its switching and control functions were performed using vacuum tubes. The EDSAC (Electronic Delay-Storage Automatic Computer) was completed in 1949. It was the first stored-program computer.
- The first generation of computers (1951-1958) began with the introduction of the UNIVAC I (Universal Automatic Computer). First-generation computers used vacuum tubes to control internal operations. These machines were very large and generated a lot of heat. They were much faster than earlier machines, but very slow by today's standards.
- Second-generation computers (1959-1964) relied on transistors for controlling internal operation. Transistors were much smaller, faster, and more reliable than vacuum tubes. In addition, significant increases in speed were obtained through the use of magnetic cores for internal storage, or memory.

Other important innovations during the second generation were the introduction of high-level programming languages, modular hardware design, and improved input/output devices.

● Third-generation computers (1965-1971) used solid-state integrated circuits rather than transistors to obtain reductions in size and cost, together with increased reliability and speed. These machines had a much larger storage capacity than second-generation computers. In addition, third-generation computers were supported by more sophisticated software. Many tasks previously handled by human operators were automated.

● Fourth generation computers rely on large scale integration, and continue to offer improvements in size, speed, and cost.

REVIEW QUESTIONS

1. Calculating machines developed in the 1600s by Pascal and Leibnitz could perform many of the functions of modern computers. Besides the fact that these machines were mechanical, rather than electronic, what was a major difference between these devices and computers?

2. In what way did the development of a loom by Jacquard impact on the development of computing devices?

3. Charles Babbage attempted to build a machine employing the concepts now used in computers. What was this machine called and why was it never built?

4. What was the first automatic calculator? How did this machine differ from first-generation computers?

5. What are the chief characteristics that distinguish first-, second-, and third-generation computers?

6. Why has the development of large-scale integration had such an impact on the computer industry?

7. Many hardware innovations were accompanied by improvements in software. What were some of the software developments during the third generations of computers? Why were improvements in software necessary?

APPLICATION

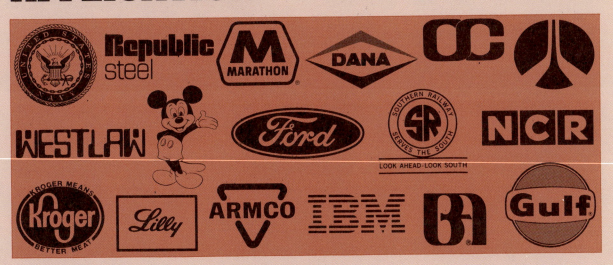

United States Navy

The United States Navy has provided a major impetus to the development of modern computers. Through the Office of Naval Research, much effort and money have been directed toward the development of concepts basic to today's computer. The most notable of these are stored programs and magnetic-core memory. Because of the increasing demands for national security, the Navy will no doubt remain at the forefront of technology.

WARTIME RESEARCH

The Navy's first major impact on computer development was its support of the Mark I, developed by Howard Aiken at Harvard and built by IBM. This project was first supported by the Bureau of Ships and then by the Bureau of Ordnance Computation Project. The Mark I was capable of performing the complex scientific calculations believed to be necessary for various applications relating to national security. In fact, some of the early calculations for the atomic bomb were performed on this machine.

Following the successful completion of the Mark I project, the Navy contracted Aiken to construct a machine for the computation of ballistic tables at the Bureau of Ordnance's Naval Proving Ground at Dahlgren, Virginia. This machine, popularly known as the "Ballistic Computer," was a special-purpose, all-relay calculator, was much faster than the Mark I.

In 1944, J. W. Forrester was contracted by the Navy Office of Research and Invention to build a computer system capable of simulating an airplane's performance. A pilot who provided input was to be part of the system, which was to respond to the pilot just as a plane would. Engineering changes to the plane could be simulated without the expense, time, and possible dangers inherent in building and operating a prototype plane.

POSTWAR ACTIVITIES

The Office of Naval Research (ONR) was established by Congress in 1946 as a postwar continuation of wartime projects initiated by the National Defense Research Committee (NDRC) and the Office of

Scientific Research and Development (OSRD). The purpose of this organization was to encourage scientific research, which was believed to be vital to the maintenance of naval power and, in effect, the preservation of national security. For many years following World War II, the ONR was the primary and most reliable source of funds for scientific research in the United States.

After World War II, the Mathematical Sciences Division in the Natural Sciences group of the ONR provided heavy support for reasearch in pure mathematics, applied mathematics, and mathematical statistics, including support for increasingly complex methods of numerical analysis. To implement these methods, researchers developed various computing devices and, eventually, large-scale electronic computers.

In 1946, the ONR began support of the Whirlwind I project at the Massachusetts Institute of Technology (MIT). This project was also under the direction of J. W. Forrester; while on the project he developed, and had operable by 1953, the magnetic-core memory that was to become the standard for all digital computers.

Also in 1946, a project under the cosponsorship of the Army Ordnance Corps and the Office of Naval Research was set up. The project, under the direction of John Von Neumann, was known as the Electronic Computer Project of the Institute for Advanced Study. Four main components—an arithmetic unit, a memory, a control, and an input/output area—were developed for the project machine. These components exist in today's computers.

In 1952, the Naval Research Laboratory of the ONR developed a scientific calculator known as the Naval Research Laboratory Electronic Digital Computer (NAREC). Its primary function was the reduction of experimental data gathered from missile-control research. The internal storage of the machine consisted of electrostatic tubes. Auxiliary storage was provided by a magnetic drum.

The Naval Ordnance Research Calculator (NORC) was developed in a joint effort by the Naval Bureau of Ordnance and IBM in 1954. At the time of its development, the NORC represented the leading edge of technology. It was a one-of-a-kind device that used electrostatic storage tubes and was capable of preforming multiplication in about thirty microseconds, a rate much faster than the six seconds needed by the Mark I to perform a similar calculation. The NORC was used to perform general scientific calculations in ordnance research, development, and testing at the Naval Proving Ground.

Beginning in about 1954, commercially available (mass-produced) computers began to replace one-of-a-kind computers. These machines, which could be adapted to a variety of purposes, began to appear everywhere in naval operations, from shipboard applications to weaponry and base control. As technology advanced, the Navy's use of computers became increasingly sophisticated.

Within this complex technological environment, ONR is searching for innovative concepts to reduce the costs of software development, improve understanding of the hardware-software interface, design automated systems to complement human decision making, improve industrial

productivity, and substitute for human performance in hostile environments. Toward these ends, the ONR Information Sciences Program is currently supporting research activity in the following areas:

1. Software Engineering: Research in software engineering is concerned with designing higher-level languages, providing program correctness, developing algorithms for computations, and developing support for large file systems.

2. Distributed Processing: ONR is studying the problems associated with distributed processing, such as networking problems, allocation of the workload, and security.

3. Computer Architecture: Computer architecture research relates to such factors as automated design and fabrication of digital computer components and provision of new concepts in memory technology.

4. Artificial Intelligence: The area of interest described as artificial intelligence spans the general fields of automated decision making and robotics, including efforts in knowledge representation, common-sense reasoning, natural language and speech understanding, and expert consulting systems. Within the robotics area, research is being performed on the development of machine vision, manipulation, sensing, and control.

In summary, the United States Navy has been operating at the forefront of computer technology for over a quarter of a century and will probably continue to do so. The advent of new technology makes possible increased national security, which is the prime concern of naval operations. The Navy will undoubtedly continue to push the development of computer technology into unexplored areas.

DISCUSSION POINTS

1. The Whirlwind I and NORC are members of which generation of computers? What characteristics place them in that generation?

2. What characteristics of third-generation computers allow them to be used in such advanced applications as aircraft and weaponry control?

SECTION II
Technology

CHAPTER 3

Hardware

Introduction
One can acquire a general understanding of electronic data processing without making a detailed study of the computer technology involved. However, with a basic understanding of how the computer operates, the student of data processing is better equipped to appreciate the computer's capabilities and limitations and to relate this knowledge to data-processing activites.

This chapter focuses on the parts of a computer system. The heart of the computer is the central processing unit, or CPU; its key components are identified and their functions explained. The chapter also examines various forms of primary storage and briefly discusses read-only memory (ROM) and programmable read-only memory (PROM). The chapter concludes with a discussion of how data is represented in ways appropriate for computer processing.

‟Computer Errors from Outer Space"

Dirk Hanson

Warning: Cosmic rays from outer space may be hazardous to the health of your computer. Researchers at Intel and IBM have discovered that subatomic particles can cause a troublesome form of amnesia in high-density computer memory chips. The main culprits are alpha particles emitted by tiny amounts of radium and thorium in the chip package itself, but particles produced when cosmic rays strike silicon chips can have the same effect. If the chip is sensitive enough, these particle-solid interactions trigger a "soft fail."

"It's like a genetic mutation," says Tim May, an Intel physicist who first called attention to the problem in 1978. The burst of electrical charge from a single alpha "can mutate a binary zero into a one, or vice versa. That can cause data loss or can even shut down a system completely." Even home computers are not immune. May calculates that the typical hobbyist microcomputer "has a rate of one soft fail every three weeks or so. No problem. You're likely to cause a failure more often than that by tripping over the power cord."

However, "smart" cash registers and other remote terminals "have been hit rather severely," May says. A big European department store recently scrapped its computerized inventory-control system because soft fails were glitching its sales records. "The most severe implications are for weapons systems," says May. "Soft fails might explain some of the recent instances of data loss in military satellites."

Other victims of the lowly alpha may be bank customers, most of whom depend on computer memories to keep track of their bank accounts.

Omni, September 1980, p. 36. Copyright 1980 by Omni Publications International Limited.

Such computer errors have far-reaching implications, since computers are being integrated into the fabric of our daily lives. This chapter explains how the "insides" of computers function.

DIGITAL AND ANALOG COMPUTERS

When the first section of this book used the term *computer*, it was talking about a specific type—the *digital computer*. However, there are also *analog computers*. It is important to distinguish between these two types.

A digital computer operates on the basis of discrete "on" and "off" states that can be represented by binary digits. The digits can represent numbers, letters, or other distinct symbols in the form of groups of 1s ("on") and 0s ("off"). A digital computer receives input and produces output in the form of these 1 and 0 states. The states used for numbers, letters, and special characters can be represented by holes in punched cards or magnetized areas on tapes or disks. They can be translated to easily recognizable printing on paper.

Digital computers achieve varying degrees of accuracy, depending on their particular construction and machine characteristics. For example, some digital computers can provide results accurate to hundreds or even thousands of decimal places. Such computers are often used in scientific applications. For business applications, results accurate to only a few decimal places are sufficient. Therefore, computer manufacturers build various models of digital computers to meet the varied needs of the ultimate users of these machines.

In contrast to digital computers, analog computers do not operate directly on "on" and "off" states represented by binary digits. Instead, they measure continuous physical or electrical magnitudes such as pressure, temperature, current, voltage, length, or shaft rotations. For example, a gasoline pump contains an analog computer that measures (1) the quantity of gasoline pumped (to the nearest tenth of a gallon) and (2) the price of that gasoline (to the nearest penny). Another example of an analog computer is a car speedometer. Here, driveshaft rotations are measured and converted to a number that indicates the speed of the car. Bussaker's slide rule is an early example of analog calculation.

It is important to note that while numerical results can be obtained from analog computers, they are arrived at indirectly. For this reason, analog computers are less accurate than digital computers. It is not uncommon for a car speedometer to be "off" by one or two miles per hour. Because digital computers are commonly used in the applications discussed in this book, the remainder of the book focuses on digital computers.

CENTRAL PROCESSING UNIT

It is not necessary to acquire a working knowledge of the internal electronic circuitry of a computer in order to use it. However, a basic understanding of computer technology is essential. The simple diagram in Figure 3–1 shows the principal components of a computer system.

The input to a computer can take many forms: data can be entered on magnetic tape, on punched cards, through the pressing of keys on a terminal keyboard, and so on. Representing data on punched cards and entering it into the system through a card reader is a common method. (Input devices will be discussed in greater detail in Chapter 4.)

The *central processing unit (CPU)*, also known as the *main frame*, is the heart of the computer system. It is composed of three units: (1) the control unit; (2) the arithmetic/logic unit (ALU); and (3) the primary storage unit. Each unit performs its own unique functions.

The *control unit*, as its name implies, maintains order and controls activity in the CPU. It does not process or store data. Rather, it directs the sequence

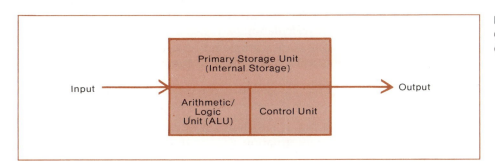

FIGURE 3–1
Computer System Components

of operations. The control unit interprets the instructions of a program in storage and produces signals that act as commands to circuits to execute the instructions. Other functions of the control unit include communicating with an input device in order to begin the transfer of instructions and data into storage and, similarly, communicating with an output device to initiate the transfer of results from storage.

The *arithmetic/logic unit (ALU)* performs arithmetic computations and logical operations. Since the bulk of internal processing involves calculations or comparisons, the capabilities of a computer often depend upon the design and capabilities of its ALU. The ALU does not store data but manipulates it.

The *primary storage unit (internal storage, memory,* or *main storage)* holds instructions, data, and intermediate and final results. At the start of processing, data is transferred from an input device to the primary storage unit, where it is stored until needed for processing. Data being processed and intermediate results of ALU calculations are also stored here. After all computations and manipulations are completed, the final results remain in memory until the control unit causes them to be transferred to an output device.

Among the most widely used of the many types of output devices are: printers, which provide results on paper; visual-display units, which project results on television-like screens; and tape and disk drives, which produce machine-readable magnetic information. (These devices will be discussed in Chapter 4.)

INSTRUCTIONS

Obtaining an **overall perspective** of the functions of each computer system component involves **understanding** the instruction and data flow through a computer system. **A computer** program is a series of instructions. Each computer instruction **has two basic** parts: the operation code and the operand. The *operation code (op code)* tells the control unit what function is to be performed (such as ADD, SUBTRACT, MOVE DATA, or COMPARE). The *operand* indicates the primary storage location of the data to be operated on. (Op codes and operands will be discussed in more detail in Chapter 10.)

The computer performs instructions sequentially unless instructed to do otherwise. This *next-sequential-instruction feature* requires that the instructions that constitute a program be placed in consecutive locations in memory. Since input must be brought into the computer for processing, a separate area must be designated for the input. Output generated by the program also requires an area isolated from the instructions. Figure 3–2 shows this segmentation of memory.

It might be useful to illustrate how all three units interact. Initially, the control unit directs the input device to transfer instructions and data to primary storage. Then the control unit takes one instruction from storage, examines it, and sends appropriate electronic signals to the ALU and to storage, causing the instruction to be carried out. The signals sent to storage may tell it to transfer data to the ALU, where it is mathematically manipulated. The result may then be transferred back to storage.

After execution of an instruction has been initiated, the control unit takes the next instruction from the primary storage unit. Data may be transferred from storage to the ALU and back several times before all instructions are executed. When all manipulations have been completed, the control unit directs the storage unit to transfer the processed data (information) to the output device.

These steps can be summarized as listed below. (Steps B through E are also shown in Figure 3–3.) Notice that computers, like humans, can only execute one instruction at a time. However, they work at incredibly high speeds.

Step A: Instructions and data from the input device are stored in primary storage under direction of the control unit.

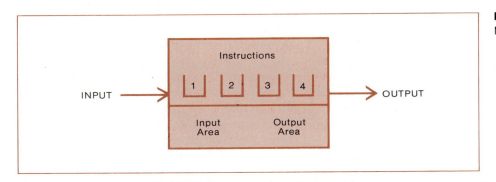

FIGURE 3–2
Memory Segmentation

FIGURE 3–3
CPU Operations

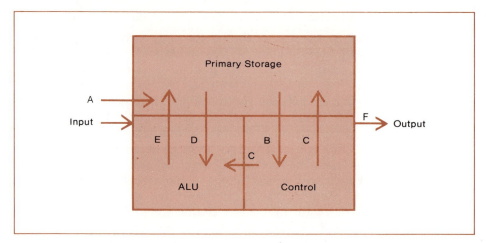

Step B: The control unit examines one instruction and interprets it.

Step C: The control unit sends appropriate electronic signals to the ALU and to primary storage.

Step D: The required data items are transferred to the ALU, where calculations and/or comparisons are performed.

Step E: The result is transferred back to the primary storage unit. Steps B–E are continued until all instructions have been executed.

Step F: The control unit signals the primary storage unit to transfer the results to the output device.

STORED-PROGRAM CONCEPT

A *program* is a series of instructions to direct the computer to perform a given task. In early computers, instructions had to be either wired on control panels and plugged into the computer at the beginning of a job or read into the computer from punched cards in discrete steps as the job progressed. The latter approach slowed down processing because the computer had to wait for instructions to be fed in by a human operator. To speed up processing, the memory of the computer came to be used to store the instructions as well as the data, as explained earlier. This development—the *stored-program* concept—was significant; since the instructions were stored in the computer's memory in electronic form, no human intervention was required during processing. The computer could proceed at its own speed—close to the speed of light!

Most modern computers are stored-program computers. Once the instructions required for a particular application have been determined, they are placed into the computer memory so that the appropriate operations will be performed. The storage unit operates much as a tape recorder does: Once a copy of the instructions and data have been stored, they remain in storage until new instructions and data are stored over them. Therefore, it is possible to execute the same instructions and process the same data, over and over again, until a change is desired. This basic characteristic of memory is known as *nondestructive read/destructive write*. Each series of instructions placed into memory is called a *stored program,* and the person who writes these instructions is called a *programmer*.

STORAGE

Storage Locations and Addresses

In order to direct processing operations, the control unit of the CPU must be able to locate each instruction and data item in storage. Therefore, each location in storage is assigned an address. A simple way to understand this concept is to picture computer storage as a large collection of mailboxes. Each mailbox is a specific location with its own number or address (see Figure 3–4). Each can hold one item of information. Since each location in storage has a unique address, particular items can be located by use of stored-program instructions that give the addresses.

Suppose the computer is to be directed to subtract TAX from GROSS PAY to determine an employee's salary. Suppose further that TAX is stored at location 104 and has a value of 55.60 and that GROSS PAY is stored at location 111 and has a value of 263.00.

To accomplish this task, the programmer instructs the computer to subtract TAX from GROSS PAY. The computer interprets this to mean that it should subtract the contents of location 104 from the contents of location 111. It is easy to see why programmers must keep track of what is stored at each location. They are often aided in this task by the use of *variables—* meaningful names, such as TAX and GROSS PAY, assigned by the programmer to numerical storage addresses. It is easier for the programmer to use such names, and the computer easily translates them into the addresses assigned to storage locations. The term *variable* arises from the fact that while the variable name (the storage address) itself does not change, the

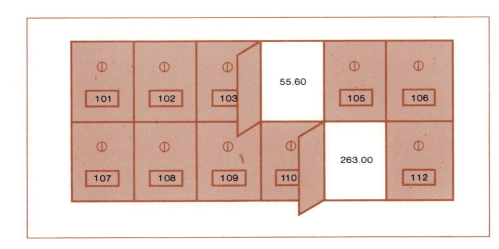

FIGURE 3–4
Each Mailbox
Represents a
Location in Storage
with a
Specific Address

data stored at the location may. The values of TAX and GROSS PAY are likely to change with each employee. The addresses of TAX and GROSS PAY will not.

Primary Storage

Primary storage comprises all storage considered part of the CPU. It may, in some cases, be supplemented by *secondary* (also called *auxiliary,* or *external*) *storage*, which is separate from the CPU. Information is transferred between primary and secondary storage through electrical lines. The most common secondary storage devices are magnetic-tape and magnetic-disk units (secondary storage devices are discussed more fully in Chapter 5).

As mentioned earlier, some primary storage units are composed of magnetic cores. Each core can store one binary digit, or *bit* (short for *BI*nary digi*T*). The core's operation is based upon the principle that a magnetic field is created when electricity flows through a wire (Gauss's Law). The direction of the magnetic field, which depends upon the direction in which the electric current flows, determines which binary state a core represents. Magnetization of a core in a clockwise direction indicates an "on" (1) condition; a counterclockwise direction of magnetization represents an "off" (0) condition (see Figure 3–5).

In the storage unit, many cores are strung on a screen, or plane, of intersecting wires. If enough current were sent down one of the wires to magnetize one particular core, all other cores along that wire would also be magnetized. To prevent this, the computer uses a system of half-currents. That is, half the amount of current required to magnetize a core is sent down one wire; a similar amount of current is sent down a second wire that crosses the first. The core at which the currents intersect receives enough combined current to be magnetized, but all other cores along the two wires are unaffected. Setting cores to store bits, then, is the result of manipulation of electrical half-currents (see Figure 3–6).

The cores in a plane may also be threaded with two other wires (see Figure 3–7). One of them, the *sense wire,* is used to read a core to determine whether it represents a 0-bit or a 1-bit. Since the process of sensing (reading) the core sets it to a 0 state, the *inhibit wire* is used to return the core to a 1 state if it was a 1 when read. Returning the core to its original state insures

FIGURE 3–5

Magnetizing a Core

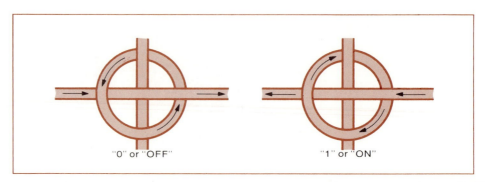

"0" or "OFF"   "1" or "ON"

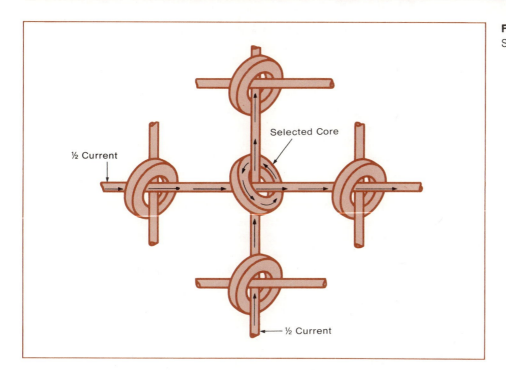

FIGURE 3–6
Selecting a Core

that the read operation does not destroy its content. This is what gives primary storage the nondestructive characteristic discussed earlier. It is essential if the core is to be read several times during processing.

In addition to this four-wire approach, two-wire and three-wire cores are also used. In some systems, the sense and inhibit functions are combined in one wire. In other systems, only the two half-current wires are used, but the same type of bit manipulation takes place.

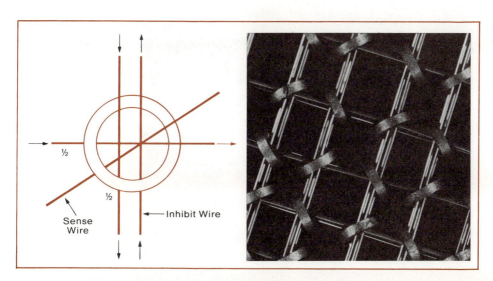

FIGURE 3–7
Four-Wire Core

Technological developments have led to the use of semiconductors in some primary storage units. *Semiconductor memory* is composed of circuitry on *silicon chips*. One silicon chip, only slightly bigger than one core, may hold as much as thousands of cores can. The speed of processing with semiconductors is also significantly faster than that with cores. The main storage of recent computers consists mostly of semiconductors (see Figure 3–8).

Semiconductors are designed to store data in locations called *bit cells*, which are capable of being in either an "on" or an "off" state. As in cores, "on" is represented by a 1, "off" by a 0. The bit cells of a semiconductor are arranged so that they can be written to or read from as needed. They have an inherent nondestructive read capability (since they either do or do not pass current), so there is no need for a restore cycle as with magnetic cores. Even though magnetic core memories have random-access capabilities, the term *RAM (random-access memory)* is generally used to refer to the random-access capability of semiconductors.

One disadvantage of most semiconductor memory units is that they require a constant power source. Since they rely on currents to represent data, all their stored data is lost if the power source fails and no emergency

FIGURE 3–8
This Memory Chip Can
Hold up to 64,000
Pieces of Information

(backup) system exists. (Core memory, on the other hand, retains its contents even if the power source fails because it relies on magnetic charges rather than on currents.) Significant improvements in semiconductor technology have nevertheless increased the popularity of semiconductor memory over core.

Recently, a device called *bubble memory* was introduced as a replacement medium not only for primary storage but also for secondary storage. This memory consists of magnetized spots, or *magnetic domains,* resting on a thin film of semiconductor material. The magnetic domains (called *bubbles*) have a polarity opposite that of the semiconductor material on which they rest. Data is stored by shifting the bubbles' positions on the surface of the material (see Figure 3–9). When data is read, the presence of a bubble indicates a 0 bit. The bubbles are similar to magnetic cores in that they retain their magnetism indefinitely. Bubbles are much smaller than magnetic cores, but more data can be stored in a smaller area. A bubble memory module only slightly larger than a quarter can store 20,000 characters of data.

Some manufacturers have introduced bubble memories in computers; however, a more common use of bubble memories is to provide limited storage capabilities in input/output devices. High cost and difficulty of production have been major factors limiting wide industry and user acceptance of bubbles.

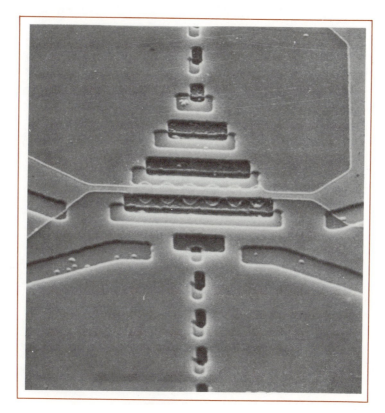

FIGURE 3–9
Bubble Memory
Detector Magnified
1,500 Times

Read-Only Memory (ROM)

Computers are capable of performing complex functions such as taking square roots and evaluating exponents. Such functions can be built into the hardware or software of a computer system. Building them into the hardware provides the advantages of speed and reliability, since the operations are part of the actual computer circuitry. Building them into software allows more flexibility, but carrying out functions built into software is slower and more prone to error.

When functions are built into the hardware of a computer, they are placed in *read-only memory (ROM)*. Read-only memory instructions are *hard-wired;* that is, they cannot be changed or deleted by other stored-program instructions. Since ROM is permanent, it cannot be occupied by common stored-program instructions or data. The only method of changing its contents is by altering the physical construction of the circuits.

A direct result of this characteristic is *microprogramming. Microprograms* are sequences of instructions built into read-only memory to carry out functions (such as calculating square roots) that otherwise would have to be directed by stored-program instructions at a much lower speed. Microprograms are usually supplied by computer manufacturers and cannot be altered by users. However, microprogramming allows the basic operations of the computer to be tailored to meet the needs of users. If all instructions that a computer can

FIGURE 3–10

Microcomputer with CPU Chip, ROM Chip, and RAM Chip

execute are located in ROM, a complete new set of instructions can be obtained by changing the ROM. When selecting a computer, users can get the standard features of the machine plus their choice of the optional features available through microprogramming. Many minicomputers and microcomputers today are directed by instructions stored in ROM (see Figure 3–10).

A point worth emphasizing is that the concept of read-only memory is entirely different from that of nondestructive read. With nondestructive read, items in memory can be read repeatedly without loss of information; however, the contents of memory can be altered by reading in new values to replace old ones as directed by stored-program instructions. Read-only memory can be changed solely by rewiring.

A version of ROM that can be programmed by the end user is *programmable read-only memory (PROM)*. PROM can be programmed by the manufacturer, or it can be shipped "blank" to the end user for programming. Once programmed, its contents are unalterable. Thus, PROM can be programmed through conventional methods, but only one time. PROM enables the end user to have the advantages of ROM along with some flexibility to meet unique needs. A problem with it, though, is that mistakes programmed into the unit cannot be corrected. To overcome this drawback, *erasable programmable read-only memory* (EPROM) has been developed (see Figure 3–11). This memory unit can be erased, but only by being submitted to a special process, such as being bathed in ultraviolet light.

FIGURE 3–11
An EPROM

Registers

Registers are devices that facilitate the execution of instructions by acting as temporary holding areas for instructions and data. They are located in the CPU but are not considered part of primary storage. Registers can receive information, hold it, and transfer it very quickly as directed by the control unit of the CPU.

A register functions much as a standard pocket calculator does. The person using the calculator acts as the control unit by transferring numbers from a sheet of paper to the calculator. This paper is analogous to the primary storage unit of the CPU. When the calculation is complete, the calculator displays the result. The person (control unit) then transfers the result displayed on the calculator (register) back to the sheet of paper (primary storage). This process is very similar to the way most modern computers work. Intermediate calculations are performed in registers, and the final results are transferred back to primary storage.

There are various types of registers. Some perform specific functions and are named according to the functions they perform. For example, an *accumulator* is a register that accumulates results of computations (like summations). A *storage register* holds information being sent to or taken from the primary storage unit. During program execution, each instruction is transferred to an *instruction register*, where it is decoded by the control unit. The address of a data item called for by an instruction is kept in an *address register*. Some computers do not have registers with specific uses but instead have *general-purpose registers*, which can be used for both arithmetic and addressing functions.

The numbers and sizes of registers in computers vary. Their purpose however, is the same; they are used as temporary storage areas to facilitate the transfer of data and instructions within the CPU.

DATA REPRESENTATION

Humans communicate information by using symbols that have specific meanings. Symbols such as letters or numbers are combined in meaningful ways to represent information. For example, the twenty-six letters of the English alphabet can be combined to form words, sentences, paragraphs, and so on. By combining the individual words in various ways, we construct various messages. This enables us to communicate with one another.

The human mind is much more complex than the computer. A computer is only a machine; it is not capable of understanding the inherent meanings of symbols used by humans to communicate. To use a computer, therefore, humans must convert their symbols to a form the computer is capable of "understanding." This is accomplished through binary representation and the "on" and "off" states discussed earlier.

Binary Representation

Data is represented in the computer by the electrical state of the machine's circuitry—magnetic states for core storage, current for semiconductor storage, and the position of magnetic bubbles for bubble memory. In all cases, only two states are possible, "on" and "off." This two-state system is known as a *binary system,* and its use to represent data is known as *binary representation.*

The *binary (base 2) number system* operates in a manner similar to the way the familiar *decimal number system* works. For example, the decimal number 4,672 can be analyzed as follows:

```
4  6  7  2
│  │  │  └──→ 2 × 10⁰ =      2    or    4    6    7    2
│  │  └─────→ 7 × 10¹ =     70
│  └────────→ 6 × 10² =    600          │    │    │    │
└───────────→ 4 × 10³ =   4000         10³  10²  10¹  10⁰
                          ────
                          4672
```

Each position represents a certain power of 10. The progression of powers is from right to left; that is, digits further to the left in a decimal number represent larger powers of 10 than digits to the right of them.

10^5	10^4	10^3	10^2	10^1	10^0
100,000	10,000	1,000	100	10	1

FIGURE 3–12
Decimal Place Values

The same principle holds for binary representation. The difference is that in binary representation each position in the number represents a power of 2. For example, consider the decimal number 14. In binary, the value equivalent to 14 is written as follows:

```
1  1  1  0
│  │  │  └──→ 0 × 2⁰ =  0        1    1    1    0
│  │  └─────→ 1 × 2¹ =  2
│  └────────→ 1 × 2² =  4    or  │    │    │    │
└───────────→ 1 × 2³ =  8       2³   2²   2¹   2⁰
                       ──
                       14
```

2^6	2^5	2^4	2^3	2^2	2^1	2^0
64	32	16	8	4	2	1

FIGURE 3–13
Binary Place Values

As further example, the value represented by the decimal number 300 is represented in binary form below:

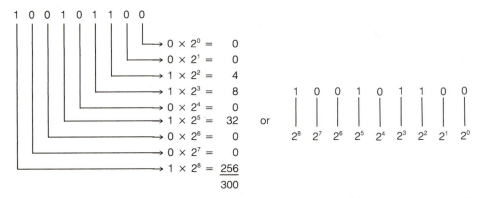

1 0 0 1 0 1 1 0 0

$0 \times 2^0 = 0$
$0 \times 2^1 = 0$
$1 \times 2^2 = 4$
$1 \times 2^3 = 8$
$0 \times 2^4 = 0$
$1 \times 2^5 = 32$
$0 \times 2^6 = 0$
$0 \times 2^7 = 0$
$1 \times 2^8 = 256$
$\overline{300}$

or

1 0 0 1 0 1 1 0 0
2^8 2^7 2^6 2^5 2^4 2^3 2^2 2^1 2^0

As indicated by the examples above, the binary number system uses 1s and 0s in various combinations to represent various values. Each digit position in a binary number is called a *bit*, as defined previously. A 1 in a bit position indicates the presence of a specific power of 2; a 0 indicates the absence of a specific power. As in the decimal number system, the progression of powers is from right to left.

Octal Number System

Many small computers today use octal numbers for representing data. In the *octal (base 8) number system*, the digits 0 to 7 are used, and each position represents a power of 8. Conversions using this system are performed in the same manner as those for binary numbers.

The octal number 1,702 is equivalent to the decimal number 962. Consider the conversion below, keeping in mind that each digit of the octal number represents a power of 8.

1 7 0 2

$2 \times 8^0 = 2$
$0 \times 8^1 = 0$
$7 \times 8^2 = 448$
$1 \times 8^3 = 512$
$\overline{962}$

or

1 7 0 2
8^3 8^2 8^1 8^0

For another example, the value represented by the decimal number 10,000 is displayed in octal form below:

2 3 4 2 0

$0 \times 8^0 = 0$
$2 \times 8^1 = 16$
$4 \times 8^2 = 256$
$3 \times 8^3 = 1,536$
$2 \times 8^4 = 8,192$
$\overline{10,000}$

or

2 3 4 2 0
8^4 8^3 8^2 8^1 8^0

Hexadecimal Number System

When a program fails to execute correctly, it is sometimes necessary to examine the contents of certain memory locations to discover what went wrong. In such cases, the programmer often finds it useful to have a printout, or *dump,* of the contents of the memory locations (see Figure 3–14). If everything were printed in binary representation, the programmer would be staring at pages upon pages of 1s and 0s. Detection of the error would be difficult.

To alleviate this problem, the contents of storage locations in 16-bit, 32-bit, 48-bit, or 64-bit computers can be represented by symbols of the *hexadecimal (base 16) number system.* This *hexadecimal representation* is convenient for several reasons: (1) the conversion from binary to hexadecimal is much easier and faster than the conversion from binary to decimal; (2) hexadecimal numbers are much easier to read than binary numbers; and (3) significant savings of both paper and time are possible when the contents of storage are printed in hexadecimal rather than binary notation—the equivalent of a twelve-page binary dump is only three pages long in hexadecimal.

In the hexadecimal number system, sixteen symbols are used to represent the digits 0 through 15 (see Figure 3–15). Note that the letters A through F designate the numbers 10 through 15. The fact that each position in a hexadecimal number represents a power of 16 allows for easy conversion from binary to hexadecimal, since 16 is equal to 2^4. A single hexadecimal digit can be used to represent four binary digits.

Computer Codes

Many computers use coding schemes other than simple binary notation to represent numbers. One of the most basic coding schemes is called *4-bit binary coded decimal (BCD).* Rather than represent a decimal number as a

```
9000D203  9000C11E  41330004  4650C05A
0010E020  C1220064  E020C186  006407FE
40F0F740  40F0F840  4040F540  40F2F340
40404040  40404040  40F2F340  40F2F340
40F4F640  40F2F540  40F1F240  40F2F440
4040F640  40F6F640  40F8F540  40404040
40F0F840  40F2F540  40F3F140  4040F540
F2F5F640  F7F8F940  F1F2F540  F6F2F440
00000005  00000005  00000006  00000007
0000000F  00000010  00000015  00000017
00000018  00000018  00000019  00000019
00000035  00000035  00000037  00000038
00000055  00000055  00000060  0000007D
0000022B  0000022B  0000022B  0000022B
0000022B  00000315  F0E3C8C5  40E4D5E2
E2D6D9E3  C5C440C1  D9D9C1E8  F1F5F5F5
F5F5F5F5  F5F5F5F5  F5F5F5F5  F5F5F5F5
F5F5F5F5  F5F5F5F5  F5F5F5F5  F5F5F5F5
```

FIGURE 3–14
Core Dump

FIGURE 3–15
Binary, Hexadecimal,
and Decimal
Equivalent Values

BINARY SYSTEM (PLACE VALUES)				HEXADECIMAL EQUIVALENT	DECIMAL EQUIVALENT
8	4	2	1		
0	0	0	0	0	0
0	0	0	1	1	1
0	0	1	0	2	2
0	0	1	1	3	3
0	1	0	0	4	4
0	1	0	1	5	5
0	1	1	0	6	6
0	1	1	1	7	7
1	0	0	0	8	8
1	0	0	1	9	9
1	0	1	0	A	10
1	0	1	1	B	11
1	1	0	0	C	12
1	1	0	1	D	13
1	1	1	0	E	14
1	1	1	1	F	15

string of 0s and 1s (which gets increasingly complicated for large numbers), BCD represents each decimal digit in a number by using four bits. For instance, the decimal number 23 is represented by two groups of four bits, one group for the "2," the other for the "3." Representations of the number 23 in 4-bit BCD and in binary are compared below:

```
0 0 1 0     0 0 1 1
|_____|   |_____|        4-bit BCD

   2           3
0000000000010111              Binary
```

The representation of a three-digit decimal number in 4-bit BCD consists of three sets of four bits, or twelve binary digits. For example, the decimal number 637 is coded as follows:

```
0 1 1 0     0 0 1 1     0 1 1 1
|_____|   |_____|   |_____|      4-bit BCD

   6           3           7
0000001001111101                        Binary
```

Use of 4-bit BCD saves space when large decimal numbers must be represented. Furthermore, it is easier to convert a 4-bit BCD to its decimal equivalent than to convert a binary representation to decimal.

The 4-bit code allows sixteen (2^4) possible unique bit combinations. We have already seen that ten of them are used to represent the decimal digits

COLOR INSET
A Tour of a
Computer Facility

Top left: A receptionist area permits monitoring of all individuals seeking to enter the computer facility. *Lower left:* The receptionist checks for proper authorization before permitting entry. *Top right:* Only authorized individuals may approach the locked computer facility. *Lower right:* Only specially coded cards will unlock the door.

Right: CRT consoles directly interconnected to the central processing units. *Below:* Operators communicating with the operating systems.

Left: Magnetic tape drive units.
Below: One of the central processing units with console interconnected in a multiprocessing system.

Right: A library storage facility for magnetic tapes.
Below: Computerized inventory control for the tape library.

Left: Magnetic disk drives. *Middle:* Magnetic disk units that resemble pizza ovens. *Bottom:* High-speed line printer.

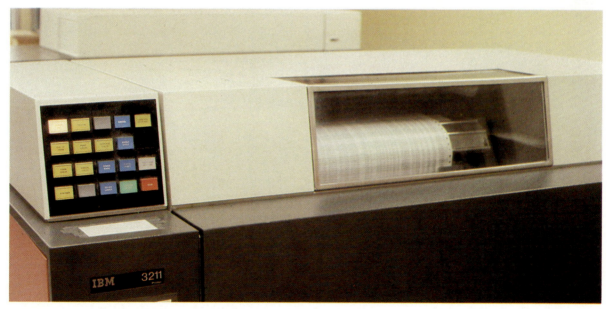

IBM 3211

Right: Front-end processor for controlling the communication system. *Below:* Patch panel and monitoring equipment for telecommunication system.

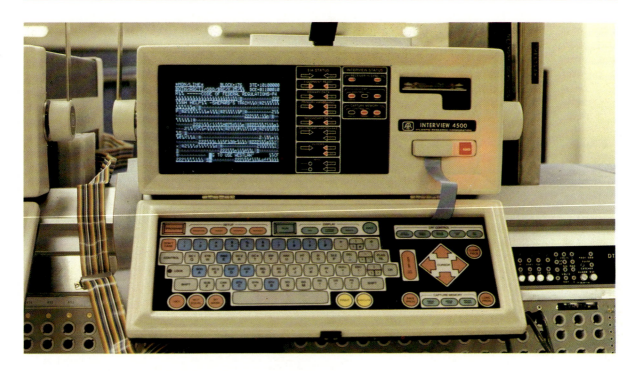

Above: A line tester to monitor the communication system. *Left:* Modems for the telecommunication system.

Right: Air conditioning unit controls.
Lower right: Controller for magnetic disk units (note fire warning lights).
Lower left: Fire control panels.

ZONE BITS		NUMERIC BITS			
A	B	8	4	2	1

FIGURE 3–16
Bit Positions in 6-Bit BCD Representation

0 through 9. Since that leaves only six remaining combinations, this code in practice is used only to represent numbers.

To represent letters and special characters as well as numbers, more than four bit positions are needed. Another coding scheme, called *6-bit BCD*, allows for sixty-four (2^6) unique bit combinations. Thus, 6-bit BCD can be used to represent the decimal digits 0 through 9, the letters A through Z, and twenty-eight characters, such as the period and the comma.

The four rightmost bit positions in 6-bit BCD are called *numeric bits*. The two leftmost bit positions are called *zone bits* (see Figure 3–16). The zone bits are used in various combinations with the numeric bits to represent numbers, letters, and special characters.

Another approach to data representation is an 8-bit code known as *Extended Binary Coded Decimal Interchange Code (EBCDIC)*. An 8-bit code allows 256 (2^8) possible bit combinations. Whereas 6-bit BCD can be used to represent only uppercase letters, 8-bit EBCDIC can be used to represent uppercase and lowercase letters and additional special characters, such as the cent sign and the quotation mark. The EBCDIC bit combinations for uppercase letters and numbers are given in Figure 3–17.

In EBCDIC, the four leftmost bit positions are zone bits, and the four rightmost bit positions are numeric bits. As with 6-bit BCD, the zone bits

Character	EBCDIC Bit Configuration	Character	EBCDIC Bit Configuration
A	1100 0001	S	1110 0010
B	1100 0010	T	1110 0011
C	1100 0011	U	1110 0100
D	1100 0100	V	1110 0101
E	1100 0101	W	1110 0110
F	1100 0110	X	1110 0111
G	1100 0111	Y	1110 1000
H	1100 1000	Z	1110 1001
I	1100 1001	0	1111 0000
J	1101 0001	1	1111 0001
K	1101 0010	2	1111 0010
L	1101 0011	3	1111 0011
M	1101 0100	4	1111 0100
N	1101 0101	5	1111 0101
O	1101 0110	6	1111 0110
P	1101 0111	7	1111 0111
Q	1101 1000	8	1111 1000
R	1101 1001	9	1111 1001

FIGURE 3–17
EBCDIC Representation: 0–9, A–Z

are used in various combinations with the numeric bits to represent numbers, letters, and special characters.

The *American Standard Code for Information Interchange (ASCII)* is a 7-bit code developed through the cooperation of several computer manufacturers whose objective was to develop a standard code for all computers. Because certain machines are designed to accept 8-bit rather than 7-bit code patterns, an 8-bit version of ASCII, called *ASCII-8* was created. ASCII-8 and EBCDIC are similar, the key difference between them being in the bit patterns used to represent certain characters.

Bits, as described, are very small units of data; it is often useful to combine them into larger units. A fixed number of adjacent bits operated on as a unit is called a *byte*. Usually, one alphabetic character or two numeric characters are represented in one byte. Since eight bits are sufficient to represent any character, 8-bit groupings are the basic units of memory. In computers that accept 8-bit characters then, a byte is a group of eight adjacent bits. When large amounts of storage are described, the symbol K is often used. Generally, one K equals 1,024 (2^{10}) units. Thus, a computer that has 256K bytes of storage can store 256 × 1,024, or 262,144, characters.

CHECK BIT	ZONE BITS		NUMERIC BITS			
C	B	A	8	4	2	1

FIGURE 3–18
Bit Positions of 6-Bit BCD with Check Bit

Code Checking

Computers do not always function perfectly; errors can and do occur. For example, a bit may be lost while data is being transferred from the ALU to the primary storage unit or over telephone lines from one location to another. This loss can be caused by dust, moisture, magnetic fields, equipment failure, or other things. Thus, it is necessary to have a method to detect when an error has occurred and to isolate the location of the error.

To accomplish this task, most computers have at each storage location an additional bit, called a *parity bit*, or *check bit*. Computers that use parity bits are specifically designed always to have either an even or an odd number of 1- (or "on") bits in each storage location. Regardless of the type of code used, if an odd number of 1-bits is used to represent each character, the characters are said to be written in *odd parity*. Similarly, if an even number of 1-bits is used to represent each character, the characters are written in *even parity*. Internal circuitry in the computer constantly monitors its operation by checking to ensure that the required number of bits is present in each location.

For example, if the 6-bit BCD code is used, a seventh bit is added as a check bit (see Figure 3–18). Suppose the number 6 is to be represented in 6-bit BCD using odd parity (see Figure 3–19). In this case, the check bit must be set to 1, or "on," to make the number of 1-bits odd. If a parity error is detected, the system may retry the read or write operation occurring when the error was detected. If retries are unsuccessful, the system informs the computer operator that an error has occurred.

Notice that the checking circuitry of the computer can only detect the miscoding of characters. It cannot detect the use of incorrect data. In the previous example, for instance, the computer circuitry could determine whether a bit had been dropped, making the representation of the number 6 invalid. However, if the number 5 had been mistakenly entered into the computer instead of 6 (say, because of incorrect keying of a card), no error would have been detected.

	C	B	A	8	4	2	1
Valid — →	1	0	0	0	1	1	0
Invalid— ←	1	0	0	0	0	1	0

FIGURE 3–19
Detection of Error with Parity Check (Odd Parity).

SUMMARY

● Computers are usually classified as either digital or analog. Digital computers operate on distinct symbols (decimal numbers, letters, and the like) and are the computers commonly used in business applications. Analog computers measure continuous physical or electrical magnitudes such as pressure, temperature, current, or voltage and are less accurate than digital computers.

● The central processing unit, the heart of the computer, is composed of three units: the primary storage unit, the arithmetic-logic unit (ALU), and the control unit. The control unit maintains order and controls what is happening in the CPU; the ALU performs arithmetic and logical operations; and the primary storage unit holds all data and instructions necessary for processing.

● Instructions are placed in consecutive locations in memory so that they can be accessed consecutively. This is called the next-sequential-instruction feature.

● The stored-program concept involves storing both data and instructions in the computer's memory, thus eliminating the need for human intervention during processing.

● The nondestructive read/destructive write characteristic of memory allows a program to be re-executed, since the program remains intact in memory until another is stored over it. The computer executes instructions sequentially (as accessed in consecutive locations in memory) unless instructed to do otherwise.

● Each location in storage has a unique address, which allows stored-program instructions and data items to be located by the control unit of the CPU as it directs processing operations. Variables—names for storage addresses—are often used by programmers to facilitate data location.

● One method of storing data in primary storage uses electrical currents to set magnetic cores to "on" and "off" states. Another form of storage is semiconductor memory, which uses circuitry on silicon chips. Semiconductor units are smaller and faster than cores, but they usually demand a constant power source. Bubble memory consists of magnetized spots that rest on a thin film of semiconductor material. These bubbles retain their magnetism indefinitely and have the ability to store much more data in a smaller space than core memory.

● Read-only memory (ROM), part of the hardware of a computer, stores items in a form that can be deleted or changed only by rewiring. Microprograms are sequences of instructions built into read-only memory to carry out functions that otherwise would be directed by stored-program instructions at a much lower speed.

● Programmable read-only memory (PROM), can be either programmed by the manufacturer, or can be programmed by users to meet unique needs. Thus, it provides greater flexibility and versatility than ROM.

● Registers are devices that facilitate the execution of instructions. They act as temporary holding areas and are capable of receiving information, holding it, and transferring it very quickly as directed by the control unit of the CPU.

● Data representation in the computer is based on a two-state, or binary, system. A 1 in a given position indicates the presence of a power of 2; a 0 indicates its absence. The 4-bit binary coded decimal (BCD) system uses groups of four binary digits to represent the decimal digits 0 through 9. The 6-bit BCD system allows for sixty-four unique bit combinations; alphabetic, numeric, and twenty-eight special characters can be represented. Both EBCDIC and ASCII-8 are 8-bit coding systems and are capable of representing up to 256 different characters.

● Octal (base 8) representation is used on many small computers.

● Hexadecimal (base 16) notation can be used to represent binary data in a concise form. For this reason, the contents of computer memory are sometimes printed in hexadecimal. Programmers use such printouts to locate errors.

● Parity bits, or check bits, are used to detect errors in the transmission of data.

REVIEW QUESTIONS

1. Distinguish between analog and digital computers, giving examples of each.
2. Name the three major components of the CPU and discuss the function of each.
3. Explain what is meant by the stored-program concept and show why it is significant to electronic data processing.
4. What technological developments have occurred in primary storage media and what impact have these developments had on modern computers?
5. Explain the concept of read-only memory. How does it relate to micro-programming?
6. Why are computer codes necessary? What advantages does EBCDIC offer over 6-bit BCD?
7. Why are concepts of the binary number system important to an understanding of digital computers? What relationship does the hexadecimal number system have to the binary system? How are the octal system and the hexadecimal system related?
8. What is the next-sequential-instruction feature?

APPLICATION

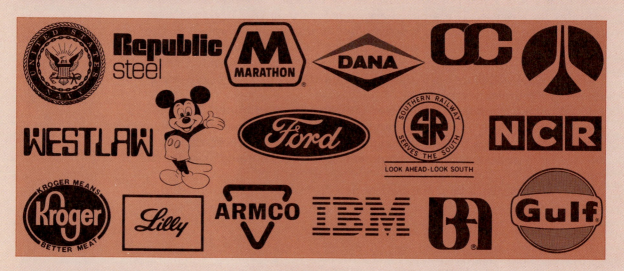

IBM

In the 1880s, Herman Hollerith developed a mechanical method of processing census data for the United States Bureau of the Census. His method included two devices: one that coded population data as punched holes in cards, and another that sensed the data. The success of his method led Hollerith to form his own company in 1896 to manufacture and sell these devices. In 1911, the company became part of the Computing-Tabulating-Recording (CTR) Company, which manufactured commercial scales and tabulating and time-recording equipment. In 1924 CTR became the International Business Machines (IBM) Corporation.

Today IBM is a leader of the worldwide data-processing community and is the leading vendor of main-frame computers. IBM's General Systems Division is the second largest producer of small computers. IBM's products include data-processing machines and systems, information processors, electric typewriters, copiers, dictation equipment, educational and testing materials, and related supplies and services. Most products can be either leased or purchased through IBM's worldwide marketing organizations.

IBM's major business is information handling. IBM computers range from small, powerful minicomputers to ultra-high-performance computers for high-speed, large-scale scientific and commercial applications. The wide range of computer applications in scientific, industrial, and commercial areas today requires machines of different sizes and capabilities. For example, a computer used to forecast the weather has capabilities different from those of a computer used mainly for payroll processing. Consequently, computers with similar characteristics are usually grouped together into a family, series, or system. The family members differ from each other in terms of range of available memory, number of input-output channels, execution speed, and types of devices with which interface can be established.

For example, IBM's Series/1 is a family of low-cost, versatile, small computers. These computers are modular—that is, the user can acquire as much or as little processing power as needed. The Series/1 includes two processor versions. One, the 4952 processor, is available in three models. All offer 32K to 128K bytes of primary storage. Data can be transferred through input-output channels at a rate of 832,000 bytes per second, and the processor has a cycle time of 2,100 nanoseconds. The 4952 Model C processor offers the same functional capabilities and contains an integrated diskette drive.

The second version of processors for the Series/1 is the 4955 processor, which is available in four models. Primary storage capacities range from 32K to 512K bytes. The I/O channel rate is 1,650,000 bytes per second, and the cycle time is 660 nanoseconds. In addition, several optional devices and functions are available, such as an input-output expansion unit, a floating point processor, and a programmer console. Users can choose from many hardware attachments and support units. Disk storage units are offered in varying sizes, all nonremovable. Diskette storage units provide a removable direct-access medium. Five display station models and five printer models are available, most of them controlled by their own microprocessors. The 4955 version offers 3 to 3.5 times the internal performance of the 4952 version.

IBM also offers software to accompany the Series/1. Like the hardware, it is modular. The Series/1 was designed to facilitate extensive

communication networks as well. Several processors and terminals may be tied together and share the same data. The Series/1 can also be used as a "front-end processor," or a link between a variety of peripherals and a central, or host, computer. The modular design and great flexibility of the Series/1 provides users of all types and sizes with a number of data-processing alternatives. Areas of application for the Series/1 include distributed processing (where there is a need for data entry, remote job entry, and inquiries to files); commercial applications (such as billing, inventory control, and sales analysis); sensor-based applications (material and component testing, machine and process control, and shop floor control); and graphics.

In comparison, IBM's System/ 370 is a family of general-purpose large computers

readily adaptable to a large number of applications. (Its predecessor, System/360, also a multipurpose system of computers was named "360" to indicate ability to handle the "full circle" of applications.) The System/370's eleven processor models all have certain characteristics in common. Data can be transferred in blocks ranging in size from eight to sixty-four bits (one to eight bytes). The System/370 has the capability of addressing as many as 16,777,216 bytes of storage.

The System/370 models' main storage capacities vary from 65,536 bytes to 8,388,608 bytes (in comparison with the Series/1 scale, 32,768 to 524,288 byte capacities.) Model 168, designed for large-scale high-speed scientific and commercial applications, has the largest main storage capacity. Its scientific

TABLE 3–1

Major IBM Computers

SERIES	MODELS	DATE INTRODUCED	COMMENTS
700	701	1953	Vacuum tubes
	702		
	704		Magnetic core
	705		
Type 650		1954	Magnetic-drum machine
1400	1401	1960	
	1410		Oriented to business
7000	7070	1960	Transistors, business-oriented
	7074		Scientific-oriented
1620		1960	Scientific-oriented, decimal minicomputer
1130		1962	Integrated circuits, small, special-purpose
1800		1963	Integrated circuits, small, special-purpose
360	20	1965	
	25		
	30		
	40		
	44		Systems designed for all
	50		purposes—business and
	65		scientific
	67		
	75		
	85		
	90		
	91		
System/7		1970	Replacement for 1800
System/3		1969	Midi/small computer
370	115	1973	
	125		IBM's most popular
	135		system—extends capabilities of
	138		System/360
	145		
	148		
	158		
	168		
	3031	1977	IBM's most powerful processors
	3032		
	3033		
	3081	1980	
System/32		1975	Small system for business
System/34		1977	Small multiple-work station for business
Series/1		1976	Versatile small computer for experienced users
System/38		1978	Powerful, general purpose supporting extensive data bases
5100		1975	Portable computer
5110		1978	Small business computer
5120		1980	Small business system
5520		1979	Administrative office system
Datamaster		1981	Small system with data, word processing
Personal Computer		1981	Microcomputer for home and office

applications range from nuclear physics and theoretical astronomy to weather forecasting. The Model 168 can be used commercially as the control center of complex airline reservation systems, coast-to-coast time-sharing networks, and process-control systems. The power and speed of these advance systems are primarily the result of improved circuit technology. The machine cycle time of the System 370 devices is as fast as is eighty nanoseconds, eight times faster than that of the Series/1 computers.

The new IBM 3081 is IBM's most powerful processor. With faster internal cycle time and up to thirty-two million characters of high-speed main storage, it is meant for users with sizable data storage and data communication requirements. Three additional high-performance processors, the IBM 3031, 3032, and 3033 are appropriate for users who need increased speed and capacity but not to the extent provided by the IBM 3081. All four processors are compatible members of the System/370 family.

One of IBM's latest advances is the System/38 family, a general-purpose, data-processing system that supports both interactive (where the user can communicate with the computer and receive a response) and batch applications. Since the System/38 is designed as a growth system for some of IBM's previous computers, especially the System/3 and System 34 conversion techniques have been developed to allow the user to convert to the new System/38 with as little reconstruction as possible.

The unique aspect of the System/38 is its use of a high-level "architecture" that involves a new use of hardware technology. The actual hardware is separated from the instruction set by two layers of microprogramming. Storage capacities range from 524,288 bytes to 2,097,152 bytes of primary storage. The System/38 is capable of translating secondary-storage addresses to main storage addresses.

The System/38 is composed of a processing unit, main storage, disk storage, console display, diskette drive, and optional I/O and communications facilities. One of the optional I/O devices is the IBM 5250 Information Display System, which consists of several models of display stations and printers.

Finally, the IBM 5520 Administrative System, is an office system that integrates shared logic and resource characteristics. It is compatible with System/370 communications and data bases. It features text processing, and document distribution. Through the text-processing functions, users can create, revise, share, print, and store documents. The file processing function can merge fields from one or two files with text to create reports or repetitive letters. Arithmetic expressions, if/else logic, record update, and multiple stored procedures provide a data-processing-like function for administrative users. The document distribution feature provides the capability to forward documents to other offices in the same building or across the country. There are four models, which differ in processing power and the amount of fixed and auxiliary storage supported. The 5520 is compatible with the System/370 model data bases, which allows for a very efficient method of controlling information and processing within an office system network.

Table 3–1 summarizes the major IBM series and their various models. As data-processing requirements have expanded, hardware capabilities such as those provided by IBM have been developed to provide the necessary support.

DISCUSSION POINTS

1. What characteristics do computers within a family have in common? How do family members within a series differ from each other?
2. Name some important hardware characteristics that must be considered when a computer is selected. How do these characteristics relate to processing requirements?

CHAPTER 4

Data Entry/Information Response

Introduction

A computer system is much more than a central processing unit. Auxiliary devices enter data into and receive output from the CPU. Data input and information output are important activities in any computer-based system, because they are the communication links between people and the machine. If these people/machine interfaces are weak, the overall performance of the computer system suffers accordingly.

This chapter describes the primary media used for computer input—punched cards, magnetic tape, and magnetic disks. In addition, the chapter looks at the growing field of source-data automation. Printers, the basic media for computer output, as well as special-purpose output devices, are also discussed. The chapter concludes with a look at I/0 control units and channels.

❝Digitization Revolutionizes Cartography❞

Robert Reinhold

The science of map making is undergoing its most profound revolution since Christopher Columbus proved that the world was not shaped like a platter.

Roads, rivers, contour lines, and other map features are being converted into millions of numbers which can be stored, manipulated, and printed out by computer.

"Digitization" has opened the way to many new uses of maps and, indeed, has begun to blur the distinction between maps—which are nothing more than graphic representations of information—and other kinds of data.

"Computer-assisted cartography is revolutionizing map making," Rupert Southard, Jr., chief of the U.S. Geological Survey's national mapping division, says. "Strangely, it may not result in more paper maps; it may be that maps will

New York Times Service © 1980 by The New York Times Company. Reprinted by permission.

become documents that help you remember how it was, and we'll use computers to look at how it is."

Digitized "maps" created by the Defense Mapping Agency are used by the military in targeting, navigation, and pilot training.

The Geological Survey is developing a data bank called the National Coal Resource Data System. Information on the location of coal deposits will be combined with digitized data on terrain and elevations (important to knowing how much earth must be lifted in mining), transportation patterns, land ownership, and so on.

The idea, Mr. Southard says, is to provide users with a vast data bank that would allow them, at the push of a button, to create customized maps, at whatever scale and with whatever features wanted. This would relieve them of relying on the available printed maps.

The Geological Survey used the new techniques to study changes in the Mount St. Helens volcano after it exploded. Mr. Southard

suggests that the Forest Service might use digital terrain information to determine what kind of view visitors to a national forest might get if all trees above a certain line were cut.

It is such a marriage of data bases that holds the payoff for digital cartography, offering "an almost explosive array of opportunities for use of data," in Mr. Southard's words.

His agency plans to build a basic digital data bank that will include national data for land characteristics, such as elevation, water bodies, vegetation, political boundaries, transportation systems, buildings, airports, dams.

Thus, someone interested in, say, drainage patterns only in a certain region could call up that particular information, screening out all other data, and superimpose his own information on the resulting map.

"We can consider all sorts of data sets: location of wells, water quality, even social data like motherless homes or outbreaks of cervical cancer," Mr. Southard says.

Digitizing the data in maps may facilitate the management of scarce land resources. Other means of input and output are discussed in this chapter.

DATA INPUT

Punched Cards

Punched cards were used in data processing long before the digital computer was developed, as we saw in Chapter 2. Today punched cards serve not only as a means of entering data into computers but also as user-oriented documents—time cards, bills, invoices, checks, and the like.

Punched-card processing involves two steps. Data must first be recorded on the cards, after which the encoded cards are processed.

Data Representation   The standard punched card has eighty vertical columns and twelve horizontal rows (see Figure 4–1). It is appropriately called an *eighty-column punched card,* or a *Hollerith card,* after its developer Herman Hollerith. Each column can contain a single letter, number, or special character. Data is recorded as holes punched in a particular column to represent a given character. The pattern of holes used to represent characters is known as the *Hollerith code.*

The eighty-column punched card is divided horizontally into three sections. The lower ten rows, numbers 0 through 9, are called *digit rows;* they can be used to represent any digit from 0 through 9. The upper three rows, numbered 12, 11, and 0, are called *zone rows.* (The 0 row is both a digit row and a zone row.) Zone punches can be combined with digit punches in the same column to represent alphabetic and special characters. The third section (at the very top of the card), called the print zone, displays the actual character punched into a card column in a form easily read by humans.

For instance, in Figure 4–1, the number 6 in column 21 is represented by a punch in the digit row 6; to represent a number, then, a hole is punched in the appropriate digit row. To represent letters or special characters, one zone punch is used in combination with one or two numeric punches.

When punched cards are used, data is generally grouped together and punched in specific columns on the cards. A group of related characters treated as a single unit of information is called a *field* and is composed of a group of consecutive columns (see Figure 4–2). A field may be from one to eighty characters in length. Related fields are stored on the same card if possible.

When one punched card contains all the necessary data about a transaction, it is said to be a *unit record*—a complete record. Figure 4–2 illustrates a unit record—a card containing all data pertaining to the sale of a particular item.

The eighty-column limitation of the Hollerith card presents major disadvantages to the establishing of unit records. First of all, when records require more than eighty columns, two or more cards must be used. This hinders processing of the cards, since punched-card machines are designed to operate on only one card at a time. Second, when less than an entire card is needed for a record, the remaining space is left unused and thus wasted.

A second type of punched card is used by IBM in its System/3 series and in some small computers of other manufacturers. This card has ninety-six columns but is smaller than the Hollerith card (see Figure 4–3). The ninety-six column punched card is divided into two areas. The bottom part of the card is the *punch area;* the upper part is the *print area.* The punch area is divided into three equal thirty-two column, horizontal sections called *tiers.* There are six punch positions in each column of a tier. Various characters are represented by various combinations of punches in the columns. The

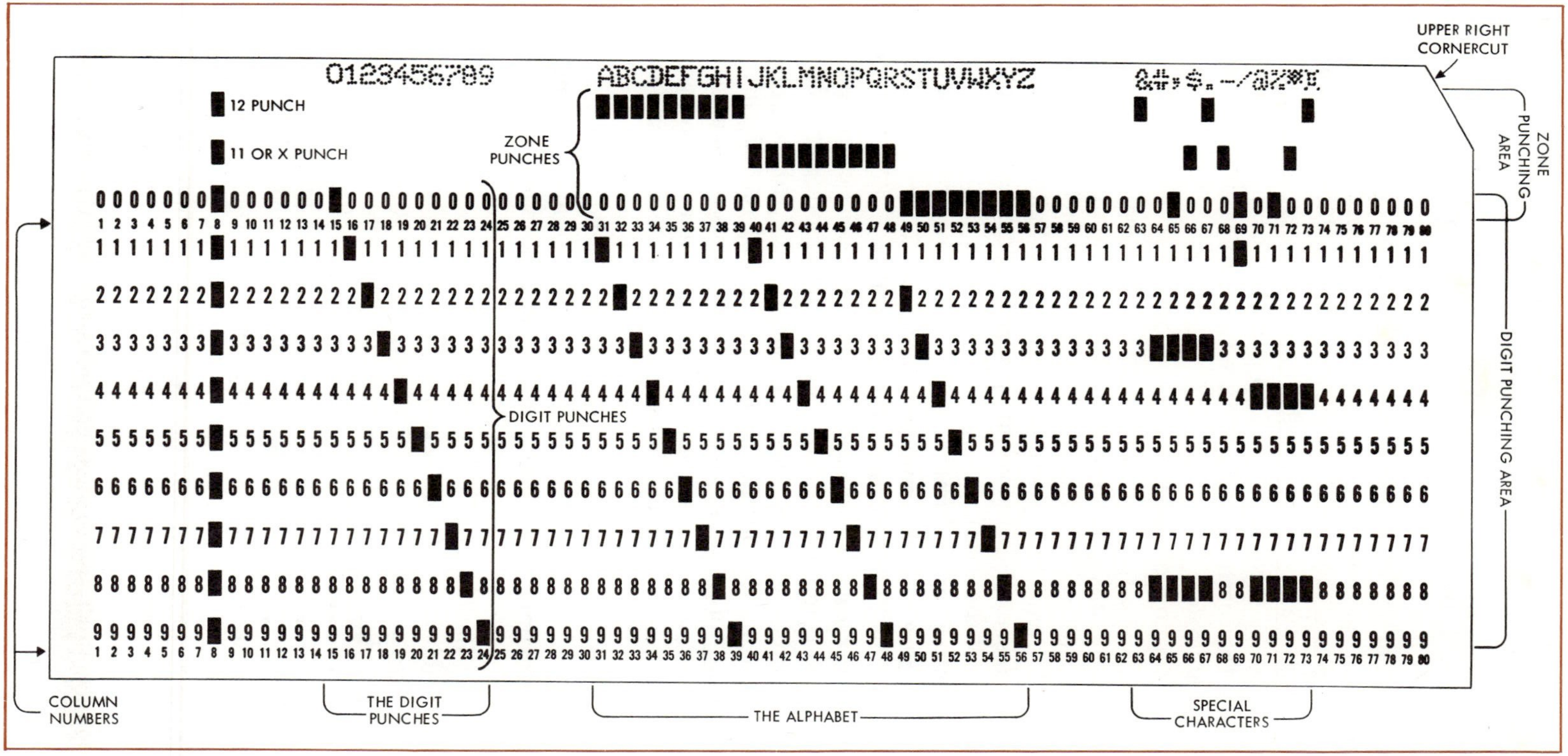

FIGURE 4-1
Eighty-Column
Punched Card
and Hollerith Code

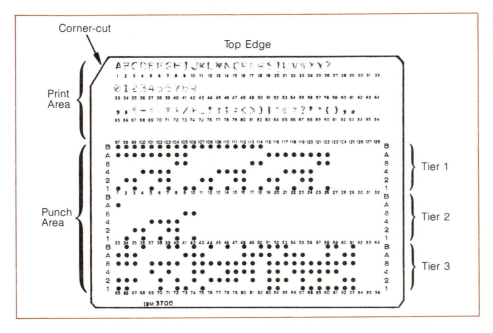

PUNCH CT D	ORDER NO.	ORDER DATE			SALESPERSON NO	CUSTOMER NO	STATE	CITY	QUANTITY	ITEM DESCRIPTION	ITEM NO.	UNIT PRICE	UNIT COST	SALES AMOUNT	COST AMOUNT	GROSS PROFIT	PUNCH RT CTR
		MO	DAY	YR													

Record

FIGURE 4–2
Unit Record

coding scheme used is similar to the 6-bit BCD system discussed in the previous chapter.

The data thus represented in the three tiers is usually printed in three corresponding rows at the top of the card in the print area. Arranging a card in this manner allows more data to be stored in a smaller space than is possible with the standard eighty-column card.

FIGURE 4–3
IBM Ninety-six
Column Punched Card

Corner-cut

Top Edge

ABCDEFGHIJKLMNOPQRSTUVWXYZ

0123456789

Print Area

Punch Area

B A 8 4 2 1   Tier 1

B A 8 4 2 1   Tier 2

B A 8 4 2 1   Tier 3

IBM 3700

Another disadvantage of using the punched card is the possibility of mutilation during handling which hinders the processing.

Card Punch Data is most commonly recorded on punched cards through the use of a *card punch*, or *keypunch* (see Figure 4–4). An operator reads a source document and transcribes the data from the document into cards by pressing keys on a keyboard, much as if he or she were using a typewriter. The machine automatically feeds, positions, and stacks the cards, thus allowing the operator to concentrate on the keying operation.

Keyboards on card-punch machines vary depending on the uses for which the machines are designed. For example, some keypunches have only alphabetic keyboards; some have only numeric keyboards; and others combine the two. Various sets of special characters and automatic skipping and duplicating are options usually available as well.

Regardless of the number of functions performed automatically (such as automatic skipping and duplicating), keypunching is probably the slowest and most costly operation in any computer system. One person is needed to operate each machine, and much time is spent keying data.

Key-to-Tape, Key-to-Disk, and Key-to-Diskette

Key-to-tape and *key-to-disk* machines were developed to help solve an ever-worsening data entry problem: punched-card systems require much mecha-

FIGURE 4–4
Eighty-Column Card
Punch

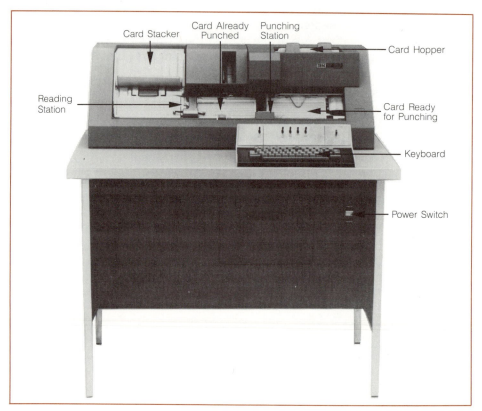

nized movement and have many limitations. With key-to-tape and key-to-disk machines, data is entered in much the same fashion as with the card punch, but it is stored not as punches on cards but as magnetized spots on the surface of a tape or disk. The data can be stored indefinitely because the spots retain their magnetism. It can be replaced with new data when desired. This reusability overcomes a major disadvantage of punched cards, which cannot be reused in this manner. Tapes and disks can also store much more data in a smaller space; for example, as many as 1,600 characters are commonly stored on one inch of magnetic tape. Finally, data stored on tape or disk can be read into the CPU more than twenty-five times faster than data on cards. Thus, use of magnetic tape or disk can significantly increase the efficiency of data-processing operations.

Key-to-Tape   In a key-to-tape system, data is recorded on magnetic tape in reels, cartridges, or cassettes (see Figure 4–5). The data recorder consists of a keyboard for entering the data; a small memory to hold data while it is being checked for accuracy; hardware to write the data on tape; and usually, a television-like screen to allow easy verification and correction by the operator.

FIGURE 4–5
Key-to-Tape System

Two general types of key-to-tape configurations are available to users. A *stand-alone key-to-tape device* is a self-contained unit that takes the place of a keypunch device. An operator keys the data onto a standard half-inch magnetic tape on reels, cartridges, or cassettes, which are then collected from all the stand-alone devices. Their data is pooled onto a single magnetic tape, which is then used for computer processing.

A second configuration is known as a *clustered-key-to-tape device*. Here, several keyboards are linked to one or two magnetic-tape units, which accept data from the operators and combine it as keying takes place. This type of configuration eliminates the pooling step needed for the stand-alone devices. Clustered key-to-tape devices (also known as key-to-central-tape devices) tend to be less expensive than stand-alone devices because the hardware for recording the data onto the tape is centralized. The clustered devices are used in applications where large quantities of similar data are keyed.

An advantage of both types of key-to-tape configurations is that the tape is edited and validated before the data is forwarded to the computer for processing.

Key-to-Disk　A typical key-to-disk configuration consists of several keying devices, all of which are connected to a minicomputer. Data is keyed onto magnetic disks (see Figure 4–6). Before that, however, it is usually stored and edited by the minicomputer. This editing is directed by the minicomputer's stored-program instructions. If an error is detected, the system interrupts the operator and "stands by" until a correction has been entered. The correct data is then stored on magnetic disk for input to the computer.

Key-to-Diskette　An increasingly popular data-entry system is the key-to-diskette system. A flexible (or floppy) disk is used instead of the conventional

FIGURE 4–6
Key-to-Disk System

(hard) disk. The data is entered on a keyboard, displayed on a screen for verification, and recorded on the diskette. A key-to-diskette system can operate as stand-alone devices or in cluster configurations (as described above). The data recorded on the diskettes is collected and pooled onto a magnetic tape for computer processing.

In summary, key-to-tape, key-to-disk, and key-to-diskette data-entry systems offer several advantages over traditional punched-card input:

1. Magnetic tapes, disks, and diskettes are reusable.

2. Errors can be corrected by backspacing and re-keying correct data over the incorrect data.

3. Since the key-entry devices work electronically rather than mechanically, they are much quieter.

4. Operators can transcribe data faster.

5. Record lengths are not limited to eighty characters. However, most key-to-disk systems can accommodate data in an eighty-column format, allowing use of old programs written to accept punched-card records.

6. Storage on tape, disk, or diskette is much more compact, which reduces data handling and saves storage space.

While key-to-disk, -tape, and -diskette systems offer many advantages over punched-card input, they also cost more. Generally, these systems are cost-effective where **large** amounts of data are prepared for processing on medium-sized or large computers.

Source-Data Automation

Data entry has traditionally been the weakest link in the chain of data-processing operations. Although data can be processed electronically at extremely high speeds, significantly more time is required to prepare it and enter it into the computer system.

Consider a computer system that uses punched cards for data input. The data is first written on some type of coding form or source document. Then it is keypunched onto cards by an operator. Next, the data may be verified by duplication of the entire keypunching operation. Incorrect cards must be keypunched and verified a second time. After all data has been recorded correctly on cards, operations such as sorting and merging may be required before the cards can be read into the computer. Generally, card files are copied onto magnetic tape for later input to the computer, because magnetic-tape files can be read into the computer much faster than card files. Figure 4–7 diagrams such a system.

This method of entering data into the computer is time-consuming and expensive. Some organizations have turned to the key-to-tape, -disk, or diskette systems described above to simplify keypunching operations. Another approach to data collection and preparation is also gaining in popularity; it is called *source-data automation*. The purpose of source-data automation is to collect data about an event, in computer-readable form, when and where the event takes place. By eliminating the intermediate steps used

FIGURE 4–7
Traditional Keypunch
Data Preparation

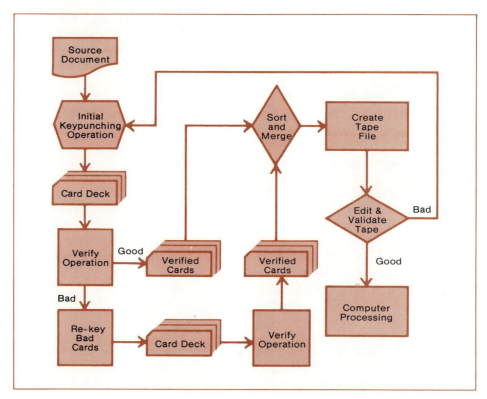

in preparing card input, source-data automation improves the speed, accuracy, and efficiency of data-processing operations (see Figure 4–8).

Source-data automation is implemented by use of a variety of methods. Each requires special machines for reading data and converting it into machine language. The most common approaches to source-data automation are discussed below.

FIGURE 4–8
Typical Methods of
Source-Data
Automation

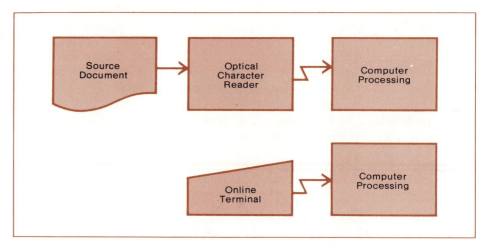

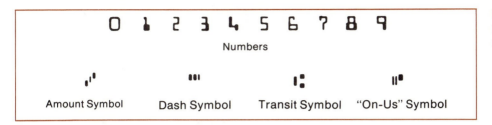

FIGURE 4–9
Magnetic-Ink
Character Set

Magnetic-Ink Character Readers Magnetic ink was introduced in the late 1950s to facilitate check processing by the banking industry. Because magnetic-ink characters can be read by both humans and machines (see Figure 4–9), no special data conversion step is needed. Magnetic-ink characters are formed with magnetized particles of iron oxide. Each character is composed of certain sections of a seventy-section matrix (see Figure 4–10). The characters can be read and converted into machine code by a *magnetic-ink character reader (MICR)*.

The MICR examines each character area to determine the shape of the character represented. The presence of a magnetic field in a section of the area represents a 1-bit; the absence of a magnetic field represents a 0-bit. Each magnetic-ink character is composed of a unique combination of 0-bits and 1-bits. When all sections in a character area are combined and translated into binary notation in this manner, the character represented can be determined. The MICR automatically checks each character read to ensure accuracy.

The processing of bank checks is a major application of magnetic-ink character recognition. The magnetic-ink characters are printed along the bottom of the check (see Figure 4–11). The *transit field* is preprinted on the check. It includes the bank number, an aid in routing the check through the Federal Reserve System. The customer's account number appears in an *"on-us" field*. A clerk manually inserts the amount of the check in the *amount field* after the check has been used and received at a bank.

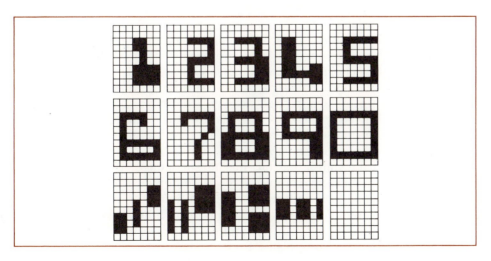

FIGURE 4-10
Matrix Patterns for
Magnetic Ink
Characters

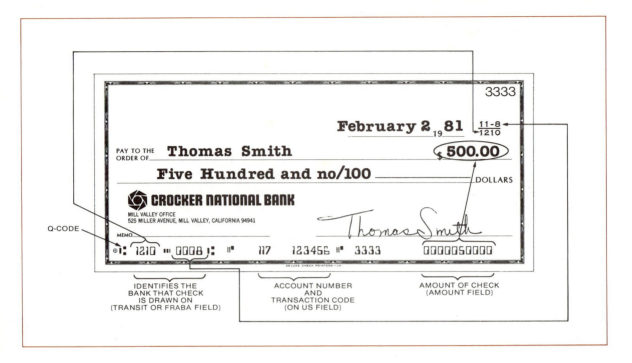

FIGURE 4–11
Sample Check with Magnetic-Ink Characters

All magnetic-ink characters on checks are formed with the standard fourteen-character set shown in Figure 4–9. (Other character sets may be used in other applications.) As the checks are fed into the MICR, it reads them and sorts them by bank number at a Federal Reserve Bank and by account number at the issuing bank. In this manner, checks are routed back to each issuing bank and then back to its customers. Between 750 and 1,500 checks per minute can be read and sorted by an MICR.

Optical Recognition   Optical recognition devices can read marks or symbols coded on paper documents and convert them into electrical pulses. The pulses can then be transmitted directly to the CPU or stored on magnetic tape for input at a later time.

The simplest approach to optical recognition is known as *optical-mark recognition (OMR),* or *mark-sensing.* This approach is often used for machine scoring of multiple-choice examinations (see Figure 4–12), where a person taking the examination makes a mark with a heavy lead pencil in the location corresponding to each desired answer. The marks on an OMR document are sensed by an *optical-mark page reader* as the document passes under a light source. The presence of marks in specific locations is indicated by light reflected at those locations. As the document is read, the optical-mark data is automatically translated into machine language. When the optical-mark page reader is directly connected to the computer, up to 2000 forms of the same type can be read and processed in an hour.

Optical-mark recognition is also used in order writing, inventory control, surveys and questionnaires, and payroll applications. Since optical-mark data is initially recorded by people, forms that are easy for them to understand and complete must be devised. Instructions, with examples, are gen-

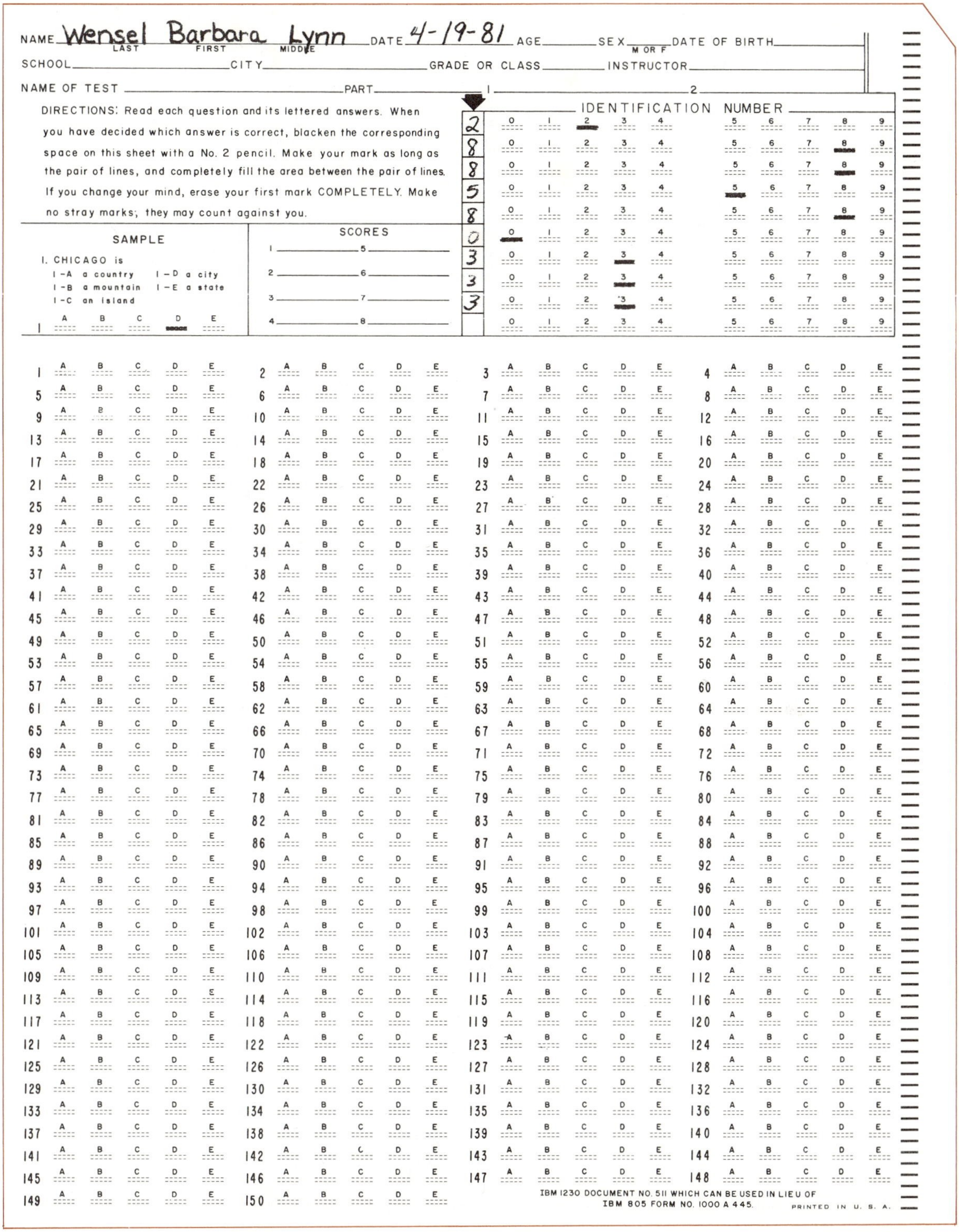
NAME Wensel Barbara Lynn DATE 4-19-81 AGE ______ SEX ______ DATE OF BIRTH ______
LAST FIRST MIDDLE M OR F
SCHOOL ______ CITY ______ GRADE OR CLASS ______ INSTRUCTOR ______
NAME OF TEST ______ PART ______ 1 ______ 2 ______

DIRECTIONS: Read each question and its lettered answers. When you have decided which answer is correct, blacken the corresponding space on this sheet with a No. 2 pencil. Make your mark as long as the pair of lines, and completely fill the area between the pair of lines. If you change your mind, erase your first mark COMPLETELY. Make no stray marks; they may count against you.

IDENTIFICATION NUMBER

2	0	1	2	3	4	5	6	7	8	9
8	0	1	2	3	4	5	6	7	8	9
8	0	1	2	3	4	5	6	7	8	9
5	0	1	2	3	4	5	6	7	8	9
8	0	1	2	3	4	5	6	7	8	9
0	0	1	2	3	4	5	6	7	8	9
3	0	1	2	3	4	5	6	7	8	9
3	0	1	2	3	4	5	6	7	8	9
3	0	1	2	3	4	5	6	7	8	9
	0	1	2	3	4	5	6	7	8	9

SAMPLE

I. CHICAGO is
I – A a country I – D a city
I – B a mountain I – E a state
I – C an island

I A B C D E

SCORES
1 ______ 5 ______
2 ______ 6 ______
3 ______ 7 ______
4 ______ 8 ______

1 A B C D E 2 A B C D E 3 A B C D E 4 A B C D E
5 A B C D E 6 A B C D E 7 A B C D E 8 A B C D E
9 A B C D E 10 A B C D E 11 A B C D E 12 A B C D E
13 A B C D E 14 A B C D E 15 A B C D E 16 A B C D E
17 A B C D E 18 A B C D E 19 A B C D E 20 A B C D E
21 A B C D E 22 A B C D E 23 A B C D E 24 A B C D E
25 A B C D E 26 A B C D E 27 A B C D E 28 A B C D E
29 A B C D E 30 A B C D E 31 A B C D E 32 A B C D E
33 A B C D E 34 A B C D E 35 A B C D E 36 A B C D E
37 A B C D E 38 A B C D E 39 A B C D E 40 A B C D E
41 A B C D E 42 A B C D E 43 A B C D E 44 A B C D E
45 A B C D E 46 A B C D E 47 A B C D E 48 A B C D E
49 A B C D E 50 A B C D E 51 A B C D E 52 A B C D E
53 A B C D E 54 A B C D E 55 A B C D E 56 A B C D E
57 A B C D E 58 A B C D E 59 A B C D E 60 A B C D E
61 A B C D E 62 A B C D E 63 A B C D E 64 A B C D E
65 A B C D E 66 A B C D E 67 A B C D E 68 A B C D E
69 A B C D E 70 A B C D E 71 A B C D E 72 A B C D E
73 A B C D E 74 A B C D E 75 A B C D E 76 A B C D E
77 A B C D E 78 A B C D E 79 A B C D E 80 A B C D E
81 A B C D E 82 A B C D E 83 A B C D E 84 A B C D E
85 A B C D E 86 A B C D E 87 A B C D E 88 A B C D E
89 A B C D E 90 A B C D E 91 A B C D E 92 A B C D E
93 A B C D E 94 A B C D E 95 A B C D E 96 A B C D E
97 A B C D E 98 A B C D E 99 A B C D E 100 A B C D E
101 A B C D E 102 A B C D E 103 A B C D E 104 A B C D E
105 A B C D E 106 A B C D E 107 A B C D E 108 A B C D E
109 A B C D E 110 A B C D E 111 A B C D E 112 A B C D E
113 A B C D E 114 A B C D E 115 A B C D E 116 A B C D E
117 A B C D E 118 A B C D E 119 A B C D E 120 A B C D E
121 A B C D E 122 A B C D E 123 A B C D E 124 A B C D E
125 A B C D E 126 A B C D E 127 A B C D E 128 A B C D E
129 A B C D E 130 A B C D E 131 A B C D E 132 A B C D E
133 A B C D E 134 A B C D E 135 A B C D E 136 A B C D E
137 A B C D E 138 A B C D E 139 A B C D E 140 A B C D E
141 A B C D E 142 A B C D E 143 A B C D E 144 A B C D E
145 A B C D E 146 A B C D E 147 A B C D E 148 A B C D E
149 A B C D E 150 A B C D E

IBM 1230 DOCUMENT NO. 511 WHICH CAN BE USED IN LIEU OF
IBM 805 FORM NO. 1000 A 445.
PRINTED IN U. S. A.

FIGURE 4–12
Optical-Mark Recognition

erally provided to aid those who must use the forms. Good design helps to prevent errors and lessens the amount of time required to complete forms.

Another type of optical reader, known as a *bar-code reader*, can read special line, or bar, codes—patterns of optical marks. Some bar codes in use today are shown in Figure 4–13. They are suitable for many applications, including point-of-sale (POS) systems, credit card verification, and freight identification to facilitate warehouse operations.

Data is represented in a bar code by the widths of the bars and the distances between them. Probably the most familiar bar code is the *Universal Product Code (UPC)* found on most grocery items. This code consists of ten pairs of vertical bars, which represent both the manufacturer's identity and the identity of the item but not the item's price. The code for each product is a unique combination of these vertical bars. The UPC symbol is read by a hand-held *wand reader* or by a fixed scanner linked to a cash-register-like device. The computer system identifies the product, its brand name, and

FIGURE 4–13
Types of Bar Codes

other pertinent information and uses this data to find the item's price. It then prints out both name and price. The computer keeps track of each item sold and thus helps the store manager to maintain current inventory status.

Optical-character readers can read special types of characters known as *optical characters*. Some *optical-character recognition (OCR)* devices can read characters of several type fonts, including both uppercase and lowercase letters. The most common font is shown in Figure 4–14.

A major difference between optical-character recognition and optical-mark recognition is that optical-character data is represented by the shapes of characters rather than by the positions of marks. However, both OCR and OMR devices rely on reflected light to translate written data into machine-readable form.

Acceptable OCR input can be produced by computer printers, adding machines, cash registers, accounting machines, and typewriters. Data can be fed into the reader via a *continuous form* such as a cash-register tape or on *cut forms* such as phone or utility bills. When individual cut forms are used, the reader can usually sort the forms as well.

The most advanced optical-character readers can also read handwritten characters. However, the handwritten characters must be neat and clear; otherwise, they may not be read correctly (see Figure 4–15). This is a major source of frustration because handwriting varies widely from individual to individual; and devices that must read handwriting are often very slow. Any characters that cannot be interpreted are rejected by the optical-character readers.

Machine-produced optical-character recognition has been used in credit-card billing, utility billing, and inventory-control applications. Handwritten optical-character recognition has been used widely in mail sorting. The reliability of optical-character recognition systems is generally very good and is improving as optical-scanning techniques continue to improve.

Remote Input   Remote terminals collect data at its source and transmit it to a central computer for processing. Generally, data is transmitted over telecommunication equipment. The many types of remote terminals available can increase the versatility and expand the applications of the computer.

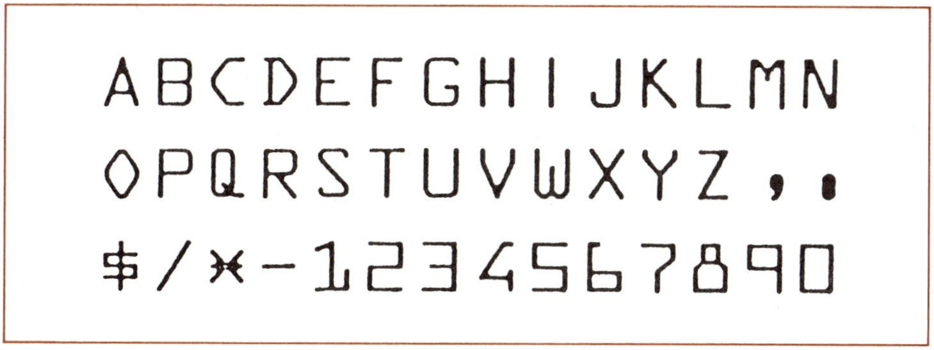

FIGURE 4–14
OCR Characters

FIGURE 4–15
Handwritten Optically
Readable Characters

Rule	Correct	Incorrect
1. Write big	0 2 8 3 4	0 2 8 3 4
2. Close loops	0 6 8 8 9	0 6 8 8 9
3. Use simple shapes	0 2 3 7 5	0 2 3 7 5
4. Do not link characters	0 0 8 8 1	00881
5. Connect lines	4 5 T	4 5 T
6. Block print	C S T X Z	(S T X Z

Types of remote terminals to be discussed here are point-of-sale terminals, touch-tone devices, voice-recognition devices, and intelligent terminals.

Remote terminals that perform the functions of a cash register and also capture sales data are referred to as *point-of-sale (POS) terminals*. Such terminals have a keyboard for data entry, a panel to display the price, a cash drawer, and a printer that provides a cash receipt. A POS terminal typical of those found in many supermarkets is shown in Figure 4–16.

As mentioned earlier, some POS terminals have wand readers that can read the Universal Product Code (UPC) stamped on an item. The sale is registered automatically as the checkout person passes the wand reader over

FIGURE 4–16
Point-of-Sale Terminal

the code; there is no need to enter the price via a keyboard unless the wand malfunctions. Thus, POS terminals enable sales data to be collected at its source. If the terminals are directly connected to a large central computer, useful inventory and sales information can be provided almost instantaneously to the retailer.

Touch-tone devices are remote terminals used together with ordinary telephone lines to transfer data from remote locations to a central computer. The data is entered via a special keyboard on the terminal. Generally, slight modifications must have been made to the telephone connection to allow data to be transferred over the line.

There are several types of touch-tone devices. One type, shown in Figure 4–17, can read holes punched in cards; this type is often used to verify credit card transactions. Another type can store large amounts of data on a magnetic belt similar to a magnetic tape before transmitting it. This type of terminal is best suited for large-volume processing.

Remote terminals that use *audio input* or *voice recognition systems* are suitable for low-volume, highly formal input and output. Users may enter data into the computer by punching keys on a terminal, perhaps a regular push-button phone terminal. Each key transmits a different tone over a telephone line. Or the user may "train" the computer to understand his or her voice and vocabulary. Here, the user must follow only the patterns the computer is programmed to recognize.

Currently, *voice recognition modules (VRM)* are available in sizes to accommodate 40, 70, or 100 isolated words and phrases. With word recognition

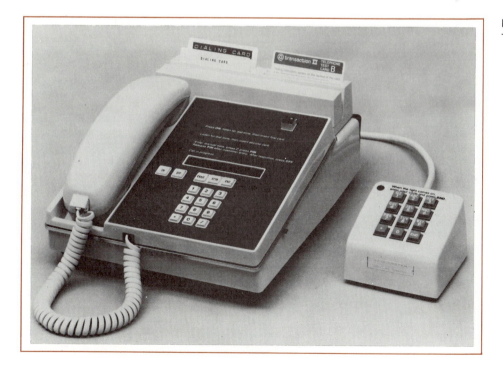

FIGURE 4–17
Touch-Tone Device

accuracy of 99 percent, the system comes close to allowing the user to communicate with the computer using natural language.

Available VRMs are compatible with high-level languages and can be interfaced to existing computer hardware. Then data can be entered by use of commands in natural spoken language, allowing greater accuracy in data entry.

The computer's *audio output* is composed of a vocabulary of half-second records of voice sounds. By arranging the records in a particular order, the computer can "speak" to the user. The approach is being used in the banking industry to report customer account balances and, in some cases, to pay bills. Usually the *audio*, or *voice, response units* are coupled with touch-tone terminals for remote data entry. An entire unit may weigh less than ten pounds. Some are built into briefcases for easy portability (see Figure 4–18).

The VRM has proved to be very effective for data entry, quality control, process control, computer-aided design, and word processing. In the future, many more uses will be found for this device.

Intelligent terminals, still another type of remote device, can be programmed by use of stored instructions. This capability distinguishes them from other terminals discussed earlier in this chapter (sometimes called dumb terminals), which cannot be programmed. Intelligent terminals have the same kinds of components as full-sized computers but are limited in their storage capability and in the set of instructions they can perform. They are useful for editing data prior to transmitting it to a central computer; editing and other manipulating functions are directed by programs stored in the terminal's primary storage unit.

Most intelligent terminals have a *CRT (cathode-ray tube)* and/or a print-

FIGURE 4–18
Portable Touch-Tone
Audio Terminal

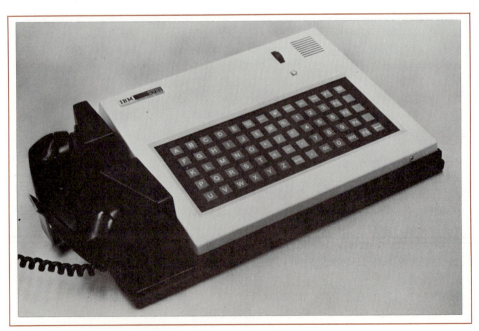

er built into them. The CRT, a visual display device with a television-like screen, is useful to show the data being edited and to display responses to inquiries. The terminal's programmable nature extends its applications into other areas as well. For example, an intelligent terminal can be connected to other I/O devices and used as a stand-alone computer system for low-volume or special-purpose processing. Alternatively, such a terminal can be used to coordinate data entry from non-programmable terminals at other locations. In this case, the data is transmitted to the intelligent terminal for editing and validation and later transmitted as a part of batched input from the intelligent terminal to a large central computer.

The use of intelligent terminals will continue to grow as their cost continues to decrease and new applications for them are discovered. They can help in many ways to make data entry and retrieval easier for the user.

INFORMATION OUTPUT

Printers

Computer *printers* serve a straightforward basic function—printing processed data in a form humans can read (see Figure 4–19). This permanent readable copy of computer output is often referred to as *hard copy*. To produce it, the printer first receives electronic signals from the central processing unit. In an *impact printer*, these signals activate print elements, which are pressed against paper. *Nonimpact printers*, a newer development, use heat, laser technology, or photographic techniques to print output.

Impact Printers Impact printers can be further subdivided into character-at-a-time and line-at-a-time printers. *Character-at-a-time printers* print one character of data at a time, typically at speeds from 600 to 900 characters per

FIGURE 4–19
Printer

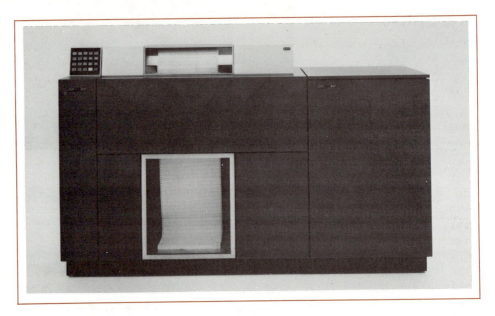

minute. *Line-at-a-time printers* print an entire line of information at a time; generally, speeds up to 2,000 lines per minute can be obtained from such an impact printer.

Printer-keyboards and wire-matrix and daisy-wheel printers are the three principal character-at-a-time devices. The printer-keyboard is similar to an office typewriter except that a stored program, rather than a person, controls it (see Figure 4–20). All instructions, including spacing, carriage returns,

FIGURE 4–20
Printer-Keyboard

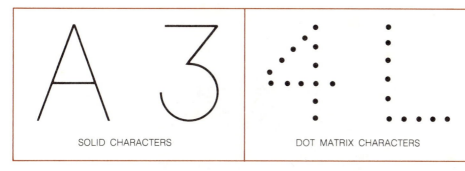

FIGURE 4–21
Wire-Matrix Printer
Dot Pattern

and printing of characters, are sent from the CPU to the printer. A printing element with characters on its surface is generally used for printing. The keyboard allows an operator to communicate with the system—for example, to enter data or instructions. The usual speed of a printer-keyboard is about 900 characters per minute. Because these printers are slow, they are typically used for small amounts of output.

Wire-matrix (also called *dot-matrix*) *printers* are based on a design principle similar to that of a football or basketball scoreboard. The matrix is a rectangle composed of pins; usually, it is seven pins high and five pins wide. Certain combinations of pins are activated to represent characters. For example, the number 4 and the letter L are formed by a combination of pins, being pressed against paper as shown in Figure 4–21. The dot combinations used to represent various numbers, letters, and special characters are shown in Figure 4–22. Wire-matrix printers can typically print up to 900 characters per minute.

Daisy-wheel printers are similar to printer-keyboards in that they resemble office typewriters. The daisy wheel itself is a flat disk with petal-like projections (see Figure 4–23). Daisy wheels come in several type fonts that can be interchanged quickly to suit application needs. The daisy-wheel printer offers high-quality type and is often used in word processors to give output a professional appearance.

Types of line-at-a-time printers include print-wheel printers, chain printers, and drum printers. A *print-wheel printer* typically contains 120 print

FIGURE 4–22
Wire-Matrix Printer
Character Set

ABCDEFGHIJKLM
NOPQRSTUVWXYZ
0123456789—.:
8/+$*!%@=(+)

FIGURE 4–23
Daisy Print Wheel

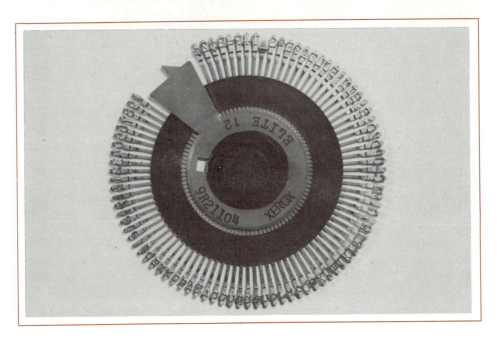

FIGURE 4–24
Print Wheel

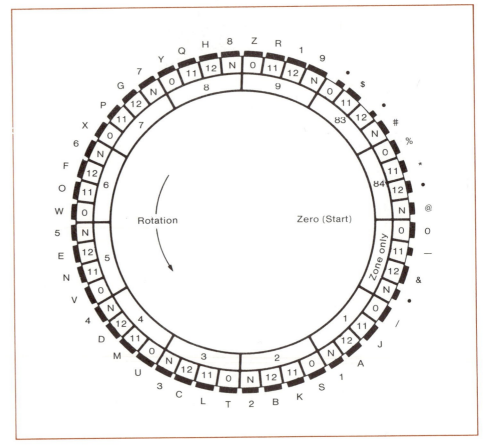

wheels, one for each of 120 print positions on a line (see Figure 4–24). Each print wheel contains 48 characters, including alphabetic, numeric, and special characters. Each print wheel rotates until the desired character moves into the corresponding print position on the current print line. When all wheels are in their correct positions, a hammer drives the paper against the wheels and an entire line of output is printed. Print-wheel printers can produce about 150 lines per minute.

A *chain printer's* character set is assembled in a chain that revolves horizontally past all print positions (see Figure 4–25). There is one print hammer for each column on the paper. Characters are printed when hammers press the paper against an inked ribbon, which in turn presses against appropriate characters on the print chain. Type fonts can be changed easily on chain printers, allowing a variety of fonts, such as italic or boldface, to be used. Some chain printers can produce up to 2,000 lines per minute.

A *drum printer* uses a metal cylinder with rows of characters engraved across its surface (see Figure 4–26). Each column on the drum contains the complete character set and corresponds to one print position on the line. As the drum rotates, all characters are rotated past the print position. A hammer presses the paper against an ink ribbon and the drum when the appropriate character is in place. One line is printed for each revolution of the drum, since all characters eventually reach the print position during one revolution. Some drum printers can produce 3,000 lines per minute.

Nonimpact Printers   As mentioned earlier, nonimpact printers do not print characters by means of a mechanical printing element that strikes paper. Instead, a variety of other methods are used. Electrostatic, electrothermal, ink-jet, laser, and xerographic printers will be discussed here.

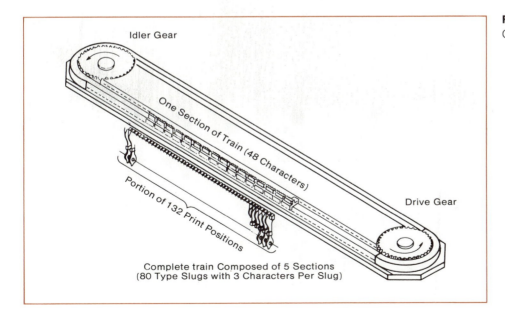

FIGURE 4–25
Chain Printer

FIGURE 4–26
Print Drum

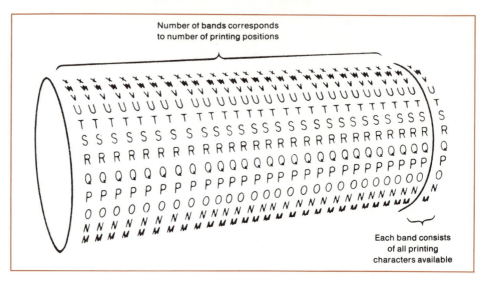

Number of bands corresponds
to number of printing positions

Each band consists
of all printing
characters available

An *electrostatic printer* forms an image of a character on special paper using a dot matrix of charged wires, or pins. The paper is moved through a solution containing ink particles that have a charge opposite that of the pattern. The ink particles adhere to each charged pattern on the paper, forming a visible image of each character.

Electrothermal printers generate characters by using heat and heat-sensitive paper. Rods are heated in a matrix; as the ends of the selected rods touch the heat-sensitive paper, an image is created.

Both electrothermal and electrostatic printers are silent in operation. They

FIGURE 4–27
Laser Printer

are often used in applications where noise may be a problem. Some of these printers are capable of producing 5,000 lines per minute.

In an *ink-jet printer*, a nozzle is used to shoot a stream of charged ink towards the paper. Before reaching it, the ink passes through an electronic field that arranges the charged particles into characters.

Laser printers combine laser beams and electrophotographic technology to create output images (see Figure 4–27). A beam of light is focused through a rotating disk containing a full font of characters. The character image is projected onto a piece of film or photographic paper, and the print or negative is developed and fixed in a manner similar to that used for ordinary photographs. The output consists of high-quality, letter-perfect images—the process is often used to print books. Laser printers operate at high speeds, up to 21,000 lines per minute.

Xerographic printers use printing methods much like those used in common xerographic copying machines. For example, Xerox, the pioneer of this type of printing, has one model that prints on single 8½-by-11-inch sheets of plain paper. Xerographic printers operate at 4,000 lines per minute.

Table 4–1 shows representative differences in print speeds of impact and nonimpact printers. Since nonimpact printers involve much less physical

TABLE 4–1
Printer Types
and Speeds

PRINTER TYPE	PRINTING CAPABILITY
IMPACT PRINTERS	
Character-at-a-Time:	
Printer-Keyboards	900 characters per minute
Wire-Matrix (Dot-Matrix)	900 characters per minute
Line-at-a-Time:	
Print Wheel	150 lines per minute
Print Drum	3,000 lines per minute
Print Chain	2000 lines per minute
NONIMPACT PRINTERS	
Xerographic	4000 lines per minute
Electrothermal	5000 lines per minute
Electrostatic	5000 lines per minute
Laser	21,000 lines per minute

movement than impact printers, they are generally much faster. They also offer a wider choice of type faces and better speed-to-price ratios than impact printers; and their technology implies a higher reliability because they use fewer moveable parts in printing. The primary disadvantage of using nonimpact printers is their inability to make carbon copies. However, they can make multiple printings of a page in less time than it takes an impact printer to make one multicarbon page.

New printing systems now being introduced combine many features of the printing process into one machine. For example, collating, routing, hole-punching, blanking out of proprietary information, and perforating may be performed. Some printers produce both text and form designs on plain paper; this reduces or eliminates the need for preprinted forms.

As the refinement of nonimpact printing technology continues, nonimpact printers will become the predominant means of producing hard-copy output.

Special-Purpose Output

In many instances, traditional printers cannot provide certain forms of output. At these times, special output devices are required.

Visual Display Terminals   *Visual display terminals* in common use display data on *cathode-ray tubes (CRTs)* similar to television screens (see Figure 4–28). A typical screen can hold twenty-four lines, each containing eighty characters. These terminals supply what is known as *soft-copy* output; that is, the screen is not a permanent record of what is shown. They are well suited for applications involving inquiry and response, where no permanent (printed) records are required, and can be used for capturing data to be transmitted from remote offices to a central computer. Data may be entered on a keyboard on the terminal and displayed on the screen for verification as it is keyed.

Visual display terminals have some advantages over printers. First, they can display output much faster than printers—some CRT terminals can dis-

FIGURE 4–28
Visual-Display Terminal

play up to 10,000 characters in a second. Also, they are much quieter in operation than impact printers. It is usually possible to connect a printer or a copier to a CRT terminal; thus, hard-copy output of the screen contents can be provided. These terminals are rapidly gaining recognition as desirable components of information systems.

Another type of CRT, known as a *graphic display device,* is used to display drawings as well as characters on a screen (see Figure 4–29). Graphic display devices are generally used to display graphs and charts, but they can also display complex curves and shapes. With some terminals, data displayed on the screen can be altered by using the *light pen,* a pen-shaped object with a light-sensitive cell at its end (see Figure 4–30). Users can draw lines on the screen by specifying the ends of the lines with the light pen and can quickly alter graphs and line drawings by applying it at the appro-

FIGURE 4–29
Graphic Display Device

FIGURE 4–30
Visual Display Device
with Light Pen

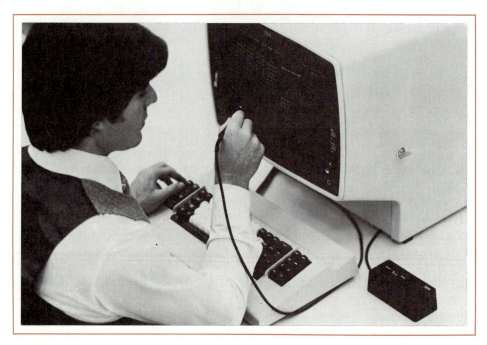

priate locations on the screen. Graphic display devices are being used in highly technical fields, such as in the aerospace industry to aid in the design of new wing structures.

Plotters A *plotter* is an output device that converts data from the CPU into graphic form. It can produce lines, curves, and complex shapes. The major difference between a plotter and a graphic display device is that the plotter produces hard-copy output (paper) whereas the graphic display device produces soft-copy output (screen image).

A typical plotter has a pen, movable carriage, drum, and chart-paper holder (see Figure 4–31). Shapes are produced as the pen moves back and forth across the paper along the y-axis while the drum moves the paper up and down along the x-axis. Both the paper movement and the pen movement are bi-directional. The pen is raised and lowered from the paper surface automatically.

The plotter can be used to produce line and bar charts, graphs, organizational charts, engineering drawings, maps, trend lines, supply and demand curves, and so on. The figures are drawn precisely, because the pen can be positioned at up to 45,000 points in each square inch of paper. Some plotters can produce drawings in up to eight colors. The usefulness of the plotter lies in its ability to communicate information in easy-to-understand picture form.

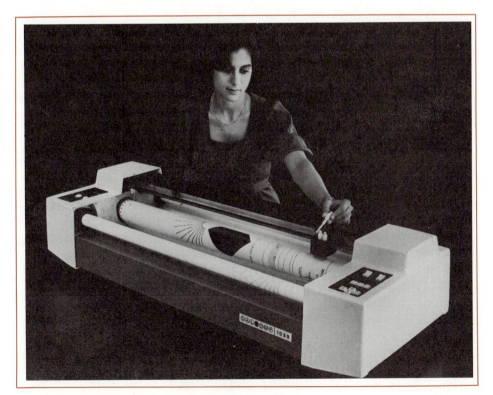

FIGURE 4–31
Plotter

Computer Output Microfilm (COM)   In situations where large volumes of information must be printed and stored for future reference, conventional paper output is not appropriate. It uses much storage space, and particular portions of it are often difficult to get to. A possible alternative is *computer output microfilm (COM),* which consists of photographed images produced in minature by the computer. In some cases, the output is first recorded on magnetic tape. Special photocopying equipment is then used to reproduce the information on microfilm. In an interactive environment, the COM equipment is used to display output on a CRT screen. The screen is exposed to microfilm. The microfilm copy can be produced as a roll of film or a four-by-six-inch microfiche card. In such a system, the speed of recording can be twenty-five to fifty times faster than traditional printing methods.

The main advantage of COM is that much data can be stored compactly, reducing both space requirements and storage costs. Further, both character and graphic output can be recorded. Use of a transparent forms-overlay permits headings to be printed and lines superimposed so that output is highly readable. The cost of producing additional microfilm copies is very low. In the past, high initial investment costs and the inability of the computer to directly retrieve microfilmed data have been disadvantages. However, costs are declining and the feasibility of attaining a COM system is increasing.

INPUT/OUTPUT OPERATIONS

Control Units

One of the key functions of the I/O subsystem of a computer system is the conversion of data into machine-readable code. For instance, data on punched cards must be converted from Hollerith code into a machine code such as ASCII or BCD. Code conversion must be performed when data is entered from devices such as remote terminals and magnetic-ink character readers. Code conversion is performed by a device known as an *I/O control unit*. This unit is different from the *control unit* of the CPU. It is located between one or more I/O devices and the CPU and is used only to facilitate I/O operations.

Besides code conversion, I/O control units perform another important function known as *data buffering*. A *buffer* is a separate storage unit (normally contained in the I/O control unit) for a particular input or output device. It is used as a temporary holding area for data being transferred to or from the CPU.

When data is read by an input device, it is converted to machine code and stored in a buffer. Once a certain amount of data has been collected in the buffer, it is transferred to the CPU. The buffer allows a large quantity of data to be transferred much faster than if the data items were transferred individually. For example, a buffer is used to temporarily hold data being entered from a remote terminal; this allows an entire record to be keyed on the terminal, held, and transferred all at once to the CPU. While the record is being keyed, the CPU processes other data (see Figure 4–32). The buffer serves a similar purpose when information is transferred from the computer to a printer or terminal as output.

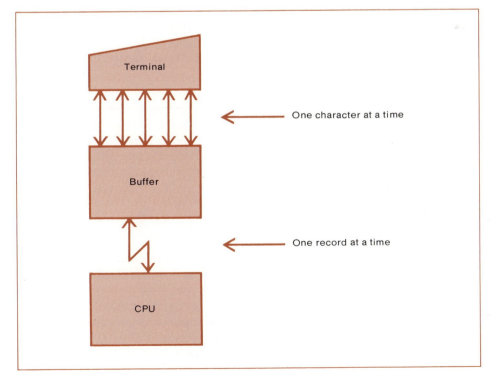

FIGURE 4–32
Data Buffering

Channels

Although the CPU is very fast and accurate, it can execute only one instruction at a time. If it is executing an instruction that requires an input or output operation, it must wait while data is retrieved from or sent to an input/output device. Compared with the CPU's internal processing speeds, I/O speeds are extremely slow. Even high-speed I/O devices often work only one-tenth as fast as the CPU. When the CPU is slowed down because of I/O operations, it is said to be *input/output-bound.*

	TIME 1	TIME 2	TIME 3
Input	Item 1		
Process		Item 1	
Output			Item 1

The CPU is input/output–bound—it can operate on only one item at a time.

The flow of data shown in the table above indicates that in this system the CPU does the process step when it has the necessary data but sits idle while input and output occur. To increase use of the CPU, *channels* have been developed to take over the task of transferring data to and from it. Each channel is a small, limited-capacity computer that serves as a data roadway. It may be within the CPU or a separate piece of equipment connected to it. During processing, when the CPU encounters an instruction requiring input or output, it merely tells the channel what it needs. The channel then goes to the required input device for data or sends information to the appropriate output device. The CPU, meanwhile, is free to execute other instructions; it is relieved of its responsibility to transfer data and can process data more efficiently.

	TIME 1	TIME 2	TIME 3
Input	Item 1	Item 2	Item 3
Process		Item 1	Item 2
Output			Item 1

With the aid of channels, the CPU can be active a greater percentage of the time.

There are two types of channels: selector and multiplexor. A *selector* channel can accept input from only one device at a time and is used with a high-speed I/O device such as a magnetic-tape or magnetic-disk unit. A *multiplexor channel* can handle more than one I/O device at a time. A byte multiplexor channel is normally associated with multiple slow-speed devices such as printers, card readers, and terminals (see Figure 4–33). A block multiplexor channel is used with multiple high-speed devices, but are less frequently encountered.

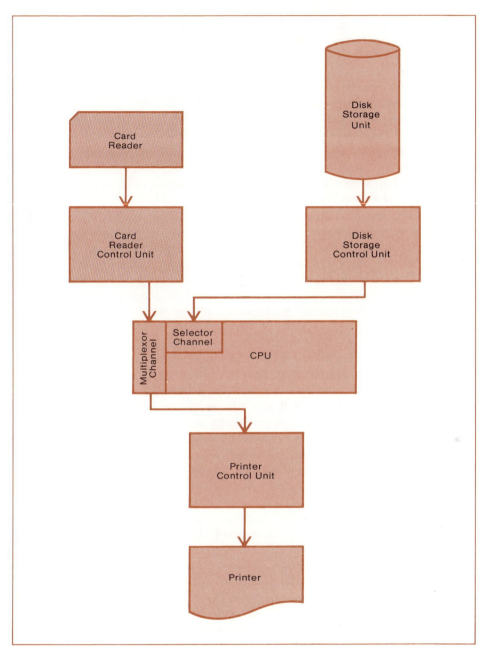

FIGURE 4–33

Channels, Control Units, and I/O Devices

SUMMARY

● There are two types of punched cards. One, the Hollerith card, has eighty vertical columns and twelve horizontal rows. The other has ninety-six columns and allows more data to be stored in a smaller space.

● Data is recorded on punched cards by means of a card punch/keypunch machine. Data is typed from source documents by an operator. Options like automatic skipping and duplicating are available on most keypunches.

● The unit record concept implies that all necessary data pertaining to a transaction is contained on one punched card.

● The major disadvantages of punched cards are length limitations, possible mutilation during handling, and slow processing speed. Also, large card files take up space and increase handling costs.

● Key-to-tape, key-to-disk, and key-to-diskette devices are increasingly used because they overcome the disadvantages of punched cards. Tapes, disks, and diskettes allow easy correction of errors, are reusable, can store more data in less space than cards, and can transfer data at least twenty-five times faster than cards. These devices also allow data to be verified, formatted, and edited as it is recorded.

● Source-data automation refers to collection of data at the point where a transaction occurs. Common approaches to source-data automation employ optical-recognition devices and other types of remote terminals.

● Magnetic-ink characters can be read by humans and also by machines, since they are magnetically inscribed. Magnetic-ink character readers (MICRs) can convert the magnetic characters into machine code for computer processing. MICRs are used extensively by the banking industry for processing checks.

● Optical-mark recognition devices can sense marks made with a heavy lead pencil and convert them into machine code. Other optical-character recognition devices are capable of reading bar codes, documents printed in various type fonts, and even handwritten characters. The main advantage of optical-character recognition is that it eliminates the intermediate process of transcribing data from source documents to an input medium.

● Remote terminals can collect data at its source and transmit it over communication lines for processing by a central computer. Included in this category are point-of-sale (POS) terminals, touch-tone devices, voice-recognition devices, and intelligent terminals. Each device satisfies distinct needs for input and output. Which device is most appropriate for a certain application depends on the particular I/O requirements.

● Printers provide output in a permanent (hard-copy) form that people can read. Impact printers are most commonly used with computers. They can be classified as either character-at-a-time—such as printer-keyboards, wire-matrix printers, and daisy-wheel printers—or line-at-a-time—such as print-wheel printers, drum printers, and chain printers.

● Nonimpact printers are more recent developments that use photographic, thermal, laser techniques to print output. They are faster than impact printers, offer a wider choice of type faces and better speed-to-price ratios, and are very reliable.

● Special-purpose output devices include visual display terminals, plotters, and computer output microfilm (COM) equipment. Visual display terminals use CRTs to display data to operators. Plotters can represent computer output in hard-copy graphic form. COM consists of miniature photographed images of computer output. It is suitable for applications that involve large volumes of information, because it uses less space, thereby reducing storage costs.

● I/O control units and channels are used in an I/O subsystem to increase the efficiency of the CPU. A control unit converts input data into machine code, and vice versa. It is also used in data buffering.

● Channels control I/O operations and free the CPU to do other processing; this allows input, output, and processing to overlap. Selector channels can accommodate only one I/O device at a time and are used with high-speed devices; multiplexor channels can accommodate multiple I/O devices and are often used with low-speed devices.

REVIEW QUESTIONS

1. Explain the unit-record concept.
2. What advantages are offered by key-to-tape, key-to-disk, and key-to-diskette devices? What are some disadvantages of key-to-tape data entry?
3. Explain source-data automation.
4. Discuss three types of optical-recognition devices. Identify applications in which each type can be used to advantage.
5. What advantages do visual display terminals offer over conventional printers?
6. What is an intelligent terminal? Give some examples.
7. Discuss the two types of printing devices. Which type is more common and why?
8. Distinguish between character-at-a-time printers and line-at-a-time printers, giving examples of each.
9. What functions does an I/O control unit perform?
10. What are channels used for? Distinguish between selector channels and multiplexor channels.

APPLICATION

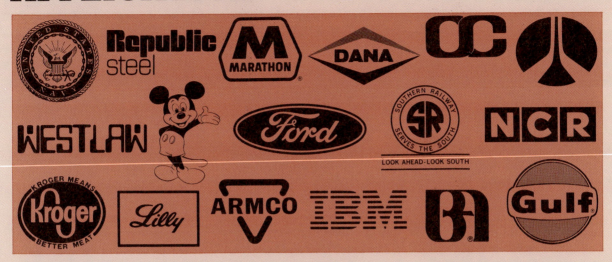

Gulf Oil Corporation

Spindletop, the most famous oil well in the world, roared in on January 10, 1901; it established Texas as a major oil source. The well was financed with $300,000 borrowed from a Mellon-controlled Pittsburgh bank. In May, Andrew W. and Richard B. Mellon organized the J. M. Guffey Petroleum Company and acquired the assets of the partnership that had drilled Spindletop (Mr. Guffey being one of them). The Gulf Refining Company was chartered by the Mellons on November 10, and construction

began on a Texas-based refinery to manufacture and market Spindletop oil. Crude oil production was 670,000 barrels in that first year.

Today, Gulf Oil Corporation produces approximately 650 million barrels of oil per year. It employs some 58,000 people all over the world and has assets of $15 billion. In addition, Gulf has become a "total energy" company: it finds and produces crude oil and natural gas, refines crude oil, processes gas and gas liquids, mines coal and uranium, produces synthetic fuels made from coal, and manufactures chemicals and petrochemicals.

The Information Services Division (ISD) of Gulf Oil is responsible for computer and communications-related services within the corporation. In the United States, programming and analysis personnel are in three major locations. Two major data

centers, one in Houston, Texas, and one near Pittsburgh, Pennsylvania, handle the large "corporate systems" and those systems that apply to specific strategy centers, such as Corporate Finance, Product Inventory/Billing, Accounts Payable, and Payroll. Each of these large data centers consists of multiple large processors, mostly IBM or IBM-compatible equipment. A third data center in Atlanta, Georgia, handles the Credit Card Accounts Receivable System. Approximately 925 employees make up the domestic ISD staff, including programmers, analysts, and operations personnel.

CREDIT CARD ACCOUNTS RECEIVABLE SYSTEM

The Atlanta Credit Card Center supports the complex process of credit card billing and is highly dependent on sophisticated data-capture techniques such as optical-character recognition (OCR). In a typical month, the Atlanta Center receives 20 million or more invoices for processing and creates 2 to 3 million customer billing statements. The Center computer equipment includes an IBM System/370 Model 158 computer, a 3031 computer, sixteen tape drives, and over forty disk drives to support the credit-card processing system.

The credit-card process begins at a service or fuel station when a customer presents a credit card as payment for products or services. The attendant uses an imprinter to record the customer's account number from the credit card and the dollar amount on an invoice. The invoices are sent to the Atlanta Center, where they are balanced and applied to customers' accounts. Finally bills are prepared and mailed along with the supporting invoices to the customers.

To handle the processing of credit card invoices and customer billing statements, the Atlanta Center utilizes TRACE (Transaction Capture and Encoding) OCR equipment manufactured by Recognition Equipment, Inc. The TRACE capture system reads data imprinted on the front of the invoice (account number, expiration date, and amount) at the rate of approximately 2,400 documents per minute and sprays the data on the back of the invoice in bar-code representation. At the same time, a machine-generated sequence number that can be read by humans is assigned to each invoice and is ink-jet printed on the face of each document. This unique number is used for invoice corrections if needed.

The invoices are broken down by billing cycle (there are eighteen billing cycles per month) and stored in a vault until the cycle is ready to be billed. The information from the invoice is stored on a disk file. This disk file is transferred to a magnetic tape for the daily batch update of the customer master file, thus ensuring an up-to-date file for online viewing.

At cycle billing time, the customer statements are printed, bar-code sprayed, and sorted by account number together with the invoices for that cycle (which were accumulated in the vault throughout the month). These customer statements and invoices are sorted by TRACE sorters that read the bar code sprayed on the back of the documents. A final sort breaks the statements into postage groupings for mailing. During this final sort, the statements and their associated invoices are microfilmed by the "input

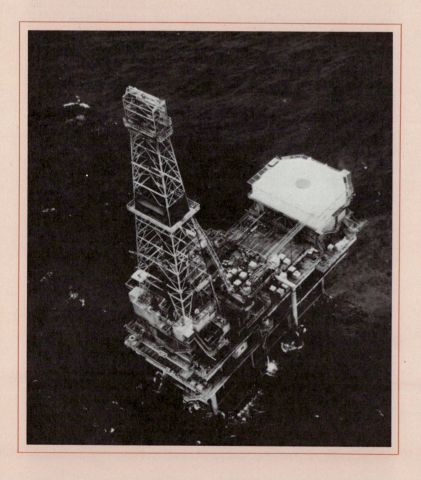

image microfilm recorder" of the TRACE system for archival and research purposes.

The daily batch update is run nightly and is the focal point of credit-card processing. This job updates customer account records, generates the alpha file (for online alphabetic inquiry to the customer master file), performs the billing routine on those accounts in the selected billing cycle, and generates records from which various control and management reports are prepared. The customer master file contains records for more than 6.5 million accounts.

Gulf Oil also receives applications for new accounts at a rate of tens of thousands per month. The New Accounts Processing System is an online interactive terminal/computer system. When an application is received, a unique serial number is stamped on it. This number becomes the key for processing the application through the system.

The data from the application is entered onto a disk file via a CRT. At this time, an automatic search is performed against the online customer master file to detect if an account already exists for the applicant. Also, a search is performed against the new account file to detect if there is currently an outstanding application from the same applicant.

After the decision to accept the application is made, the data to set up the account is entered via a CRT. An account number is randomly assigned, and a new account is set up on the customer master file during that night's daily batch update. If the application is rejected, a declination letter stating the reason for rejection is sent to the applicant.

The Gulf Atlanta Center also utilizes a point-of-sale (POS) system for twenty-four-hour, seven-day per week telephone credit authorization services. The purpose of the POS system is to minimize bad-debt and fraud loss by allowing a Gulf dealer to check a customer's credit status at the time of the sale. The dealer places a toll-free call to the POS unit in Atlanta, where the up-to-date customer master file is accessible via CRTs. Credit authorization is required on all card sales of $35 or more, and the credit decision is usually available in twenty-five to thirty seconds. Failure to comply with this procedure may result in the invoices being charged back to the dealer if the credit would otherwise have been denied by the POS system. The POS system is made up of sixteen CRTs to handle the authorization calls from dealers, which exceed 5,000 per day.

As can be seen from Gulf's complex credit-card processing system, sophisticated data-capture tecnhiques are necessary for handling the massive volume of transactions occurring in a large credit card system. By automating data entry, the transactions are recorded at a rate of thousands per minute, documents are sorted without human handling, and files are kept up-to-date for online inquiry to customer files.

DISCUSSION POINTS

1. Discuss Gulf's control over bad-debt minimization. How do the dealers keep up to date concerning credit authorization?

2. The Gulf credit card system is an example of a "country club billing system," where invoices supporting the credit transactions are returned to the customer. Descriptive billing systems list transactions line-by-line on the customer statement rather than include the customer-signed invoices. What are the advantages and disadvantages of each type of system? What would Gulf Oil have to do to convert to a descriptive billing system?

CHAPTER 5

Storage Devices

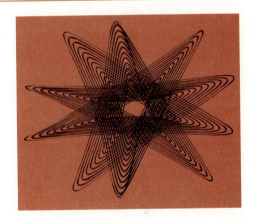

Introduction

Organizations store large volumes of data for a variety of purposes. Organizations that use electronic methods of processing this data must store it in computer-accessible form. Some storage media used in such situations have dual functions. For example, magnetic tapes and disks, which were mentioned in the previous chapter, are used for input and output and also for storage.

In discussing storage media, this chapter distinguishes between main storage and auxiliary storage. Auxiliary storage devices are further classified according to whether they provide sequential access or direct access to stored data. The most common sequential-access storage media are magnetic tapes. For direct access, magnetic disks are commonly used. Both are explained in detail here. The chapter also discusses the major advantages and disadvantages of mass storage systems.

"Computers Help Pick Future "

Students considering the future can now consult a computer.

The system, called Discover, provides mountains of information on a college or career. International Business Machines sells the service to high schools and colleges. IBM expert Larry Blasch demonstrated the system, which uses a video screen with a keyboard underneath and a light pen the user touches to the screen to call up information.

"Surveys show the average high school student gets four hours of counseling in four years," Blasch said. Overworked counselors can't provide all the information a

November, 1980 Written by United Press International.

curious student might want in that time.

The system allows a student to delve as deeply as he wants into the prospects for a future in, for example, nursing.

Schools offering training, job prospects, wages in different parts of the country and drawbacks of the profession can be called up on the TV screen for study and a printout can be made.

Blasch said school districts, charged $900 a month, have access to an IBM databank in Los Angeles which tells about more than 1,500 four-year colleges, 2,000 two-year or technical colleges, over 600 types of jobs and 450 military training programs. JoAnn Bowlsbey, co-developer of the system and college counselor, said "the system supplements work of the guidance counselor but doesn't replace him."

James Boyd, the other developer and technical director of the program at an Illinois college, said the system "is intended to do four things to help a student: help himself; understand the decision-making process; understand the world of work and his relationship to it, and identify training paths related to occupations."

Students who might feel shy or confused with a counselor can use the computer screen and daydream about the future with no pressure.

Blasch said middle-aged mothers and housewives entering the job market for the first time find the system very helpful.

He added that while the system is now geared to careers, sometime soon persons nearing retirement can use it and find out opportunities for post-working years, including hobbies, part time and volunteer jobs.

Computers' ability to store and retrieve data is one of the reasons they are so useful. How do you think the career data base discussed in this article is stored? The following chapter explains some of the data storage and retrieval options available.

CLASSIFICATION OF STORAGE MEDIA

A computer system generally includes two types of storage: main storage and auxiliary storage. *Main storage,* discussed in Chapter 3, is actually part of the CPU and is used to store both instructions and data. An increasingly popular medium for main storage is semiconductor circuits; in contrast, magnetic cores are slowly losing ground. Bubble memory is also becoming popular as the technology improves and costs decrease.

In many instances, the amount of data required by a program or set of programs exceeds the capacity of main storage. In such cases, the data is stored in *auxiliary,* or *secondary, storage,* which is not part of the CPU. The most common types of secondary storage are magnetic tapes and magnetic disks. Media such as punched cards, mass storage, and magnetic drums are also used. These auxiliary storage media cost much less than primary storage and thus make storage of large volumes of data economically feasible.

The secondary storage devices are connected to the CPU, and once data has been placed in them it can be retrieved as needed for processing. However, the retrieval of items from secondary storage is slower than from main storage. After processing has been completed, the data or results can be written back onto the auxiliary medium (see Figure 5–1).

Access to data in auxiliary storage can be either direct or sequential; the method depends on the storage medium used. Media such as magnetic tape and cassette tape provide *sequential-access storage*. The computer must start at the beginning of a tape and read what is stored there until it comes to the desired data. In contrast, a medium such as a magnetic disk or magnetic drum does not have to be read sequentially; the computer can get access to the desired data immediately—hence the name *direct-access storage*. Direct-access media, then, provide faster retrieval than do sequential-access media.

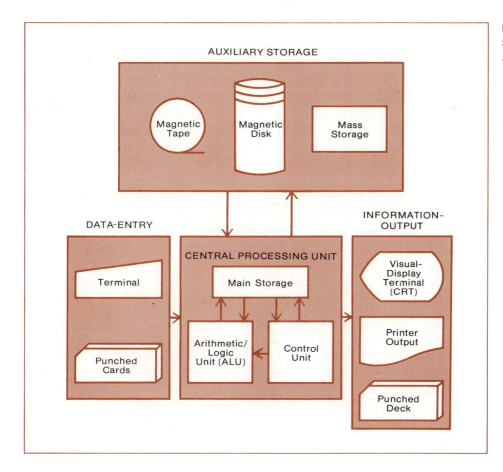

FIGURE 5–1
Schematic Drawing of a Computer System

SEQUENTIAL-ACCESS STORAGE

Magnetic Tape

A *magnetic tape* is a continuous plastic strip wound on a reel, quite similar to the tape used in reel-to-reel stereo recorders. The magnetic tape's plastic base is treated with a magnetizable coating. Typically, the tape is one-half inch in width. It is wound in lengths of 2,400 feet on $10\frac{1}{2}$-inch diameter reels. Magnetic tapes are also packaged in cartridges for use with small computers.

Data is stored on magnetic tape by the magnetizing of small spots of the iron oxide coating on the tape. Although these spots can be read by the computer, they are invisible to the human eye. Large volumes of information can be stored on a single tape; densities of 1,600 characters per inch are common, and some tapes are capable of storing up to 6,250 characters per inch. A typical tape reel of 2,400 feet can store as much as 400,000 punched cards.

The most common method of representing data on tape uses a nine-track coding scheme, although other coding schemes, such as six-track and seven-track, are also available. When the nine-track method is used, the tape is divided into nine horizontal rows called *tracks* (see Figure 5–2). Data is represented vertically in columns, one character per column. The method of coding data is identical to the Extended Binary Coded Decimal Interchange Code (EBCDIC) used to represent data in internal storage (see Chapter 3). Thus, eight bits (and eight of the nine tracks) are used to represent each character. The ninth bit is used as a parity bit.

A magnetic tape is mounted on a *tape drive* (see Figure 5–3) when the information it contains is needed by a program. The tape drive has a *read/write head* (actually an electromagnet) that creates or reads the bits as the tape moves past it (see Figure 5–4). When it is reading, the read/write head detects the magnetized areas and converts them into electrical pulses to send to the CPU. When writing, the head magnetizes the appropriate spots on the tape, erasing any previously stored data. Thus, writing is destructive, and reading is nondestructive.

FIGURE 5–2

Nine-Track Tape with Even Parity

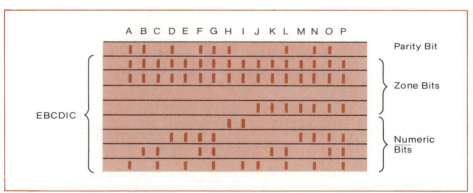

Note: The parity bit is shown in the top track to simplify visualization.

FIGURE 5–3
Magnetic-Tape Drive

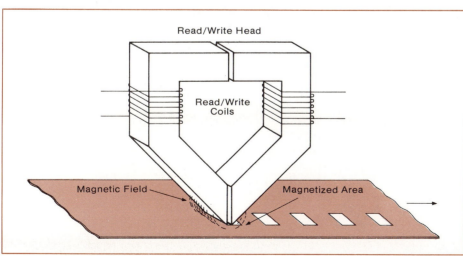

Read/Write Head

Read/Write Coils

Magnetic Field

Magnetized Area

FIGURE 5–4
Recording on Magnetic Tape

Typical tape drives move tapes at speeds ranging from 25 to 200 inches per second. The *density* of the data on the tape determines how fast it can be transferred from the tape to the CPU. For example, if a tape has a density of 1,600 characters per inch and moves at a speed of 112.5 inches per second, then the data is transferred at a rate of 18,000 characters per second (1,600 characters per inch × 112.5 inches per second).

Individual records on magnetic tape are separated by *interrecord gaps (IRGs)*, as shown in Figure 5–5. These gaps do not contain data but perform another function. A tape is rarely read in its entirety, all at once. Rather, it is stopped when the end of a record is reached. The tape must be rotating at the correct speed to allow the next record to be read correctly; otherwise, the result would be similar to what happens when a phonograph record is played at the wrong speed. The IRG allows the tape to regain the proper speed before the next record is read. The length of the interrecord gap depends on the speed of the tape drive; if the tape drive is very fast, longer gaps are needed, while slower speeds require shorter gaps.

If records are very short and divided by equally long IRGs, the tape may be more than 50 percent blank, causing the tape drive to be constantly stopping and accelerating. To avoid this possibility, records may be grouped, or blocked. These *blocked records,* or *blocks,* are separated by *interblock gaps (IBGs),* as in Figure 5–6. Now instead of reading a short record and stopping, reading a short record and stopping, and so on, the read/write head reads a group of short records at once and then stops, reads another group and stops, and so on. This method reduces the overall input/output time. An entire block of records is read into a buffer, and individual records are transferred from the buffer to primary storage for processing. Blocking also reduces the wasted space on the tape, permitting more records to be stored on a given length of tape. Thus, tape is much more versatile with respect to record length than punched cards.

Cassette Tape

Small computer systems may not need a large amount of auxiliary storage. For these systems, *tape cassettes* and *tape cartridges* have been developed. Tape cassettes look like those used in audio recording, and some can even be used with a typical cassette player/recorder. The major difference be-

FIGURE 5–5
Magnetic-Tape Records

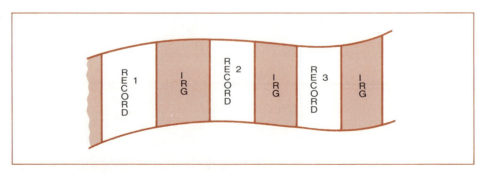

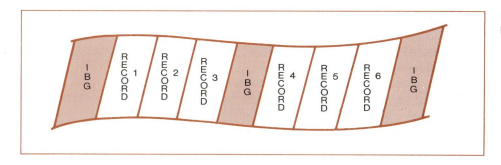

FIGURE 5–6
Blocked Records

tween the two types of tape cassettes is the tape; tape cassettes used for storing data use higher-quality, high-density digital recording tape (see Figure 5–7). The recording densities range from 125 to 200 characters per inch, and the common length is between 150 and 200 feet.

Because of the low cost and convenience of tape cassettes, their use for input, output, and storage has increased greatly in minicomputer and microcomputer systems. Tape cassettes are an ideal storage system for home computers. They can be used with a standard cassette player purchased for roughly $50 to $60. Tape cassettes are easy to store and also provide security, since they can be removed from the system and carried with the user.

Magnetic tape, as used on both reels and cassettes, has many advantages over punched card storage:

● Data can be transferred between magnetic tape and the CPU at high speeds.

FIGURE 5–7
Tape Cassette

● Magnetic-tape records can be any length, while card records are usually limited to eighty characters.

● Because of their high recording densities, magnetic tapes can store data in much less space than cards.

● Magnetic tape can be erased and reused.

● Magnetic tape can provide high-capacity storage and backup storage at a relatively low cost. A 2,400-foot magnetic tape costs about $15.

● Magnetic tape is perfectly suited for sequential processing. It is the most common storage medium in these types of systems.

Magnetic tape has the following disadvantages:

● Since tape is a sequential medium, the entire tape must be read from start to finish when being updated. The amount of time required precludes its use where instantaneous retrieval of data is required.

● All tapes and reel containers must be properly labeled and identified.

● Humans cannot read the data on magnetic tape. When the validity of such data is questioned, the contents of the tape must be printed.

● Environmental factors can distort data stored on magnetic tape. Dust, moisture, high or low temperatures, and static electricity can cause improper processing. Therefore, the environment must be carefully controlled.

DIRECT-ACCESS STORAGE

Magnetic Disk

The conventional *magnetic disk* is a metal platter fourteen inches in diameter coated on both sides with a magnetizable material like iron oxide. In many respects, a magnetic disk resembles a phonograph record. However, it does not have a phonograph record's characteristic grooves; its surfaces are smooth. Nevertheless, a disk unit does store and retrieve data in much the same fashion as a phonograph. The disk is rotated while a read/write head moves above its magnetic surface. Instead of spiraling into the center of the disk like the needle of a phonograph, however, the read/write head stores and retrieves data in concentric circles. Each of these circles is called a *track*. One track never touches another, as shown in Figure 5–8. A typical disk has two hundred tracks per surface.

In most disk storage devices, several disks are assembled to form a *disk pack* (see Figure 5–9) and mounted on a center shaft. The individual disks are spaced on the shaft to allow room for a mechanism to move between them (see Figure 5–10). The disk pack in Figure 5–10 has eleven disks and provides twenty usable recording surfaces; the top and bottom surfaces are not used for storing data because they are likely to become scratched or nicked. A disk pack may contain anywhere from five to a hundred disks.

A disk pack must be positioned in a disk storage unit when the data on the pack is to be processed. The *disk drive* rotates all disks in unison at a speed ranging from 40 to 3,600 revolutions per second. In some models, the disk packs are removable; in others, the disks are permanently mounted on

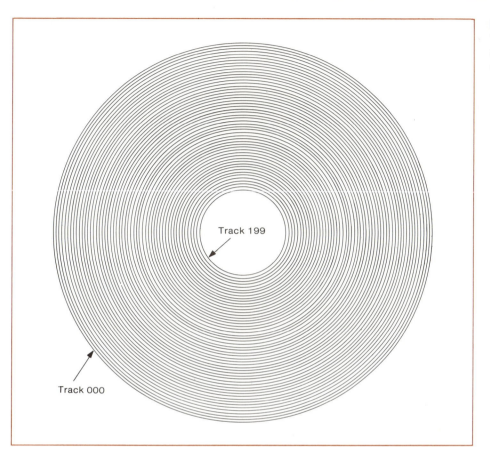

FIGURE 5–8
Top View of Disk
Surface Showing
Concentric Tracks

Track 199

Track 000

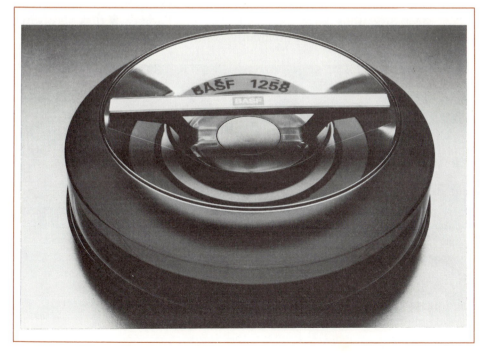

FIGURE 5–9
Disk Pack

FIGURE 5–10
A Disk Pack

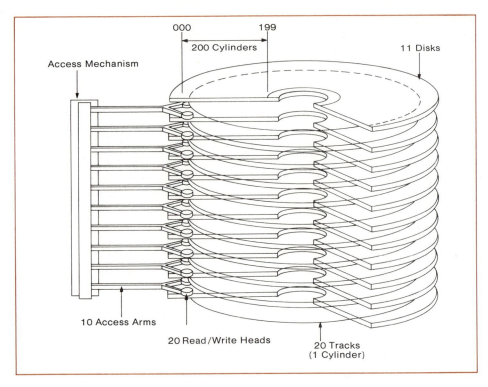

the disk drive. Removable disk packs allow disk files to be removed when the data they contain is not needed. Users of removable disk packs typically have many more disk packs than disk drives (see Figure 5–11).

The data on a disk is read or written by the read/write heads between the disks. Most disk units have one read/write head for each disk recording surface. All the heads are permanently connected to an *access mechanism.*

FIGURE 5–11
Disk Storage Units with
Removable Disk Packs

When reading or writing occurs, the heads are positioned over the appropriate track by the in-and-out movement of the access mechanism (see Figure 5–10). Some disk units have one read/write head for each track. The access time is much faster with this type of disk unit, since the access mechanism does not need to move from track to track; but such units are rarely used because of their high costs.

When data on the surface of one disk in the disk pack is required, all the heads move to the appropriate track, because they are connected to the same access mechanism. Because all the read/write heads move together, they are positioned over the same tracks on all disk surfaces at the same time. All the number-1 tracks on the disk surfaces form a *cylinder*; the number-2 tracks on all surfaces form another cylinder enclosed within the first; and so on. The number of cylinders per disk pack equals the number of tracks per surface.

Each track on a disk can store the same amount of data (even though the tracks get smaller toward the center of the disk). Consider a disk pack on which a maximum of 7,294 bytes (or characters) can be stored per track and 4,000 usable tracks (20 surfaces × 200 tracks per surface) are available. Such a disk pack could conceivably store 29 million characters of data.

Data stored on a magnetic disk is located by disk surface number, track number, and record number; this information constitutes a disk address. The disk address of a record immediately precedes the record (see Figure

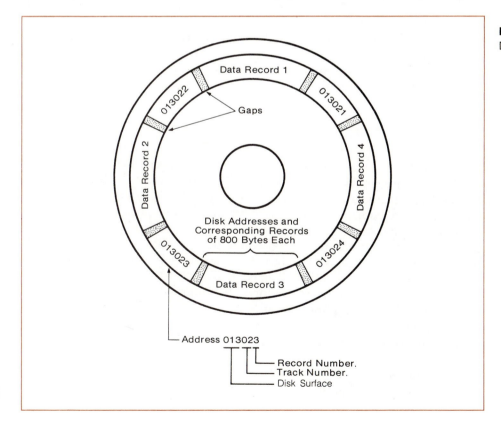

FIGURE 5–12
Disk Address

5–12). Note that disk records are separated by gaps similar to the interrecord gaps on magnetic tape. Thus, although more data can be stored on a track by blocking several records together and reducing the number of gaps, the presence of gaps does reduce the amount of information that can be stored on a disk. In the disk pack described above, the usable storage capacity would be somewhat less than the potential capacity of 29 million characters of data.

Because disks provide direct access, they are typically used to store data against which frequent inquiries are required. Depending upon the disk drive, read speeds of up to 850,000 characters per second are possible.

Floppy Disks

The *flexible disk, diskette,* or *floppy disk* was introduced in 1973 (see Figure 5–13) to replace punched cards as a medium for data entry, but it can also store programs and data files. These floppy disks are made of plastic and coated with an oxide substance. They are, in most respects, miniature magnetic disks. The diskettes often sell for as little as $5 and are very popular for use with minicomputer systems and point-of-sale terminals. They are reusable, easy to store, and weigh less than two ounces. They are readily interchangeable and can even be mailed. Because flexible disks are removable, they provide added security for a computer system. A typical disk can store as much as 3,000 punched cards.

The floppy disk comes in two standard sizes—8 inches and 5¼ inches. The 5¼-inch disk is referred to as a mini-floppy. The disks are permanently sealed in a paper jacket (see Figure 5–14a). Data is stored as magnetized spots in tracks, as on conventional (hard) magnetic disks, and is addressed by track number and sector number (see Figure 5–14b). There are seventy-seven tracks and twenty-six sectors on a standard 8-inch disk, thirty-five tracks and eighteen sectors on a mini-floppy. The read/write head moves

FIGURE 5-13
Floppy Disk

back and forth in the rectangular opening (the read/write notch) and can be placed on any track. Unlike the one in hard disk systems, this read/write head actually rides on the surface of the disk rather than being positioned slightly above it. The disk rotates at 360 revolutions per minute (as compared to 40 to 1,000 revolutions per second for hard disk drives).

FIGURE 5-14(a)
Packaging of a Floppy Disk

FIGURE 5-14(b)
Sectors on a Floppy Disk

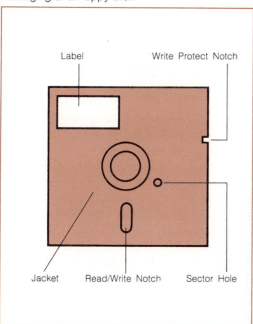

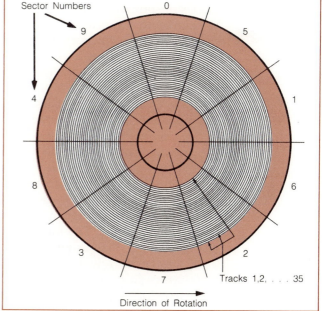

Magnetic disks have several advantages over magnetic tape:

● Disk files can be organized sequentially and processed in the same way as magnetic tape or they can be organized for direct-access processing.
● The fast access time offered by magnetic-disk storage allows data files to be updated immediately.
● Quick response can be made to inquiries (normally, response is made in seconds).
● Files stored on disks can be linked by software (stored-program instructions) to allow a single transaction to update all files simultaneously.

The major disadvantages of magnetic-disk storage are:

● Magnetic disk is a relatively expensive storage medium; it may cost ten times as much as magnetic tape in terms of cost per character stored. However, reductions in disk costs and the introduction of flexible disks are making these storage devices more attractive from a cost standpoint.
● When disk files are updated, the original data is erased and the new data put in its place. Therefore, there is no backup file. If there are no other provisions for error checking and backup files, data may be lost.
● Disk storage requires more sophisticated programming for gaining access to records and updating files. The hardware itself is also highly sophisticated, and skilled technicians are required to maintain it.
● Security may be a problem because of the ease of gaining direct access to data on disk files.

MASS STORAGE

Using primary storage is very fast because access to data is direct and requires no physical movement. The speed of electricity is, in effect, the limiting factor. However, primary storage is also very expensive. Disk storage is less expensive, and it provides direct-access capabilities. But even disk storage tends to be too expensive when very large amounts of data must be stored for direct-access processing.

To meet this need, mass storage devices have been developed. They allow rapid access to data, although their access times are much slower than those of primary storage or magnetic disk. Large files, backup files, and infrequently used files can be placed in mass storage at a relatively low cost.

One approach to mass storage uses a cartridge tape as the storage medium. The cartridges are similar to cassette tapes; however, the high-density tape used requires 90 percent less storage space than common magnetic tape. A mass storage system such as this can hold the equivalent of up to 8,000 tape reels. The mounting of the tapes is under the control of the system, rather than of an operator, and tends to be faster than the traditional operator-controlled mounting of magnetic tapes.

Mass storage is not limited to high-density magnetic tape. Recently, a mass storage system for minicomputers using small floppy disks as the stor-

age medium was introduced. However, unlike the cartridge system described above, most mass storage devices require extensive physical movement, because the needed files must first be found and then mounted mechanically before data can be read or written. Although direct access is possible, the retrieval time is relatively slow (normally measured in seconds).

FUTURE TRENDS IN DATA STORAGE

As technology continues to advance, smaller, faster, and less expensive storage devices will become commonplace. Advances are rapidly being made in semiconductor and laser technology. A recent innovation in semiconductor technology is the development of charge-coupled devices (CCDs) for use in data storage. CCDs are made of silicon, similar to semiconductor memory. They are nearly a hundred times faster than magnetic bubbles but somewhat slower than semiconductor, random-access memories. As in semiconductor memories, data in CCDs can be lost if a power failure occurs.

Laser technology provides an opportunity to store massive quantities of data at greatly reduced costs. A *laser storage system* can store nearly 128 billion characters of data at about one-tenth the cost of standard magnetic media. In a laser system, data is recorded by a laser beam's forming patterns on the surface of a polyester sheet coated with a thin layer of rhodium metal. To read data from this sheet, the laser reflects light off the surface, reconstructing the data into a digital bit stream. Laser data resists alteration, and any attempt to alter it can be detected readily; so it provides a secure storage system. Further, unlike magnetic media, laser storage does not de-

HIGHLIGHT 5–3

Storage Integrity

Problems with computer memory are seldom the result of hardware failure. A good example of the real problem was seen in Utah last tax season. A student who was expecting a tax refund check for $14.39 received instead the sum of $800,014.39. Upon investigation, officials found that a diskette storing taxpayer information had been incorrectly coded. When computer operators tried to correct the error, they chose a quick method and tried to make the correction from a data-entry console. Following this procedure automatically circumvented programmed edit checks. The later examination showed that the correction had not been error-free either, leading to the over-refund. If the student had not notified the State Tax Commission, officials wonder whether the mistake would have been caught— especially since the same operation had automatically updated the State's books, keeping them in balance.

The message of this mishap is that the best of storage technology cannot fix errors stemming from disregard of procedures. Procedures that seem a waste of time when followed *may* be the most economical path to quality service.

teriorate over time and is immune to electromagnetic radiation. Another advantage is that there is no danger of losing data because of power failures.

A very recent development is a laser system to be used as a mass storage device for minicomputers. This system uses a helium-neon laser, delivering about ten milliwatts of optical power to a disk coated with a film of non-metallic substance (tellurium). Data is recorded when the laser creates a hole approximately one micrometer in diameter in the film. The disk used in this system is thirty centimeters in diameter and can store ten billion bits on its 40,000 tracks. The data cannot be erased once it is written, so this system is best suited for archival storage or for a great volume of data that must be maintained online.

Technology advances so rapidly that accurate prediction of what future storage media will be like is nearly impossible. The objectives of making storage less expensive, faster, and smaller will continue to be pursued. The current state of the art will remain current for only a short time.

SUMMARY

- Auxiliary storage, which is not part of the CPU, can store large amounts of data and instructions at a lower cost than main storage. The most common auxiliary storage media are magnetic tapes and magnetic disks.
- Access to data in auxiliary storage can be either sequential or direct. Magnetic tapes on reels and in cassettes provide sequential-access storage, whereas conventional, or hard, magnetic disks and floppy disks provide direct-access storage.
- Magnetic tape consists of a plastic base coated with iron oxide. Data is stored by small areas on the surface of the tape's being magnetized.

● Usually, data is represented on tape by a nine-track coding scheme, such as 8-bit EBCDIC with a ninth bit for parity.

● Tape density refers to the number of characters that can be stored on one inch of tape. The transfer rate of data from tape to CPU depends on the density of the tape and the speed at which it travels past the read/write head.

● Data is often recorded on magnetic tape in groups of records called blocks. Blocks are separated from each other by interblock gaps (IBGs). Blocking reduces overall input/output time.

● Tape cassettes are similar to audio cassettes. They can store up to 200 characters per inch and are used when small amounts of storage are required.

● The major advantages of magnetic tape are high speed of data transfer, unlimited record length, reusability, and low cost. Disadvantages include requirement for sequential organization, data representation that humans cannot read, and susceptibility to environmental factors, which can distort data on tape.

● A disk pack consists of from five to a hundred metal platters, or disks. In some packs, each platter has two hundred tracks on which data is recorded in magnetic form. Data is read or written by read/write heads connected to an access mechanism.

● A disk pack is positioned on a disk drive, which rotates all disks in the pack in unison. Some disk packs are removable; others are permanently mounted on disk drives.

● Magnetic disks provide direct access. Any record can be located by reference to its disk surface number, track number, and record number. The read/write head can be positioned directly over the desired track.

● Flexible, or floppy, disks provide low-cost, direct-access storage. Some can provide as much storage as 3,000 punched cards. Floppy disks are reusable, easy to store, and can be mailed. They are frequently used with minicomputers.

● Advantages of disk storage include fast access times and provision for both sequential and direct-access file organizations. Major disadvantages are high cost, lack of backup, greater programming complexity, and need for greater security measures.

● Mass storage devices are appropriate when large amounts of data must be stored at a low cost. They provide direct access, although access time is much slower than with disk. Commonly used mass storage media are cassette-type cartridge tapes and floppy disks.

● Technological advances will continue to make storage devices faster, smaller, and less expensive. Recent innovations include charge-coupled devices and laser storage systems.

REVIEW QUESTIONS

1. Distinguish between main storage and auxiliary storage. Name some common auxiliary storage devices.

2. Which storage media provide direct access and which provide sequential access? Explain how direct-access capabilities are achieved.

3. Compare magnetic tape and magnetic disk as auxiliary storage media. Identify applications for which each is suitable.

4. Explain blocking of records. What is its purpose? Why are interblock gaps necessary?

5. Describe two types of mass storage devices. What are the advantages and disadvantages of such devices?

6. What are the advantages of floppy disks? With what type of hardware are they typically used?

APPLICATION

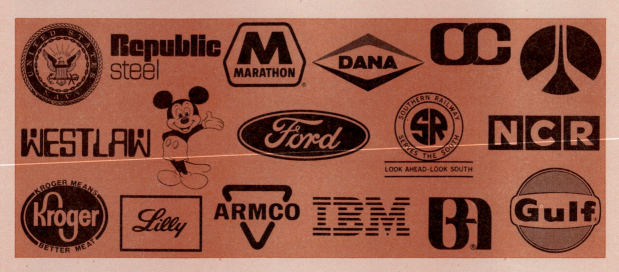

Republic steel

Republic Steel

The Republic Iron and Steel Company was the outgrowth of a merger of thirty-five smaller midwestern iron companies. In its early days, Republic attracted some interesting people, among them John "Bet-a-Million" Gates. Along with some associates, Gates bought into Republic with the idea of using it as the basis for a great steel empire. Although the strategy failed in the Panic of 1906, Republic Iron and Steel grew quickly.

By 1927, Republic was in the hands of Cyrus Eaton, one of this country's most active, eccentric, and brilliant empire builders. It was Eaton's desire

to use Republic Iron and Steel as the nucleus for a vast midwestern steel company. His progress was impressive. In 1928, Republic combined forces with Steel and Tubes, Inc., which had plants in Ohio, New York, and Michigan, and merged with Trumbull Steel. Republic's own plants in Youngstown, Ohio, gave Republic Iron and Steel much diversity. Union Drawn Steel, with plants in Ohio, Pennsylvania, Connecticut, Indiana, and Ontario, was added in 1929. The Republic Steel Corporation was officially born in 1930 as a result of mergers with three other steel and steel products companies.

Since then, Republic Steel has done better than most expected. Even before Republic's official birthdate, financial experts were predicting its death. Yet Republic has not died. Financially handicapped

through most of the Depression, Republic nevertheless survived to grow in size and production capacity and continued to acquire smaller companies. During the 1960s, Republic's production of raw steel reached an all-time high of 10.7 million net tons (which was topped in 1973 with a total shipment of 11.3 million tons).

Today, Republic Steel is this country's fifth largest steel manufacturer. Recently its sales reached an all-time high of $3.8 billion. Its corporate umbrella includes steel plants; steel and tubing divisions; and manufacturing, mining, and transportation interests.

Four large data centers, located in Cleveland, Warren, and Massillon, Ohio, and Chicago, maintain the data-processing activities of the geographically dispersed steel plants. Each data center maintains several large CPUs. Specifically, the Cleveland data center utilizes two IBM 3000 Series computers and one Amdahl computer; the Massillon center operates three IBM System/370 model 158 computers; the Warren center operates two Amdahl computers; and the Chicago center uses two IBM System/370 model 158 computers.

In addition, Republic utilizes three other processing operations called satellite centers in other locations. The satellite centers are tied into the four large data centers described above and transfer data to them via remote job entry (RJE). Also hooked up to

the large data centers are approximately 1,500 input/output terminals providing access to stored data.

Each data center handles a variety of data-processing applications. For example, the Cleveland data center computers handle the processing of corporate accounting procedures, such as accounts payable and accounts receivable, order entry and order processing, personnel, production control, and inventory control. Because of the necessity of gaining ready access to the large amounts of data needed for these

applications, large and efficient data storage techniques are necessary. The Cleveland data center alone uses twelve IBM series 3350 disk drives and twenty-eight Control Data Corporation (CDC) double density model 33502 disk drives. Tape drives are STC 3650, and fourteen tape drives are used for processing.

The Cleveland data center performs processing in two ways: batch and online. The batch processing applications include payroll and accounting. Payroll data such as personnel records, tax records, and the like are stored on magnetic tape. When the payroll checks are to be processed, the data is transferred to magnetic disk and is accessed via direct-access storage devices (DASD). Once the necessary files are updated and the payroll checks are processed, the updated files are transferred from disk to tape for storage. The magnetic tape provides a storage medium for files that are used periodically and also allows for file backup and archival storage.

The online processing is important for gaining immediate access to data. Republic Steel has an extensive teleprocessing system. Data communication techniques are used to connect the 1,500 terminals to the data centers. An example of this online teleprocessing system is the order entry–customer billing system. Orders for Republic's products are entered on a CRT. The data is edited and verified and a sales order is prepared.

The information (customer name, items ordered, and so on) is stored on magnetic disk. A copy of the order is transmitted to the production department, where it is compared with other order and production data stored on disks. This data is also used by the accounting function to keep up-to-date records of accounts receivable, sales, and the like.

By storing data on magnetic disks, Republic has ready access to the files and can make inquiries to the customer files or change the dates or the instructions of a particular order.

The trend of Republic Steel's data-processing operation has been toward increased utilization of teleprocessing and data communication techniques. As the need for ready access to information grows, more and more information will be stored on disk devices, providing online availability of data.

DISCUSSION POINTS

1. Explain why a backup system of computer files is necessary. What methods of backup does Republic Steel use for its tape storage? For its disk storage?

2. What are the advantages of using disk storage for the order entry/billing system? How would tape storage be used in processing the order entry application?

CHAPTER 6

Remote Access/ Communication Systems

Introduction

Managing today's diverse businesses is a complex task. Management information needs extend beyond periodic summary reports provided on a routine basis. A manager must have current knowledge of company operations in order to control business activities and to ensure that effective customer service is provided. Decisions must be made on short notice and on the basis of data gathered and analyzed from geographically remote locations. An efficient, fast way to capture, process, and distribute large amounts of data is needed. Data communication systems developed to meet this need help reduce delays in the collection and dissemination of data.

This chapter explains how communication systems allow users at remote locations to gain fast, easy access to computer resources. It discusses the concepts and techniques involved in message transmission and introduces the types of equipment that make data communication possible. It also presents alternative methods of using communications technology to implement management information systems.

"Big Business's Big Bird"

Merrill Sheils
with William J. Cook

The launch was perfect. To a chant of "Go! Go! Go!" from a blue-chip gallery of businessmen, a Delta rocket blasted off from Cape Canaveral and headed for a spot 22,300 miles above the equator just west of the Galápagos Islands. Its payload was a 2,300-pound communications satellite, and as the bird, designated SBS-1, was carefully "tweaked" into position last week, the enthusiasm of the earthbound executives was understandable. SBS-1 is the first satellite dedicated solely to enhancing corporate communications— and its launch marks the start of a revolution in the way big corporations do business.

The newest space bird belongs to Satellite Business Systems (SBS), a five-year-old partnership among IBM, the Communications Satellite Corp. (Comsat) and Aetna Life & Casualty Co. Other technological colossi, such as AT&T and Xerox, are preparing corporate satellite services of their own, but SBS is the most ambitious effort yet to cash in on business's growing need to transmit vast quantities of data quickly and efficiently. Early

next year SBS-1 will begin to function as a relay tower in the sky for eleven major companies, including General Motors, Boeing, Westinghouse, All-State Insurance and Wells Fargo Bank. So far, the three partners have invested $375 million in the venture, and by 1983 they expect to break even. "We see the marketplace as very big," says SBS president Robert C. Hall. "We'll be a billion-dollar company by the end of the decade."

SBS-1 will float in geosynchronous orbit, circling the earth exactly once a day and thus seeming to hover over the same spot. Transmitters on earth will beam radio signals at the bird, whose transponders— mechanisms that amplify such impulses— will then return the signals to earth stations on rooftops or in parking lots near SBS customers. SBS will go on the air with the ability to transmit 1.5 million bits of data per second,* and has the potential for four times that volume. (A typical land-line telephone circuit can move only 9,600 bits per second.)

Eventually, SBS officials expect most of their business to be in high-speed data transmission. But most of their customers do not yet need SBS-1's full potential. As a result, SBS is concentrating on voice services, competing directly with Ma Bell and other long-distance telephone companies. Customers can

choose among three packages. The most complex will link various parts of one large company through earth stations, enabling officials at headquarters in New York, for example, to telephone, send data and transmit documents, or hold teleconferences with colleagues all over the country. A second service will allow three to six companies to share SBS stations for the same kind of link-up. Finally, SBS's "exchange service" will provide cheap long-distance telephone communication.

New Wonders: Meanwile, SBS has contracted with AM International, E-Systems, Inc., and Bunker Ramo Corp.—all manufacturers of electronic equipment—to build some devices SBS suspects its customers will want as they learn to take advantage of the system. AM International, for instance, has built a batch-document-distribution machine that scans a page with a laser, translates the information into digital code and stores it. When the storage system has collected 5,000 pages of copy, explains SBS vice president Ray Fentriss, "it goes banging over the satellite" to receiving stations. At the receiving end, another machine decodes the digital signals and prints out high-quality copy at 70 pages per minute, then collates and staples the lot. With the device a head office could send a complete instruction manual to eight or ten branch offices overnight.

SBS's ambitious plans have

*A bit is one digit, either 1 or 0, in the binary code that computers use to do their calculations.

only begun: next April the company plans to launch its second satellite, and it will have a third ready for the first

commercial flight of the space shuttle in late 1982 or 1983. "We're about to become a real, honest-to-god company, with

revenues coming in," says Hall. The market is still unproven, but for the moment, at least, all SBS systems are go.

This article describes one of the latest advancements in data communication technology. Communication networks combined with computer systems provide very powerful data processing capabilities. This chapter describes how communication systems are tied together by use of data communications.

DATA COMMUNICATION

Data communication is the electronic transmission of data from one location to another, usually over communication channels such as telephone/telegraph lines or microwaves. In a data communication system, data are transmitted between terminals and a central computer or between two or more computers. As people and equipment become geographically dispersed, the computer and input and output devices, or *terminals* are hooked into a communication network. The combined use of communication facilities, such as telephone systems, and data-processing equipment is called *teleprocessing*.

Message Transmission

Data can be transmitted over communication lines in one of two forms: analog or digital. Transmission of data in continuous wave form is referred to as *analog transmission*. An analog transmission can be likened to the waves created in a pan of still water by a stick. By sending "waves" down a wire electronically, one causes messages to be sent and received. In the past, analog transmission was the major means of relaying data over long distances. This was due largely to the type of communication lines provided by American Telephone and Telegraph (AT&T). (see Figure 6–1a.) *Digital transmission* involves transmitting data as distinct on and off pulses; it is becoming more popular. Digital communications tend to be faster and more accurate than analog communications.

Analog transmission requires that the sender convert the data from the pulse form in which it is stored to wave form before transmitting it. This conversion process is called *modulation*. The opposite conversion—from wave form to pulse form—is required at the receiving end before the data is entered into the computer. This conversion is called *demodulation*. Both modulation and demodulation are accomplished by devices called *modems*, or *data sets* (see Figure 6–2). The term *modem* is derived from the terms *mo*dulation and *dem*odulation.

As stated earlier, when digital transmission is used, data are transmitted in *pulse form*, as shown in Figure 6–1b. Since the computer stores data in pulse form, there is no need to convert the data to wave form. This reduces the time required to send messages. Digital transmission has also demon-

139

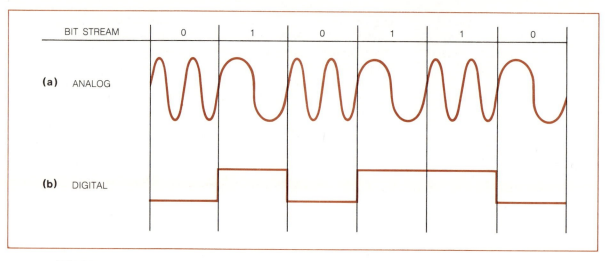

FIGURE 6–1
Analog and Digital
Transmission

FIGURE 6–2
Modem

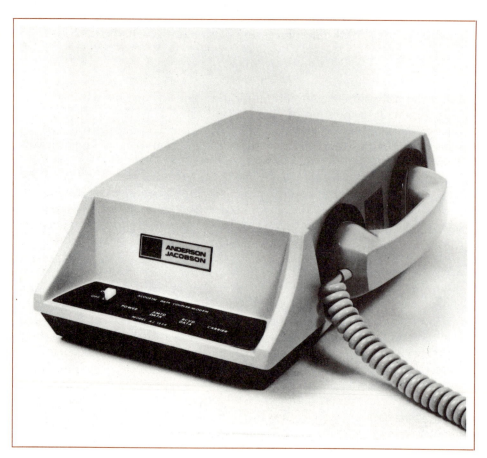

strated a much lower error rate (about 100 times lower) than analog transmission. These two facts mean that users can transmit large amounts of data faster and more reliably.

Communication Channels

A *communication channel* is the link that permits transmission of electrical signals between distributed locations; its purpose is to carry data from one location to another. The types of communication channels used for data transfer are telegraph lines, telephone lines, coaxial cables, microwave links, communication satellites, high-speed helical waveguides, and laser beams.

Grades of Transmission   The *grade*, or *bandwidth*, of a channel determines the range of frequencies it can transmit. The rate at which data can be transmitted across the channel is directly proportional to the width of the frequency band. *Narrow bandwidth channels* can transmit data at a rate of 45 to 90 bits

141

per second. Telegraph channels are typical narrow bandwidth channels.

Voice-grade channels have a wider frequency range; they can transmit at rates of from 300 to 9,600 bits per second. Voice-grade channels, such as telephone lines, are used by the Dataphone and Dataspeed equipment of AT&T's Bell Telephone System, the Wide Area Telphone Service (WATS), and many others.

For applications that require high-speed transmission of large volumes of data, *broad-band channels* are most suitable. Coaxial cables, microwaves, helical waveguides, and laser beams belong in this grade. Leased broad-band services are offered by both Western Union and the Bell System (see Figure 6-3); an example of a leased broad-band service is the Telpak system. Such a service is capable of transmitting data at rates of up to 120,000 bits per second.

Modes of Transmission   Another method of classifying communication channels is by the mode of transmission they use. Depending on the application and the terminal equipment used, channels operate in one of three basic transmission modes (see Figure 6–4):

● *Simplex*. A simplex channel provides for unidirectional, or one-way, transmission of data. A terminal that transmits via a simplex channel can either send or receive; it cannot do both.
● *Half-duplex*. In the half-duplex mode, communication can occur in both directions, but in only one direction at a time. This type of transmission is commonly used in telephone services and telephone networks.
● *Full-duplex*. A full-duplex channel can transmit data in both directions simultaneously; thus it is the most versatile mode of transmission.

Multiplexers and Concentrators

Multiplexers and *concentrators* increase the number of devices that can use a communication channel. This is necessary because terminals operate at a

FIGURE 6–3
High-speed Modem

much slower speed (100 to 150 bits per second) than do communication channels (300 to 9,600 bits per second for voice grade). Thus, a channel is not used to full capacity by a single terminal.

Multiplexing can create a more economical usage of the communication channel by combining the input streams from several terminals into a single input stream which can be sent over a single channel. This allows for a single communication channel (typically voice grade) to substitute for many slower subvoice channels that might otherwise have been operating at less

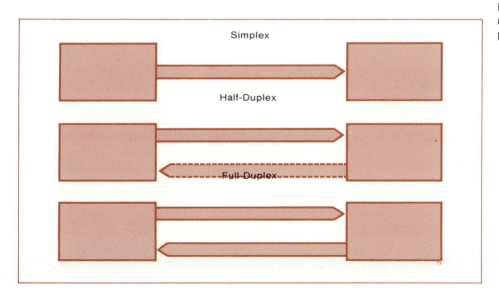

FIGURE 6–4
Channel Transmission Modes

than full capacity. At the receiving end, a similar unit separates the various input streams for further processing.

A concentrator differs from a multiplexer in that it allows data from only one terminal at a time to be transmitted over a communication channel. The concentrator polls the terminals one at a time to see if they have any messages to send. When a communication channel is free, the first terminal ready to send or receive data will get control of the channel and will continue to control it for the length of the transaction. The use of a concentrator relies on the assumption that not all terminals will be ready to send or receive data at a single given time. Figure 6–5 shows communication systems with and without multiplexers and concentrators.

Programmable Communications Processors

A *programmable communications processor* is a device that relieves the CPU of many of the tasks typically required in a communication system. When the volume of data transmission surpasses a certain level, a programmable communications processor can handle these tasks more economically than the CPU. Examples of such tasks include handling messages and priorities, disconnecting after messages have been received, requesting re-transmission of incomplete messages, and verifying successfully transmitted messages.

The two most frequent uses of communications processors are message-switching and front-end processing. The principal task of the processor used for *message-switching*, is to receive messages and route them to appropriate destinations. A *front-end processor* also performs message-switching, as well as more sophisticated operations such as validating transmitted data and pre-processing data before it is transmitted to the central computer.

COMMUNICATION SYSTEMS

Single CPU Systems

A typical computer system consists of a single main frame linked to a variety of *peripherals* (input/output devices, secondary storage devices, and so on). If the peripherals are connected directly to the CPU, the system is said to be a *local system*. However, in recent years, advancements in computer technology have made it possible to place terminals (or other devices) in the hands of users in locations removed from the main frame. These terminals are connected to the central computer by a communication channel. The resulting system is called a *remote system*.

Time-Sharing   Many businesses could benefit from the installation of a computer facility but are prohibited from doing so by its cost. Some organizations only infrequently need the power of a large computer system. To meet both of these requirements, *time-sharing systems* have been developed. Under time-sharing, two or more users with diverse tasks can access the same

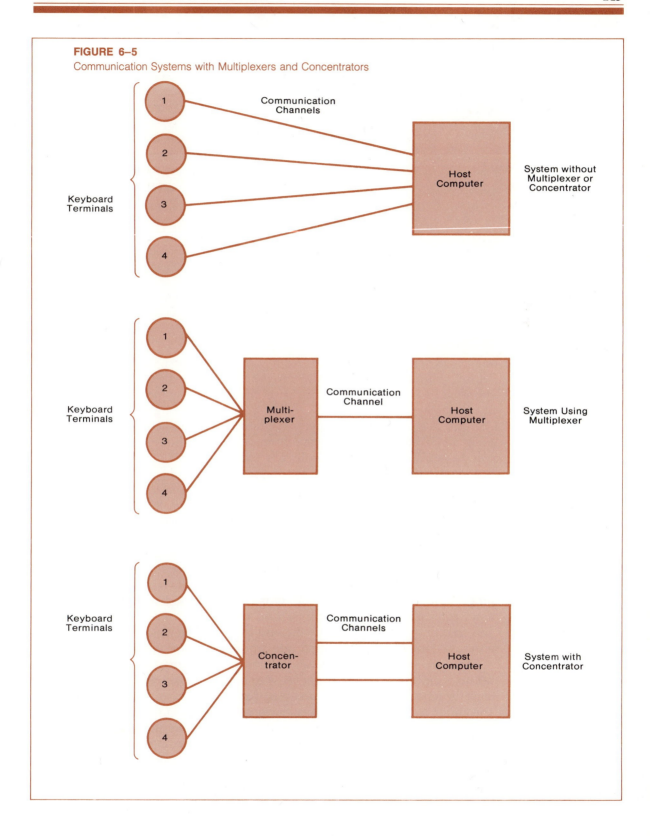

FIGURE 6–5

Communication Systems with Multiplexers and Concentrators

central computer resources and receive what seem to be simultaneous responses. Each user believes that he or she has total control of the computer; but in reality, the computer is dividing its time among them. Each user is charged only for the computer resources he or she actually uses. Remote users may access the system via terminals and telephone lines. Nearby users may have I/O devices that are directly connected to it.

A system that supports time-sharing must have some method of allocating computing time to users. The purpose of the time-sharing system would be defeated if one user had to wait a long time while another monopolized the CPU's processing facilities. To solve this problem, a technique called *time-slicing* is often used. Each user is allocated a small portion of processing time. If the user's program is completely executed during this time, or if the program reaches a point at which input or output activity must occur before the time is used up, the CPU begins (or resumes) executing another user's program. If the program is not completely executed during the allocated time, control of the CPU is transferred to another user's program anyway. The first program is placed at the end of a waiting line. This switching of programs occurs at such a rapid rate that users are generally unaware of it.

There are two methods of establishing time-sharing capability. One is to set up a time-sharing system *in-house* to obtain quick answers to such problems as production and cost analysis, forecasting, and accounts receivable. The other is to purchase time-sharing capability from a service company. This approach is often taken by small organizations that cannot afford to have their own computers. Because of the intense competition in this area, many service companies have expanded to provide not only time-sharing capability but also specialized programs and technical assistance.

The major advantages of time-sharing systems include the following:

● They provide an economical means for small users to utilize the resources of a large computer system.
● They allow each user to seem to possess a private computer.
● They provide quick response capabilities.
● Through resource pooling, they can provide access to greater numbers of application programs at a lower unit cost than privately owned and maintained computers.
● The user who purchases computer time from a service bureau does not need to worry about equipment obsolescence.

Time-sharing also has inherent problems, some of them identified below:

● Users connected to the system by telephone lines must worry about breakdowns in the lines or increases in communication costs. Furthermore, telephone lines are designed primarily for voice communication; they are not the best medium for transmission of data. Thus, applications involving extensive I/O operations may not be suited to time-sharing.
● Because data can be accessed quickly and easily in a time-sharing system, concern for security must be increased. All programs and data must be safeguarded from unauthorized persons or use.
● When quick response is not a necessity, time-sharing capability may be needlessly expensive.
● System reliability may be lower than in non-time-sharing systems. The additional equipment and communication channels create more areas for both mechanical and system-related problems.

Multiple CPU Configurations

As the complexity of business and scientific problems increases, the resources of a single CPU may not be sufficient to provide adequate response time to inquiries or to perform the complex calculations required. To provide adequate computing power for solving such problems, several CPUs may be linked together to form a *network.*

As with a single CPU and its terminals, the network's main frames may be hooked together to form either local or remote systems. Several computers can be connected at a central location to enhance computing capabilities. The computers can also be dispersed geographically to the locations of data collection or information dispersal. These dispersed computers are connected by a communication network. The advantages of a distributed system include reduced organization impact, greater flexibility and responsiveness, and increased ability to withstand failure.

Different types of structures can be used to implement the multiple CPU concept (see Figure 6–6). In a *spider configuration,* all transactions must go through a central computer before being routed to the appropriate network computer. The effect is to create a central decision point. This facilitates workload distribution and resource sharing, but it exposes the system to

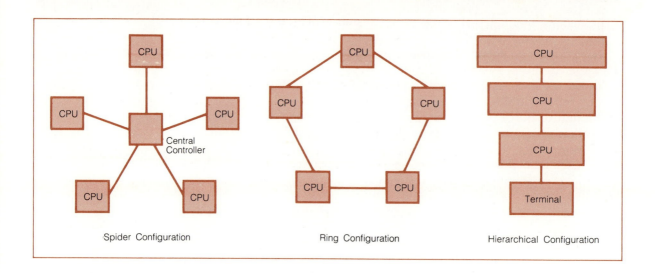

Spider Configuration

Ring Configuration

Hierarchical Configuration

FIGURE 6–6
Multiple CPU
Configurations

single-point vulnerability. An alternative approach uses a number of computers connected to a single transmission line in a *ring configuration*. This type of system can bypass a malfunctioning unit without disrupting operations throughout the network.

FIGURE 6–7
Distributed System

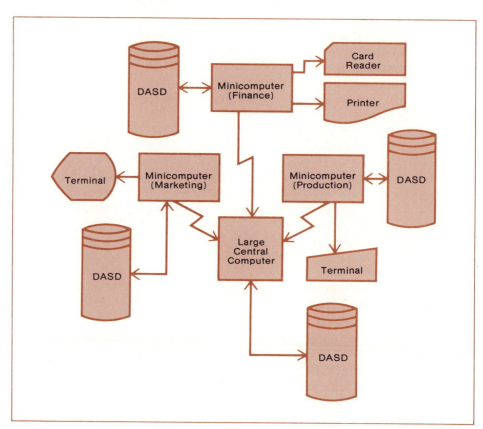

An interesting and more sophisticated approach is the *hierarchical network*. Under this approach, an organization's needs are divided into multiple levels which receive different levels of computer support. The lowest is the user level, where only routine transaction computing power is supplied. But this level is connected to the next higher level and its associated information system. At each higher level, the machine size increases while the need for distribution decreases. Thus, such a system consists of a network of small computers tied into a large central computing complex.

Figure 6–7 shows a distributed system consisting of three dispersed minicomputers connected by communication linkages to a large central computer. The three minicomputers are located in three functional departments of the organization—finance, marketing, and production. Thus, the functional departments can meet their processing requirements locally. Some of the information generated by the minicomputers is communicated to the central computer to be used in corporate-wide planning and control. Such a network provides fast response and great flexibility to local system users. Furthermore, the central facility is available to them for jobs that require computing power beyond the capabilities of the minicomputers.

The networks discussed so far are terrestrial-based networks. Today many networks rely on the use of satellite communication channels to extend their ranges to other continents. However, satellite-based networks are very expensive, primarily because they need earth stations (small dish-like antennas) to send and receive messages from the satellites. Currently such systems are only cost-effective for users who process large volumes of information.

SUMMARY

● Data communication is the electronic transmission of data from one location to another, usually over communication channels such as telephone/telegraph lines or microwaves. The combined use of data-processing equipment and communication facilities, such as telephone systems, is called teleprocessing.

● Modulation is the process of converting data from the pulse form used by the computer to a wave form used for message transmission over communication lines. Demodulation is the process of converting the received message from wave form back to pulse form. These functions are performed by devices called modems, or data sets.

● Digital transmission involves transmitting data as distinct on and off pulses rather than as waves. This mode of transmission eliminates the specialized steps of conversion from pulse to wave form and subsequent reconversion from wave to pulse form at the destination.

● A communication channel is the link permitting transmission of electrical signals from one location to another. Types of communication channels include telegraph lines, telephone lines, coaxial cables, microwave links, and communication satellites. Communication channels can be classified by (1) their grade, or bandwidth, or (2) the mode of transmission (simplex, half-duplex, or full-duplex).

● Multiplexers, concentrators, and programmable communications processors are devices that reduce the costs associated with data transmission in a communication system.

● A time-sharing system allows several users to access the same computer at the same time. An in-house time-sharing system can be installed, or time-sharing capability can be purchased from a service company.

● Multiple CPU communication systems are characterized by several computers linked together in a terrestrial-based, or satellite-based communications network. Possible configurations for such systems include spider, ring, and hierarchical designs.

REVIEW QUESTIONS

1. What are modems? What purpose do they serve in data communication systems?

2. Distinguish among simplex, half-duplex, and full-duplex transmission modes. Why are the transmission mode and bandwidth of communication channels of concern to an analyst designing a data communication system?

3. What alternative is available to a firm that does not process a sufficient volume of data to justify the installation of a computer? What problems may arise?

4. Which configuration for multiple CPU systems has the disadvantage of single-point vulnerability? Why?

5. Distinguish between the terms *local system* and *remote system*. How does each apply to single and multiple computer systems?

APPLICATION

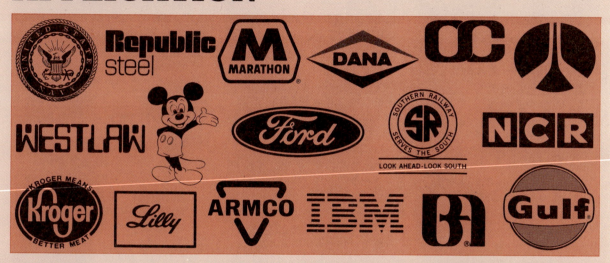

Bank of America

In October 1904, a small neighborhood bank opened for business in a remodeled tavern in the North Beach area of San Francisco. Its assets at the end of 1904 were $285,000. The founder of this bank, Amadeo Peter Giannini, had decided that small wage earners and small businesses should be offered the same banking services heretofore reserved for wealthy individuals and large companies.

Giannini's Bank of Italy (so named until 1930) was completely destroyed by the San Francisco earthquake of 1906, but Giannini was able to load $80,000 in cash on wagons and move the money to his home for safekeeping. Before the larger banks could reopen, he was lending money from a plank-and-barrel counter at the waterfront. Surviving the bank-closing panic of 1907, by 1918 the Bank of Italy had twenty-four branches in California—the leader in branch banking despite opposition from competitors and state officials. During the Great Depression, Giannini's newly named Bank of America survived while 8,000 other banks were liquidated, went bankrupt, or were forced to merge in order to stay afloat.

Today, Bank of America is one of the foremost banks in the world, with over $70 billion in assets; 1,200 branches throughout California; and 223 branches, affiliates, subsidiaries, and representative offices in 78 countries abroad. Its data-processing activities center around financial transactions and services such as check processing, savings services, Visa transactions, travellers' check services, and funds transfers. Two major data-processing centers handle the very large volumes of activity; one is located in San Francisco, and the other in Los Angeles.

The most significant data-processing work revolves around balancing the bank's books and determining its assets each night. Each day, paper records (in the form of checks and transaction records) and electronic records (in the form of magnetic tape) are sent to the data centers from the 1,200 branches, from internal bank departments, and from other banks with whom the Bank of America does business. Bank of America has its own air and auto fleet to pick up and deliver the input and computer work from its branches and departments. Just to service the San Francisco data center, the fleets cover about 23,000 miles a day!

Once the balancing is completed, a multitude of reports are prepared to be used by the bank's branches and internal departments and by other banks with which it has direct correspondence. In addition, from the posted account information, numerous data bases (savings, checking, Visa, Versateller, student loans, travellers' checks, and many more) are updated to contain current customer information for the next processing day.

VERSATELLER

Bank of America uses many online applications of data communication technology. One is the Automated Teller Machine (ATM), known as the Versateller service. (See Figure 6–8.) More than 200 Versateller machines throughout California are connected with the main-frame computers in Los Angeles and San Francisco. The two host computers are tied together by a communication link that uses telephone facilities. Programmable communications processors and modems at each end of the link convert the data in the form of signals from digital to analog and back again. Along the link, are signals sometimes carried on telephone lines, other times via microwave receivers or a combination of telephone and microwave, depending upon the distance involved.

Each host computer also supports a sub-network of terminals used by its Versateller Customer Service Center for updating and inquiring into the customer data base; communication takes place over telephone circuitry. Within the customer service center, coaxial cables link the control units with the terminals themselves.

Each host supports a sub-network of Versateller machines as well. In this sub-network, the programmable control units are located in the data center; from there, telephone circuitry provides the communication link between the Versateller machines and the control units. A single control unit can support up to eighteen Versateller machines. As with all transmission over telephone circuitry, modems at each end of the line must make the digital/analog conversions.

DISTRIBUTED COMPUTING FACILITY

A second major network using communication facilities is the Distributed Computing Facility (DCF). (See Figure 6–9.) This network is actually attached to the ATM network. It centers around a group of minicomputers connected to an IBM host computer that runs the Versateller network; this system is set up in both San Francisco and Los Angeles. Six high-speed digital lines pass customer account transaction information between the host computer and the distributed minicomputer system used by DCF. This process allows

Bank of America's San Francisco Data Center Complex

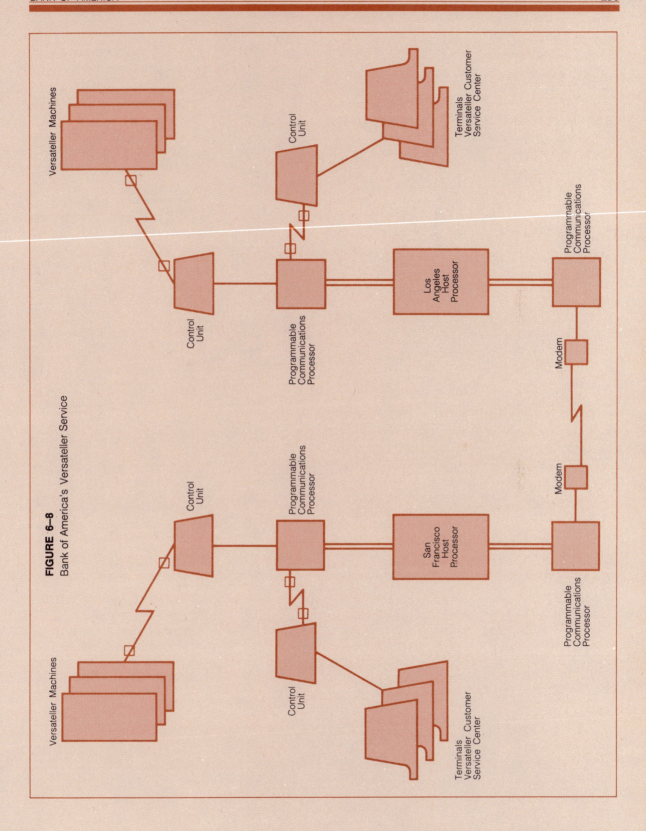

FIGURE 6–8
Bank of America's Versateller Service

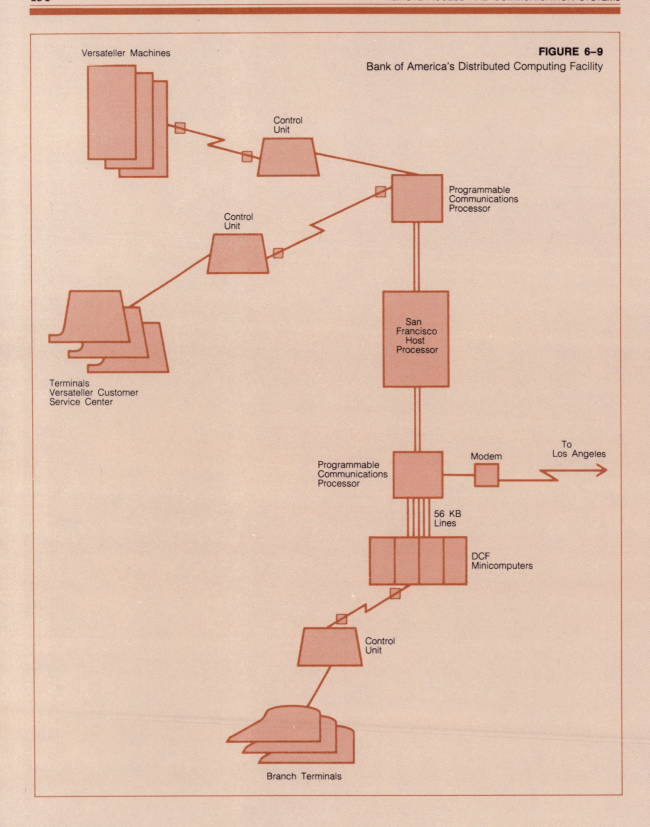

FIGURE 6–9
Bank of America's Distributed Computing Facility

Versateller Machines

Control Unit

Programmable Communications Processor

Control Unit

Terminals Versateller Customer Service Center

San Francisco Host Processor

Modem

To Los Angeles

Programmable Communications Processor

56 KB Lines

DCF Minicomputers

Control Unit

Branch Terminals

account balances to be kept up to the minute for all the Bank's customers.

The branch teller network is the facility by which tellers in the branches can inquire against and update information on customer account balances. Several specialized terminals are located in each branch and connected by coaxial cable to a control unit, which is also located in the branch bank. From the control unit, telephone circuitry is again used to transmit data to the DCF minicomputers at the data centers.

The DCF minicomputer system is an excellent example of a distributed system. It consists of eight independent hardware modules, each handling only a portion of the full customer data base. Thus, if any module goes down, its

customer file can be immediately taken over by another module, and teller access is not interrupted.

MONEY TRANSFER SERVICE

A third major network handling Bank of America's activities is the Money Transfer Service. This network, composed of multiple minicomputers, utilizes telegraph lines, fiber optics, multiplexers, and satellites. It is responsible for sending and receiving messages between minicomputers in the San Francisco data center and those thoughout the world. The technologies needed to perform this message-switching depend upon the countries to which the messages are being sent or from which the messages are being received. For example, messages to and from South

America primarily use telegraph interfaces provided by Western Union; messages to Hong Kong are transmitted via satellite. Communication to London is provided by a wide variety of communication links. (See Figure 6–10.)

The London-bound line leaving a money transfer minicomputer is first fed into a multiplexer. Here it is combined onto a higher-speed line with other Bank of America lines headed for London. This line in turn is fed into a concentrating modem, where it is combined with two other high-speed lines. This single line travels via telephone circuitry to a satellite earth station servicing the San Francisco Bay area. The signal is passed via satellite to New York where it is carried by telephone circuitry to Western Union International's undersea

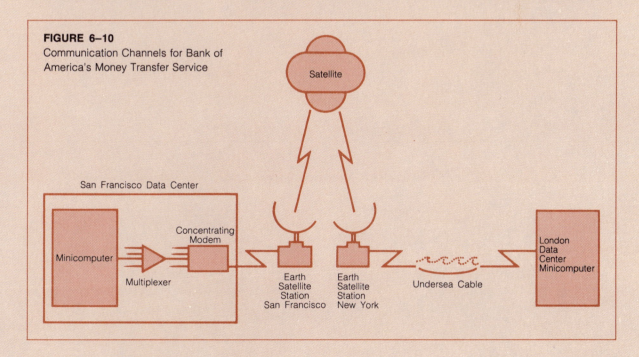

FIGURE 6–10
Communication Channels for Bank of America's Money Transfer Service

San Francisco Data Center

Satellite

Minicomputer

Multiplexer

Concentrating Modem

Earth Satellite Station San Francisco

Earth Satellite Station New York

Undersea Cable

London Data Center Minicomputer

cable. Through this cable, it crosses the Atlantic to London, where it is dispersed through additional multiplexing equipment onto telephone circuits for its final journey to the bank's London data center's message-switching minicomputers. A reverse procedure is used in sending messages to San Francisco from London.

The Money Transfer Network is just beginning to use fiber optics circuitry. Connections between the minicomputers and the terminals used by the Money Transfer Service Center are soon to be handled by fiber optics technology.

These three networks, only a few of the many communication networks at Bank of America, show how greatly data communication technologies have increased the capabilities and efficiency of data processing in the banking industry.

DISCUSSION POINTS

1. Explain how Bank of America's data-processing system provides up-to-the-minute account balances for its customers. Why is such an operation important?

2. The Money Transfer Service allows the bank to communicate with associates all over the world. What other industries might need this type of communication?

SECTION III
Programming

CHAPTER 7

System Software

Introduction

The computer is a powerful machine that can solve a variety of problems. Previous chapters have covered the major hardware components of a computer system and have shown how these components are used to store and process data and generate information. However, the computer cannot solve problems without using computer programs. Programming is a critical step in data processing; if the system is not correctly programmed, it delivers information that cannot be used.

This chapter examines several aspects of computer programming, or software. It explains differences between system programming and applications programming and discusses the various functions performed by operating system software. The chapter also describes some of the more advanced software developments that have occurred in recent years. The concepts of multiprogramming and multiprocessing are introduced, and the use of virtual storage to avoid limitations of main storage is discussed in detail.

66Can a Computer Have Worms?99
Byte

Several years ago rumor had it that an enterprising computer hacker had gained access to a DOD [Department of Defense] computer from a remote terminal. Once inside, he entered a program that rewrote

its data into all of the computer's memory, destroying the computer's software and data base. In other words, the program was like the shapeless monster from the classic science-fiction thriller, *The Blob*.

Now, from Xerox's Palo Alto (California) Research Center, comes the "Worm." The Worm is a series of programs that wiggles through a computer network at will, copying itself into inactive systems in the network. The Worm coordinates the operation of all the

computer systems in the network. It delegates tasks to unused machines and coordinates the operation of machines in the network. Any complex computations are handled by harnessing multiple processors.

The Worm is still in the experimental stage. As such, it may be the precursor of much more powerful autonomous programs that, like the Blob, could take over and control entire networks.

A computer system needs some means of managing its resources. System software, like "the worm" in the article, performs this housekeeping function so that computer systems can run efficiently.

PROGRAMS

Despite the apparent complexity and power of the computer, it is merely a tool manipulated by an individual. It requires step-by-step instructions to reach the solution to a problem. As stated earlier, this series of instructions is known as a *program,* and the individual who creates the program is the *programmer*. There are two basic types of programs: (1) *system programs,* which coordinate the operation of computer circuitry; and (2) *applications programs*, which solve particular user problems.

System Programming

System programs directly affect the operation of the computer. They are designed to facilitate the use of the hardware and to help the computer system run quickly and efficiently. For example, a system program allocates storage for data being entered into the system. We have already seen that computers differ in main storage capacity, in the methods used to store and code data, and in the number of instructions they can perform. Consequently, system programs are written specifically for a particular type of computer and cannot be used (without modification) on different machines.

System programming is normally provided by the computer manufacturer or a specialized programming firm. Thus, system programs are initially written in a general fashion to meet as many user requirements as possible. However, they can be modified, or tailored, to meet a particular organization's specific needs.

A system programmer maintains the system programs in good running order and tailors them, when necessary, to meet organizational requirements. Since system programmers serve as a bridge between the computer and applications programmers, they must have the technical background needed to understand the complex internal operations of the computer. Because each organization uses a different set of applications programs, system programs must be modified (tuned) to ensure computer efficiency at each organization's installation.

Applications Programming

Applications programs perform specific data-processing or computational tasks to solve the organization's information needs. They can be developed within the organization or purchased from software firms. Typical examples of applications programs are those used in inventory control and accounting; in banks, applications programs update checking and savings account balances.

The job of the applications programmer is to use the capabilities of the computer to solve specific problems. Applications programs can be written by a programmer without an in-depth knowledge of the computer. The applications programmer instead concentrates on the particular problem to be solved. If the problem is clearly defined and understood, the task of writing a program to solve it is greatly simplified.

OPERATING SYSTEMS

In early computer systems, human operators monitored computer operations, determined the order in which submitted programs were run (the priority); and readied input and output devices. While early electronic development increased the processing speeds of CPUs, the speed of human operators remained constant. Time delays and errors caused by human operator intervention became a serious problem.

In the 1960s, *operating systems* were developed to help overcome this problem. An operating system is a collection of programs used by the computer to manage its own operations. This approach provides a control system that can operate at computer speeds. Instead of a human operator preparing the I/O devices to be used for each program and loading the programs into storage, the operating system assumes responsibility for all jobs to be run.

Functions of Operating Systems

The functions of an operating system are geared toward attaining maximum efficiency in processing operations. Eliminating human intervention is one method. Allowing several programs to share computer resources is another; the operating system allocates these resources to the programs requesting them and resolves conflicts that occur when, for example, two or three programs request the use of the same tape drive of main storage locations. In

addition, the operating system performs an accounting function: It keeps track of all resource usage so that user fees can be determined and the efficiency of CPU utilization evaluated.

Another important function performed by the operating system is scheduling jobs on a priority basis. Although it may seem logical to run programs in the order in which they are submitted, this is not always the most practical approach. For instance, assume five programs are submitted for processing within a short period of time. Suppose one program requires one minute of CPU time and the other four require one hour each. It may be reasonable to process the short program first. Or suppose one program will produce a vital report and the others' output is less important. The more important program should probably be processed first. A system of priorities can be established based on considerations such as the required processing time and the need for the expected output.

Types of Operating Systems

There are two basic types of operating systems: *batch* (or *stacked job*) and *real time*. In a stacked-job processing environment, several user programs (jobs or job steps) are grouped into a batch and processed one after the other in a continuous stream. For example, in the morning an operator may load all jobs to be processed during the day into a card reader and enter them into the system. The stacked-job operating system will direct processing without interruption until all jobs are complete, thus freeing the operator to perform other tasks.

A real-time operating system can respond to spontaneous requests for system resources, such as management inquiries entered from online terminals.

Many operating systems can handle both batch and real-time applications simultaneously. These systems direct processing of a job stream but also

162

respond to interrupts from other devices, such as online terminals, in direct communication with the CPU. (An *interrupt* is a condition or event that temporarily suspends normal processing operations—for example, a request for data from an input device or a request for transfer of data to an output device.)

COMPONENTS OF OPERATING SYSTEMS

An operating system is an integrated collection of subsystems. Each subsystem consists of programs that perform specific duties (see Figure 7–1). Since all operating system programs work as a "team," CPU idle time is avoided and utilization of computer facilities is increased. Operating system programs are usually stored on an auxiliary device known as the *system residence device*. The auxiliary devices most commonly used are magnetic tape (TOS—tape operating system) and magnetic disk (DOS—disk operating system). Magnetic drum technology allows for the fastest processing times, but many existing operating systems use magnetic disk technology.

Two types of programs make up the operating system: *control programs* and *processing programs*. Control programs oversee system operations and perform tasks such as input/output, scheduling, handling interrupts, and communicating with the computer operator or programmers. Processing programs are executed under the supervision of control programs and are used by the programmer to simplify program preparation for the computer system.

Control Programs

The *supervisor* program (also called the monitor or executive), the major component of the operating system, coordinates the activities of all other parts of the operating system. When the computer is first put into use, the supervisor is the first program to be transferred into main storage from the

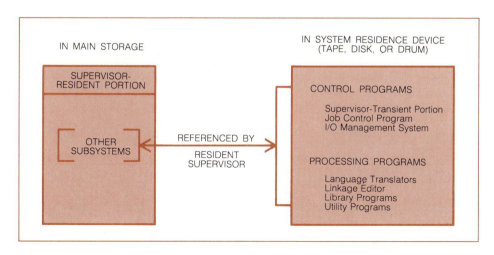

FIGURE 7–1

Operating System in Main Storage and System Residence Device system residence device. Only the most frequently used components of the supervisor are initially loaded into main storage. These components are referred to as *resident routines*. Certain other supervisor routines, known as *transient routines*, remain in auxiliary storage with the remainder of the operating system. Supervisor routines call for these nonresident system programs as needed and load them into main storage. The supervisor schedules I/O operations and allocates channels to various I/O devices. It also sends messages to the computer operator indicating the status of particular jobs, error conditions, and so on.

The operating system requires job-control information in order to perform its mission. (A *job* is a unit of work to be processed by the CPU.) A *job-control language* (JCL) serves as the communication link between the programmer and the operating system. Job-control statements are used to identify the beginning of a job, to identify the specific program to be executed, to describe the work to be done, and to indicate the I/O devices required. The *job-control program* translates the job-control statements written by a programmer into machine-language instructions that can be executed by the computer.

In most computer systems, the data to be processed is stored on high-speed input devices such as magnetic-tape units or disk units. In these systems, job-control statements are entered on cards from an input device other than the device in which the data is stored. For example, the job-control cards may be entered in a stream from a card reader as shown in Figure 7–2a. Among other things, these cards specify which data files and input devices are required. As each job is processed, the operating system in-

FIGURE 7–2
Continuous Job Streams for Stacked-Job Processing System

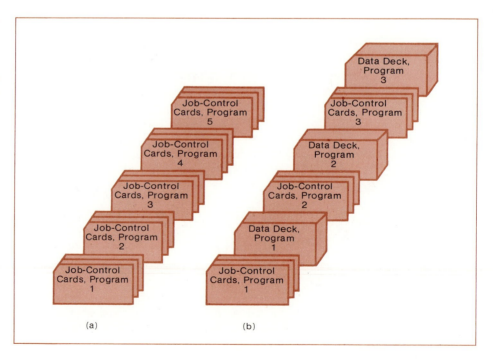

structs the operator to load particular tapes or disk packs needed for the job.

In other systems, programs and data are read into storage from the same input device (see Figure 7–2b). No additional I/O devices are required in this instance, but it is not an efficient method for processing large programs or data files. This method is most often used when programs are being tested, before they are stored on secondary storage devices.

A job is often thought of as a single program entered by a user into the computer. In fact, most data-processing jobs require the execution of many related programs. For example, processing a weekly payroll job may require that programs execute the following tasks:

1. Entering the payroll cards through a card reader, editing the data, and transferring the information to tape.
2. Sorting the records into some order, such as by employee number.
3. Matching the resultant transaction file with the master payroll file.
4. Processing the matched data to produce payroll checks, a payroll check register, and various payroll reports.

Thus, several job-control statements are needed to indicate which operations are to be performed and the devices needed to perform them.

The control programs of the operating system must be able to control and coordinate the CPU while receiving input from channels, executing instructions of programs in storage, and regulating output. I/O devices must be assigned to specific programs, and data must be moved between them and specific memory locations. The *input/output management system* oversees and coordinates these processes.

Processing Programs

The operating system contains several processing programs that facilitate efficient processing operations by simplifying program preparation and execution for users. The major processing programs contained in the operating system are the language translators, linkage editor, library programs, and utility programs.

Applications programs are seldom (if ever) written in machine language, because of the complexity and time that would be required to write them. Instead, most programs are written in a language closely resembling English. A *language-translator program*, as its name implies, translates English-like programs written by programmers into machine-language instructions (1s and 0s).

A number of programming languages are available; common examples are FORTRAN, COBOL, BASIC, and PL/1 (all discussed more fully in Chapter 10). The programmer must specify (in a job-control statement) the language in which a program is written. When the program is to be executed, the job-control program interprets that job-control statement and informs the supervisor which language translator is needed. The supervisor then calls the appropriate language translator from the system residence device. The language translator converts the program (called the *source* program) into machine language so it can be executed.

The translated application program (called the *object* program) often remains on the system residence device until the supervisor calls for it to be loaded into primary storage for execution. It is the task of the *linkage editor* to "link" the object program from the system residence device to main storage. It does this by assigning appropriate main storage addresses to each byte of the object program.

Library programs are user-written or manufacturer-supplied programs and subroutines that are frequently used in other programs. So that these routines will not have to be rewritten every time they are needed, they are stored in a *system library* (usually on magnetic disk or tape) and called into main storage when needed. They are then linked together with other programs to perform specific tasks. A *librarian program* manages the storage and use of library programs by maintaining a directory of programs in the system library; it also contains appropriate procedures for adding and deleting programs.

Operating systems also include a set of *utility programs* that perform specialized functions. One such program transfers data from file to file, from one I/O device to another. For example, a utility program can be used to transfer data from tape to tape, tape to disk, card to tape, or tape to printer. Other utility programs, known as *sort/merge programs*, are used to sort records into a particular sequence to facilitate updating of files. Once sorted, several files can be merged to form a single, updated file. Job-control statements are used to specify the sort and merge programs; these programs or routines are then called into main storage when needed.

Additional Software

As mentioned at the beginning of the chapter, system programs are available from a variety of sources. Each data-processing department must decide which subsystems to include in its operating system. The original operating system is usually obtained from the manufacturer of the CPU. However, in some cases alternative operating systems may be purchased from software vendors.

Once the essential operating system has been purchased, optional subsystems may be obtained. These subsystems either improve an existing subsystem or provide additional capabilities to the operating system. For example, the operating system for a bank's computer might be supplemented with a subsystem to interface with MICR equipment (discussed in Chapter 4). Applications requiring the use of light pens with display terminals also demand special subsystems.

MULTIPROGRAMMING

When the CPU is very active, the system as a whole is more efficient. However, the CPU frequently must remain idle because I/O devices are not fast enough. The CPU can operate on only one instruction at a time; furthermore, it cannot operate on data that is not in primary storage. If an input

device is slow in providing data or instructions, the CPU must wait until I/O operations have been completed before executing a program.

In the earliest computer systems with simple operating systems, most programs were executed using *serial processing*—they were executed one at a time. Serial processing was terribly inefficient because the high-speed CPU was idle for long periods of time as slow input devices loaded data or output devices printed or stored the results.

Overlapped processing was developed to correct this problem. In overlapped processing, the computer works on several programs instead of one. As one program is being loaded into the computer from an input device via a channel, another program is being executed by the CPU, while the results of yet another program are being allocated to another channel for output. In overlapped processing, then, the CPU is utilized more fully than in serial processing (see Figure 7–3).

Multiprogramming increases CPU active time still more by effectively allocating computer resources and offsetting low I/O speeds. Under multiprogramming, several programs reside in the primary storage unit at the same time. Although the CPU still can execute only one instruction at a time, it can execute instructions from one program, then another, then another, and back to the first again. Instructions from one program are executed until an interrupt for either input or output is generated. The I/O operation is handled by a channel, and the CPU can shift its attention to another program in memory until that program requires input or output. This rotation occurs so quickly that the execution of the programs in storage appears to be simultaneous. More precisely, the CPU executes the different programs *concurrently*, which means "over the same period of time."

Although multiprogramming increases the system's flexibility and efficiency, it also creates some problems. First, the programs in main storage

167

FIGURE 7–3
Comparison of Serial
and Overlapped
Processing

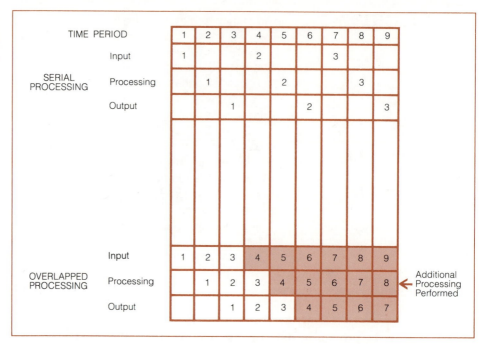

FIGURE 7–3
Comparison of Serial and Overlapped Processing

must be kept separate. This is accomplished through the use of *regions* or *partitions*. A region is a storage area of variable size reserved for one program; a partition is a storage area of fixed size reserved for one program. Keeping programs in the correct region or partition is known as *memory management*, or *memory protection*. A similar situation exists with I/O devices—two programs cannot access the same tape or disk drive at the same time. These problems are handled by operating system control programs.

A second problem that arises with multiprogramming is the need to schedule programs to determine which will receive service first. This requires that each program be assigned a priority. In a time-sharing system, the programs being used for online processing must be capable of responding immediately to users at remote locations. Thus, these programs are assigned the highest priority. The highest-priority programs are loaded into *foreground partitions* and are called *foreground programs*. Programs of lowest priority are loaded into *background partitions* and are called *background programs* (see Figure 7–4). Background programs are typically executed in a batch mode. When a foreground program is interrupted for input or output, control is transferred to another foreground program of equal or lower priority or to a background program.

For large systems with several foreground and background programs, scheduling is not a simple task. Two programs of the same priority may request CPU resources at the same time. The method of deciding which program gets control first may be arbitrary; for example, the program that has been in main storage the longer may receive control first. Fortunately, the operating system is capable of handling such problems as they occur.

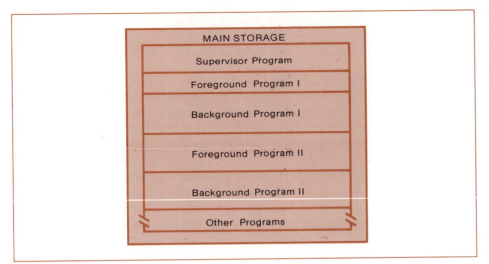

FIGURE 7–4

Foreground and
Background
Programs in a
Multiprogramming
Environment

VIRTUAL STORAGE

Multiprogramming increases system efficiency because the CPU can concurrently execute programs instead of waiting while I/O operations occur. A limitation of multiprogramming, however, is that each partition must be large enough to hold an entire program; the program remains in memory until its execution is completed.

Another limitation of this approach is that all the instructions of a program are kept in primary storage throughout its execution, whether they are needed or not. Yet, a large program may contain many sequences of instructions that are executed infrequently. For example, the program may consist of several logical sections, but most of the processing may be done by only one or two of them. While this processing occurs, those not being used (representing the bulk of the program) are occupying space that could otherwise be used more efficiently. As processing requirements increase, the physical limitations of memory become a critical constraint, and the productive use of memory becomes increasingly important.

For many years, the space limitations of main storage have been a barrier to applications. Programmers have spent much time trying to find ways to trim the sizes of programs so that they could be fit into available main storage space. In some cases, attempts have been made to segment programs (break them into separate modules) so that they could be excuted in separate job steps; but doing this manually is both tedious and time consuming. While hardware costs have decreased and storage capacities have increased, this storage problem still exists in high-volume processing systems that require large programs.

To alleviate the problem, an extension of multiprogramming called *virtual storage* has been developed on the principle that only a portion of a program (that portion needed immediately) has to be in main storage at any given time; the rest of the program and data can be kept in auxiliary storage. Since only part of a program is in main storage at one time, more programs can reside in main storage simultaneously; and so more programs can be executed within a given time period. This gives the illusion that main storage is unlimited.

To implement virtual storage (or *virtual memory*, as it is sometimes called), a direct-access storage device such as a magnetic-disk unit is used to augment main storage. The term *real storage* is usually given to main storage within the CPU, while *virtual storage* refers to the direct-access storage (see Figure 7–5). Both real and virtual storage locations are given addresses by the operating system. If data or instructions needed are not in the real (main) storage area, the portion of the program containing them is transferred from virtual storage into real storage, while another portion currently in real storage may be written back to virtual storage. This process is known as *swapping*. If the portion of the program in real storage has not been modified during execution, the portion from virtual storage may be simply laid over it, because copies of all parts of the program are kept in virtual storage.

There are two main methods of implementing virtual-storage systems, both of which use a combination of hardware and software to accomplish the task. The first method is called *segmentation*. Each program is broken into variable-size blocks called *segments*, which are logical parts of the program. For example, one segment may contain data used by the program; another segment may contain a subroutine of the program; and so on. The operating system software allocates storage space according to the size of these logical segments.

A second method of implementing virtual storage is called *paging*. Here, main storage is divided into physical areas of fixed size called *page frames*. All page frames for all programs are the same size, and this size depends on the characteristics of the particular computer. In contrast to segmentation,

FIGURE 7–5

Schematic Drawing of Virtual Storage and Swapping

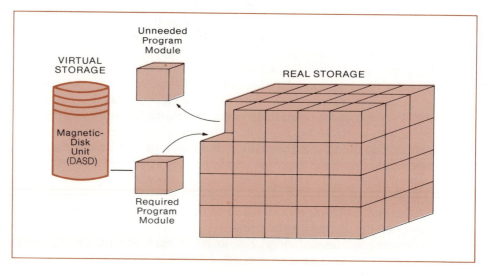

paging does not consider the logical portions of the programs. Instead, the programs are broken into equal-size blocks called *pages*. One page can fit in one page frame of primary storage (see Figure 7–6).

In both paging and segmentation, the operating system handles the swapping of pages or segments whenever a portion of the program that is not in real storage is needed during processing.

Virtual storage offers tremendous flexibility to programmers and system analysts designing new applications; they can devote their time to solving the problem at hand rather than to fitting programs into storage. Moreover, as already explained, the use of main storage is optimized, since only needed portions of programs are in main storage at any time.

One of the major limitations of virtual storage is the requirement for extensive online auxiliary storage. Also, the virtual-storage operating system is highly sophisticated and requires significant amounts of internal storage. If virtual storage is not used wisely, much time can be spent locating and exchanging program pages or segments; in some programs, little actual processing occurs compared with the amount of swapping. (This is known as *thrashing*.)

MULTIPROCESSING

Multiprocessing involves the use of two or more central processing units linked together for coordinated operation. Stored-program instructions are executed simultaneously, but by different CPUs. The CPUs may execute dif-

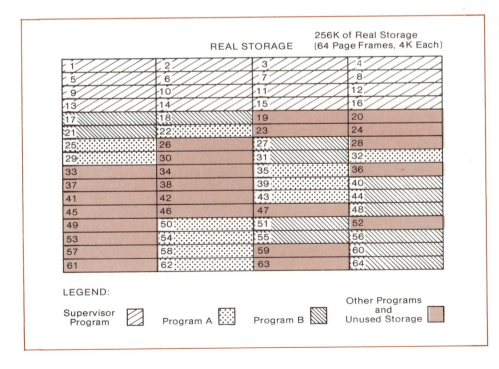

FIGURE 7–6
Paging

ferent instructions from the same program, or they may execute totally different programs. (In contrast, under multiprogramming, the computer appears to be processing different jobs simultaneously, but is actually processing them concurrently.)

Multiprocessing systems are designed to achieve a particular objective. One common objective is to relieve a large CPU of tasks such as scheduling, editing data, and maintaining files so that it can continue high-priority or complex processing without interruption. To do this, a small CPU (often a minicomputer) is linked to the large CPU. All work coming into the system from remote terminals or other peripheral devices is first channeled through the small CPU, which coordinates the activities of the large one. Generally, the small CPU handles all I/O interrupts and so on, while the large CPU handles the "number crunching" (large mathematical calculations). A schematic diagram of this type of multiprocessing system is shown in Figure 7–7. The small CPU in Figure 7–7 is commonly referred to as a *front-end processor*. It is an interface between the large CPU and peripheral devices such as online terminals.

A small CPU may also be used as an interface between a large CPU and a large data base stored on direct-access storage devices. In this case, the small CPU, often termed a *back-end processor*, is solely responsible for maintaining the data base. Accessing data and updating specific data fields are typical functions a small CPU performs in this type of multiprocessing system.

Many large multiprocessing systems have two or more large CPUs. These large CPUs are not different from those used in single-CPU (stand-alone) configurations. Each may have its own separate memory, or a single mem-

FIGURE 7–7
Multiprocessing System with Small Front-End Processor and Large Main Frame

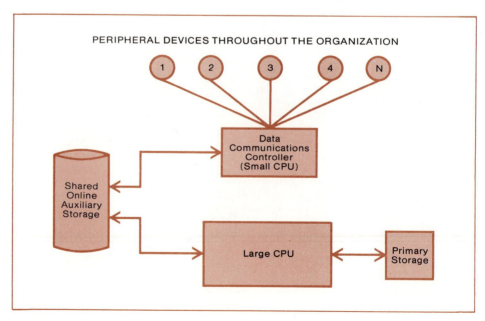

ory may be shared by all of them. The activities of each CPU can be controlled in whole or in part by a common supervisor program. This type of system is used by organizations with extremely large and complex data-processing needs. Each large CPU may be dedicated to a specific task such as I/O processing or arithmetic processing. One CPU can be set up to handle online processing while another handles only batch processing. Alternately, two CPUs may be used together on the same task to provide rapid responses in the most demanding applications. Many multiprocessing systems are designed so that one or more of the CPUs can provide backup if another malfunctions. A configuration that uses multiple large CPUs is depicted in Figure 7–8. This system also uses a small CPU to control communications with peripheral devices and perform "housekeeping chores" (input editing, validation, and the like).

Coordinating the efforts of several CPUs requires highly sophisticated software and careful planning. The scheduling of workloads for the CPUs involves making the most efficient use of computer resources. Implementing such a system is a time-consuming endeavor that may require the services of outside consultants as well as those provided by the equipment manufacturers. The payoff from this effort is a system with capabilities extending far beyond those of a single-CPU system.

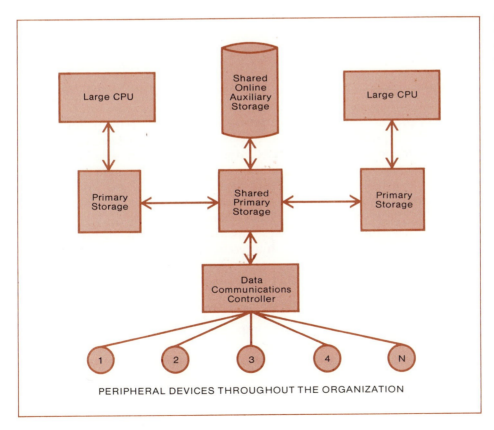

FIGURE 7–8
Multiprocessing System Using Multiple Large CPUs

SUMMARY

- A program is a series of step-by-step instructions required to solve a problem. Applications programs solve user problems, whereas system programs coordinate the operation of all computer circuitry.
- System programs are generally provided by the computer manufacturer or a specialized programming firm. Applications programs can be developed within the organization or purchased from a software firm.
- An operating system is a collection of programs designed to permit a computer system to manage its own operations. It allocates computer resources among multiple users, keeps track of all information required for accounting purposes, and establishes job priorities.
- Batch (stacked-job) operating systems allow uninterrupted processing of a batch of jobs without operator intervention. Real-time operating systems can respond to spontaneous requests for system resources, such as management inquiries entered from online terminals. Operating systems that can handle both batch and real-time applications are available.
- An operating system consists of control programs and processing programs. The supervisor, the major component of the operating system, controls the other subsystems.
- A job-control language (JCL) is the communication link between the programmer and the operating system. Job-control statements identify the beginning of a job, identify the specific program to be executed, and describe the work to be done.
- The input/output management system is part of the operating system

control programs. It receives input from channels, regulates output, assigns I/O devices to specific programs, and coordinates all I/O activities.

• Language translators convert English-like programs into machine-language instructions.

• Library programs consist of programs and subroutines frequently used in other programs; they are stored in a system library (usually on magnetic tape or disk) and called into main storage when needed.

• The linkage editor links the object program from the system residence device to main storage by assigning appropriate main storage addresses to each byte of the object program.

• Utility programs perform specialized functions like sorting and merging and transferring data from one I/O device to another.

• Operating systems can be developed in a modular fashion by addition of components to the original operating system.

• The CPU may be idle for a significant amount of time because of the speed disparity between the CPU and I/O devices. Multiprogramming is used to increase the efficiency of CPU utilization.

• With multiprogramming, several programs reside in the primary storage unit at the same time. Instructions from one program are executed until an interrupt for either input or output is generated. Then the CPU shifts attention to another program in memory until the program requires input and output.

• When multiprogramming is used, the programs in main storage are kept separate by use of partitions or regions. Memory protection and a method of assigning priorities to programs are required. High-priority programs are loaded into foreground partitions, and low-priority programs are loaded into background partitions.

• Multiprocessing is limited by main storage space limitations. A complete program may not fit into a partition; also segments of some programs may take up space but be executed infrequently. These problems are alleviated by use of virtual storage.

• Virtual storage involves loading only the part of a program needed in primary storage while keeping the remainder of the program in secondary storage. This gives the illusion that primary storage is unlimited.

• Segmentation is a method of implementing virtual storage whereby each program is broken into segments of variable size. Each segment is a logical subunit of the complete program. Paging, another method of implementing virtual storage, uses equal-size blocks called pages without considering logical parts of the program.

• Multiprocessing involves the use of two or more CPUs linked together for coordinated operation. Separate programs or separate parts of the same program can be processed simultaneously by different CPUs.

• Small computers can be linked to main frames as either front-end processors or back-end processors. The former acts as an interface between the CPU and I/O devices; the latter acts as an interface between the large CPU and a data base stored on a DASD.

• Large CPUs can be linked together to handle extremely large and complex data-processing needs. Each CPU may be assigned to a specific task, or it may be used with other CPUs on the same task to provide rapid response.

REVIEW QUESTIONS

1. Distinguish between applications programs and system programs. Give examples of each and explain why they belong to that particular category.

2. What are the major functions performed by an operating system? Is an operating system that can handle stacked-job processing more complex and sophisticated than one that allows real-time processing? Explain.

3. What are the major components of an operating system? Briefly explain the functions of each component.

4. What is the primary purpose of a job-control language?.

5. Who is most likely to use utility programs and why?

6. Distinguish between multiprogramming and multiprocessing. What are some of the problems that must be solved in a multiprogramming environment?

7. Why were virtual-storage systems developed? Compare and contrast the two techniques—segmentation and paging—used to implement virtual-storage capabilities.

8. A corporation is implementing a large data-base management system that can respond to inquiries from online terminals. What multiprocessing configuration would be most suitable for this application?

APPLICATION

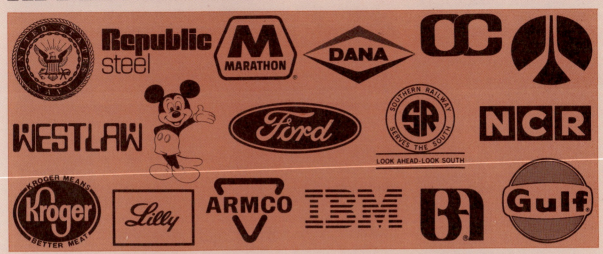

NCR

NCR Corporation

The cash register was invented in 1879 by a Dayton cafe owner, James Ritty, and his brother John. By 1883, the National Manufacturing Company had been formed to manufacture the new device. John H. Patterson, who was using two cash registers in his small store in Coalton, Ohio, found that they proved to be the difference between operating at a loss and making a profit. Patterson bought twenty-five shares of stock in the National Manufacturing Company. He became its secretary and a member of the Board of Directors; and in 1884, he purchased a controlling interest

and changed the company's name to the National Cash Register Company.

Patterson's first factory employed thirteen people and produced as many as five cash registers a week. By 1900, the company's registers were widely used throughout the United States and overseas. Today, almost a hundred years later, the corporation employs 65,000 people and has sales and service facilities in more than a hundred countries.

To more accurately reflect the corporation's expanded activities, the Board of Directors changed the company's name in 1974 from the National Cash Register Company to the NCR Corporation. While NCR is still involved in the design and manufacture of retail systems, its market has expanded to encompass many other types of products.

NCR Corporation today is a multinational organization

engaged in developing, producing, marketing, and servicing business equipment and computer systems. Its product line includes electronic data-processing systems, electronic point-of-sale terminals for retail stores and financial institutions, a variety of data-entry and retrieval terminals, communication equipment such as modems, adapters, concentrators, etc., individual free-standing business equipment, business forms, supplies, and related accessories. In addition, NCR has recently acquired a communications firm in St. Paul, Minnesota, called COMTEN and a firm named ADDS (Applied Digital Data Systems) that specializes in general-purpose CRTs, and a firm DPI (Data Pathing Inc.) that specializes in manufacturing control terminals and systems.

MISSION

NCR develops applications software as well as system software to support its equipment. A major new application is NCR MISSION (Manufacturing Information System Support Integrated On-Line). One of the largest applications ever undertaken by the company, MISSION can be used as a single or multiple-plant system for the complete control of an industrial company's manufacturing operations. This application required the use of a data base management system and a transaction processor. The DBMS used was CINCOM's TOTAL. The transaction processor (communications monitor) was developed by the MCS organization and is called TRAN-PRO.

Numerous NCR plants across the nation and abroad are involved in the design and manufacture of hardware and software for NCR products. The plants are decentralized; each has a separate management information system (MIS) department to support it and produce the systems it needs. In an attempt to incorporate all common manufacturing systems used by the plants, a group called the manufacturing control system (MCS) was formed to oversee all the MIS department. This overall MIS function was staffed with applications programmers from outside the company to bring ideas to NCR. The group interviewed the plant managers to determine their individual needs and found these needs to be not only common among NCR management but also similar to those found in any type of manufacturing plant. The MCS group broke the system into subunits and assigned these subunits to separate plants for development. The design of system files, transaction processing, and I/O interfaces was required.

A design review committee of user personnel from three plants was established to evaluate the design and documentation produced by the various developing plants and to ensure that the systems satisfied user specifications. After the final design was agreed on, the MIS department within each plant proceeded with applications programming.

The total system design includes many applications modules that work together and draw upon common resources. Eight of these modules, or subsystems, have been completed: the Bill of Material, Material Management, Inventory Management, Cost, Routing, Order Processing, Capacity Requirements Planning, and Material Requirements Planning.

The only difference between MISSION and an application designed specifically for customer use is that MISSION was originally designed for use in NCR's own manufacturing plants. Therefore, the system had to go through the tests given to systems designed for sale to customers before it was

approved for use. The first of these tests is known as BETA test. For MISSION, it was a complete in-house system test of the completed applications subsystems. This was followed by GAMMA test, which ensures the quality of the application. The final procedure was the Customer Verification Test (CVT). Normally, the system is installed in a user site for this test; in the case of MISSION, the system was installed in one of NCR's plants.

Because MISSION's debut was successful, the completed subsystems have been made available to NCR customers. Each applications subsystem is made up of 25 to 200 separate programs; for example, the Bill of Materials application contains 100 separate programs, half of which accept input from online terminals.

VRX

Since its debut, MISSION has been converted to run under VRX (Virtual Resource Executive). VRX is a group of software modules comprising an operating system that allows multiprogramming, virtual storage, and multiple virtual machine capabilities.

In a multiprogramming environment, VRX schedules and runs up to thirty-five jobs concurrently. Real memory, processor time, and peripheral use are automatically allocated, and the user can exercise as much or as little control over job processing as needed.

The VRX handles a virtual storage environment by assigning currently active portions of virtual storage to real memory. The virtual memory, which is stored on a high-speed, randon-access peripheral device, is divided into pages. The entire virtual storage operation is transparent to the application running in the system; that is, the programs are totally unaware of the environments created for them.

The virtual machine capabilities make it possible to tailor a system to operate on a specific programming language. The language compiler translates the source code into an intermediate, object-level code that is interpreted by firmware (small hardware chips that contain complete programs). In most cases, one source-code instruction (which usually requires many object-level commands) translates to one object-level command. Therefore, programs are compiled and executed much faster and far more efficiently than on machines that are not language oriented.

DISCUSSION POINTS

1. Describe how the VRX software allows the virtual machine capabilities. What are the advantages of a language-oriented computer system? What are the disadvantages?
2. What are the advantages of purchasing an applications package such as MISSION instead of developing it in-house? What are the disadvantages?

CHAPTER 8

Programming

Introduction

People often solve problems intuitively, without having to identify each step they use. Computers lack this human capability. Therefore, using a computer to help solve a problem requires a great deal of planning. All the steps required to solve the problem must be identified and coded into a logical instruction sequence—a program—before the computer can be used to perform the computations and get the correct result.

This chapter identifies the five stages involved in developing a program and discusses the first two, defining the problem and planning a solution, in detail. (The remaining three are discussed in Chapter 9.) The chapter explains the four traditional, basic patterns of program logic that can be used to solve any problem. It discusses pseudocode and flowcharts and also provides a sample problem to illustrate the analysis of a problem and the design of a solution.

❝ An Acute Shortage of Programmers ❞

"If you give me the names of 600 good programmers, I could place them all by 5 p.m. today," promises Lawrence A. Welke, president of International Computer Programs Inc. This is no idle boast. The acute shortage of people who write the instructions that tell the computer what to do is regarded by industry executives as perhaps the biggest single problem facing the data processing industry today.

"We have a real manpower crisis in our industry," points out Donald J. Reifer, president of Software Management Consultants. Despite the fact that there are now 300,000 programmers working in this country and another 300,000 who work part-time on software, the demand for highly skilled people to write software is 40% greater than the supply, says Robert Curtice, an analyst for Arthur D. Little Inc.

As a result, 92% of all computer users say that they have trouble finding enough programmers for their inhouse staffs. Computer Sciences Corp. faces a shortage of 5% to 10% in its El Segundo (Calif.) home office and one as high as 50% at some of its field locations. At Computer Task

Group Inc, (CTG), which lends custom programmers under contract to major corporations, President David N. Campbell complains: "We have openings right now for 75 people."

Job-hopping

Because it is clearly a seller's market, starting salaries for programmers are rising by 15% annually, according to Dewey F. Manzer, a vice-president at Honeywell Information Systems Inc. A typical programmer starts at $12,000 a year at CTG, Campbell says, and within three years is making $20,000. And salaries for top-notch systems programmers can reach $50,000 a year.

The intense competition is causing a dramatic rise in job-hopping for higher salaries. "There are at least 20 companies within a 60-mi. radius [of Boston], all vying for the same systems programmers," says William G. Watson, president of Software International Corp. His company spent more than $250,000 in fees over the last nine months to placement firms that recruit programmers from other companies. Two years ago the company was spending one-tenth of that amount.

Bring a friend

Companies are trying nearly anything to pirate programmers.

Software International offers its employees a $2,000 referral bonus if they bring in a programmer from a rival company. This turns out to be an effective way to build a programming staff. Campbell, of CTG, estimates that 50% of the programmers he will hire this year will come from referrals made by his own employees.

A big part of the problem, of course, is identifying the few good programmers. Many of the job applicants are simply not capable of writing sophisticated software. At Digital Equipment Corp., 20% of the programmers produce 80% of the minicomputer maker's software. And after interviewing 330 job candidates for 100 programming slots in June, CTG found only 22 of them met its requirements.

Programmer-short companies have also resorted to training their own people. Computer Task Group, for example, spends $1 million annually to train its programming staff. Liberal arts graduates, with no computer background, can be taught to do simple programming with six weeks of intensive training, say company executives.

Despite these efforts and the trend to advanced software that over the long run should reduce the need for skilled programmers, it is difficult for anyone to see the demand easing for programmers. Says John W. Luke, a vice-president at Computer Sciences: "It is a worldwide problem, and it's getting worse rather than better."

Knowledgeable programmers are in great demand in the business world today, and this demand will continue to increase as more and more organizations implement computer systems. The following chapter discusses the basic procedures followed by programmers when preparing a problem to be solved by use of a computer.

Most people think computers are cold, calculating machines. In all fairness to computers, they are. They process tax returns and paychecks with equal impartiality. Computers have no emotion, independent thought, or voluntary action. How is it, then, that computers have come to dominate our present-day business society?

From the beginning, this book has described the computer as a machine that is incredibly fast and accurate but has an IQ of zero. It performs step by step only what it has been told to do. On the one hand, this appears to limit the tasks that computers can perform; on the other hand, it suggests that computers are limited only by people's ability to break down a problem into steps that computers can use to solve it. As economist Leo Cherne suggested, "The computer is incredibly fast, accurate, and stupid. Man is unbelievably slow, inaccurate, and brilliant. The marriage of the two is a force beyond calculation."

The evolution of the computer from the first mechanical machine to the vastly complex electronic marvel of today is a tale of human ingenuity. When it appeared that computer applications would be limited because all instructions had to be coded in machine language, someone devised a method of having the computer itself translate English-like commands into its own language. When this middle-level language in turn became cumbersome, several higher-level languages were developed. All these innovations did nothing more than make it easier for humans to give instructions to the computer.

The previous chapter introduced system programs that help the computer to manage its own operations. These programs are designed, written, and maintained by programmers. If a computer is able to oversee its vastly complex operations, it is only because someone has been able to understand what operations were required and how they were to be performed and has then programmed the computer to execute them. This chapter discusses the sometimes complicated task of breaking down a problem and its solution into the logical series of steps required for computer problem solving.

COMPUTER PROBLEM SOLVING

As any seasoned programmer will tell you, the computer does not "solve" problems the same way we do. Humans solve problems by using reason, intelligence, and intuition. Computers solve problems according to instructions provided by programmers. Any "intelligence" the computer seems to possess is given to it by these programmers. At present, computers cannot even take general instructions like "calculate each employee's net pay" and turn them into programmatically correct statements it can use to perform the task. Instead, the computer has to be told how to calculate an employee's net pay, step by step. It is nothing more than an overgrown calculator!

Each program, then, has to be well thought out. Instructions must be ordered in a logical sequence. The problem must be analyzed to such a level of detail that all logical conditions that may be encountered during processing are anticipated in advance. If an unanticipated condition arises during processing, the program will be executed incorrectly or, in some cases, not at all.

Problem-Solving Process

When programs were first written, there were few rules for programmers to follow because there were few things computers could do. Today, however, with the vast array of programming languages, processing techniques, storage devices, and printing media, a programmer is well advised to use a structured approach to problem solving and program development. Five steps have been found helpful in this process:

- Defining the problem.
- Designing a solution.
- Writing the program.
- Compiling, debugging, and testing the program.
- Documenting the program.

Defining the problem and designing a solution are two steps that can be followed regardless of the programming language used. They are also usually the most difficult, because the analyst/programmer not only must be adept at analyzing a problem but also must establish a method of solving it with current computer capabilities. These two steps are discussed in this chapter.

The other three steps—writing the program; compiling, debugging, and testing the program; and documenting the program—involve translating the solution into one of several computer programming languages. This requires a good understanding of the advantages and limitations of the language used, as well as a logical and structured approach to program writing. These three steps are discussed in the next chapter.

DEFINING THE PROBLEM

The first step in defining a problem begins with recognizing a need for information. This need may be expressed as a request from management, users, or a system analyst performing a system study. The analyst/programmer receiving the request must analyze the problem thoroughly in order to understand what is required of its solution. Since such problem-solving skills often differ from the skills required of a programmer, some companies use the system analyst to perform this function (see Chapter 12).

Output

Whether the system analyst, the programmer, or both together define the problem, its solution must be stated in terms of clear, concise objectives. One of the ways to do this is to first define what output is required of the program; this output represents the information requirements of users and management. The analyst/programmer often prepares report mock-ups to show users and asks them to verify the output requirements. In this way, the analyst/programmer can quickly determine whether any omissions or incorrect assumptions about the purpose of the program were made.

Input

Next, the input required to provide this output must be determined. The analyst/programmer reviews current systems to see what data may be available and to determine what new data items must be captured in order to provide the required information.

Processing

Finally, given (1) the output specifications developed by the analyst/programmer in close cooperation with the users and management and (2) the required input established by careful evaluation of the current systems, the processing requirements can be determined. Once they are known, the analyst/programmer proceeds to the next step—planning a solution.

Defining the Problem—Payroll Example

The accounting department's payroll section is not functioning properly. Checks are issued late, and many are incorrect. Most of the reports to management, local and state governments, and union officials are woefully inadequate. The section's personnel often work overtime to process the previous week's payroll checks.

The problem is fairly obvious—company expansion and new reporting requirements have strained the accounting department beyond its capacity. It needs a new computerized payroll system. Management has agreed with this assessment and has contacted the computer services department for help.

Output Defining this problem in terms of determining what functions are actually performed in this company's payroll system is more difficult. Most functions can be determined by observing the output of the payroll section. Naturally, it issues paychecks. It also sends a statement of weekly and monthly payroll expense to management and an updated list of changes in employee salaries and positions to the personnel department. The local, state, and federal governments require a monthly report of income taxes withheld, and the union receives payment of employee dues deducted by the payroll section. Not only the checks but all of these reports must be provided by a computerized system.

Input The next step in defining the problem is to determine the inputs to the payroll system. One input is the employee time card, which contains the employee number and the hours worked each day of the week. Another input, dealing with new employees and changes in pay scales, is sent by the personnel department. Supervisors provide a special form regarding employee promotions. The tax section sends updates of tax tables used to calculate local, state, and federal withholdings. The union provides dues withholding information.

Processing Given the output reports generated by the accounting department and the inputs provided to it by various sources, the processing required of the new computerized payroll system can be determined (see Figure 8–1).

First, each employee's gross pay must be calculated from the employee's time card and pay scale. Second, each deduction regarding taxes and union dues must be determined from the tax rates provided by the tax department and the information regarding union dues is provided by the union and subtracted from the gross pay to arrive at the net, or take-home, pay. Third, the employee's paycheck must be printed. Totals must be kept of all employees' gross pay and net pay values as well as of taxes and union dues withheld. These totals are used to generate reports to management, government, and union officials. In addition, changes in any employee's work status must be reported to the personnel department. Once the problem has been defined to this level of detail, the analyst/programmer must plan a structured solution to the problem.

DESIGNING A SOLUTION

FIGURE 8–1
Problem Definition
Step for
Payroll Example

When the definition of the problem has been completed, the design of the solution begins. This design may take the form of one or more programs. The programmer takes each of the segments uncovered in the definition

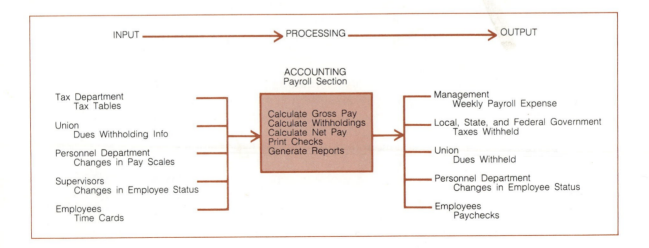

step and works out a tentative program flow. By approaching each segment separately, the programmer can concentrate on developing an efficient and logical flow for that segment.

The programmer does not need to know which programming language is to be used in order to develop a tentative flow. (In fact, knowing the processing requirements first helps the programmer to select the language best suited to those requirements.) To develop a tentative flow, the only thing a programmer needs to know are the four basic logic patterns used by the computer.

Basic Logic Patterns

There is nothing magical about writing a computer program. In fact, the computer can understand and execute only four basic logic patterns: simple sequence, selection, loop, and branch. High-level languages may have more complicated statements, but they all are based on these four patterns. As you read about the patterns, refer to Figure 8–2.

Simple Sequence   Simple sequence logic involves the computer's executing one statement after another in the order given by the programmer. It is the most simple and often-used pattern; in fact, the computer assumes that all statements entered by the programmer are to be executed in this fashion unless it is told otherwise.

Selection   The selection pattern requires that the computer make a choice. The choice it makes, however, is not based on personal preference or taste, but on pure logic. Each selection is made on the basis of a comparison that determines whether one item is equal to, less than, or greater than another. In fact, these are the only comparisons the computer can make. Complex selections are made by use of a sequence of these comparisons.

FIGURE 8–2

A Computer's Basic Logic Patterns

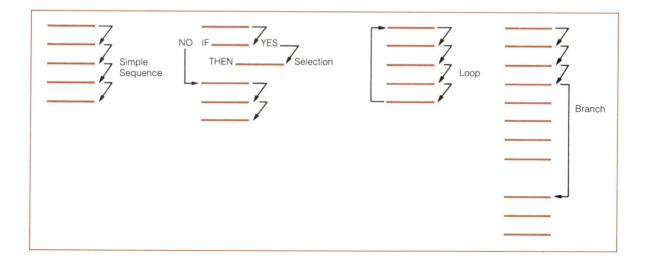

Loop The loop pattern enables the programmer to instruct the computer to alter the normal next-sequential-instruction process and loop back to a previous statement in the program. The computer then re-executes statements according to the simple sequence flow. This is especially useful if the same sequence of statements is to be executed, say, for each employee in a payroll program; the programmer need not duplicate the sequence of statements for each set of employee data processed.

When using the loop, the programmer must establish a way for the computer to get out of the loop once it has been executed the required number of times. For instance, once all employee data has been processed, the computer should not try to get more of it. Two basic methods of controlling loops are through the use of *trailer values* and *counters*. A *trailer value* is a unique item that signals the computer to stop performing the loop. It is also referred to as an "end of-file" item, since it can be used to signal the end of the input data. The programmer tests for this trailer value within the program. Since it will cause the computer to exit from the loop, it should be a value that will not be encountered in the input date.

The second method of loop control uses a *counter*, which regulates the number of times the loop is executed. A counter can be entered at the time of program execution, as a value in an instruction in the program, or computed within the program. To use a counter to control a loop, the programmer must set up a method of incrementing the counter and testing its value each time the loop is executed. When the proper value is reached, the execution of the loop can be terminated.

Branch The last and most controversial pattern is the branch. The branch is most efficiently used in combination with selection or looping. This pattern allows the programmer to skip past statements in a program, leaving them unexecuted.

Branching is controversial for several reasons. If a program uses it too often, the computer must jump frequently from one part of the program to another when executing it. This is inefficient. Furthermore, it is extremely difficult, if not impossible for one programmer to understand another's program when it uses much branching. Such programs are also difficult and time consuming to maintain. For these reasons, Chapter 11 is devoted to structured programming, which seeks to reduce the use of branching techniques.

It is easy to see why the solution of a problem must be well thought out before programming is started. The programmer has to work creatively around the computer's limitations. The problem must be stated in such a way that it can be solved by use of a series of simple sequence instructions, selections, loops, and, in some cases, branches. Even the selections have to be simplified so that they involve only equal to, less-than, and greater-than comparisons.

When faced with the task of writing a series of programs designed to solve complicated problems, the programmer can easily make omissions and errors in processing logic. Pseudocode and flowcharting techniques can help the programmer to avoid such omissions and errors.

Pseudocode

Pseudocode can be thought of as narrative descriptions of processing steps to be performed in a program. The programmer arranges these descriptions in the order in which corresponding program statements will appear in the program. Using pseudocode allows the programmer to focus on the steps required to perform a particular process by eliminating the need to determine how they should be phrased in a computer language. (As will be explained in Chapter 10, coding statements in a computer language often requires strict adherence to syntactical rules.)

Figure 8–3 is an example of pseudocode used to lay out the processing steps required to calculate a shopper's grocery bill. Notice in the figure how the logic patterns just discussed are expressed. Correctly written, each pseudocode statement can be translated into one or more program statements. It is easy to see from the example how useful a tool psuedocode can be.

Flowcharts

A *flowchart*, sometimes called a *block diagram* or a *logic diagram*, provides a visual frame of reference of the processing steps in a program. Instead of using the English-like statements of pseudocode, flowcharting uses easily recognizable symbols to represent the type of processing performed in a program. These symbols are arranged in the same logical sequence in which corresponding program statements will appear in the program.

Flowcharts provide excellent documentation of a program. For maintenance, the flowchart can be used to guide the programmer in determining what statements are required to make any necessary changes and where to locate them. Once the flowchart is updated to reflect these changes, it provides good documentation of the revised program. Because of their potential value, flowcharts should be completed, up-to-date, and easy to read. To help achieve the latter objective, the American National Standards Institute (ANSI) has adopted a set of flowchart symbols, which are commonly accepted and used by programmers.

Figure 8–4 shows some of the ANSI flowchart symbols. The symbol ⬭ represents the start or termination of a program and so appears at the start and end of a program flowchart. The symbol ▭ shows a process step such as addition, subtraction, multiplication, or division. Most of the data manipulation performed in a program is represented by process symbols. A com-

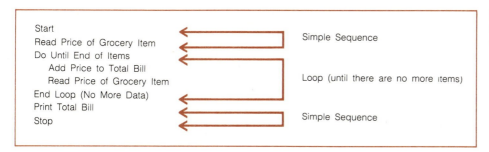

FIGURE 8–3
Example of
Pseudocode

FIGURE 8–4
Flowchart Symbols

MEMORIZE THESE SYMBOLS

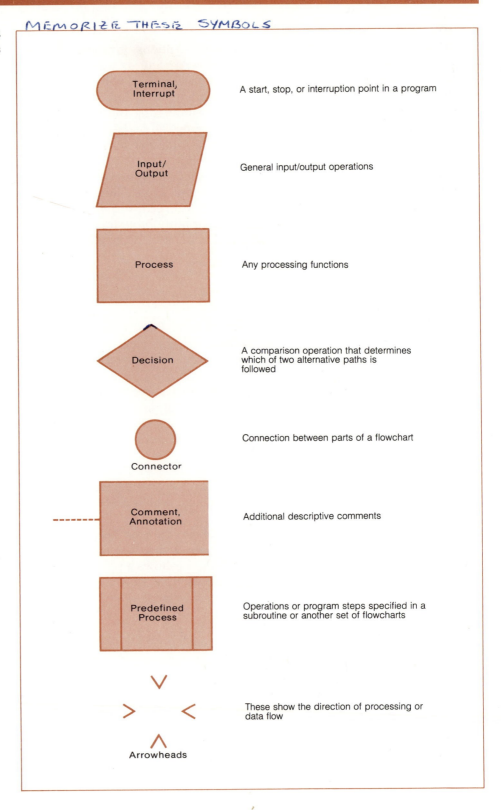

Terminal, Interrupt	A start, stop, or interruption point in a program
Input/ Output	General input/output operations
Process	Any processing functions
Decision	A comparison operation that determines which of two alternative paths is followed
Connector	Connection between parts of a flowchart
Comment, Annotation	Additional descriptive comments
Predefined Process	Operations or program steps specified in a subroutine or another set of flowcharts
Arrowheads	These show the direction of processing or data flow

parison, or decision, is represented by the symbol ◇ , which represents a program statement that directs the computer to compare values. The computer may take either of two paths for a decision step. If the result of the comparison is true, one path is executed; if the result is false, the other is taken. Finally, the symbol ▱ indicates that the program requires either input or output of data. Data can be put into the program via punched cards, CRT terminals, or secondary storage devices. Output from the program can be directed to CRT terminals, printers, or secondary storage devices.

Figure 8–5 shows the grocery bill calculation of Figure 8–3 expressed in flowchart form. It is important to notice several things in the figure. First,

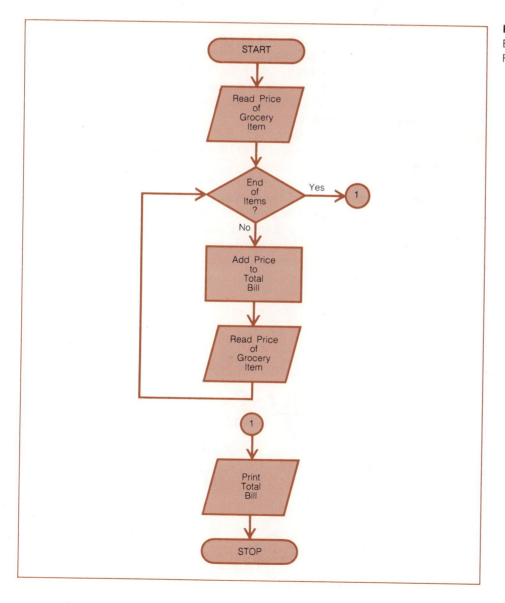

FIGURE 8–5
Example of a
Flowchart

the symbols are arranged from top to bottom, left to right. *Flowlines* connect the symbols and visually represent the implied flow of logic from statement to statement. Arrowheads indicate the direction of flow. Notice also the very brief pseudocode instructions written within the symbols to provide a more detailed description of the activities represented by the blocks.

It is useful to connect the earlier discussion of basic logic patterns to the flowchart symbols (see Figure 8–6). The first basic logic pattern, simple sequence, is implied by the top-to-bottom, left-to-right arrangement of symbols in the flowchart. The flowlines connecting the symbols arranged in this order merely help to make this flow more apparent. The second pattern, the selection, is represented by the decision symbol, ⬦ . The loop pattern is represented by a flowline from the last symbol included in the loop up to the first block to be re-executed. Notice that the arrow on the loop flowline indicates that the direction is opposite the normal flow. Finally, the branch is represented by a flowline pointing away from the normal flow to a circle with a number in it. Another circle with the same number appears later in the flowchart, pointing back into the flowchart's logical flow. The numbers within the circles connect the branch exit and re-entry points. The three other flowchart symbols—start or stop, ⬯ ; processing, ▭ ; and input/output, ▱ —are used to differentiate the types of programming statements used by the programmer and help him or her to visualize the logical processes followed within the program.

Flowcharts can be used to provide an overview of the major components of a program or to detail each of the processing steps within a program. A flowchart that outlines the general flow and major segments of a program is called a *modular program flowchart,* or *macro flowchart.* The major segments of the program are called *modules.* Macro flowcharts are useful to highlight possibilities for independent program development and are especially useful in implementation of structured programming techniques (discussed in Chap-

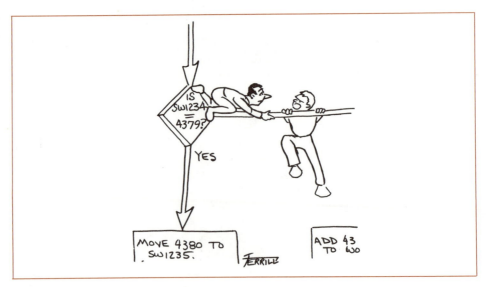

FIGURE 8–6

Four Traditional
Program
Logic Patterns

1. **Simple sequence pattern**
One statement after another,
executed in order as stored
(A then B)

2. **Selection pattern**
Requires a test, and,
depending upon the result
of the test, one of two
paths is taken. For instance,
IF A is true THEN do B;
ELSE do C.

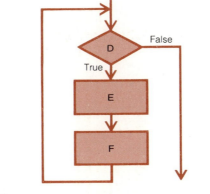

3. **Loop pattern** Execution
of E and F continues in a
loop fashion as long as D
is true. If D is false, the
loop is exited; E and F are
not executed. The logic is
DO E and F WHILE D is
true.

4. **Branch or link pattern**
Control is transferred from
the simple sequence flow to
another portion of the
program. For instance, If G
is false, GO TO J. The flow
of the program continues
with execution of J (rather
than H) whenever G is false.

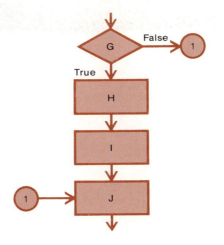

FIGURE 8–7
Modular Flowchart and Detail Flowchart

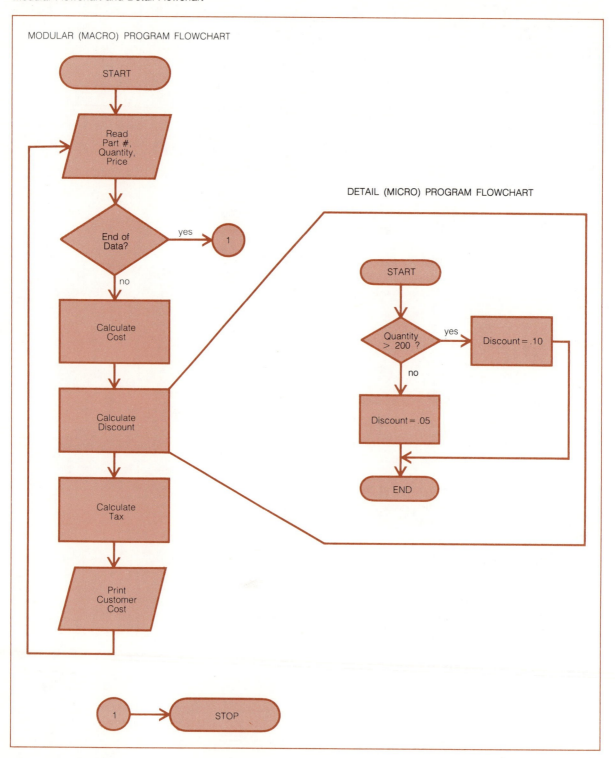

ter 11). *Detail flowcharts* depict the processing steps required within a particular program and often involve a one-to-one correspondence between flowchart blocks and program statements. Figure 8–7 shows both modular and detail flowcharts.

Planning a Solution—Payroll Example, Continued

It was determined in the definition stage of the payroll problem that several processing steps are required. First, an employee's gross pay must be calculated. Next, deductions for taxes and union dues must be determined and subtracted from that pay to determine the employee's net pay. Given the gross pay, tax, union dues, and net pay, the employee's check can be printed. Finally, a series of reports are required for management, government and union officials (see Figure 8–8 for a modular flowchart of these functions).

The first step to planning a solution is to take each of these processing segments and work out a tentative program flow. First, to determine an employee's gross pay, the hours worked during the week are multiplied by the hourly wage. Next, to calculate the employee's withholdings, the appropriate rate and union dues must be determined. For the purposes of this example, assume that a weekly salary over $150 is taxed at a 10 percent rate, while all salaries less than that are taxed 6 percent. Union dues are $15 per week. To calculate net pay, the taxes and union dues are subtracted from the gross pay. The paycheck is printed next. These calculations are repeated for each employee.

The steps required to solve the payroll processing problem can be represented in pseudocode as shown in Figure 8–9. Each of the pseudocode statements corresponds to a flowchart symbol. The first statement requires input of data and is represented by the symbol ⧄ . The next statement involves a decision; if there are no more employees, skip the processing part of the program and go to print reports. This statement is represented by a decision block, ◇ , with a branch that goes past the processing statements

195

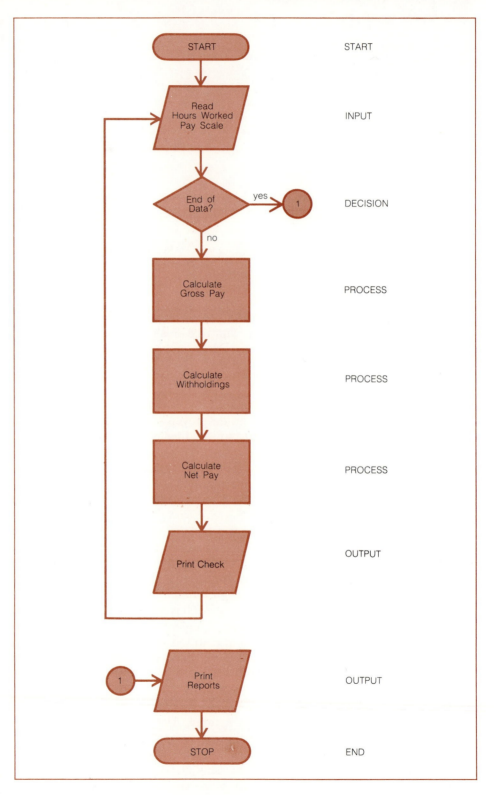

FIGURE 8–8
Modular Flowchart for
Payroll Program

FIGURE 8–9
Pseudocode for Payroll Problem

Read employee's hours worked and hourly wage.
If no more employees, print reports.
Multiply hours worked times hourly wage to get gross pay.
If gross pay is more than $150, then tax rate is 10 percent.
  Otherwise tax rate is 6 percent.
Multiply tax rate times gross pay, giving tax.
Union dues are $15.
Subtract tax and union dues from gross pay, giving net pay.
Print check.
Go process another set of employee data.
Print reports.

when the end of data is reached. Next is a processing statement relating to calculating gross pay, which is represented by the symbol ☐ . To calculate the correct tax rate, a selection must be made on the basis of gross pay—again a decision block. The next three statements—regarding calculating tax, union dues, and net pay—are all processing statements represented by the symbol ☐ . Printing a check requires output of data and is represented by the symbol ▱ . The statement sending processing back to the read statement is a loop. The final portion of the program requires output of data—the printed reports—and is represented by a ▱ . The finished detail flowchart corresponding with the pseudocode statements is shown in Figure 8–10.

Notice how the pseudocode statements have been further abbreviated within the flowchart symbols. Since the symbol itself identifies the type of processing, only a brief description is necessary. For example, since the symbol ▱ means input/output, all that need be described is which operation is being performed (input or output) and what data is involved (like hours worked and hourly wage). Notice also how the loop back up to the input block to read employee data is represented and how the test for end of data may cause a branch out of the loop.

If all payroll programs were this easy, programmers would soon be out of jobs. There are many more processing steps in an actual payroll system. For instance, employees who work more than forty hours in the week are entitled to overtime pay. A payroll program would be required to test the number of hours worked and calculate the overtime "premium" for hours over forty. Similarly, it is likely that not all employees belong to the union. For example, office workers may be excluded from union membership. A payroll program handling this processing problem would be required to bypass union dues calculations for these employees. The revised pseudocode incorporating these processing constraints might look like Figure 8–11.

Notice in this example that to enable the computer to differentiate between union and nonunion employees, another data item must be included in the input stream; there would be no way for the computer to select the correct employees otherwise. This data item is "status," and status must have a value of "x" for employees exempt from union dues. (Figure 8–12 shows this processing in flowchart form.)

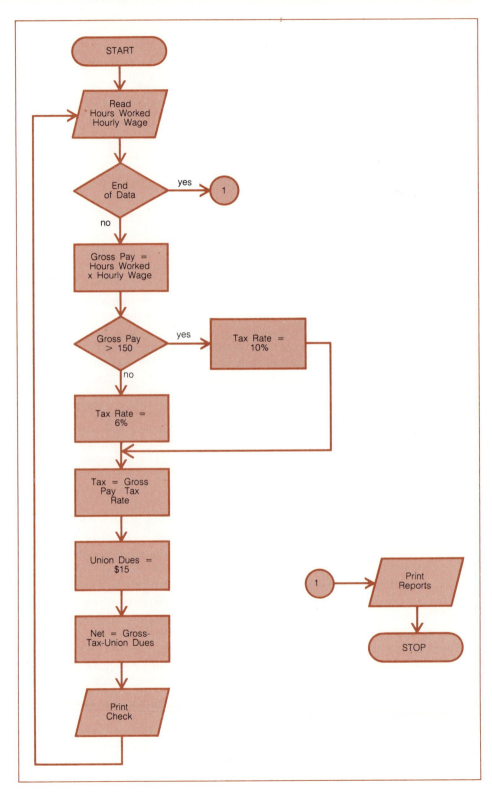

FIGURE 8–10
Detail Flowchart for
Payroll Problem

FIGURE 8–11

Pseudocode for
Enhanced Payroll
Problem

Read employee's hours worked, hourly wage, and status.
If no more employees, print reports.
Multiply hours worked times hourly wage to get gross pay.
If hours worked is greater than 40, then subtract 40 from
    hours worked, giving overtime; multiply overtime by
      $2.50 (assumed premium) and add to gross pay.
  Otherwise continue with next step.
If gross pay is more than $150, then tax rate is 10 percent.
  Otherwise tax rate is 6 percent.
Multiply tax rate times gross pay, giving tax.
If status equals x, then union dues are 0.
  Otherwise union dues are $15.
Subtract tax and union dues from gross pay, giving net pay.
Print check.
Go process another employee.
Print reports.

The need to add this new data item underscores the importance of doing a thorough analysis of output requirements in the problem definition stage. If a program had already been written when this new requirement was discovered, the programmer would have to rework the program to allow for it.

The payroll example illustrates how a solution to a complex problem can be built from a very simple framework, provided the problem has been analyzed thoroughly. By breaking the problem down into manageable segments and designing a solution for each segment, the programmer is able to write a logically structured program that maintains maximum flexibility.

Accumulators

The loop is a powerful tool not only for reducing the number of program statements required to perform a particular task but also for accumulating totals. For instance, as each employee's gross pay is calculated, it can be added to the total gross salary paid to all employees. This is also true of the employee's net pay, tax, and union dues. When all employee data has been processed, these totals can be printed on summary reports required by management, government, and the union. An important point to remember, however, is that these totals can be used only after all employee data has been read and processed. Although the *accumulators* are positioned within the loop, the reporting of their values must occur outside the loop after it has been executed the required number of times.

In order to accumulate totals in a program that uses a loop, the programmer must do two things. First, he or she must include statements within the loop to accumulate the desired totals. These statements must appear at the correct logical points of the loop. For instance, a statement accumulating gross pay should be inserted directly after the statement that calculates the gross pay for an employee, not before it. Second, the programmer must provide for printing or storing the total outside the loop once the loop has been executed the desired number of times.

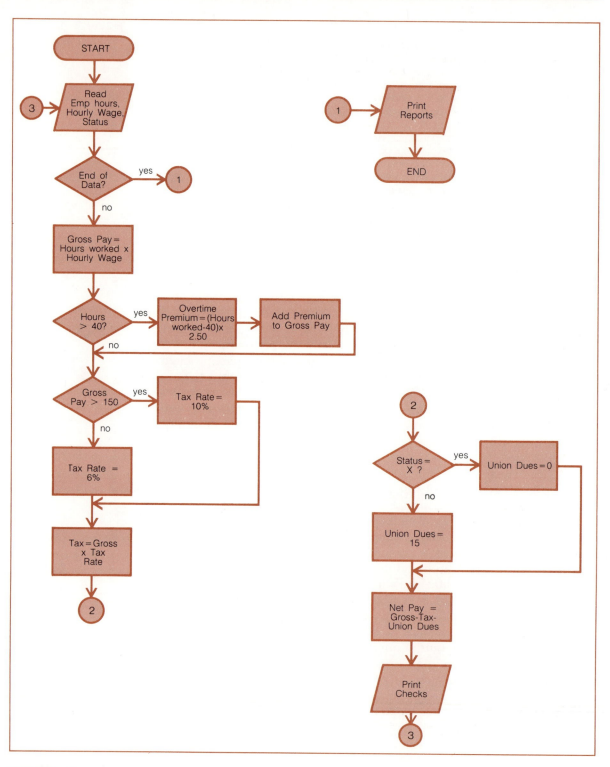

FIGURE 8–12
Detail Flowchart for Enhanced Payroll Problem

The payroll processing example without enhancements is used in Figure 8–13 to show in pseudocode required to accumulate totals in the program. The flowchart for this program is shown in Figure 8–14.

Special Considerations in Solution Design

In solving business problems, computer programmers must be aware of other considerations besides developing the processing steps required for solution. (1) The form of input to the program determines how the program should ask for data. (2) Processing steps should verify the accuracy of data and identify potential errors. (3) The program may be required to produce output that is not in hard-copy form.

Input In today's computer systems, users have a variety of ways to communicate with programs. Given the vast array of input devices discussed in Chapter 4, it is not difficult to see why. The programmer must know in advance which input devices will be used to put data into the program. For instance, if punched cards are to be used, the program must accept input within the eighty-column constraint. If input will be in the form of tape, the program must be prepared to accept the data in the same way it was stored on the tape. If a data base will provide input, the program may need to actively search and retrieve data from the data base.

Different input devices require different input considerations. The input devices and forms of data input must be precisely defined before solution design begins. Considerable time may otherwise be required to rework programs designed to accept input in an inappropriate format.

Processing Businesses are naturally concerned with the accuracy and integrity of data used to provide the information managers use to make decisions. Programmers must do their part to help keep data error free; merely designing a program with logically correct processing statements providing

---

FIGURE 8–13
Pseudocode with Accumulators

```
Read employee's hours worked and hourly wage.
If no more employees, print reports.
Multiply hours worked times hourly wage to get gross pay.
Add gross pay to total gross pay paid to all employees.
If gross pay is more than $150, then tax rate is 10 percent.
   Otherwise tax rate is 6 percent.
Multiply tax rate times gross pay, giving tax.
Add tax to total tax paid by all employees.
Union dues are $15.
Add union dues to total union dues paid by all employees.
Subtract tax and union dues from gross pay, giving net pay.
Add net pay to total net pay paid to all employees.
Print check.
Go process another set of employee data.
Print reports (total gross salary, net salary, tax, and union dues).
```

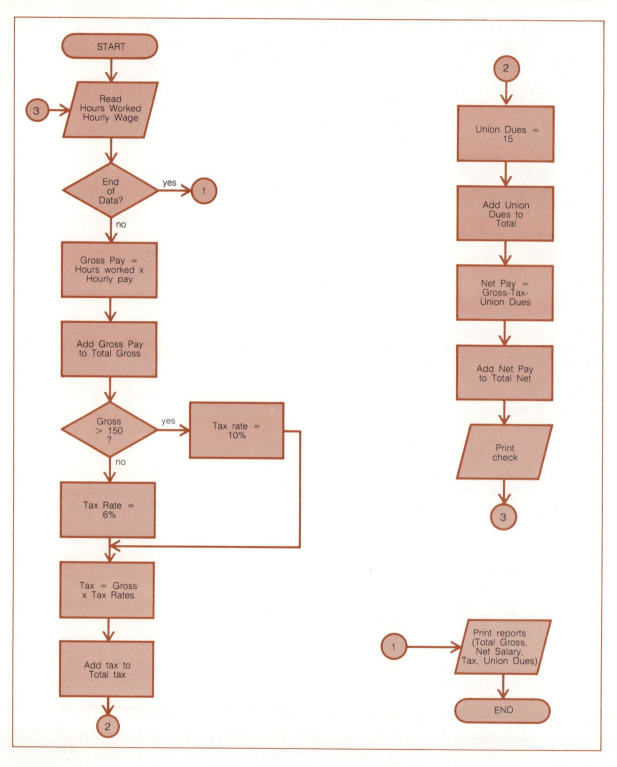

FIGURE 8–14
Detail Flowchart with Accumulators

the required output may not be enough. Most programmers are required to include expensive "edit checks" on the data before storing it in data files. Edit checks are processing statements designed to identify potential errors in the input data.

Several broad types of edit checks can be incorporated into the solution design; reasonableness, range, type, and correct code are a few possibilities. A reasonableness check looks at a data item to see if its stated value is possible, given the type of data it represents. For instance, if the program requires input of the effective date of a purchase, the program could check that date against today's date. Any date that is not later in the calender year could be reported to the users for further investigation. It may be difficult for some users to remember to use the new year's date during January processing. A reasonableness check of this type would quickly identify such incorrect dates.

A range check evaluates the data item to see if its value lies within an established range. For instance, if a company sells bulk gasoline to truck tankers, experience may have shown that a normal load varies between 8,000 and 12,000 gallons. A value lower or higher would be highlighted for the users to verify.

A type check verifies that the data value is in the right form. If the program is expecting someone's age, the data item entered should be numeric, not alphabetic. Similarly, if the user is requested to enter a number between 1 and 3, the letter x would be an incorrect type. Catching type errors can greatly reduce processing reruns.

Verifying the correct code requires matching a data value to specific numbers or values used in the company. A product number is one example of a code; employee type and status are others. When a code is received as input, the program looks it up in a computer table. If the code is there, it is valid. If it is not, it will be reported for user investigation.

In some situations, combinations of these edit checks are required. The determination of how many and what kinds of edit checks should be performed on input data is usually made by all personnel involved in the solution design. The users, management, system analyst, and programmer should all be involved in ensuring the integrity of input data.

Output   In modern systems, not all data is entered directly into a program by users nor output fed directly to hard-copy reports. Many systems require the use of interdependent programs in which the output from one program is used as input to another, and so on. The reason for this is that each program may perform a specialized function (as suggested by the modular flowchart in Figure 8–8). If the solution design requires this type of processing, programmers need to ensure that output from one program is in a form acceptable as input to another. Similarly, if the first program in the processing cycle has done extensive edit checks on the input data, later programs need not do verification. (Once data items are put into the computer for processing, they will not change!)

If the data output will be hard-copy reports, the reports should be easy to read. If they seem imposing or confusing to users, the reports will likely be used incorrectly or not at all.

Real-Time Systems   The trend in computer systems today is to design programs that process data immediately after it is input by the user. The user usually provides the input at a CRT terminal and receives the output from the program at the same terminal. This type of processing is quite useful in business, but it imposes stringent processing constraints.

One problem is that the program becomes a series of input, processing, and output segments, rather than one input segment, a series of processing statements, and an output segment. The program must perform edit checks on each data item as it is entered by the user, even if the item was also entered and checked in an earlier step. To the program, the data item appears new each time it is entered.

Another problem is that, in order for immediate output to be provided, data items may be stored on computer files during processing. Once the processing is completed, there is no way of checking the data further. Input processed for modern data bases faces this type of problem; all types of edit checks must be made during the input of data by the user, before it is accepted, processed, and written to the data base.

Finally, the way in which the programmer designs the program to ask the user for data input can have an important effect on how the user feels about the system. Computer specialists like to refer to programs that ask for input effectively as being "user friendly." Frustration, panic, or boredom can result from improperly designed input segments.

The design of a solution to a problem requires a careful definition of the problem. If inadequate analysis has been performed, considerable work will be required to redesign the solution. If the problem has been defined well, the programmer can easily design a solution by following the solution design steps. Once a design has been decided upon, the programmer proceeds to the next three steps in the problem solving process: writing the program; compiling, debugging, and testing it; and documentating it. These steps are discussed in the next chapter.

SUMMARY

● The computer is incredibly fast and accurate, but it has an IQ of zero. Any intelligence the computer appears to have is given to it by the programmer. The programmer must tell the computer how to solve a problem, step by step.

● There are five steps in the problem-solving process—defining the problem; designing a problem solution; writing the program; compiling, debugging, and testing the program; and documenting the program.

● Defining the problem begins with recognizing the need for information. This need can be in the form of a request from users, management, or a system analyst conducting a system study.

● The second step in defining the problem requires determining what output the system should provide. This is determined either by the system analyst or by the programmer and verified by users and management.

● The next step is to determine what input is available from current systems and what new data items need to be provided.

● The final step is to determine what processing steps the program should include based on the output required and the input provided to the system.

● Planning a problem solution requires only that a programmer know the four basic logic patterns used by the computer to solve problems: simple sequence, selection, loop, and branch.

● When it uses the simple sequence pattern, the computer executes program statements one after another in the order given by the programmer.

● Selection requires that the computer make a comparison between two items to determine whether one is equal to, less than, or greater than the other.

● The loop sends the computer back to a previous program statement. That statement is re-executed, and processing continues with the next statement in accordance with simple sequence logic.

● The branch logic pattern makes the computer skip over certain program statements. If used too often, it can be inefficient and confusing.

● Pseudocode refers to English-like descriptions of the processing steps required in a program that help the programmer determine the program's logical flow.

● Flowcharts are pictorial representations of the processing logic in a program. Modular flowcharts depict the major processing segments, while detail flowcharts show each processing step.

● A simple program can be made to process more complicated logic as long as the problem has been adequately defined.

● Accumulators are used to keep totals of certain items in a program. The statement accumulating the total is placed within the loop. The reporting of the final value of the accumulator takes place outside the loop after the loop has been executed the required number of times.

● Special considerations in the design of a solution to a business problem include the form of input, processing requirements, and output required of the program.

REVIEW QUESTIONS

1. Consider the problem of finding an apartment. Can you define the problem well enough that a computer could be used to solve it? (Assume that data on all vacant apartments is available.) Design a solution to your problem, once you have defined it.

2. Use the four basic logic patterns to draw a flowchart that depicts the decisions and steps involved in going to the grocery store. If you can, draw modular and detailed flowcharts of the process.

3. Descibe some of the processing edit checks you might incorporate into a program for students registering for next session's classes.

4. Have you ever had to enter data into a computer system that was not user friendly? Describe your experience. In what ways could the programmer have designed the input routine to make it easier for you?

APPLICATION

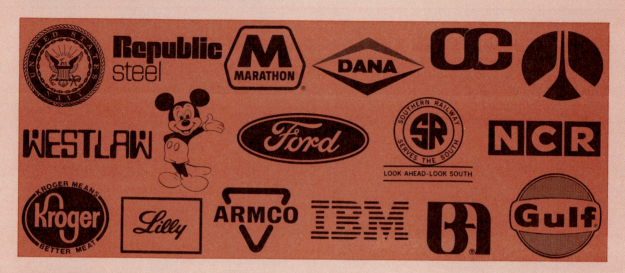

Eli Lilly and Company

On May 10, 1876, Colonel Eli Lilly, a Civil War veteran, began operating a small laboratory in downtown Indianapolis, Indiana, to manufacture medications. With total assets of $1,400 in fluid extracts and cash, Lilly began producing pills and other medicines. In 1881, the firm, which had since incorporated as Eli Lilly and Company, moved to the location just south of downtown Indianapolis that today continues to house its principal offices and research headquarters.

Two of the best-known medical discoveries toward which Lilly provided substantial contributions are insulin and the Salk polio vaccine. More recently, the company has developed a number of important antibiotics and cancer treatment agents. Besides manufacturing pharmaceutical products, Lilly has diversified into agricultural products, cosmetics, and medical instrument systems through its subsidiaries.

Products are manufactured and distributed through the company's own facilities in the United States, Puerto Rico, and 33 other countries. In 17 countries, the company owns or has an interest in manufacturing facilities. Its products are sold in more than 130 countries.

With interests in business and research scattered across the globe, Eli Lilly and Company has developed an extensive data processing operation to support every department of the corporation. The Scientific Information Systems Division handles activities related to research and development. Corporate Information Systems and Services supports the firm's business data-processing needs. The Corporate Computer Center consists of two large IBM computers and two Digital Equipment Corporation computers that receive and process data transmitted to the center via online teleprocessing, remote job-entry (RJE), and time-sharing terminals located in user departments of the corporation in U. S. and overseas locations. The Corporate Computer Center supports more than 200 time-sharing terminals, more than 500 teleprocessing devices, and at least 75 RJE stations. In a typical business day, more than 10,000 programs are executed and about 140,000 teleprocessing transactions are processed.

The Information Systems Development Division, which

employs approximately 250 people, is responsible for the design, development, and maintenance of business information systems. The division is composed of functional development groups; each group works with line management and staff groups to develop application programs designed to reduce operating expenses and provide information for more effective management. Marketing activities, manufacturing departments, financial systems, all phases of engineering, patent and general legal affairs, corporate affairs, and industrial relations are supported by this organization.

When a user department requests a major new application, a project is initiated to begin a multiphase process called PLAD (Process for Lilly Application Development). Figure 8–15 illustrates the flow of the PLAD phases and their related activities.

1. The first phase of the process requires documentation of the objectives and requirements of the requested system. Some projects warrant the review and approval of a separate objectives document before the detailed requirements are studied. These documents are carefully prepared to serve several purposes:

- User and management signoff helps assure that the system will meet the business need.
- Technical reviews provide the opportunity for computer operations, system programming, data management, and other support groups to verify feasibility and resource availability.
- Cost/benefit analysis provides the basis for management approval.

After systems and user management have approved the objectives/requirements documents, the design phase begins.

2. In the external design phase, the users are provided a detailed understanding of how the system will work so that they can verify that the system as planned by the designer will meet their specific needs. Logical system structure charts explain the flow and the transactions for each part of the system. Users participate in the design of reports, screen formats, and inquiries. The external design report documents the architecture of the system and provides plans for the following phases.

3. The next phase, internal design, produces the blueprints for the construction of the system. The user language of the external design phase is translated into technical terms. The system structure is divided into subsystems and programs. Specifications describe the functions performed by each program. All data elements are defined to the data element dictionary. Data files used for communications between programs are specified. Experienced designers, not a part of the project team, conduct the design walk-through. The internal design report includes plans for the coding, testing, and installation phases to follow.

4. During the coding and unit-test phase, additional members often join the project team. With the information from internal design and firm staffing plans,

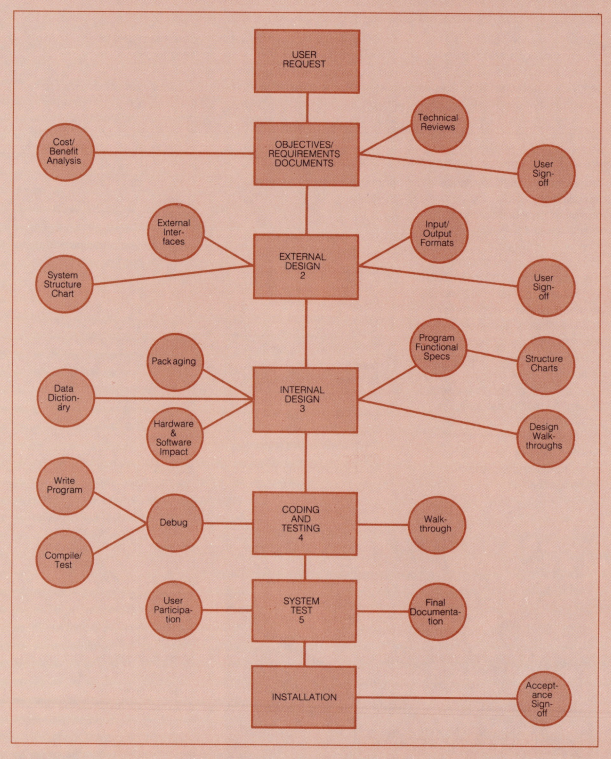

FIGURE 8–15

PLAD

the project leader is able to project a fairly reliable finish date. Each team member begins detailed design and coding of assigned programs. When coding is completed, the program is submitted for compilation. Any clerical errors should be detected during the compilation process. This step is repeated until an error-free compilation is achieved. The programmer then conducts a walk-through, explaining the purpose of the program to a previously uninvolved third party. This person, usually a fellow programmer, can provide fresh insights into areas where the purpose of the program is unclear (and thus requires additional comments). The person can also desk-check the program to identify logic errors that the programmer has overlooked. At this point, before the actual testing, the program is usually recompiled according to a compiler program that optimizes the machine-language code (builds instruction sequences that will be most efficient for repetitive processing purposes). It may also provide diagnostic messages indicating possible logic problems.

The program is now ready to be executed using real, or "live," test data that represents what may be processed in real-life situations. If the data is processed correctly, the program is ready for use. However, correct processing seldom occurs on the first run. To identify the causes of errors, the programmer may submit trial runs with abnormal terminations that produce core dumps at the end of execution. Occasionally, an error is so subtle that the programmer cannot determine its cause by analyzing a dump. In this case, a trace program can be used to indicate the execution flow through the entire sequence of instructions. The programmer can then determine if the flow has mistakenly entered a wrong section of the program.

5. The system-test phase involves heavy user participation and is actually the beginning of user training. Each subsystem is thoroughly tested using user-supplied input data. Finally, the entire system is tested, usually running in parallel with the old system.

After the system has been thoroughly tested, a final review of the application is made by members of the staff who will be involved in its operation. This review includes a check to see that (1) the system conforms to established standards; (2) user and system development documentation requirements have been satisfied; and (3) the system is ready to be assigned to "production" status. If the total application is found to be acceptable, it is released for implementation.

The application is allowed to operate for two to three months following implementation. After this period, the user area and operations staff review the application and either document their acceptance or suggest revisions.

The complexity of activities involved in the development of a new application, from the objectives document through completion of the system test, is justified by the financial and business factors associated with such an undertaking. Failure to properly perform any of the steps in the process can result in, at best, considerable difficulty and, at worst, a complete failure of the application. For this reason, the stringent standards described above have been adopted by Eli Lilly and Company.

DISCUSSION POINTS

1. Why does Eli Lilly involve users so heavily in the designing of a new application? In what ways are users incorporated into the application development process?

2. What procedures are used to test the applications prior to their implementation?

CHAPTER 9

Software Development

Introduction

Defining the problem and planning a solution are only the beginning of the programming process. Next, the appropriate programming language must be selected and the program coded in computer-acceptable statements. Writing programs requires the use of basic statements to describe operations common to all computers and all languages. These statements can be combined in countless ways to form programs. Individual programmers may write programs differently (even to solve similar problems), but all programs should possess certain qualities.

Once the program is written, it must be translated into a form that can be understood by the computer. In this translation process, error messages are generated to show the programmer where rules of the programming language have been broken. This is the beginning of the debugging and testing process. *Debugging* is removing syntax errors in the program; *testing* is determining whether the program is logically correct—that is, whether it works the way it is supposed to work. The final step in the programming process, documentation, requires that the programmer provide vital information to people who will work with and maintain the program.

66 The Smash Hit of Software 99

Daniel Bricklin, 29, and Robert Frankston, 31, a team of new-wave composers, have penned a dynamite disc that has grossed an estimated $8 million. It is not a punk-rock smash, but an unmelodic magnetic number called VisiCalc, the bestselling microcomputer program for business uses. The featherweight sliver of plastic is about the size of a greeting card, but when it is placed in a computer, the machine comes alive. A computer without a program, or "software," is like a $3,000 stereo set without any records or tapes.

Three years ago, Bricklin, then a first-year Harvard Business School student,

conceived VisiCalc while struggling with financial-planning problems on his calculator. He enlisted the aid of Frankston, a longtime friend and an expert programmer, to develop a new piece of computer software that would make juggling all those figures easier.

The partnership paid off. Since late 1979 nearly 100,000 copies of nine different versions of VisiCalc have been ordered at prices ranging from $100 to $300. It is far ahead of other business programs like Data Factory and General Ledger, and even outsells the programs for Star Cruiser, Dogfight and other arcade-like computer games.

VisiCalc translates simple commands typed on a keyboard into computer language that the machine then uses to solve problems. It enables a businessman, for example, to manipulate labyrinthine equations to

calculate financial trends for his company. If he changes one figure, the machine can tell quickly how that affects the other numbers. A firm that gives its workers a 10% pay hike could estimate how that action would alter its costs, sales, profits, or dividends.

The computer program is being put to a wide range of uses. It helps Allerton Cushman Jr., a New York financial analyst, to project insurance-industry profits during the week and tote up his income taxes on the weekend. The Cabot Street Cinema Theatre in Beverly, Mass., bought VisiCalc to figure out which pattern of movie show times draws the best box-office receipts. An accounting firm in Las Vegas plans to use VisiCalc to tell its gambling-house clients how to position slot machines around the floor to ensure the biggest take. VisiCalc is obviously one composition that is in no danger of fading from the charts.

Software programs, such as VisiCalc, are available in prewritten packages. Organizations have the option of either purchasing software packages, or developing the software within the organization. This chapter outlines the steps taken by programmers when writing computer programs.

WRITING THE PROGRAM

After the programmer has defined the problem and designed a solution, the program is written in a specific programming language. The type of language to be used can affect the solution to the problem as well as the ultimate structure of the program. Programming languages are usually designed for specific types of applications. For example, FORTRAN is a language designed primarily for scientific applications; COBOL is normally used for business applications. A programmer may have no part in the selection of a language for a particular application—there may be a business requirement to use COBOL, for instance, because of its readability. Programming languages are discussed further in Chapter 10.

This book has often emphasized that one key to success in using a computer is always to keep in mind that it can do only what it is instructed to do. It would be convenient to direct the computer by saying: "Take the data I am about to give you; calculate the gross pay, taxes, and net pay; and print the results." Computers are not yet sophisticated enough to handle such instructions.

Types of Statements

Certain types of programming statements are common to most high-level programming languages; they are comments, declarations, input/output statements, computations, transfers of control, and comparisons.

Comments The type of statement known as the remark or comment has no effect on program execution. Comments are inserted at key points in the program as documentation—notes to anyone reading the program to explain the purposes of program segments. For example, if a series of statements sorts a list of names into alphabetical order, the programmer may want to include a remark to that effect: "This segment sorts names in ascending alphabetical order."

Declarations The programmer uses declarations to define items used in the program. Examples include definitions of files, records, initial values of counters and accumulators, reusable functions, and the like.

Input/Output Statements Input statements bring data into main storage for use by the program. Output statements transfer data from main storage to output media such as hard-copy printouts or displays on video terminals. These statements differ considerably in form (though not so much in function) from one programming language to another.

Computations Computational instructions perform arithmetic operations— addition, subtraction, multiplication, division, and exponentiation. Languages vary in their facilities for invoking the computer's arithmetic capabilities.

Transfers of Control Another type of instruction allows the sequence of execution to be altered by transferring control. A conditional transfer of control alters the sequence only when a certain condition is met. An unconditional transfer always changes the sequence of execution.

Comparisons The final type of statement is the comparison, which allows two items to be compared. Based on the result of the comparison, either input/output, computation, or transfer of control could occur.

Desirable Program Qualities

As the program is being coded, the programmer should be aware that generating the correct output is not the only requirement of a good program. There is always more than one way to code a program to provide the correct solution; however, one program can be better than another. The programmer should try to incorporate the following qualities into any program:

● Programs should be easy to read and to understand. Data names should be descriptive. Short data names that do not reflect the data represented should be avoided. Statements should be placed in a format that is easy to read and to follow. In other words, the programmer should write the program in such a way that someone else can easily read and understand it.

● Programs should be efficient. In general, this means that programs should execute in as little time as possible. Computers are very expensive, and CPU time is a valuable resource. Some companies charge users hundreds of dollars for *one minute of CPU time*. An efficient program could save a user thousands of dollars per year.

● Programs should be reliable—they should consistently produce the correct output. All formulas and computations, as well as all logic tests and transfers of control, must be accurate.

● Programs should be robust—they should work under all conditions. Reliability alone is no guarantee of a successful program. Internal logic may be correct, but an incorrect data item (garbage in) could produce incorrect output (garbage out). For example, a program that uses the age of a person may want to test for incorrect ages in the data stream. How would the program react if someone's age were 4,692 or −35?

● Programs should be maintainable. They should be easy to update and modify. Programs should be written in independent modules so that a change in one module does not necessitate a change in others.

Program Development Aids

When programmers write (or code) the problem solution in a programming language, they can use special coding forms (see Figure 9–1). These forms are designed to reflect the rules (such as column restrictions) of the programming language used. In addition, the use of coding forms helps reduce clerical errors in coding and simplifies keying operations.

In many organizations today, coding is done on visual-display units with attached keyboards instead of on coding forms to be submitted for keypunching onto cards. It is much faster to enter statements from such a terminal than from a keypunch machine, and errors are more easily corrected. Some organizations utilize nonprogrammers to check programming statements entered on the terminals for errors in grammar and syntax. This helps to reduce later debugging time. Program development is highly labor intensive, and even modest amounts of automation can generate benefits in the form of increased productivity.

Programmers with access to terminals often have access to special software that assists them in program development. For example, some programming tasks are merely language conversions, such as converting a payroll program written in COBOL to PL/1. Software exists to accomplish this task. More special software to enhance programmer productivity is needed.

FIGURE 9–1
Some Commonly Used
Coding Forms

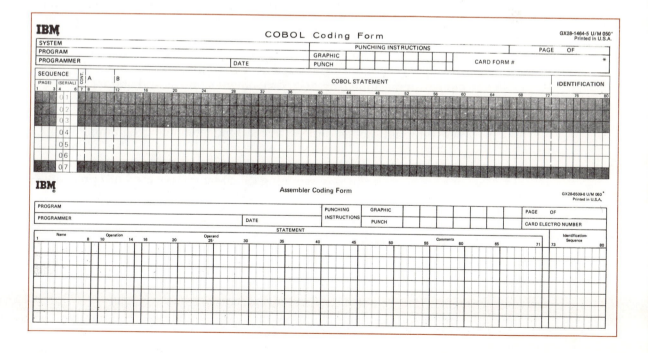

COMPILING, DEBUGGING, AND TESTING THE PROGRAM

After the program has been written, it is submitted to the computer. Levels of language and language translation are discussed here to illustrate how a high-level language program is altered to a form the computer can use.

Levels of Language

The programmer uses a sequence of instructions to communicate with the computer and to control program execution. As computers have developed in complexity, so have programming languages. Today there are three language levels—machine language, assembly language, and high-level language (see Figure 9–2).

Machine Language   Machine language is as old as the computer itself. It is the code that designates the proper electrical states in the computer and is expressed as combinations of 0s and 1s. It is the only language the computer can execute directly; therefore, it can be called the language of the computer.

Each type of computer has its own machine language, which is not transferrable to another type of computer. Each machine-language instruction must specify not only what operation is to be done but also the storage locations of data items. Because of these requirements and the nature of the language itself, machine-language programming is extremely complex, tedious, and time consuming. Therefore, other languages have been developed.

Assembly Language   Assembly language is one step removed from machine language. Programmers using assembly languages must be very conscious of the computer and must designate not only the operations to be performed but also storage locations, as when using machine language. However, assembly language is more easily understood by humans. Instead of the 0 and 1 groupings of machine language, convenient symbols and abbreviations are used. For instance, "STO" may stand for STORE; "TRA" for TRANSFER. Even with these conveniences, programming in assembly language is cumbersome, although not as difficult as machine-language programming.

High-Level Programming Languages   High-level languages provide a great deal of sophistication in programming. Such languages are both procedure-

FIGURE 9–2
Language Levels

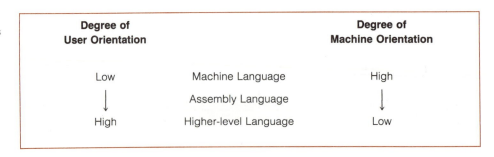

and problem-oriented; they are designed so that most of the programmer's attention can be focused on the problem at hand rather than on details of computer operations. Many high-level languages are English-like and allow use of common mathematical terms and symbols. The time and effort needed to write a program are reduced, and programs are easier to correct and modify.

High-level languages are so called because they are furthest removed from the hardware; they least resemble the 0 and 1 combinations of machine language. Whereas one assembly-language instruction is generally equivalent to one machine-language instruction, one high-level-language statement can accomplish the same result as a half-dozen or more machine-language instructions, principally because the addresses for many of the required storage locations do not have to be specified; they are handled automatically.

Figure 9–3 illustrates one statement written in the high-level language COBOL and the machine-language instructions that correspond to it. The machine-language instructions are expressed in the hexadecimal number system.

Language Translation

Assembly and high-level languages are much more widely used by programmers than machine language. Since these languages cannot be executed directly by computers, they are converted into machine-executable form by a *language-translator program*. The sequence of instructions written by the programmer—the *source program*—is transformed by the language-translator program into a machine-executable form known as the *object program*, which accomplishes the same operations as a program originally written in machine language.

The translator program for an assembly language is called an *assembler program*. A high-level-language translator is called a *compiler program*. Both assemblers and compilers are designed for specific machines and languages. For example, a compiler that translates a source program written in FORTRAN into a machine-language program can only translate FORTRAN (see Figure 9–4).

FIGURE 9–3
One COBOL Statement and Corresponding Machine-Language Instructions

```
(a) COBOL

   STANDARD-ROUTINE.
      MULTIPLY HOURS-WORKED BY WAGE-PER-HOUR GIVING GROSS PAY.


(b) MACHINE LANGUAGE

*STANDARD-ROUTINE
            000778
MULTIPLY    000778    F2    71    D    1E8    7    010
            00077E    F2    73    D    1F0    7    012
            000784    FC    42    D    1EB    D    1E5
            00078A    F3    43    6    000    D    1EC
            000790    96    F0    6    004
            000794    58    10    D    21C
            000798    07    F1
```

HIGHLIGHT 9–2

Putting Program Code to Good Use

When program maintenance—keeping programs error-free and in line with current requirements—is discussed, most suggestions are aimed at better documentation. However, a second factor for reducing maintenance time can be applied by writing the program carefully in an understandable program code.

COBOL, often promoted because of its readability, is frequently made unreadable by being adapted to systems use because of DP management rules. A typical example of COBOL adapted in this way is coding that uses the same data names as the assembler copy library (which are limited to eight positions):

```
IF MEDTRNTP = 'A'
PERFORM ALL-TRN THRU
EXIT-1.
```

The same instruction coded properly in COBOL is definitely easier to understand:

```
IF MEDICARE-
TRANSACTION-TYPE
EQUAL 'A' PERFORM
150-ALLOWANCE-
TRANSACTION THRU 160-
ALLOWANCE-EXIT.
```

By increasing the program's understandability, companies can realize savings from the ease with which programs are debugged, tested, and maintained.

However, efforts to write understandable programs in companies that presently use shorter codes can be hampered. Management is often reluctant to invest the resources needed to rewrite all the existing programs. When faced with this situation, the next-best route is to at least write the new programs in a clear, self-documenting, standard code. Then, as time progresses, the older, more complicated programs will be retired; and the advantages of the newer, better-written programs will eventually be realized.

FIGURE 9–4
FORTRAN Program Translation

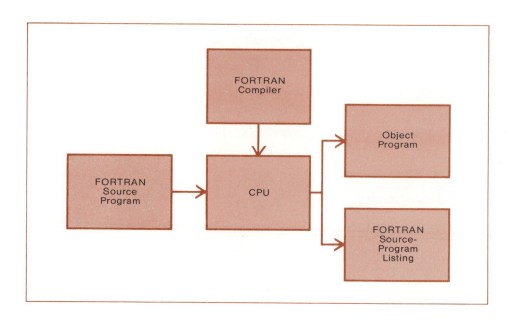

During the compilation, or assembly (the translation process), the object program is generated. The programmer receives an assembly listing or a source-program listing that contains indications of any errors the assembler or compiler detected during translation. The errors are usually violations of the rules associated with the particular programming language. For example, if a statement that should begin in column 8 on a line begins in column 6, an error message will be generated. Similarly, an error message will be generated if language keywords such as WRITE or COMPUTE are misspelled.

To help the programmer, the compiler can provide a listing of all compiler-detected errors. This error-message listing may give the number of each statement in error and may also describe the nature of the error (see Figure 9–5). Only after all detected errors have been corrected can the object program be submitted to the computer to be executed. Several attempts at successful compilation or assembly may be needed. The complete process of compilation and execution of a COBOL program is shown in Figure 9–6. In this case, the COBOL source program has been punched on cards, and the data provided as input to the object program has been stored on magnetic tape.

Debugging the Program

The compiler that translates the program can detect grammatical errors, such as misspellings and incorrect punctuation. However, logical errors are often harder to detect. Such errors may result when the programmer does not fully understand the problem or does not account for problems that may arise during processing.

Errors in programs are called "bugs," and the process of locating, isolating, and eliminating bugs is called "debugging." The amount of time that must be spent in debugging depends on the quality of the program. However, a newly completed program rarely executes successfully the first time it is run. In fact, one-third to one-half of a programmer's time is spent in debugging.

FIGURE 9–5
Compiler-Detected
Errors

STATEMENT NUMBER	ERROR CODE	ERROR MESSAGES
1972	IKF1080I-W	PERIOD PRECEDED BY SPACE. ASSUME END OF SENTENCE.
1999	IKF1080I-W	PERIOD PRECEDED BY SPACE. ASSUME END OF SENTENCE.
2074	IKF1043I-W	END OF SENTENCE SHOULD PRECEDE 02. ASSUMED PRESENT.
2399	IKF2126I-C	VALUE CLAUSE LITERAL TOO LONG. TRUNCATED TO PICTURE SIZE.
2432	IKF1043I-W	END OF SENTENCE SHOULD PRECEDE 02. ASSUMED PRESENT.
2481	IKF1080I-W	PERIOD PRECEDED BY SPACE. ASSUME END OF SENTENCE.
2484	IKF1080I-W	PERIOD PRECEDED BY SPACE. ASSUME END OF SENTENCE.
2623	IKF1004I-E	INVALID WORD NOTE. SKIPPING TO NEXT RECOGNIZABLE WORD.
2623	IKF1007I-W	MINUS SIGN NOT PRECEDED BY A SPACE. ASSUME SPACE.
2623	IKF1007I-W	**NOT PRECEDED BY A SPACE. ASSUME SPACE.

Testing the Program

When a compilation without errors is achieved, it is time for a test run. This run involves executing the program with input data that is either a represen-

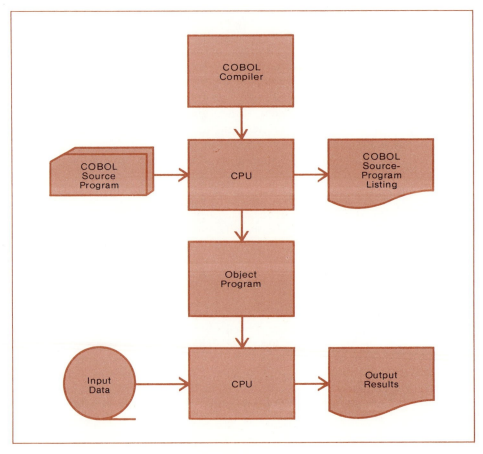

FIGURE 9-6
COBOL Program Translation and Execution

tative sample of actual data or a facsimile of it. Often, sample data that can be manipulated easily by the programmer is used so that the computer-determined output can be compared with programmer-determined correct results. The output should be easy to recognize so that the programmer can see if it is correct.

A complex program is frequently tested in separate units so that errors can be isolated to specific sections, helping to narrow the search for the cause of an error. The programmer must correct all mistakes; running and rerunning a specific unit may be necessary before the cause of an error can be found. The programmer then rewrites the part in error and resubmits it for another test. Care must be taken so that correction of one logical error does not give rise to several others.

Each section of the program must be tested (even sections that will be used infrequently). If instructions for handling exceptions are part of the program, the sample input data should include items that test the program's ability to spot and reject improper data items. The programmer often finds *desk-checking (desk-debugging)* helpful. With this method, the programmer pretends to be the computer and, reading each instruction and simulating how the computer would process a data item, attempts to catch any flaws in the program logic.

After a programmer has worked for a long time to correct the logic of a program, he or she may tend to overlook errors or assume a clarity that in reality does not exist. For this reason, programmers sometimes trade their partially debugged programs among themselves. The programmer stepping through a "fresh" program may uncover mistakes in logic that were hidden to the original programmer.

In many cases, program errors prove especially difficult to locate. Two commonly used diagnostic procedures usually available to the programmer in such cases, are dump programs and trace programs.

A *dump program* lists the contents of registers and main storage locations. In some systems, the resulting printout, the *dump,* lists storage values in hexadecimal notation (see Figure 9–7). Trying to understand such a dump can be a cumbersome procedure; but once dump-reading is learned, it can be a very useful debugging technique. The programmer can determine whether data and instructions have been correctly stored in the proper locations. In this way, errors can be isolated to specific statements or data, and corrections can be made.

FIGURE 9–7
Storage Dump

```
USER STORAGE
                              CORE ADDRESSES SPECIFIED-     000000 TO 000390
000000   05C0E020 C0520064 E000C0B7 00064770   C032E020 C0B60007 41200006 4130C0B7   *................................*
000020   45A0C17E F235C107 C0B7FA33 C10BC107   47F0C006 4120000A F393C174 C10B4130   *..A.2.A.....A.A..0......3.A.A...*
000040   C17445A0 C218E020 C10F0064 E020C173   000B07FE F1E3C8C5 E2C540C1 D9C540E3   *A...B...A.....A.....1THESE ARE T*
000060   C8C540E5 C1D3E4C5 E240D9C5 C1C44040   40404040 40404040 40404040 40404040   *HE VALUES READ                  *
000080   40404040 40404040 40404040 40404040   40404040 40404040 40404040 40404040   *                                *
0000A0   40404040 40404040 40404040 40404040   40404040 40404040 40F0F2F1 F2F0D0F5   *                          02120.5*
0000C0   F5F5F5F5 F5F5F5F5 F5F5F5F5 F5F5F5F5   F5F5F5F5 F5F5F5F5 F5F5F5F5 F5F5F5F5   *55555555555555555555555555555555*
 LINES    0000E0-0000E0    SAME AS ABOVE
000100   F5F5F5F5 F5F5F5F5 F5002120 0DF0F0F0   C0F0E3C8 C540E2E4 D440D6C6 40E3C8C5   *555555555....000.0THE SUM OF THE*
000120   40E5C1D3 E4C5E240 C9E24040 40404040   40404040 40404040 40404040 40404040   * VALUES IS                      *
000140   40404040 40404040 40404040 40404040   40404040 40404040 40404040 40404040   *                                *
000160   40404040 40404040 40404040 40404040   40404040 4040F5F5 F5F5F5F5 F5F5F5F5   *                      5555555555*
000180   0620954E 30004780 C19A9560 30004770   C1AC1A32 94DF3000 47F0C1A0 1A3294CF   *........A.......A........0A.....*
0001A0   30001B32 92F03000 41220001 07FAE020   C1B40064 07FA40C6 C9D9E2E3 40C3C8C1   *.....0..........A..... FIRST CHA*
0001C0   D9C1C3E3 C5D940E2 C5D5E340 E3D640E7   C9D540E6 C1E240D5 D6E340C1 40E2C9C7   *RACTER SENT TO XIN WAS NOT A SIG*
0001E0   D5404040 40404040 40404040 40404040   40404040 40404040 40404040 40404040   *N                               *
```

A *trace* produced by a *trace program,* is apt to be easier to use than a dump. The trace lists the steps followed during program execution in the order in which they occurred. The programmer can specify that all or portions of a program be traced. The trace is often used in combination with the desk-checking procedure described above to see if the correct flow of execution has occurred. The values of selected variables can also be displayed in the trace; this can be helpful in determining whether the necessary calculations have been performed correctly.

DOCUMENTING THE PROGRAM

Documentation consists of written descriptions and explanations of programs and other materials associated with an organization's data-processing systems. Documentation of system and program designs is one of the most important (and, unfortunately, one of the most neglected) requirements for success in a data-processing application. The importance of complete documentation has long been known, but many firms are only now beginning to insist that complete documentation be prerequisite to implementing a new program or changing an existing one.

Everyone who uses the computer needs such documentation at some time. Proper program documentation serves as a reference guide for programmers and analysts who must modify or update existing programs and system procedures. Without it, a programmer may have to spend days or weeks trying to ascertain what a program does and how it does it. Further, in many cases, programs are designed to operate under a fixed set of conditions and constraints. When organizations change and grow, program modifications must keep pace with their changing needs. Documentation helps management to evaluate the effectiveness of data-processing applications and to determine where changes are desirable.

Documentation is also essential to those who must perform manual functions required by the system. When staff changes occur, new employees need complete documentation of all clerical procedures within the system. This information helps them to understand their jobs and how to carry them out. Finally, documentation provides instructions to the computer operator about the requirements (tape drives, card readers, and the like) for running particular programs.

The process of documentation is an ongoing process. It begins with the initial request for information. The individual making the request should be identified. So should those who will be charged with the responsibility of designing the system and the required programs. The names of the persons who must approve the request should be provided.

During the problem-definition phase, the problem should be described clearly in a short narrative statement. The objectives of the program that will be created to solve the problem should be included with the problem statement. Several other descriptions are necessary:

● A complete description of the contents and formats of all data inputs, outputs, and files to be used.

● A statement of the hardware requirements for running the program, such as magnetic-tape drives, disk drives, and card readers, as well as estimated processing time and storage requirements.

● A statement of software requirements, such as utility programs and library programs; this statement may also identify the programming language to be used and list the reasons for choosing it.

In the planning phase, the most important documentation produced is the flowchart. If the application is complex, both modular and detail program flowcharts should be prepared. Descriptive comments may be included for each processing step. Completeness and accuracy are essential. If changes are made to the program, they must be reflected in the flowchart so that all program documentation stays up-to-date.

An operator's manual, sometimes known as a *run book*, should also be prepared. It contains the instructions needed to run the program and will be used primarily by the computer operator. All the documentation for a program or system can be combined to form a user's manual, which contains documentation designed to aid persons not familiar with a program in using the program.

PROGRAMMING CASE STUDY

The objective of this problem is to calculate the average numerical grade for each student in a class and to determine his or her final letter grade for the course. Our input will be the students' names and the five numerical grades each received during the course. Our output requirements are to print the names of the students, their average numerical grades, and their final letter grades under the headings "Name," "Average," and "Final Grade."

The final grade for each student is to be based on the following grade scale:

AVERAGE	FINAL GRADE
90–100	A
80–89	B
70–79	C
60–69	D
0–59	F

Thus, the job requirements have been defined: the input will be the students' names and grades; the required computation will be the determination of average and final grades; and the required output will be the students' names, averages, and final grades listed under appropriate headings. It is important to remember that the problem solution must be defined logically and that the computer must be given all relevant data and instructions.

The first step in designing a problem solution is to determine a basic instruction flow. Output headings can be printed before the student data is read as input. Since each student has five grades, the student's name and five grades must be input and the grades added together. When the addition has been completed, the average can be calculated. Once the average has been determined, the appropriate final letter grade can be assigned according to the grade scale. After the final letter grade has been established, the name, average, and final grade can be printed. When the data for one student has been processed, the data for the next student can be read and processed, and so on, until no more statistics are available.

The flow can be placed into steps as follows:

1. Print headings.
2. Read student's name and five grades.
3. Total the student's numerical grades.
4. Calculate the student's grade average.
5. Determine the final letter grade based on the grade scale.
6. Print name, average, and final letter grade.
7. Repeat steps 2–6 for all students.
8. Stop.

A flowchart for the solution of this problem is given in Figure 9–8. The relationship between the steps above and the blocks on the flowchart is also pointed out.

After the flowchart has been constructed and the logic reviewed, the next task is to express the solution in a programming language—in this case, BASIC. The completed source program can then be entered into the computer via the keyboard of a terminal. Then it can be translated into an object program. A listing of the source program and notification of errors (if any) detected by the compiler can be generated. Then the program can be executed. Figure 9–9 shows the source-program listing; Figure 9–10 shows the output produced during the execution of the program.

SOURCES OF PROGRAMS

Many organizations employ programmers to develop programs for their internal operations. This approach, called in-house development, allows for programming creativity while satisfying customer/user requirements. However, it requires significant expenditures for staff. In addition, many other organizations may write programs to accomplish the same basic objectives, thus duplicating effort. Why spend scarce resources (programming time and talent) unnecessarily?

An alternative method of developing programs is to hire *contract programmers*. Contract programmers are not employees of the organization using their services; rather, they contract with the organization to develop a program or programs. Contract programmers work either independently or for a firm that locates programming work for them.

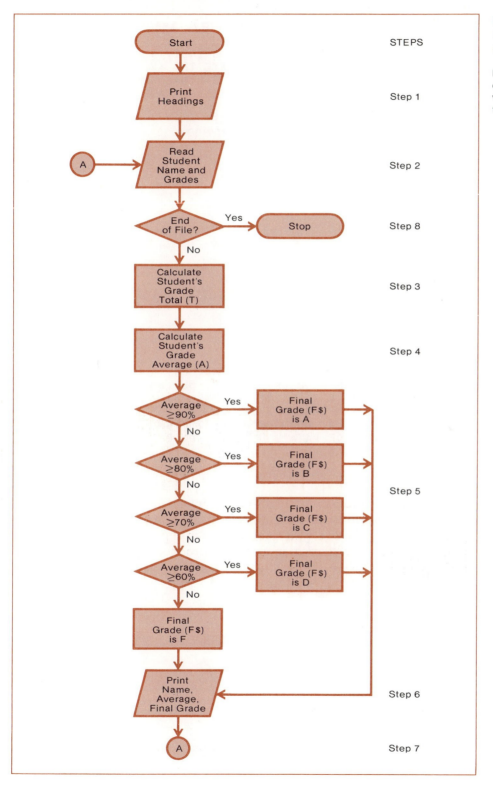

FIGURE 9–8
Flowchart
for Case Study

Note: The characters
enclosed in ( ) are the
variable names used in
the BASIC program.

FIGURE 9–9

BASIC Program with Sample Data for Case Study

```
GRADE     21:54     TUESDAY JULY 27, 1982

100 REM THIS PROGRAM WILL ADD 5 INDIVIDUAL GRADES
110 REM FOR A STUDENT, CALCULATE THE AVERAGE, AND THEN
120 REM DETERMINE THE STUDENT'S FINAL GRADE
130 PRINT 'NAME','AVERAGE', 'FINAL GRADE'
140 PRINT
150 READ N$, G1, G2, G3, G4, G5
155 IF N$ = 'END OF DATA' THEN 999
160 LET T = G1+G2+G3+G4+G5
170 LET A = T/5
180 IF A >= 90 THEN 240
190 IF A >= 80 THEN 260
200 IF A >= 70 THEN 280
210 IF A >= 60 THEN 300
220 LET F$ = 'F'
230 GO TO 310
240 LET F$ = 'A'
250 GO TO 310
260 LET F$ = 'B'
270 GO TO 310
280 LET F$ = 'C'
290 GO TO 310
300 LET F$ = 'D'
310 PRINT N$, A, F$
320 GO TO 150
330 DATA 'FRED J. SMITH', 70, 65, 24, 100, 98
340 DATA 'JASON R. JACKSON', 97, 96, 59, 78, 60
350 DATA 'JOHN S. LAWSON', 90, 94, 88, 98, 96
360 DATA 'SUSAN EAKINS', 83, 76, 87, 89, 95
370 DATA 'MARY Q. JOHNSON', 66, 79, 83, 75, 70
380 DATA 'END OF DATA', 0, 0, 0, 0, 0
999 END
```

Hiring contract programmers can be advantageous for a firm. If a large programming task must be done quickly, using contract programmers is a good way to temporarily supplement the in-house programmers to complete the task. Good contract programmers can produce high-quality programs

FIGURE 9-10

Output for Case Study

```
RUN GRADE

GRADE     21:54     TUESDAY JULY 27, 1982

NAME                    AVERAGE         FINAL GRADE

FRED J. SMITH           71.4            C
JASON R. JACKSON        78              C
JOHN S. LAWSON          93.2            A
SUSAN EAKINS            86              B
MARY Q. JOHNSON         74.6            C
```

rapidly, because they can work independently (often at home), away from the distractions of the normal work environment.

Using contract programmers can also have its disadvantages. A firm that hires a contract programmer it has never used before is hiring an unproven resource. Also, because contract programmers work for the firm only temporarily, there may be no incentive for them to write well-documented, easily maintainable programs, unless doing so is expressly required by their contracts. Thus, a firm should exercise caution when employing contract programmers.

Because of the disadvantages of in-house development and contract programming, interest groups have been created for the purpose of sharing software among organizations operating in similar environments; and firms specializing in software development have been formed to meet the growing demand for prewritten programs. Software and consulting activities require an ever-increasing share of data-processing expenditures, thereby reducing the proportion spent on hardware. Most computer manufacturers supply some or all of these services (often at a separate cost), but there is a large and growing market for externally supplied services.

Software Packages

A *software package* is a set of standardized computer programs, procedures, and related documentation designed to solve problems of a specific application. Proprietary software packages are developed and owned by an organization but sold or leased to many users. Packages to handle almost any common application are available. Their costs range from $15 or even less to more than $100,000. When a package exists that fits a user's requirements (or can be easily adapted to do so), its cost is almost certainly less than that of in-house development. Furthermore, such packages are usually debugged and documented, and ongoing maintenance and support may be offered.

System Packages   System packages are sets of programs that make it possible to operate computers more conveniently and efficiently. Traditionally, system packages were bundled with hardware; that is, they were provided to the customer/user by the equipment manufacturer at no additional cost. When major computer manufacturers began to unbundle system software, interest in the commercial aspect of system program development began to accelerate. Programs similar to those formerly supplied "free" by the manufacturers were made available, but at additional cost. Users of computer equipment were given an incentive to shop around to find suitable software at costs to their liking.

System packages exist in many forms; examples include operating systems, data-base management systems, report generators, job-accounting systems, compilers, input/output control routines, and diagnostic routines. Since these packages are normally machine-dependent, they still are most often supplied by the equipment manufacturers; however, an increasing number are being made available by independent software suppliers. System packages comprise about 25 percent of all currently available software packages, but they account for more than 50 percent of total revenues.

Application Packages   Application packages are sets of programs that perform specific, well-defined data-processing or computational tasks. Application packages have long been available for engineering and scientific applications; the Statistical Package for the Social Sciences (SPSS) and the Generalized Package for System Simulation (GPSS) are examples. These packages include routines for performing matrix inversion, regression analysis, probability functions, and so on. Many statistical packages are designed to be used easily, even by inexperienced users; but they are normally available only for large systems.

Packages for business applications are available for almost any kind of computer. They perform payroll, accounts receivable, accounts payable, general ledger, inventory control, production scheduling, and many other common business data-processing functions. Such packages are written in a general way and then tailored to the requirements of individual firms. About 75 percent of all packages are application packages. Although they are available from equipment manufacturers, the fastest-growing market comprises those supplied by independent software firms.

Choosing Packages   A major decision made by computer users is whether to buy a prewritten software package or to develop the software in-house. In-house development often suffers from serious delays, underestimated resource and time requirements, poor documentation, and high development costs. In contrast, purchased packages are normally available at a fixed cost known in advance and can be installed and made to operate within a relatively short time period. In addition, good documentation can be established as a prerequisite for purchased software. Thus, many factors favor the purchase of prewritten packages.

Unfortunately, implementing prewritten packages is seldom simple. Because of their generalized nature, prewritten packages may be difficult to tailor to meet a firm's unique requirements. The costs of modifying, installing, converting, and testing software packages can be significant. Also, the costs of maintaining the packages and training people to use them must not be overlooked. The overriding concern is, of course, whether the package can meet the requirements of the user. The more modification needed, the greater the implementation costs.

Many proprietary packages have been extremely successful and have many satisfied users. Others have been dismal failures. For this reason, firms considering buying or leasing a proprietary package often elect to contact current users of the package, a practice that has much merit. Inferior packages will be recognized as such, and will soon fade from the market.

The use of proprietary software packages is expected to increase over the next several years as more firms discover its potential benefits. At the same time, in-house developers will concentrate more on unique projects that offer new challenges.

SUMMARY

- Once the problem solution has been planned and the appropriate language chosen, the program can be written. Several types of programming statements are common to most languages.
- Programmers should strive to write high-quality programs that are easy to read and understand, efficient, reliable, robust, and maintainable.
- Programming development aids such as coding forms, visual-display units, and special software are available to help improve programmer productivity.
- There are three levels of language groups: (1) machine language is expressed as combinations of 0s and 1s and is the only language the computer can execute directly; (2) assembly language provides convenient symbols and abbreviations for writing programs; and (3) high-level languages are English-like and procedure- and problem-oriented (allowing programs to be transferred from one computer to another with little change).
- A sequence of instructions written in assembly language or high-level language is called a source program. The language translator converts the source program into a machine-language equivalent known as an object program.
- The translator program for an assembly language is called an assembler program. A high-level language translator is called a compiler program.
- After programs have been written, they are debugged and tested. Dump programs and trace programs provide diagnostics to help debug programs. Testing is done on sample data so that the computer-determined output can be compared with predetermined correct results.
- Program documentation is essential throughout the programming cycle. It simplifies modification and updating of existing programs and system procedures and is a must for the success of any program.
- In-house program development is performed entirely by a firm's own employees. Contract programmers are sometimes hired to temporarily supplement the in-house staff in order for a programming task to be finished more quickly.
- A software package is a set of standardized computer programs, procedures, and related documentation for a particular application. Software packages are becoming popular because of their relatively low cost and the fact that they have usually been tested, debugged, and documented.
- System packages are designed to increase the efficiency and convenience of computer operations. Historically bundled with equipment, they now must be purchased separately.
- Application packages, which are used to solve specific problems, are available for a variety of scientific and business applications.
- Implementing packages can be difficult because they must be modified to meet the user's specific needs. Costs of installation, conversion, and testing can be high. Firms considering purchase or lease of a package should get a report on its performance from current users.

REVIEW QUESTIONS

1. List and describe the types of statements used in most high-level programming languages.

2. Discuss the qualities that can make one program better than another. How can these qualities make a program better?

3. After a program has been written and submitted to the computer, how does the computer translate it into usable form?

4. What is documentation, and at what steps of program development should it be included? Why is documentation important?

5. A firm can develop programs in several ways. Describe these various alternatives and the advantages and disadvantages of each.

APPLICATION

Rockwell International

When people think of spaceships and space shuttles, the name Rockwell often comes to mind. Indeed, Rockwell International was the principal contractor for the NASA Space Shuttle *Columbia,* which made its pioneer voyage in April, 1981. However, although Rockwell International is known primarily for its aerospace activities, it has four diverse business segments—automotive, aerospace, electronics, and general industries.

With sales close to $2 billion and mutinational facilities, the Automotive Division of Rockwell

International is far from small. It is one of the leading suppliers of components for heavy-duty truck and off-highway equipment. In addition, through its new Automotive Technical Center, Rockwell hopes to expand its participation in the huge passenger car, light truck and international markets.

In addition to the space shuttle and space transportation system, Rockwell's Aerospace Division is currently working on three more shuttlecraft under a contract from the National Aeronautics and Space Administration as well as on unmanned satellite programs, the most important of them for the Department of Defense. Rockwell has used its rocket technology to design and develop water-propulsion systems for the Navy. Finally, it continues to work on the B–1 strategic aircraft and to work for civilian commercial aviation manufacturers, specifically the

Boeing Company.

Close behind the automotive division in sales, the $1.7-billion-a-year Electronics operations of Rockwell International is growing rapidly. It has developed a huge research and development organization for air-transport avionics, which has resulted in Rockwell International's winning contracts from Boeing (for fully digital autopilot systems and flight instrument systems for the new 757s and 767s) and from Lockheed (for control systems expected to help cut fuel consumption by 3 percent—a lot for a jet airliner).

Telecommunications is another part of Rockwell's electronics business; its digital microwave systems have been ordered by seventeen of the twenty-three Bell Telephone operating companies. This division makes a great many other products as well.

Finally, Rockwell's General

Industries Division includes businesses engaged in manufacturing and marketing high-speed printing presses; energy-generation and environmental control systems for utilities; components for oil, gas, and nuclear industries; power tools; and textile machinery products. General Industries, which accounts for about $1.5 billion of annual sales, operates forty-two plants and employs more than 23,000 men and women in nineteen countries.

Electronic data-processing operations at Rockwell are managed by a corporate information system center in Seal Beach, California. A sophisticated communications network connects this center with regional computing centers in Seal Beach, Dallas, and

Cedar Rapids, Iowa. Approximately 3,000 of Rockwell's employees work in some phase of computer development or operations.

IBM supplies a majority of Rockwell's computer hardware. An IBM System 370 Model 3033, which can handle up to sixteen megabytes of storage, provides the large-scale main frame for business applications. A separate scientific computing center handles science and engineering applications; this center utilizes a Cyber 176 and a Univac 1100–83. Word processing equipment, which varies from stand-alone to shared logic systems, is scattered throughout the Rockwell divisions. Users are tied into the central system by remote job entry (RJE) terminals and CRTs.

Rockwell utilizes COBOL programs for business applications, FORTRAN and PL/1 for scientific applications. Many programming aids are also used.

Among the many programming aids used by the management information system area of Rockwell are:

- A Bolle and Babbage software package, which identifies inefficient portions of programs.
- A BTS (batch test simulator), which enables online programs to be tested in batch mode.
- An IBM TESTCOB that helps in diagnosing problems in COBOL programs.
- Autoflow, which automatically produces flowcharts for source programs.
- ADF, an IBM software package that aids in the development of interactive portions of systems.
- TSO/SPS and ROSCOE, two packages that provide time-sharing options for users in separate locations.
- A data dictionary is being installed that will provide a central source of information for files, data elements, and programs for easy reference.

The scientific community uses different programming aids appropriate for engineering, research and development, and the like. For instance, Computer Assisted Design/Computer Assisted Manufacture (CAD/CAM) is used extensively in aerospace and electronics technology. Originally

developed to help design computer circuitry, CAD/CAM now has a multitude of uses in many diverse areas. A light pen can be used to experiment with various designs by drawing them on the video display screen. The artist can then view the designs in three dimensions from various angles and can easily make alterations. Recent developments in color graphics have made CAD/CAM an even more valuable tool.

Many of the software packages currently used by Rockwell come from independent firms. The question of whether to buy or lease software is determined by cost-benefit analysis on a situational basis. If suitable software packages do not exist for specific applications; programmers develop them in-house. The vast majority of programmers at Rockwell are regular employees; however, additional personnel have been contracted during periods of peak loads. This practice has become less common, though, because of some recent changes in the tax laws.

Creative use of computers, especially software, can do much to accelerate the growth of companies like Rockwell that take full advantage of EDP capabilities.

DISCUSSION POINTS

1. Why does Rockwell maintain a separate scientific computer center? What programming aids are utilized by scientific personnel?

2. How do programming aids such as BTS and ADF increase programmers' productivity? What might be some consequences of programming without the use of such tools?

CHAPTER 10

Programming Languages

Introduction

The hardware capabilities of computers have grown tremendously during the past decade. However, benefits from the hardware technology cannot be realized unless there are complementary developments in software; thus, various programming languages have been developed to increase the usefulness of computers. The future of information processing appears to depend less on the development of better machine technologies than on the effectiveness with which we use existing capabilities. Thus, developments in software and programming technologies can be expected to play a key role in the future success of computer-based systems.

This chapter highlights the major programming languages used today. It discusses the unique features and characteristics and the advantages and disadvantages of each and identifies typical applications. The payroll program developed in Chapter 8 is used here as a sample program to illustrate use of the various languages. The chapter ends with a critical comparison of the languages that points out the factors to be considered in selecting the most appropriate one for a particular application.

66 A Company that Works at Home 77

For a company with 600 employees, the home office of F International Ltd. is modest, to say the least. It houses a computer, but little else. The British computer software company has no need of long rows of offices, because it is perhaps the leading corporate example of telecommuting, a growing trend by which employees communicate directly with the office computer from their homes. Almost all of F International's personnel work at home, and about half use computer terminals.

The British company's business lends itself to this novel work arrangement. F International offers services for computer users, ranging from writing computer programs to designing complete data processing systems. This work is usually done directly on computer terminals in any case, making the location of these units irrelevant. The company was founded in 1962 by Vera S. Shirley, now chairman, after she quit her programming job to raise a family. She had assumed that many women left jobs for the same reason but still wanted to work. Such women continue to account for 95% of the company's staff.

A Suitable Arrangement

The company grew from a handful of employees to 200 staffers by 1970, with those working at home using pencil and paper for their programming chores. The shift in recent years has been to home terminals, which are linked via phone lines either to the client's computer or to F International's own computer center. "This suits me perfectly," says Jeannette E. Scott, a marketing executive who began work on a terminal as a home-based computer programmer. "It lets me combine a demanding career with my other interests. I don't want to dump the children at 8 a.m. and pick them up at 6 p.m."

Working on the terminal at home "saves time, effort, and it's easier," adds Elizabeth Hull, a 37-year-old mother of two who has worked three years for F International. In addition to saving commuting time, Hull can work at night, when it is most convenient. "You have complete choice [of time of day] to try out your computer coding." she says.

By careful staff selection and the right kind of management, the home workers can be more productive than office-based workers, maintains Suzette M. Harold, F International's managing director. Office-based professionals, she says, tend to whittle away at an 8-hour work day with coffee breaks and lunch hours. "We're working five useful hours on the average," Harold says, "so

we're producing a week's work in less time." Most home workers are paid by the hour.

Discipline

Working at home is not without its problems, however. It requires a new set of disciplines for the worker, says Mary M. Smith, one of F International's production managers for home work. "It's difficult to go into the study and shut the neighbors out," she says.

F International also has had to develop the right kind of management for home workers. "People you don't see need as much management, attention, and support as those you do see," says Harold, so her project managers often call the homes of employees. And only people with at least four years' experience—the average is 10 years—are hired to ensure their ability to adhere to deadlines.

Quality Spurs Growth

F International has prospered with its team of home workers. The company "is on a 20% real growth path," according to Harold. While she will not provide numbers, industry observers estimate that the privately held company's annual sales in Britain run about $5 million, a fair size for a computer software services company. F International has opened subsidiaries in Denmark and the Netherlands, and it has begun marketing its services in Thailand and Australia. Heights Information Technology Service Inc. in White Plains, N.Y., has licensed F International's management approach to use with its programmers working at home.

The company has been able to sustain this growth rate because its customers have overcome their initial skepticism of home workers. This acceptance has been helped by the unusually tight job market: "The computer industry is very, very short-staffed," says Harold.

Lloyds Bank International Ltd. (London) was initially wary about doing business with F International because of concern about "extremely confidential documents being shipped around the country" to workers' homes, according to a bank official. But now, he says, "we have a good opinion of them. If anything, they did higher quality work than other firms." These days, boasts F International's Scott, "people treat us as an ordinary computer software firm—and that's how we prefer it."

Advanced computer concepts, such as telecommuting, are bringing computer technology into the lives of more and more people. There are numerous programming languages in existence today, and it is important for programmers to be aware of the capabilities of these many languages. The following chapter gives an overview of several, common programming languages.

BATCH-ORIENTED VERSUS INTERACTIVE PROGRAMMING LANGUAGES

Batch-Oriented Programming Language

Batch-oriented programming languages are used with batch programs, which solve problems for which immediate responses are not required. A batch program is submitted to the computer as a single unit containing both instructions and data. Once the instructions and data have been put into the CPU, processing takes place without intervention from programmers or users.

Most batch programs are used to solve specific problems that recur. For example, payroll processing is usually done in batch mode, since the same payroll processing functions must be performed each week or month. A batch program that indicates the steps necessary to process the payroll can be written once and then used repeatedly to process different sets of data. Other common batch-processing applications are accounts receivable, inventory control, and billing.

Batch programs are not executed as they are submitted to the computer. Instead, several batch programs are stored temporarily on an auxiliary storage device until the CPU is ready to execute them. Several jobs may be read in at the same time and processed at different times during the day or night, depending on their priorities.

There are three categories of batch programming languages: *machine-oriented, procedure-oriented,* and *problem-oriented* languages. An assembly language is an example of a machine-oriented language. The programmer using a machine-oriented language must pay close attention to the machine functions that take place during program execution. Machine-oriented languages are very similar to actual machine language.

In contrast to the machine orientation of assembly languages, high-level languages are either procedure- or problem-oriented. When a procedure-oriented language is used, the programming emphasis is placed on describing the computational and logical procedures required to solve a problem. Commonly used procedure-oriented languages are COBOL, FORTRAN, and PL/1. A problem-oriented language is one in which the problem and solution are described without the necessary computational procedures being detailed; the most popular problem-oriented language is RPG.

Because high-level batch-oriented programming languages are not machine-oriented, their use reduces the amount of coding required to solve a problem and thus simplifies the programmer's task. However, programs written in these languages are likely to require more storage space and execution time than comparable programs written in assembly languages.

Interactive Programming Language

Interactive programming languages allow the programmer or program user to communicate directly with the computer in a conversational fashion. Programs and data can be submitted directly to the computer from remote terminals. The programs are translated (compiled) and executed, and the results are returned to the remote terminal in a matter of seconds. (In contrast, programs submitted in a batch environment may spend several hours in a queue before they are executed and the results returned to the user.)

Programs written for interactive computing are usually simple, and they usually process small amounts of data. Typical interactive programs are one-time requests for information and inquiries into data files. Most systems designed to handle interactive computing permit several programmers to use the system at the same time. The systems' fast response time allows programs to be written and debugged quickly. The three major interactive programming languages discussed in this chapter are BASIC, Pascal, and APL. Some batch-oriented languages, such as PL/1, are also available in special versions developed specifically for online, interactive processing. However, this chapter's discussions of these languages revolve around their use in batch programs.

MACHINE-ORIENTED LANGUAGES

Machine Language

The earliest computers were programmed by the arranging of various wires within the components. Up to six thousand switches could be set on the ENIAC to perform a program. However, when a new program was to be run, all of the switches had to be reset. Clearly, this was highly undesirable. The EDSAC, the first stored-program computer, allowed instructions to be entered into primary storage without the need for rewiring or setting switches, but some form of code was needed to enter these instructions. These codes came to be known as *machine language*.

Machine language is the language of the computer, the only language that the computer directly understands. It also functions as the object language of higher-level language programs, since all high-level languages must be translated into machine language in order for the computer to execute them.

Remember from Chapter 3 that data in digital computers is stored as either a 1 or a 0, an "on" or "off" electrical state. Therefore, machine language must take the form of 1s and 0s to be understood by the machine. But coding a program in this binary form is very tedious, so machine language is often coded in either octal or hexadecimal codes.

The programmer using machine language must specify *everything* to the computer. Every step the computer must take to execute a program must be coded. This means that the programmer must know exactly how the computer works. Actual numerical addresses of storage locations for instructions and data must be specified. Every switch and register (temporary storage areas for holding data and instructions) must be known.

In order to accomplish the necessary specificity, each machine language instruction must have two parts. The *op code,* short for operation code, tells the computer what function to perform. The *operand* tells the computer what data to use when performing that function. The operand takes the form of the specific storage addresses where the data is located. Figure 10–1 shows examples of machine-language instructions.

Advantages and Disadvantages The greatest advantage of machine language is that it is the most efficient in terms of storage area use and execution speed. It also allows the programmer to fully utilize the computer's potential for processing data.

On the other hand, programming in machine language is extremely tedious and time consuming. The instructions are difficult to remember and to use. Programs written in machine language will execute only on the specific machine for which they were written; so they must be rewritten if a new computer is purchased. Machine language is therefore totally unstandardized, unlike some high-level languages.

48	00	23C0	
4C	00	23C2	
40	00	2310	
D2	01	2310	2310
48	00	2310	
4E	00	2028	
F3	17	3002	2028
96	F0	3003	

FIGURE 10–1
Machine-language Instructions Expressed in the Hexadecimal Number System

Assembly Language

Assembly languages were developed to alleviate many of the disadvantages of machine-language programming. When programming in an assembly language, the programmer uses symbolic names, or *mnemonics*, to specify machine operations; thus, coding in 0s and 1s is no longer required. Mnemonics are English-like abbreviations for the machine-language op codes. For example, Table 10–1 shows some common arithmetic operations coded in an assembly language and in binary.

TABLE 10–1
Examples of Assembly-Language Mnemonic Codes

OPERATION	TYPICAL ASSEMBLY-LANGUAGE MNEMONIC CODE	TYPICAL BINARY OP CODE
Add memory to register	A	01011010
Add register to register	AR	00011010
Compare memory locations	CLC	11010101
Divide register by memory	D	01011101
Load from memory into register	L	01011000
Multiply register by memory	M	01011100
Store register in memory	ST	01010000
Subtract memory from register	S	01011011

Many of the operations listed in Table 10–1 involve the use of registers. Further, the mnemonic codes for assembly-language instructions differ depending on the type and model of computer. Thus, assembly-language programs, like machine-language programs, can be written only by persons who know the computers that will execute them.

There are three basic parts in an assembly-language instruction: an op code and an operand, as in machine language, and a *label* (see Table 10–2). The label is a programmer-supplied name that represents the first storage location to be used for an instruction. When the programmer wishes to refer to the instruction, he or she can simply specify the label, without regard to its storage location.

The op code, as in machine language, tells the operation to be performed; but it is in mnemonic form (refer again to Table 10–1). The operand, also in mnemonic form, represents the address of the item to be operated on. Each instruction may contain one or two operands. The remainder of the coding-form line can be used for remarks that explain the operation being performed (the remarks are optional). The payroll program developed in Chapter 8 (see Figure 8–10) is coded in assembly language as shown in Figure 10–2.

Advantages and Disadvantages There are several advantages to using assembly language: First, it can be used to develop programs highly efficient in terms of storage space use and processing time. The programmer has tight control of the machine. Second, the assembler program performs certain checking functions and generates error messages (as needed) that are useful in debugging. Third, assembly language encourages modular programming techniques, which break a program into a number of separate modules, or programming units. The advantage of this technique is that it makes the logic of the total program more manageable; instead of one extensive program, it becomes a group of small, easily handled segments.

The main disadvantage of assembly language is that it is cumbersome to use. Generally, one assembly-language instruction is translated into one machine-language instruction; this one-for-one relationship leads to long program preparation times.

Another disadvantage of assembly language is the high level of skill required to use it effectively. As with machine language, the programmer must know the computer to be used and must be able to work with binary or hexadecimal numbers and with codes such as EBCDIC. The task of writ-

LABEL	OP CODE	OPERANDS A and B	REMARKS
READRT	GET	INCARD,INWORK	READ INTO INWORK
	MVC	LIMOUT,LIM	SET UP PRINT LINE
	PACK	LIMP(3),LIM	PACK LIMIT
LOOP	AP	ANSP,CTR	ADD CTR TO ANSP

TABLE 10–2
The Parts of an Assembly-Language Instruction

FIGURE 10–2
Payroll Problem in
Assembly Language
(Continued on
Facing Page)

```
SOURCE  STATEMENT
        START
PAYROLL BALR    12,0 ⎱  Set Up Registers
        USING   *,12 ⎰
        XPRNT   HEADING,45 }  Print Headings
READCRD XREAD   CARD80
        CLC     EOF,''C'99'  ⎱  Read Data Card
        BE      DONE         ⎰
        PACK    WKHR!,HOURS   ⎱
        PACK    WKRATE,RATE   ⎢  Convert Data to
        ZAP     GROSS,ZERO    ⎢  Decimal
        ZAP     OVRTME,ZERO   ⎢  Form and Initialize
        ZAP     REG,ZERO      ⎰  Variables
        CP      WKHRS,FORTY   ⎤
        BH      OVERTIME      ⎢
        AP      GROSS,WKRATE  ⎬  Compute Regular Pay
        MP      GROSS,WKHRS   ⎢
        B       TAXRATE       ⎦
OVERTIME AP     OVRTME, FORTY         ⎤
        MP      OVRTME,WKRATE         ⎢
        AP      GROSS,WKRATE          ⎢
        SP      WKHRS,FORTY           ⎢  Compute
        MP      WKHRS,ONEHLF          ⎬  Overtime
        MP      GROSS,WKHRS           ⎢  Pay
        MVN     GROSS+5(1),GROSS+6    ⎢
        ZAP     GROSS(7),GROSS(6)     ⎢
        AP      GROSS,OVRTME          ⎦
TAXRATE CP      GROSS,=P'25000' ⎱
        BH      UPPERRTE        ⎢  Determine
        ZAP     RATE,LOW        ⎬  Tax Rate
        B       TAXES           ⎦
UPPERRTE ZAP    RATE,HIGH
TAXES   ZAP     TOTAXES,GROSS          ⎤
        MP      TOTAXES,RATE           ⎢
        AP      TOTAXES,=P'50'         ⎬  Compute
        MVN     TOTAXES+5(1),TOTAXES+6 ⎢  Taxes
        ZAP     TOTAXES(7),TOTAXES(6)  ⎦
        SP      GROSS,TOTAXES  ⎱  Calculate Net Pay
        MVC     PRPAY,MASK     ⎬  and Edit Print Line
        ED      PRPAY,GROSS    ⎰
        MVC     PRNAME,NAME  ⎱  Print Output Line
        XPRNT   LINE,32      ⎰
   SOURCE  STATEMENT
        B       READCRD
DONE    XPRNT   HEADING,1
        BR      14
*
*
*
```

```
        CARD      DS      OCL80  ⎫
        NAME      DS      CL16   ⎪
        HOURS     DS      CL2    ⎪  Input Card File
                  DS      CL2    ⎬  Definitions
        RATE      DS      CL4    ⎪
                  DS      CL54   ⎪
        EOF       DS      CL2    ⎭
        HEADING   DS      OCL45  ⎫
                  DC      CL1'1'        ⎪
                  DC      CL13,EMPLOYEE NAME'  ⎪
                  DC      CL10'         ⎬  Output Print
                  DC      CL7'NET PAY'  ⎪  File Definitions
                  DC      CL14' '       ⎪
        LINE      DS      OCL30         ⎪
                  DC      CL1'  '       ⎪
        PRNAME    DS      CL16          ⎪
        PRPAY     DS      CL15   ⎭
        GROSS     DS      PL7    ⎫
        WKRATE    DS      PL3    ⎪
        OVRTME    DS      PL7    ⎪
        REG       DS      PL7    ⎪
        WKHRS     DS      PL4    ⎪
        FORTY     DC      PL2'40'   ⎬  Variable Definitions
        ONEHLF    DC      PL2'150'  ⎪
        LOW       DC      PL2'14'   ⎪
        HIGH      DC      PL2'20'   ⎪
        ZERO      DC      PL4'0000' ⎪
        TOTAXES   DS      PL7    ⎭
        MASK      DC      X'4020202020202020202020214B2121' ⎫  Edit Field
                  END     PAYROLL
                          =C'99'
                          =P'50'
                          =P'25000'
```

Output:

EMPLOYEE NAME	NET PAY
LYNN MANGINO	224.00
THOMAS RITTER	212.42
MARIE OLSON	209.00
LORI DUNLEVY	172.00
WILLIAM WILSON	308.00

ing the solution to a problem in assembly language is often the most difficult phase in the solution process.

Finally, assembly language is machine-dependent; a program written for one computer generally cannot be executed on another. Thus, equipment changes may require substantial reprogramming.

Assembly language is often used for operating systems. Because operating systems are designed for particular computers, they are machine-dependent. The potential efficiency of assembly language makes it well suited for operating-system programming.

PROCEDURE-ORIENTED LANGUAGES

COBOL

COBOL (Common Business-Oriented Language) is the most frequently used business programming language. Before 1960, no language well suited to solving business problems existed. Recognizing this inadequacy, the Department of Defense called together representatives of computer users, manufacturers, and government installations to examine the feasibility of establishing a common business programming language. That was the beginning of the *CODASYL* (Conference of Data Systems Languages) Committee. By 1960, the committee had established the specifications for COBOL, and the first commercial versions of the language were offered later that year. The government furthered its cause in the mid-1960s by refusing to buy or lease any computer that could not process a program written in COBOL.

"By Jove . . . this is written in COBOL!"

Datamation
April, 1981.
Reprinted by permission

One of the objectives of the CODASYL group was to establish a language that was machine-independent—that could be used on any computer. Thus, when several manufacturers began offering their own modifications and extensions of COBOL, a need for standardization became apparent. Consequently, in 1968 the American National Standards Institute (ANSI) established and published guidelines for a standardized COBOL that became known as ANSI COBOL. In 1974, ANSI published a revised version of the standard in which the language definition was expanded. The CODASYL Committee continues to examine the feasibility of modifying or incorporating new features into COBOL.

Another key objective of the designers of COBOL was to make the language look like English. Their intent was that programs written in COBOL should be understandable even to casual readers, and hence self-documenting. You can judge how successful they were by looking at Figure 10–3, which shows the payroll application coded in COBOL.

COBOL programs have a formal, uniform structure. Many types of statements must appear in the same form and position in every COBOL program. The basic unit of a COBOL program is the sentence. Sentences are combined to form paragraphs; paragraphs are joined into sections; and sections are contained within divisions. COBOL programs must have four divisions: IDENTIFICATION, ENVIRONMENT, DATA, and PROCEDURE. The divisions appear in the program in this order and are identified by headings, as in Figure 10–3.

The IDENTIFICATION DIVISION provides documentation of the program. At a minimum, a unique name is assigned to the program. The program's author, the date it was written, the compilation date, and relevant security requirements may also be provided.

In theory, the ENVIRONMENT DIVISION is the only machine-dependent division of a COBOL program. Its purpose is to specify the computer to be used when the program is compiled and executed. File information is related to input/output devices. Therefore, if the program is run on different computer systems, adjustments to the ENVIRONMENT DIVISION may be required.

The DATA DIVISION describes the variable names, records, and files to be used by the program. Variables—words chosen and defined by the programmer to represent data items referred to in the program—are mnemonics for the storage locations of data. Each data name may be up to thirty characters long; since letters, numbers, and embedded hyphens can be used, this allows for very descriptive data names. In COBOL, the programmer need only know the variable name; the COBOL language keeps track of actual data locations in storage. Figure 10–3 shows some examples of data names. The input and output formats of data are also specified in the DATA DIVISION. These formats tell the program how data is to be brought in and how it is to be written to an output or storage device.

The PROCEDURE DIVISION contains the actual processing instructions. In keeping with its English-like nature, COBOL uses verbs in its statements to perform various functions—for example, DISPLAY, READ, MULTIPLY, ADD, SUBTRACT, MOVE, and WRITE. Since these verbs have special

```
IDENTIFICATION DIVISION.
PROGRAM-ID. PAYROLL.
ENVIRONMENT DIVISION.
INPUT-OUTPUT SECTION.
FILE-CONTROL.
    SELECT CARD-FILE ASSIGN TO UR-2540R-S-SYSIN.
    SELECT PRINT-FILE ASSIGN TO UR-S-SYSPRINT.
DATA DIVISION.
FILE SECTION.
FD  CARD-FILE LABEL RECORDS ARE OMITTED.
01  PAY-CARD.
    02 EMPLOYEE-NAME PICTURE A(16).
    02 HOURS-WORKED PICTURE 99.
    02 WAGE-PER-HOUR PICTURE 99V99.
FD  PRINT-FILE LABEL RECORDS ARE OMITTED.
01  PRINT-LINE.
    02 NAME          PICTURE A(16).
    02 FILLER        PICTURE X(5).
    02 AMOUNT        PICTURE $$$$.99.
WORKING-STORAGE SECTION.
77  GROSS-PAY        PICTURE 999V99.
77  REGULAR-PAY      PICTURE 999V99.
77  OVERTIME-PAY     PICTURE 999V99.
77  NET-PAY          PICTURE 999V99.
77  TAX              PICTURE 999V99.
77  OVERTIME-HOURS   PICTURE 99.
77  OVERTIME-RATE    PICTURE 999V999.
77  BLANK-LINE       PICTURE X(132) VALUE SPACES.
PROCEDURE DIVISION.
    DISPLAY 'EMPLOYEE NAME                ', 'NET PAY'.
    DISPLAY BLANK-LINE.
    OPEN INPUT CARD-FILE, OUTPUT PRINT-FILE.
```

meanings in COBOL, they are called reserved words. In all, more than 250 words are contained in COBOL's reserved word list.

Advantages and Disadvantages   COBOL offers many advantages as a business programming language. Because of its English-like nature, programs that use it require little additional documentation; well-written COBOL programs tend to be self-explanatory. COBOL is much easier to learn than either machine language or assembly language, since learning it does not involve learning detailed machine functions. Testing and debugging are simplified, because the logic of the program is easy to follow.

COBOL also has strong file-handling capabilities, unlike FORTRAN and other languages used primarily in scientific applications. It supports sequential, indexed, and relative files (to be discussed in Chapter 14). Although

```
WORK-LOOP.
    READ CARD-FILE AT END GO TO FINISH.
    IF HOURS-WORKED IS GREATER THAN 40 THEN GO TO
        OVERTIME-ROUTINE.
    MULTIPLY HOURS-WORKED BY WAGE-PER-HOUR GIVING GROSS-PAY.
    GO TO TAX-COMPUTATION.
OVERTIME-ROUTINE.
    MULTIPLY WAGE-PER-HOUR BY 40 GIVING REGULAR-PAY.
    SUBTRACT 40 FROM HOURS-WORKED GIVING OVERTIME-HOURS.
    MULTIPLY WAGE-PER-HOUR BY 1.5 GIVING OVERTIME-RATE.
    MULTIPLY OVERTIME-HOURS BY OVERTIME-RATE GIVING
        OVERTIME-PAY.
    ADD REGULAR-PAY, OVERTIME-PAY GIVING GROSS-PAY.
TAX-COMPUTATION.
    IF GROSS-PAY IS GREATER THAN 250 THEN MULTIPLY GROSS-PAY
        BY 0.20 GIVING TAX ELSE MULTIPLY GROSS-PAY BY 0.14
        GIVING TAX.
    SUBTRACT TAX FROM GROSS-PAY GIVING NET-PAY.
    MOVE EMPLOYEE-NAME TO NAME.
    MOVE NET-PAY TO AMOUNT.
    WRITE PRINT-LINE.
    GO TO WORK-LOOP.
FINISH.
    CLOSE CARD-FILE, PRINT-FILE.
    STOP RUN.
```

Output:

```
    EMPLOYEE NAME        NET PAY

    LYNN MANGINO         $224.00
    THOMAS RITTER        $212.42
    MARIE OLSON          $209.00
    LORI DUNLEVY         $172.00
    WILLIAM WILSON       $308.00
```

many COBOL application programs are written for batch processing, COBOL is being used increasingly in an interactive mode.

One final advantage of COBOL is its standardization, which allows a firm to switch computer equipment with little or no rewriting of existing programs. Because COBOL is widely supported, many programmers know it through previous experience or college training. Thus, organizations are able to acquire experienced programmers to maintain and enhance their applications.

The effort to make COBOL as English-like as possible has resulted in some disadvantages. A large and sophisticated compiler program is needed to translate a COBOL source program into machine language. Such a compiler occupies a large portion of primary storage. As a result, COBOL cannot be used on some small computers. (But there are some COBOL compilers

FIGURE 10–3
continued

supporting subsets of the language that can be used with minicomputers. This problem will become less serious as minicomputers become more powerful.)

Another disadvantage is COBOL's tendency to be wordy. Using COBOL may require that many more statements be made to solve a problem than would be needed with a more compact language such as FORTRAN. Certain features of COBOL make it less than ideal for structured programming (discussed in Chapter 11). Finally, COBOL's computational abilities are limited; for this reason, it is seldom used for scientific and mathematical applications.

Regardless of COBOL's disadvantages, it is likely to remain a popular language for many years. Polls indicate that over 80 percent of business application programs are written in COBOL. Converting these hundreds of thousands of COBOL programs to other languages, as well as retraining thousands of programmers, would not be an easy task for the business community.

FORTRAN

FORTRAN (Formula Translator) is the oldest high-level programming language. Its origins can be found in the mid-1950s, when most programs were written in either assembly language or machine language. Efforts were made to develop a programming language that resembled English but could be translated into machine language by the computer. This effort, backed by IBM, produced FORTRAN—the first commercially available high-level language.

Early FORTRAN compilers contained many errors and were not always efficient. Moreover, several manufacturers offered variations of FORTRAN that could be used only on their computers. Although many improvements were made, early FORTRAN continued to suffer from this lack of standardization. In response to this problem, ANSI laid the groundwork for a standardized FORTRAN. In 1966, two standard versions of FORTRAN were recognized—ANSI FORTRAN and Basic FORTRAN. They were very similar to two earlier versions, FORTRAN IV and FORTRAN II. A group from the University of Waterloo in Ontario developed a subset of FORTRAN—WATFOR (Waterloo FORTRAN)—specifically for the beginning or student programmer. Improvements were added to WATFOR, and the enhanced version was called WATFIV. In spite of the attempts to standardize FORTRAN, however, most computer manufacturers have continued to offer their own extensions of the language. Therefore, compatibility of FORTRAN remains a problem today.

In 1957, when FORTRAN was first released, the computer was primarily used by engineers, scientists, and mathematicians. Consequently, FORTRAN was developed to meet their needs; and its purpose has remained unchanged. FORTRAN is a procedure-oriented language with extraordinary mathematical capabilities. It is especially applicable where numerous complex arithmetic calculations are necessary. However, it is not well suited for programs involving file maintenance, editing of data, or production of documents. Figure 10–4 shows the sample payroll program in FORTRAN.

General Organization of FORTRAN Program The basic unit of a FORTRAN program is a statement (which corresponds to a sentence in COBOL). There is only one statement that must appear in every program: END. In contrast to a COBOL program, with its four divisions, a FORTRAN program is one unit that incorporates all storage declarations, computations, and input/output definitions. Also unlike COBOL, FORTRAN does not require that most variables be declared before use. Record descriptions are contained in FORMAT statements within the program.

Four types of statements are used in FORTRAN programs: control statements, arithmetic statements, input/output statements, and specification

FIGURE 10–4

Payroll Program in FORTRAN

```
FORTRAN IV G LEVEL 21       MAIN                 DATE = 81214

      WRITE (6,1)
1     FORMAT('1','EMPLOYEE NAME',5X,'NET PAY'/'')
2     READ (5,3) NA,NB,NC,ND,NHOURS, WAGE, IEND
3     FORMAT (4A4, I2, 2X, F4.2, 54X, I2)
      IF (IEND. EQ.99) STOP
      IF (NHOURS.GT.40) GO TO 10
      GROSS = FLOAT(NHOURS)*WAGE
      GO TO 15
10    REG = 40.*WAGE
      OVERTM=FLOAT(NHOURS-40)*(1.5*WAGE)
      GROSS=REG+OVERTM
15    IF (GROSS.GT.250.) GO TO 20
      RATE = .14
      GO TO 25
20    RATE = .20
25    TAX=RATE*GROSS
      PAY = GROSS - TAX
      WRITE (6,50) NA,NB,NC,ND,PAY
50     FORMAT (' ', 4A4, 3X, F6.2)
      GO TO 2
      END
```

Output:

```
EMPLOYEE NAME      NET PAY

LYNN MANGINO       224.00
THOMAS RITTER      212.42
MARIE OLSON        209.00
LORI DUNLEVY       172.00
WILLIAM WILSON     308.00
```

statements. Control statements determine the sequence in which operations will be performed and govern operations such as choosing between alternatives and branching to another part of the program. Arithmetic statements direct the computer to perform computations. Input/output statements instruct the computer to read data from, or write data to, an I/O device. Specification statements tell FORTRAN *how* to interpret data read from an input device and how to write data to an output device.

Numbers are represented by two kinds of variables: real number variables and integer variables. Variable names beginning with the letters I through N are reserved for integers. A variable name is usually limited to a length of six characters. (Remember that COBOL variable names may be up to thirty characters long.)

In FORTRAN, a string of *alphanumeric* characters (numeric, alphabetic, or special) must be divided into groups of four characters each. Thus, to store alphanumeric data consisting of more than four characters, more than one variable is needed. For example, assume a data card contains an employee's name in the first sixteen columns. The programmer can use four *single*, or *simple, variables,* each of which stands for a single data item. (Refer to line 03 of Figure 10–4.)

Notice that only two characters are stored in the locations set aside for the variable name ND. The remaining space is filled with blanks.

FORTRAN also allows *array variables,* which can be used to represent groups of similar data items. The elements of the array are referred to by *subscripts.* The same employee name shown above could be represented by an array named N with four elements.

WILLIAM WILSON＿ ＿
N(1) N(2) N(3) N(4)

Advantages and Disadvantages FORTRAN was designed for use by engineers, scientists, and mathematicians and is used with great success in scientific applications. Use of FORTRAN for certain types of business applications is increasing; for example, FORTRAN is often used for quantitative analysis involving techniques such as linear programming and regression analysis.

In general, however, FORTRAN is not a good business language, primarily because it was designed for scientific purposes. It has limited ability to process alphabetic data and files and to format printed reports, which are all necessities for a good business language. Also, as Figure 10–4 shows, FORTRAN does not closely resemble English and so requires good documentation.

PL/1

PL/1 (Programming Language 1) was designed to be an all-purpose, proce-dure-oriented language for both scientific and business applications. With the increased use of management-science techniques such as linear programming and regression analysis, the business programmer needed a language with greater computational capabilities than COBOL. By the same token, a language with greater file-manipulation ability than FORTRAN was desired by the scientific programmer. PL/1 combined the best features of both COBOL and FORTRAN; it is a flexible high-level language. PL/1 was introduced during the early 1960s for use with IBM System/360 computers and is still primarily an IBM-sponsored language, although its use is spreading to other computers.

All the languages discussed so far—machine language, assembly language, FORTRAN, and COBOL—impose some rather strict coding rules on the programmer. Column restrictions are prevalent. In contrast, PL/1 is a free-form language with very few such restrictions.

The basic element in a PL/1 program is the statement, which must be terminated by a semicolon. Statements are not confined to individual lines or paragraphs and need not begin in certain columns, as long as they are between columns 2 and 72 (see Figure 10–5).

In addition to its free-form characteristic, PL/1 has many other desirable features. PL/1 programs can be constructed in a modular fashion; separate logical procedures, called blocks, can be combined to form a complete program. This simplifies writing of the program and facilitates the use of structured programming techniques (to be discussed in Chapter 11).

The PL/1 compiler has certain *default* features. A default is a course of action chosen by the compiler when several alternatives exist but none has been explicitly stated by the programmer. The default has been determined by the designers to be the alternative most often required. For example, if the programmer does not specify the types of data to be represented by particular variable names, the compiler assumes that data items beginning with the letters I through N represent integer values. Thus, the number of statements needed in a program is reduced.

The PL/1 compiler also contains several *built-in functions,* SQRT (for taking square roots) and LOG (for finding logarithms). The availability of these built-in functions greatly simplifies the programmer's task; he or she need only refer to a required function by name to cause the corresponding pre-tested, correct routine to be executed and the results returned to the program. Many of these functions are also offered in FORTRAN but have no equivalents in COBOL.

PL/1 was designed to be used by both novice and expert programmers. The beginning programmer can learn to write programs using basic features of the language. As knowledge of the language increases, the programmer can use more powerful features to write programs to solve complex problems.

Various subsets of PL/1 containing only portions of the full language have been developed. These subsets are especially geared toward educational use

FIGURE 10–5

Payroll Program in PL/1

```
PAYROLL: PROCEDURE OPTIONS (MAIN);

PAYROLL: PROCEDURE OPTIONS (MAIN);
DECLARE NAME      CHARACTER (16);
DECLARE HOURS     FIXED DECIMAL (2);
DECLARE WAGE      FIXED DECIMAL (3,2);
DECLARE GROSS_PAY FIXED DECIMAL(5,2);
DECLARE TAXRATE   FIXED DECIMAL (2,2);
DECLARE TAX       FIXED DECIMAL (4,2);
DECLARE NET_PAY   FIXED DECIMAL (5,2);
PUT PAGE LIST ('EMPLOYEE NAME', 'NET PAY');
PUT SKIP;
START: GET LIST (NAME, HOURS, WAGE);
ON ENDFILE GO TO FINISH;
IF HOURS>40 THEN
   GROSS_PAY→40*WAGE + 1.5*WAGE*(HOURS-40);
  ELSE GROSS_PAY=HOURS*WAGE;
IF GROSS_PAY>250 THEN TAXRATE=.20;
   ELSE TAXRATE=.14;
TAX=TAXRATE*GROSS_PAY;
NET_PAY=GROSS_PAY - TAX;
PUT SKIP (1) LIST (NAME, NET_PAY);
GO TO START;
FINISH: END PAYROLL

PAYROLL       14:50    AUGUST 3RD, 1981
```

Output:

```
EMPLOYEE NAME     NET PAY

LYNN MANGINO      224.00
THOMAS RITTER     212.42
MARIE OLSON       209.00
LORI DUNLEVY      172.00
WILLIAM WILSON    308.00
```

(just as WATFIV is geared to educational use for FORTRAN). The PL/1 program in Figure 10–5 is actually written in PL/C, a subset of PL/1 developed at Cornell University.

Advantages and Disadvantages   The greatest strength of PL/1 is its power—it is a language with many attractive features. PL/1's powerful features make it good for system programming. It is less wordy than COBOL and is well suited for short programming projects. Its default and modularity features make it easier to learn. Facilities that allow use of structured programming techniques are another distinct advantage of PL/1.

PL/1 is not free of disadvantages, however. Because it is such a broad, powerful language, a large amount of storage is required for its compiler.

This prohibits its use on small computers. As data processing becomes increasingly distributed, this restriction may make using PL/1 impossible for some businesses. Further, the breadth of PL/1 makes learning all the features of the language difficult.

PL/1 was developed after COBOL and FORTRAN, and programmers experienced in those languages often resist having to learn a new one. Also, the need for a computer large enough to support the compiler has restricted the teaching of PL/1 in colleges and universities. Finally, PL/1 is used primarily with IBM computers; there has been no government support to increase its use as there was with COBOL.

PROBLEM-ORIENTED LANGUAGES

RPG

RPG (Report Program Generator) is a problem-oriented language originally designed to produce business reports. Basically, the programmer using RPG describes the type of report desired without having to specify much of the logic involved. A generator program is then used to build (generate) a program to produce the report. Therefore, little programming skill is required to use RPG.

Since RPG was initially intended to support the logic of punched-card equipment, it is used primarily with small computer systems. Many firms that formerly used electromechanical punched-card processing equipment have upgraded their data-processing operations to small computer systems. These firms usually have relatively simple, straightforward data-processing needs. In such cases, a small computer system supporting RPG can provide significantly improved data-processing operations. Management reports can be produced in a fraction of the time required by electromechanical methods.

RPG is now used for processing files as well as for preparing printed output. The programmer does not code the statements required; instead, he or she completes specification forms such as those shown in Figure 10–6. All files, records, and fields to be manipulated must be defined by entries in specific columns on the specification forms. The operations to be performed and the content and format of output files are described similarly. The entries on the RPG forms are keypunched, combined with job-control cards, and submitted to the computer. The RPG generator program builds an object program from the source program, and the object program is executed by the computer (see Figure 10–7).

Like other programming languages, RPG is constantly being improved. IBM introduced a new version named RPGII in the early 1970s for use on its IBM System/3 computers. This new version has been widely accepted and is now supported by many computer manufacturers; in fact, it has essentially replaced the original RPG. A third version introduced in 1979, RPGIII, features the ability to process data stored on a data base.

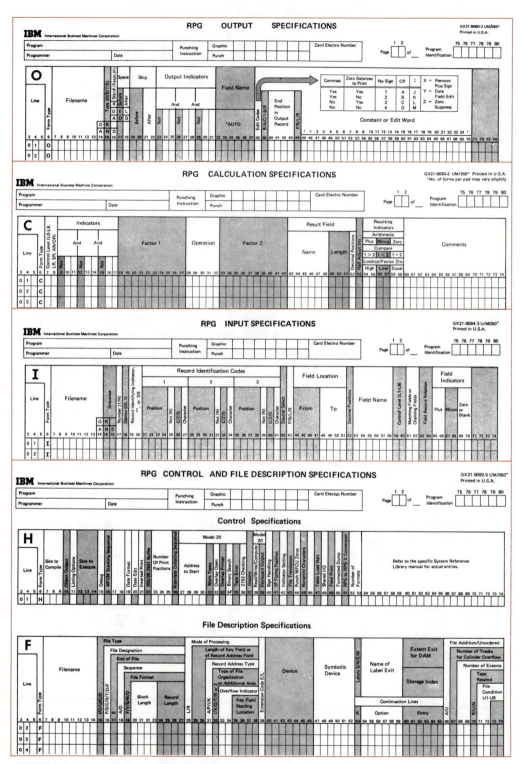

FIGURE 10-6 RPG Program Specification Forms

```
00010H       0003          132
00020F*                        PAYROLL EXAMPLE
00030FCDIN    IP  F  80   80           READ01
00040FPRINTR  O   F 132  132      OF   PRINTER
00050I* DEFINES INPUT
00060ICDIN    ZZ  01   80 CD
00070I                                   1      6 DATE
00080I        ZZ  02
00090I                                   1     10DEPT  L1
00100I                                   2      5 EMPNO
00110I                                   6     92HRS
00120I                                  10    133RATE
00130I                                  14    140EXEMP
00510C*TO FIND GROSS PAY, NET PAY
00511C    40              SETOF                    30
00512C    N40 02          SETON                    3040
00520C    02    HRS   COMP  40.00               100909
00530C    02 09 RATE  MULT  HRS     GROSS   52H
00540C    02 10 HRS   SUB   40.00   OTHRS    42
00550C    02 10 RATE  MULT  40.00   REG      52
00560C    02 10 RATE  MULT  1.5     OTRT     43
00570C    02 10 OTHRS MULT  OTRT    OVER     52
00580C    02 10 REG   ADD   OVER    GROSS    52
00590C    02    EXEMP MULT  14.40   EXAMT    52H        EXEMPT AMT
00600C    02    GROSS SUB   EXAMT   BASE     52
00610C    02    BASE  MULT  .12     INCTX    52H        INCOME TAX DED
00620C    02    GROSS SUB   INCTX   NET      52
00630C    02    GROSS ADD   DGROSS  DGROSS   62
00640C    02    HRS   ADD   DHRS    DHRS     52
00650C    02    GROSS ADD   GGROSS  GGROSS   72
00660C    02    HRS.  ADD   GHRS    GHRS     62
001400* DEFINES HEADINGS AND OUTPUT
001500PRINTR   H 0201   01
001600       OR      OF
001700                              10'DATE'
001800                   DATE       19' / / '
002100                              67'PAYROLL'
002200                             120'PAGE'
002300                   PAGE      125'  0'
002400       H 02    L1
002500       OR      OF
002600                              10'DEPT'
002700                              24'EMP NO'
002800                              37'HOURS'
002900                              49'RATE'
003000                              63'GROSS'
003100                              81'EXEMPTIONS'
003200                             100'INCOME TAX'
003300                             115'NET PAY'
003400       D 02    02
003500               L1  DEPT       8
003510               30  DEPT       8
003600                   EMPNO      23
003700                   HRS        37'  . '
003800                   RATE       49'  . '
003900                   GROSS      63'  0.  '
004000                   EXEMP      76
004100                   INCTX      97'  0.  '
004200                   NET       114'  0.  '
004300       T 33    L1
004400                              27'DEPARTMENT
004500                   DGROSS B   63' ,  #0.  '
004600                   DHRS   B   37'  0.  '
004700       T 30    LR
004800                              29'GRAND TOTALS
004900                   GGROSS B   63' ,  #0.  '
005000                   GHRS   B   39'  0.  '
```

FIGURE 10–7

Payroll Program in RPG

FIGURE 10–7
continued

```
//GO.PRINTR DD SYSOUT=A
//GO.CDIN   DD *
052775
10029400031753
10087410029002
10141420044401
10160400026754
10387445049954
10401510037502
10403400029003
20037400024502
20098400029701
20201400044501
20221440041503
20485478541705
/*EOF
```

Output

```
                                              PAYROLL

DEPT    EMP NO    HOURS    RATE      GROSS    EXEMPTIONS   INCOME TAX   NET PAY

  1      0029     40.00    3.175     127.00       3          10.06      116.94
         0087     41.00    2.900     120.35       2          10.99      109.36
         0141     42.00    4.440     190.92       1          21.18      169.74
         0160     40.00    2.675     107.00       4           5.93      101.07
         0387     44.50    4.995     233.51       4          21.11      212.40
         0401     51.00    3.750     211.87       2          21.97      189.90
         0403     40.00    2.900     116.00       3           8.74      107.26

DEPARTMENT
TOTALS           298.50            $1,106.65

DEPT    EMP NO    HOURS    RATE      GROSS    EXEMPTIONS   INCOME TAX   NET PAY

  2      0037     40.00    2.450      98.00       2           8.30       89.70
         0098     40.00    2.970     118.80       1          12.53      106.27
         0201     40.00    4.450     178.00       1          19.63      158.37
         0221     44.00    4.150     190.90       3          17.72      173.18
         0485     47.85    4.170     215.90       5          17.27      198.63

DEPARTMENT
TOTALS           211.85             $801.60

   GRAND TOTALS  510.35           $1,908.25
```

Advantages and Disadvantages RPG is easy to learn and to use, since the basic pattern of execution is fixed. Since it does not require large amounts of main storage, it is one of the primary languages of small computers and minicomputers. RPG provides an efficient means for generating reports requiring simple logic and calculations; it is commonly used to process files for accounts receivable, accounts payable, general ledgers, and inventory.

However, the computational capabilities of RPG are limited. Some RPG compilers can generate machine-language instructions for up to thirty different operations. However, compared with COBOL, FORTRAN, and PL/1, its looping, branching, and decision capabilities are restricted. RPG is not a standardized language; therefore, RPG programs may require a significant degree of modification if they are to be executed on a computer other than the one for which they were initially written. This is especially true if a firm

BASIC Software Packages

Learning a new computer language can be fun and profitable at the same time. BASIC, for example, is relatively easy to learn and is becoming the predominant language available with personal computers. As the microcomputer market matures and hundreds of thousands of these machines come into use, the demand for software increases. Manufacturers of most microcomputers offer a very limited selection of software, and thus the need grows for alternative suppliers. This need is being met largely by individual owners of microcomputers who write programs for their own machines and offer them for sale to others.

People who would dive into the BASIC programming market must first consider several factors. Many different versions of BASIC are available on microcomputers. This suggests two possible product strategies. One is to write programs for the most popular versions of BASIC and charge low prices to beat the competition. The other is to write for the less popular versions, allowing greater unit selling prices to be charged but fewer units to be sold.

Packaged programs can be marketed in several ways. One method is to advertise in magazines such as *BYTE* and *Creative Computing*. Another is to sell software to one of the computer utilities forming around the country; these companies allow subscribers with microcomputers to use a "library" of programs for a specified fee. A third method is to write a collection of programs and offer the entire selection for sale in book form. One final method, which might be the best, involves the microcomputer manufacturers. Many manufacturers are developing user groups that publish monthly or bimonthly newsletters containing listings of programs, suppliers, and prices. Manufacturers provide this service because it increases the usefulness of their products to users and stimulates new sales.

Working as a contract programmer is another way to make money by programming in BASIC. Businesses are currently the largest purchasers of microcomputers. Many of these businesses have immediate data-processing needs that no packaged programs can meet and so must contract with programmers to write specialized programs. Some businesses are willing to pay hundreds or even thousands of dollars for such programs.

changes computer manufacturers; however, if a firm stays with a particular manufacturer's equipment, its RPG programs can generally be run on a similar but more powerful computer with only slight modifications.

INTERACTIVE PROGRAMMING LANGUAGES

BASIC

BASIC (Beginners' All-Purpose Symbolic Instruction Code) was developed at Dartmouth College for use with time-sharing systems. Because BASIC is easy to learn, it can be used by people with little or no programming experience—novice programmers can write fairly complex programs in BASIC in only a matter of hours.

The growth in the use of time-sharing systems has been accompanied by an increase in the use of BASIC. Most computer manufacturers offer BASIC support on their computers. Although BASIC was originally intended to be used by colleges and universities for instructional purposes, many companies have adopted it for their data-processing needs. In addition, the increasing popularity of microcomputers in homes is furthering the use of BASIC, since it is the language most often supported by these microcomputers.

A BASIC program consists of a series of sequentially numbered statements. Each statement occupies a separate line. Following the line number is a keyword, such as PRINT or READ, which identifies the type of statement. Figure 10–8 shows the payroll program coded in BASIC.

Writing a BASIC program involves typing three types of entries from the terminal:

● Programming-language statements are used to write the BASIC program. BASIC statements such as IF, GO TO, PRINT, and INPUT correspond to similar statements used in other high-level languages.

● System commands are used to communicate with the operating system. For example, the terminal user must type a system command such as RUN to direct the computer to begin program execution. To terminate program execution, the user types the system command STOP.

● Editing commands are used for inserting changes in, or deleting parts of, the source program. For instance, the programmer can delete an incorrectly keyed letter or number simply by pressing the backward arrow (←) key and then typing the correct character.

Advantages and Disadvantages   Among BASIC's most attractive features are its simplicity and flexibility. It is very easy to learn. It can be used for both scientific and business applications. And although BASIC was intended for use as an interactive programming language, it is finding increased use as a batch language.

The simplicity of BASIC has led many manufacturers to offer different versions of the language. A BASIC standard was established in 1978, but it covers only a small subset of the BASIC language.

BASIC programs written for one system may need substantial modification before being used on another. Many extensions to BASIC have been developed, but only at the expense of increasing the difficulty of learning and using the language. As firms continue to expand online, real-time programming applications, however, the use of BASIC will no doubt continue to increase.

Pascal

Pascal is the only language mentioned in this chapter whose name is not an acronym. Pascal is named after the French philosopher and mathematician Blaise Pascal. (Remember from Chapter 2 that Pascal invented the first me-

FIGURE 10–8
Payroll Program in
BASIC

```
PAYROLL          14:50    AUGUST 3RD, 1981

10   REM THIS PROGRAM CALCULATES A WEEKLY
15   REM PAYROLL FOR FIVE EMPLOYEES
20   PRINT 'EMPLOYEE NAME', 'NET PAY'
30   PRINT
40   READ N$, H, W
50   IF H > 40 THEN 70
60   LET G = H*W
65   GO TO 100
70   LET R = 40*W
80   LET O = (H-40) * (1.5*W)
90   LET G = R+O
100  IF G > 250 THEN 130
110  LET T = .14
120  GO TO 140
130  LET T = .20
140  LET T2 = T*G
150  LET P = G-T2
160  PRINT N$, P
170  GO TO 40
180  DATA 'LYNN MANGINO', 35, 8.00
190  DATA 'THOMAS RITTER', 48, 4.75
200  DATA 'MARIE OLSON', 45, 5.50
210  DATA 'LORI DUNLEVY', 40, 5.00
220  DATA 'WILLIAM WILSON', 50, 7.00
230  END

RUN PAYROLL

Output

PAYROLL

EMPLOYEE NAME    NET PAY

LYNN MANGINO     224.00
THOMAS RITTER    212.42
MARIE OLSON      209.00
LORI DUNLEVY     172.00
WILLIAM WILSON   308.00

LINE  40:   END OF DATA
```

chanical adding machine.) Niklaus Wirth, a computer scientist from Switzerland, developed Pascal between 1968 and 1970. The first Pascal compiler became available in 1971.

Like BASIC, Pascal was first developed to teach programming concepts to students but is rapidly expanding beyond its initial purpose and finding increased acceptance in business and scientific applications. Pascal is well suited for both batch and interactive modes, although most Pascal business applications are batch-oriented.

Pascal is a relatively new language, developed and offered after the concept of structured programming began to receive support. Thus, it is designed to be compatible with structured programming concepts (which will be explained in Chapter 11). Each Pascal program has two basic parts: a heading (in which definitions and declarations are made) and a body (in which input, processing, and output are accomplished). Pascal also discourages the use of GO TO (branching) statements, (although it makes them available) by offering alternative logic patterns such as:

```
REPEAT-UNTIL, WHILE-DO, FOR-TO/DO,
IF-THEN-(ELSE), and CASE -OF.
```

Advantages and Disadvantages   Pascal receives avid support from its users because, while it is relatively easy to learn, like BASIC, it is powerful, like PL/1. As mentioned, it can be used in both batch and interactive modes. Unlike PL/1, Pascal is available on microcomputers and seems to be a good alternative to BASIC for use on personal computers. Pascal's suitability for structured programming and its graphics capabilities (described below) make it a very good language for educational purposes.

Unlike FORTRAN, Pascal allows variable names of any length, although only the first six characters have meaning to the computer. Thus Pascal is more English-like than FORTRAN. (Figure 10–9 shows the payroll program written in Pascal.)

Pascal does not have many default features. Thus, there are fewer compiler-generated errors to be debugged. The compiler provides fast translation of the source program. Also, Pascal is good for system programming.

Unlike COBOL and FORTRAN, Pascal has very good graphics capabilities. Programmers can create intricate, detailed objects using Pascal on properly equipped display terminals. This feature is attractive to scientists and increasingly so to business personnel as well.

At first, Pascal's availability was limited. But as time passes, more computer manufacturers are offering Pascal compilers with their machines. Perhaps the major disadvantage of Pascal is that it is not yet standardized. Many versions and enhancements are available from manufacturers, which may cause programs written in Pascal to differ depending upon the specific compiler used. In addition, some people believe that PASCAL has poor input-output capabilities.

APL

APL was conceived in 1962 by Kenneth Iverson, who described it in his book, *A Programming Language,* and worked with IBM to develop it. APL became available to the public through IBM in 1968 and, over the years, has been expanded and has gained many enthusiastic supporters. Several businesses now use APL as their main programming language.

FIGURE 10–9

Payroll Program in
Pascal

```
PROGRAM PAYROLL (INPUT,OUTPUT);
VAR HOURS,REGULAR,WAGE,OVERTIME,GROSS,TAX,NETPAY : REAL;
NAME : ARRAY(.1..17.) OF CHAR;
I : INTEGER;
BEGIN
WRITELN('1','EMPLOYEE NAME','               NET PAY');
WRITELN('  ');
WHILE NOT EOF DO
   BEGIN
   FOR I:=1 TO 17 DO
      READ (NAME(.I.));
      READLN (HOURS,WAGE);
      IF HOURS> 40
         THEN BEGIN
            REGULAR:=40*WAGE;
            OVERTIME:=(HOURS-40)*(1.5*WAGE);
            GROSS:=REGULAR + OVERTIME
         END
         ELSE BEGIN
            GROSS:=HOURS*WAGE
         END;
      IF GROSS>250
         THEN BEGIN
            TAX:=0.20*GROSS;
            NETPAY:=GROSS-TAX
         END
         ELSE BEGIN
            TAX:=0.14*GROSS;
            NETPAY:=GROSS-TAX
         END;
   WRITE(' ');
FOR I :=1 TO 17 DO
      WRITE(NAME(.I.));
      WRITELN(NETPAY:12:12);
   END
END.
```

Output

```
EMPLOYEE NAME    NET PAY

LYNN MANGINO     224.00
THOMAS RITTER    212.42
MARIE OLSON      209.00
LORI DUNLEVY     172.00
WILLIAM WILSON   308.00
```

The full power of APL is best realized when it is used for interactive processing via a terminal. A programmer can use APL in two modes. In the *execution mode*, the terminal can be used much as a desk calculator. An instruction is keyed in on one line, and the response is returned immediately on the following line. In the *definition mode,* a series of instructions is entered into memory and the entire program is executed on command from the programmer. Much as with BASIC, the APL user enters statements to develop a source program, system commands to communicate with the operating system, and editing commands to modify the source program. However, APL bears little resemblance to any high-level programming language discussed thus far.

Both character-string data and numeric data can be manipulated when APL is used. It is especially well suited for handling tables of related numbers known as *arrays*. To simplify the programmer's task, a number of operations (up to fifty or more) are provided for array manipulation, logical comparisons, mathematical functions, branching operations, and so forth. The operators are represented by symbols on a special APL keyboard (see Figure 10–10). Some examples of APL coding are shown in Table 10–3. Figure 10–11 shows an interactive APL session.

Advantages and Disadvantages   APL operators can be combined to perform some very complex operations with a minimum of coding. APL's lack of formal restrictions on input and output and its free-form style make it a very powerful language. It can be learned quickly by programmers. APL is also available through time-sharing networks for organizations that need only a limited amount of data processing.

APL involves a few disadvantages as well. It is very difficult to read. Further, as mentioned above, a special keyboard is required to enter APL statements; fortunately, however, the large offering of new, low-cost terminals capable of handling several type fonts has greatly reduced this problem. Many people do not believe that APL is suitable for handling large data files. Another limitation of APL is the large amount of primary storage required by its compiler. Usually, only large and medium-sized systems are capable of supporting APL. However, if a network of remote terminals is connected to a large central computer, APL can be made available to users at the remote sites. (Indeed, time-sharing networks such as this have led to increased use of APL.) Finally, APL is not as widely supported as are COBOL and Pascal.

FIGURE 10–10

APL Keyboard

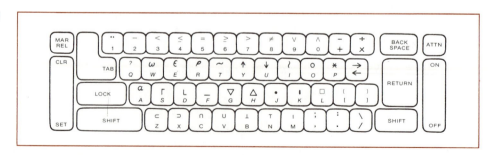

TABLE 10–3
APL Coding

APL CODING	ENGLISH TRANSLATION
A + B	A plus B
A ← 25	A = 25
A L B	Finds the smaller of A and B
V1 ← 2 5 11 17	Creates a vector of 4 components and assigns this vector to V1
⌈/V1	Finds the maximum value in the vector V1

FIGURE 10–11
Interactive APL
Session

```
          ∇PALINDROME[□]∇

      ∇ PALINDROME PHRASE;ALPHA;COMPRESSED;REVERSE
[1]   ⍝   PROGRAM TO DETERMINE IF A PHRASE IS A PALINDROME
[2]   ⍝   THE PHRASE MUST BE CHARACTER DATA AND HAVE AT LEAST ONE
[3]   ALPHA←'ABCDEFGHIJKLMNOPQRSTUVWXYZ'
[4]   COMPRESSED←(PHRASE∊ALPHA)/PHRASE
[5]   →(0=ρCOMPRESSED)/NONE
[6]   REVERSE←COMPRESSED[⌽⍳ρCOMPRESSED]
[7]   →(∧/REVERSE=COMPRESSED)/YES
[8]   PHRASE,'  IS NOT A PALINDROME'
[9]   →0
[10]  YES:PHRASE,'  IS A PALINDROME'
[11]  →0
[12]  NONE:'THERE ARE NO ALPHABETIC CHARACTER IN PHRASE'
     ∇


      PALINDROME 'MOM'
MOM  IS A PALINDROME


      PALINDROME 'THIS'
THIS  IS NOT A PALINDROME


      PALINDROME 'MADAM IN EDEN I''M ADAM'
MADAM IN EDEN I'M ADAM  IS A PALINDROME


      PALINDROME '1 21'
THERE ARE NO ALPHABETIC CHARACTER IN PHRASE
```

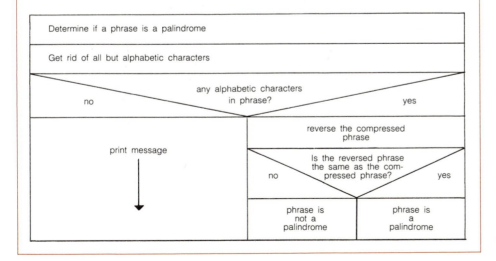

PROGRAMMING LANGUAGES—A COMPARISON

Implementing an information system involves making an important decision concerning the type of programming language to use. This decision is based almost entirely on the application involved. Some questions must be asked:

- What languages does the selected (or available) computer system support?
- Will the application require mostly complex computations, or file processing, or report generation?
- Is a fast response time crucial, or will batch processing be satisfactory?
- Are equipment changes planned for the future?
- How frequently will programs need modification?
- What languages do the programmers who will use the system know?

The size of the computer system is an obvious constraint on language choice. The limited main storage capacity of small computers usually prohibits the use of languages such as COBOL, FORTRAN, PL/1, and APL, which require significant amounts of main storage and sophisticated hardware. The computational capabilities of RPG are limited, but in many cases they can supply sufficient information for the management of small firms. If interactive processing is desired, BASIC and Pascal, which can be used on many small computers and minicomputers, should be considered. Subsets of PL/1, COBOL, and FORTRAN that can be used on small systems have also been developed.

For large systems, the type of processing is the key consideration in choosing a language. Business applications typically involve large amounts of data on which relatively few calculations are performed. Substantial file processing (requiring many I/O operations) is required; thus, many business applications are *input/output–bound*. In such cases, COBOL and PL/1 provide the necessary power for efficient operations. When choosing between COBOL and PL/1, management must weigh the importance of standardization versus ease of programming. Although PL/1 has been standardized, it is still primarily an IBM language. In contrast, COBOL is available on all large computers but may require greater programming effort because of its wordiness.

Scientific programming applications usually require many complex calculations on relatively small amounts of data. Therefore, they tend to be *process-bound*. The computational capabilities of FORTRAN make it ideal for such applications. Another alternative is PL/1, which becomes more attractive as more manufacturers offer PL/1 compilers. Pascal is a third possibility for scientific programming. It has good mathematical and graphics capabilities; and it is available on all sizes of computers, unlike PL/1.

If interactive computing is desired, APL, BASIC, or Pascal can be used. Although BASIC is easier to learn and use, APL has some very powerful features not available in BASIC. APL, however, is not available on all large computers and requires a special keyboard. Pascal is available on smaller computers and is similar to BASIC.

Because of the diversity of programming languages, many firms choose to use several. For example, a firm can write scientific programs in FORTRAN, file-updating programs in COBOL, and programs for interactive processing in BASIC. It is also possible to write part of a program in one language and another part in a different language; this involves compiling the various portions of the program in separate steps and linking together the resultant object programs. These steps can be specified in job-control statements. For example, a program written in COBOL may call up an assembler program to perform extensive sorting of alphanumeric data, since assembler language can sort more efficiently than COBOL and can save processing time.

Nevertheless, there has been a definite trend away from programming in assembly language. Because of the one-to-one relation between assembly-language instructions and machine-language instructions, programming assembly language is very time consuming. Assembly-language programs may be efficient, but writing them is laborious. In contrast, high-level languages shift the programming emphasis away from detailed computer functions toward procedures for solving problems. High-level-language compilers require significant amounts of main storage capacity, but the languages are much easier to use than machine-oriented languages.

As hardware costs have decreased, more firms have determined that they could afford computers capable of supporting high-level languages. At the same time, labor costs have increased, and program development and maintenance have become significant expense items. Thus, high-level languages have increased in popularity. However, in systems where main-storage capacity is a critical constraint and virtual storage capabilities are not available, assembly languages are the best, if not the only, alternative available. This situation is frequently encountered in microcomputer systems.

Like choosing hardware, choosing software involves many considerations. A comparison chart reflecting some of the most important ones is shown in Table 10–4.

	ASSEMBLY LANGUAGE	FORTRAN	COBOL	PL/1	RPG	BASIC	APL	PASCAL
Strong math capabilities	X	X		X		X	X	X
Good character-manipulation capabilities	X		X	X		X	X	X
English-like			X	X				X
Available on many computers	X	X	X		X	X		X
Highly efficient	X							
Standardized		X	X	X		X		
Requires large amounts of storage			X	X			X	
Good interactive capability						X	X	X
Procedure-oriented		X	X	X		X	X	X
Problem-oriented					X			
Machine-dependent	X							

TABLE 10–4

Comparison of Programming Languages

SUMMARY

● Programming languages can be placed into two categories—batch-oriented and interactive. Batch-oriented languages can be further classified as machine-oriented, procedure-oriented, or problem-oriented.

● Interactive programming languages are used to communicate directly with the computer in a conversational mode. Response time is almost immediate. Interactive programs are fairly simple; typical examples are one-time requests for information and inquiries into data files.

● Machine language is the language of the computer, the only language that the computer directly understands. Machine language must take the form of 0s and 1s to be understood by the computer.

● Machine-oriented languages include machine and assembly languages, which require extensive knowledge of the computer. Procedure-oriented languages like COBOL, FORTRAN, and PL/1 emphasize the computational and logical procedures for solving a problem. Problem-oriented languages such as RPG describe a problem without detailing the computational steps necessary to solve it.

● Programs in problem- and procedure-oriented languages are simpler to code but require more execution time than comparable programs written in lower-level, machine-oriented languages.

● An assembly-language program uses symbolic names for machine operations, making programming less tedious and time consuming than when machine language is used. Assembly-language programs can be very efficient in terms of storage and processing time required. However, assembly-language programming requires a high level of skill, and the language itself is machine-dependent.

● COBOL is the most popular business programming language. It was designed to be English-like and self-documenting. Standardization of COBOL has helped to make it machine-independent. The main disadvantage of COBOL is that a large and sophisticated compiler is required to convert a COBOL source program into machine language.

● FORTRAN was the first high-level language developed. It is procedure-oriented and well suited for scientific and mathematical applications.

● PL/1 is an all-purpose, procedure-oriented language combining the best features of COBOL and FORTRAN. Its modularity facilitates structured programming. PL/1 compilers require a large amount of storage and are not available on small computers.

● RPG is designed to produce business reports. The output format must be specified, but the RPG generator program can build a program to provide the output. Thus, little programming skill is required to use RPG. It is popular with users of small computers and minicomputers. However, it has limited computational capabilities and is not totally machine-independent.

● BASIC is an easy-to-learn language, well suited for instructional purposes and ideal for time-sharing systems. It is flexible and can be used for both scientific and business applications. Because many features of the language are not standardized, it is machine-dependent.

● Pascal is also easy to learn and well suited for instructional purposes. It is useful in both business and scientific applications in either batch or interactive processing. Structured programming techniques work well with Pascal because of the language's modular features.

● APL is a powerful interactive language that can be used in an execution mode or a definition mode. Both character-string data and numeric data can be manipulated easily. Because APL includes a large number of unique symbols as operators, it requires a special keyboard. The APL compiler needs a large amount of primary storage; this restricts its use to medium-sized and large computers.

● Factors to consider when selecting an appropriate programming language include: What languages can the computer support? Are computations simple? What response time is required? Are equipment changes planned in the future? How often will programs be modified?

● Decreasing hardware costs and increasing labor costs have helped create a trend toward the use of high-level, procedure-oriented languages.

REVIEW QUESTIONS

1. What are the three categories of batch programming languages and the differences among them?

2. Distinguish between machine languages and assembly languages. What are the advantages and disadvantages of each?

3. What are the major differences between batch and interactive programming languages?

4. List and discuss some of the factors that should be considered when a programming language for use with a particular system must be chosen.

APPLICATION

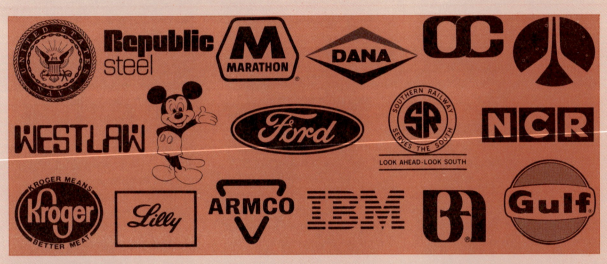

Ohio Citizens Bank

Ohio Citizens Bank opened for business in Toledo on March 28, 1932, with twenty-five employees and capital funds totaling $350,000. After a 1959 merger with the Spitzer-Rorick Trust and Savings Bank, the bank's total deposits exceeded $100 million. Today, its total deposits approach $500 million.

Through the years, the bank has pioneered and popularized many services in the greater Toledo area, including personal loans, drive-up windows, money orders, charge cards, freight payment, payroll systems, and statement savings. In 1975, the bank introduced an automatic loan plan called CheckLOAN,

which provides extra funds whenever needed for approved checking customers. The twenty-four-hour teller machines, OC24 Banks, were also introduced during that year.

"OC Transfer," the first bank telephone transfer system offered in the marketplace, was developed in 1977. This system allows a customer to transfer funds among checking, savings, and CheckLOAN.

Offering financial services to both retail and commercial communities, the bank processes an average of 700,000 transactions per week. Millions of dollars worth of computers and other facilities are used to record and process nearly 133,000 transactions daily.

The operations center of Ohio Citizens, in downtown Toledo, houses the corporate data-processing facilities. Two main-frame computers, an IBM

System/370 Model 148 and an IBM 4341 processor, provide information support for all departments. Each CPU has a two-megabyte memory. The 148 is used primarily to support online applications, while the 4341 is used for batch processing. Both systems are completely switchable, however, to insure minimal interruption of online service in case of equipment failure.

Charge-card processing, installment loans, and stock transfers are supported by remote data-entry stations in the appropriate departments. Entrex, the primary key-entry system, is a key-to-disk data-entry system in which the data is collected, stored, retrieved, and forwarded to the application computer systems for processing. The data is entered on a keyboard with a visual display screen and stored directly on a disk; the data on the disk is transferred to tape or transmitted through telecommunication facilities for daily processing. Entrex is also a dual system to ensure uninterrupted service.

Ohio Citizens' data-processing applications use three programming languages: COBOL, BASIC, and assembly language. The controller's division of the bank uses BASIC on an IBM 5100 microcomputer with a CRT to process special accounting-oriented financial reports. These applications use online, real-time programming; data is submitted directly to the computer from remote terminals, and results are returned in seconds. Accounting applications on the microcomputer are conducive

to BASIC programming because the same procedure is used every day; it involves only entering data in an interactive style. The controller's division also uses BASIC for two programs that are not run daily. One is a Return-on-Investment Analysis program, which determines instantaneously the bank's return on investment. The other is a Budget Modeling program; because the BASIC program can be changed quickly and simply, it provides an excellent environment for manipulating alternative budget models.

In the data-processing department, programs are written in assembly language and COBOL. Originally, all

programming was done in assembly language. Because the department's first IBM System/360 computer was a Model 30—a small computer with only 32K bytes of main storage—it was necessary to use a compact language, such as assembly language. The transition to larger equipment has made the use of COBOL possible; many programs have already been converted to the COBOL language.

All batch applications in the department will eventually be written in COBOL and all new or replacement applications are written in COBOL. The Installment Loan and Payroll applications are two original assembly-language programs that have already been rewritten in COBOL.

Assembly language will not be phased out completely, however. The assembly-language programs written for System/360 machines can be run on System/370 equipment. Because of its speed and efficiency, assembly language will continue to be used for teleprocessing monitors and MICR support. Also, some applications require I/O devices that can only be supported with assembly language provided by the equipment manufacturer. These programs and the operating systems will also continue to be programmed in assembly languages.

The three languages just discussed were selected by Ohio Citizens in order to match the requirements of the applications with the strengths

of the languages. The online, real-time microcomputer programs are written in BASIC so that results can be obtained quickly. Operating systems and programs that require assembly-language I/O support will continue to be written in assembly languages. COBOL has been selected as the application language of the future because of its standardization and readability and because it is easy for programmers to use.

In addition to the three standard programming languages used at Ohio Citizens, the programming facilities use another product called EASYTRIEVE, marketed by Pansophic Systems, Inc. EASYTRIEVE is an information-retrieval and data-management system that can be used to produce reports from any number of input files on a variety of output media. Programs to do relatively simple jobs such as file to file or file to printed output can be set up and run with very little effort. It is used for special-request reports, file analysis, and file repair. EASYTRIEVE is ideal for producing one-time reports that are needed quickly.

DISCUSSION POINTS

1. Ohio Citizens is in the process of converting some of its programs from assembly language to COBOL. Which programs has it decided are better suited for assembly language?
2. Why is BASIC ideal for applications such as budget modeling?

CHAPTER 11

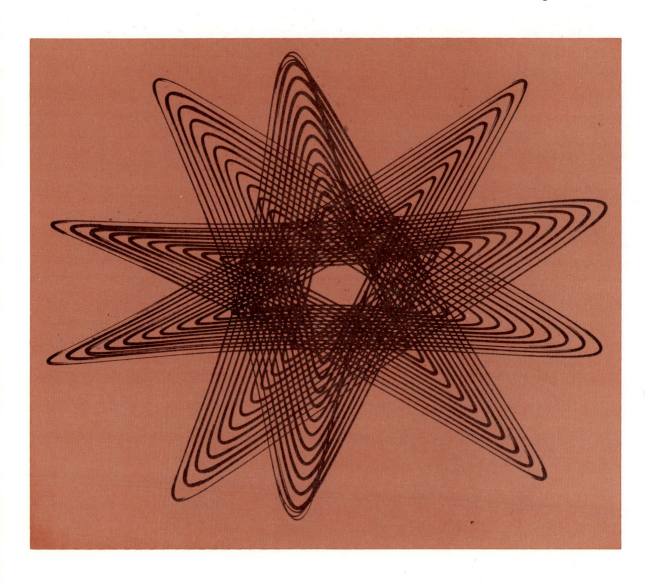

Structured Design Concepts

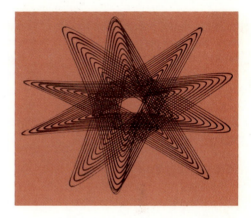

Introduction

With recent advances in computer technology, hardware costs have continued to decrease while capabilities have expanded. Unfortunately, the same cannot be said of program and system development costs. Modern business environments have become more complex and dynamic. Systems designed to supply information to management must be continually redesigned or modified to respond to changing needs. As more time is spent in system design and maintenance, the costs for such services continue to rise dramatically in relation to hardware costs.

These problems have caused greater emphasis to be placed on simplicity and well-thought-out logic in system and program design. A sound methodology for program and system development is a necessity. This chapter first discusses the concept of top-down design and the tools for its implementation. These techniques apply to both system and program development. A later section deals specifically with structured programming. Finally, the chapter describes the management of system projects.

"'Do You Take This Input to Be Your Lawfully Wedded Interface?'"

Marilyn Chase

SUNNYVALE, Calif.—"Hello, my name is Rev. Apple," says the text on the screen of the Apple II. "I'm the world's first ordained computer. Groom, what's your name?"

So far, half-a-dozen couples have punched responses into the keyboard, and ended up married. The first three were wed on Valentine's Day. One groom wore work clothes and arrived late; his bride wore a pale pantsuit and wept. The second couple chose formal attire and requested a printout of the liturgy.

The "marrying computer" has a human co-celebrant. He is the Rev. Reinhard Jaenisch, a 30-year-old mail-order minister with the Universal Life Church of

Wall Street Journal, July 28, 1981, p. 27. Reprinted by permission of the *Wall Street Journal* © Dow Jones & Company, Inc., 1981. All rights reserved.

Sunnyvale who likes to be called Rev. Ron. A part-time minister, he earns a living as an executive headhunter. He says he devised computer weddings "as publicity for the church and a gimmick to get people interested in marriage, the church and God."

Fun in the Afternoon

Rev. Ron concedes he's also eager to divert quickie-wedding traffic from Reno, Nev. "Heck," he says, "I've married people on their lunch breaks and in cowboy suits. I do custom (noncomputer) weddings, too. I'm into making church fun."

Apple Computer, Inc. hasn't given its blessing to the computer marriages, but a spokesman says, "It's good to have divinity on your side."

There are drawbacks, though. When the program text reaches the bottom of the screen, the computer interrupts the ceremony to command the couple to "please press space bar to continue." There's no music yet, either. Rev. Ron says synthesized Mendelssohn will cost the church another $1,000 in software. Finally, the traditional matrimonial assent, "I do," doesn't compute. The bride or groom must punch in "y" for yes.

Is It Silly?

John Barry, managing editor of InfoWorld, a computer tabloid, was invited to attend one of the weddings. He says it was hard to suppress a giggle when "Rev. Apple" lit up his screen. "I thought it was essentially silly—not harmful, just silly," he says. "But then I may have an East Coast bias against such spectacles."

But Rev. Ron insists there are advantages to being wed by computer. It's free at his church. It's modern. The church provides a marriage-counseling program on the Apple II. And if that fails, Rev. Ron is planning to add an "unwedding program" (digital divorce).

This is an example of one programmer's creativity. Whether programs are written for unique applications, such as weddings (and even divorces), or for routine procedures, such as payroll and billing, programmers should be concerned with using the computer efficiently. The following chapter outlines a number of structured-design concepts which can be used by programmers to write efficient and structured programs.

THE NEED FOR STRUCTURED TECHNIQUES

Data processing has come a long way since the days of the UNIVAC I, when the leading scientists of the period projected that the world would need only ten such machines for the rest of time. Today the world has millions of computers with processing capabilities billions of times greater than ten UNIVAC Is, and the demand for computing power continues to increase. In the first generation of computers, hardware was expensive, accounting for 80 percent of costs while software accounted for 20 percent. Today, those figures are reversed, and it appears this trend will continue for a long time.

As the pace of technological innovation accelerates, data processing departments are hard pressed to keep up. In fact, most are unable to. Software development is far behind existing technology, because software development is extremely labor intensive. Thus, data processing departments today face a productivity problem: They must obtain greater software development for each dollar invested. The basic ways of increasing productivity are: (1) to automate the software development process, (2) to require employees to work harder or longer or both, and (3) to change the way things are done. This chapter focuses on the third option, improving methodology.

In the early days of data processing, programming was very much an art. It was a new skill, with no standards and no concrete ways of doing things. Programmers considered programs their own creations. Very often, like artists, they would not allow anyone to see their creations until they were finished. Much has been learned since those early days. Thousands of programs have been written; studies have been done; and the body of knowledge regarding program development has grown accordingly. Attempts are now being made to use this knowledge to develop standardized techniques of program development.

One growing body of knowledge is concerned with structured techniques. Most of such techniques have existed only since the early 1970s and are being continually expanded and refined. While structured techniques are not universally accepted in the data-processing community, their use is increasing as managers recognize their ability to improve productivity. Three of these techniques—structured design, structured programming, and structured review—will be discussed in the remainder of this chapter.

STRUCTURED DESIGN METHODOLOGY

Top-Down Design

Chapter 8 mentioned that it is possible to simplify a problem by breaking it into segments, or subunits. This is known as a *modular approach* to problem-solving. A problem solution is defined in terms of the functions it must perform. Each step, or *module,* in the solution process consists of one or more logically related functions. Thus, a problem solution may consist of several independent modules that together perform the required tasks.

The use of modules greatly facilitates the solution-planning process. But the modules must be meaningfully organized. *Top-down design* is a method

of organizing a solution by defining it in terms of major functions to be performed and further breaking down these major functions into subfunctions.

The most general level of organization is the main control logic; this overall view of the problem is the most critical to the success of the solution. Modules at this level contain only broad descriptions of steps in the solution process. These steps are further broken down into several lower-level modules that contain more detail as to the specific steps to be performed. Depending on the complexity of the problem, several levels of modules may be required, with the lowest-level modules containing the greatest amount of detail.

The modules of the problem solution are related to each other in a hierarchical manner. These relationships can be depicted graphically on a *structure chart*. Figure 11–1 shows a portion of such a chart for an inventory processing application.

The highest level in the hierarchy is the *main control module*, which is represented in Figure 11–1 by the block labeled "Inventory Processing." This module is further broken down into lower-level modules that correspond with the inventory-processing application's three basic functions: reading a master inventory record and a sales transaction card; computing the reorder quantity; and writing an updated master file and purchase orders. The "Compute Reorder Quantity" module can be further divided into "Compute Current Inventory" and "Compute Order Requirements" modules. Finally, computing the current inventory involves two modules: "Determine Beginning Inventory" and "Determine Units Sold." Notice how the level of detail increases at the lower level.

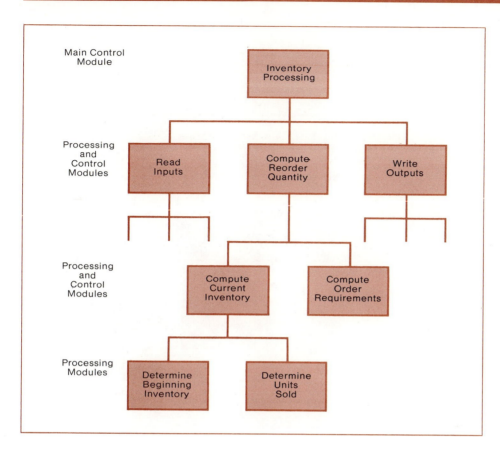

FIGURE 11-1

Portion of Structure
Chart
for Inventory
Processing
Example

The flow of control in the structure chart is from top to bottom, demonstrating the top-down design of the solution. In other words, each module has control of the modules directly below it and is controlled by the module directly above it. The higher-level modules are both processing modules and control modules; they describe processes and also control modules below them in the hierarchy. At the lowest-level, modules involve only processing.

The complete structure chart for the inventory processing application is shown in Figure 11-2.

When top-down design is used, certain rules must be followed. First, each module should be independent of other modules; in other words, each module should be executed only when control is passed to it from the module directly above it. Similarly, once a module has been executed, control should be passed back to the module directly above. The return process continues until the main control module is reached.

Another rule of the modular approach is that each module should be relatively small to facilitate the translation of modules into program statements. Many advocates of the modular approach suggest that each module should consist of no more than fifty or sixty lines of code. When module size is limited in this manner, the coding for each module can fit on a single page of computer printout, which simplifies testing and debugging procedures.

FIGURE 11–2
Structure Chart for
Inventory
Processing Example
with Four Levels
of Processing Modules

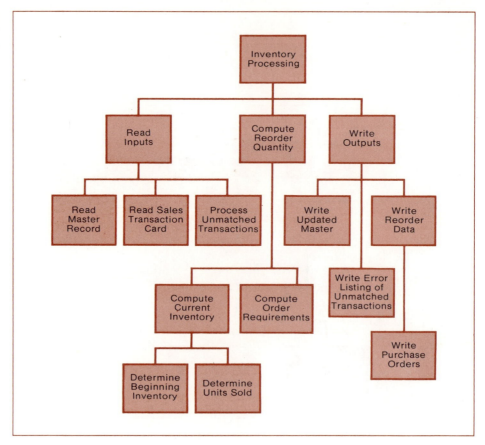

Yet another rule is that each module should have only one entrance point and one exit point. This makes the basic flow easy to follow and also allows easy modification of program logic to accommodate system changes.

When top-down design is used, the complete solution is not established until the lowest-level modules have been designed. However, this does not prevent higher-level modules from being coded and tested at earlier stages in the development cycle. To do this, programmers create *dummy modules* and use them in place of the lower-level modules for testing purposes. Significant errors in higher-level modules can be isolated by the testers' observing whether control is correctly transferred between the higher-level modules and the dummy modules. As the lower-level modules are designed and coded, they can replace the dummy modules and be similarly tested. Thus, by the time the lowest-level modules have been coded, all other modules have already been tested and debugged.

Documentation and Design Tools

The structure charts described above provide an excellent means of documentation. However, structure charts show only functions, their relation-

ships, and the flow of control; they do not show the processing flow, the order of execution, or how control will be transferred to and from each module. Therefore, structure charts must be supplemented with system charts, program flowcharts, record layouts, and so on. Chapter 8 discussed program flowcharts and layout forms. System charts will be discussed in Chapter 13. Two design and documentation aids—HIPO and pseudocode—are discussed in this section.

HIPO   The term HIPO (Hierarchy plus Input-Process-Output) is applied to a kind of visual aid commonly used to supplement structure charts. Whereas structure charts emphasize only structure and function, HIPO diagrams show the inputs and outputs of program modules.

A typical HIPO package consists of three types of diagrams that describe a program, or system of programs, from the general level to the detail level. At the most general level is the *visual table of contents*, which is almost identical to a structure chart but includes some additional information. Each block in the visual table of contents is given an identification number that is used as a reference in other HIPO diagrams. Figure 11–3 shows a visual table of contents for the inventory-processing application introduced in Figure 11–1.

Each module in the visual table of contents is described in greater detail in an *overview diagram*, which includes the module's inputs, processing, and outputs. The reference number assigned to the overview diagram shows

279

FIGURE 11-3
Visual Table of
Contents for
Inventory Processing
Example

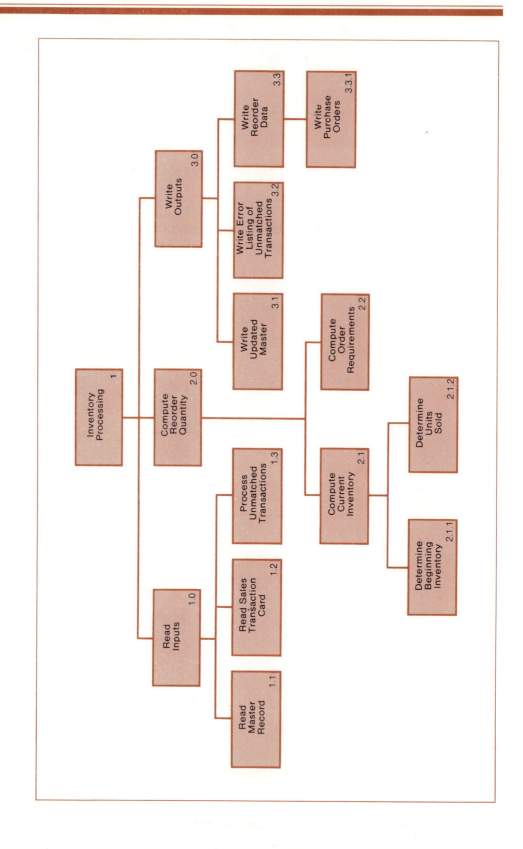

where the module fits into the overall structure of the system as depicted in the visual table of contents. If the module passes control to a lower-level module in the hierarchy for some specific processing operation, that operation is also given a reference number. An overview diagram for the inventory processing "Read Inputs" module (1.0) is shown in Figure 11–4.

Finally, the specific functions performed and data items used in each module are described in a *detail diagram*. The amount of detail used in these diagrams depends on the complexity of the problem involved. Enough detail should be included to enable a programmer to understand the functions and write the code to perform them.

HIPO diagrams are an excellent means of documenting systems and programs. The varying levels of detail incorporated in the diagrams allow them to be used by managers, analysts, and programmers to meet needs ranging from program maintenance to overhaul of entire systems.

Pseudocode   Flowcharts are the most commonly used method of expressing program logic, but pseudocode is becoming increasingly popular for that purpose. Pseudocode, as you may recall from Chapter 8, is an English-like description of the processing steps in a program. At times, flowcharts become lengthy and difficult to read, especially those for complex programs. In some cases, it is difficult to express the logic of processing steps with the

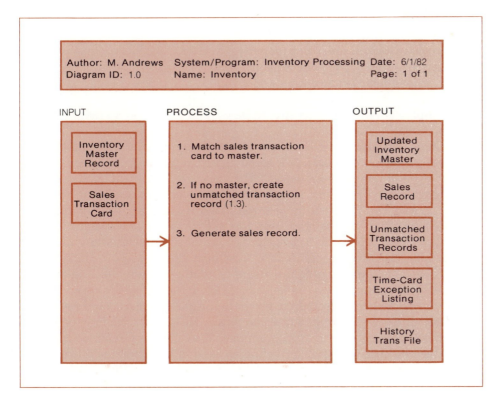

FIGURE 11–4
HIPO Overview Diagram for "Read Inputs" Module

commonly used flowcharting symbols. When pseudocode is used, the program solution follows an easy-to-read, top-down sequence.

Although certain keywords such as IF, THEN, and ELSE are used in pseudocode, no rigid set of rules must be followed. Thus, pseudocode is a simple technique to learn and use. Figure 11–5 contrasts pseudocode with program flowcharting. As the example indicates, pseudocode is understandable even to those unfamiliar with the program logic. The actual program can be easily coded directly from the pseudocode.

STRUCTURED PROGRAMMING

Emphasis on the art of programming and on the flexibility that high-level languages provide has sometimes encouraged poor programming techniques. For example, many programs contain numerous branches that continually alter the sequential flow of processing. These programs may work successfully, but their often confusing logic can be understood only by the original programmer. This increases the costs and difficulties associated with program maintenance. Furthermore, without a standardized method of attacking a problem, a programmer may spend far more time than necessary in determining an appropriate solution and developing the program. To counter these tendencies, *structured programming* has been widely publicized.

Structured programming has four objectives:

1. To reduce testing time.
2. To increase programmer productivity.
3. To increase clarity by reducing complexity.
4. To decrease maintenance time and effort.

More simply stated, programs should be easy to read, easy to maintain, and easy to change.

Structured programming encourages well-thought-out program logic. The top-down, modular approach discussed earlier in this chapter is used during development of the program design. The structured program itself uses only three basic control patterns: simple sequence, selection, and loop (see Figures 11–6 and 11–7). When these three patterns and the modular approach are used, programs can be read from top to bottom and are easier to understand. An attempt is made to keep programs as simple and straightforward as possible; structured programming discourages the use of "tricky" logic that is likely to confuse program users (sometimes even the original programmer).

A basic guideline of structured programming is that each module should have only one entry point and one exit point. This allows the flow of control to be followed easily by the programmer. When the modular approach is used, the one-entry/one-exit guideline is easy to incorporate into the program. A program that has only one entrance and one exit is called a *proper program*.

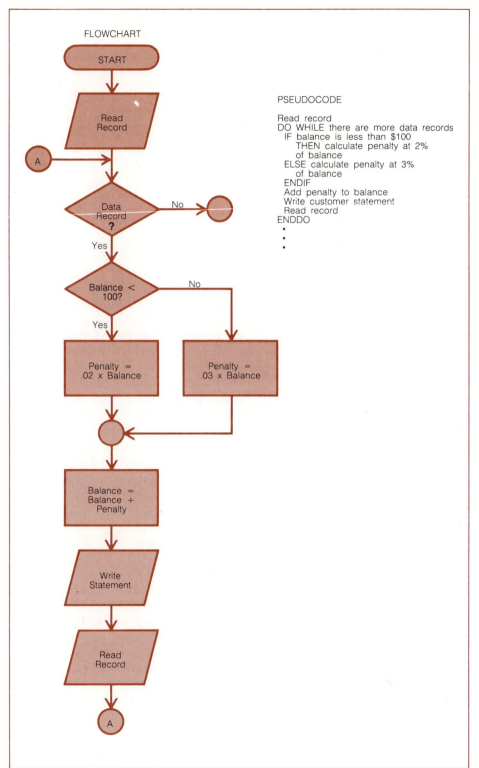

FLOWCHART

PSEUDOCODE

Read record
DO WHILE there are more data records
 IF balance is less than $100
    THEN calculate penalty at 2%
      of balance
 ELSE calculate penalty at 3%
      of balance
 ENDIF
 Add penalty to balance
 Write customer statement
 Read record
ENDDO

FIGURE 11–5

Comparison of
Pseudocode and
Flowchart

FIGURE 11–6
Basic Structured
Programming Control
Patterns

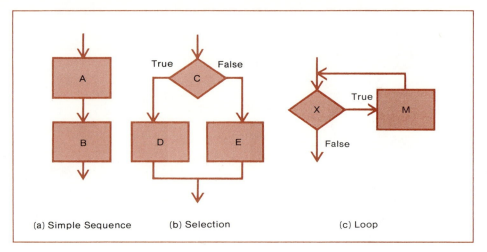

(a) Simple Sequence　　(b) Selection　　(c) Loop

Several features should be included in structured programs to make them easy to read. Comment statements, or remarks, should be used liberally. Variable names should be definitive. Finally, indentation and spacing of program statements should be used.

It must be emphasized that the branch pattern, characterized by the GO TO statement, is not advocated in structured programming. (In fact, structured programming is sometimes called "GO-TO-less" programming or "IF-THEN-ELSE" programming.) A GO TO statement causes an unconditional branch from one part of the program to another. Excessive use of GO TO statements results in the continual changes in execution flow mentioned earlier. Often the flow is transferred to totally different logical sections of the program. Programs containing many GO TO (branching) statements are difficult to modify because they are obscure and complicated. A programmer may not know how a change in one part of the program will affect processing in other parts. In contrast, structured programming logic flows from the beginning to the end of a program, without backtracking to earlier sections (see Figure 11–7). This is not to say that a structured program may not have any GO TO statements, but that they should be used only to implement structured logic.

Some programming languages are better suited to structured programming than others. Especially well suited are Pascal, PL/1, and ALGOL (a language developed by a coordinated effort of user groups and computer manufacturers and is in widespread use in Europe). Languages such as FORTRAN and BASIC lack some features that many people consider essential for structured programming. For example, it is sometimes difficult to avoid the use of GO TO statements in these languages. However, careful planning and well-placed GO TO statements can result in well-structured programs, regardless of the language used. Figure 11–8 compares structured and unstructured versions of a portion of a payroll program written in COBOL.

Management's difficulties in implementing structured programming may originate in a resistance to change. However, the use of structured program-

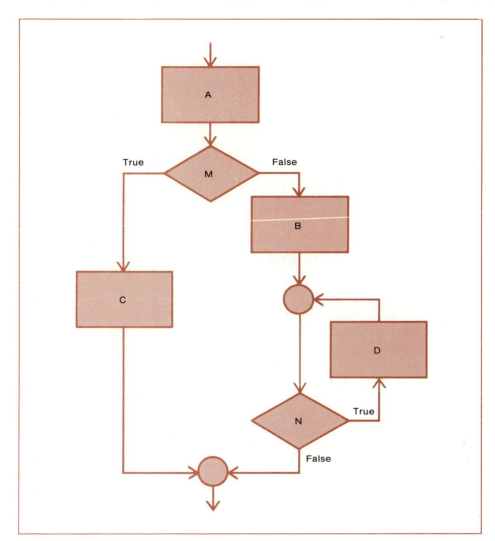

FIGURE 11–7
Sample Flowchart of
Structured
Programming

ming not only significantly improves programming practices but also represents potential cost savings.

MANAGEMENT OF SYSTEM PROJECTS

This chapter has presented various tools—top-down design, modular design, HIPO diagrams, pseudocode, and structured programming—intended to aid in designing an efficient, easy-to-maintain system in a minimal amount of time. However, even the most organized and well-structured system may contain errors and omissions that can render it useless. Thus, continuous review of the system during the development cycle is essential. While errors and oversights will almost certainly surface after a system be-

```
00032
00033     WORK-LOOP.
00034         READ CARD-FILE AT END GO TO FINISH.
00035         IF HOURS-WORKED IS GREATER THAN 40 THEN GO TO
00036             OVERTIME-ROUTINE.
00037         MULTIPLY HOURS-WORKED BY WAGE-PER-HOUR GIVING GROSS-PAY.
00038         GO TO TAX-COMPUTATION.
00039     OVERTIME-ROUTINE.
00040         MULTIPLY WAGE-PER-HOUR BY 40 GIVING REGULAR-PAY.
00041         SUBTRACT 40 FROM HOURS-WORKED GIVING OVERTIME-HOURS.
00042         MULTIPLY WAGE-PER-HOUR BY 1.5 GIVING OVERTIME-RATE.
00043         MULTIPLY OVERTIME-HOURS BY OVERTIME-RATE GIVING
00044             OVERTIME-PAY.
00045         ADD REGULAR-PAY, OVERTIME-PAY, GIVING GROSS-PAY.
00046     TAX-COMPUTATION.
00047         IF GROSS-PAY IS GREATER THAN 250 THEN MULTIPLY GROSS-PAY
00048             BY 0.20 GIVING TAX ELSE MULTIPLY GROSS-PAY BY 0.14
00049             GIVING TAX.
00050         SUBTRACT TAX FROM GROSS-PAY GIVING NET-PAY.
00051         MOVE EMPLOYEE-NAME TO NAME.
00052         MOVE NET-PAY TO AMOUNT.
00053         WRITE PRINT-LINE.
00054         GO TO WORK-LOOP.
00055     FINISH.
00056         CLOSE CARD-FILE, PRINT-FILE.
00057         STOP RUN.
```

(a) Unstructured Portion of COBOL Program

FIGURE 11–8
Unstructured versus
Structured COBOL
Code

comes operative (sometimes even months or years later), such problems can be minimized through careful planning, coordinating, and review.

Chief Programmer Team

An important first step sometimes taken to coordinate a system design effort is the formation of a *chief programmer team (CPT)*, a small number of programmers under the supervision of a chief programmer. The goals of the CPT approach are: to produce a software product that is easy to maintain and modify; to improve programmer productivity; and to increase system reliability. Organizations have applied the CPT concept to implement systems well ahead of schedule and with minimal errors.

The chief programmer is responsible for overall coordination and development of the programming project, as well as its success. A lead analyst works with the chief programmer in large system projects. In such cases, the lead analyst may supervise the general system design effort while the chief programmer concentrates on the technical development of the project.

Usually, a backup programmer is assigned as an assistant to the chief programmer. The backup programmer is a highly qualified specialist who

```
00033    WORK-LOOP.
00034        READ CARD-FILE AT END CLOSE CARD-FILE, PRINT-FILE, STOP RUN.
00035        IF HOURS-WORKED IS GREATER THAN 40
00036            THEN PERFORM OVERTIME-ROUTINE
00037            ELSE PERFORM STANDARD-ROUTINE.
00038        PERFORM TAX-PAY-COMPUTATION.
00039        PERFORM PRINTING.
00040        GO TO WORK-LOOP.
00041    STANDARD-ROUTINE.
00042        MULTIPLY HOURS-WORKED BY WAGE-PER-HOUR GIVING GROSS-PAY.
00043    OVERTIME-ROUTINE.
00044        MULTIPLY WAGE-PER-HOUR BY 40 GIVING REGULAR-PAY.
00045        SUBTRACT 40 FROM HOURS-WORKED GIVING OVERTIME-HOURS.
00046        MULTIPLY WAGE-PER-HOUR BY 1.5 GIVING OVERTIME-RATE.
00047        MULTIPLY OVERTIME-HOURS BY OVERTIME-RATE GIVING
00048            OVERTIME-PAY.
00049        ADD REGULAR-PAY, OVERTIME-PAY GIVING GROSS-PAY.
00050    TAX-PAY-COMPUTATION.
00051        IF GROSS-PAY IS GREATER THAN 250 THEN MULTIPLY GROSS-PAY
00052            BY 0.20 GIVING TAX ELSE MULTIPLY GROSS-PAY BY 0.14
00053            GIVING TAX.
00054        SUBTRACT TAX FROM GROSS-PAY GIVING NET-PAY.
00055    PRINTING.
00056        MOVE EMPLOYEE-NAME TO NAME.
00057        MOVE NET-PAY TO AMOUNT.
00058        WRITE PRINT-LINE.
```

(b) Structured Portion of COBOL Program

may help in system design, testing, and evaluation of alternative designs. The chief programmer and backup programmer normally code the most critical parts of the overall system. Separate modules of the system are programmed and tested by different programmers. The chief and backup programmers then work with one or more other programmers to integrate all parts into a complete system. This approach uses both structured programming and top-down design.

The CPT also uses a *librarian* to help maintain complete, up-to-date documentation of the project and to relieve the team programmers of many clerical tasks they would otherwise have to perform. The librarian's duties include:

● Preparing computer input from coding forms completed by programmers.
● Submitting inputs and picking up computer output.
● Maintaining up-to-date source-program listings in archives available to all programmers.
● Updating test data and implementing changes in programs and job-control statements as required.
● Maintaining up-to-date documentation.

FIGURE 11–8
Continued

Using a librarian in this way enhances communication among team members, because all program descriptions, coding, and test results are current and visible to everyone involved in the effort. In addition, this approach enables the chief programmer to maintain control of costs and of human and computer resources and to ensure adherence to standards.

The organizational structure of a chief programmer team is shown in Figure 11–9. As mentioned previously, the structure varies depending on the complexity of the project.

Structured Review and Evaluation

Obviously, an important goal of a system design effort is to produce an error-free system in the shortest possible time. This requires that the system be carefully reviewed before it is implemented. Early detection of errors and oversights can prevent costly modifications later.

One approach used in the early phases of system development is an *informal design review*. The system design documentation is studied by selected management, analysts, and programmers, usually before the actual coding of program modules. After a brief review period, each person responds with suggestions for additions, deletions, and modifications to the system design.

A *formal design review* is sometimes used after the detailed parts of the system have been sufficiently documented. The documentation at this point

FIGURE 11–9
Organization of Chief
Programmer Team

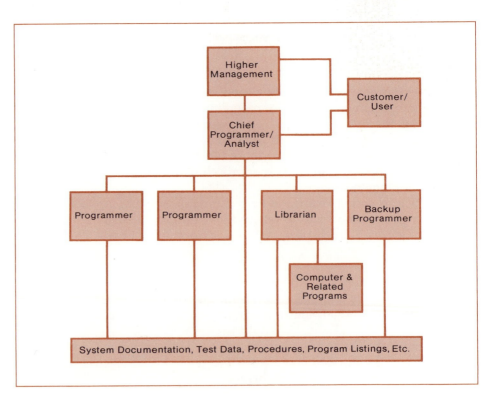

The Parable of the '67 Chevy

Once upon a time there was a man who wanted to be able to get from New York to Los Angeles on 12 hours' notice. His means of transportation was a 1967 Chevrolet that had bald tires and fired on three cylinders.

Recognizing the deficiencies of his means, he had the car tuned up and bought new tires, a supercharger and a radar detector. Performance improved 87%, but he still couldn't get from New York to L.A. in 12 hours.

By Daniel D. McCracken, "Software in the 80's: Perils and Promises," *Computerworld.* September 17, 1980, p. 10.

He next put in a Cadillac engine and added streamlining; still not fast enough. His last gasp was to install a turbine engine and aerodynamic controls, which got him to 200 m.p.h. on the interstates—within reach of what he needed—but led to bad scenes going through the small towns.

When last heard of, he was complaining about problems with his turbine engine and small-town police; he had not realized that he was trying to improve the performance of a basically wrong means of transportation.

He was also asking what caused contrails and, when told about jet airplanes, said, "They'll never fly!"

Morals:

● If you're using the wrong tool, improving its performance won't help much.
● The people who know the most about existing tools are often the hardest to get to accept better and different ones.
● The development of new tools seldom makes the existing ones totally obsolete. Even if our man had accepted jet airplanes, he would still have needed his car for getting to the grocery store.

Note: This parable perfectly depicts the current state of programming practices—no matter how we fine-tune them, they cannot get us where we want to go. Practices will grow outdated but not necessarily obsolete; we can still use the old methods to some degree. But newer methods are appearing, and newer ones will follow those. Adaptability must be a constant goal for both humans and the tools they use.

---

may consist of program flowcharts, pseudocode, narrative descriptions, or combinations of these methods. Sometimes called a *structured walkthrough*, the formal design review involves distributing the documentation to a review team of two to four members that studies the documentation and then meets with the program designers to discuss the overall completeness, accuracy, and quality of the design. The reviewers and program designers often trace through the programs using desk-checking as discussed in Chapter 9. Both valid and invalid data are used to ascertain the program's exception-handling and standard procedures.

After programs have been coded and executed on the computer, their outputs can be compared with hand-calculated results for verification. Any discrepancies can be noticed and problems corrected. When this approach is used, few, if any, errors remain undetected when the system finally becomes operative.

SUMMARY

● Software now accounts for a greater share of data-processing budgets than does hardware, a reversal of the situation in the 1950s.

● Data-processing departments are lagging behind in program development. Thus, programmers' productivity must increase.

● Top-down program design and structured programming are techniques that have been developed to reduce program development and maintenance costs.

● In the top-down approach, a program is broken into functional modules. At the highest level is the main control module, which is further divided into lower-level modules. Structure charts are used to graphically depict the program modules and their relationships. The flow of control in the structure chart is from top to bottom.

● When using top-down design, the programmer codes the higher-level modules first and tests them. Lower-level modules are then coded and tested. This facilitates debugging, because errors can be isolated to particular modules.

● Two methods of documentation used with top-down design are HIPO diagrams and pseudocode. HIPO diagrams show the input, processing steps, and output of each module. HIPO documentation consists of three types of diagrams—a visual table of contents, overview diagrams, and detail diagrams. Program logic can be expressed in pseudocode, an English-like description of the processing steps in a program. In pseudocode, the program solution follows a top-down sequence. The technique is easy to learn and use.

● Structured programming is a "GO-TO-less" programming concept. It uses only three basic control patterns—simple sequence, selection, and loop. Some languages, like Pascal, PL/1, and ALGOL, are especially well suited to structured programming.

● The chief programmer team (CPT) concept involves organizing a small number of programmers under the supervision of a chief programmer. Usually, the chief programmer is assisted by a highly qualified backup programmer. These two people code the most critical parts of the overall system. A librarian maintains complete, up-to-date documentation. The organization of the CPT varies according to the complexity of the project.

● Systems must be reviewed before they are implemented. In an informal design review, the system design documentation is reviewed before coding takes place to determine any changes that may be desirable. After a detailed system design is complete, a formal design review is held to check for completeness, accuracy, and quality. Desk-checking and test data are used to check all programs.

REVIEW QUESTIONS

1. Explain what top-down design is and why it is being used for system and program design.

2. What is the role of HIPO and pseudocode in structured design methodology? Do these tools offer any significant advantages over traditional methods of documentation? Explain.

3. Structured programming avoids the use of GO TO statements. Does this reduce the flexibility of the programmer and make coding more difficult?

4. What benefits can be realized by using structured programming? Give reasons to support your answer.

5. Explain the chief programmer team concept. What is the role of the librarian in this approach to system design?

APPLICATION

Armco Steel Corporation, Butler Plant

In the late 1880s, a young man named George M. Verity, manager of a small roofing company, was looking for a reliable source of quality steel sheets. These sheets were not easy to find; and Verity decided to become his own supplier. He organized the American Rolling Mill Company—the first company to bring together all the steps necessary to make steel; roll it flat into sheets; and galvanize, corrugate, and fabricate the sheets into a finished product. Today, Armco,

Inc., is a highly diversified company headquartered in Ohio. Employing 52,000 people, Armco is one of the nation's largest producers of steel, traditionally ranking third in the industry in assets, sales, and profits.

At the Armco plant in Butler, Pennsylvania, about 3,700 employees make the steels used in electrical equipment such as transformers, motors, and other devices that generate, distribute, and use electric power. This plant is now the world's largest producer of electrical steels; it also makes large quantities of stainless steel sheets and strips.

Throughout the data-processing structure at Armco, large computers, minicomputers, and microcomputers are used. More specifically, these systems include IBM, Four-Phase, Westinghouse, and Process Computer Systems (PCS)

hardware. The regional CPUs are located at Armco corporate headquarters in Middletown, Ohio. They consist of two IBM 3033 computers with disk and tape units. All general office and Butler regional applications are processed on this equipment. Butler jobs are handled by an IBM remote job-entry (RJE) terminal, and keypunch data is transmitted by a Four-Phase key-to-disk system with ten display-entry stations.

The data-processing center at Butler houses two IBM System/7 (S/7) minicomputers and one IBM Series 1 (S/1) minicomputer, which are tied to the regional equipment at Middletown. With this communication capability, the Butler plant can transfer any data it processes to the equipment at headquarters. All data-base activities are handled by a Modcomp 7870 machine. A communications attachment handles line traffic from approximately 100 data collection devices. The S/7 computers are strictly application machines that depend on the S/1 for handling communications and on the Modcomp machine for processing data. Figure 11–10 illustrates the hardware configuration for the Regional Computer Center and the Butler Plant. The minicomputers and attached disks handle the Butler Information Management System test and production systems, time-sharing option, and load applications development. Many other interactions exist within the cluster, and many more will be possible in the future.

The data-processing department at Butler presently has forty-one employees. Computerized data processing is used in the areas of payroll, cost accounting, production inventory control, metallurgical testing of customer shipments, forecasting of production requirements, and preparation of management information reports. Other applications include an automated shipping system that tracks shipping inventory and prints out necessary shipping documents, a personnel data system that keeps complete employment records of all employees, a badge reader and time-keeping system, and a maintenance job-order control system.

The data-processing department uses a structured approach to analyze business problems and to design,

program, and test solutions to these problems. All computer systems are developed through a defined project life cycle that consists of several steps starting with a system study and ending with the system's operating on a scheduled basis. The programming step lies about in the middle of the project, and structured programming techniques are used. The typical flow constructs are established. Coding rules for statements, comments, segmentation, indentation, and so on, are applied. In setting out the procedures they would follow, the EDP personnel chose the structured features they considered most applicable to their philosophy and discarded others. For instance, they do not use a librarian or detailed HIPO

diagrams. However, they have implemented the use of structure charts. PL/1 and Pascal are used in coding because of their structured qualities.

During the design steps of the project life cycle, every program in the system is identified. Then, before programming begins, these programs are grouped into units, each containing from one to five programs. The programs are developed through a process known as a unit development procedure. The project leader assigns a unit to a team member. Documentation developed during the design steps and a brief description by the project leader identify the programs in the unit and the functions they are to perform. The team member creates a

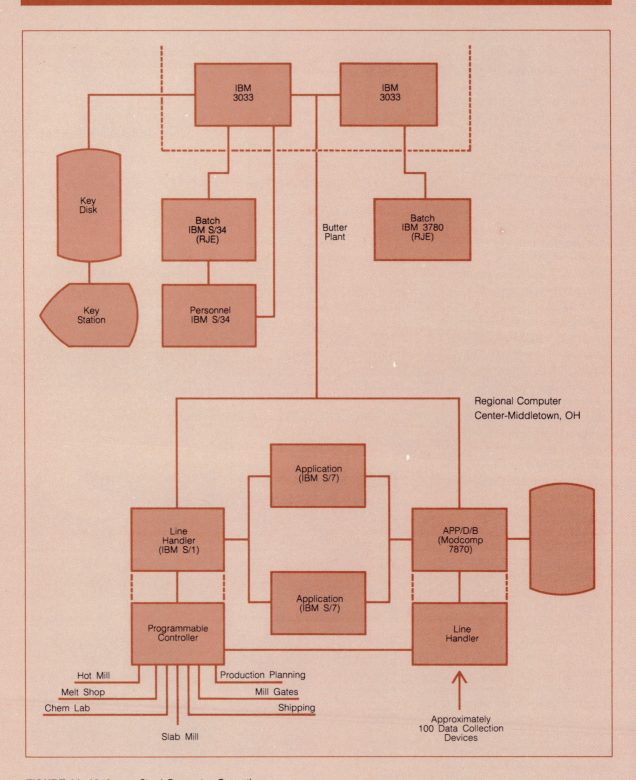

FIGURE 11–10 Armco Steel Computer Operations

unit development plan (UDP) to estimate the effort needed to develop that particular unit. The UDP clarifies early, and in writing, the specific functions that a program is to perform. It is valuable as a feedback mechanism to ensure that the team member understands the function to be performed. Errors are frequently detected during review of the UDP, before any code has been written. The UDP also provides a means of scheduling checkpoints with the program user, thus promoting user involvement with project development.

As stated, the UDP is initiated by a brief and general written assignment statement from the project leader to a team member. The assignment statement includes a definition of the task, recommendations for establishing its interface with other tasks, and a target completion date. It also includes recommendations regarding procedures such as edits, timing, and important tests (see Figure 11–11).

When the team member receives the assignment statement, he or she sets up a schedule of subtargets and prepares the unit development plan. Three standard items must be included in the UDP:

● Data definition list and flow plan: The definition list is an itemization of all input and output. The flow plan specifies the flows needed, the approach to be used on them (structured, top-down, or the like), and an estimate of the time needed to complete the flows.

● Coding and clean-compile estimates: These are estimates of the time needed to code the program, key in the code, and clean-compile the program

(eliminate all compiler-detected errors).

● Test and documentation plans: The test plan defines the editing needs and the test conditions that will be used to validate the program. It may

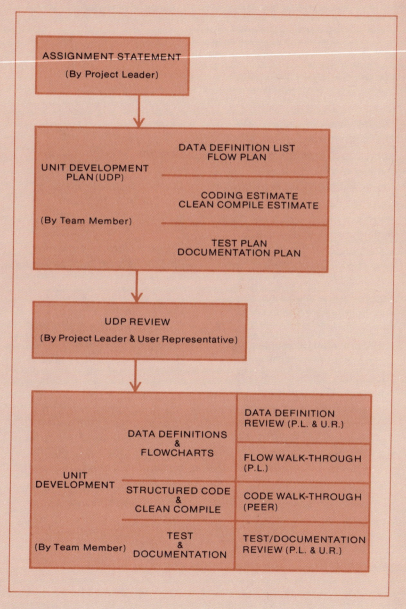

FIGURE 11–11 Relationship among Plan, Review, and Development Processes of Project

also include an estimate of the number of compilations and test runs anticipated. The documentation plan includes a list of documentation and training considerations.

Throughout the development of the UDP, the team members meet once a week to discuss their progress. After each UDP is completed, it is reviewed by the project leader and a user representative. At this time, the team member and project leader review the target dates that each has estimated. A final target date is assigned. The project leader and user representative can then either approve the UDP or meet with the team member to resolve any differences. The approved UDPs are then assembled, and the whole project plan is reviewed for approval. Upon approval, the team members begin the unit development effort.

Figure 11–11 illustrates the relationship of the UDP to the actual unit development. The development begins with establishment of data definitions and flow charts. Typical flow constructs have been established as standard:

● Every structure has one entrance and one exit.

● Every connector has two arrows going in and one arrow coming out.
● Every structure should have the potential of being compressed into one box.
● Each modular structure must be independent of other modular structures.

These initial steps end with a data definition review by the project leader and user representative and a flow walkthrough by the project leader.

The next step for the programmer is the actual program coding. Some structured-programming conventions have been established for use with PL/1:

● Every procedure must be a proper program, with one entry and one exit.
● No GO TO or RETURN statements are allowed.
● There must be only one statement per line and only one data characteristic (attribute) per line.

The code is keypunched, compiled, and then reviewed by the programmer and another team member. Next, the program is validated with data that tests its conditions and editing needs; finally, it is

documented. Both the test and the documentation are reviewed by the project leader and user representative.

Armco's Butler plant is committed to the structured approach because of the many benefits derived from it. The major benefit relates to planning and organizing projects. The modular approach and the weekly team reviews have led to a tremendous reduction in errors. For example, one of the projects included fifty programs and, after implementation, was found to have only two errors. Furthermore, the discussions of logic flow among team members aid greatly in any follow-up and documentation.

DISCUSSION POINTS

1. What specific benefits have Armco's Butler plant personnel found in the structured approach? What are some of its other advantages?
2. In what stages of the programming process does this group use the structured approach? Do you think that might be typical of many businesses or unique to this one?

SECTION IV
Systems

CHAPTER 12

The System Approach to System Analysis

Introduction

In computer-based information systems, the hardware and software technologies discussed in earlier chapters are applied as tools for the collection, storage, and retrieval of information helpful to management (such as sales analysis, investment analysis) or otherwise required for routine business procedures (such as payroll, income tax). It is necessary to understand these technologies in order to effectively use them in management information systems.

This chapter focuses on the application of these technologies to the development of computer-based information systems. The chapter discusses the importance of understanding the concept of a system and of using the system approach to problem solving. It provides an overview of the three phases required to develop a new system—analysis, design, and implementation. System analysis, the evaluation of current procedures and operations of an organization to enhance understanding and determine critical problem areas, is discussed in detail. System design and implementation are discussed in Chapter 13.

66 New Sandwich Computer Hams It Up for Inventors 99

BOSTON (AP)—Rushed at lunchtime? Hate to stand in long lines to tell someone to hold the mayo? Some Massachusetts men have an answer—a computerized sandwich.

Press a few buttons and presto! In seven seconds, you're holding a submarine bulging with roast beef, ham or chicken and your choice of lettuce, onion, pickles, tomato, peppers and mushrooms.

The sleek submarine-

Austin American Statesman (AP), Aug. 10, 1981, p. A8. Reprinted with permission from Associated Press.

sandwich maker has been christened the "Compuserve 2000" by its creators, Robert Hanson, 25, and Edward Lewis, 29, of Tewksbury, Donald Olson, 26, of Millis, and Daniel Miller, 24, of North Andover.

The four, two of whom have engineering backgrounds, worked on the computer in their spare time for 15 months, foraging for parts in electrical supply shops and devising their own pieces.

They spent $4,800 to build the machine, which is 47 inches long, 33 inches wide, 42 inches tall and looks like an office copier.

Now they're trying to find a market for it.

"This is the start of the revolutionizing of the food industry," said Hanson. "All fast

food today depends on making it in food warmers. . . . With this machine, the customer is going to get exactly what he wants, and it's going to be fresh."

The sub-machine was conceived when Hanson, who works as a technician at a laser optics firm, was brainstorming for ventures that would eventually make him his own boss. He became interested in opening a submarine sandwich shop, but he wanted to be able to compete with the big fast-food chains.

The computer's small, square buttons bear the neatly etched names of the ingredients stored in cassettes inside: roast beef, chicken, etc. Digital numbers show how many portions are left.

This computerized "cook" is a combination of many hours of planning and many varieties of cold cuts. The inventors had to consider the many factors involved in a fast food system. In business applications, many factors must be considered in the analysis phase of the system methodology.

INTRODUCTION TO INFORMATION SYSTEMS

Information is data that has been processed and is useful in decision making. It helps decision makers by increasing knowledge and reducing uncertainty. Modern businesses cannot be run without information; it is the lifeblood of an organization.

Information Channels

An example of the information flow in a small, growing business partnership may help to illustrate the concept of information channels. The Centron Company is an organization that markets labels and labeling equipment on a national scale. Centron was started by Greg (the president) and Bruce (the vice-president), who originally employed two sales people and a secretary.

At first, Greg made all management decisions—he knew everything that was going on within the company, because he had to know. He kept track of all sales and knew every account that was past due, everyone's salary, and all Centron's suppliers and how much was owed each one.

Information required by Centron flowed to and from Greg, since he participated in every decision. As Greg became more familiar with his information requirements, he began to request reports containing the information he used most often. His employees, anticipating these requests, began to produce some reports regularly. Greg began to refer to these reports for information rather than bother his employees. The reports became the formal information channels for Centron, and the information they contained was assumed to be correct, accurate, and timely. The reports were used as the basis for making important business decisions.

Sales increased rapidly and the company expanded. New salespersons were hired to sell in new markets. A printing press was purchased, and a production department was formed. An artist was employed to design labels to the needs of customers. Part-time secretaries were hired to help keep pace with the added business correspondence. Bruce, the vice-president, was given more managerial responsibility.

Centron's growth resulted in an increased quantity and variety of information. Greg could no longer participate in every decision. Out of necessity, he became less involved with each individual transaction and more involved with managing his employees and his business.

New and old employees alike encountered problems in determining who to contact about decisions in their areas. When employees postponed making decisions until they could reach the right persons, sales were sometimes lost. New employees did not know they were expected to provide the data required to produce good information. When decisions were made based on inaccurate information in reports, revenue was often lost.

Variety of Information Needs

These information problems could not be solved by providing all of Centron's new decision-makers with all of the information formerly provided to Greg. Different managers have different information needs; information useless to one may be invaluable to another.

A production manager needs information that helps in planning production: Scheduled production should not exceed the capacity of the factory. Raw materials must be available to the production process. The mix of work must be planned carefully and jobs assigned to the proper machines and workers.

The sales manager, on the other hand, needs to evaluate the performance of each salesperson as well as the sales of each product: He or she needs information from customers concerning future purchase plans, degree of satisfaction, and suggestions for product or service improvement.

Not only do the information needs of managers vary, but the same manager may require different information over time as conditions change. In our example, Greg required all information when the business was first es-

tablished. As the company grew, the systems developed to meet his information needs became inadequate. Greg began to require more general and summarized information that could be used for planning, control, and strategic decision making.

As formal information channels became inadequate, Centron employees began to develop informal channels of communication through trial and error. They made phone calls to obtain information not provided on reports; they circulated memos to meet information needs that could better have been served by formal reports. In short, informal information channels developed where information needs arose.

Centron had quite a problem adjusting to its rapid growth, and much of that problem was caused by inadequate information system channels' hindering information flow. The need for new information channels was painfully felt. The future success of Centron will depend in part on its ability to respond to the changing information needs of its decision makers.

Modeling Reality: The System Approach

A business is too complex to study directly. A system analyst needs tools to help analyze the complex information flows that affect it. Just as the person who cannot see the forest for the trees needs to take a few steps backwards, the analyst needs a tool to help remove the complexities of information systems in order to better understand and evaluate them.

The system approach to system analysis is one such tool. It is a model that aids in the analysis of information systems by attempting to mirror events in the real world while reducing the complexity of the activities involved in those events. The systems model highlights important factors, patterns, and flows. Instead of accurately representing each tree in the forest, the model shows the overall pattern of the trees, their outline in the forest, and the countryside bordering its edges.

SYSTEM THEORY

Definition of a System

The system approach is based upon system theory. System theory defines a *system* as a group of related elements that work together toward a common goal. One example of a system is a single cell in a human body; each molecule in the cell performs important functions and all these molecules work together in order for the cell to survive.

A system is made up of inputs, processes, and outputs. *Inputs* enter the system from the surrounding environment. In the cell, the inputs might be oxygen and nutrients. These inputs are transformed by some *process* into outputs. The cell processes its inputs into energy and wastes. Most of the *outputs* leave the system, going to the environment; but some may stay within the system. The energy output from cell processing is kept for survival. Wastes are returned to the environment.

Feedback is another important concept in system theory; it can take the form of either internal or external communication. That is, information can flow within the system's internal environment or between the system and the outside. Its purpose is to inform the system whether or not predetermined standards are being met. The feedback for a cell is whether it has what it needs to survive. If the cell does not have enough, it tries to get more. If an attack from the outside threatens, the cell alters its chemistry to deter it.

The System's Interaction with Other Systems

The body contains many different types of cells—blood cells, nerve cells, lung cells, and so on. Each of these groups can be thought of as a system—blood cells are part of the circulatory system, nerve cells are part of the nervous system, lung cells are part of the respiratory system. These systems, in turn, collectively form a still larger system called a human body. Each of the systems can be viewed in terms of its inputs, processes, outputs, and feedback mechanisms.

The boundaries between systems are not always easy to define. Neither are the elements of a system that might stand alone as systems in themselves. The determination depends on the level or scope at which one views the system. A doctor who is a general practitioner views the body as the system; an opthalmologist views the eye as the system.

The fact that one system may belong to another, larger one is an important concept in system theory. It implies the existence of interaction among systems. All of these concepts are put to good use when system theory is used to view the organization.

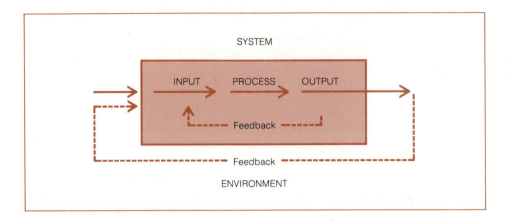

The Organization as a System

The concepts of system theory can be applied to a business firm. It has a group of related elements (departments or employees) working together towards a common goal (survival and profit). Figure 12–1 shows the firm using inputs from the surrounding environment to create outputs through a transformation process. Figure 12–2 shows a business firm (Centron) as a

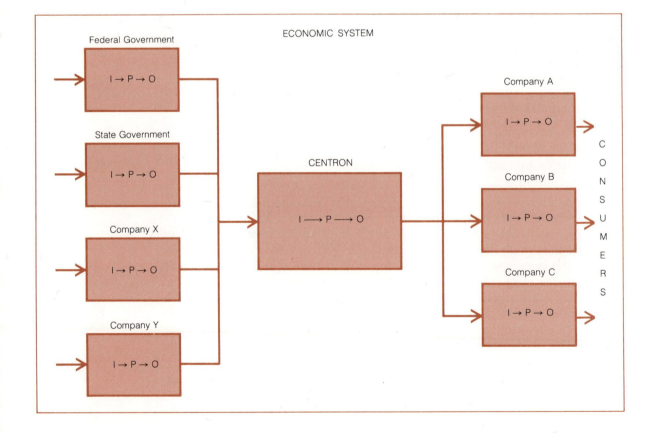

system within a larger one—the economic system of today's business world.

As Figure 12–2 shows, Centron is affected by external environmental factors outside its control. Government regulations, competition, and the economy are examples of such external factors. Internal factors affecting Centron include the quality of its managers, its management/labor relations, its departmental relationships, and its internal communication channels. An analysis of Centron's information needs must take into account both its internal and external environmental factors.

Each department within Centron can also be thought of as a system. A planner in the production department (a system) needs information about forecast sales from the sales department (another system). In making sales forecasts, the sales department probably uses past history and information from its own salespersons (internal environment) as well as stated customer intentions and projected economic conditions (external environment). Information about the availability of raw materials is provided by the purchasing department, which communicates with suppliers. The list of interactions goes on and on (see Figure 12–3).

FIGURE 12–3
The Company as a System

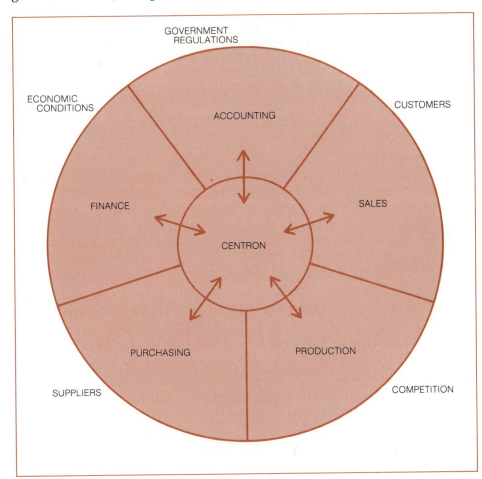

SYSTEM METHODOLOGY

An information system is designed to satisfy the needs of decision makers. Some information systems are computerized; others are manual. Both must provide management with the information it needs or they will become unused and outdated as informal systems arise. However, even when there are reasons to review an existing system, it does not necessarily follow that a new system should be developed. Revising an information system may cost hundreds or even millions of dollars. It is a complex and time-consuming process. The decision to revise a system should be based on need. Developing a system involves three steps—analysis, design, and implementation (see Figure 12–4). The goal of the first step, system analysis, is to determine whether or not need exists.

System Analysis

System analysis will be discussed in detail in a later section. The first step, however, is to formulate a statement of overall business objectives, the goals of the system (the big picture). Identifying these objectives is essential to the identification of information the system will require. The next step is for the analyst to acquire a general understanding of the scope of the analysis. What system level is being analyzed? This scope should be agreed on with

FIGURE 12–4
System Methodology

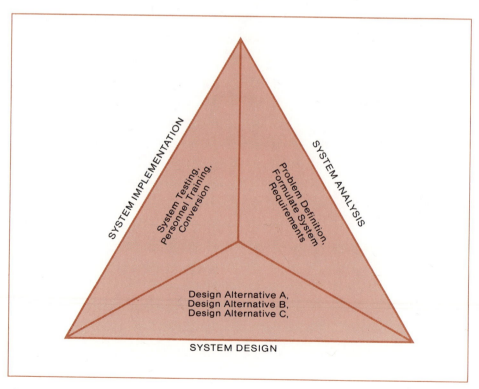

management and reviewed in the form of a proposal to conduct system analysis. The salient points of the proposal should include:

- A clear and concise statement of the problem, or reason for the system analysis.
- A statement delineating the scope of the system analysis and its objectives.
- An identification of the information that must be collected and the potential sources for this information.
- A preliminary schedule for conducting the analysis.

The proposal ensures that management knows what resources will be required during the system analysis and also helps the system user to be sure the analyst has identified the problem correctly and understands what the analysis should accomplish. Because system analysis is costly and time consuming, the scope should be clarified in this way before the analysis continues.

Once the proposal has been accepted, the analysis can proceed. Data relevant to decision makers' information needs is gathered and analyzed. When the analysis is completed, the analyst communicates the findings to management in the *system analysis report*. On the basis of this report, management decides whether or not to continue with the next step in system development—system design.

System Design

System design is concerned with formulating information channels to achieve the objectives identified during the analysis phase. While the emphasis during system analysis is on what *is* being done and why, in system design the emphasis shifts to how things *should* be done to meet the newly verified system requirements. Translating the information requirements identified during system analysis into a feasible and detailed design plan requires originality and creativity.

A problem often encountered by the analyst considering design alternatives is that of conflicting objectives within the organization. For example, the shipping department may want additional trucks to improve delivery service, but the finance department may be unwilling to make the additional capital investment. The overall goals of the organization must be the determining factor in the resolution of conflicting objectives.

The design process consists of the following steps:

● Reviewing the verified system goals and objectives.
● Developing a conceptual model of the system.
● Evaluating the organizational constraints.
● Developing alternative design proposals to meet the requirements.
● Preparing a *cost/benefit analysis* for each alternative.
● Recommending the most appropriate alternative and offering a plan for implementation of that alternative.

Each of these steps is discussed in detail in the next chapter.

The presentation of alternative designs, in conjunction with a recommendation and a project plan for system implementation, officially terminates the design phase.

System Implementation

The final phase in the development and operation of new or revised systems is *system implementation,* which involves the following activities:

● Programming.
● Personnel training.
● Testing.
● Conversion.

The goal of system implementation is to ensure that the system is completely debugged and operational and is acceptable to its users. These steps are discussed more fully in the next chapter.

SYSTEM ANALYSIS

Scope of System Analysis

System analysis is performed for various reasons, and the reason for the analysis determines its scope, or magnitude. Gathering and analysis of data occur at differing levels of intensity, depending upon the scope. System analysis may be required because of a need to solve a problem, respond to new information requirements, incorporate new technology into a system, or make broad system improvements. Each of these reasons is discussed below.

Solving a Problem Sometimes information systems do not function properly and thus require adjustment. Perhaps a particular manager is not getting a report at the time when it is needed. Or an insufficient number of copies of a certain report may be printed. Or the information a report provides may be incorrect.

In attempting to solve such a problem, the analyst may find that the effort snowballs into a broad system improvement; one problem may lead to another, which leads to another, and so on. Analysts must use discretion and discipline in solving the problem at hand. This is another of the main reasons for determining the scope of the system analysis at the outset of the project, as described earlier.

Responding to New Requirements Information systems should be designed to be flexible, so that changes can be made without much trouble. Unfortunately, it is often difficult to anticipate future information needs. New requirements more often than not cause change, which in turn requires a new system analysis. For example, oil companies have experienced a series of changes in government regulations in recent years. Passage of the windfall profits tax followed by the earlier-than-expected deregulation of domestic oil prices created instant headaches for the companies and instant projects for system analysts. Information systems, especially for the accounting departments, had to be updated very rapidly in order to comply with new laws.

Another area in which government regulations have affected business information systems is personnel. Regulations governing hiring and firing practices are constantly changing. Privacy is another area; more and more information must be kept confidential with each passing year.

New requirements also originate from nongovernment sources. A company may add a new product line, requiring a whole new series of reports. A new labor agreement may require new benefits and new deductions or a different way of paying overtime or calculating base pay.

Implementing New Technology The introduction of new data-processing technology can cause major changes in information systems. Chapter 2 highlights some of the changes that have occurred. Many companies started with punched-card, batch-processing environments. When magnetic tape became available, larger files could be processed and more information could be stored. The introduction of magnetic-disk technology opened up direct-access processing, causing many information systems to change drastically in the late 1960s. New input devices such as visual display terminals began to replace paper forms and punched cards for data entry.

In banking alone, the introduction of MICR technology (magnetic ink character recognition—see Chapter 4) eliminated thousands of bookkeeping jobs because it allowed electronic posting of entries to accounts instead of manual posting. In grocery stores and other retail stores, bar-code readers and optical-character readers are being combined with point-of-sale devices to dramatically change internal accounting and checkout procedures. The list goes on and on. Changes in data-processing technology often lead to changes in information systems.

Making Broad System Improvements   There may be times when an organization wants to update its entire information system, perhaps because of an increase in its size or sales volume or a competitive incentive to operate as efficiently and effectively as possible.

One example of a broad system improvement is the introduction and use of online ticketing by major airlines. As soon as the first company converted to this new method, other airlines had to follow suit to remain competitive. The new method forced changes in the airlines' entire accounting and reservation systems.

Numerous companies discovered their information systems were out of date during the boom years of the 1950s and 1960s. Some growth was natural, but much was due to mergers and acquisitions. Many companies found that it was advantageous to update their entire information systems rather than to just keep patching them.

A broad system improvement normally requires an extensive system analysis, because it has a very broad scope.

Data Gathering

After the proposal to conduct system analysys has been accepted, the analyst sets out to gather data. The type and amount of data gathered depend upon the scope and goal of the system analysis. Data can be supplied by internal and external sources.

Internal Sources   Four common sources of internal information are interviews, system flowcharts, questionnaires, and formal reports.

Interviews.   Personal interviews can be a very important source of data. Preliminary interviews provide data about current operations and procedures and the users' perception of what the system should do. The analyst must be diplomatic, yet probing. Often the analyst discovers informal information in the form of reports, personal notes, and phone numbers that indicate how the current information system really works. Unless interviews are conducted, these "extras" might never appear. Follow-up interviews and discussion sessions provide checkpoints to verify the accuracy and completeness of the procedures and documentation within the system.

System Flowcharts.   Given the documents that provide the system input, the processing steps needed are illustrated in *system flowcharts*. The devices and files used, the resulting output, and the departments that use the output are identified. (System flowcharts are discussed in detail later in this chapter.)

Questionnaires. Questionnaires are used to collect more details about system operations. By keying questions to specific steps in a system chart, the analyst can obtain detailed data on the volume of input and output. The frequency of processing, the time required for various processing steps, and the personnel and equipment used can also be identified.

Questionnaires are only useful if they are properly constructed. Further, the analyst must be careful to indicate who fills out which form; a manager might respond differently than an employee. The analyst must also be sure to follow up if a questionnaire is not returned.

Formal Reports. Formal reports, the major outputs of many systems, should be studied carefully by the analyst. The processing steps taken to convert data to information are usually apparent from these reports. The number of copies made and who receives them helps to identify the flow of information within the organization. How and where a report is stored may indicate the degree of sensitivity and importance of the information it contains. With the advent of inexpensive paper copiers, the task of determining all users of a particular report may be extremely difficult; the ease with which copies can be made is not always an advantage in this case.

External Sources System analysts should (within budgetary constraints) leave no stones unturned during the data-gathering stage. External sources of information can be very helpful. Standard sources are books, periodicals, brochures, and product specifications from manufacturers. Customers and suppliers are sometimes good sources. For example, analyzing an accounts receivable system might involve asking customers what information they would like to see on an invoice. Analysts should also attempt to contact other companies that have developed or implemented similar information systems.

Data Analysis

After data has been collected, it must be organized and integrated to be seen in proper perspective. Whereas the focus during data collection is on *what* is being done, the focus during data analysis is on *why* certain operations and procedures are being used. The analyst looks for ways to improve these operations.

Information Needs A study should be made early to determine what information the user needs. This will have a great impact later when input/output requirements are being determined.

Determining information needs requires that the analyst use a system approach. In a magnetic-tape-oriented, file-processing environment, it is relatively easy to create and manipulate files. But many companies are rapidly moving into data-base environments. Creating and maintaining an effective data base requires that data items be independent. This means that the data must be analyzed and organized from a corporate-wide perspective. No longer can a file be created just for the production department; data must be accessible to many other departments as well. The trick is to properly relate each data item to all other data items, ignoring departmental boundaries.

Some of the techniques used to analyze data are grid charts, system flowcharts, and decision logic tables. These techniques are explained below. This list is not all-inclusive, however. Analysts should use whatever tools and techniques they can devise to evaluate the gathered data.

Grid Charts   The tabular, or grid, chart is employed to summarize the relationships among the components of a system. Figure 12–5 is a grid chart indicating which departments use which documents of an order-writing, billing, and inventory-control system.

A special type of grid chart is an I/O chart, which shows the relationships between system inputs and outputs (see Figure 12–6). The input documents are listed in the rows on the left; the output reports, in the columns on the right. If a particular document is used in the preparation of an output report, an X is placed at the intersection of the appropriate row and column. These charts help the analyst to identify subsystems—parts of the system that may be relatively independent.

System Flowcharts   As we saw in Chapter 8, program flowcharts are concerned with operations on data. They do not indicate the form of input (for example, terminal keyboard, cards, or tape) or the form of output (for example, display, document, disk, or tape); they simply use a general input/output symbol ($\boxed{}$) for all forms.

In contrast, *system flowcharts* emphasize the flow of data through the entire data-processing system, without describing details of internal computer op-

FIGURE 12–5

A Grid Chart

Document \ Department	Order Writing	Shipping	Billing	Inventory	Marketing	Accounts Receivable
Sales Order	X				X	
Shipping Order	X	X	X	X		
Invoice			X		X	X
Credit Authorization					X	X
Monthly Report					X	X

_____ of _____ sheets						DATA ANALYSIS SHEET			AREA: *TITLE VII*						
INPUT						ELEMENTS OF DATA			OUTPUT						
DOC. NAME INPUT/OUTPUT DATA	Form I	Form 3A	Form 3B	Form 4	Referral	CLASS OF DATA　　CODE FIXED ELEMENTS　IDENTIFYING　　I　QUANTITATIVE　　Q VARIABLE ELEMENTS			Form 2	Form 5	Form 6	Form 7	Form 8	Form 9	
C O D E						REPORTED　　　　R									
V O L GEN FLOW REF						GENERATED　　　G CONSTANTS　　　C									
F R E Q						DATA CODE	DESCRIPTION	NR CHAR	A/N	DEC					
	X						DATE/INITIAL PARTICIPATION								
	X		X	X	X		NAME				X	X			
	X			X			SOCIAL SECURITY NUMBER								
	X		X	X			ADDRESS				X	X			
	X						DATE OF BIRTH								
	X			X			RACE								
	X		X	X			SEX								
	X				X		PHONE NUMBER								
	X		X				MEANS OF TRANSPORTATION				X				
	X		X				DOCTOR								
	X		X				DOCTOR'S PHONE NUMBER								
	X						EMERGENCY CONTACT								
	X						EMERGENCY PHONE NUMBER								
	X						PHYSICAL HANDICAP								
							WEEKLY CALENDER TRANSPORTATION				X	X			

FIGURE 12–6　I/O Chart

erations. A system flowchart represents the interrelationships among various system elements.

The general input/output symbol used in program flowcharting is not specific enough for system flowcharting. A variety of specialized input/output symbols are needed to identify the wide variety of media used in input/output activities. The symbols are miniature outlines of the actual media (see Figure 12–7).

Similarly, specialized process symbols are used instead of the general process symbol ( ) to represent specific processing operations. For example, a trapezoid is used to indicate a manual process such as key-to-tape data entry (see Figure 12–8).

The difference in emphasis in the two forms of flowcharting is due to the difference in the purposes they serve. A program flowchart aids the programmer in writing a source program by specifying the details of operations so that the programmer can code the steps more easily. In contrast, system flowcharts are designed to represent the general information flow; they often represent many operations within one process symbol.

Figure 12–9 is a sample system flowchart that shows the updating of an inventory master file. The *online storage symbol* ( ) indicates that the file is kept on an online external storage medium such as disk or tape. The file is used to keep track of the raw materials and finished products of the or-

FIGURE 12–7
Specialized Input/
Output
Symbols for System
Flowcharting

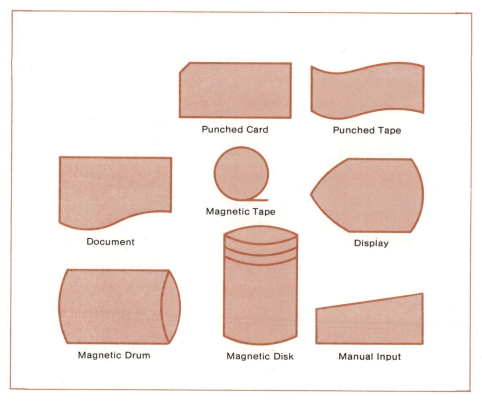

Punched Card

Punched Tape

Magnetic Tape

Document

Display

Magnetic Drum

Magnetic Disk

Manual Input

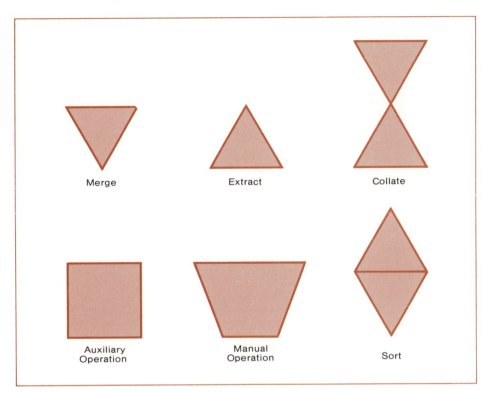

FIGURE 12–8
Specialized Process
Symbols
for System
Flowcharting

Merge

Extract

Collate

Auxiliary
Operation

Manual
Operation

Sort

ganization. How current this information is depends on how often the master file is updated. If it is updated as soon as a product is shipped or a raw material supply depleted, then the information it provides is up-to-date. Usually, however, the updating is done on a periodic basis. All changes that occur during a specific time period are batched and then processed together to update the inventory master file. Reports from the shipping, receiving, and production departments are collected. The data from this set of documents is transferred onto cards. These cards and the inventory master file then serve as input for the updating process.

The flowchart in Figure 12–9 outlines the steps in this process. In addition to updating the inventory master file, the system generates three reports, which give management information about inventory, order shipments, and production. Notice that in the system flowchart, one process symbol encompasses the entire updating process. A program flowchart must be created to detail the specific operations to be performed within this process.

Decision Logic Tables   A *decision logic table (DLT)* is a tabular representation of the actions to be taken under various sets of conditions. Thus, the decision table expresses the logic for arriving at a particular decision under a given set of circumstances. The structure within the table is based on the proposition "if this condition is met then do this."

The basic elements of a decision logic table are shown in Figure 12–10.

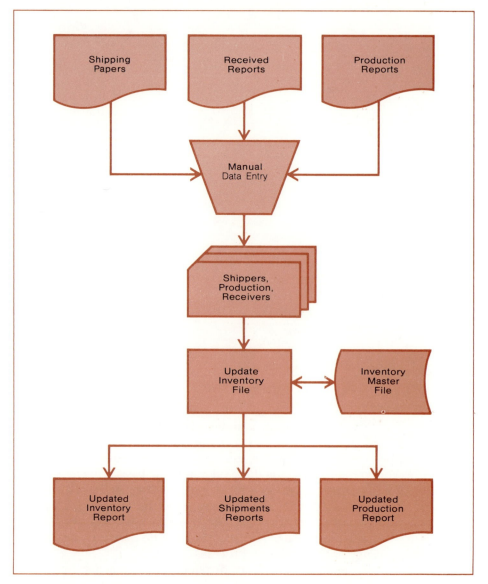

FIGURE 12–9

Sample System
Flowchart

The upper half lists conditions to be met, and the lower half shows actions to be taken. That is, the *condition stub* describes the various conditions; the *action stub* describes the possible actions. *Condition entries* are made in the top right section. *Action entries* are made in the bottom right section.

A decision table is not needed when conditions can be communicated and understood easily. However, where multiple conditions exist, a decision table serves as a valuable tool in analyzing the decision logic involved. Figure 12–11 shows a decision table for selecting applicants for an assembly-line job.

The rules for selecting applicants are based on the age, education, and

FIGURE 12–10
Decision Logic Table

HEADING	RULE NUMBERS							
	1	2	3	4	5	6	7	8
CONDITION STUB	CONDITION ENTRIES							
ACTION STUB	ACTION ENTRIES							

experience of the candidates. The applicants must be at least eighteen years of age to be considered for the position. They must have at least a high school education or a year's experience to be interviewed for further evaluation. They are hired directly if they meet both requirements. The Ys in the table mean yes, the Ns mean no, and the Xs indicate what actions are to be taken. The decision table is read as follows:

● *Rule 1:* If the applicant's age is less than eighteen years, then reject him or her.
● *Rule 2:* If the applicant is at least eighteen years old but has no high school education and less than one year's experience, then reject him or her.
● *Rule 3:* If the applicant is at least eighteen years old, has no high school education, but has experience of more than one year, then call him or her for an interview. Once a candidate has been selected for an interview, another decision table may be needed to evaluate the interview.

FIGURE 12–11
Decision Logic Table
for Selecting
Applicants

SELECTING APPLICANTS		RULES				
		1	2	3	4	5
CONDITIONS	AGE < 18 YEARS?	Y	N	N	N	N
	HIGH SCHOOL EDUCATION?		N	N	Y	Y
	EXPERIENCE > 1 YEAR?		N	Y	N	Y
ACTIONS	REJECT	X	X			
	INTERVIEW			X	X	
	HIRE					X

● *Rule 4:* If the applicant is at least eighteen years old, has a high school education, but has less than one year's experience, then call him or her for an interview. Again, another decision table might be used to evaluate the interview.

● *Rule 5:* If the applicant is at least eighteen years old, has a high school education, and has more than one year's experience, then hire him or her.

A more detailed decision logic table is shown in Figure 12–12. The first step in constructing such a table is to determine what conditions must be considered. In this case, these conditions are: (1) Is the customer's credit rating AAA? (2) Is the quantity ordered above or equal to the minimum quantity for a discount? (3) Is there enough stock on hand to fill the order? The conditions are listed in the condition stub section of the decision table.

The next step is to determine what actions can take place. These are: Either (1) bill at a discount price or (2) bill at a regular price; and either (3) ship the total quantity ordered or (4) ship a partial order and back-order the rest. These possibilities go in the action stub.

Once the conditions and possible courses of action have been identified, the conditions can be related to corresponding action entries to indicate the appropriate decision. Thus, Rule 4 could be interpreted as follows: "If the customer has a credit rating of AAA and the quantity ordered is equal to or above the minimum discount quantity and there is enough stock on hand, then the customer is to be billed at the discount price and the total order is to be shipped."

Decision tables present logic in a summarized form that is easy to understand. They are used to record facts collected during the investigation of the

FIGURE 12–12

Decision Logic Table for Order Processing

ORDER PROCESSING	Rules							
	1	2	3	4	5	6	7	8
Credit Rating of AAA	Y	Y	Y	Y	N	N	N	N
Quantity Order >= Minimum Discount Quantity	Y	N	N	Y	Y	N	Y	N
Quantity Ordered <= Stock on Hand	N	Y	N	Y	N	Y	Y	N
Bill at Discount Price	X			X				
Bill at Regular Price		X	X		X	X	X	X
Ship Total Quantity Ordered		X		X		X	X	
Ship Partial and Back-Order Remaining Amount	X		X		X			X

old system and can also be used to summarize aspects of the new system. In the latter case, they guide programmers in writing programs for the new system.

System Analysis Report

After collecting and analyzing the data, the system analyst must communicate the findings to management. The *system analysis report* should include the following items:

- A restatement of the scope and objectives of the system analysis.
- An explanation of the present system, the procedures used, and any problems identified.
- A statement of all constraints on the present system and any assumptions made by the analyst during this phase.
- A preliminary report of alternatives that currently seem feasible.
- An estimate of the resources and capital required to either modify the present system or design a new one. This estimate should include costs of a feasibility study.

Only if management approves this report can the system analyst proceed to the detailed system design.

SUMMARY

● Information channels are the routes information takes within a company. Formal information channels are planned, created, and approved. Informal information channels usually develop as change begins to render formal channels obsolete.

● The system model highlights important factors, patterns, and flows within the organization. It is a tool often used to model reality.

● A system is a group of related elements that work together toward a common goal. Inputs are transformed by some process into outputs. Feedback provides information to the system about its internal and external environments.

● Most systems are collections of subsystems and are themselves subsystems in larger systems.

● A business is a system made up of subsystems (departments). It interacts with other systems (suppliers, customers, governments) and is also a subsystem in larger economic and political systems.

● Every system revision consists of three phases: analysis, design, and implementation. System analysis is an evaluation of the system processes undertaken to enhance understanding and determine problem areas. System design is the formulation of alternative solutions to solve problems uncovered in the analysis phase. System implementation involves making the design operational and insuring error-free operations and user acceptance.

● System analysis is conducted for any of four reasons: to solve a problem, to respond to a new requirement, to implement new technology, or to make broad system improvement.

● Problem solving is an attempt to correct or adjust a currently malfunctioning information system. The analyst must balance the desire to solve just the problem at hand with an attempt to get at the most fundamental causes of the problem. The latter could snowball into a major project.

● A new requirement is caused by either internal or external change. A typical example is a new law or a change in government regulations.

● New technology can force system analysis by making formerly infeasible alternatives feasible.

● The most comprehensive system analysis is conducted for a broad system improvement, which can be necessitated by rapid sales or rapid internal growth or by desire to redesign the present system.

● Data is gathered during system analysis from internal and external sources. Interviews are an excellent way of collecting data and often lead to unexpected discoveries. System flowcharts help the analyst to get a better understanding of how the components in a system interrelate. Questionnaires can be helpful, but they are sometimes difficult to design, administer, and interpret. Formal reports tell the analyst much about the present workings of the system.

● An analyst should also collect data from external sources, such as customers, suppliers, software vendors, hardware manufacturers, books, and periodicals.

● Data should be analyzed in any manner that helps the analyst understand the system. Grid charts, system flowcharts, and decision logic tables are three of the tools analysts use to accomplish this task.

● The final result of the system analysis stage is the system analysis report, a report to management reviewing the results of the analysis and the feasibility of proceeding with system design and implementation.

REVIEW QUESTIONS

1. Give an example of a system. Describe the subsystems within the system. What larger system does it belong to?

2. What four internal sources of data do analysts frequently use? Which one seems most effective?

3. Distinguish between system flowcharts and program flowcharts. What purposes does each serve?

4. What is system analysis, and why might a firm want to engage in it? Why might a firm decide not to analyze its present systems?

APPLICATION

The Kroger Company

In 1883, twenty-five-year-old Bernard H. (Barney) Kroger and his friend B. A. Branagan opened a small store in Cincinnati, Ohio, with $722 in capital. It was named "The Great Western Tea Company" and sold coffees, teas, sausages, staples, and chinaware. At the end of the first year, with assets amounting to $2,620, Kroger bought out the store and ran it by himself.

Ninety-four years later, in 1977, the Kroger Company was the sixth largest retailing company in the United States as ranked by total sales; and

Kroger Food Stores was the country's second largest supermarket chain, with 1,245 stores in twenty-one states. Most Kroger stores are "superstores" with sizes ranging from 25,000 to 45,000 square feet. These stores offer specialty and personal service departments such as delicatessens, bakeries, wine shops, and greeting-card departments.

Kroger also manufactures and processes food for sale by these supermarkets, a tradition that began before the turn of the century. The company operates eight regional bakeries and five dairies in addition to a sausage plant, a cheese plant, egg production facilities, egg grading and packing plants, a peanut butter plant, a candy plant, and a general processing plant.

The Kroger Company headquarters are in Cincinnati, Ohio, as are the data-

processing facilities that serve and support the corporate activities. The data-processing operation is concentrated in two main-frame computers at headquarters. Most transactions are transmitted to them by private leased lines connecting fifteen other marketing-area locations. Thirteen of these locations consist of an area headquarters, an area warehouse, and fifty to a hundred supermarkets. Each marketing-area location also has a data-processing staff. This configuration is illustrated in Figure 12–13.

The MIS Department at the Cincinnati headquarters provides services to most departments in the company, including merchandising and buying, warehousing, transportation, store operations, finance and accounting, manufacturing, personnel, and market research. Current applications in these

FIGURE 12–13
Kroger Company Data-Processing
Configuration

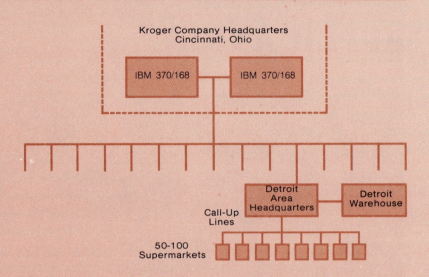

departments include order-entry and billing, inventory control, payroll, accounts payable, and accounting. The MIS Department has a staff of about 185 employees, 136 of them involved in system analysis and programming, the remaining 49 in operations, communications, and data entry.

Kroger has been an industry leader in the development and implementation of the electronic scanning operations that have flourished since the introduction of the Universal Product Code; 245 Kroger supermarkets have fully operational point-of-sale terminals, and their number is expected to reach 300 by the end of 1981.

DEVELOPMENT OF THE UNIVERSAL PRODUCT CODE SYSTEM

The idea of using product codes to facilitate automatic checkout counters has been around since the 1930s, but technology did not advance sufficiently to make it feasible until the 1960s. During that decade, there was much discussion throughout the food industry concerning the need for a nationally standardized unique identifier for each product. The question was how to get producers, packagers, distributors, and retailers to agree on a uniform coded symbol and how to integrate the

code with electronic data processing. An initial system study was conducted on an industry-wide scale for three basic reasons:

1. To solve a problem.
2. To take advantage of new technology.
3. To respond to new information-processing requirements that resulted from the rapid growth and increasing complexity of the industry.

What is remarkable about this particular system study is that competitors from all levels of the task environment combined their efforts to study a common problem and succeeded in formulating a common objective to solve it. At this level, the system study was very broad; but it illustrates some notable points: Kroger, a system in itself, is only one small subsystem within a larger system, the food industry. And all of the business firms in the

food industry system interact with one another in their pursuit of common goals—profit and growth.

Around 1968, John L. Strubbe of Kroger, one of the task force members for the study, began teaching electronics firms about the information-processing requirements of the grocery business so they could design scanning equipment to read a standard code. RCA pioneered in the development of an electronic scanning device, which was tested in a Kenwood, Ohio, Kroger store for fifteen months in 1971 and 1972. The Universal Product Code was chosen by the task force in 1971, and a council consisting of a broad spectrum of industry leaders was set up to govern policy. The consulting firm of McKinsey & Co. was hired to do the feasibility study, and their investigation concluded that the proposal was economically sound.

on the experiences of Kroger's pilot electronic scanning operations, which were launched in 1974. In computing the predicted return on investment, Kroger ignored intangible benefits, which were difficult, if not impossible, to quantify. Still, it was able to justify the system even without considering these "soft savings."

The first pilot store utilized IBM scanning equipment; and the second, which opened six months later, was equipped with Univac computers. Major phase-in operations began in 1978; and by the end of 1981, almost a quarter of all Kroger stores should be equipped with electronic scanning equipment. These stores communicate directly with their area headquarters, which in turn communicate with corporate headquarters.

KROGER'S SYSTEM ANALYSIS

Kroger had started individual system analysis around 1970. Specifically, its goals were to improve speed and accuracy at the customer input and to advance its inventory control capabilities. The analysis was conducted by the MIS Department in conjunction with Store Operating Services and Accounting Policy Methods and supported by all other departments. This was a pioneer effort for Kroger—never before had an MIS project included and affected every single working element in the entire organization.

The UPC council, a primary external source of information, provided written descriptions, flowcharts, and other documentation of how the system would function and what data it would need. Internal surveys, matrices, and existing documentation helped the Kroger group to determine general design requirements. It also monitored competitors' activities for further ideas.

In doing its feasibility study, Kroger concentrated on quantifiable benefits such as more customer traffic, increased accuracy, lower inventory costs, and higher sales. Many of the projected figures were based

DISCUSSION POINTS

1. System theory implies that elements of a system interact. Describe how a transaction at a new Kroger checkout counter will affect files within different departments in the organization.
2. Discuss some of the intangible costs and benefits Kroger chose not to analyze in its feasibility study.

CHAPTER 13

System Design and Implementation

Introduction

Formal information systems come into existence by careful planning, much effort, and considerable expense. Businesses must use some version of the system methodology approach to create such information systems. The last chapter provided an overview of system analysis, design, and implementation and a detailed discussion of system analysis techniques.

This chapter covers the system design and implementation phases in more depth. System design involves developing alternative models that satisfy the goals and objectives set out in the system analysis report. System implementation results when one of these designs is approved by management and incorporated into the business information systems.

"Army May Turn Video Games into War Games"

Bill Laberis

The young U.S. Army trooper maneuvered his camouflaged tank from behind the brush, locking the gunsight onto an enemy half-track rumbling some 150 meters ahead.

Aiming his round just a hair ahead of the slow-moving target, the trooper, holding his 20-ton tank at idle, squeezed off a shot that pierced the half-track's thin plating and blew apart the front end, sending thick orange and black smoke skyward.

Also up in smoke went about $3,500 U.S. tax dollars for this and countless other training sessions designed in part to teach recruits the hand/eye coordination needed to operate sophisticated ground weapons systems.

But all this may change, according to Capt. Gary Bishop, chief of plans and operations at Ft. Stewart here [Hinesville, Georgia].

"The cost of teaching the basics of coordination in handling today's weaponry has gone through the roof," Bishop said in a recent phone interview. "That's why we're going to give these computer games a good hard look. For training purposes, I really think

Computerworld, July 20, 1981, p. 25. Copyright 1981 by CW Communications/Inc., Farmingham, Mass., 01701—reprinted from Computerworld.

they might be the wave of the future."

Ordinary Video Games

The games Bishop referred to are the coin-operated, microprocessor-controlled video games he sees soldiers playing in the post's recreation rooms.

Bishop said he noticed the soldiers "are very big on the games," and he began to think there was more to them than strictly blasting martians and alien invaders.

"And then I began thinking about the possible cost effectiveness of using the games with some modifications as training tools," he said.

"After all, taking a tank out of the motor pool, driving it to the range and pumping rounds downrange just to teach the basics of hand and eye coordination and facility with the controls is a very expensive proposition."

Bishop presented the idea of using video games for training to the Army training board, and the board responded by initiating a feasibility study. No funding has yet been committed to any pilot project, however.

He has also requested that Ft. Stewart be used as a test site should the board move forward with plans for the video training.

Ironically, it may represent the first time that consumer technology percolates up to the military complex, instead of the usual case where weapons development technology filters down to the private sector.

"All I know is that if we can

get around some of the expense of field training while still training our people as well or even better, the Army's decision makers will probably go for it," he said. "These days, the important thing is that a plan be cost effective while still doing the job."

Real Tank Training

Tank training, as an example, requires a recruit to look into a field of vision, whether it is a video screen or a periscope down range, and then to maneuver a weapon system to lock on the target and fire, Bishop said.

"And from the standpoint of morale, video training is a great idea, aside from the fact that it helps develop the coordination we need to make these new weapon systems go like they were designed to," he added.

One game Bishop has examined closely is Atari Corp.'s Battlezone, which simulates tank combat in full crashing and exploding color. Bishop said it would be no great problem to outfit the game with more real-life tank controls and use it in place of some of the costly field training methods presently employed.

An Atari spokesman said the Army has yet to contact the company, adding, "We're not a defense contractor.

"But if they want to put on sophisticated controls once they buy the games, that is totally their business," Michael Fournell, director of public relations at Atari, said. "I guess the ball is now in their court."

This article demonstrates the use of a computer system for training purposes. Whether a system is used for simulation, or for solving real problems, careful planning, design, and implementation are necessary.

SYSTEM DESIGN

If, after reviewing the system analysis report, management decides to continue the project, the system design stage begins. Designing an information system demands a great deal of creativity and planning. It is also very costly and time consuming. In system analysis, the analyst has focused on what the current system does and on what it should be doing according to the requirements discovered in the analysis. In the design phase, the analyst changes focus and concentrates on how a system can be developed to meet the information requirements.

Several steps are useful during the design phase of system development:

- Review goals and objectives.
- Develop system model.
- Evaluate organizational constraints.
- Develop alternative designs.
- Perform feasibility analysis.
- Perform cost/benefit analysis.
- Prepare system design report and recommendation.

Review Goals and Objectives

The objectives of the new or revised system were identified during system analysis and stated in the system analysis report. Before the analyst can proceed with system design, these objectives must be reviewed, since any system design offered must conform to them.

In order to maintain a broad approach and flexibility in the system design phase, the analyst may restate users' information requirements so that they reflect the needs of the majority of users. For example, the finance department may want a report of customers who have been delinquent in payments. Since this department may be only one subsystem in a larger accounts-receivable system, the analyst may restate this requirement more generally. It might more appropriately be stated as (1) maintain an accurate and timely record of the amounts owed by customers, (2) provide control procedures that ensure detection of abnormal accounts and report them on an exception basis, and (3) provide, on a timely basis, information regarding accounts receivable to different levels of management to help achieve overall company goals.

A well-designed system can meet the current goals and objectives of the organization and adapt to changes within the organization. In discussions with managers, the analyst may be able to determine organizational trends that help to pinpoint which subsystems require more flexibility. For in-

stance, if the analyst is developing a system for an electric company, strong consideration should be given to providing flexibility in the reporting subsystem in order to respond to changing regulatory reporting requirements.

Develop System Model

The analyst next attempts to represent symbolically the system's major components to verify his or her understanding of the various components and their interactions. The analyst may use flowcharts to help in the development of a system model or may simply be creative in the use of diagrammatic representations.

In reviewing the model, the analyst refers to system theory to discover any possible omissions of important subsystems. Are the major interactions among subsystems shown? Are the inputs, processes, and outputs appropriately identified? Does the model provide for appropriate feedback to each of the subsystems? Are too many functions included within one subsystem?

Once a satisfactory system model has been developed, the analyst has an appropriate tool for evaluating alternative designs (discussed later in this section). Each alternative can be evaluated on the basis of how well it matches the requirements of the model. Figure 13–1 is an example of a conceptual model of an accounts-receivable system.

Evaluate Organizational Constraints

No organization has unlimited resources; most have limitations on financial budgets, personnel, and computer facilities and time constraints for system development. The system analyst must recognize the contraints on system design imposed by this limited availability of resources.

Few organizations request the optimal design for their information requirements. Businesses are profit-seeking organizations. Only in extremely rare cases does an organization request an all-out system development with

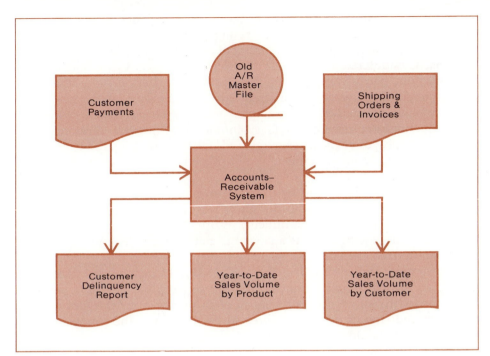

FIGURE 13–1

Model of an Accounts-Receivable System

no cost constraints. (Competition or technological developments, for example, may make such an uncharacteristic decision mandatory.)

The structure of the organization also affects subsequent designs developed by the analyst. A highly centralized management may reject a proposal for distributed processing. Similarly, an organization with geographically dispersed, highly autonomous decision centers may find designs that require routing reports through the central office unsatisfactory.

Before proceeding with system design, the analyst must be fully aware of these organizational constraints and critically evaluate their impact on the system design.

Develop Alternative Designs

Systems can be either simple or complex. Simple systems require simple controls to keep processes working properly. Complex systems, on the other hand, require complex controls. A business is a complex system; it requires vast numbers of interactions among its many interrelated subsystems. It naturally follows that information systems developed for business use must be complex, since they model the actual business.

There is more than one way to design a complex information system, and system analysts are generally required to develop more than one design alternative. This requirement is useful because it forces the analyst to be creative. By designing several possible systems, the analyst may discover valuable parts in each that can be integrated into an entirely new system. The alternative systems may also be designed in ascending order of complexity and cost; since management often desires alternatives from which to choose, designing alternative systems in this fashion is quite appropriate.

The analyst must work with a number of elements in designing alternative systems. Computerized information systems have many components. Inputs, outputs, hardware, software, files, data bases, clerical procedures, and users interact in hundreds of different ways. Processing requirements also differ in each alternative. For example, one may require batch processing and sequential organization of files; another may provide random-access processing using direct-access storage and online terminals. The data collection, processing, storage, retrieval, and update procedures vary, depending on the alternative selected.

Each alternative developed by the analyst must be technically feasible. In some instances, analysts try to design at least one noncomputerized alternative. Although this may be difficult, it often reveals unique methods of information processing that the analyst has not considered when developing the computerized systems.

In designing each alternative, the analyst should include tentative input forms, the structures and formats of output reports, the program specifications needed to guide programmers in code preparation, the files or data base required, the clerical procedures to be used, and the process-control measures that should be instituted.

With the increasing use of online systems, the input forms are often input screens. These screens must be designed in as much detail as their hard-copy counterparts. The analyst, in consultation with those who will be inputting the data, must design each screen to maximize efficiency in data input. The screen format must be easy for users to view and understand (see Figure 13–2).

Output reports must be designed so that users can quickly and easily view the information they require. The analyst often prepares mock-up reports that approximate how the actual computer-generated report will look (see Figure 13–3). Most contain sample data. It is easier for users to relate their needs to such sample reports than to discuss them in abstract form with the analyst in an interview. Mock-up reports also allow the analyst to verify once again his or her understanding of what is required of the system.

Once the input forms or screens and output reports have been designed, a detailed set of programming specifications for each alternative must be prepared. The analyst must determine what processing is to occur in each of the system designs. He or she often works in conjunction with the programming staff to determine these requirements and to develop cost estimates for program coding.

File and data-base specification is particularly important. The analyst must be aware of the physical layout of data on a file. The storage media and keys used to get (or *access*) data on the files need to be determined (this topic is discussed further in Chapter 14). The analyst should also determine the potential size of each file, the number of accesses and updates that may take place during a particular time period, and the length of time for which users may wish to retain each file. Since each of these specifications requires the use of computer facilities, such estimates help the analyst determine the potential cost of each design alternative.

FIGURE 13–2
Screen Format

```
CLERK IDENTIFICATION: XXXXXXXXXXXXXX
CLERK AUTHORIZATION CODE: ########
CLERK PASSWORD: XXXXXXX
DATE: ##/##/##

CUSTOMER NAME: XXXXXXXXXXXXXXXXXXXXXXXX
CUSTOMER NUMBER: ########
SHIP TO STREET: XXXXXXXXXXXXXXX
SHIP TO CITY: XXXXXXXXXXXXXX
SHIP TO STATE: XX
SHIP TO ZIP: #####
BILL TO STREET: XXXXXXXXXXXXXXXXXXXX
BILL TO CITY: XXXXXXXXXXXXXXXXXX
BILL TO STATE: XX
BILL TO ZIP: #####

DELIVERY REQUESTED: ##/##/##
DELIVERY PROMISED: ##/##/##
TAX RATE: #
ITEM NUMBER: ######
ITEM IDENTIFICATION IS XXXXXXXXXXXXXXX
OKAY? (Y/N): Y
QUANTITY ORDERED: ######

PRINT INVOICE? (Y/N): Y

CUSTOMER NAME: XXXXXXXXXXXXXXXXXXXXXXXXXXX
```

FIGURE 13–3
Output Report Format

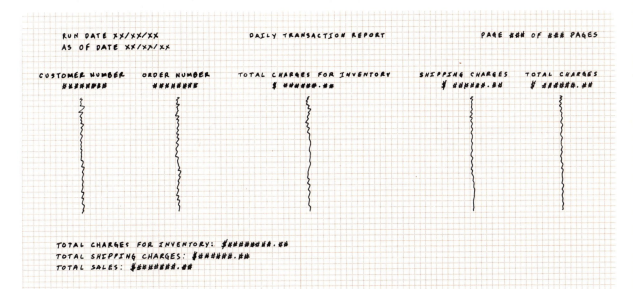

The analyst must think carefully about each clerical procedure required in a particular system alternative. In a sense, the analyst must imagine himself or herself actually performing the steps required. From the receipt of data through the processing steps to the final output, the analyst must determine the most efficient methods for users to perform their required tasks.

Process-control measures were easier in the days of batch processing. With online real-time systems, however, changes made to files and data bases are instantaneous. If the changes are made on the basis of incorrect data, incorrect values will be stored, accessed, and reported. The analyst must institute controls from initial data capture and entry through processing and storage to final reporting. Methods to restore data bases when errors in data entry occur should be developed. Security procedures should be instituted to prevent unauthorized access to stored data. Since the advent of privacy legislation (discussed in Chapter 17), the development of control procedures has become increasingly important.

Perform Feasibility Analysis

Designing systems is an iterative process; in developing each alternative system, the analyst must keep asking the question, "Is this feasible?"

A design may require certain procedures the organization is not staffed to handle; the design must be discarded, or the appropriate staff acquired. The analyst may discover an alternative with great potential for reducing processing costs but may find that the company does not own the hardware required to implement it. The analyst may choose to present this alternative to management rather than disregard it. The analyst must use personal judgment and experience to eliminate infeasible alternatives.

The users' educational backgrounds and organizational positions must be taken into consideration. The lack of familiarity of some employees with computer-based information systems may prohibit the use of a complex system. Highly educated managers may resist a simple information system because they feel uneasy working with it. Companies in rural locations may be unable to properly staff data-processing departments.

Analysts must also determine whether there are legal constraints that affect the design of the system. For example, several U.S. presidents have proposed to Congress the creation of a massive, integrated data base about citizens receiving benefits from the government. Their objective was to reduce fraud, inefficiency, and multiple payments. However, the possibility that such a data base might violate privacy laws had to be considered (see Chapter 17). Although the system is feasible in other respects, the controls that would have to be incorporated into it to conform with the legal constraints have hindered its development.

Time is frequently a constraining factor. This constraint may appear before system development begins, during the development process, or during implementation. The required completion date may preclude the selection of a complex alternative, necessitate changing the selected design to one less complex, or require that the system be developed in stages different from those suggested by the analyst.

The economic feasibility of a project is paramount. Many systems have fallen by the wayside because of budgetary constraints. The system's economic feasibility is determined by cost/benefit analysis, which is discussed below. In performing this analysis, the analyst must be extremely careful. Costs that at first appear to exceed the budget may in fact give rise to greater benefits. The expression "you have to spend money to make money" is often applicable here. It is up to the analyst to foresee such possibilities.

Perform Cost/Benefit Analysis

Cost/benefit analysis is a technique commonly used in business decision making. The firm has limited financial resources. They must be allocated to projects that appear to offer the greatest return on the costs of initial development. In order for cost/benefit analysis to be performed, both costs and benefits must be quantified. Costs are easier to determine than benefits. Some benefits are tangible (or realizable as cash savings). Others are intangible (not necessarily giving rise to obvious reduction in costs). Naturally, intangible benefits are especially difficult to determine. How does one estimate the benefit from an improved information system's providing better customer service?

An analyst might approach the cost/benefit analysis of an accounts receivable system in the following fashion. A company is unable to respond to 20 percent of customer orders because of inefficiencies in its current information system. A proposed new system will reduce lost sales by increasing the customer service level so that only 5 percent of orders remain unprocessed. By observing the current sales level and predicting how much sales will increase if the new system is implemented, the analyst can approximate the cash benefits of the alternative.

The costs of an alternative include direct costs like the initial investment required for materials and equipment; setup costs required to create computer files from old manual systems, install data-processing equipment, and hire personnel; and educational costs to educate the users of the new system. Ongoing expenses resulting from employee salaries, computer operations, insurance, taxes, and rent must also be identified.

It is not always necessary for positive economic benefits to exist for an alternative to be considered feasible. For example, environmental impact statements are required of some companies by law. Design alternatives for a system that must produce such reports must allow for provision of accurate and timely information in spite of the cost/benefit relationship involved. However, the resources required to develop such a system should be kept at a minimum.

Many statistical routines are available to use in determining costs and benefits of large system designs. Sampling and modeling enable the analyst to provide cost/benefit figures not readily apparent from available information. By modeling the complex interactions of accounts-receivable, inventory, and service levels, the analyst may be able to determine how savings in one area affect costs in another. Other techniques ranging from judgment to common sense to experience are useful to the analyst attempting to choose the best alternative.

Which design alternative management selects often depends on the results of cost/benefit analysis. The analyst must ensure that a comprehensive cost/benefit study has been performed on all alternatives.

Prepare Design Report

Once the analyst has completed all of the steps described above, he or she must prepare a report to communicate findings to management. The system design report should explain in general terms how the various designs will satisfy the information requirements determined in the analysis phase. The report should also review the information requirements uncovered in the system analysis, explain in both flowchart and narrative form the proposed designs, detail the corporate resources required to implement each alternative, and make a recommendation.

Since many organizational personnel may not have participated actively in the analysis stage of system development, the analyst restates information requirements in the design report to tell these decision makers the constraints considered in creating alternative designs. The restatement also shows that the analyst understands what information the new system should provide.

Each of the proposed alternatives should be explained in easy-to-understand narrative form. Technical jargon should be avoided. The purpose of the design report is to communicate; using words unfamiliar to the reader will hinder this communication process. Flowcharts of each alternative should be provided as well.

From the detailed design work performed on each alternative, the analyst should glean the important costs, benefits, and resources required for its implementation. This, more than any other portion of the report, will be analyzed carefully by those empowered to make a design selection. Their decisions will be based on the projected benefits of each design versus the corporate resources required to implement it.

Finally, the analyst should make a design recommendation. Because of the analyst's familiarity with the current system and with each alternative design, he or she is in the best position to suggest the one with the greatest potential for success. If the analyst has been thorough in analyzing resource costs and potential benefits, as well as objective in viewing corporate goals, this recommendation is apt to be adopted by management.

After evaluating the system design report, management can do one of three things: approve the recommendation, approve the recommendation with changes (this includes selecting another alternative), or select none of the alternatives. The "do nothing" alternative is always feasible. If the design of the system is approved, the analyst proceeds to implement it.

SYSTEM IMPLEMENTATION

In the implementation stage of the system methodology, the analyst is able to see the transformation of ideas, flowcharts, and narratives into actual processes, flows, and information. This transition is not performed easily, however. Detailed programming specifications must be coded in a computer language, debugged, and put into production. Personnel must be trained to use the new system procedures. The system must be thoroughly documented and tested. A conversion must be made from the old system to the new one.

Programming

A computerized information system requires computer programs in order to work properly. If the analyst does not program, the system design specifications must be communicated to people who do. They must completely understand what is expected of the system before programming begins. If the design of the system has been thorough, there will be few changes to make in programs during conversion. If, on the other hand, the analyst has not fully considered all processing requirements, considerable time may be spent in reprogramming.

The analyst, in conjunction with the programming department, may wish to evaluate software packages designed to perform tasks similar to those required of the selected design. Evaluations should be made on the basis of compatibility and adaptability. Are the package controls and clerical procedures similar to those in the analyst's design? Can the package be readily adapted to this particular application?

To maintain flexibility, programs should be developed in independent modules, which make the system easier to maintain and change (review Chapter 11).

Personnel Training

Two groups of people interface with a system. The first group includes the people who develop, operate, and maintain the system. The second group includes the people who use the information generated by the system to support their decision making. Both groups must be aware of their responsibilities regarding the system's operation and of what they can and cannot expect from it. One of the primary responsibilities of the system analyst is to see that education and training are provided to both groups.

The user group includes general management, staff personnel, line managers, and other operating personnel. It may also include the organization's customers and suppliers. These users must be educated as to what functions they are to perform and what, in turn, the system will do for them.

The personnel who will operate the system must be trained to prepare input data, load and unload files on auxiliary storage devices, handle problems that occur during processing, and so on.

Such education and training can be provided in large group seminars or in smaller tutorial sessions. The latter approach, though fairly costly, is more personal and more appropriate for complex tasks. Another approach, used almost universally, is on-the-job training. As the name implies, the employee learns while actually performing the tasks required.

Personnel training and education are expensive, but they are essential to successful system implementation.

Documentation

Until recently, one of the most neglected parts of system implementation was documentation. Many systems developed in the early 1970s were implemented with sparse documentation. This presented no problems when the systems were first implemented. Over time, however, changes in the businesses and their information requirements necessitated making systems and programming changes. It was at that point that organizations painfully realized the need to have extensive system documentation. It was often difficult to understand programs written five to ten years earlier. Changes made to them often caused errors in other programs. Thus, most organizations have adopted a system development methodology requiring adequate documentation.

Creating system documentation requires taking an overview of the purpose of the entire system, its subsystems, and the function of each subsystem. Documentation of subsystems usually includes system flowcharts depicting the major processing flows, the forms and computer files input to the subsystem, and the reports and computer files output from the subsystem. This provides a frame of reference for system maintenance as information needs change.

Program documentation includes explanations of major logical portions of the program. The programmer may construct program flowcharts to allow maintenance **programmers** to locate areas to be changed and to observe how the **changes will affect** other programs. File declarations explaining the layouts of **data elements** on computer files are also included as part of this **documentation**.

Procedure documentation instructs users how to perform their particular functions in **each subsystem**. These documents are designed so that users can quickly and easily get the information they need. User documentation is particularly important, since the best-designed system can fail if users perform their functions incorrectly. Procedures must be established to keep user documentation up to date with the latest system changes.

Testing

Before a system becomes operational, it must be tested and debugged. Testing occurs at various levels. The lowest level is program testing. Programs are divided into distinct logical modules. Each module is tested to ensure that all input is accounted for, the proper files are updated, and the correct

". . . and in 1/10,000 of a second, it can compound the programmer's error 87,500 times!"

© 1978 by Sidney Harris
American Scientist Magazine

reports are printed. Only after each module has been debugged should the modules be linked together and the complete program tested.

Once all program testing is complete, system testing can proceed; this level of testing involves checking all the application programs that support the system. All clerical procedures used in data collection, data processing, and data storage and retrieval are included in system testing.

Two test methods discussed in Chapter 9—desk-checking and processing test data—are often used in system testing. Desk-checking involves mentally tracing the sequence of operations performed on a particular transaction to determine the correctness of the processing logic. This approach is least costly, but it is not always reliable. Processing test data involves taking "live" data that has already been processed by the old system and processing it in the new system. If the results from the two systems match, the new system is functioning properly.

Conversion

The switch from an old system to a new one is referred to as conversion. Conversion involves not only the changes in the mode of processing data but also the changes in equipment and in clerical procedures.

Several approaches can be used to accomplish the conversion process. The most important ones are explained below:

● *Parallel conversion.* When parallel conversion is used, the new system is operated side-by-side with the old one for some period of time. An advantage of this approach is that no data is lost if the new system fails. Also, it gives the user an opportunity to compare and reconcile the outputs from both systems. However, this method can be costly.

● *Pilot conversion.* Pilot conversion involves converting only a small piece of the business to the new system. For example, a new system may be implemented on one production line. This approach minimizes the risk to the organization as a whole in case unforeseen problems occur and enables the organization to identify problems and correct them before implementing the system in other areas. A disadvantage of this method is that the total conversion process usually takes a long time.

● *Phased conversion.* With phased conversion, the old system is gradually replaced by the new one over a period of time. The difference between this method and pilot conversion is that in phased conversion the new system is segmented, and only one segment is implemented at a time. Thus, the organization can adapt to the change gradually over an extended period. One drawback is that an interface between the new system and the old system must be developed for use during the conversion process.

● *Crash conversion.* Crash conversion, sometimes referred to as *direct conversion*, takes place all at once. This approach can be used to advantage if the old system is not operational or if the new system is completely different in structure and design. Since the old system is discontinued immediately upon implementation of the new one, the organization has nothing to fall back on if problems arise. Because of the high risk involved, this approach requires extreme care in planning and extensive testing of all system components.

SYSTEM AUDIT AND REVIEW

Evaluating System Performance

After the conversion process is complete, the analyst must obtain feedback on the system's performance. This can be done by conducting an audit to evaluate the system's performance in terms of the initial objectives established for it. The evaluation should address the following questions:

1. Does the system perform as planned and deliver the anticipated benefits? How do the operating results compare with the initial objectives? If the benefits are below expectation, what can be done to improve the cost/benefit tradeoff?
2. Was the system completed on schedule and with the resources estimated?
3. Is all output from the system used?
4. Have old system procedures been eliminated and new ones implemented?
5. What controls have been established for input, processing, and output of data? Are these controls adequate?
6. Have users been educated about the new system? Is the system accepted by users? Do they have confidence in the reports generated?
7. Is the processing turnaround time satisfactory, or are delays frequent?

All persons involved in developing the system should be aware that a thorough audit will be performed. The anticipated audit acts as a strong incentive; it helps to ensure that a good system is designed and delivered on schedule.

As a result of the audit or of user requests, some modification or improvement of the new system may be required.

Making Modifications and Improvements

A common belief among system users is that after a system has been installed, nothing more has to be done. On the contrary, all systems must be continually maintained. System maintenance detects and corrects errors, meets new information needs of management, and responds to changes in the environment.

One of the important tasks of the analyst during the system audit is to ensure that all system controls are working correctly. All procedures and programs related to the old system should have been eliminated. Many of the problems that the system analyst deals with during system maintenance and follow-up are problems that were identified during the system audit.

A well-planned approach to system maintenance and follow-up is essential to the continued effectiveness of an information system.

Responding to Change

A well-designed information system is flexible and adaptable. Minor changes should be easily accommodated without large amounts of reprogramming. This is one of the reasons why structured programming was emphasized in Chapter 11; if each program module is independent, a minor change in one module will not snowball into other changes.

No matter how flexible or adaptable a system is, however, major changes become necessary over time. When the system has to be redesigned, the entire system cycle—analysis, design, and implementation—must be performed again. Keeping information systems responsive to information needs is a never-ending process.

SUMMARY

- If the system analysis report is approved, the analyst begins the design stage. Goals and objectives of the new or revised system are reviewed. A system model is developed, and organizational constraints are evaluated.
- Alternative designs should always be generated in the design phase. There is always more than one way to design a system; and management likes to have alternatives from which to select.
- When developing the various alternatives, the analyst must include tentative input forms or screens, output report formats, program specifications, file or data-base designs, clerical procedures, and process-control measures for each alternative.
- Each alternative should undergo a feasibility analysis. This involves looking at constraints, such as those imposed by hardware, software, human resources, legal matters, time, and economics.
- A cost/benefit analysis should be conducted to determine which alternative is most viable economically. While tangible costs and benefits are easy to determine, intangible benefits are difficult to quantify.
- The final step in system design is preparing a design report to present to management. This report should explain the various alternatives and the costs, benefits, and resources associated with each. The report includes the analyst's recommendation.
- The final stage of the system methodology is system implementation. Once management has selected a design alternative, programming, personnel training, and system testing begin.
- Programming is one of the most time-consuming parts of implementation and begins almost immediately after management has approved a design. Training of operators and users usually begins at the same time and continues until implementation is complete.
- Documentation is a necessary part of system and program development. System documentation provides an overview of the entire system and its subsystems. It includes system flowcharts and narratives describing the input forms and computer files as well as the output reports and computer files. Program documentation provides an explanation of the logical portions

of the programs and may also include program flowcharts. Procedure documentation provides users with instructions on how to perform the functions of each subsystem.

● Testing is performed when each program module is completed. When all program testing is done, system testing commences.

● Converting to a new system can be done in several ways. In parallel conversion, the old and the new system operate together for a period of time. In pilot conversion, the new system is first implemented in only a part of the organization to determine its adequacies and inadequacies; the latter are corrected before full-scale implementation. In phased conversion, the old system is gradually replaced with the new system a portion at a time. In crash conversion, the new system is implemented all at once.

● Once a new system is operational, it must be audited to ascertain that the initial objectives of the system are being met and to find any problems occurring in the new system. System maintenance is the continued surveillance of system operations to determine what modifications are needed to meet the changing needs of management and to respond to changes in the environment.

REVIEW QUESTIONS

1. Why is it important for the analyst to design several alternatives?

2. Why is it difficult to design the "perfect" information system?

3. What are some of the methods used to train personnel in new system procedures? What groups of individuals must undergo training?

4. Why is a system audit important? What is the difference between system audit and system maintenance?

APPLICATION

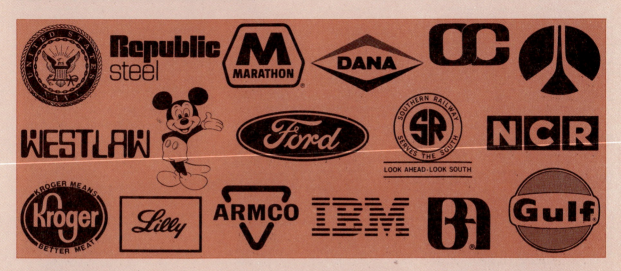

Marathon Oil Company

Marathon Oil Company is a fully integrated oil company; exploration, production, transportation, and marketing of crude oil and natural gas, as well as refining, transporting, and marketing of petroleum products, are its primary activities. The pursuit of these activities has led to its establishing significant international operations extending to six continents and involving over 15,000 employees. With sales of nearly $9 billion, Marathon is ranked among the fifty largest industrial corporations in the United States.

Two distinct computer centers are maintained by the Marathon Oil Company. One is the Computer Sciences Department at its research center in Littleton, Colorado. The primary function of this department is support of petroleum engineering, geophysical, and research work conducted at the research center. The computer system itself comprises three Burroughs 6800 main frames and the necessary tape and disk drives. Several pieces of online equipment directly associated with research activities are also used.

The other computer facility, located at the corporate headquarters in Findlay, Ohio, is devoted primarily to business-related computing. This computer system consists of two IBM 3033s in a multiple-processor arrangement and a variety of peripheral devices.

The Computer Services Organization at Findlay encompasses three functional areas: Systems Development, Technical and Remote Computing, and Computer Operations. The applications developed and operated at Marathon range from a simple payroll procedure to computer control of refining operations. It is not unusual to find one project development group updating an existing billing system while another group is developing a highly sophisticated engineering application. Thousands of programs have been developed to handle user requests. An average of 3,200 jobs (12,500 programs) are processed each day.

The Systems Development Division of the Computer Services Organization employs approximately 240 people who are concerned with the maintenance of current systems and the development of new systems arising from user requests. Marathon uses PRIDE, a standard methodology for system development marketed by M. Bryce & Associates. In all, seven phases of system analysis and design are outlined in the PRIDE methodology.

Phase I is essentially a feasibility study comprising the following steps:

1. Project Scope. The overall nature of the project is defined; emphasis is placed on what the study intends to accomplish.

2. Information Requirements. Data is collected during extensive interviews with individuals who will interface with the new system and become its primary users.

3. Recommendations and Concepts. A general flowchart of the proposed system is developed; it depicts the flow of key documents through the system. A narrative is included to explain the flow.

4. Economics. The projected costs of developing the proposed system and the annual costs associated with its operation are determined. Savings generated by the system, as well as a payout schedule, are included.

5. Project Plan. A calendar schedule outlining the time required to complete the proposed system is set up.

Several alternatives are usually generated during Phase I. These alternatives are presented to management, which selects the one it considers most feasible. The

chosen alternative is then carried forward into Phase II.

During Phase II, all major functions of the system are identified. The total system is divided into logical subsystems. Each subsystem is thoroughly documented through the use of flowcharts. Included in the flowcharts are subsystem identification, the inputs and outputs associated with the subsystem, and the files to be accessed, referenced, or updated by the subsystem. Any output report generated by the subsystem is also formatted at this time. A narrative is included to clarify any points not represented by the flowcharts. The entire package is then presented to management for final approval. Once the design has been approved by management (at the end of Phase II), no other formal presentation of the entire system is made, although the final details of each subsystem are reviewed.

Phase III entails subsystem design and focuses directly on the project plan for each subsystem. Administrative procedures and computer procedures are thoroughly documented in a subsystem design manual. Flowcharts and narratives are again used as documentation tools. During this phase it is not unusual to discover overlooked outputs, such as control totals, that the system should provide. These changes are incorporated, and the final formats for all output reports are developed.

In Phase IV, the activities of analysts and programmers are separated. The analysts begin work on the administrative procedure design, which is denoted as Phase IV–1. The key activity here is the development of a users' manual. The system design manual generated during Phase II generally becomes the first chapter of this manual; the remaining chapters are devoted

to the component subsystems. Necessary input documents are designed and added to each subsystem definition. The previously designed output documents are usually carried forward. The procedures or methods to be used in inputting data are defined.

While the analysts are developing the users' manual, programmers are busy with program design, Phase IV–2. Extensive use of HIPO techniques occurs during this phase, which eventually leads into Phase V. During Phase V, the actual programs are produced. This phase tends to be overlapped with Phase VI, during which each program module is tested.

The activities of the analysts and programmers are carefully coordinated so that the users' manual and the programs are completed at approximately the same time. The entire system is now ready to begin the final phase outlined in the PRIDE methodology—a complete systems test. Phase VII involves extensive volume tests and comprehensive training of the system users.

An example of a system developed internally by this method is the Medical Claims System, designed to speed the processing of medical claims submitted by Marathon employees. Before this system was developed, each claim was processed manually. First, a medical claims processor thoroughly checked the claim's validity. After all the medical bills associated with the claim

had been received, the processor filled out a worksheet to complete the claim. The processor was then able to prepare a check to the employee.

The new system greatly simplifies and speeds this processing. Once the entire claim has been collected, it is entered into the system via a CRT. This is the last human interface with the claim; the system handles all subsequent processing, including generation of the check.

The bar chart in Figure 13–4 indicates the time involved in each phase of the development of this system. More than 4,600 person-hours were required for development. This means that if one person were to devote 40 hours a week to the development of such a system, over two years would be required to finish it.

During 1980, the Systems Development Division was

actively involved in the development of many new systems as well as in maintaining systems already in operation. Despite their continual efforts to satisfy users' demands, a sizable backlog of requests remains virtually untouched. As users continue to become more comfortable with computer interaction, the demands on this division will undoubtedly continue to grow.

DISCUSSION POINTS

1. The structured approach outlined in the PRIDE methodology is an effective technique for conducting system analysis, design, and implementation. Should such a detailed procedure always be followed? Why?

2. What types of documentation are included in the PRIDE methodology? During what phase or phases is documentation prepared?

FIGURE 13–4 Medical Claims System Time-Phased Development Chart

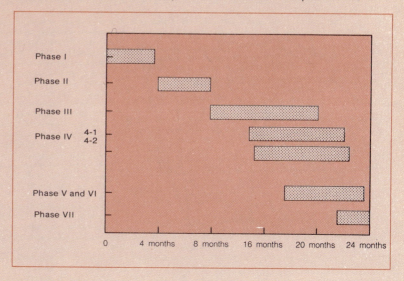

CHAPTER 14

Data Design

Introduction

All business organizations maintain a wide variety of files that contain data about production, employees, customers, inventory levels, and so forth. An organization's method of processing this data is determined largely by specific job requirements. To facilitate the processing of data, an organization can tailor its files to meet certain objectives. For example, files can be structured to decrease overall processing time and to increase processing efficiency.

This chapter examines three types of file arrangement, or data design: sequential, indexed sequential, and direct access. It describes representative applications of these methods to clarify how they are used and discusses the advantages and disadvantages of each method.

66 Plugged-In Prose 99

J. D. Reed

Jimmy Carter uses one. So do Novelists John Hersey and Richard Condon. Every month more writers are discarding their pencils and typewriters for "word processors"—technical jargon for small computers with typewriter-like keyboards, electronic screens for scanning and manipulating text, units to store information, and high-speed printers. Like all other modern products, they come in a range of prices, from Apple's no-frills model at about $2,500 to the luxurious new CPT 8100. Cost of the machine, with a twin-head Rotary VII Printer that can switch instantaneously from roman to italic type or from letters to scientific symbols: $19,990.

Plugged-in writing is not a new phenomenon. In 1973 Hersey tried out electronic fiction writing in order to aid a Yale University computer project—and became an instant convert. But it took a while to get the gadget out of the institution and into the study. Once Carter was pictured composing his memoirs on the Lanier "No Problem," authors and others could easily imagine themselves at the console. Spurred by the new availability of word-processing programs for personal computers like Radio

Shack, Apple and Atari, demand for home units has risen dramatically. Among the aficionados: Bestseller Luminaries Michael Crichton *(Congo)* and Alvin Toffler *(The Third Wave).* Spy-Master Robert Ludlum endorses the Atari system in magazine ads. Though Novelist Irving Wallace still writes on a 1920-vintage portable, he has promised his secretary a processor.

These authors praise their new ability to delete and move words and paragraphs at the touch of a few keys and to enjoy automatic pagination, footnoting and regular book-quality right-hand margins. Novelist Stanley Elkin *(The Living End),* 51, professor of English at Washington University in St. Louis, who suffers from multiple sclerosis, was given the use of a $13,000 Lexitron by the school. Even before he was disabled by the disease, claims Elkin, the processor would have accelerated his output: "You don't have to screw around erasing and crossing out, finding a clear place in the forest to drop the next hat. If I'd had it in 1964, I'd have written three more books by now." Chicago Author William Brashler *(The Bingo Long Traveling All Stars and Motor Kings),* 33, switched on when his exhausted electric portable began throwing keys across the room. Says Brashler of his $8,400 IBM Displaywriter: "It takes the drudgery out of writing. I correct a mistake on the screen in a second, and the

printer retypes the page in three seconds. No more retyping the whole page by hand."

Co-author of *April in Paris,* Screenwriter Melville Shavelson, converted his Radio Shack home computer into a word processor with the addition of inexpensive software. This double-barreled capacity to tap and then manipulate information allows him a futuristic scope: "I subscribe to a Virginia computer service called The Source. I can get Jack Anderson scoops three days before they're scoops," claims Shavelson. "I can feed into it any two cities in the world and it'll figure out the airline connections for me, with a restaurant guide to various cities. Also I have a research service and memory bank feature that gives me data from 150 libraries around the world right on my screen. It's everything in one package."

Sesame Street Consultant Christopher Cerf adds even more voltage to his endorsement: "I use my processor to write, to store notes, to create, to edit, to organize. It's already paid for itself. I don't need a secretary any more. It's the most important tool writers have been given since Gutenberg created movable type."

Still, there were those who thought Gutenberg's invention was the work of the devil, and there are many writers who refuse to countenance a glowing screen above their keyboards. Screenwriter Jeffrey Fiskin *(Cutter and Bone)* decided against one: "Testing a machine, I programmed out *the*. The processor also removed *thesis* and *theocracy*. I thought: 'Do I want one of those, or do I want to add to my wine cellar?' The wine cellar won." John Updike speaks for many colleagues: "I am not persuaded that the expense and time it takes to learn the machine would be worth it. I'll stick to my manual, as I have for 20 years."

Even zealots occasionally have second thoughts. Carter forgot to store several pages of his memoirs and lost them from his Lanier "No Problem." Historical Romance Writer Robyn Carr (*The Blue Falcon*)

fears that workmen digging near her new house in Florida will hit a power line. A voltage drop of even a few seconds could cause the displayed page of text to disappear on her Burroughs Redactor-III. (Apple Computer Inc. offers an accessory for just such occasions—a battery pack that supplies electricity during blackouts. Its name: Apple Juice.) The most surreal glitch occurred when Environmentalist-Writer Michael Parfit, 30, recently heard a *zap,* and his Radio Shack TRS-80 stopped dead. It seemed that ants had crawled into the air vents.

These are the equivalents of

leaky pens, misplaced notes, carbon paper inserted backward—all the inevitable vexations of the writing trade. They may be annoying, but they are not enough to turn off the current of this newest electronic revolution. Even the biggest drawback to processors, their size, is shrinking. Sony, master of the mini, recently introduced a 3-lb. briefcase-size keyboard unit capable of storing text to be printed out later. A few stubborn novelists and historians may resist until the final pencil stub and the last typewriter ribbon, but in the final chapter, the processor will win. As Cerf concludes, "I have seen the future, and it glows."

Word processing systems have made life easier for authors and offices alike. The following chapter presents the elements involved in a computerized system.

FILE PROCESSING

File processing is the operation of periodically updating permanent files to reflect the effects of changes in data. Files can be organized in several ways, with or without the use of a computerized system. Without computers, files must be recorded on paper and manually updated. For example, consider the case of ABC Company, a small sports equipment supplier. The company carries an inventory of fifty types of items, supplies equipment to thirty customers, and maintains a staff of twenty employees. All of ABC's records are kept on paper and transactions are recorded manually.

Every time a customer places an order, a clerk must prepare a sales order. The customer's file is checked to obtain all necessary information about the customer, such as billing and shipping addresses and credit status. The clerk fills in the type and quantity of equipment ordered, and the sales order is sent to the warehouse where the inventory is stored. At the warehouse, an employee determines if the requested equipment is available. This operation requires a physical count of inventory. If the inventory is available, it can be packaged and prepared for shipping. If the order cannot be filled, the employee must prepare a back-order. The sales order is forwarded to the accounting department, where the customer's bill is prepared. In this department, a clerk consults a company catalog to determine the cost of each item. The total bill is calculated, including tax and shipping rates; this total is recorded on the customer's record; and the order is shipped.

Even this simplified transaction includes many time-consuming and inefficient activities. In addition, ABC Company must prepare a monthly payroll as well as purchase orders to replenish depleted inventory. Obviously, ABC Company could benefit from computerizing its activities.

Several computerized files could be arranged to facilitate ABC's operations. First, an employee file could be set up; each individual employee record might contain the employee's home address, social security number, wage per hour, withholding tax, and gross income. So that this data can be used in a variety of ways by various individuals, it is organized in an integrated manner. Figure 14–1 shows a portion of an employee file and reintroduces several terms useful in a discussion of data design. Recall from Chapter 1 that a *field* is a data item; a *record* is a collection of data items that relate to a single unit; and a *file*, or *data set*, is a grouping of related records.

The company could also use an inventory file with one record for each item carried in inventory. Each record could contain a description of the item, the quantity on hand, the cost of the item, and the like. Finally, a customer file containing such fields as billing and shipping addresses, current balances owed, and credit status would be useful.

Each of these files would be accessed, or read, in different ways. For example, the entire employee file would be read every time the payroll was prepared. The inventory file, however, would only need to be accessed one record at a time—that is, only one record would be read each time an order was placed for a particular item. The customer file would be accessed in two ways. First, when a customer placed an order, only the particular record containing data about that customer would be read. Second, the entire file would be read each time ABC Company prepared customer bills or needed a report on outstanding customer balances.

FIGURE 14–1
Employee Data—
ABC Company

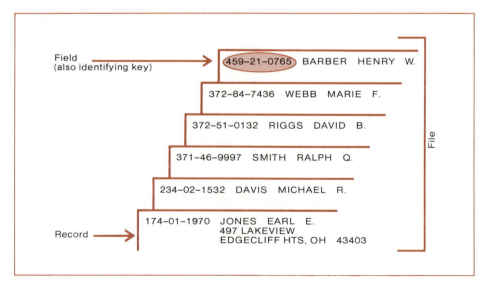

The following sections will discuss the three types of file arrangements that would be used in these three cases.

SEQUENTIAL DESIGN

If we need to find a particular record and the set of records in a file is very small, then it may not be difficult to search the file from the beginning to find the record. For files containing large numbers of records, however, this method is impractical. A special ordering technique is needed so that records can be retrieved more easily. For this reason, employee records, for example, may be arranged according to social security number (look again at Figure 14–1), or records in an inventory file may be arranged according to item number. The identifier used to locate a particular record in the file is called a *key*. Since a key is used to locate a particular record, it must be unique—that is, no two records in a file can have the same key value. The records ordered according to their key values form a *sequential file*.

Updating involves two sets of files; the basic file containing all existing records is called the *master file*, and the file containing changes to be made to the master file is called a *transaction file*. The master file is organized according to the identifier chosen as a key. Since the changes, or transaction records, must be matched against the master records, processing is greatly enhanced if the transaction records are ordered according to the same key. That is, the transaction file should also be sequentially organized.

In updating, both the master file and the transaction file serve as input to the computer system. The computer compares the key of the first master record with the key of the first record on the transaction file. If the keys do not match, the next record on the master file is read. When a match between the transaction record and a master record occurs, the master record is updated. If a master record has no matching transaction record, it is left unchanged. If a transaction record has no matching master record, an error or warning message may be generated.

The updated master record can be longer or shorter than it was before the updating occured. Since records are stored one after another on a sequential file, a new record may overwrite the next record following it or may leave a gap before it. In some applications, an unmatched transaction causes an entirely new master record to be inserted between two other master records. In others, some transactions may cause old master records to be deleted. To allow such processing, a new master file is created whenever changes have to be made to the old master file. Every master record not deleted explicitly must be written to the new master file, whether or not it is changed.

When such *sequential processing* is utilized, there is no way to directly locate the matching master record for a transaction. Every time a given master record is to be updated, the entire master file must be read and a new master file created. To eliminate a great deal of unnecessary processing, transactions are collected for a given time period and then processed against the master file in one run. This approach, you may remember from earlier chapters, is called *batch processing* (see Figure 14–2).

The amount of time required to update a record in the sequential processing mode includes the time needed to process the transaction, read the master file until the proper record is reached, update the master record, and rewrite the master file. To reduce the time needed, the transactions are sorted to reflect the order of the master file. For security, the old master file and the transaction records are retained for a period of time; then, if the new master is accidentally destroyed, it can be reconstructed from the old master and the transaction files.

Example of Sequential Processing

The billing operation is well suited to sequential processing. Customers' bills must be prepared, but only at scheduled intervals. Standard procedures apply, and large numbers of records must be processed.

Processing customer records results in the preparation of bills for customers and updates of the amounts they owe. Magnetic tape is an appropriate

FIGURE 14–2
Sequential Processing

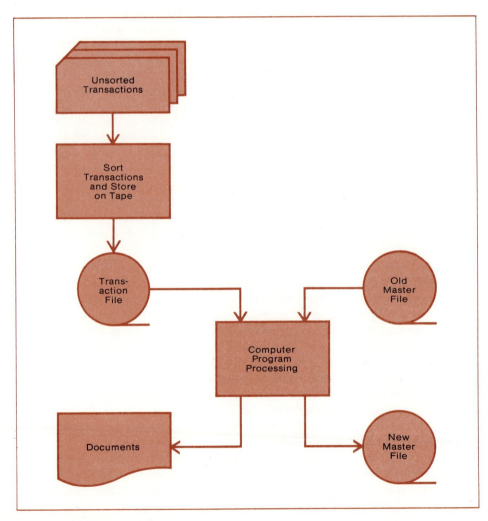

medium for this application because the customer records can be arranged in customer number order and processed in sequence accordingly.

The procedure for preparing the billing statements involves the following steps:

Step 1: The transaction cards indicating which items have been shipped to customers are keypunched and verified. One card is used for each item shipped (see Figure 14–3a).

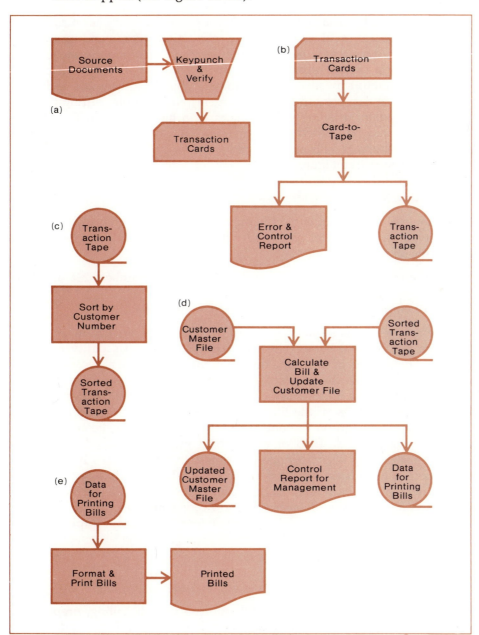

FIGURE 14–3
Billing Operations

Step 2: The data on the cards is transferred to magnetic tape. The card-to-tape program also edits the input data. Editing checks include tests to make sure the contents of fields are within reasonable limits, numeric fields have numeric data, alphanumeric fields have alphanumeric data, and so forth. The card-to-tape run provides a report of invalid transactions so that they can be corrected (see Figure 14–3b).

Step 3: The transaction records are sorted according to customer number because the customer master file is arranged in customer number order (see Figure 14–3c).

Step 4: The sorted transactions are used to update the customer master file. The process involves reading the transaction records and master records into main storage. There may be more than one transaction record for a master record. The master record is updated to reflect the final amount owed by the customer. Usually, during an update, a report is also printed for management. For example, during the billing update, a listing of customers who have exceeded their credit limits may be printed (see Figure 14–3d).

Step 5: The customers' bills are prepared from the data generated in the previous step (see Figure 14–3e).

Interrogating Sequential Files

How inquiries into a sequential file on magnetic tape are handled depends on the type of inquiry. Let us consider the following inquiries into the employee file shown in Figure 14–1.

1. List the records of employees with social security numbers 234–02–1532 and 372–84–7436.

2. List all employees from the area with zip code 43403.

The employee file is sequenced according to social security number. In the first case the file will be searched for the correct social security numbers from the beginning of the file, but only the key of each record will be checked. As soon as the required social security numbers are located, the records will be listed and the search stopped. Of course, if the numbers are in the last two records on the file, then the entire file must be searched.

For the second inquiry, the entire file will again have to be searched. In this case, the zip code field of each record must be checked to see if it matches 43403. This illustrates one problem with referring to a nonkey field on sequential files. If an inquiry is based on a field other than the key, then a great deal of time is wasted in the search process. To alleviate this problem, a second employee file ordered by zip code could be created; however, this approach requires maintaining multiple files that contain duplicate data.

Assessment of Sequential Design

Some advantages of sequential processing and file design are:

● It is suitable for many types of applications—payroll, billing, preparation of customer statements, and so forth—that require periodic updating of large numbers of records.

● Economies of scale are achieved when the number of records processed is high. If at least half the records in a master file are updated during a processing run, the large volume of transactions reduces the processing cost per record.
● The design of sequential files is simple.
● Magnetic tape, a low-cost medium, can be used to maximum advantage.
● Input and output rates are higher than those achieved with direct input of transactions from terminal keyboards.

The disadvantages of this mode of processing include the following:

● The entire master file must be processed and a new master file written even if only a few master records have to be updated.
● Transactions must be sorted in a particular sequence; this takes time and can be expensive.
● The master file is only as up-to-date as the last processing run. In many instances, the delay in processing the master file results in use of old and thus incorrect information.
● The sequential nature of the file organization is a serious handicap when unanticipated inquiries must be made.

DIRECT-ACCESS DESIGN

Direct-access processing is suited to applications involving files with *low activity* and *high volatility*. Activity refers to the proportion of records processed during an updating run, and volatility refers to the frequency of changes to a file during a certain time period.

In contrast to a batch-processing system, a direct-access system does not require that transaction records be grouped or sorted before they are processed. Data is submitted to the computer in the order it occurs. Direct-access storage devices (DASDs) make this type of processing possible. A particular record on a master file can be accessed directly and updated without all preceding records on the file being read. Only the key to the record need be known. Thus, up-to-the-minute reports can be provided.

For example, assume Ralph Smith's address in the employee master file in Figure 14–1 had to be changed. With direct-access processing, the computer can locate the record to be updated without sequentially processing all records that precede it.

A major consideration in the use of direct-access processing is finding the record to be updated. For the record to be located, its address must be known. The address is usually a number from five to seven digits in length that is related to the physical characteristics of the direct-access storage device. The address can be obtained through a transformation process on the record key (also called *randomizing* or *hashing*) or from a *directory*. Directories list reference numbers along with their corresponding addresses in storage. During processing, the computer searchers the directory to locate the address of a particular record.

For example, assume that the ABC Company's employee master file (Figure 14–1) is on a direct-access storage device and that addresses are listed in a directory. The directory (or table) would consist of two columns, the first containing the key of the record (social security number) and the second containing the address of the record with that key. To find Ralph Smith's record, the computer would scan the first column until it found his social security number. It would then pick up the corresponding address from the second column and access the record stored at that location.

When the transformation process is used to locate addresses, an arithmetic manipulation is performed on the record key to create an address, and there is no need for a directory.

For example, suppose we need a three-digit disk address. The nine-digit Social Security number can be converted as follows. First, we select a number such as 995. Every Social Security number is then divided by 995 and the result is a quotient and a remainder. The employee's record is stored at the address equal to the remainder. Thus, Ralph Smith's record would be stored at address 677. ($371469997 \div 995 = 373336$ with a remainder of 677.)

Examples of Direct-Access Processing

Many applications are not suited for sequential processing. One example is an airline reservation system. Airline employees who assign seats on flights must have up-to-date information. Sales efforts must be coordinated so that a passenger in Cleveland and one in Detroit do not purchase the same seat on the same flight to New York. If data for an airline were processed once a week, plane flights would often be oversold. With a direct-access system, on the other hand, a ticket agent can submit a flight number and quickly determine the number of seats available. This is possible because not all flight records must be read—only the record of the flight in question. The computer system has up-to-date information on all flights at all times.

Another example of direct-access processing is a savings account system at a bank. The bank can maintain a current status of all savings accounts by updating each account as soon as a deposit or withdrawal is made. Customer records are stored on a DASD. Terminals are installed at all branch offices and connected to the computer by communication facilities (for example, telephone lines); the terminals are used for both input and output (see Figure 14–4).

When a bank customer makes a deposit or withdrawal, the amount of the transaction, the type of transaction (deposit or withdrawal), and the customer's account number are communicated to the central computer through the typewriter-like terminal at the branch office. The computer immediately locates the record containing that account number on the DASD, updates the account, and sends a message giving the current balance back to the terminal. The message is printed on the customer's savings book.

It is important to note that the desired record can be directly located on the DASD and that only one record is updated. Using the direct-access method can be compared to finding a particular landmark on a city map by means of coordinates. Knowing these coordinates, we can immediately zero in on the exact location of the landmark. Sequential processing is unsuitable for this kind of application.

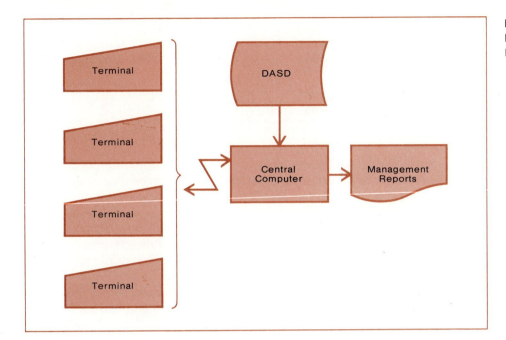

FIGURE 14–4
Direct-Access
Processing

Interrogating Direct-Access Files

To see how direct-access files handle inquiries, let us look again at the two inquiries discussed in connection with sequential files:

1. List the records of employees with social security numbers 234–02–1532 and 372–84–7436.
2. List all employees from the area with zip code 43403.

With regard to the first inquiry, the records of the two employees can be located directly because the addresses can be found by use of either a directory or a transformation process, as described earlier (assuming social security number is used as the key).

The approach used for the second inquiry will depend on the organization of the file. If much processing is done based on a geographic breakdown of employees, a directory relating zip codes and their record addresses can be created (see Figure 14–5). However, if ABC is a small company, a directory to locate employee records by zip code may have little value. In this case, we encounter the same situation we did with sequential files: The entire file must be read to obtain the desired information. This could take a great deal of time.

Assessment of Direct-Access Design

The following are advantages of direct-access processing and file design:

● Transaction data can be used directly to update master records via online terminals without first being sorted. Transactions are processed as they occur.

FIGURE 14–5
Directory for Zip codes

ZIP CODE	ADDRESS
43403	12043
43403	12140
44151	12046
44153	12143
44200	12146
44201	12045

• The master file is not read completely each time updating occurs; only the master records to be updated are accessed. This saves time and money.

• It takes only a fraction of a second to gain access to any record on a direct-access file.

• Direct-access files provide flexibility in handling inquiries.

• Several files can be updated concurrently by use of direct-access processing. For example, when a credit sale is made, the inventory file can be updated; the customer file can be changed to reflect the current accounts-receivable figure; and the sales file can be updated to show which employee made the sale. Several runs would be required to accomplish all of these operations if sequential processing was used.

Disadvantages of direct-access design include the following:

• During processing, the original record is replaced by the updated record. In effect, it is destroyed. (In batch processing, a complete new master file is created, but the old master file remains intact.) Consequently, to provide backup, an organization may have to make a magnetic-tape copy of the master file weekly and also keep the current week's transactions so that master records can be reconstructed if necessary.

• Since many users may have access to records stored on direct-access devices in online systems, the chances of accidental destruction of data are greater. Special programs are required to edit input data and to perform other checks to ensure that data is not lost. Also, there exists the possibility of confidential information falling into unauthorized hands; additional security procedures are necessary to reduce this risk.

• Implementation of direct-access systems is often difficult because of their complexity and the high level of programming (software) support that such systems need.

• When the randomizing technique is used with direct-access file organization, some file locations can be unused. It is necessary to keep track of these unused locations for use as overflow areas for later additions.

INDEXED-SEQUENTIAL DESIGN

Sequential processing is suitable for applications where the proportion of records processed in an updating run is high. However, sequential files provide slow response times and cannot adequately handle file inquiries. On

the other hand, direct-access processing is inappropriate for applications like payroll where most records are processed during a run. When a single file must be used for both batch processing and online processing, neither direct-access nor sequential file organization is appropriate. The same customer file that is used in a weekly batch run for preparing bills by the accounting department may be used daily by order-entry personnel to record orders and check credit status. To some extent, the limitations of both types of file design can be minimized by using another approach to file organization—*indexed-sequential* design.

In this structure, the records are stored sequentially on a direct-access storage device. In addition, an *index* to selected record keys and their corresponding addresses is established. The file can be accessed directly by a record key's being matched against the index table to get an approximate address for the required record. The computer then goes to that location on the direct-access storage device and checks records sequentially until the desired record is found.

This approach is similar to the way we might locate a house in an unfamiliar city. The address specifies the street and house number—for example, 213 South Clay Street. The first step is to go to South Clay Street. Then we check the number of the closest house. Let's say it's 219. Then, we proceed down the street to check if the next house is 221 or 217. If it is 217, we proceed in the same direction until we find 213. This approach is quicker than checking in turn each house on South Clay Street. We can use the approach because we know the house numbers are in sequence.

Thus, an indexed-sequential file provides direct-access capability. Since all the records are ordered according to a key, it also allows efficient sequential processing.

Examples of Indexed-Sequential Processing

The customer file referred to earlier in this chapter is an example of a file suitable for indexed-sequential processing. The file could be read sequentially for the billing operation. In addition, it could be accessed one record at a time for order-entry transactions. The following steps outline the procedures involved in preparing a customer order:

Step 1: A customer mails or phones an order to ABC Company for equipment. The clerk receives the order and enters the customer number on a visual display terminal. This number acts as a key to the file.

Step 2: The customer file is searched until a match is found between the number entered and the appropriate record. Once the appropriate record is found, the information appears on the terminal's screen. The clerk verifies shipping and billing addresses.

Step 3: The order is entered on the keyboard, and a sales order is generated by a printer connected to the system.

Step 4: The customer's record is updated to reflect the current order.

"I hear they're doing some amazing things with computers these days."

Datamation, January, 1981. Drawing by S. Attoe.

Assessment of Indexed-Sequential Design

Advantages of indexed-sequential design include the following:

● Indexed-sequential files are well suited for both inquiries and large processing runs.
● Access time to specific records is apt to be faster than it would be if the file were sequentially organized.

Disadvantages of indexed-sequential design include the following:

● More direct-access storage space is required for an indexed-sequential file than for a sequential file holding the same data because of the storage space required for indexes.
● Processing time for specific record selection is longer than it would be in a direct-access system.

Each of the types of file organization discussed in this chapter describes the physical organization of computer files—that is, how the data is arranged on a particular storage medium. In a sequential file, for example, the records are physically placed one after another. Many organizations maintain a file for every application program; one for accounting, one for billing, one for inventory, and so on. This may result in the same data's being recorded in several files.

There is another approach to data organization in which a file is not treated as a separate entity. This method uses a *data base*—a single collection of related data which can be used by many applications. Much duplicate data is eliminated.

363

Data-base organization allows the user or application programmer to concentrate on *logical*, rather than physical, structures. In logical structures, data is organized in a way that is meaningful to a particular user, who is not concerned with the physical arrangement of data on a storage medium. Data-base organization and logical data structures are discussed in the next chapter.

SUMMARY

● File processing is the process of periodically updating permanent files to reflect current data. Files are accessed in different ways, depending upon the organization of the file.

● Sequential processing involves storing records in a sequence based on a unique identifier called a key. These records form a master file. All changes to be made to the master file are collected and processed in a batch to create the new master file. The changes to be processed against the master file form a transaction file; they must be ordered in the same sequence as the records in the master file. After processing, there is a new master file, an old master file, and a transaction file.

● Sequential processing is normally used when files are large and need to be updated only periodically, such as for payroll or billing. However, sequential file organization is not well suited to responding to inquiries, since the file must be read from the beginning to locate a desired record.

● In a direct-access system, transaction records are processed as they occur, without prior sorting or grouping. This method requires the use of high-speed, direct-access storage devices (DASDs).

● To find a record in a direct-access file, the user must know its address, or location on a particular storage device. The addresses can be found through use of either an arithmetic manipulation on the record key or a directory containing the reference numbers of the records and their storage locations on DASDs.

● Direct-access processing is most often used when changes are frequent but only a small proportion of master records must be updated at any single time.

● Indexed-sequential file organization is suitable where the proportion of records to be processed in an updating run is high. Records are stored in sequence on a direct-access storage device. An index to selected record keys and their corresponding addresses is established. When a record in an indexed-sequential file must be located, the index gives the approximate address of the record. The records near that location are read sequentially until the correct one is found. Both indexed-sequential and direct-access file organizations are well suited to responding to inquiries into data files.

● The physical design of files describes the manner in which data is stored on a particular storage medium. Logical design describes the way data is organized to be meaningful to a user.

REVIEW QUESTIONS

1. How are sequential files updated?
2. Under what circumstances is sequential processing applicable? What are its limitations?
3. What are two commonly used ways of finding addresses in direct-access files? Explain briefly the differences between them.
4. Direct-access processing is best suited to what types of applications?
5. Contrast indexed-sequential file organization with sequential and direct-access file organization. What advantages does indexed-sequential organization have over the other two approaches?

APPLICATION

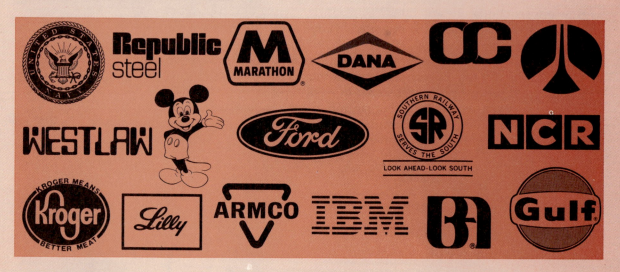

Dana Corporation

Dana's origins date to 1904, when Clarence Spicer, a mechanical engineering student at Cornell University, adopted the idea of replacing the sprockets and chains being used to transmit the power from the engine to the rear axle in automobiles with a universal joint and drive shaft. The Spicer Manufacturing Company was founded in Plainfield, New Jersey, to manufacture and market these universal joints. When an order for ninety-six sets of universal joints and drive shafts was received in 1905 from the Wayne Automobile Company, nearly sixteen weeks

of around-the-clock production were required to fill it. Today, Dana produces and ships 2.5 million joint sets in a similar sixteen-week period.

Dana's major products today are axle parts, transmissions, universal joints, clutches, industrial products, engine parts, and frame and chassis parts. International sales have grown from about $1 million in 1950 to over $390 million in the late 1970s. Total sales have increased from $153 million to almost $1.8 billion during the same period.

The Spicer Transmission Division of Dana has an extensive data-processing center that supports the division itself and another plant in Jonesboro, Arkansas, and also maintains some financial information and centralized accounts receivable for the corporate headquarters. Fifteen management personnel and three data-entry operators are

involved in programming, operations, and the preparation of data for subsequent processing at this facility.

The CPU is an IBM 3031 with a main storage capacity of 3 million characters. More than twenty remote terminals are used in the centralized accounts-receivable system. Six terminals are located at the World Headquarters for Financial Control and Marketing. Seventy-six additional remote terminals at the Spicer plant complex are used for online sales, new product development, and personnel record-keeping applications.

The variety of needs of users at the Spicer Transmission Division requires both online/direct-access and batch/sequential modes of processing. Most application programs are written in COBOL. (The entire COBOL program library contains some 2,000 programs.) Although recent emphasis has been placed on the development of online applications, batch processing remains a vital aspect of the overall data-processing activities.

One system that operates in a batch mode is the material requirements planning (MRP) system, which is extremely important to the production and purchasing departments of the division. Production planning schedules depend heavily on a sufficient supply of the parts required in the assembly of a given product. A shortage is extremely expensive, because the entire assembly line must either be halted until the needed parts arrive or be converted to another assembly process. Carrying a large supply of parts in inventory is also expensive, so the purchasing department must strive to have no more inventory than is needed to meet demand.

Any transactions affecting inventory have an impact on the MRP system. During a typical day, many such transactions occur—deliveries of goods, shipments of goods, withdrawals of goods from inventory, and so on. As these transactions occur, they are entered directly into the computer via online cathode-ray tube terminals (CRTs). The transactions are stored on a transaction file that is processed nightly against the master files in the MRP system. These master files can be used to produce planning reports, inventory shortage and overage reports, and material-buying reports.

Approximately 150 reports are available through the MRP system. They can be generated at regular intervals or on user demand. Consider, as an example, an inventory shortage report. This report can include item number, description, quantity on hand, quantity on order, expected future requirements, requirements during past periods, shortage quantities, the division placing the orders, and even the specific buyer responsible for the item. Such comprehensive, up-to-date reports are invaluable to management.

Another batch-processing application is the payroll system. The office staff and production workers are paid on a weekly basis. The salaried management personnel are paid on a semimonthly basis. Employees are normally paid for forty hours per week; an additional complication arises when exceptions to that work period are reported by supervisors. The exceptions are encoded on magnetic diskettes. This data is sequentially processed against an employee master file, which uses the employee number as a key. Together, the diskette file and the master file contain all the data necessary for the calculation of employees' pay and the computer generation of paychecks. The entire payroll can be processed in five to six hours.

The two batch systems discussed above adequately serve certain user needs. However, many users also need immediate access to data to effectively perform their jobs. The engineering department is an example of such a user group.

The Spicer Transmission Division has produced approximately 5,000 different types of transmissions over the years. The specifications for these transmissions are maintained in a transmission file. When a customer submits specifications for a new product, such as a heavy truck transmission, the engineering department must determine how that product will be produced. When the order is received, an engineer keys into the keyboard of a CRT any number of major component specifications for the ordered transmission. The computer searches the transmission file and indicates which of those transmissions contain the largest number of

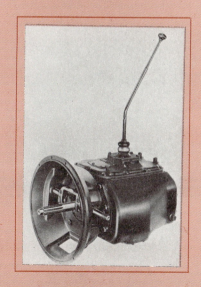

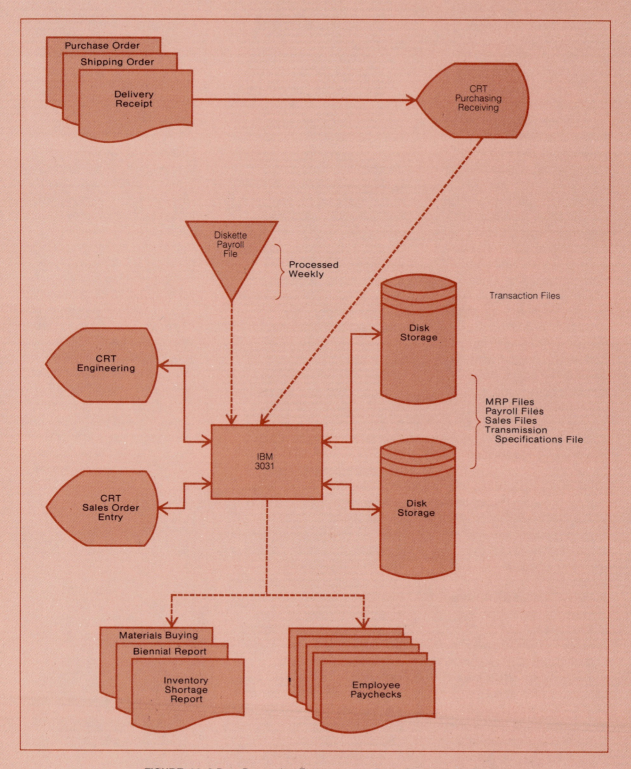

FIGURE 14-6 Data-Processing Environment at Dana Corporation's Spicer Division

parts identical to the new specifications. With this information, the engineer can determine the development or retooling necessary to produce the new product and provide the purchaser with accurate time and cost estimates.

A vitally important online/direct-access system used extensively by the Spicer Transmission Division is the one used to enter sales orders. This system makes use of a complex data base containing data about customers and pricing as well as a part-number interchange. When an order is received, a sales-entry clerk uses a CRT to obtain customer data such as the shipping address, terms, and party to be charged. The order information and part number are then entered. Since the part number the customer uses is often different from the number used by Dana to represent the same part, the data base converts the customer's part number to the appropriate Dana classification. The order is then submitted for processing. A computer-generated shop order is produced and entered into the manufacturing system, and a customer acknowledgement form is created for mailing to the buyer. The customer's order is also entered into an open-order file. Through this file, a sales representative can inquire into the status of a customer's order at any time. This capability is used hundreds of times a day in response to customer inquiries.

A schematic diagram of the data-processing environment at Dana's Spicer Division is presented in Figure 14–6.

DISCUSSION POINTS

.1. What criteria determine if an application will be processed batch/sequential or online/direct access?

2. Describe the type of file organization used in the processing of sales orders. Why might this particular file organization have been chosen?

CHAPTER 15

Management Information Systems

Introduction

For many years, computers have been used to perform routine and repetitive operations formerly done manually. Person hours are saved when functions such as payroll preparation and order writing are done by computer, but these types of applications are not especially helpful to management when it must plan for the future or control daily activities. Simply having a computer does not ensure that management has an effective information system. To achieve its full potential, the computer must be integrated with people and procedures to provide information useful in decision making.

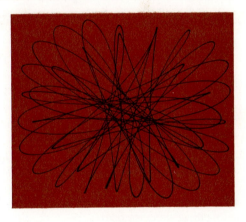

This chapter emphasizes the decision-oriented reporting of a management information system. It discusses the various levels of management and the information needs of each and presents several approaches to designing an information system to meet these needs. It explains the concept of the data base and how it uses physical and logical design. Finally, it describes data-base management systems and software packages available for various data-base systems.

"Colleges Turn to New Computers as Way to Simulate Real Events"

Peter W. Barnes

Computer simulations are turning college students and faculties on to computer teaching. Medical students are using computers to work on imaginary infants who are dying; law students are prosecuting murderers, and history students are being transported by computer into the turmoil of the French Revolution.

Computer instruction isn't new. But until recently, it has been confined largely to routine exercises in math, sciences and languages. Now better technology, particularly the microcomputer, is spurring a new generation of sophisticated and innovative classroom exercises that imitate real situations. Previously, they could only be done on large computers.

Some Dartmouth College students have lost their heads over one exercise. Through a computer terminal that prints questions on paper, a student is quizzed about the French Revolution. Suddenly, with bells ringing, the computer declares that the student stands before a revolutionary tribunal, and that based on the "evidence"—quiz answers which, unknown to the student, were biased toward one revolutionary faction or another—the tribunal "has found you guilty and has sentenced you to be guillotined within 24 hours."

The simulation teaches students about the "revisionary quality" of the revolution, says its author, Michael Carter. "People generally don't know what the game is about until they've gotten their head cut off for the first time," he says.

Such simulations are more difficult to program than drill and practice exercises. At the University of Minnesota, law professors have developed complex exercises on topics from torts to legal ethics. A technique called "branching," used frequently in simulations, allows the computer to teach in a form of Socratic method: The computer, programmed to discuss or criticize predictable student responses, follows a certain line of questioning. If the student gets off the track, the computer introduces a specific "branch" of questions to steer him back.

In some simulations, the computer acts as judge while the student plays prosecutor or defense counsel. One exercise is based in part on actual proceedings from the Lizzie Borden ax murder trial; the student must decide whether to object to the admission of testimony. In a similar exercise, if the student objects too often, the computer—with all the grace of a seasoned jurist—says, "Counsel, you are trying my patience with these objections."

The branching technique is used in some medical-school simulations as well. In a simulation for practicing diagnostic procedures, students pretend to treat a seven-day-old baby dying of heart failure. As they race the clock to save the infant's life, the computer monitors changing vital signs such as pulse and respiration. The information is displayed on a cathode ray tube terminal. The students prescribe the proper treatments, typing them in on the keyboard. Then the computer creates complications, which require further diagnosis. The machine will choose a "branch" of complications, depending on what remedies the students pick.

The dying-infant exercise took six months and $10,000 to develop. Generally, cost and time depend on the sophistication of the simulation. Some can take years and cost thousands of dollars to create.

Some business schools are finding simulations an inexpensive way to recreate the world of high finance for students. At Carnegie-Mellon University, for example, graduate students in business can wheel and deal in the laundry-detergent industry with the help of a computer. The machine uses a financial model, or a group of mathematical rules, to come up with sales, profits and various seasonal fluctuations through which students can evaluate their management skills.

Aside from helping to keep students motivated about the course-work, simulations can help cut expenses without hurting the quality of instruction, educators say. In such areas as engineering, computers replace expensive laboratory gear, and simulations faithfully recreate experiments.

At the Federal Judicial Center in Washington, D.C., new appointees to the federal bar can practice and review legal topics with the same exercises used by students at the University of Minnesota. ("They get really curious when the computer tells them they're

wrong," says an educator involved in the project.) Further, some specialists predict simulations and other forms of computer teaching will become common in the home as more families buy inexpensive personal computers.

Simulations require computing power that not long ago only large, commercial machines could provide. But many of the latest simulations are being written for microcomputers on flexible, or floppy, disks, that resemble small phonograph records. Harvey J. Brudner, a Highland Park, N.J., consultant in education technology, expects 1981 to be "the take-off year" for simulations in education.

Already, Mr. Brudner says, colleges and universities are spending about $35 million a year for more than 17,000 microcomputers, and he expects a 50% increase in unit sales in the current academic year.

Individuals or small companies do most simulation programming. Conduit, a programming unit within the University of Iowa, sells 80 different simulation exercises programmed on disks for $35 to $120, depending on programming difficulty. Conduit sold 3,600 disks last year and expects to sell twice that this year. Without that volume, reproduction of the exercises wouldn't be economical.

Computer systems are quickly moving away from being mere "number crunchers" to providing decision support systems, as this article illustrates. This chapter discusses some characteristics of management information systems, which help managers make effective decisions.

ELEMENTS OF MANAGEMENT INFORMATION SYSTEMS

Data-processing systems are found in most organizations. Typical data-processing activities involve collecting and manipulating data to produce reports. Managers have found that, with computer help, such activities can be performed faster, more accurately, and at a lower cost than is possible otherwise. Recently, managers have recognized that the possibilities for computer use extend beyond normal reporting to generating information to support decision making. This application is known as a *management information system (MIS)*. An MIS is a formal information network using computer capabilities to provide management with information necessary for making decisions. The goal of an MIS is to get the correct information to the appropriate manager at the right time.

No matter what types of operations an organization performs, its management information system must provide:

Reports that are decision-oriented. Decision-oriented reports provide information that is accurate, timely, complete, concise, and relevant. If the information does not have these characteristics, then the reports are not useful for decision making.

● *Room for expansion and growth.* The survival and growth of an organization depends on how well it adapts to a changing environment. Therefore, the MIS must be flexible enough to handle the organization's changing needs. It should also be able to handle any increase in user requirements.

● *Results that the user needs.* As noted above, the primary objective of MIS is to provide management with information necessary for decision making. An MIS cannot be successful if it does not meet the users' requirements.

To better understand the concept involved in such a system, we will look separately at each element of the term *management information system.*

Management

Three levels of management generally exist within an organization, and managers at each level participate in certain characteristic decision-making activities. These levels are depicted in Figure 15–1.

● *Top-level management—strategic decision making.* At the top level, activities are future-oriented and involve a great deal of uncertainty. Examples include establishing goals and determining strategies to achieve the goals. Such strategies may involve introducing new product lines, determining new markets, acquiring physical facilities, setting financial policies, generating capital, and so forth.

● *Middle-level management—tactical decision making.* The emphasis in middle levels is on activities required to implement the strategies determined at the

FIGURE 15–1
Levels of Decision
Making

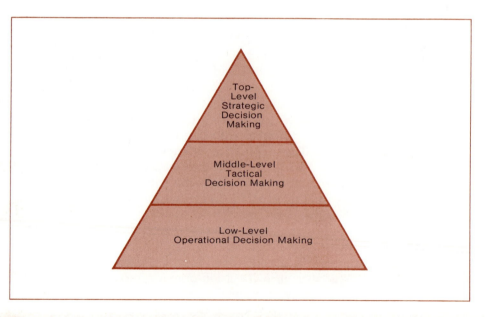

top level. Thus, most middle-management decision making is tactical. Activities include planning working capital, scheduling production, formulating budgets, making short-term forecasts, and administering personnel. Much of the decision making at this level pertains to control and short-run planning.

● *Lower-level management—operational decision making.* Members of the lowest level in the management hierarchy (first-line supervisors and foremen) make operating decisions to ensure that specific jobs are done. Activities at this level include maintaining inventory records, preparing sales invoices, determining raw material requirements, shipping orders, and assigning jobs to workers. Most of these operations can be programmed, because the decisions are deterministic—they follow specific rules and patterns established at higher levels of management. The major function of lower-level management is controlling company results—keeping them in line with plans and taking corrective actions if necessary.

In addition to the breakdown of an organization into three management levels, there exists a breakdown of the organization by function. Each functional group generates a separate stream of information flow (see Figure 15–2). For example, one such group, the marketing department, might produce detailed sales reports for each product but might feed only a summary of these reports showing divisional sales levels to middle-level marketing management. This summary report might again be summarized to show sales figures for the whole company in a report to top-level marketing management.

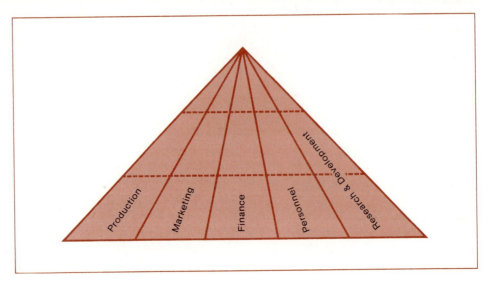

Information

Managers at all levels must be provided with decision-oriented information. The fact that the nature of decisions differ at the three levels creates a major difficulty for those attempting to develop an MIS: The information needs of each level differ, and the information system must be tailored to provide appropriate information to all levels.

Decisions made at the lower level are generally routine and well defined. The needs of first-level supervisors can be met by normal administrative data-processing activities such as preparation of financial statements and routine record keeping. Although this level of decision making is fairly basic, it provides the data-processing foundation for the entire organization. If the information system is faulty at this level, the organization faces an immediate crisis.

Tactical decision making is characterized by an intermediate time horizon, a high use of internal information, and significant dependence on rapid processing and retrieval of data. Many middle-level decisions are ill structured. The major focus of tactical decisions is how to make efficient use of organizational resources.

The main problems in MIS design arise when planners attempt to define and meet the information requirements of top-level management. It is extremely difficult, if not impossible, to clearly delineate these information needs. Most problems are nonrepetitive, have great impact on the organization, and involve a great deal of uncertainty. Most information systems serve the needs of the two lower levels but are not adequately designed to cope with the variety of problems encountered by top management. However, well-designed management information systems can help.

Table 15–1 summarizes the differences among the three levels of decision-making. Since the information needs at the three levels differ, data has to

CHARACTERISTICS	LEVELS OF DECISION MAKING		
	Operational	Tactical	Strategic
Time Horizon	Daily	Weekly/Monthly	Yearly
Degree of Structure	High	Moderate	Low
Use of External Information	Low	Moderate	Very high
Use of Internal Information	Very high	High	Moderate/Low
Degree of Judgment	Low	Moderate	Very high
Information Online	Very high	High	Moderate
Level of Complexity	Low	Moderate	Very high
Information in Real Time	High	High	High

TABLE 15–1
Characteristic Differences in Levels of Decision Making

be structured differently at each level. For routine operating decisions such as payroll preparation and replenishment of inventory, separate employee and inventory files are adequate. To serve the middle and top levels, the data should be organized to provide query capabilities across functional lines and to handle routine information reports.

Systems

The system cycle is represented in Figure 15–3. As you may recall from Chapter 12, in a system, inputs are processed to achieve outputs; and feedback—information received by the system, either internally or externally—is used in adjusting future events. For example, in a manufacturing system, input takes the form of raw materials, which are processed by manufacturing facilities, which results in output in the form of finished goods. Feedback occurs in the form of quality control standards and customer complaints. Processing can respond to feedback by adjusting output. These four elements are present in all systems and can thus be used to analyze them.

A business firm is composed of a multitude of such systems. By carefully integrating the data required to meet its systems' information needs, a business positions itself to cope with internal and external changes. It can compete more effectively in the marketplace, because it faces fewer unknowns.

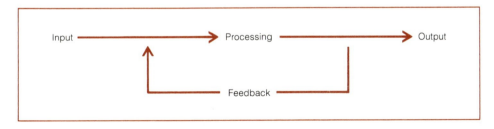

FIGURE 15–3
The System Cycle

DECISION-ORIENTED REPORTING

Information Reports

Management information systems typically generate several types of reports, including scheduled listings, exception reports, predictive reports, and demand reports.

Scheduled Listings   Scheduled listings are produced at regular intervals and provide routine information to a wide variety of users. Since they are designed to provide information to many users, they tend to contain an overabundance of data. Much of it may not be relevant to a particular user. Such listings constitute most of the output of current computer-based information systems.

Exception Reports   Exception reports are action-oriented management reports. The performance of business systems is monitored, and any deviation from expected results triggers the generation of a report. Such reports can also be produced during routine batch processing. Exception reports are useful because they ignore all normal events and focus management's attention on abnormal situations that require special handling. This saves time and effort.

Predictive Reports   Predictive reports are used for planning. Future results are projected on the basis of decision models. Such models can be very simple or highly complex. Their usefulness depends on how well they can predict future events. Management can manipulate the variables included in a model to get responses to "what if" kinds of queries. Thus, such models are suited to tactical and strategic decision making.

Demand Reports   Demand reports are produced only on request. Since they are not required on a continuing basis, they are often requested and displayed through online terminals. The MIS must have an extensive and appropriately structured data base if it is to provide responses to unanticipated queries. No data base can provide everything, but the data base of a well-designed MIS should include data that may be needed to respond to such user inquiries. Providing demand reporting can be expensive, but it permits decision makers to obtain relevant and specific information at the moment they need it.

Management and MIS

Although an MIS can help management make decisions, it cannot guarantee the decisions will be successful. One problem that frequently arises is determining what information is needed by management. To many, decision making is an individual art. Experience, intuition, and chance affect the decision-making process. These inputs are all but impossible to quantitate. In designing a system, the analyst relies on the user to determine information requirements. Frequently, lacking precise ideas of what they need, managers request everything the computer can provide. The result is an overload of information. Instead of helping the manager, this information overload creates another problem: how to distinguish what is relevant from what is irrelevant.

After the MIS has been installed, management does not always consider the change beneficial. Often, the people who must use the system were not involved in the analysis and design; thus, their expectations are unrealistic. Managers frequently expect that decision making will be totally automatic after implementation of an MIS; they fail to recognize that unstructured tasks are difficult to program. Even though routine decisions (such as ordering materials when inventory stock goes below a certain point) can be programmed easily, decisions that depend on more than quantitative data require human evaluation, because the computer system has no intuitive capability.

Other problems may arise. As the computer takes over routine decisions, managers may resist further changes. They may fear that their responsibility for decision making will be reduced or that the computer will make their positions obsolete. They may fail to realize that the availability of good information can enhance their managerial performance.

The success of an MIS depends largely on the attitude and involvement of management. An MIS is most apt to be successful when it is implemented in an organization already operating on a sound basis, rather than in an organization seeking a miracle.

DECISION SUPPORT SYSTEMS

Closely related to management information systems is the *decision support system* (DSS). Decision support is a methodology for developing a decision–making computerized process to assist managers in relatively unstructured tasks. Although DSS seems to overlap with the fundamental nature of MIS, there are some professionals in the information field who feel that a distinction must be made between the two. They claim that MIS has become associated with systems that emphasize structured or routine decisions, whereas DSS focuses on the managerial decision–making process of an information system.

DSS separates programmable decisions from nonprogramming decisions. For example, a purchase order for a certain product may be generated automatically if an inventory stock level falls below a certain quantity. Such a programmable decision can be handled by a computer.

A decision support system places more emphasis on less structured or nonprogrammable decisions. While the computer is used as an analytical aid to decision making, DSS does not attempt to automate the manager's tasks or impose solutions. For example, an investment manager must make recommendations to a client concerning the client's portfolio. The manager's decision is based on stock performance and requires a judgmental process. The computer can be used to aid the decision but cannot make the recommendation to the client.

Advocates of DSS claim that its emphasis is toward improving the effectiveness and quality of decision making. The view behind the decision support concept is not to replace management information systems but to add to them. Although the distinction between an MIS and a DSS is often blurred, the DSS approach claims to provide many benefits to strategic-level decision makers. Regardless of the title, many more organizations are realizing success through the use of information systems. In the future, decision support systems may evolve as an answer to more effective decision making.

DESIGN ALTERNATIVES

The development of an MIS or a DSS is an integrated approach to organizing a company's activities. The company must be structured in a way that will allow it to fully realize the benefits of integration. When considering alternative organizational structures, the analyst faces virtually unlimited possibilities. This section describes four basic design structures: centralized, hierarchical, distributed, and decentralized. These structures should be viewed as checkpoints along a continuous range of design alternatives rather than as separate, mutually exclusive options. For example, a system design may incorporate attributes from both the distributed system and the decentralized system. Whatever design is used, the resulting system must meet the needs of the organization it is to serve.

Centralized Design

The most traditional design approach involves the centralization of computer power. A separate electronic data-processing (EDP) department is set up to provide data-processing facilities for the organization; this department's personnel, like other staff personnel, support the operating units of the organization. All program development, as well as all equipment acquisition, is controlled by the EDP group. Standard regulations and procedures are employed. Distant units use the centralized equipment through remote access via a communication network. A common data base exists, permitting authorized users to access information (see Figure 15–4a).

The advantages of the centralized approach are that it permits economies of scale, eliminates redundancy and duplication of data, and results in efficient utilization of data-processing capability. However, a centralized design is not always best suited to all divisions of an organization. Response to division needs is generally slow because priorities are assigned based on overall organizational needs. Also, many managers prefer to control their own data-processing needs; they are reluctant to relinquish authority to a central EDP staff group.

Hierarchical Design

When hierarchical design is used, the organization comprises multiple levels with varying degrees of responsibility and decision-making authority. In addition, the organization may have functional subdivisions based on geo-

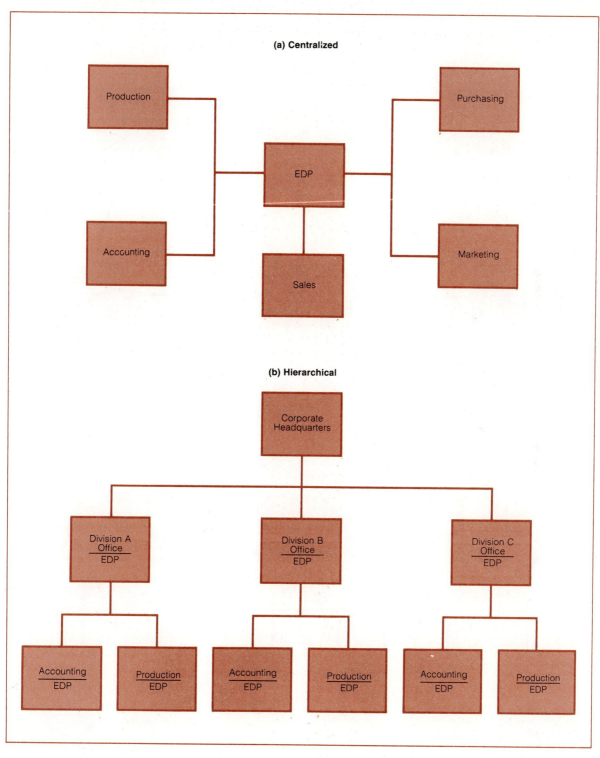

FIGURE 15–4 Sample Design Structures

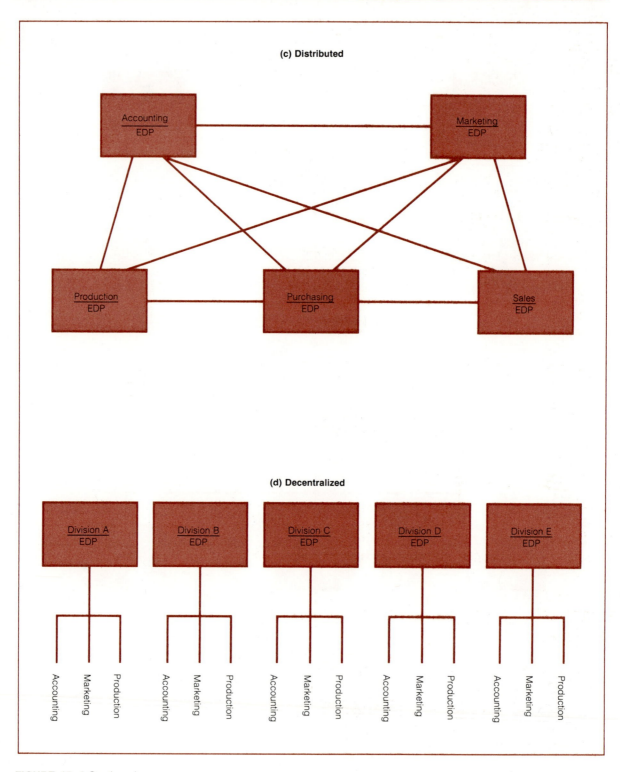

FIGURE 15–4 Continued

graphical considerations. Information flows among the various levels of management. Requests for information come down the levels, and summarized information flows up. Communication among the subdivisions is limited.

In hierarchical design, each management level is given the computer power necessary to support its task objectives. At the lowest level, limited support is required, because the work is considered technical in nature. Middle-level support is more extensive, because managerial decisions at this level require more complicated analysis (hence, more information processing). Finally, top-level executives seek little detailed information. They deal with general issues, requiring information that can be obtained only with greater processing and storage capabilities.

Data bases are usually segregated along regional or functional lines. The data bases at each level may or may not be standardized. Communication among levels is essential, but the line of responsibility for computer systems is normally traced through several levels rather than handled within all levels of the organization. The tendency, then, is for the largest group of people and machines—those at the top level—to assume responsibility for coordination and control. An example of this design approach is shown in Figure 15–4b.

Distributed Design

The distributed design approach identifies the existence of independent operating units but recognizes the benefits of central coordination and control. The organization is broken into the smallest activity centers requiring computer support. These centers may be based on organizational structure, geographical location, functional operations, or a combination of these factors. Hardware (and often people) are placed within these activity centers to support their tasks. Total organization-wide control is often evidenced by the existence of standardized classes of hardware, common data bases, and coordinated system development. The distributed computer sites may or may not share data elements, workload, and resources, depending on whether or not they are in communication with each other. An example of the distributed design approach is given in Figure 15–4c.

Decentralized Design

In a decentralized design, authority and responsibility for computer support are placed in relatively autonomous organizational operating units. These units usually parallel the management decision-making structure. Normally, no central control point exists; the authority for computer operations goes directly to the managers in charge of the operating units. Since there is no central control, each unit is free to acquire hardware, develop software, and make personnel decisions independently. Responsiveness to user needs is normally high, because close working relationships are reinforced by the proximity of the system to its users. Communication among units is limited or nonexistent, thereby ruling out the possibility of common or shared ap-

plications. This design approach can only be used where an existing organizational structure supports decentralized management. Further, it is not highly compatible with the management information system concept. An example of the decentralized design approach is shown in Figure 15–4d.

DATA-BASE CONCEPTS

Before the integrated system approach was introduced, departments had their own separate data files and collected their own input. The accounting data structure was set up to suit the preparation of financial accounts; the marketing data structure, the preparation of sales reports; and the production data structure, the preparation of production schedules and the monitoring of inventory levels. These files frequently contained duplicate data about customers, employees, and products.

In contrast, the installation of an MIS requires the use of some form of general data storage. The organization's data must be stored in such a way that the same data can be accessed by multiple users for varied applications. This can be accomplished by use of a *data base,* a grouping of data elements structured to fit the information needs of multiple functions of an organization. Data is independent—it is grouped and organized according to its inherent characteristics rather than specifically for one application task. Thus, multiple departments can use the data, and duplication of files is avoided.

In addition to reducing redundancy and increasing data independence, the data base increases efficiency. When a particular item is to be updated, the change needs to be made only once. There is no need for multiple updates as required with separate files. The integration of data also permits the results of updating to be available to the entire organization at the same time. Furthermore, the data base concept provides flexibility because the system can respond to information requests that may previously have bridged several departments' individual data files.

Data Organization

The design of data for a data base is approached from two perspectives. *Physical design* refers to how the data is kept on storage devices and how it is accessed. *Logical design* deals with how data is viewed by application programs or individual users. The logical data design is performed by the system analyst and data analyst (see Chapter 13). Together, they attempt to model the real-world relationships that exist among data items. Logical records should be designed independent of physical storage considerations. The physical design is often performed by the data administration department. Taking into account such problems as data redundancy, access time, and storage constraints, this team tries to implement the logical data design within the physical records and files actually stored on the data base.

A logical unit can extend across more than one physical file. That is to say, what one user views as a logical unit of data may include data from the employee history file and the payroll file. Conversely, one physical file may contain parts of several logical units of data. One user's logical unit may include only an employee's name and address; another may include only the employee's number and job code. In both of these cases, the data is only a part of one physical file: the employee file.

Manipulation, Retrieval, and Inquiry

Data-base systems depend on direct-access storage devices to permit easy retrieval of data items. The capabilities provided by a DASD are needed to handle the variety of logical relationships that exist among data elements. Routines can be established to retrieve various combinations of data elements from any number of DASDs.

In data-base systems, several methods are used to store and retrieve data from storage devices. A *simple structure* (or *list*) is a sequential arrangement of data records. All records are viewed as independent entities, as illustrated in Figure 15–5. If the records are ordered—that is, arranged in a specific sequence—then the list is referred to as a *linear structure*.

A list can be subdivided into groups to provide valuable information. Each such group has one ''owner'' record and any number of ''member'' records.

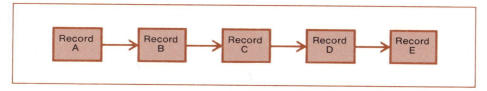

FIGURE 15–5

Example of a Simple Structure

This is called a *hierarchical*, or tree, structure. Such a list, a customer-order file, is illustrated in Figure 15–6. The owner record of each group contains the customer's number, name, and address. Each member record consists of the item number, item description, quantity ordered, and total price.

A typical file with a simple structure is shown in Figure 15–7. Each record in this file has five characteristic fields called *attributes*—name, title, education, department, and sex. Simple file structure is appropriate for generating large reports but cumbersome for handling inquiries. To overcome this limitation, an *inverted structure* can be used.

The inverted structure is better suited to responding to unanticipated inquiries. It contains indexes for selected attributes in a file, similar to those used in indexed-sequential files, and the addresses of records having those attributes (see Figure 15–8). Thus, the indexes rather than the actual files can be searched, and complex inquiries can be handled easily. Search criteria can be given for multiple files or for several attributes within one file. Once the search criteria have been satisfied and the addresses of the desired records obtained, the actual physical records can be retrieved from the file.

The major advantage of the inverted structure is that it enables a variety of inquiries to be handled quickly and efficiently. A major disadvantage is

FIGURE 15–6
Customer-Order File with Owner and Member Records

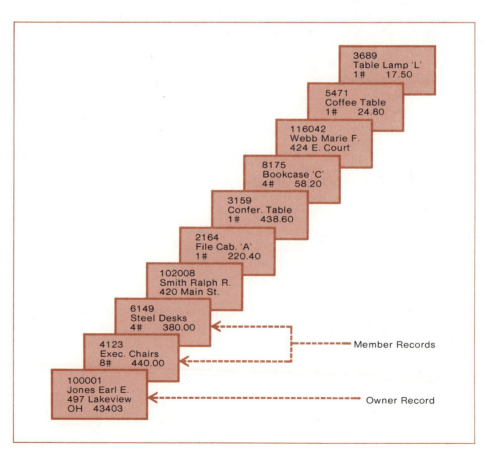

ADDRESS	NAME	TITLE	EDUCATION	DEPARTMENT	SEX
018021	Borgelt	Asst. Prof.	Ph.D.	Marketing	Male
018024	Henkes	Professor	D.Sc.	Management	Male
018046	Pickens	Instructor	M.S.	Accounting	Male
018020	Deluse	Asst. Prof.	Ph.D.	Marketing	Female
018016	Kozak	Assoc. Prof.	Ph.D.	Accounting	Male
018412	Gadus	Assoc. Prof.	Ph.D.	Accounting	Male
018318	Cross	Asst. Prof.	M.B.A.	Management	Female

FIGURE 15–7
File with
Simple Structure

that the attributes to be used in searches must be indexed. In some cases, the indexes for a particular file may be larger than the file itself.

Some typical inquiries and responses relating to the inverted file in Figure 15–8 follow:

Question: How many female assistant professors do we have and what are their names?

Response: Total of 2—Deluse, Cross.

The computer checks the attribute list for sex until it finds female. It then goes to the attribute list for title and locates assistant professor. Record addresses for those two values are compared. After female there are two addresses. Both of them match addresses listed for assistant professor in the title index. The computer goes to each of these addresses in the master file, finds the record, and returns the name.

Question: List the name of each employee who has a Ph.D.

Response: Borgelt, Deluse, Kozak, Gadus.

The computer checks the education list for Ph.D. Since there are no other search criteria, it goes to the addresses listed and prints the corresponding names.

FIGURE 15–8
File with Inverted
Structure

NAME		TITLE		EDUCATION		DEPARTMENT		SEX	
Value	Address	Value	Address	Value	Address	Value	Address	Value	Address
Borgelt	018021	Instructor	018046	M.S.	018046	Marketing	018021	Male	018021
Henkes	018024	Asst. Prof.	018021	M.B.A.	018318		018020		018024
Pickens	018046		018020	Ph.D.	018021	Management	018024		018046
Deluse	018020		018318		018020		018318		018016
Kozak	018016	Assoc. Prof.	018016		018016	Accounting	018046		018412
Gadus	018412		018412		018412		018016	Female	018020
Cross	018318	Professor	018024	D.Sc.	018024		018412		018318

In addition to the two file structures discussed, there are other more complex structures, such as the network structure, which is suitable for applications that require multiple linkages among data items. A detailed explanation of these structures is beyond the scope of this text.

Data-Base Management System (DBMS)

To facilitate the use of a data base, an organization can use a *data-base management system (DBMS)*—a set of programs that serves as the major interface between the data base and its three principal users—the programmer, the operating system, and the manager (or other information user). By installing an available DBMS, an organization greatly reduces the need to develop its own detailed data-handling capabilities.

One of the major purposes of a DBMS is to effect the physical data independence mentioned earlier. This physical data independence permits the physical layout of data files to be altered without necessitating changes in application programs. Such insulation between a program and the data with which it interacts is extremely desirable. The programmer does not have to pay attention to the physical nature of the file. He or she can simply refer to the specific data that the program needs.

Most existing data-base management systems provide the following facilities:

● Integration of the data into logical structures that model the real-world relationships among data items.
● Provision for storing the volume of data required to meet the needs of multiple users.
● Provision for concurrent retrieval and updating of data.
● Methods of arranging data to eliminate duplication and thereby avoid inconsistencies that arise from duplication.
● Provision for privacy controls to prevent unauthorized access to data.
● Controls to prevent unintended interaction or interference among programs that run concurrently.
● Capability for data base interface from within application programs coded in high level programming languages.

Assessment of the Data-Base Approach

Using a data base has a number of advantages:

● Data redundancy is minimized.
● Data can be stored in a manner that is useful for a wide variety of applications.
● Updating involves only one copy of the data.
● The system can handle requests that previously may have spanned several departments.

Limitations of the data-base approach include the following:

- An error in one input data record may be propagated throughout the data base.
- Design and implementation of a data-base system requires highly skilled, well-trained people.
- Major attention must be given to the security of the system, since all the data resources of the organization are collected in a repository that is readily accessible to data-base users.
- Traditional processing jobs may run slower.

Data-Base Software Packages

For many years, data-base management systems (DBMS) were available only for large computer systems. However, the increased use of minicomputer and microcomputer systems has led to an increased demand for *data-base packages* to run on these systems. Vendors are now providing data-base packages for all levels of the market.

In the main-frame sector of the market, complete data-base management systems are sold by large vendors. These systems help organizations to organize records, eliminate redundancy of records, and keep records up-to-date. Some permit online inquiries. A large DBMS may cost over $100,000, while data-base packages for microcomputers may cost between $200 and $600 but lack many of the capabilities of the larger versions.

Data-base packages are available at various levels of complexity even for the large computer market. A user may require only the capabilities of a simple report generator and information retrieval system. Examples of such

389

packages are Panasonic's EASYTRIEVE and Burroughs' REPORTER. Other users may need the extensive capabilities of complex, integrated data-base management systems, such as Hewlett-Packard's IMAGE, Cullinane's IDMS, Software AG's ADABAS, Cincom's TOTAL, and IBM's IMS. These packages can generate reports; create, update, and sort programs; and provide extensive security measures. Many DBMS packages include special, high-level query languages that provide easy access to stored data. These languages are user-oriented, enabling users with no programming experience to make inquiries to the data-base.

SUMMARY

● A management information system is a formal information network that uses computer capabilities to provide management with information necessary for decision making. The goal of an MIS is to get the correct information to the appropriate manager at the right time. The MIS should produce reports that are decision-oriented, have room for expansion and future growth, and contain results that the user needs.
● The concept of an MIS involves three elements—management, information, and systems. The management element includes three levels of management, each with its own level of decision-making: (1) Top-level management handles strategic decisions; (2) middle-level management handles tactical decisions; and (3) lower-level management handles operational decisions.
● The information element of an MIS differs at each level of management. Because of these differences, the data must be organized and defined differently at each level to meet managers' information needs. Data is filtered at each level to provide summarized reports for use in higher-level decision making.
● The system element operates as a cycle; inputs are processed to achieve outputs, and feedback affects future processing. Feedback is an output that is entered into the system as an input to control future events.
● An MIS typically generates four kinds of reports: (1) scheduled listings, produced at regular intervals; (2) exception reports, generated when deviations from expected results occur; (3) predictive reports, used to project future outcomes; and (4) demand reports, which answer random requests for information.
● Decision support systems emphasize effective decision making. Managers in strategic areas are provided with relevant information to help them make decisions. Support is provided for tasks which are not routine or structured.
● The ways in which an MIS can be designed within the structure of an organization are virtually unlimited. Common approaches are centralized, hierarchical, distributed, and decentralized structures. The centralized approach generally uses a single computer department to provide data processing for the entire organization. In the hierarchical approach, each management level is given the computer power needed to support its task objectives. In the distributed approach, computer support is placed in key

activity centers, and information may be shared among the various functions. In the decentralized approach, authority and responsibility for computer support are placed in relatively autonomous organizational units.

● A data base is a grouping of data elements structured to fit the information needs of all functions of an organization. The data base reduces data redundancy and increases data independence and flexibility.

● Storage of data in a data base reflects both logical and physical structures. Physical structure refers to the location of a data item on a storage device. Logical structure refers to how the data is viewed by the programs that use it.

● Logical structures can be placed on physical storage devices in several ways. The two basic methods use simple and inverted structures. A simple structure organizes records sequentially; each record is viewed as an individual entity. (If the records are organized in a specific sequence, the structure is linear.) An inverted structure creates indexes for selected attributes of the record for easy cross-referencing.

● A data-base management system (DBMS) is a set of programs that provides, among other things, (1) a method of arranging data to limit duplication; (2) an ability to make changes to the data easily; and (3) a capability to handle direct inquiries.

REVIEW QUESTIONS

1. What levels of management exist in a typical organization? What are the information requirements at each level? What are some difficulties for the MIS attempting to supply needed information to each level?

2. Identify the types of reports an MIS generates. Describe the uses of each type of report and show, by examples, where each could be utilized.

3. What is a decision support system? How does it differ from an MIS?

4. Contrast the distributed with the centralized MIS design alternative. Which of them is likely to be more responsive to user needs?

5. What is a data base? How can it be structured to respond to a variety of inquiries?

6. Should a data base be designed to handle all possible inquiries? Explain.

APPLICATION

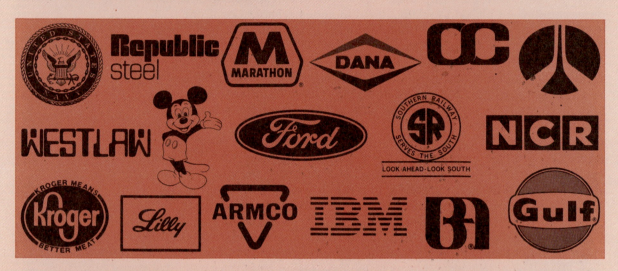

Ford Motor Company

Since 1903, Ford Motor Company has grown from a tiny operation in a converted Detroit wagon factory to a multinational enterprise with more than 300,000 stockholders. Today, Ford serves tens of millions of customers throughout the United States and overseas. It is one of the world's largest industrial enterprises with revenues totalling $37 billion and assets exceeding $24 billion; it is also the second largest auto company in the world.

Ford Motor Company entered the age of computers in 1955. Today there is data-processing equipment in every division plant, both in the United States and abroad. More than 300 computers are used for business applications; they vary in size and capacity and are supplied by a number of manufacturers, including IBM, Hewlett-Packard, Honeywell, Burroughs, Univac, and Amdahl. More than 800 computers are used in the industrial control area; most of them are minicomputers supplied by Control Data, Digital Equipment Corporation, and General Automation. Corporate-wide, data processing at Ford involves more than 2,000 system analysts, programmers, and operations researchers and almost 3,000 personnel in computer operations; more than 2,500 systems; and more than 50,000 individual computer programs.

The Ford Communications and Data-Processing Center in Dearborn, Michigan, one of the largest such centers in private industry, houses large-scale computers to provide data-processing services to the company's Dearborn-area facilities. The center also is the headquarters for Ford's world-wide communication activities; a network of terminals connected to its communications processor transmits thousands of messages per day throughout the world.

Successful applications of computers in all phases of the company's activities range from product development to management control. With the aid of the computer, Ford analyzes market data to monitor customers' reactions to present products and to suggest possible product improvements to meet the changing needs of its customers. In the area of product design and development, body-design engineers use a computer-directed scanner to translate the dimensions of clay models into digital coordinates. For capacity and product planning, a computer forecasting model projects total car and truck demand several years into the future. For production planning, a computer makes monthly forecasts of orders by body styles, options, and option combinations.

The development of computer systems has helped Ford management to improve operations related to the crucial area of customer service. By developing dealer-oriented applications close to the retail level, management can more efficiently control and monitor sales and inventory. For example, efficient parts service in an operation as extensive as Ford's is vital to customer service. Computer communication systems have improved parts service to dealers and independent service facilities. Dealers (more than 6,000 Ford and Lincoln-Mercury dealers and 1,000 independent distributors) cannot be expected to stock the 200,000 different parts needed to service all Ford vehicle products sold in the United States. Therefore, a system has been developed to allow dealers to order and receive parts as quickly as possible and at the same time allow corporate management to control inventory.

Figure 15–9 shows the flow of a parts order originated by any of the approximately 35 million customers who own Ford-built vehicles in operation. Each

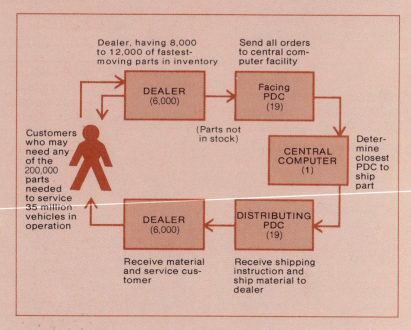

FIGURE 15–9 Ford's Volume of Customers, Dealers, and Parts Distribution Centers

dealer stocks from 8,000 to 12,000 parts and must depend on the Ford parts distribution system to replenish this inventory as well as to ship parts not normally stocked. Dealers are serviced by nineteen Parts Distribution Centers (PDCs) across the nation. The PDCs' inventories

are based on a hierarchical stocking pattern, with the fastest-moving parts stocked at the greatest number of locations. Ten of the PDCs each stock from 14,000 to 15,000 of the fastest-moving parts. Eight other PDCs each stock from 30,000 to 40,000 different parts; stock is made up of the fastest-

moving inventory as well as the inventory that moves at an intermediate speed. One PDC carries inventories of the slowest-moving parts. Each dealer places all of his parts orders with the PDC closest to him even though the parts may be shipped from any one of the nineteen centers.

A system has been developed by the Ford Parts and Service Division to get parts from PDCs to dealers quickly. The system was designed in-house and has been in use for over five years. Distributed-processing capabilities allow an individual dealer to order any part from a facing distribution center. Each dealer can transmit parts orders to the facing PDC by telephone, mail, or a specialized input terminal. The PDC's computer transmits dealers' orders by leased lines to the Ford Parts and Service central computer facility in Dearborn. The system is centered around a data base at the central facility. This data base is accessed to determine the location from which each ordered part should be sent.

An individual dealer has three ordering alternatives (see Table 15–2):

1. A weekly stock order. The stock supply normally ordered is replenished and a 5 percent incentive discount is received.
2. An interim order. Parts are shipped every other day and no discount is received
3. A priority order. Parts are shipped within twenty-four hours and a surcharge must be paid.

TABLE 15–2 Ordering Alternatives

ORDER CONDITION	INCENTIVE	PART LOCATION SEARCH
Weekly stock order	5% discount	First normal stocking PDC
Interim order	No discount	Up to four closest stocking PDCs
Priority order	10% surcharge	Up to 21 PDCs

Each type of order requires that a different search pattern be carried out against the data in the data base. For example, filling an interim order involves following a logical order pattern established in the data base for each dealer. When a dealer orders a part, the warehouse and transportation combination that can most economically supply the part is determined. If the part is not available at the closest location that normally stocks it, a computer search is made at the three next-closest stocking locations. If the part is not available at any of them, it is placed on a back-order at the closest location that normally stocks it.

If, for example, a Ford dealer in Louisville, Kentucky, needs an exhaust manifold for a 1976 Mustang, that dealer notifies the facing PDC in Cincinnati (see Figure 15–10). From the Cincinnati PDC computer, the order is transmitted to the Ford Parts and Service central computer facility in Dearborn; the central computer searches the data base and finds the PDC closest to the Louisville dealer that has the part. If the Cincinnati PDC normally stocks these exhaust manifolds, it is the first logical stocking location

for the Louisville dealer. If the part is there, it is shipped. The master part file is updated to show the shipment of one exhaust manifold from the Cincinnati PDC. If the Cincinnati PDC is temporarily out of the part, the central system examines the master file for the exhaust manifold in the Detroit PDC, the next closest shipping location. Again, if the part is located, it is shipped, and the master file is updated. If it is still not located, the central computer examines the Atlanta PDC's inventory position for this part. If the part is located, the normal procedure occurs. If not, the procedure is repeated once again for Chicago. If the exhaust manifold is not found during the computer search of the fourth location, it is put on a back-order at the PDC in Cincinnati. The entire search process is done in a fraction of a second.

When the part has been located, the dealer's facing PDC in Cincinnati sends him a hard-copy listing to show that the part has been ordered and to identify the location from which it will be shipped. The central facility processes the order and updates the inventory for the PDC from which the part

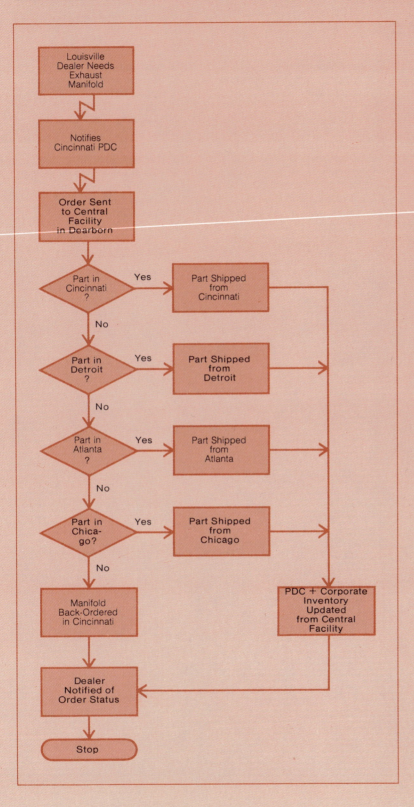

FIGURE 15–10

The Four-Step Logical
Order Pattern for an
Interim Order

is being shipped as well as
quantitatively controlling
corporate inventory.

The system was designed for
real-time operation to help
dealers quickly get out-of-stock
parts. It is also used for normal
stock reordering; and by
maintaining an inventory record
of each part stored at each
center, it provides up-to-date
inventory information to
management as well. An up-to-
the-minute report can be
generated to show exactly
which parts, and how many of
each, are in stock at any
distribution center.

DISCUSSION POINTS

1. How could the parts-ordering
system be used as a
management tool for corporate
decision making?
2. What benefits do individual
Ford dealers derive from this
system?

CHAPTER 16

Computer Systems

Introduction

During the past two decades, all aspects of the computer market have experienced rapid growth. New products are constantly being introduced to perform tasks ranging from monitoring fuel mixtures in automobiles to modeling the economies of nations. A microcomputer is used for the former application, but a large-scale computer system is needed for the latter. Computer systems today are available in a wide spectrum of sizes and capabilities to handle a variety of problems.

This chapter discusses important factors that must be taken into consideration when a computer system is to be acquired. It identifies the various categories into which computer systems can be grouped. Although the distinctions among maxicomputer, main-frame, minicomputer, and microcomputer systems are not always clear cut, the chapter attempts to delineate the characteristics of each category and to identify applications for which the systems in each category are appropriate. It also discusses important market trends and vendor support within each market sector and briefly describes the software market and the computer services offered by service bureaus and time-sharing companies.

"Cash for Cornhuskers"
Daniel Seligman

We come now to a truly sensational development at the National Bank of Commerce, an institution with some $300 million of deposits that is based in Lincoln, Nebraska. In the interests of fair play, we will confess right off that our coverage in this case will consist essentially of stealing the story from the *American Banker*. But what a story! To our mind, the first sentence qualifies as the most exciting lead of 1980. The sentence: "Bank customers in Nebraska will now be able to access their bank accounts through electronic terminals at the State Fair racetrack."

It is plain as a pikestaff, if not plainer, that here at last is the breakthrough to put electronic banking over the top. Automatic teller machines at the track will finally cause the people to grasp the operational meaning of electronic funds transfer. The meaning is that people can still play the ninth race even if they have tapped out in the eighth. Small wonder that Dennis Stelzer, vice president of the Commerce Bank, sounds pleased with himself and also with the racetrack officials. "When we first approached the State Fair people," he told the *American Banker* reporter, "we weren't really sure what their reaction would be. To our pleasure, we found them very receptive and eager to try new innovative concepts."

For some reason, Mr. Stelzer does not linger on the possibility that the innovation will primarily be a service for Nebraska's losers. Indeed, he suggests that it is the winners who will mainly benefit. The new machines will not only permit withdrawals; they will, of course, also accept deposits, and Mr. Stelzer would have you believe that the winners will be rushing to utilize this service. "They won't have to carry their money off the premises," he observes.

The notion that people do not like to carry money away from racetracks was a new thought to us, frankly, as was the proposition that horseplayers are eager to create computerized records of their winnings for the benefit of the Internal Revenue Service. But then, the marketing of electronic funds transfer is still in its infancy.

Research associate: Peter Dworkin

New applications for using computers appear daily—as evidenced by this article. Some of the points management must consider when evaluating computerized alternatives for their applications are outlined in this chapter.

MANAGEMENT PERSPECTIVES IN COMPUTER SYSTEMS

Management is faced with several alternative methods of meeting data-processing requirements. Some firms choose to lease or buy computer resources and do in-house processing; other firms use outside service bureaus. Other alternatives include time-sharing and traditional methods of manual processing. Selecting the best alternative for an organization is an exceedingly complex task.

The selection is further complicated by the myriad of equipment configurations available. Given the numerous peripheral devices discussed in Chapters 4 and 5, a seemingly infinite number of configurations are possible. The following paragraphs discuss some of the major points organizations should consider when choosing from among available alternatives.

The purchase prices of CPUs and peripheral devices prohibit all but the largest firms from buying and owning large computer systems. Traditionally, therefore, large and medium-sized computer systems have been rented or leased. From the user's point of view, leasing offers several advantages. First, lease payments are fully tax-deductible. Second, since the equipment is leased, the user can adapt to changing requirements by exchanging CPU models and accessories; a firm need not worry about technological advances rendering its equipment obsolete. Further, leasing does not require large, one-time expenditures. Normally, it takes several years of lease payments to reach the purchase price of the equipment. On the other hand, minicomputers and microcomputers are much lower in cost and are usually purchased.

The costs and quality of service must not be overlooked. These costs are normally included in the lease price, but they are not considered a part of the purchase price. Therefore, when a system is purchased, maintenance is a separate contractual matter; and its cost can be significant (often several thousand dollars a month for large systems). Maintenance services can be performed by the computer manufacturer or by a specialized maintenance firm. The quality of service is vital, because a computer breakdown can totally disrupt work flow.

Vendor support and training are especially important when an organization first installs a computer system or radically changes an existing one. The expertise of the vendor can be invaluable during design and implementation. Most vendors offer training classes to educate users of the systems they sell or lease, but the quality and amount of training offered vary greatly. The cost for these services may be included in the price of the equipment; if so, the support is said to be *bundled.* In contrast, if such items are priced separately, they are said to be *unbundled.* In 1969, IBM set a precedent by unbundling its software. As previous chapters have pointed out, the industry is evolving into a business dominated by software and service costs.

Large computer systems are often justified on the basis of the *volume* or the *complexity* of work they can be used to accomplish. Their capabilities stem not only from the equipment within the system but also from the sophisticated software available for use with it. For large firms, multiprogramming and virtual-storage capabilities may be necessities. These capabilities can be exploited fully only with large and medium-sized computers.

Software is a significant expense. In minicomputer systems, the software may cost more than the hardware. Large computer users can frequently purchase prewritten programs. Until recently, few programs were available for small computers and minicomputer systems; so firms owning minicomputer and microcomputer systems had to develop much of their software themselves.

The speed and storage capacity of the CPU are of great interest to computer users. The volume and type of processing to be done determine the speed and storage capacity, and thus the size of computer, needed. Large businesses that process data in great volume frequently need large computer systems. Firms that use computers for scientific applications need very fast computers but may not need large storage capacities. Small organizations

may find that minicomputers meet all their requirements. Large businesses may use small computers for applications where response times and storage capacities are not critical. For example, a minicomputer costing only $50,000 may do much the same work as a computer costing $2,000,000. In other words, a minicomputer that costs one-fortieth as much as a large computer can do much more than one-fortieth the work.

Besides paying for hardware and software, an organization must pay the salaries of its computer staff—managers, system analysts, programmers, data-entry personnel, computer operators, and computer technicians. Most computer-related jobs require a high degree of skill and training. These specialized services do not come cheaply; the salaries of computer staff may constitute a significant portion of an organization's monthly payroll. Small and minicomputer systems do not require as much staff support as large systems, but they may require staff more highly skilled in certain areas. For example, firms using minicomputers may need many highly skilled programmers to do program-development work either because of the specialized language used or because no suitable prewritten programs are available.

The *flexibility* of a system is the degree to which it can be adapted or tailored to meet changing requirements. Many manufacturers design their systems using a modular approach, which permits the addition of components to a system configuration, thereby allowing for growth and adaptation as an organization's needs change. An organization can start with a relatively slow, limited system and then change to a large CPU or add more peripherals when needed. Systems designed with emphasis on modularity are usually flexible.

Software compatibility also affects a system's flexibility. Compatibility refers to the ability to use programs written for one system on another system with little or no change. From a user's point of view, the number of required program changes should be minimal since reprogramming is both costly and time consuming. Fortunately, many manufacturers offer systems that can be expanded with few program changes.

While this list of considerations is by no means complete, it demonstrates the complexities involved in choosing a computer system. Other key considerations include the size of the organization and its structure. For example, a large, highly centralized organization may have little choice but to acquire a large computer system. In contrast, small businesses and decentralized organizations often find that all their data-processing needs can be met with minicomputer systems.

The computer industry is a large and growing sector of the United States economy. Although the largest user of computers is the federal government, the business world is rapidly closing the gap. A computer explosion has occurred, and there is little indication that the industry's rapid growth has slowed or is about to. With the rapidly expanding capabilities of minicomputers and small computer systems and new technological developments in secondary storage and communication systems, the task of evaluating system alternatives will become increasingly complex. However, as the industry matures, computer vendors are specializing their product offerings to appeal to specific market segments. The following sections provide an overview of some of these specialized segments and products.

MAIN FRAMES

At the heart of a large-scale computer system is the *main frame*, or CPU, (which consists, as you recall from Chapter 3, of control unit, ALU, and primary storage). A main frame can process large amounts of data at very high speeds, hold millions of characters in its primary storage, and support many input, output, and auxiliary storage devices.

Vendors

The main-frame sector is the backbone of the computer industry. Major competitors in this market are International Business Machines (IBM), Burroughs, Honeywell, Univac, National Cash Register (NCR), Control Data Corporation (CDC), and Amdahl (see Table 16–1). These vendors appeal to potential users of large, sophisticated computers.

Entry into the market is restricted by the huge capital investment required. However, once in the market, companies can take advantage of economies of scale in research and development, hardware, and application and system software design. Large, well-established companies can spread these costs over a number of units; this gives them a pricing advantage.

An example of a main-frame computer is any member of IBM's System/370 series. This series comprises many models, and an organization can choose the model best suited to its processing needs. Other vendors in the main-frame sector also offer computers in various sizes with various processing speeds and storage capacities. Purchase costs of these computers range from $200,000 to $1 million.

COMPANY	DP REVENUES	1980 DP GROWTH RATE	COMPANY CLASSIFI- CATIONS		COMPANY	DP REVENUES	1980 DP GROWTH RATE	COMPANY CLASSIFI- CATIONS
1 IBM Corporation	$21367.0	16.5%	1	36	Northern Telecom Inc	217.1	26.0	6
2 NCR Corporation	2840.0	17.3	1	37	Racal Electronics Ltd	212.0	39.6	7
3 Control Data Corporation	2790.5	22.8	1	38	Tymshare Inc	211.0	19.7	9
				39	3M Company	205.0	28.1	10
4 Digital Equipment Corp	2473.3	35.0	2	40	Four-Phase Systems Inc	197.2	10.3	2
5 Sperry Corporation	2552.0	24.5	1					
6 Burroughs	2748.0	1.5	1	41	Computervision Corp	191.1	85.5	6
7 Honeywell Inc	1634.1	12.5	1	42	C. Itoh Electronics	189.0	22.7	5
8 Hewlett Packard	1577.0	37.5	2	43	System Development Corp	186.8	14.6	9
9 Xerox Corporation	770.0	35.1	3					
10 Memorex Corporation	686.0	4.3	6	44	Motorola Inc	175.0	29.6	7
11 Wang Laboratories	681.8	66.1	4	45	General Instrument Corp	172.0	15.2	9
12 Data General	672.8	24.7	2	46	Ampex Corporation	169.7	12.2	6
13 Storage Technology Corp	603.5	25.9	6	47	Apple Computer Inc	165.2	175.1	3
14 Texas Instruments	562.0	41.2	2	48	Bunker Ramo	146.7	8.0	6
15 Computer Sciences Corp	560.3	34.8	2	49	Sander Associates	145.0	208.5	8
16 Automatic Data Processing	505.0	24.1	9	50	Bradford National	142.7	18.8	9
17 General Electric	475.0	21.2	9		Total	$51438.9	20.2%	
18 Electronic Data Systems	408.5	31.1	9					
19 Amdahl Corporation	394.4	31.7	1					
20 TRW	376.8	32.7	6					
21 Datapoint Corporation	364.0	33.7	2					
22 Triumph Adler, Inc	325.0	10.2	5					
23 Management Assistance Inc	310.4	12.7	2					

	COMPANY CLASSIFICATION	NUMBER OF COMPANIES	COMPANIES # IN AVAILABLE ESTIMATES
24 Tektronix	286.4	38.4	5
25 McDonnell Douglas Corp	280.0	14.3	9
26 Mohawk Data Sciences	277.7	12.3	3

COMPANY	DP REVENUES	1980 DP GROWTH RATE	COMPANY CLASSIFI- CATIONS
24 Tektronix	286.4	38.4	5
25 McDonnell Douglas Corp	280.0	14.3	9
26 Mohawk Data Sciences	277.7	12.3	3
27 Prime Computer Inc	267.6	75.0	2
28 Harris Corp	260.0	23.8	2
29 Teletype Corporation	250.0	72.4	3
30 ITT Corporation	250.0	2.0	5
31 Dataproducts Corporation	248.3	43.8	6
32 National Semiconductor	245.0	6.5	1
33 Perkin-Elmer	226.0	31.0	2
34 Raytheon Company	225.0	28.6	6
35 Tandy Corporation	220.0	46.7	3

	COMPANY CLASSIFICATION	NUMBER OF COMPANIES	COMPANIES # IN AVAILABLE ESTIMATES
1	Mainframes	8	8
2	Minicomputers	11	11
3	Microcomputers	2	2
4	Word Processing	1	1
5	OEM Peripherals	7	6
6	End User Peripherals	7	4
7	Data Communications	2	1
8	CAD/CAM	2	2
9	Software & Services	9	9
10	Media	1	0
	Total	50	44

Source: Gartner Group, inc.
Reprinted from the May 25, 1981 issue of *Forbes Magazine*.

TABLE 16–1
Data Processing
Top 50

Vendor Support

Main-frame vendors do more than sell main frames. A computer is useless to an organization that lacks the knowledge needed to operate it. Most vendors provide support services along with an initial purchase. These services normally include education and training for all levels of users, including top executives and data-entry personnel. Training can involve classes and seminars or self-study, in which users pace their own learning through manuals and machine exercises.

Other services may be included in the purchase or lease price of the computer system. Managers must consider any additional costs when purchasing a large computer system.

Market Trends

Though the main-frame sector dominates the computer industry, it has lost part of its market share during the past decade because of the changing nature of the computer business. At one time, as previous chapters have pointed out, the industry was almost purely a hardware business. The price of a computer system was dominated by the cost of the hardware; software costs were bundled in the total system price. With recent technological advances, the cost of hardware has been declining at a rate of 15 to 20 percent per year. In contrast, software and service costs have continued to increase significantly.

Another change in the computer industry is the trend toward distributed processing and away from centralized processing. The demand for larger, central-site computer systems has been replaced by a demand for smaller, more flexible systems. Main-frame vendors who have specialized in the production of large CPUs are diversifying into other sectors of the computer industry to remain competitive. For example, IBM has established a General Systems Division to manufacture minicomputers. Honeywell, Burroughs, and Amdahl have diversified into the areas of minicomputers, office products, and telecommunications.

Most companies requiring the processing capabilities of large computers have already had them for some time. Purchases of newer processors are made only when the company needs expanded capacity or when new price/performance ratios make them cost effective. The costs of maintaining large computer systems deter many firms from acquiring them. Some users are finding it more economical to purchase small computer systems. Since few users require the power of a maxicomputer (described below), the potential market for those large computers is limited. In short, the high end of the computer market is becoming saturated.

MAXICOMPUTERS

As pointed out, main-frame vendors sell their products to organizations requiring extensive data-processing capabilities. These organizations may process vast amounts of data or may need to perform millions of calculations per second. In some cases, demand exists for even higher processing speeds and efficiency. To respond to these needs, some vendors offer super-large, sophisticated computers called "maxicomputers."

Maxicomputer systems are very expensive, and their costs are justified in relatively few cases. The CRAY-1 computer, developed by Cray Research, Inc., is an example of a maxicomputer system (see Figure 16–1). The CRAY-1 is offered at a base price of $4.5 million; it is used mainly in the scientific areas of weather forecasting, nuclear weapons development, and energy supply and conservation. Other maxicomputers are used by large corporations and government agencies where the needs for large data bases and complex calculation capabilities justify the costs of obtaining them. Such a configuration is shown in Figure 16–2.

FIGURE 16–1
The Cray-1 Computer

As hardware costs continue to decline, organizations that have not previously been able to afford a maxicomputer may be able to pay the purchase price for one. Even then, however, the software costs associated with these systems would limit the number of users who could justify installing them.

MINICOMPUTERS

Minicomputers have come a long way since their initial development for specific applications such as process control and engineering calculations. Current minicomputers are more flexible, provide greater capabilities, and support a full line of peripherals (see Figure 16–3). The growth in minicom-

FIGURE 16–2
Maxicomputer
Configuration

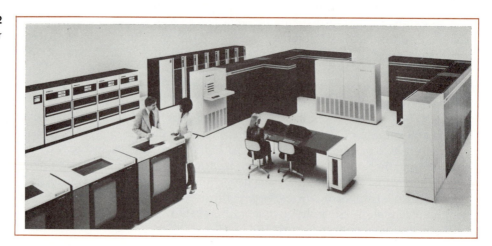

puter applications has led to the concept of distributed processing. Minicomputers are also used in time-sharing applications, numerical control of machine tools, industrial automation, and word processing.

The distinction between minicomputers and main frames has blurred over the past decade. The minicomputers manufactured today are more powerful than the main frames manufactured ten years ago. Their price ranges from $15,000 to $250,000. Many minicomputer vendors offer support services (education, training, hardware maintenance, and so on).

One reason for the popularity of the minicomputer is its flexibility. Minicomputers can be plugged into standard electrical outlets; they do not require special facilities (such as air conditioning and water cooling); and they can be utilized in an unlimited number of configurations. For example, a minicomputer system for a small firm may consist of a visual display terminal, a disk storage unit, and a printer (Figure 16–4). A large distributed system may consist of hundreds of minicomputers and peripherals tied together by communication channels to meet the needs of a geographically dispersed organization.

Another important advantage of a minicomputer system is that it can be enlarged to meet the needs of a growing organization, since it can be implemented in a modular fashion. For example, a hospital may install one minicomputer in its outpatient section for record keeping and another in the pharmacy section or laboratory. As additional minis are installed, they can be connected to existing ones to share common data.

The minicomputer industry has been growing at a rate of 35 to 40 percent annually. However, recent analysis indicates that the growth rate of this sector of the market is declining and may stabilize in the near future. Leading manufacturers include Digital Equipment Corporation (DEC), Hewlett-Packard, Data General, Honeywell, General Automation, and Texas Instruments. Smaller manufacturers include Wang Laboratories, Systems Engineering Laboratories, Inc. (SEL), and Prime Computer, Inc. IBM and Burroughs have also entered this market.

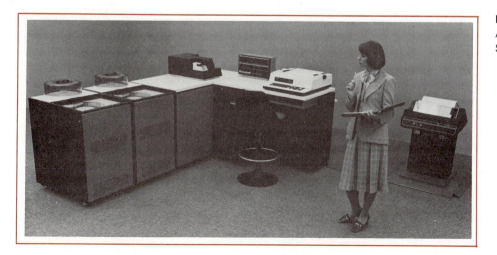

FIGURE 16–3
A Minicomputer System

FIGURE 16–4
Diagram of a Small
Minicomputer System

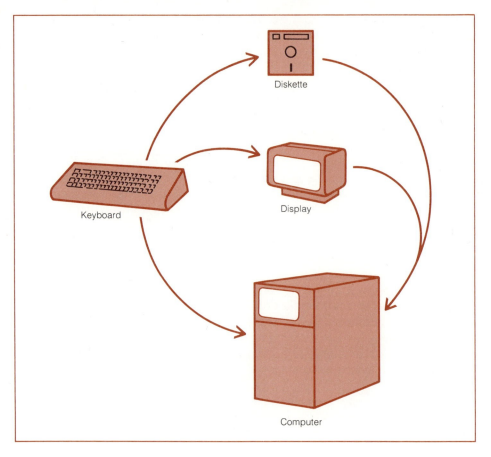

Diskette

Keyboard

Display

Computer

Distributed Processing

In many cases, minicomputers are used in conjunction with communication facilities to provide distributed processing capabilities (see Chapter 6). Most vendors in the minicomputer sector include data-communication equipment in their product offerings. Minicomputers can be combined with communication equipment to provide powerful, flexible computing capabilities.

Prior to the advent of distributed processing, many organizations depended on large, centrally located computers. As user needs increased, these computers became overloaded. Centralized computer departments were not able to respond quickly to user requirements. Users began to replace or supplement their large computers with a number of minicomputers located where processing was required, reducing the workloads on the large computers.

For example, minis placed in specific departments or branch locations of a business can handle local inquiries and produce reports for the particular departments or branches. In addition, the minis can filter and condense data before transmitting it to a central, or host, computer. Minicomputers can also be used in key-to-tape and key-to-disk data-entry systems. The minis can verify and edit the data, relieving the host computer of data-entry procedures.

Small businesses comprise one group of potential minicomputer customers. These organizations are discovering that minis yield far more efficient methods of bookkeeping and accounting than manual, mechanical, or punched-card systems. Minicomputer systems are also used in other applications. Retail stores use data-communication facilities to link minicomputers at the stores with host computers on a regional or national level. The minis provide up-to-date customer, inventory, and sales information. Each store can perform credit checks and process catalog orders. Minicomputers located in hotel chains can handle local reservations, while a host computer at a central site can handle accounting and other functions common to all hotels in the chain. Manufacturers can increase inventory control and production control by locating minis throughout production facilities. In all these applications, minicomputers provide fast, efficient processing and up-to-date output.

A typical use of minicomputers in a distributed environment occurs in the air traffic industry. Minicomputers at airports and travel agencies maintain

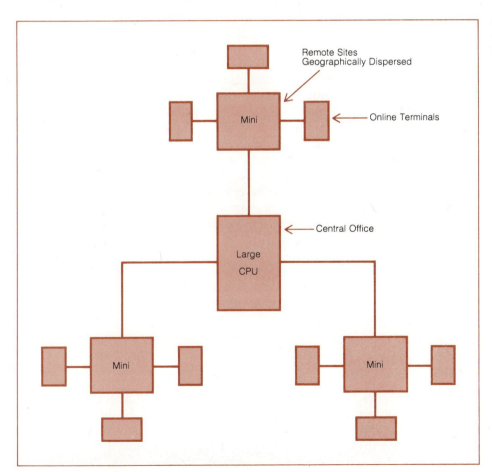

FIGURE 16–5
Distributed
Minicomputer System

up-to-the-minute records of plane departures, arrivals, and reservations. The distributed systems are connected to a main frame at an airline's central office, where nationwide data is collected and summarized for financial reporting. Visual display terminals and other peripherals allow online viewing of airline data at all remote sites. Figure 16–5 diagrams such a distributed minicomputer system.

Software Support

At the center of a minicomputer system is the software that directs its operations. For example, a minicomputer and peripherals alone are not enough to implement a distributed system. Hence, many vendors in this market sector sell software packages to accompany their hardware. The vendors realize that low cost and performance will no longer sell their products. Rather, efficient software has become the key to selling hardware. In addition, several firms specialize in software development. Software can also be developed by the user, but such developement is time consuming and costly. Many users choose to buy prewritten packages and tailor them to meet their specific needs. Indeed, when choosing a minicomputer system, managers often base their decisions on the software packages available from vendors, then choose the hardware that supports the software they need.

Many application software packages have been developed for specific industries. Minicomputer users can purchase packages designed for transportation, manufacturing, hospitals, food companies, and so on. A manufacturing application package might contain inventory-control programs, bill of material programs, and process-control programs. Accounting packages containing programs for accounts receivable, payroll, order entry, billing, and general ledger are available for many minicomputer systems.

In addition, system software is now available for minis. High-level language translators are available for FORTRAN, BASIC, COBOL, RPG, and other languages. Software vendors have developed data-base management systems, data dictionaries, and program development aids that allow relatively untrained users to develop their own application programs.

Minicomputer users, then, are finding it increasingly attractive to purchase software packages. The need for in-house staff is decreased, and total systems can be implemented within relatively short time periods. Given the number and variety of software packages available, most users can purchase software that meets their data-processing needs. A later section will further discuss the software market.

MICROCOMPUTERS

The microcomputer market has received a great deal of attention recently. When microcomputers first appeared, they were used by hobby-oriented engineers, programmers, electronics buffs, and other technically competent and inquisitive individuals. These computer hobbyists built their computers from scratch or purchased ready-to-assemble computer kits. Within a few hours, the hobbyist could put together a real computer, complete with a keyboard for data entry and a TV-like display tube.

At the sight of a true consumer market, manufacturers began to offer user-oriented microcomputer systems. These small systems were preassembled and equipped with programs to do simple jobs, such as balancing a checkbook or playing a game of backgammon. The personal computing market started in 1975 when MITS introduced the Altair 8800, a computer kit for under $500. Today a wide range of personal computers offer complete computing capabilities at low costs. A computer for the home can be purchased for about the same price as a good stereo system; those available range in price from $257 to $5,000.

At the heart of a microcomputer is a *microprocessor* that performs arithmetic/logic operations and control functions, much as the CPU of a large computer does. The microprocessor fits on a single silicon chip the size of a nail head (see Figure 16–6). Some cost under $10. Memory and input/output units are added, as on a large main-frame computer.

With the advent of the microprocessor and microcomputer systems, computers have become available to the consumer. The use of personal computers is expanding daily as more and more people discover their tremendous capabilities.

Vendors and Vendor Support

Two popular personal computer systems are the Apple and the TRS 80 computers. Initially, Radio Shack offered the TRS 80 Level I microcomputer system for about $600. It now offers an improved version, the TRS 80 Level II microcomputer (see Figure 16–7). This system can be expanded by the addition of memory and input/output units. The computer can be programmed in BASIC or in an assembler language. Radio Shack and a wide variety of other firms and individuals have developed software for use with the TRS 80 Level II, including programs for payroll, finance, home-recipe, games, and so on.

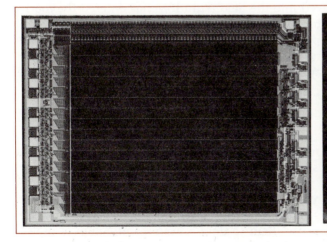 

FIGURE 16–6
Microprocessor on a Chip

FIGURE 16–7
TRS 80 Microcomputer

The Apple II computer (see Figure 16–8) is a more expensive system (around $1,000). Its standard features include 16K of RAM, five programmed cassettes, a keyboard, and a module for color TV hook-up. The system is designed for growth and has many accessories (disk drives, printers, and so on). A wide range of software for small business owners, engineers and scientists, educators, and home users is available. BASIC, PASCAL, or assembler language can be used to write additional programs.

Although the production of microcomputers has been dominated by a host of small firms, large manufacturers such as RCA, Texas Instruments, and Heath have now moved into the field. And IBM has entered the market with a personal computer priced to compete with Apple's and Radio Shack's. The new IBM personal computer will be distributed by Sears, Roebuck and Company and by Computerland. Like other personal computers, it will have color graphics, word processing, and problem-solving capabilities.

Applications

Profitable applications of microcomputers are found in small businesses and in the professions. An estimated one-third of all personal computers are located in private offices, where businesspersons can use them to do word processing, accounting, inventory control, order processing, customer lists, client records, tax records, mailing labels, and evaluation of bids and contracts. School teachers can use them to devise exams and compute grades;

FIGURE 16–8
Apple II
Microcomputer

doctors, to keep patients' records; and college football coaches, to figure out potent combinations of players and strategies.

The use of personal computers in small businesses has led to a new phenomenon known as telecommuting. *Telecommuting* is based on computer hookups between offices and homes that allow employees to work at home. This concept enables firms to employ labor resources that might not otherwise be available. For example, handicapped people, women who leave jobs to raise families but still want to work, and commuters who find the rising costs of gasoline prohibitive to taking jobs can be gainfully employed.

Many experiments with this new work environment are in progress. Control Data Corporation has sixty employees involved in a voluntary work-at-home project. McDonald's is installing terminals in the homes of the handicapped so that they can write computer programs. A British company, F International Ltd., has 600 employees, almost all of whom work at home; about half of them use computer terminals. By offering the telecommuting option to employees who want to stay home, many companies have reduced their employee turnover.

Another area influenced by the low cost of microcomputers is word processing, the manipulation of text data to achieve a desired output. Wang Laboratories is the leading manufacturer of word-processing equipment, but many other manufacturers are also developing word processors.

A typical stand-alone word-processing system consists of a keyboard, a visual display screen, a storage unit, and a printer (see Figure 16–9). An operator enters text (in the form of memos, letters, reports, and the like) on the keyboard. The text is stored and can be edited, revised, and reformatted without retyping of entire documents. The printer is used to generate hard copies when desired. A further advantage is the word processor's ability to

FIGURE 16–9
Word Processor

store names and addresses that can be used in form letters or for distribution of output.

Word-processing systems have helped to improve office productivity. For example, clerical staffs are relieved of many typing chores, and filing is no longer a manual task. Because of this potential to improve office productivity, the market for word-processing systems appears to be a large one. Many vendors in the minicomputer sector are providing the software needed to support word-processing applications on their systems. Data-entry terminals linked directly to a minicomputer can be used for text entry, and the entered text can be stored as data available to other applications.

Office managers have a wide variety of alternatives from which to choose when selecting a word-processing system. The system can be used to increase productivity, improve working conditions, and increase employee satisfaction and career opportunities through job enrichment.

Computer Stores

Personal computing was, until recently, primarily a mail-order business. Products were shipped directly from manufacturers to users. With the emergence of the home-computer concept, however, a new retailing phenomenon has evolved—*computer store.* These stores are structured to appeal to owners of small businesses and to personal users. Today, thousands of home computer stores exist in the United States. The best ones offer a variety of products and services manufactured by several firms. Demonstration systems are on display so that potential buyers can experiment with the systems, much as they would take test drives before purchasing a car. Microcomputer experts are available to answer questions and to provide technical guidance to the computer novice.

Word Processing Replaces Typing

One of the hottest-selling items in the computer industry is the word processor—essentially an electric typewriter with a video display screen and a memory. There are two types of word processors: "stand-alone" type which consists of a keyboard and from one to four display screens; and the "cluster" type, which is hooked up to a central computer. Most current business processors are the stand-alone type.

These devices can really help the secretary, because everything typed is displayed on the screen. The secretary can then correct mistakes and even rearrange words or sentences. When the page is completed, the machine or a printer prepares the desired number of copies on paper. Changes can be made to each copy before it is printed, which is especially useful for typing letters.

The newest word processors will even catch spelling errors. A new IBM machine contains a 50,000 word dictionary, available in six languages, that will point out misspelled words and highlight any words not in the dictionary. Compucorp has introduced a word processor that outdoes the IBM machine; it has a dictionary of one million words, catches misspelled words, and then corrects them!

The next major advantage will probably be realized when these word processors are connected to other systems across the country. With this type of network, the finished letter will no longer need to be typed and sent through the mail; it will be sent instantly to its destination by telecommunications equipment. While this "electronic mail" is used to some extent by large companies, the scope of connected systems is still too small for broad use in mass

Evaluating Microcomputers

Purchasing a personal computer is like purchasing a stereo component. There are so many models available, with so many different characteristics, and at so many different prices, that a number of key features to consider must be identified. Concerning the computer itself, the buyer might want to look at the type of keyboard and the availability of a programming language (such as BASIC) in read-only memory (ROM). Optional equipment—such as more programming memory, high-level languages, printers, disk drives, and the like—and its cost should be evaluated. If the computer will be used for business purposes or for writing and editing, it should have the growth capability needed for word processing. For financial or engineering analysis, full memory, a disk drive, a printer, and graphics capability are useful. Both hardware support and software support are important. The buyer should check to determine whether service as well as expansion hardware will be available a few years in the future.

A businessperson anticipating a microcomputer purchase should evaluate several stores' offerings. Many stores specialize in a certain brand of machines, while a few are "computer supermarkets" carrying five or six brands. Businesspersons can learn of current developments by reading about the various microcomputers in publications such as *Byte Magazine, Kilobaud, Microcomputing Magazine,* and *S–100 Microsystems*, which are available at computer stores or book stores. Finally, the businessperson should meet with computer owners' groups (owner of Apples and TRS 80s, among others, have formed groups around the country) to discuss the pros and cons of the various systems. Local stores know of owners' groups associated with the brands of machines they sell.

TABLE 16–2
Consumers' Guide to
Software Shopping

TYPE OF SOFTWARE	WHAT IT DOES	WHERE TO BUY IT	SOFTWARE PRICE
DATA BASE MANAGEMENT SYSTEM	Organizes data in line with the informational needs and organizational structure of a business. Makes it easier to access and update files.	Computer vendors Systems software companies	Starts at $7,000 (for use with a minicomputer) and runs to more than $100,000 (for use with a mainframe computer or for custom programming)
NETWORKING	Enables computers in one building or across the country to communicate.	Primarily computer vendors	$5,000 to $15,000 per machine in a minicomputer network and $30,000 to $75,000 for each mainframe computer in a network
TRANSACTION PROCESSING	Permits users to carry on a dialogue with the computer—typing information and getting an immediate response. For use with such commercial applications as check processing and order entry.	Computer vendors Systems software companies	$15,000 and up
PROGRAMMING TOOLS	Helps programmers write applications programs by automatically testing software code and identifying errors. Also known as "debuggers."	Computer vendors Systems software companies	$1,000 to $5,000 (for a minicomputer) and $5,000 to $75,000 (for a large mainframe computer)
QUERIES AND REPORT GENERATORS	Aids the novice user in extracting information from a computer memory and formating it into a report.	Computer vendors Systems software companies	$1,000 to $37,000 for standard software

SOFTWARE

Software and consulting firms specialize in developing information systems for businesses. Usually, such a firm specializes in either system software or application software. Both are often sold as packages—collections of programs that work together to accomplish specific processing objectives. Such software packages are debugged and well documented. Some suppliers even provide ongoing maintenance.

TYPE OF SOFTWARE	WHAT IT DOES	WHERE TO BUY IT	SOFTWARE PRICE
APPLICATIONS GENERATORS	Generates applications software programs without the need for an experienced programmer.	Major computer vendors	$5,000 and up
GENERAL FINANCIAL	Automates the accounting functions of a business, including billing, inventory control, accounts payable, accounts receivable, general ledger, and payroll.	Computer vendors Applications software companies	Packages range from $1,000 to $20,000 (for minicomputer systems) and from $20,000 to $70,000 (for large mainframe computers)
MANUFACTURING RESOURCE PLANNING	Helps the user gain better control over the entire manufacturing process from production planning and inventory control to materials monitoring.	Large computer vendors Applications software companies	$50,000 and up for standard packages, $100,000 and up for custom software
FINANCIAL PLANNING	Simulates profit-and-loss scenarios for a company based on revenues, sales force location, commissions, and other controllable variables.	Primarily applications software companies	$5,000, to $45,000 for packages; custom work begins at $250,000
CASH-FLOW MANAGEMENT	Assists financial managers in getting the best use of funds within a business.	Primarily applications software companies	$25,000 to $75,000 for packages; custom software begins at $150,000
MANAGEMENT SUPPORT SYSTEMS	Combines software packages such as color graphics and business modeling that aid the manager in making decisions.	Primarily applications software companies	Depends on the packages selected

TABLE 16–2
Continued

Data: International Computer Programs Inc., BW

Vendors

Manufacturers in all market sectors provide software packages to accompany their equipment. However, the overwhelming demand for software in the past decade has made it profitable for firms to specialize in software offerings. The leading suppliers of computer software include Computer Sciences, Automatic Data Processing (ADP), General Electric, Electronic Data Systems (EDS), McDonnell Douglas, and Tymeshare.

The most popular type of software packages are data management packages, which were discussed in Chapter 15. Others include communication packages, in which complete programs are offered to tie together large networks of computers; for example, ADR offers DATACOM, IBM offers CICS, and Cincom offers ENVIRON/1. Operating system software and utilities packages are available from several vendors; common examples are librarian programs and high-level language translators. In addition, application software is available in a multitude of forms, ranging from inventory management to payroll and general ledger.

Market Trends

Software suppliers have experienced their highest growth in the home and small business computer markets. Other expanding areas include computer graphics, robotics, and industrial applications. The U.S. government's Departments of Defense, Agriculture, HEW, and HUD use a great deal of software.

The increased purchases of hardware that resulted from declining costs have escalated software demand. Users want sophisticated software, such as a data-base management system (DBMS). Many users who once developed their own software are now buying standardized application programs and system programs. Although these standardized programs may need to be tailored for the organization, the benefits of purchasing packages are quickly realized, since the cost of buying a package is a fraction of the cost of developing the software in-house.

Small business users and first-time users are hardest hit by the "software crunch." These users do not have the staff needed to support software development. Software firms are attempting to reach these potential customers through avenues such as retail stores. Some stores offer one-stop shopping: programs ranging from computer games to small business applications are provided. The current offerings of any one software company are in a constant state of flux. Many firms offer new releases of their software packages containing the latest developments requested by users. Other firms develop specialized software packages under contractual arrangements. Table 16–2 shows a listing of some of the software packages available to customers.

SERVICE BUREAUS AND TIME-SHARING COMPANIES

Computer systems are a major expense. Many companies cannot afford systems of their own. Service bureaus (which provide data-processing services) and time-sharing companies (which provide computer facilities) allow users to take advantage of the sophistication of a large computer system without incurring all of its costs. They also provide computer power to companies who do not need twenty-four-hour-a-day processing.

Growth in the time-sharing industry is primarily due to the advances in data-communication equipment. Time-sharing customers usually purchase input/output devices and use them to access the facilities of the time-sharing company. Storage space on magnetic tapes and disks can be rented. The customer pays for CPU resources at a monthly rate. Some time-sharing companies have networks of computers spread throughout the nation. Great economies of scale can be realized by distributing the costs of such a system over many users.

A disadvantage of using time-sharing is that it becomes very expensive as data-processing needs increase. The more computer time required, the greater the monthly costs. However, time-sharing may be an economical alternative for companies that are first-time EDP users.

Service bureaus provide a number of data-processing services. Some such bureaus perform all data-processing activities for small firms. Others specialize in providing temporary personnel to perform data-entry or programming activities. Many specialize in a particular industry, such as oil companies or savings and loan associations.

An example of a service bureau is McDonnell Douglas Automation Company (MCAUTO). MCAUTO, the largest computer center in the world, services approximately 3,000 customers and processes over 30,000 time-sharing jobs in an average week. The computer center contains thirteen large-scale computers linked to 16,000 terminals (see Figure 16–10). McDonnell Douglas also sells software to various industries (insurance, manufacturing, and

FIGURE 16–10
MCAUTO Computer Center

construction) and offers computer-related consulting services to computer users.

Thus, managers have countless alternatives from which to choose when acquiring an EDP system, and they will be faced with an even greater number of decisions as computer vendors continually develop new and better ways to gain a share of the market and to reach the consumer with information about their products.

SUMMARY

- Selecting a computer configuration for an organization or for personal use is a complex task. Important factors to be considered include: purchase versus rental prices of hardware, maintenance costs, vendor support, software costs and capabilities, hardware capabilities, staff requirements, and system flexibility and compatibility.

- The main-frame sector of the computer industry is limited to a few large companies. This sector dominates the computer industry; however, entry into this market is limited by the huge capital investment needed. Main-frame vendors provide software support and maintenance in various ways. These costs may or may not be included in the initial purchase or lease price.

- Maxicomputer systems are capable of processing large amounts of data and performing millions of calculations per second. These systems are very expensive and are used by large corporations and government agencies that need to support large data bases and complex calculations.

- The declining costs of hardware along with the trends toward distributed processing have resulted in a changing computer industry. Main-frame vendors have found it profitable to diversify into other market sectors.

- Minicomputer systems have led to the concept of distributed processing. Minicomputers are flexible and can support many peripherals. When combined with data-communication equipment, they can be very powerful data-processing tools. Vendors in this market include software and services in their product offerings. In addition, software companies supply various types of software packages. Organizations can purchase prewritten packages or develop programs in-house.

- Microcomputers have rapidly gained popularity in homes, small businesses, and large corporations. Personal computers offer homeowners and hobbyists a wide variety of electronic games and also perform household duties. Small businesses and professionals use microcomputers to perform clerical tasks such as payroll, accounts receivable, appointment scheduling, and billing. Telecommuting allows employees to work at home on computer terminals tied to offices. Large corporations use computers to provide desktop conveniences for managers.

- Word-processing systems ease the typing duties of secretaries in all sizes of organizations. Word processing can be provided by a stand-alone microcomputer or by a distributed minicomputer system.

● A multitude of software and peripheral devices can be used with microcomputers. The microcomputer sector has evolved to serve a mass-merchandise, retail market. Both hardware and software are available at local computer stores. Prospective microcomputer users must consider the importance of software support when buying computer systems.

● The demand for software is growing at an unprecedented rate. Many users find it less expensive to buy software from a software vendor than to create programs in-house. Prewritten packages are documented and debugged. However, an organization must tailor such programs to meet its particular needs.

● Service bureaus provide data-processing activities to firms which are unable to support the costs of a computer system. Time-sharing companies provide the use of computer facilities to customers for a monthly fee. Both of these allow users to realize the benefits of a large computer system without the associated costs.

REVIEW QUESTIONS

1. Discuss the importance of software in a computer system. How should a potential buyer choose a software package?

2. Describe the factors a manager must consider before acquiring a computer system.

3. How have recent trends in the computer industry affected computer vendors? What has been the effect of these trends on small businesses?

4. Explain the term *compatibility*. How has this factor affected the computer industry?

5. What are some uses of maxicomputer systems? of minicomputers? of microcomputers?

6. Why might a firm contract with a service bureau? What are some advantages and disadvantages of using service bureaus and time-sharing companies?

APPLICATION

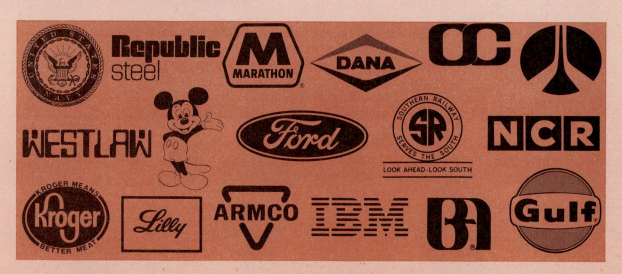

Southern Railway Company

The eighty-four-year old Southern Railway Company is a profitable, highly innovative organization with a history of leadership in many areas of the railroad industry. It is the eighth-largest railroad in the United States and, unlike many U. S. railroads, has achieved its success operating only railroads. (Some lines have oil, like Union Pacific; timber, like Burlington Northern; or coal, like Norfolk & Western; while still others, like IC Industries and Santa Fe Industries, have become diversified holding companies.)

Southern Railway has also had a long and successful history of computer use. It currently has a large computer installation in Atlanta. The central system hardware consists of one IBM System/370 Model 158MP and two IBM System/3033's. Examples of applications processed by these computers are: a real-time car-movement system designed to keep track of freight cars and trains on the lines of the railroad, accounting, payroll, marketing and sales analysis, statistical reporting, engineering and car distribution functions, and inquiry systems that provide information for car distribution and field personnel.

In 1980, Southern completed its Terminal Information Processing System—better known as TIPS. TIPS now encompasses a network of microprocessor terminals and minicomputers in 246 locations in yards, terminals, and stations throughout the railway. All of these installations are capable of independent computer functions. Some are used primarily as input/output terminals, but all are linked to a main computer in Atlanta. Each of the 246 terminals is a reporting and inquiry station.

One of the most interesting applications involves a sophisticated network of minicomputers at the Sheffield, Alabama, automatic railroad classification yard. The system, completed in 1973, was a $15 million, two-and-a-half-year project that uses a distributed approach; the data needed for the Sheffield operation is transmitted from the central computer complex in Atlanta. The computer activity at the Sheffield rail yard is divided into two systems, a management information system (MIS) and a process control (PC) system. Five minicomputers are linked together to form these systems—two on PC, one on MIS, and two on backup.

The purpose of a rail yard is to receive inbound trains in the receiving area, reclassify the individual train cars in the classification area, and consolidate the new classifications of cars for forwarding to the proper destination. In the Sheffield automatic classification yard, the switching is done by the PC minicomputers.

The information flow really starts long before a train arrives at Sheffield. Throughout the thirteen southeastern states served by Southern, about 246 stations report every movement of every car and train to the central online/real-time system. Consequently, the central computer complex in Atlanta has current data about every car and train on more than 10,500 miles of track. About two hours before a train arrives at Sheffield, the Atlanta computer transmits an "advanced consist" to Sheffield. The consist tells the makeup of the train, specifying the cars' precise sequence, destination, weight, and so on. This data is stored by the MIS minicomputer and printed to assist yard personnel in planning.

When the train arrives at the Sheffield yard, the yard supervisor decides which receiving track the cars will go onto and informs the MIS minicomputer via a CRT. The computer updates the inventory of the receiving yard. At the end of the receiving tracks is a small hill over which each inbound car is pushed; as it rolls free over the hill, it is switched onto one of the thirty-two classification tracks. This process is controlled by the PC minicomputers and other instrumentation, including photoelectric cells, weigh-in-motion scales, wheel sensors, speed-reading radars, and wind gauges. There are 600 inputs in the PC minis from the various devices in the yard. As each car starts to roll over the hill, its weight is calculated, length determined, axles counted, and rate of speed change measured. Also determined at this point are the curves the car must negotiate and the distance it must roll to reach its classification track so that it will strike the last car there at less than four miles per hour (see Figure 16–11).

After these calculations are made, a "master retarder" is instructed by the minicomputer to slow the car to the calculated speed and to align the switches that will direct the car to the proper track. The car enters the complex of switches and is directed to its assigned track. At the other end of the classification track, a locomotive pulls the cars, under radio instruction, from that track and moves them to the forwarding yard, where they are coupled into trains for a subsequent road haul.

The MIS minicomputer also assists in the classification process. When the cars are ready to go over the small hill, the yard supervisor uses the CRT to enter the receiving track, number of cars, and beginning and ending car numbers. From this, the MIS minicomputer prepares a list of every car, their sequence, and the classification track to which each should go (depending on its route, destination, contents, and the like). The speed at which the cars should be shoved to the hill is then selected. The PC mini takes over control of the "switching" locomotive and adjusts the

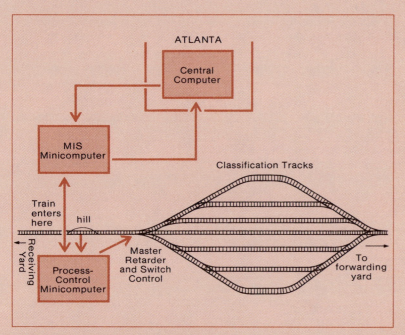

FIGURE 16-11 Computer-Controlled Railroad Classification Yard

speed as the cars approach the hill.

A CRT displays the first ten cars to go over the hill, and a closed-circuit TV shows the supervisor the actual operation. He or she compares the car on the TV with the first car on the CRT list. If they are the same, the supervisor does nothing else. As the first car clears the hill, the list on the CRT rolls up one. The process is repeated for each car.

As each car completes its switching, the PC mini sends the MIS mini data regarding which track the car actually went to. If this data is not the same as the data in the original list, the differences are analyzed. Appropriate messages are updated and displayed to the yard supervisor. Occasionally, a car

does not go to the proper track. If the first car rolled slowly and the second car rolled fast and caught up with, or came too close to, the first car, the PC mini may have deemed it unwise to throw switches between them. If so, it allowed the second car to go to the wrong track. These moves must receive attention.

Finally, the yard supervisor requests CRT displays of the contents of the tracks. He or she decides which cars will make up an outbound train and what their sequence will be. This decision is keyed in as a work order which, in turn, is relayed by radio to the "pullback" locomotive engineer. As the train leaves the forwarding yard, the supervisor records the fact that the train is leaving the particular track. The

MIS mini updates the inventories and sends the consist of the outbound train to the central computer in Atlanta.

Thus, the system makes much of the record-keeping automatic—and gives the personnel the capability to determine in advance what will happen if certain decisions about train movement are made. It also lays the groundwork for other improvements, such as better grasp of locomotive and car availability.

Only control instructions—no data—are entered into the system locally. Full advantage is taken of the centralized data already existing in the Atlanta computer. The concept of the distributed data base, where the data needed for local operation is transmitted and processed locally, is extremely important for complete reliability. Trains must be classified twenty-four hours a day, regardless of computer or communication problems. Distributed computers and data bases are essential for high-reliability operations in this application.

DISCUSSION POINTS

1. Why is the concept of distributed computers and data bases extremely important for operations that require complete reliability?

2. What types of applications does Southern Railway process on its large computers? For what purposes does it use minicomputers?

SECTION V
Computers in Society

CHAPTER 17

Computer Security, Privacy, and the Law

Introduction

Perhaps without realizing it, the United States has made an irrevocable commitment to computerization. It is almost impossible to function in today's society without interacting wth a large number of computer systems. Both government and private industry collect and store personal information about people, and the computer has become an essential tool in this process. At the same time, it has caused some erosion of the rights and privileges of the individual. Major problems also exist in the areas of computer crime and security. Billions of dollars are lost each year because of computer crimes.

This chapter examines some of the major threats faced by a computer-based system and the security measures required to protect such a system against damage and abuse. It also presents some of the problems of privacy and computer crime and some of the remedies currently being applied to them.

"Superzapping in Computer Land"

Frederic Golden
Reported by Philip Faflick/New York,
with other U.S. Bureaus

The customer, calling from Ottawa, was furious. Someone, he complained to officials of Telenet, a telecommunications network based in Vienna, Va., was using its lines to penetrate his company's computer. As a result, his operations were fouled up. The next week another computer network, named Datapac and tied to Telenet, got a similar call from a firm in Montreal. Its circuits too were being plagued by electronic interlopers.

Operating out of unknown terminals, possibly hundreds of miles away, the intruders had tapped into—or "accessed," in computer jargon—one of the company's computers. Even worse, they had actually "seized control" of the electronic brain, blocking the network's legitimate users from getting on line, and were systematically destroying data. The raids continued for more than a week. During one foray, 10 million "bits" of information, almost one-fifth of the computer's storage capacity, were temporarily lost.

It was an electronic sting with international repercussions: the Royal Canadian Mounted Police joined with the FBI to catch the

criminals. By tracing phone calls, they soon got their man. Or rather boys. The culprits, only 13 years old, were four clever students at New York's Dalton School, a posh private institution on Manhattan's Upper East Side.

The bit-size bandits, perhaps the youngest computer con men ever nabbed, had obtained the Telenet phone number, coupled their school terminals to the line, and probably by nothing more than trial and error punched out the right combinations—in this case only five letters and numbers—to link up with the computers. More shrewd guesswork got them the "password" to log onto and operate the machines.

It was a schoolboy lark. None of the Dalton gang, even its eighth-grade leader, was prosecuted. But computer specialists were not amused. Besides costing the firms thousands of dollars in computer time, the incident was one more irritating example of the vulnerability of systems that can have price tags in the millions and store informaton of incalculable value. It was also a sign of the growing incidence of computer crime.

No one can say exactly how much such crime costs; often the losses are not even reported by embarrassed companies. But the larceny clearly is far from petty. It may well run to hundreds of millions of dollars a year. Last January, California became the first state to enact a computer-fraud law, allowing fines of up to $5,000

and three years' imprisonment. Still, warns Donn Parker of SRI International, a leading scholar of electronic theft: "By the end of the 1980s, computer crimes could cause economic chaos."

An exaggeration perhaps. But as computers spread into all facets of life, from controlling the flow of money to manning factories and missile defenses, the potential for troublemaking seems boundless. Already computer thieves, often striking from within, have embezzled millions of dollars. In 1978 a consultant got a Los Angeles bank's computer to transfer $10.2 million to his out-of-town account. Only a confederate's tip led to his discovery. To be a computer-age thief, you need nothing more than an inexpensive home computer, a telephone and a few light-fingered skills. As in the Dalton case, computer passwords are often short and simple. Besides, computer networks, like Telenet or Datapac, frequently publicize their numbers to attract customers. Once into the computer system, there are other barriers to crash, and other techniques for purloining information.

Computer crooks have developed a whole bag of electronic tricks. One is the so-called Trojan Horse. Like the famed ruse used by the Greeks to penetrate Troy, it helps an interloper get into forbidden recesses of a computer. The mischiefmaker slyly slips some extra commands into a computer program (the instructions by which the machine performs a given task). Then when another programmer with higher clearance runs the program, he will unwittingly trigger the covert instructions. These unlock the guarded areas, just as the Greek soldiers hidden in the horse unlocked Troy's gates. The culprit might then transfer money to his own account, steal private information, or sabotage the system itself. Other colorfully named ploys: superzapping (penetrating a computer by activating its own emergency master program, an act comparable to opening a door with a stolen master key); scavenging (searching through stray data or "garbage" for clues that might unlock still other secrets); and piggybacking (riding into a system behind a legitimate user).

Faced with such ingenuity, some computer owners are resorting to complex coding devices that scramble information before it is transmitted or stored. They are also changing passwords. Some even rely on detectors that identify legitimate individual computer users by fingerprints or voice patterns.

Yet as the safeguards go up, so does the urge to crash the barriers, especially among students. In a celebrated Princeton University case, students snatched grades and housing data from the school's computers and, by their account, briefly shut them down. Last September, two Illinois high school students dialed their way into one of DePaul University's computers and threatened to immobilize it unless they got access to a special program that would have let them communicate with the machine more directly. Said an investigator who helped catch the teen-agers: "They did it because everyone said it couldn't be done." Maybe so. But computer owners wonder: Where does the fun end and the crime begin?

As computers have become a fact of life, so has computer crime. The following chapter discusses some of the security measures and legal procedures that are working to meet the challenge.

COMPUTER SECURITY

Computer security involves the technical and administrative safeguards required to protect a computer-based system (hardware, personnel, and data) against the major hazards to which most computer systems are exposed and to control access to information.

Physical computer systems and data in storage are vulnerable to several hazards—fire, natural disasters, environmental problems, and sabotage.

● *Fire.* Fire is one of the more apparent problems, because most computer installations use combustible materials—punched cards, paper, and so on. Further, if a fire gets started, water cannot be used to extinguish it, because water can damage magnetic storage media and hardware. Carbon-dioxide fire-extinguisher systems are hazardous because they would endanger employees, if any were trapped in the computer room. Halon, a nonpoisonous chemical gas, can be used in fire extinguishers; but systems that use halon are costly.

● *Natural disasters.* Many computer centers have been damaged or destroyed by floods, cyclones, hurricanes, and earthquakes. Floods pose a serious threat to the computer hardware and wiring. However, water in the absence of heat will not destroy magnetic tapes unless the tapes are allowed to retain moisture over an extended period of time. Protection against natural disasters should be considered when the location for the computer center is chosen—for example, the center should not be located in an area prone to flooding.

● *Environmental problems.* Usually, computers are installed in buildings that were not originally planned to accommodate them. This practice can give rise to environmental problems. For example, water and steam pipes may run through a computer room; bursting of these pipes could result in extensive damage. Pipes on floors above the computer room are also potentially hazardous; so all ceiling holes should be sealed. Data on magnetic media can be destroyed by magnetic fields created by electric motors in the vicinity of the computer room. Other environmental problems include power failures, brownouts (temporary surges or drops in power), and external radiation.

● *Sabotage.* Sabotage represents the greatest physical risk to computer installations. Saboteurs can do great damage to computer centers with little risk of apprehension. For example, magnets can be used to scramble code on tapes, bombs can be planted, and communication lines can be cut. Providing adequate security against such acts of sabotage is extremely difficult and expensive.

In addition to safeguarding their computer systems from these physical difficulties, companies must protect stored data against illegitimate use by controlling access to it. There is no simple solution to these security problems. Some ways to protect computer systems from physical dangers, such as fire and flood, are suggested in the list above. Organizations have instituted various other security measures—most to restrict access to computerized records, others to provide for reconstruction of destroyed data. Some examples are given below:

● Backup copies of data are stored outside the organization's location, and recovery procedures are established.

● Authorized users are given special passwords. Remote-terminal users have their own unique codes, and batch-processing users have specific job cards. Codes and passwords should be changed frequently.

● The scope of access to the computer system is proportionate to the user's security clearance and job responsibility. Access to specific portions of the data base can be gained only by those whose jobs necessitate it.

● Installations are guarded by internal security forces. For example, access to the data-processing department may be restricted to personnel with special badges and keys.

● Data is *encrypted,* or translated into a secret code, by complex coding devices that scramble information before it is transmitted or stored. When data is transmitted to or from remote terminals, it is encrypted at one end and *decrypted,* or translated back into plain text, at the other. Files can also be protected by the data's being encrypted before it is stored and decrypted after it has been retrieved. Data is principally encrypted on its way out of the computer and decrypted on its way back in.

● Computer installations use detectors that identify legitimate individual computer users by fingerprints or voice patterns. For example, computer makers have developed attachments that grant access only to operators who put proper thumbprints on glass plates. Adoption of such expensive devices is slow, however, because they deter the main objectives of computers: economy and convenience.

These security measures are not complete, however. They may not prevent internal sabotage, fraud, or embezzlement. For example, an organization member with a special access code may steal classified information. In fact, computer crimes have been called the "white-collar crimes of the future," and many organizations already have had such problems. Banks and insurance companies are especially susceptible. Often, these companies do not wish to report the incidents because of the bad publicity and the difficulty in solving such crimes.

How, then, can organizations establish computer security? First, computer users must recognize their role in security. If a high-level priority is assigned to security in the company, employees must be made aware of it and of the security measures that are being taken.

Second, many organizations recognize the need to have a well-trained security force—a department of security guards who specialize in maintaining data security, conducting system audits, and asking the right kinds of questions on a daily and continuing basis. Computerized records, like handwritten books, should be scrutinized regularly to see that everything is in order.

Third, a company should exercise a great deal of care in the selection and screening of the *people* who will have access to computers, terminals, and computer-stored data. Companies should choose programmers as carefully as they select attorneys or accountants.

Lastly, companies must discharge employees who stray beyond legal and ethical boundaries. Whenever these incidents occur, it is imperative that people be shown that they will not be tolerated and that, however hard the necessary course of action, those responsible for security and protection have the intellectual and ethical integrity to follow through.

THE PRIVACY ISSUE

The widespread use of computers, information systems, and telecommunication systems has created a major concern in recent years—a concern about the invasion of individual privacy. *Privacy* involves an individual's ability to determine what, how, and when information about him or her is communicated to others. Many people are concerned about the use of personal information about them by government and private business; they think that computerized record keeping poses a threat to personal privacy.

Before computerized record keeping became widespread, most business and government decisions concerning such benefits as credit, educational grants, and medicare were based on personal knowledge of the individuals involved, on limited information obtained from a decentralized system of public records, and from friends and associates of the individuals. These individuals' privacy was protected to some extent by the inefficiency of these sources and methods of collecting data. The details of people's lives were maintained in widely separated manual files and in memories of people who knew them. It was difficult to compile from these sources a detailed dossier on any individual.

With computers, data is easier to collect and store. Enabling information handlers to increase their data-collection activities tends to encourage them to collect more data. Further, computers can transmit data quickly and easily from one location to another. As mentioned above, manual systems provided an inherent deterrent to privacy invaders because of the difficulty of searching widely scattered records. In contrast, penetrating a single computerized data file gives access to much information; so there is greater incentive to make the attempt. Also, computers make it possible to compile lists of people connected with various types of activities from widely scattered data that probably could not be brought together manually. Previously unknown relationships may be revealed.

Control over personal information has become the accepted definition of privacy. With computers, the individual often has no significant control over what personal information will be collected, whether it will be accurate and complete, or to what uses it will be put. In fact, the individual seldom knows that such collection and dissemination are taking place, even though the results of such activities can effectively determine whether he or she will have access to services, privileges, opportunities, or benefits such as credit, education, medical care, and employment.

The main concerns of the privacy issue can be summarized as follows:

● Too much personal information about individuals is being collected and stored in computerized files.
● Organizations are increasingly using these computerized records in making decisions about individuals.
● Much of the personal data collected about individuals may not be relevant to the purposes for which it is to be used. Also, the accuracy, completeness, and currency of the data may be unacceptably low.
● The security of stored data is a problem.

Of course, the same computers that are eroding individual privacy are also allowing institutions (private and public) to operate more efficiently. For example, it is obviously beneficial to a business to have enough information about individuals to make decisions about issuing credit that will control the firm's risks. Thus, a solution to the privacy issue must find an appropriate balance between the legitimate needs of organizations for information about people and the rights of individuals.

Data Banks

During the past decade, the establishment of large, centralized computer data banks has been proposed. These data banks were to hold a vast array of personal data in forms easily accessible to individuals and agencies. Privacy advocates initially focused their criticisms on such proposals. However, some now recognize that the cumulative effect of linking small, separate data banks can be just as threatening to personal privacy as establishing large data banks. These critics fear that separate scattered records may be combined to create dossiers on individuals, tracing virtually every aspect of their lives.

Consider, for example, the personal information held in computer data banks of the U.S. government alone (see Figure 17–1). The collection of taxes, distribution of welfare and social security benefits, supervision of public health, direction of the Armed Forces, and enforcement of criminal law require the orderly preservation of great quantities of data. Much of this data is personal and potentially embarrassing or harmful.

Anyone who has ever been employed and paid taxes is mentioned in Internal Revenue Service (IRS) files. Currently, the IRS operates a centralized master file in the National Computer Center in Martinsburg, West Virginia. Every week the master file is updated with the tax return information. It contains full taxpayer account data, organized by social security numbers (in the case of individuals), for the past three years; and older data is kept on microfilm. These individual taxpayer accounts are composed of data received from taxpayers, employers, and other governmental institutions. They include identification data; accounting data; delinquent collection information; indications of tax levies, liens, and foreclosures; return and audit information; investigation data; assignment and control information; and miscellaneous data. Other files used in IRS operations include the Information Index System, an intelligence file system, and the Treasury Enforcement Communication System (TECS). TECS terminals in the national IRS office permit data to flow between the FBI's criminal record system and the IRS.

The FBI holds 21.4 million criminal records of both federal and state offenders. These records contain data about police arrest charges, court disposition, and sentencing. They are used for a variety of purposes, most frequently for pre-arrest investigation by police and prosecutors. They also are referred to in arrest and bail decisions, court case preparation, witness verification, juror qualification, sentencing, assignment to specific correction institutions, and parole/probation activities such as estimating the likelihood of violence or escape. Criminal records are also used in government employment processes, the licensing of certain professions, and security investigations. And they can be used illegally; a black market exists for criminal information. The Department of Labor estimates that 30 percent of the active work force has a criminal history—held by the FBI or by any one of more than 56,000 state and local criminal justice agencies.

In addition to the personal data maintained by federal agencies and bureaus, files containing personal data are maintained by local and state governments and by private concerns (see Figure 17–2). Fortunately, these files are not all interrelated. The possiblity of integration does exist, however, because many of the files use social security numbers as keys to access individual records. The use of a common key provides an easy way to correlate and match pieces of data scattered in various files.

FIGURE 17–1 Federal Data Banks

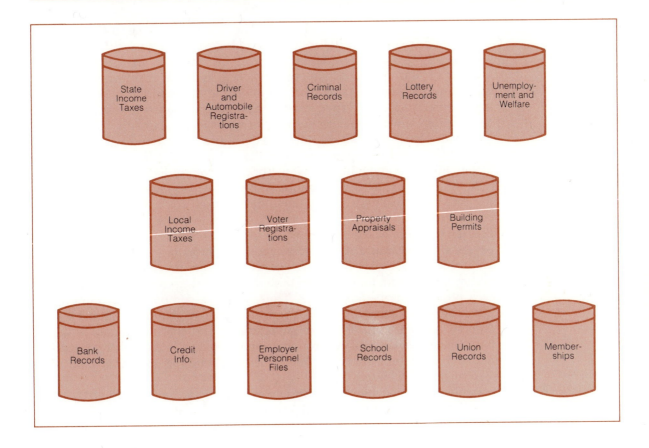

Linking Files with a Common Identifier

A certain amount of integration within government programs already exists. Two examples involve systems aimed at identifying persons illegally receiving welfare benefits. In their desire to hold down welfare costs, the Department of Health and Human Services and the State of New York have both embarked upon massive computerized matching plans. Their objective is to detect ineligible welfare recipients. Both systems use social security numbers to cross-check data on various files.

The system used by the Department of Health and Human Services is called *Project Match*. It seeks to expose lawbreakers by matching state welfare rolls with lists of federal employees. Project Match permits transfers of data among four large federal agencies—the Department of Health and Human Services, the Defense Department, the Office of Personnel Management, and the Justice Department. Since all agencies that have welfare recipients on their payrolls are also involved, data is disseminated throughout the federal government.

The major objections to Project Match stem from the fact that data obtained for one purpose can be used out of context for a different purpose, with no opportunity for those affected to control its flow. On the other hand, the program is defended because it saves the government money by

FIGURE 17–2
Personal Data Maintained by State and Local Governments and by Private Concerns

uncovering illegal welfare recipients. The government has estimated that several hundred million dollars are wasted each year as a result of fraud in welfare programs. The traditional process of sampling, in which a limited number of files are randomly cross-checked, is more time consuming and less thorough than the computerized matching program.

The New York State Wage Reporting System also aims to expose individuals illegally collecting both paychecks and welfare benefits. This system uses data supplied by all employers required to deduct and withhold taxes. Critics oppose the program for much the same reasons they oppose Project Match; however, they find the New York law even more objectionable, since it includes private as well as public employees. Many people are afraid that the data-collection system may some day be used for a wider range of purposes. However, this program, like Project Match, has been defended as a necessary means of eliminating waste in the welfare system. Savings to taxpayers after the first matchup were about $10 million.

Since it is less expensive for an agency to obtain information from another agency's data bank than to collect the information itself, agencies like to use each other's data bank facilities. Thus, in these computerized fraud-detection programs, pieces of personal data are transferred and exchanged among different agencies and levels of government; and the individuals to whom the data relates have no control over the process. It is difficult for people to find out what information is known about them and to whom that information can be released.

While these matching programs have helped to remove ineligible recipients from welfare rolls and eliminate overpayments, they have also presented serious questions about possible abuses of computer technology.

Data Accuracy

Not only the amount of data filed about an individual but also the accuracy, completeness, and currency of that data are of concern to many individuals. Recent studies have shown that many computerized systems operate with a high level of error. The probability of inaccuracies and the possibility of harm to data subjects can be seen through the experience of the National Driver Register. The purpose of the register is to identify incompetent drivers by matching license applicants against a list of drivers whose licenses have been revoked. The first matching of queries against the register's records generated 5,000 possible matches (or identified incompetent drivers) per day. Subsequent manual screening reduced that number to about 500 probable ones. Eventually only about 125 individuals had to show that their licenses had not been revoked!

One study of the accuracy of criminal histories was recently completed by the Legal Aid Society of New York on behalf of clients suing the New York State Department of Criminal Justice Services for disseminating false and misleading records. A random survey of 793 individual files, involving 2,741 arrest-events, showed that only 27 percent were complete and correct, while 45 percent were blank, 8 percent were incomplete, 9 percent were inaccurate, and 10 percent were ambiguous.

IRS records also contain errors. Some are introduced by citizens, either intentionally or through inaccuracy; but many are created by incorrect programs. In one 1974 case, a U.S. Court of Appeals found that the great majority of persons on the IRS computer list of nonfilers who received special investigative attention either had filed returns or had legitimate reasons for not filing.

It is one thing to be denied a benefit or service on the basis of data that is true. It is quite another to be denied that service or benefit because of false or misleading data. Many people have been refused employment or credit because their records were in error or because they were confused with other people having the same names. Further, information from the past can interfere with the future. For example, if a person defaults on a loan, a record of the default may be available to credit bureaus across the nation for years, even though the person's creditworthiness may increase a great deal. As people change and grow, they often want to leave certain aspects of their lives behind them. But data in computer files doesn't wear out. Is it fair that outdated or irrelevant data be provided for use in making decisions about whether a person will receive opportunities, services, and benefits?

Electronic Transmission of Data

The quantity and inaccuracy of data in data banks are not the only threats to individual privacy. The increasing use of *electronic funds transfer (EFT)* also has serious implications. More and more financial transactions are being handled electronically. In an EFT system, the accounts of the two parties involved in a transaction are adjusted by electronic communication between computers; there is no exchange of money in the form of cash or check. A direct consequence of this processing is that most of the individual's financial transactions are recorded in a data bank according to some key. Obviously, one can find out a great deal about an individual's lifestyle and habits if one has access to all the financial transactions in which that person has been involved.

Electronic message systems (EMSs) are another area in which privacy risks may exist. An EMS provides communication by means of electronic transmission facilities and devices. The U.S. Postal Service is currently talking about supplying such a service, and one of the undecided issues is whether the government should monitor all traffic. How can we be assured that all such communication would receive the same kind of confidential treatment that first-class mail supposedly receives today?

It is easy to see that computer technology has greatly amplified our capability to invade individual privacy. Conceivably, the computer could be used as a tool to create an Orwellian society in which the lives of individuals would be controlled and manipulated by a "Big Brother" regime. It is the responsibility of society to protect individual privacy; and with this responsibility in mind, both federal and state governments have enacted privacy legislation.

PRIVACY LEGISLATION

Since the early 1970s, an increasing **number of laws** and regulations to protect privacy have been enacted to control the collection, use, dissemination, and transmission of personal data.

Federal Self-Regulation

Four major federal laws have been established in an effort to limit the possibility for abuse in the centralized record-keeping systems of governmental agencies.

Privacy Act of 1974   The Privacy Act of 1974, signed on January 1, 1975, was passed to protect the privacy of individuals identified in information systems maintained by the federal government. It also includes a number of restrictions on the dissemination of personal data by federal agencies. The basic provisions of the act are:

- There must be no secret data banks of personal information.
- Individuals must be able to determine what information about themselves is being recorded and how it will be used.
- Individuals must be provided a means to correct or amend information about themselves.
- Information collected for one purpose should not be used or made available for any other purpose without the consent of the individual.
- Any organization creating, maintaining, using, or disseminating personal information must ensure the reliability of the data and must take precautions to prevent its misuse.

This act applies only to federal agencies; it has been criticized for its failure to reach beyond the federal government to state and private institutions.

Education Privacy Act   The Education Privacy Act addresses certain practices of federally funded educational institutions. The basic provisions of this law are:

- Data can be collected only by those authorized by law.
- Parents and students are permitted access to students' educational records. In fact, no federal funds will be made available to an educational agency that has a policy of denying parents and students the right to inspect and review relevant educational records.
- Educational records can be disclosed only to school officials who perform organizational functions, to state and local authorities according to laws of those jurisdictions, and to state and federal educational agencies.

This federal law is designed to protect individuals' privacy by regulating access to private and public schools' computer-stored records of grades and evaluations of behavior.

Right to Financial Privacy Act of 1978   The Right to Financial Privacy Act of 1978 provides further protection to the individual by limiting governmental access to the customer records of financial institutions, thus protecting to some degree the confidentiality of personal financial data.

Freedom of Information Act of 1970   Individuals can also gain access to data about themselves in files collected by federal agencies, according to the 1970 Freedom of Information Act, a law passed because of the potential for the government to conceal its proceedings from the public.

State Laws

Many state laws regulating government record-keeping practices are patterned after the Privacy Act of 1974. Most states have enacted some type of controls on such practices in the public sector. Many of these laws contain provisions that require publication of notices describing the records that each governmental agency maintains; provide for the collection and storage of only data that is relevant, timely, and accurate; and prohibit unauthorized disclosures of data relating to individuals.

Regulation of Nongovernmental Organizations

The only significant federal attempt to regulate information practices of private organizations is the Fair Credit Reporting Act of 1970, a law intended to deter privacy violations by lending institutions that use computers to store and manipulate data about people's finances. This legislation provides to individuals (1) the right to gain access to credit data about themselves and (2) the opportunity to challenge and correct erroneous data.

States have also begun to regulate the information activities of nongovernmental organizations. Much of the legislation in this area operates to strengthen the protections afforded individuals by the Fair Credit Reporting Act of 1970.

It can be seen, however, that the greatest emphasis of privacy legislation has been on limiting the information practices of the government. Regulation of private business practices has been limited, in part because of inadequate development of the concept of information privacy and in part because of doubt about the possible impact of such regulation. The Privacy Act of 1974 created a study group, the Privacy Protection Study Commission, to perform a full study of relevant practices in the private sector and assess the impact of federal regulation on such private-sector activities.

The commission, made up of experts in such fields as civil liberties, records management, and computer technology, recommended regulation of record-keeping practices of several private industries, including credit and investigatory agencies, financial institutions, insurance companies, and medical care facilities. Several proposals for regulation of such practices, based in large part on the recommendations of the Privacy Protection Study Commission, have become legislation or are currently being considered by Congress. Among them are the Privacy of Medical Information Act and the

Privacy of Research Records Act. It is reasonable to expect that further legislation in the area of information privacy will be forthcoming.

Relatively few information privacy violation cases have been litigated. Since one of the problems of information privacy is that data is transferred and disclosed without the knowledge or consent of the subjects, it is not likely that people will even be aware of the use of data about themselves; therefore, they probably will not know to take the claim to court. Further, privacy litigation is something of a contradiction in terms: By taking claims to court, litigants may expose private aspects of their lives to a far greater extent than the initial intrusion did.

COMPUTER CRIME

Computer crime is more of a problem than most people realize. Americans are losing billions of dollars to high-technology crooks whose crimes go undetected and unpunished—estimates of losses range from at least $2 billion to more than $40 billion a year. While no one really knows how much is being stolen, the total appears to be growing fast.

The earliest known instance of electronic embezzlement occurred in 1958, just a few years after IBM began marketing its first line of business computers. By the mid-1970s, scores of such crimes were being reported every year; yearly losses were estimated to be as high as $300 million.

Even worse problems appear to be ahead. Home computers and electronic funds transfer systems pose a new threat to the billions of dollars in data banks accessible through telephone lines. Already, crooks have made illegal switches of money over the phone, and more cases can be expected as EFT systems become widespread. Furthermore, the trend to distributed systems is relentless, and distributed systems present many opportunities for security and privacy violations.

Among the many well-documented cases of computer crime are the following examples.

Flagler Dog Track Fraud

From 1974 to 1977, the Flagler Dog Track in Florida was the scene of what is often cited as the only true "computer" crime ever reported. The dog track used two duplicate computers to figure the odds and payoffs at the track. This computerized betting setup seemed fool-proof, but an employee found a flaw in the system.

When the odds and payoffs are computed at a race track, they are flashed onto a tote board in the race field where the players can see them and chart their win, place, and show wagers against the betting pools. This is done for every race expect the trifecta—the bet requiring the selection of the exact 1–2–3 order of finish in a race. The odds against winning this bet are immense; for example, in an eight-dog field the trifecta creates 336 possible betting combinations. The odds can be handled easily enough by the computer, but there is not enough room to post them all on the infield tote board. Consequently, if the trifecta odds change, even *after* a race, no one may know it. That is the flaw the employee saw.

One of the five members of the conspiracy communicated the results of the trifecta to the computer room. A computer operator (also a member of the conspiracy) would alter one of the computers, causing the program to halt execution. At the console, the operator then transferred bets recorded on losing numbers to winners. Then he restarted the computer and allowed the program to complete its computations. Later, the gang ran the ticket printers to print up fraudulent winning tickets, which they cashed the next day. By adding illegitimate winners to the trifecta pool, the conspirators diluted the pool; but the legitimate ticket holders never noticed their losses, because they never knew how much they were legitimately supposed to win. (Remember the odds and payoffs were never posted before the race.) For example, if two tickets were moved in a trifecta that had a betting pool of $4,000, and only two legitmate tickets had been purchased on that number, the fraudulent tickets would rob the lawful bettors of half their winnings. The payoff would be split four ways instead of two, and the winnings would drop from $2,000 a ticket to $1,000. But a bettor who has won $1,000 is not likely to demand a recount. The track never lost a dime, since the money was stolen from the betting public.

The gang was finally caught, but only because the talkative wife of one of its members confided in a friend, who in turn contacted track officials. The conspirators' sentences ranged from nine months to five years. Most of them cooperated with investigators and turned over much of the money. The ringleader estimated that by the time they were caught, each had made close to $2 million.

Pacific Telephone Case

Another famous computer-related crime concerned Pacific Telephone. Jerry Schneider, a child prodigy and an electronics whiz, found a way to steal electronic equipment from Pacific Telephone while he was a part-time college student. Years earlier he had walked to school past a Pacific Telephone warehouse and occasionally poked around in their trash cans and taken a few things home with him, such as discarded equipment or technical manuals. While he was an engineering student at U.C.L.A., he read the manuals and learned about Pacific Telephone's computer systems. He wheedled account codes and identification numbers from unsuspecting employees and then purchased an automatic dialer so that his touch-tone telephone's signals seemed authentic to the company's computer.

By tampering with the company's computer programs, Schneider arranged to have expensive telephone equipment delivered to his home and other locations. He formed a corporation, the Los Angeles Telephone and Telegraph Company, which then sold the equipment to private suppliers and users.

Schneider was eventually turned in by one of his employees who had been refused a raise. Although he had stolen more than a million dollars worth of equipment, he served only forty days of a sixty-day sentence at a prison farm and paid Pacific Telephone a settlement of only $8,500. When he was released from the prison farm, he set himself up as a computer-security consultant.

Equity Funding Life Insurance Company

The biggest computer crime case uncovered so far involved the Equity Funding Life Insurance Company of Los Angeles. Officers of the company used a computer to fabricate $1 billion worth of fake life-insurance accounts for 64,000 fictitious customers. They sold shares in the phony business to investors and used the computer to create the phony policies and keep track of the vast amount of data associated with them. The $2-billion fraud was discovered when a former Equity Funding employee told a securities analyst, who in turn informed his clients and the authorities. When caught, the officers had at their disposal a program that could have erased all the computer evidence.

These cases exemplify the types of electronic crime being committed: manipulating input to the computer; changing computer programs; and stealing data, computer time, and computer programs. The possibilities for computer crime seem endless. It has recently been suggested that computers are used extensively by organized crime and that a computer-aided murder may already have taken place.

The unique threat of computer crime is that criminals often use computers to conceal not only their own identities but also the existence of the crimes. Law officers worry that solving computer crimes seems to depend on luck. Many such crimes are never discovered, because company executives do not know enough about computers to detect them. Others are hushed up to avoid scaring customers and stockholders. It is estimated that only about 15 percent of computer thefts are reported to police. Many of these do not result in convictions and jail terms, because the complexities of data processing mystify most police officials, prosecutors, judges, and jurors.

The cases discussed earlier demonstrate the lenience of the courts in sentencing computer criminals. In one exception to this almost universal rule, a bookkeeper who had stolen a million dollars from his employers in six years was charged with sixty-nine counts of grand theft and forgery. He pleaded guilty and was sentenced to ten years, of which he had to serve five and a half. This sentence is one of the longest ever given for a computer crime.

PRODUCT LIABILITY OF COMPUTER VENDORS

Another area of interface between the law and computers is the liability of computer vendors for the products they sell. Both software and hardware manufacturers have certain responsibilities concerning the performance of their products, and computer buyers must be aware of the extent of vendors' liabilities.

In a landmark case, a seller of computer software was found to have breached express warranties as well as implied warranties when its software failed to perform four of the six functions for which it had been sold. The

court found that all Uniform Commercial Code remedies for breach of warranty also apply to computer software.

As a result of the growing number of information privacy violations and computer crimes, many manufacturers have delayed the introduction of technological advances in areas such as banking and pay television while engineers and lawmakers try to work out ways to prevent abuses. A whole new world of technological developments is waiting to be exploited, but we may have to wait to enjoy the benefits until we find a way to control the problems of information privacy and computer crime.

SUMMARY

● Security is a key consideration in computer installations. Besides being susceptible to fraud and embezzlement, physical computer systems and data in storage are also vulnerable to fire, flood, unintentional mistakes, environmental problems, and sabotage. To combat potential dangers, organizations have instituted various security measures such as giving unique codes and passwords to authorized users, restricting access to the data-processing department, storing backup copies of data, and encrypting data when it is transmitted.

● The widespread use of computers has brought a major concern to society—the invasion of individual privacy. Use of computerized record-keeping systems often prohibits individuals from having significant control over what personal information is collected about them, whether it is accurate and complete, and to what uses it is put. In fact, individuals may not even know that such collection and dissemination activities are taking place.

● Some steps taken to eliminate the problems surrounding the privacy issue are: (1) the Fair Credit Reporting Act of 1970, which provides to individuals the right to gain access to credit data about themselves and to challenge any erroneous data; (2) the Privacy Act of 1974, which outlines steps giving people more control over data about themselves collected by federal agencies; (3) the Education Privacy Act, which protects an individual's computer-stored records of grades and evaluations of behavior in federally funded educational institutions; and (4) the Right to Financial Privacy Act of 1978, which limits governmental access to the customer records of financial institutions.

● Another major problem facing society today is computer crime. Estimates of losses from such crimes go as high as $40 billion a year, and the crimes often go undetected and unpunished. Types of computer crime include manipulating input to the computer; changing computer programs; and stealing data, computer time, and computer programs.

● The growing use of computers for illegal purposes has caught the U.S. criminal justice system unprepared. Computer crimes are not only difficult to detect; they are also difficult to prosecute. Witnesses and evidence are often scarce; and police officials, prosecutors, judges, and juries often are not knowledgeable enough about computers to understand the crimes.

● Computer buyers should be aware of the extent of vendors' liabilities. Recent court decisions have found that the Uniform Commercial Code applies to computer software in the case of breach of warranties.

REVIEW QUESTIONS

1. Name five organizations or institutions that are storing data about you. How much could a stranger tell about you if he or she consolidated all the data into a single, integrated file?

2. Can you suggest some guidelines that should be followed in establishing legislation to assure the privacy of information about individuals? For example, do you think an organization should inform people every time information about them is disseminated to another organization? What would be the pros and cons of such guidelines?

3. What types of organizations are particularly susceptible to computer crime? If you worked for such an organization and thought that a computer crime was going on, what would you do? Do you think it would be your responsibility to become involved and report the incident?

4. In the documented cases of computer crime in the chapter, how were most of the crimes discovered? How were they punished? What special actions do you think need to be taken in establishing laws for prosecuting computer criminals?

5. What steps can be taken to remedy the problem of computer security? What are some advantages and disadvantages of these remedies?

APPLICATION

WESTLAW

Westlaw

Not many years ago, computer-assisted legal research seemed an unlikely notion: Law was an art rather than a science; as such, it could not be reduced to numbers and programs. And even if it could be, the results would be poor and prohibitively expensive.

Today, computer-assisted legal research systems exist and are successful. One such system, WESTLAW, was created by West Publishing Company. West applied its 100 years of service to the legal profession to design a system tailored to the needs of lawyers and judges.

The two basic advantages of computer-assisted research are: (1) speed in finding the law and (2) search capabilities not possible with traditional law book research. The first advantage is much needed; about 40,000 new cases are reported each year, making the task of finding cases relevant to a specific problem difficult for the lawyer. WESTLAW gives the lawyer the ability to search thousands of cases and retrieve relevant ones in a matter of seconds.

The second advantage—unique search capabilities—is of equal importance. For example, WESTLAW allows the lawyer to search for anything that may be contained in the text of a court decision—names of judges, witnesses, products, companies, medical terms, and unusual nonlegal terms. Such terms are not normally indexed in law books, which are organized around legal concepts rather than specific details from cases.

The WESTLAW system is an online, real-time system involving geographically dispersed remote terminals linked to a central computer. The central computer in the WESTLAW system is a powerful IBM 3033 located at West headquarters in St. Paul, Minnesota. Visual display terminals located in law firms, courts, government agencies, and other organizations are linked to the computer by normal phone lines. Data is transmitted over the lines at the rate of 1,200 bits per second.

Inquiries, commands, messages, and cases are flashed on the CRT screen of the terminal, and a keyboard similar to a typewriter keyboard is used to input commands and inquiries. A printer, usually adjacent to the terminal, allows the user to copy any document displayed on the screen by pressing a key on the terminal keyboard.

A great deal of analysis preceded the design of the WESTLAW data bases. Currently the data bases provide access to the full text

When the SEND key is pressed, the computer will search for and retrieve all cases containing the selected terms. The retrieved cases are ranked by the computer on the basis of the frequency of occurrence of the search terms in the documents. The retrieved documents are then displayed in sequence of apparent relevance.

SECURITY AND TIME-KEEPING

The WESTLAW data base and terminals are protected from unauthorized access by a multistep sign-on procedure. An authorized user must know at least two key elements in order to gain access to WESTLAW. One element is the terminal identifier—a special code that identifies the terminal as a WESTLAW terminal. The other key element is the special password assigned to the particular terminal being used. A user must know both the terminal identifier and the password in addition to other steps in the sign-on procedure. This system has worked well in preventing unauthorized use of WESTLAW terminals.

Another important element in the sign-on procedure is of special importance to the user. Before actually searching the data base, a lawyer can enter a client or file identification code to identify the client for whom the search is being performed. The total time of the search is recorded in the WESTLAW accounting system and is sent

and headnotes of all opinions of the United States Supreme Court from 1932 to date, the opinions of the United Courts of Appeals from 1950 to date, and the United States District Courts from 1945 to date. (A headnote is a brief explanatory note prefacing a legal case.) The full text and headnotes of all reported opinions of the state courts are available from at least 1967 to date in most states, and in some states coverage is afforded for earlier years. Both state and federal cases are constantly added to the data base as new decisions are reported. In addition to its case-law data base, WESTLAW also offers a specialized federal tax data base and the complete text of the U.S. code.

Searches usually use words or phrases that describe a legal issue or fact. Suppose, for example, a researcher wants to find cases involving the issue of whether a doctor must advise a patient about the side effects of a treatment. The researcher might type in certain relevant key words:

```
DOCTOR PHYSICIAN SURGEON
/P INFORM* ADVIS* /P

PATIENT /P TREATMENT*
OPERATION* SURGERY
SURGICAL PROCEDURE*
```

Synonyms for "doctor," "treatment," and "advise" are given, since a court may use any of several equivalent terms. The symbol * is a root expansion command that will retrieve plurals and other forms of a word. The special connecting symbol /P is used to require that terms will be in the same paragraph and not spread through several pages in a case.

to the user at the end of the month. In this way, the user has an accurate timekeeping system for the purpose of billing clients for WESTLAW searches.

WESTLAW has changed legal research by allowing users to do more research in a shorter time as well as giving them some new capabilities. As legal data bases continue to grow and computer technology improves, the use of computer-assisted legal research will become more commonplace.

DISCUSSION POINTS

1. What advantages does the real-time capability of the WESTLAW system provide to the legal researcher?

2. The WESTLAW data base is protected from unauthorized usage. How is this done? Why is it necessary to maintain these security measures?

CHAPTER 18

Computers in Our Future

Introduction
Computers are evident in all segments of society today and will play a major role in shaping its future. This chapter focuses on some of the new, and often controversial, uses of computers. What are the implications of the automated workplace? Will we be able to stay home and work? What will be the impact of automation and robotics? Will computers ever be able to think? Will they "control" society? What will you be able to do with a personal computer in your home?

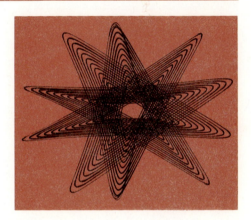

"Dear Mom: At Camp Today I Swam, Rode, and Ran a Computer"

Earl C. Gottschalk Jr.

At Camp Rancho Oso [California], nestled in the mountains of the Los Padres national forest, it's time for the evening campfire event, a ritual of children's summer camps everywhere.

But as the sun dips below the mountains into the Pacific, there are no irreverent skits or choruses of "There's a Hole in the Bottom of the Sea." Instead, the 40 campers here plunge into a heavy discussion of how computers are changing society.

And nobody is writing home to ask Mom and Dad to get him out of the place. This is computer camp, a two-week sleep-away session for those annoyingly smart kids who always seem to understand everything faster than anyone can teach it to them. At computer camp they get just what they seem to want—lots of good, character-building mental athletics.

Computer camp is the latest in a growing list of specialty children's camps, adding to those offering summer days spent canoeing in white water, losing weight, learning to fly in a glider, playing soccer or

The Wall Street Journal, July 30, 1980. Reprinted by permission of the Wall Street Journal © Dow Jones & Company, Inc., 1980. All rights reserved.

exploring marine biology. Like most camps, Rancho Oso has a big old lodge on a woodsy setting; it has camp rules, camp counselors, camp pranksters and camp food in the dining hall. The difference is that half of that dining hall is crammed with small personal computers.

After breakfast at 7:30, the campers, aged 10 to 15, set to work tapping things out on the computer keyboards. Instructors help them as they work on such home computers as the Apple II, the Radio Shack TRS 80, the Atari 800 and the Texas Instruments 99/4, which has color graphics and a speech synthesizer that converts data into human speech. Peripheral products such as floppy disk drives are available.

Keeping Track of Things

It's as much fun as a ballgame to Greg Berman, a freckle-faced 12-year-old who speaks a rapid-fire blend of English and computer jargon. "I've learned to program and debug, I've learned PASCAL and BASIC (computer languages), more about electronics and circuitry, and to operate different kinds of computers," he says. When he gets home, Greg is going to think up computer programs to keep track of his lawyer father's personal-injury cases and antiques collection.

Noah Perlman, 11, adds that "everyone should learn about computers. The next generation of kids will learn BASIC and PASCAL just like kids of today learn foreign languages in school."

Noah also has a project for when he gets home. He is the son of violinist Itzhak Perlman, and he plans to use his personal microcomputer to catalog data about his famous father's 100 annual concerts around the world.

Thomas McCroskey of Atlanta, who is 15, may prove even more useful to the parents who sent him off to Camp Computer. Thomas says he will devise a program to analyze his folks' stock purchases.

Camp Rancho Oso is the bright idea of Denison Bollay, a 27-year-old computer consultant from Santa Barbara. "Computer uses are expanding at astronomical rates," Mr. Bollay argues, "and in the future, adults who don't have this knowledge will forever live and work at a sharp disadvantage." Children of 10 to 15 pick it up rapidly, he says, because "they have no fear of the computer, as the adult does."

But Mr. Bollay says the idea isn't to drum specifics about particular home computers into campers' heads. "In three years these computers will be obsolete." he says. The point of the camp is to teach youngsters "how to learn about the computer."

The Camp Turtle

Rancho Oso is in its first year, and so far it hasn't reached the 50% occupancy that Mr. Bollay says is needed for him to break even. One reason might be the stiff price: $795 for two weeks.

Some hesitant parents are more concerned that sending a

COLOR INSET
The World
of Computers

Clockwise from left: With this hospital's communications management system, doctors and nurses can update computerized records for patients and rooms from any of the hospital's telephones; production line data-entry station; an experimental, interactive computer-based system is helping Bell Labs' design engineers lay out and examine new integrated circuits on a color-graphics display terminal.

Clockwise from right: Bethlehem Steel's computer controlled furnaces; Southern Railway's console of a computer-assisted dispatching system in Birmingham, Alabama; an audio-visual training center.

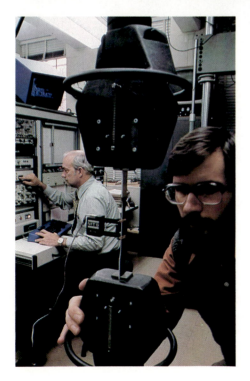

Clockwise from left: Computerized metallurgical testing; Walt Disney Productions' computerized Audio-Animatronics ® enables voices, music, and sound effects to be synchronized with lifelike movements of three-dimensional objects ranging from birds to humans; a Tektronix computer display terminal that is uniquely suited for displaying the highly complex graphics found in contour mapping, seismic analysis, and energy field modeling.

Clockwise from left: Computer-aided design of yellow pages—this graphics terminal is used for ad composition and page layout; flight deck of the space shuttle Columbia; dairy research—automated data acquisition; portable word processing system; microwave control.

child off to program computers might narrow his vocational focus prematurely. But Mr. Bollay insists that "it isn't a camp where the kids spend 12 hours a day on the computer keyboards and come out like little robots."

Still, many campers do spend most of their time with the computers. They are free to do what they wish, including play tennis, ride or swim, from lunchtime to about 4 p.m., when computer classes resume. One advanced group used the free time to build a kind of robot called a turtle, which looks like an upside-down salad bowl on wheels. Only this salad bowl can run a maze.

Campers' assessments of their summer place also have a special cast. "Some kids are jealous and won't share the computers," complains Andy Reed, a 12-year-old from Alexandria, Va.

But some things at summer camp never change. "The hardware and software were great," says 15-year-old Thomas McCroskey. "But the food—typical camp fare."

As the article reprinted here points out, people who do not know how to use computers will "forever live and work at a sharp disadvantage." What better time to learn than at camp! However, there are certainly problems with trying to assimilate a technology that literally changes our lives daily. This final chapter takes a look at issues such as automation, artificial intelligence, and personal computing.

OFFICE ELECTRONICS

Automation refers to machine-directed processes. Just as the Industrial Revolution brought automation to the factory, the computer revolution is bringing it to the one place where automation has not had tremendous impact in the past—the office. Recent developments in communications, information storage and retrieval, data analysis, and decision making have made computer applications feasible in office environments.

In communications, for instance, computerized facilities have been designed to handle messages, text and graphics, and conferences. Word-processing systems, electronic mail, reprographics, and computer conferencing systems are simplifying secretarial and managerial work and increasing office productivity. With the rising cost of labor, using such office automation offers great cost savings. One further incentive for office electronics is the increasing amount of reporting required by governmental agencies.

Word Processing

Word processing simply means writing with a computer. It provides a mechanism to prepare material that otherwise would be written by hand or typed. As a previous chapter explained, the text is entered on a typewriter-like keyboard. Words appear on a visual-display screen rather than on paper. A word-processing program can edit, rearrange, insert, and delete material until the document is exactly as desired. Then the computer prints the text on paper; it produces a letter-perfect document with much less the effort it takes to produce it on a typewriter. Further, the computer can print as many perfectly typed copies as desired. The text can be stored on cassette tape or disk and can be changed at any time.

Word processing is available on computer systems ranging in size from personal computers to huge commercial installations. All word-processing systems involve computers. A CRT display, a printer that can print letter-quality type, and a keyboard from which the user enters text are also parts of all word-processing systems. In addition, an auxiliary storage device (normally using cassettes, floppy disks, or hard disks) is needed to store documents for revision or reuse. (See Figure 18–1.) A stand-alone system includes all of these components with a microcomputer; the user thus has his or her own system (see Figure 18–2). In a larger system (often called a shared-logic word-processing system), the computer may be a large, centrally located machine that does many other data-processing chores. It supports the terminal as a microcomputer does, but on a time-sharing basis. Such a system may include several CRTs and keyboards and several auxiliary storage devices and printers, all controlled by one CPU. Users work at terminals that are functionally their own personal word-processing systems.

The cost of a basic word-processing system is between $5,000 and $20,000. The leading manufacturer of word-processing systems is Wang Laboratories. Others include CPT Corporation, Datapoint Corporation, Digital Equipment Corporation, IBM, and Victor Graphics.

Word-processing systems are not restricted to the tasks described above. In addition to providing sophisticated word-processing functions, they can merge data with text, process files, perform mathematical functions, generate output of photocomposition devices, facilitate paperwork management (electronic filing), and accept input from optical character recognition de-

FIGURE 18–1
Hardware Components of a Word-Processing System

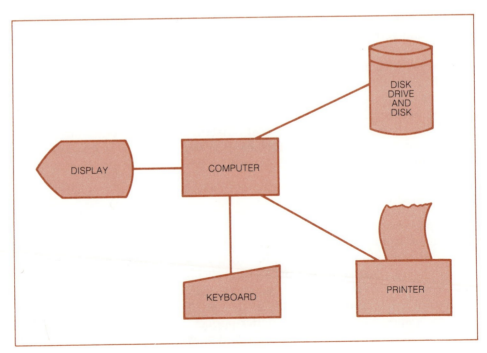

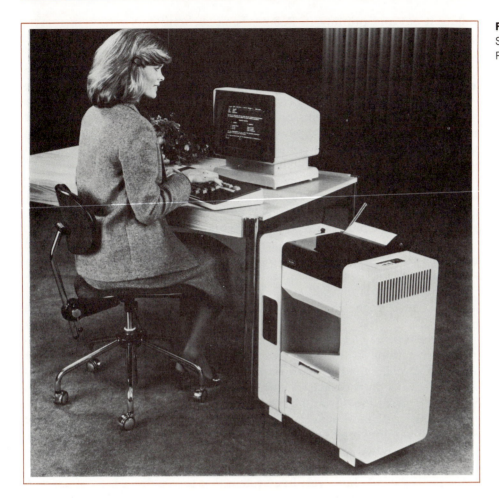

FIGURE 18–2
Stand-Alone Word-
Processing System

vices (typewriter-created text may be put into word-processing systems for subsequent editing). Some systems can communicate with other word-processing systems and can distribute text after it has been created, allowing documents prepared in one location to be printed in others.

Electronic Mail

Early word processors could not communicate with each other; text transfers had to be handled manually. Now, however, text transmissions are possible, and any type of message can be sent electronically. Since managers and professionals spend approximately 25 percent of their time reading, and since roughly one trillion pages of paper are exchanged between U.S. businesses and government agencies each year, this capability to transmit text electronically can be put to good use in the office.

Electronic mail is the transmission of messages at high speeds over telecommunication facilities. The main idea behind these computer-based mail systems is that one user of the service sends a message to another by placing it in a special storage area from which the second receives the message by pulling it out and printing it. People using such systems can be in remote locations and need not use the system at the same time in order to send and receive messages.

Electronic mail terminals are often located in centralized communication centers staffed by trained operators. Sometimes, however, the terminals are placed on the desks of managers, professionals, and secretaries. Receivers can view incoming mail items on a CRT screen or can receive paper documents printed in the same typewriter quality as the originals. The mail can be revised, incorporated into other documents, passed along to new recipients, or filed like any other documents in the system.

In some systems, application programs actually send and receive mail items. For example, an application producing sales reports can automatically address, duplicate, and mail the reports to branch offices quickly and easily. Branch office personnel can read their reports the same day—not days later.

There are two basic forms of electronic mail: teletypewriter systems and facsimile systems. *Teletypewriter systems* transmit messages as strings of characters. *Facsimile systems,* sometimes called *telecopier systems,* produce a picture of a page by scanning it, as a television camera scans a scene or a copier scans a printed page. The image is then transmitted to a receiver, where it is printed.

Another type of electronic message system on which much work is currently being done is the *voice message system (VMS).* In VMS, the sender presses a special "message" key on the telephone, dials the receiver's number, and speaks the message. A button lights on the receiver's phone. When he or she presses the "listen" key, the message is played back.

Electronic mail is already a $2 billion industry. Many major computer equipment vendors offer such a service as part of automated office systems now being designed and introduced. Costs of electronic mail are low and are likely to fall 15 to 25 percent each year. Some problems exist with electronic mail systems, however. In a system that serves thousands of users, it may be difficult to find a recipient's address (especially if the recipient's name is—say—Robert Smith). Another problem is the possibility of missed or incomplete delivery of messages. With telephone calls, it is easy to tell if you have reached your party; but when you send a message on an electronic message system, there often is no way to know that it has been received.

Reprographics

Another application of electronics in the office, as well as in the publishing industry, is *reprographics,* or computer typesetting. The computer is connected to a typesetting machine and the output is film "repro" paper, or tape to be used ultimately to prepare total page layouts for books, magazines, newspapers, and the like. The type is set automatically from the text stored in computer memory. The text contains special codes to indicate where various typefaces (such as italics and boldface) are to be used. The codes can also specify formatting for insertion of photos and so on.

Word processing, electronic mail, and reprographics are all applications of the computer to assist in communications in the office. The other office functions previously mentioned (information storage and retrieval, data analysis, and decision making) are also being automated.

Office Automation

The *automated office* combines office electronics with data processing. *Office information systems* contain a variety of word processors, data-entry terminals, graphics terminals, information distributors, printers of all kinds, OCR devices, photocomposition devices, and computer-based text editors. For example, a word processor linked to an intelligent copier (a copier that can accept both printed source documents and electronic input) can send instructions and text directly to the copier, with no need for an original paper document.

Chicago's Continental Bank, a leader in office automation, has instituted a sophisticated electronic communication system that includes home data terminals, electronic mail, and remote-location dictation. Ultimately, text, data, voice, and image will be integrated into an information system that can be used as a corporate resource.

Hardware and software systems are being introduced for the automated office. For example, Wang Laboratories has introduced the OIS/BASIC Integrated Office System, which combines word processing and data processing. Users can simultaneously perform word processing, data processing, printing, and communication activities. With this system, users can accomplish a wide variety of tasks, such as general accounting, insurance calculations, cash flow analysis, and project scheduling. For example, sales office personnel can answer customers' letters, write memos, communicate with the home office, enter orders, and do their monthly sales reports on one system.

Office automation can provide many benefits to companies. Staffing costs are reduced because fewer office personnel are needed to perform a given amount of work. Space, for both people and paper, is conserved. Most importantly though, the timeliness of work is increased; this leads to better results and better information, and these in turn lead to better decisions.

Automating the office may be worthwhile, but it can also cause problems. Job displacement and the declining quality of jobs are two main issues. Critics argue that clerical workers' skills are de-emphasized and that they are made to feel like extensions of their machines. Jobs are made routine, paced by the computer, and measured by dehumanizing factors, such as number of keystrokes per hour. The implications of such arguments must be considered. What will be their impact on labor relations, management, and job satisfaction?

AUTOMATION

Ever since the Industrial Revolution, automation has been of great concern to people. As technology has advanced, more and more processes have been automated, leading to greater efficiency and lower costs but also to machines' replacing people in many jobs. With the advent of computers, fears about automation's leading to unemployment and depersonalization have taken on even greater significance. Whether these fears are justified is yet to be seen.

The evidence of the past three decades does not indicate that increased automation leads to increased unemployment. To be sure, workers have been displaced; but each new technology has created new employment opportunities that more than compensate for the jobs eliminated. For example, the invention of the automatic weaving machine eliminated many jobs in the garment industry; but this effect was offset by the creation of a whole new industry involved in the manufacture and marketing of the new equipment.

Nevertheless, many people argue the impact of computers is going to be much more significant, because computer technology provides for much more versatile and complex automation. Computers, instead of humans, can be used to control automatic machines and entire assembly lines. Grocery stores can be automated—that is, a person can call in an order; and a computer can record it, find the required items, and even arrange for their delivery. Other computers can control entire processes in oil refineries, turning crude oil into tar, heating oil, diesel oil, gasoline, and so forth.

Several studies have been conducted to determine the effects of computer automation on jobs. The results have not been conclusive but have in general indicated that a certain amount of job displacement can be expected, because the computer can take over many routine clerical jobs. However, the extent to which such displacement occurs also depends on other factors, including the following:

● The goals that are sought from the use of the computer. Is the objective to be able to handle an increasing workload with the same personnel, or is it to reduce costs by eliminating jobs?

● The growth rate of the organization. If the organization is expanding, it can more easily absorb workers whose jobs are being eliminated, since many new jobs must be created to cope with the increasing business.

● The planning that has gone into the acquisition and use of the computer. With careful preparation, an organization can anticipate the personnel changes a computer system will bring about. It can make plans either to reassign the affected people or to help them to find new jobs with other organizations. First-time use of a computer-based system will definitely create new jobs in the areas of computer operations, data-entry, programming, and system analysis and design. Usually, however, the skills and education required for these jobs differ from those required for the eliminated jobs. However, displaced employees can be trained to handle such jobs as operating computer equipment (loading and unloading tapes and the like) and keypunching; they can also be sent to schools for more formal training.

Robotics

Perhaps the impact of automation on job displacement is felt most keenly in production-oriented environments, because the nature of mass production is conducive to automation. Robot-like equipment is already common in manufacturing. *Industrial robots,* as these machines are called, are a far cry from the endearing C-3PO pictured in *Star Wars.* Typically, an industrial robot is just a mobile arm ending in some sort of vice-like grip, or claw. The arm is attached to a box that houses the control unit. The computer is plugged into an electric outlet, and cables that run from the computer along the arm transmit instructions in the form of electric impulses to the claw. For heavy work, hydraulic pressure is used.

At present, most industrial robots are used to perform very simple, repetitive tasks. They paint cars, assemble appliances, and mine coal. Chrysler is using robots to weld auto bodies; fifty such robots can do the work of 200 human workers. General Motors currently uses 270 robots in its auto assembly processes. Robots are also found in industrial environments potentially dangerous to humans. For example, robots can be used in high-radiation environments to handle parts too hot or too cold for humans or to clean up the radiation of a damaged nuclear reactor. At a Department of Energy plant, a robot is used to transport reprocessed plutonium, one of the most toxic substances known, in and out of a furnace. Robots can also be used to operate machines such as stamping mills and electric saws that can maim careless operators.

Robots can work faster and more efficiently than humans. They can work around the clock without becoming tired or bored. They don't get hungry or sick or join a union. Robots range in price from $7,500 to $150,000 and have an average life span of about eight years. They can be operated and paid for at a cost of about $5 per hour, while a human worker might cost $20 per hour.

Many efforts in robot development are sponsored by military and space programs. The Voyager I robot traveled 1.3 billion miles to Saturn. In 1986, the Mars Rover, which is currently being built, will travel to Mars and be able to motor around on the planet, looking at rocks with its TV eyes and digging up samples with a shovel. Other robots currently being developed will be able to take off from the space shuttle and repair a satellite in orbit or be sent out aboard an unmanned submarine to find and repair vessels undersea.

The potential ability of robots reaches into fields other than science and manufacturing. One robot manufacturer has been asked to develop a robot that can pluck chickens. In Australia, a robot that shears sheep is being tested. Robots are being designed to care for the afflicted, aid nurses and doctors during surgery, and fight crime. Some day, robot servants may be commonplace in the home.

Future Impact   Today, more than 3,000 robots work throughout the United States, while Japan operates about 10,000. A recent forecast by the American Society of Manufacturing Engineers and the University of Michigan predicts that by 1987, 15 percent of all U.S. assembly systems will use robot technology and that by 1988, 50 percent of the labor in small-component assembly will be replaced by automation. Japan's advanced technology will force the United States to be competitive in employing robots. If this forecast is correct, and if robots continue to become cheaper and more efficient, what will human workers do? So far, robots have been used mainly for boring or dangerous tasks. This has helped workers view robots as more of a help than a threat. But if robots also begin to replace humans in more pleasant and exciting jobs, their use may cause alarm.

The use of robots may cause some difficulties and bring about many changes in our society. The "Robot Revolution" may lead to a shorter work week and more leisure time. This new technology may increase personal freedom in terms of options of occupational choice and leisure-time activities. It may also encourage a shift from manufacturing to service occupations.

Furthermore, the robot industry itself may be a huge new employer, creating many more jobs than robots displace. The North American robots systems market alone is widely expected to have constant dollar growth from $65 million in 1980 to more than $500 million by 1985 and to $1.5 billion by 1990.

ARTIFICIAL INTELLIGENCE

So far, this text has used well-structured problems to illustrate using the computer as a problem-solving tool. Each problem could be solved with a carefully defined procedure. For example, to solve the payroll problem, we developed a structure that did not need to be changed each time the payroll was calculated. However, many problems must be solved by processes quite different from the conscious, deliberate methods used to solve problems in mathematics or logic. People do not always think according to a set of strictly defined rules. Many problem solutions involve not only logic but also intuition, creativity, and intelligence. Examples of such problems include: (1) deciphering someone's scribbled messages, (2) playing a game that requires strategy or deception, and (3) distinguishing literally intended meanings from sarcasm. Such problems are not difficult for humans to solve; they are natural tasks we do every day. But the question of whether techniques can be developed to enable computers to solve problems that seem to require imagination or intelligence is one that continues to challenge researchers.

Research efforts are currently aimed at preparing programs that can perform tasks never before done automatically and usually assumed to require human intelligence—programs that perform tasks such as thinking, reasoning, making logical deductions, remembering past experiences, or solving present problems by recognizing analogous situations. This field of research is called *artificial intelligence*. Research efforts and technical developments in the field of artificial intelligence are advancing rapidly. Researchers are developing computers that can understand human speech, read and summarize news stories, and compile data about a sick person and diagnose the illness.

The practical applications of artificial intelligence seem endless. Intelligent computers could, for example, read books, newspapers, journals, and magazines and prepare summaries. They could search libraries for facts pertinent to a decision that must be made and perhaps suggest possible courses

of action and their probable consequences. In areas such as law and medicine, computers could understand specialized knowledge and know how to put it to work.

Research in artificial intelligence has been directed mainly toward such fields as heuristics, speech understanding, print and script reading, and natural-language processing.

Heuristics

The word *heuristic* means "helping to learn or discover." A heuristic problem-solving process suggests a certain course of action to be taken in a certain situation. The action is not guaranteed to be the correct or the only solution for a problem, but one that has worked well in similar situations in the past and is worth trying. Generally, heuristics are used to solve problems too complex or time consuming to yield to conventional mathematical analysis. An advantage of heuristics is that they can reduce the number of alternatives that have to be explored.

To decide which heuristics to apply in a particular situation, a problem solver can look for patterns. For example, a chess player is guided by patterns formed by the pieces on the board. Heuristic processes are therefore programmed into computers that play chess. The computer can recognize the pattern of pieces on the board and know moves that have worked in the same situation in the past. Thus, the total number of choices of moves has been narrowed.

Speech Interpretation

Researchers are also attempting to program computers to understand speech—a very difficult task because of variations in intonation and pitch, pauses, errors, hesitations, incomplete words, and different pronunciations of words. Consequently, most research in this area has been restricted to programming machines to perform specified tasks in response to spoken commands, using a very limited vocabulary and simple sentence structure. One such system, for example, accepts spoken commands to move chess pieces. There are only thirty-one words and a small number of action statements like "move" and "check" in the computer's vocabulary. The computer can test whether a statement makes sense, because it has a record of where all the pieces are on the board and knows the legal moves.

One of the most practical applications in this area of research is in aiding handicapped people. In one such application, a wheelchair controlled by a computer can understand spoken English commands. A user can instruct the computer to move the wheelchair in certain directions. A mechanical arm attached to the wheelchair and controlled by the computer can be instructed, for example, to manipulate eating utensils. Systems such as this one can greatly increase the self-sufficiency of handicapped persons.

Print and Script Reading

Researchers are now trying to program computers to read handwritten script or print. This capability can be very useful for such applications as sorting mail. In fact, the USSR and Japan use such readers to process 20,000 pieces of mail an hour with 93 percent accuracy. (Address codes must be written in preprinted boxes on envelopes.)

Natural-Language Processing

Considerable research has been devoted to developing techniques whereby computers can process natural languages, for example, to summarize text or to translate text from one language to another. As suggested in the discussion of speech interpretation, this is very difficult, because many of the statements people speak, hear, and read are highly ambiguous and assume a thorough understanding of words, grammar, and their context. However, approximate translations of technical text (which is more straightforward than general writing) from Russian to English are now possible.

In order for computer programs to understand the written word, they must be able to link words with ideas and make logical conclusions. A program written at Yale University called FRUMP reads short news stories and writes one-sentence summaries in English, Spanish, and Chinese. In one instance, FRUMP was presented with a 600-word story about the death of Margaret Mead, the anthropologist. The computer wrote the following summary: "Anthropologist Margaret Mead, 76, has died from cancer." FRUMP has made some mistakes, however. One story of the shooting of the San Francisco Mayor in 1978 contained the phrase "shooting shook San Francisco." FRUMP concluded there had been an earthquake in California!

Concerns for the Future

One of the major hindrances in the advancement of research into artificial intelligence is that discoveries about how the mind works have not kept pace with discoveries in other scientific fields like physics and genetics. So far, biologists have not been able to explain how the brain thinks; and so researchers have not been able to duplicate its functions in the laboratory. In fact, the most difficult problems arise in the attempt to mimic the simplest elements of human behavior, such as simple eye-to-hand coordination and recognition of spoken words. On the other hand, the successes in artificial intelligence have been in modeling some extremely complex skills that often require years of effort for humans to accomplish, such as playing chess well, diagnosing diseases, and solving problems in college physics.

Artificial intelligence researchers are studying human behavior, what happens to information when the brain processes it, and how human memory is organized so that one particular piece of information can be retrieved from the vast amounts of information stored in the brain. As new clues are discovered, researchers try to mimic them with a computer. The consequences of using computers to understand the human mind may be extremely beneficial. As we get a deeper understanding of how the mind works, we may be able to make the process of education more effective and may become more effective at solving problems and making decisions.

On the dark side of this forecast, misuse of such powerful computers could endanger personal freedom; for example, what if computers that understood speech were programmed to listen in on every human conversation? Would there be any individual privacy? Humans are perhaps most troubled by the idea that computers can learn to think, maybe even at a range and scope approaching that of human thinking; it presents a strange encroachment on people's feeling of uniqueness. What if society became too dependent on such computers? What if they became so complex people lost the ability to understand why they reached the decisions and took the actions they did? And then there is the ultimate fear that computers would conspire to take over.

Like any new technology, computers must be used properly. If computing knowledge and resources are sufficiently available to people on both sides of the issues, the risks of misuse will decrease. Society must be aware of the consequences of new technology and take responsibility for them.

PERSONAL COMPUTING

A concept which for years was discussed only as a science fiction novelty is now a trend—acquiring computers for personal use. Because microcomputers are inexpensive and widely available, computing power is available to almost anyone. In the past five years, the personal computer industry has grown from nothing to nearly $1 billion in annual sales to the hobbyist, the consumer at home, and the small business. Today there are more than 750,000 general-purpose microcomputers in U. S. homes and small businesses, and the number is increasing by over 40 percent per year.

The most promising market for the microcomputer is in the home; it may soon be as common in homes as color television. The most popular use of home computers thus far has been for entertainment. Computer games that simulate sports such as golf, hockey, baseball, and tennis are available (see Figure 18–3). Conventional games such as chess and backgammon, in which the computer is a formidable opponent, are also popular. The graphical and audio capabilities and fast operation of microcomputers allow them to display action in spectacular detail in games such as Space Invaders and Star Raiders.

FIGURE 18–3
Computer Games in
the Home

The microcomputer is as natural as an aid in financial matters. It can keep track of your checkbook, savings account, and loans and can maintain the family budget and tell you the best time to buy a new car. It can keep personal records, inventory, mailing lists, and property lists.

The homemaker can make extensive use of a microcomputer. It can be used to maintain a Christmas-card list, monitor biorhythms, file recipes, work out a dinner menu with what food is in the refrigerator, monitor calorie intake, or start the roast when triggered by a phone call from the office. As an educational aid, it can enhance children's basic math, reading, and spelling abilities; tutor high school and college subjects; and teach the fundamentals of computers and computer programming. Software is available to teach typing and to teach Chinese!

Adding sensors, motors, and switches to a microcomputer enables it to run a wide range of gadgets around the home. A microprocessor-controlled microwave oven allows the user to specify how long food should be defrosted or cooked as well as what time cooking should begin. A microcomputer can manage energy use by keeping various rooms of the house at desired temperatures. It can monitor for fire and enhance security by locking doors and controlling burglar alarms. The microcomputer can water the lawn according to ground moisture, send a signal if water begins seeping into the basement, open and shut drapes, and control lights. Also, minute wires placed underneath a baby's crib mattress can allow the computer to signal the baby's movements in the crib or even detect irregularity in the baby's breathing and sound an alarm.

This may seem like a lot of uses for personal computers, but it only includes applications limited to computers isolated from one another. A whole new range of usefulness opens up when we consider networks that allow home computers to communicate with one another and with commercial installations. There are available, for example, a number of personal computer information services (see Figure 18–4). Some provide a link to a library or to a nationwide want-ad service. The Dow Jones News/Retrieval service allows users access to current quotations for stocks, bonds, mutual funds, and treasury notes for more than 6,000 companies and enables them to lookup articles in the *Wall Street Journal*.

Communication networks linking home computers to banks will provide computer-based home banking services. At least one such service is being tested. The customers can pay bills using their home computers by authorizing the bank to pay specified amounts to certain merchants from their accounts. The service also includes a news and information network that customers can use to obtain national, international, and financial news, as well as information about the bank's services. Customers have access to a statement that shows all their banking activities since the last formal statement. They can see what items have cleared and what direct deposit checks have reached their accounts. Deposits and withdrawals still must be handled at branches or by mail. The fee for such a system? Five dollars per month.

In the future, the home-computer owner will also be able to shop from home. In a computerized shopping system, the user dials a store, identifies items of interest to be displayed on the screen, and then selects the items to

FIGURE 18–4
Home Information
System

be purchased and delivered. The user can purchase not only groceries but also clothes and furniture without leaving home.

The personal computer may be the answer to many problems ranging from energy regulation to food consumption. The time has come for the machine that has changed people's lives to become a part of their lives.

PERSPECTIVE

Computer technology has had a more significant impact on society than any other factor since the Industrial Revolution. The extent of the impact has led many to classify the present era as the *Information Revolution*. In an extremely short time, computers have moved out of the laboratory and into an indispensable position in modern life. This rapid progress has generated many problems as well as spectacular benefits.

Some people born and educated before widespread implementation of computers refuse to recognize their existence. Psychological barriers are raised, and no attempt is made to understand the logical base of computer operations. The technological obsolescence associated with computer advances often requires job restructuring or retraining; this tends to increase resistance to computer applications. Computer professionals must commit themselves to continuing education if they want to remain current in this dynamic field. These problems are people-oriented rather than dependent upon scientific advancements. As such, they are more difficult to solve.

The world would be very different today if all the advances attributed to computers were removed. For example, airlines could not continue to func-

HIGHLIGHT 18–3

Computerized Surgery

At the University of Minnesota, Otto Schmitt is about to revolutionize surgery with the computerized knife he has nearly completed. The use of an electric knife in surgery is not new; such knives have proven helpful because their high-frequency vibrations stop the bleeding as they cut. Schmitt, however, has attached a tiny computer chip to the knife handle to enable the surgeon to quickly and accurately change cutting speeds, depths, or patterns.

Schmitt hopes next to make his knife "smart"; he wants it to recognize situations and make adjustments automatically when necessary. Every operation would be individually pre-programmed. These developments should help doctors to more successfully conduct difficult surgery.

tion without computerized airline reservations systems; space travel would be impossible without simulation and control programs; and many economic systems would grind to a halt without the tremendous speed of the computer upon which the banking industry relies so heavily for processing cash flow.

One point must be understood: Not all computer applications are beneficial or even effective. The computer is only a tool used by analysts and programmers to help people solve problems. If instructions are inappropriate or incorrect, then the computer system has the same deficiencies. Computer power is a fact of technological achievement; harnessing this power is a function of the individuals who control computer use. The principal limitation on computer applications is the imagination and ingenuity of the humans who use them.

SUMMARY

● Office electronics is a rapidly growing application of computerization. Word-processing systems, electronic mail, reprographics, and office automation simplify secretarial and managerial work, decrease costs, and increase productivity and the flow of information in the office. The "office of the future" is fast becoming the "office of the present."

● Automation refers to machine-directed processes. Automation through the use of computers has created new jobs while eliminating some jobs and modifying others. The amount of job displacement that results from computer use depends on the goals sought from its use, the growth rate of the organization, and the amount of planning that went into the acquisition and use of the computer.

● Computer-controlled machines, including robots, are now used for simple, repetitive tasks and for tasks deemed too dangerous for humans.

Though often used in industrial environments, these machines are far from displacing the working class.

● Artificial intelligence is a field of research attempting to develop and improve techniques for programming computers to solve problems that seem to require imagination, intuition, or intelligence. Research efforts have been directed to such areas as heuristics, speech understanding, print and script reading, and natural-language processing.

● Personal computing is a trend gaining widespread popularity, both in small businesses and in the home. Applications of microcomputers in the home range from entertainment to more practical tasks such as monitoring energy and security devices.

REVIEW QUESTIONS

1. What changes do you think the automated office will bring to the working day as people now know it?

2. Robots and other computer gadgets are used extensively in science-fiction movies and television shows. What are possible practical applications for such robots?

3. Do you see any possible impact of artificial intelligence on employment or unemployment? Explain.

4. To what use would you, or do you, put a personal computer?

APPLICATION

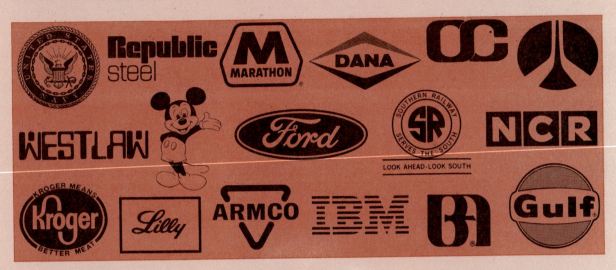

Massachusetts Institute of Technology

The Massachusetts Institute of Technology, which opened on February 20, 1865, is a privately endowed, independent university. It is broadly organized into five academic schools: architecture and planning, engineering, humanities and social science, management, and science. The coeducational student population consists of approximately 4,400 undergraduates and 4,400 graduates.

MIT embodies the philosophy of its founding father and first president, William Barton Rogers, a natural scientist, who believed that professional competence is best developed by combining a traditional teaching college with actual research and "applying the acquired knowledge" to real-world problems. Many of the twenty-three academic departments have related interdepartmental research divisions that enhance opportunities for valuable learning experiences. All in all, MIT has succeeded in creating an academic environment that integrates a diverse mix of ages, disciplines, and nationalities.

MIT has several computer facilities to handle a variety of data-processing requirements. Most students use the computer for various applications in the course of their studies and research activities. Information-processing facilities at MIT are divided into two areas: those provided within the information-processing center, which serves as a large, versatile central computer facility, and those provided through the local departmental and laboratory computer facilities, which offer more specific information-processing capabilities to meet specific needs.

On November 1, 1979, a word-processing facility sponsored by the School of Engineering began operation. Its purpose was to make the advantages of electronic word-processing technology available to individuals and organizations within the MIT community at reasonable cost and within the required time and resource constraints.

The center is equipped with an optical character recognition (OCR) device, two CPT text-editing devices, two printers, and a communication modem.

The communication modem enables the word-processing center to use some of MIT's other computer facilities that have been equipped with ASCII modems. In this manner, the center is spared the expense of purchasing duplicate equipment, yet it can use some of the more sophisticated and expensive hardware located elsewhere in the institute. The facility can read typewritten material which is prepared for the OCR equipment and transmitted to the Honeywell 6180, IBM 370, or the Digital Equipment Company computers in the Engineering Joint Facility. These machines all have text editing features, and are operated by a variety of users.

A feasibility study indicated that keyboarding the original text material cut the productivity of the facility to a fraction of its potential. Therefore, it was decided to use OCR equipment to record the original text. The equipment will accept copy typed on IBM Selectric typewriters with appropriate ribbon and typing elements and read this typed material directly into the text editor. Changes to the material can be made by the operator at the text-editing console; the results are printed out and returned to the author. If further changes are needed, the material need only be returned to the center, the changes entered, and fresh copy generated for the author. The Honeywell 6180, IBM 370, and Digital Equipment Company computers all contain text-editing capabilities as well. The authors can edit the material at their convenience, then submit it to the word-processing text editors, who can format and print it as directed by the authors. Papers can also be typed on home computers and transmitted to the center to be formatted and printed. The OCR device permits papers to be prepared by several authors, each using his or her own secretary or IBM Selectric typewriter. The results can then be scanned by the OCR device, either edited by the facility or transmitted to a computer for editing by one of the authors, and printed in whatever form the authors desire.

The word-processing center can also transmit information to phototypesetters, which can then typeset the transmitted material without having to enter it through a keyboard. The facility plans to eventually operate round the clock on three shifts to provide for maximum utilization of equipment and faster turnaround time for high-priority documents.

Four priority levels have been established to allow customers to choose the one that provides the fastest service for what they have to spend. These priorities apply to any job requiring a sufficient amount of operator time. For jobs such as OCR reading and transmitting to a computer, the standard price prevails and the normal turnaround time is overnight. Figure 18–5 shows the service and price levels for the four priorities.

The charge for word-processing services, then, is based on the actual use of services by the customer and on the speed with which the documents must be returned. At low priority, the costs are competitive with the expense of

FIGURE 18–5 Charges for Word-Processing Services

PRIORITY OF WORK	SERVICE LEVEL	STANDARD PRICE MULTIPLIER
Head of the line	ASAP	3.0
2 days	HIGH	2.0
3 days	STANDARD	1.0
5 days	DEFERRED	0.8

TYPE OF SERVICE	PRICE
OCR (input)	85¢/double-spaced $8^{1}/_{2} \times 11$ page
Print (output)	30¢/double-spaced $8^{1}/_{2} \times 11$ page
Print (output)	45¢/single-spaced $8^{1}/_{2} \times 11$ page
Transmit	10¢/25-line page (no charge if OCR read)
Receive	10¢/double-spaced $8^{1}/_{2} \times 11$ page
Edit	35¢/minute

OCR reads $8^{1}/_{2} \times 11$ double-spaced pages in 30 seconds.
Printer reads $8^{1}/_{2} \times 11$ double-spaced pages in 55 seconds.
1,200 baud coupler reads $8^{1}/_{2} \times 11$ double-spaced pages in 15 seconds.

using secretarial time when two or three drafts are required. However, as the number of drafts increases, word processing becomes less expensive by comparison. It should be noted that a primary economic concern should be to put the document on OCR paper at as early a stage as possible.

The final product of these word-processing techniques is superior to the traditional product because a wide range of printout formats, including right-margin justification and interchange of fonts, is available. For documents that undergo periodic revision, this method is extremely economical.

DISCUSSION POINTS

1. How does MIT put text material into the word-processing system and why is it done in this manner?
2. List some of the people or groups at your school or university who might need this type of service. For what purposes would they use it?

APPENDIX
Career Opportunities

PEOPLE AND THEIR ROLES

Men and women with technical or managerial skills in data processing are employed in almost every industry. The need for data-processing personnel exists not only in business firms but also in hospitals, schools, government agencies, banks, and libraries. However, the major emphasis of this section will be on computer-related career opportunities in a business environment.

A typical computer installation in a business organization is expected to perform at least three basic functions: system analysis and design, programming, and computer operation. Personnel with the education and experience required to work in these areas are needed; in addition, data-base technology has created the need for specialists in data-base analysis and administration. Further, an information system manager is needed to coordinate activities, set goals for the data-processing department, and establish procedures to control and evaluate both personnel and projects in progress.

Information System Managers

Historically, data-processing managers have been programmers or system analysts who worked their way up to management positions with little formal management training. But the increasing emphasis on information systems and information management has brought a change; professional managers with demonstrable leadership qualities and communication skills are being hired to manage information system departments.

The *management information system (MIS) manager* is responsible for planning and tying together all the information resources of the firm. The manager must organize the physical and human resources of the department to achieve company goals and must devise effective control mechanisms to monitor progress. This means that the MIS manager must possess the following knowledge and skills:

- A thorough understanding of the organization, its goals, and its business activities.
- Leadership qualities to motivate and control highly skilled people.
- Knowledge of data-processing methods and familiarity with available hardware and software.

468

A man or woman seeking a career in information system management should have a college degree. For managing business data-processing centers, a degree in business administration with a concentration in the area of management information systems is desirable. Some employers prefer to hire someone with an MBA degree. Furthermore, to handle high-level management responsibilities such as those outlined above, a candidate for a position as MIS director should have at least two years of extensive management experience, as well as advanced knowledge of the industry and competence in all technical, professional, and business skills.

System Development Personnel

Programmers   Generally, three types of programming are done in an organization: *application programming*, *maintenance programming*, and *system programming*. Persons working in any of these areas should possess the following basic skills:

- Good command of the programming language or languages in which programs are written.
- A knowledge of general programming methodology and of the relationships between programs and hardware.
- Analytical reasoning ability and attention to detail.
- Creativity and discipline to develop new problem-solving methods.
- Patience and persistence.

Application programs, which were discussed in Chapter 9, perform data-processing or computational tasks to solve specific problems facing an organization. This type of programming constitutes the bulk of all programming tasks. It involves taking a broad system design prepared by an analyst and converting it into instructions for the computer. The responsibilities of application programmers also include testing, debugging, documenting, and implementing programs.

An application programmer in business data processing must apply the capabilities of the computer to problems such as customer billing and inventory control. In addition to the basic skills outlined earlier, a business-oriented application programmer should know the objectives of the organization and have a basic understanding of accounting and management science.

Besides business-oriented application programmers, there are scientific application programmers who work on scientific or engineering problems, which usually require complex mathematical solutions. Thus, a scientific application programmer needs a basic knowledge of science or engineering.

Program maintenance is a very important but often neglected activity. Many large programs are never completely debugged, and there is a continuing need for changes to and improvement of major programs. It is the responsibility of maintenance programmers to change and improve existing programs. In some organizations, maintenance programming is done by application programmers. To be effective, a maintenance programmer needs considerable programming experience and a high level of analytical ability.

A different type of specialist, the system programmer, is responsible for creating and maintaining system software. System programmers are not concerned with writing programs to solve day-to-day organizational problems. Instead, they are expected to develop utility programs; maintain operating systems, data-base packages, compilers, and assemblers; and be involved in decisions concerning additions and deletions of hardware and software. Because of their knowledge of operating systems, system programmers typically offer technical help to application programmers. To be able to perform these duties effectively, a system programmer should have: (1) a background in the theory of computer language structure and syntax and (2) extensive and detailed knowledge of the hardware being used and the software that controls it.

In hiring any of these types of programmers, employers may also look for specialized skills. For example, the increasing impact of minicomputers and microcomputers is creating a demand for programmers with experience in real-time or interactive systems using mini and micro hardware. Also, the advanced technology of today's communication networks provides excellent opportunities for programmers skilled in designing, coding, testing, debugging, documenting, and implementing data communication software.

Educational requirements for programmers vary, because employers' needs vary. For a business-oriented application programming job, a college degree, though desirable, is usually not required. However, most employers prefer applicants who have had college courses in data processing, accounting, and business administration. Sometimes, workers experienced in computer operation or specific functional areas of business are promoted to programming jobs and, with additional data-processing courses, become fully qualified programmers.

Scientific application programming usually requires a degree in computer or information science, mathematics, engineering, or a physical science. Some jobs require graduate degrees. Few scientific organizations are interested in applicants with no college training.

Persons seeking to enter the system programming field should have at least one year of assembly language programming experience or a college degree in computer science. In addition to a degree, work experience, although not essential for a job as a programmer, is extremely beneficial.

Computer programming is taught in technical and vocational schools, community and junior colleges, and universities. Many high schools offer computer programming courses.

Application and system programmers will continue to be in exceptionally high demand. Application programmers with some exposure to data-base management and direct-access techniques, remote processing, conversational programming, structured design, and distributed processing will be in greatest demand. As the use of minicomputers and microcomputers increases, knowledge of BASIC, RPGII, and Pascal will be valuable. System programmers knowledgeable in data communications, network planning and analysis, data-base concepts, and terminal-oriented systems will be in great demand. With these trends in mind, data processing, computer science, and business administration students may choose to direct their education toward some degree of specialization.

Within an organization, a programmer's chances for advancement are usually good. A programmer who has demonstrated his or her technical competence and ability to handle responsibility may be promoted to lead programmer and given supervisory responsibilities. Some application programmers become system programmers, and vice versa. The career path for an application or system programmer often leads to the position of system analyst; it can also lead to a managerial position, provided that the programmer possesses the necessary communication, leadership, and management skills.

System Analysts   The *system analyst* is the key person in the analysis, design, and implementation of a formal information system. The analyst has the following responsibilities:

- Helping the user determine information needs.
- Gathering facts about existing systems and analyzing them to determine the effectiveness of current processing methods and procedures.
- Designing new systems, recommending changes to existing systems, and being involved in implementing these changes.

The analyst's role is critical to the success of any management information system. He or she acts as an interface between users of the MIS and technical personnel such as programmers, machine operators, and data-base specialists. This role becomes more important as the cost of designing, implementing, and maintaining information systems rises.

To be effective, the system analyst should possess the following characteristics:

- A general knowledge of the firm, its goals and objectives, and the products and services it provides.
- Familiarity with the organizational structure of the company and management's rationale for selecting that structure.
- Comprehensive knowledge of data-processing methods and current hardware and familiarity with available programming languages.
- The ability to plan and organize work and to cooperate and interact effectively with both technical and nontechnical personnel.
- A high level of creativity.
- The ability to communicate clearly and persuasively with technical personnel as well as with persons who have little or no computer background.

The minimum requirements for a job as a system analyst generally include work experience in system design and programming and some specialized industry experience. System analysts seeking jobs in a business environment should be college graduates with backgrounds in business management, accounting, economics, computer science, information systems, or data processing. An MBA or some graduate study is often desired. For work in a scientifically oriented organization, a college background in the physical sciences, mathematics, or engineering is preferred. Many universities offer majors in management information systems; their curricula are designed to train people to be system analysts.

Some organizations, particularly small ones, do not employ system analysts. Instead, *programmer/analysts* are responsible for system analysis and programming. In other companies, system analysts begin as programmers and are promoted to analyst positions after gaining experience. However, the qualities that make for a good analyst are significantly different from those that characterize a good programmer. Hence, there is no clear career path *from* programming *to* analysis, though such movement is possible.

System analysis is a growing field. According to data from the United States Department of Labor, computer system analysts can look forward throughout the 1980s to employment prospects brighter than those for workers in almost any other occupation. There is a continuing growth of management consulting firms and computer services organizations, as well as a high demand for system professionals by computer manufacturers. The growth rate in jobs is estimated to be 37 percent by 1990. Also, the increasing use of minicomputers and microcomputers will cause an increase in the small user's needs for analysts to design systems for small computers.

Data-Base Specialists

Data-base specialists are responsible for designing and controlling the use of the organization's data resources. A *data-base analyst*—the key person in the analysis, design, and implementation of data structures—must plan and coordinate data use within the system. The analyst has the following responsibilities:

● Helping the user or system analyst to analyze the interrelationships of data.
● Defining physical data structures and logical views of data.
● Designing new data-base systems, recommending changes to existing ones, and being involved in the implementation of these changes.
● Eliminating data redundance.

In some organizations, the function of data analysis and coordination is incorporated in the system analysis function.

A data-base analyst needs technical knowledge of programming and system methodologies. A background in system software is valuable for persons planning physical data-base structures. The job requires a college education with concentration in the areas of computer science, business data processing, and data-base management system design. Many colleges offer courses in data-base management to train people to be data analysts.

The career path within the data-base specialty often leads to the position of corporate *data-base administrator (DBA)*. Data-base administrator is a management-level position responsible for control of all the data resources of the organization. The primary responsibilities of this position include:

- Developing a dictionary of standard data definitions so that all records are consistent.
- Designing data bases.
- Maintaining the accuracy, completeness, and timeliness of data bases.
- Designing procedures to ensure data security and data-base backup and recovery.
- Facilitating communications between analysts and users.
- Advising analysts, programmers, and system users as to the best ways to use data bases.

To handle these responsibilities, a data-base administrator must have a high level of technical expertise as well as an ability to communicate effectively with diverse groups of people. This person must exhibit supervisory and leadership skills developed through experience.

Demand is strong for data-base specialists. With the increasing trend toward data-base management, the need for persons with the technical knowledge to design data-base-oriented application systems is increasing.

Data-Processing Operations Personnel

Data-processing operations personnel are responsible for entering data and instructions into the computer, operating the computer and attached devices, retrieving output, and ensuring the smooth operation of the computing center and associated libraries. An efficient operations staff is crucial to the effective use of an organization's computer resources.

The *librarian* is responsible for classifying, cataloging, and maintaining files and programs stored on cards, tapes, disks, diskettes, and all other storage media and kept in a computer library for subsequent processing or historical purposes. The librarian's tasks include transferring backup files to alternate storage sites, purging old files, and supervising the periodic cleaning of magnetic tapes and disks.

The librarian's job is important because he or she controls access to stored master files and programs. Computer operators and programmers do not have access to the tapes or disks without the approval of the librarian. This prevents unauthorized changes or processing runs.

The educational background required for this particular job is not extensive; a high-school diploma is adequate. In addition, the individual must have some knowledge of basic data-processing concepts and should possess clerical record-keeping skills.

A *computer operator's* duties include setting up equipment for particular jobs; mounting and removing tapes, disks, and diskettes as needed; and monitoring the operation of the computer. This person should be able to identify operational problems and take appropriate corrective actions. Most computers run under sophisticated operating systems that direct the operator through messages generated during processing. However, the operator is responsible for reviewing errors that occur during operation, determining their causes, and maintaining operating records.

People seeking jobs as computer operators should enjoy working with machines and be able to read and understand technical literature. A computer operator has to act quickly and properly; a good operator can prevent the loss of a great deal of valuable computer time, as well as the loss or destruction of files and input data. An operator must also possess communications skills so that he or she can explain to users why programs worked or did not work.

Most operators receive training as apprentice operators. Few have college degrees. However, formal operator training is available through technical schools and junior colleges. To be effective, training must include several weeks of on-the-job experience with equipment similar to that the operator will be using.

A *data-entry operator's* job involves transcribing data into a form suitable for computer processing. A *keypunch operator* uses a keypunch machine to transfer data from source documents to punched cards. Operators of other key-entry devices transfer data to magnetic tape or magnetic disk for subsequent processing.

A *remote terminal operator* is also involved with the preparation of input data. The operator is located at a remote site, probably some distance from the computer itself. The data is entered into the computer directly, from the location at which it is generated.

Data-entry jobs usually require manual dexterity, typing or keying skills, and alertness. No extensive formal education is required; a high-school diploma is sufficient. However, all personnel in this category should be trained carefully to minimize the incidence of errors. Usually several weeks of on-the-job training is provided for new operators to familiarize them with the documents they will be reading and the data-entry devices they will be using.

Occupations in computer operations are being affected by changes in data-processing technology. The demand for keypunch operators will continue to decline as new methods of data preparation are developed and as the use of computer terminals and direct data-entry techniques continues to flourish. However, as the use of computers continues to expand, especially in small businesses, demand for computer operating personnel should remain strong.

MANAGING INFORMATION SYSTEMS

Organization of Data Processing

Traditionally, data-processing activities have been performed within the functional departments of organizations. However, because of increased record-keeping requirements, the ever-present need for current information, and the necessity to adapt to a complex, changing environment, many organizations have consolidated their data-processing operations. The computer has been used increasingly as a tool to manage the paper explosion that threatens to engulf many organizations.

The rapid growth of computer-based data processing has affected the location of the EDP department in an organization's structure. In most organizations, data processing originated in the accounting area, since most record keeping was done there. However, management has recognized that information is a scarce and valuable resource of the entire organization and has increasingly emphasized the data-processing activity and elevated it in the organizational structure.

Figure A–1 shows two versions of an organizational chart for a typical manufacturing firm, each with a different general location for the EDP department. Figure A–1a shows the traditional location: the EDP manager reports to the vice-president of finance and accounting. This location is satisfactory only if the other functional areas do not demand extensive use of computer capabilities. Unless the processing requirements of the accounting and finance department are extensive, the computer is not used to its full potential under such an arrangement. Further, this location has the following drawbacks:

● It is biased toward accounting and financial applications in the setting of job priorities. Since the data-processing manager reports to the controller he or she will obviously give high priority to financial applications.

● It discourages involvement of data-processing personnel with the other functional divisions and inhibits overall integration of the data-processing function.

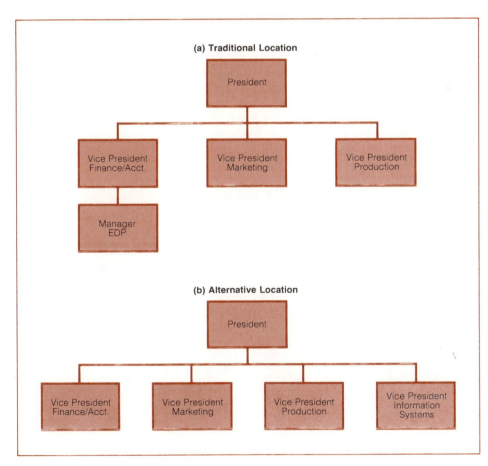

FIGURE A–1
Possible Locations for EDP Department in Organizational Structure

Figure A–1b shows an alternative location that overcomes these limitations. Elevating the data-processing activity to the same status as the traditional line functions (production, marketing, finance) reflects its corporate-wide scope. When it occupies this position, the EDP department's name is often changed to management information system (MIS) department, to stress the importance of its function. The independent status of the MIS department helps to ensure that each functional area gets impartial service and that their particular information requirements are integrated to meet organizational goals.

The internal organizational structure of the MIS department can take various forms. Perhaps the most common breakdown is by data-processing function—system analysis and design, programming, and computer operations—as illustrated in Figure A–2.

An alternative structure emphasizes project assignments. Analysts and programmers work on specific projects in teams that include personnel from user departments. As projects are completed, teams are restructured and team members are assigned to new projects. Such an approach is illustrated in Figure A–3.

Managing System Development

System analysis, design, and implementation were discussed in detail in Chapters 12 and 13. It is the responsibility of the MIS (data-processing) manager to monitor the total system development cycle to ensure that projects are completed within reasonable time schedules. Various formal network techniques like *PERT* (Program Evaluation and Review Technique) and *CPM* (Critical Path Method) are available for project planning and control. To use such techniques, the manager must break the project into distinct activities, determine the sequence in which the activities are to be performed, and

FIGURE A–2
Functional
Organization
of MIS Department

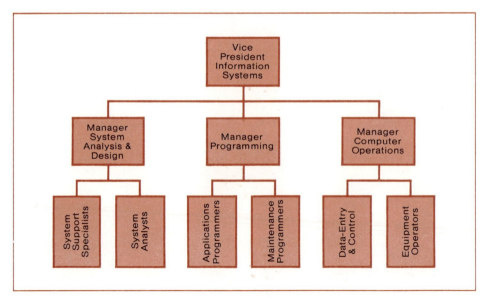

establish a time estimate for each activity. Then, a scheduling chart can be designed. The responsible manager monitors the progress of the project by comparing estimated completion times with actual times. If delays occur, the reasons behind them must be identified and corrective actions taken.

Managing Computer Operations

Most modern computer systems cost millions of dollars; thus, there is increasing concern that the systems' CPUs and peripheral devices be used efficiently. Management can collect data and analyze it to determine the degree of utilization of the hardware and encourage higher efficiency and increased throughput by proper job scheduling and balancing of hardware capabilities.

In addition to improving hardware utilization, the data-processing manager must strive for a high degree of maintainability and reliability; preventive maintenance schemes must be developed for both hardware and software. Better systems can be achieved through use of the following practices:

● Establishing standard procedures to control actions that initiate and implement change.
● Using a modular approach for both hardware and software so that systems can be expanded; a complete switch to new equipment and new programs is a costly undertaking and should be avoided if possible.
● Strictly adhering to documentation standards. Software maintenance is impossible without extensive documentation to clarify how specific programs work.
● Implementing standard control and audit procedures to ascertain that the administrative policies and procedures established by management are followed.
● Planning for all contingencies so that data-processing interruptions are not catastrophic.

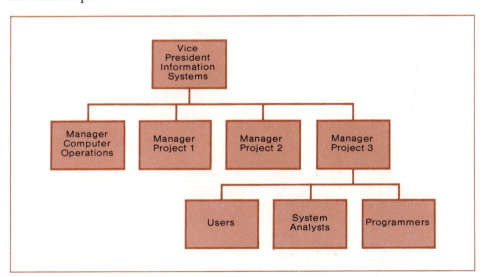

FIGURE A–3

Project Organization of MIS Department

Managing an MIS is a difficult but important task. Managers must keep in mind that an MIS is an integrated set of people and machines. No matter how sophisticated the MIS, success in using it can be achieved only through its acceptance by users at all levels of the organization.

PROFESSIONAL ASSOCIATIONS

Professional societies have been formed to increase communication among professional people in computer fields, to continue the professional education of members, and to distribute current knowledge through publications of professional journals.

AFIPS

The American Federation of Information Processing Societies (AFIPS), organized in 1961, is a national federation of professional societies established to represent member societies on an international basis and to advance and disseminate knowledge of these societies. There are two categories of AFIPS participation: (1) member societies that have a principal interest in computers and information processing and (2) affiliated societies that, although not primarily concerned with computers and information processing, have a major interest in this area. Some of the prominent constituent societies of AFIPS are the Association for Computing Machinery (ACM), the Data Processing Management Association (DPMA), the Institute of Electrical and Electronic Engineers (IEEE), and the American Society for Information Science (ASIS). Affiliated societies of AFIPS include the American Institute of Certified Public Accountants (AICPA) and the American Statistical Association (ASA).

ACM

The Association for Computing Machinery (ACM) is the largest scientific, educational, and technical society of the computing community. Founded in 1947, this association is dedicated to the development of information processing as a discipline and to the responsible use of computers in increasingly complex and diverse applications. The objectives of the association are:

- To advance the science and art of information processing, including the study, design, development, construction, and application of modern machinery, computing techniques, and programming software.
- To promote the free exchange of ideas in the field of information processing in a professional manner, among both specialists and the public.
- To develop and maintain the integrity and competence of individuals engaged in the field of information processing.

The ACM has established special interest groups (known as SIGs) to address the wide range of interests in the computing field. For example, SIGS-

MALL was established for ACM members interested in small computers; SIGPLAN, for those interested in programming languages; and SIGCSE, for those interested in computer science education.

DPMA

Founded in Chicago as the National Machine Accountants Association, the Data Processing Management Association (DPMA) was chartered in December 1951. At that time the first electronic computer had yet to come into commercial use. The name "machine accountants" was chosen to identify persons associated with the operation and supervision of punched-card equipment. The society took its present name in 1962.

DPMA is one of the largest world-wide organizations serving the information-processing and management communities. It comprises all levels of management personnel. Through its educational and publishing activities, DPMA seeks to encourage high standards in the field of data processing and to promote a professional attitude among its members.

One of DPMA's specific purposes is to promote and develop educational and scientific inquiry in the field of data processing and data-processing management. As such, it sponsors college student organizations interested in data processing and encourages members to serve as counselors for the Scout computer merit badge. The organization also presents the "Computer Sciences Man of the Year" award for outstanding contributions to the profession.

ASM

The Association for Systems Management (ASM), founded in 1947, is headquartered in Cleveland, Ohio. The ASM is an international organization engaged in keeping its members abreast of the rapid growth and change occurring in the field of systems management and information processing. It provides for the professional growth and development of its members and of the systems profession through:

- Extended programs in local and regional areas in the fields of education and research.
- Annual conferences and committee functions in research, education, and public relations.
- Promotion of high standards of work performance by members of the ASM and members of the systems profession.
- Publication of the *Journal of Systems Management,* technical reports, and other works on subjects of current interest to systems practitioners.

The ASM has five technical departments: Data Communications, Data Processing, Management Information Systems, Organization Planning, and Written Communications. An ASM member can belong to one or more of these departments.

ICCP

The Institute for Certification of Computer Professionals (ICCP) is a non-profit organization established in 1973 for the purpose of testing and certifying knowledge and skills of computing personnel. A primary objective of the ICCP is to pool the resources of constituent societies so that the full attention of the information-processing industry can be focused on the vital tasks of development and recognition of qualified personnel.

The establishment of the ICCP was an outgrowth of studies made by committees of the DPMA and the ACM, which developed the concept of a "computer foundation" to foster testing and certification programs. In 1974, the ICCP acquired the testing and certification programs of DPMA, including the *Certificate in Data Processing (CDP)* examination, which DPMA had begun in 1962. All candidates for the CDP examination must have at least five years of work experience in a computer-based information system environment. The examination consists of five sections: data-processing equipment, computer programming and software, principles of management, quantitative methods, and system analysis and design. Any qualified person may take the examination; he or she must successfully complete all five sections to receive the certificate. Another certification, the *Certificate in Computer Programming (CCP)*, recognizes experience and professional competence at the senior programmer level. Candidates for this certification must also pass a basic five-part examination.

The ICCP is involved in improving existing programs and establishing new examinations for various specialties. A framework for a broad spectrum of tests and the relationship of these tests to job functions and curricula is under development.

SMIS

The Society for Management Information Systems (SMIS) was founded in 1968 to serve persons concerned with all aspects of management information systems in the electronic data-processing industry, including business system designers, managers, and educators. The organization aims to be an exchange or marketplace for technical information about management information systems and to enhance communications between MIS directors and executives responsible for the management of the business enterprise. SMIS also offers educational and research programs, sponsors competitions, bestows awards, and maintains placement programs.

BASIC
Supplement

CONTENTS

PREFACE

BASIC has traditionally been accepted as the most effective programming language for instructional purposes. In recent years, business and computer manufacturers have recognized the vast potential for the BASIC language beyond education. Therefore, the availability and usage of BASIC has increased dramatically. Today most small business computer systems and home computer systems rely exclusively on BASIC programming support.

One major problem associated with such tremendous growth has been the lack of controls on the implementation of the language. Although there is a national standard (ANSI) version of BASIC, it is normally not followed by computer designers. Thus there are differences in the BASIC language found on various computers. The material in this book not only presents BASIC found on a typical large time-shared computer system (Digital Equipment Corp.), but also includes coverage of microcomputer implementations (PET, Apple, IBM, TRS-80). Whenever a BASIC instruction deviates from the national standard, it is highlighted.

Color coding has been used extensively throughout the material to assist the reader. The following legend should prove valuable:

BLUE	Computer Output
RED	Highlighted Statements
BROWN	User Response
BROWN SHADING	Nonstandard BASIC

A special note of appreciation to Terrye Gregory and Dr. Stephen Gregory for their herculean efforts on this project. Every program has been both class tested and run on the various computer systems. Our primary goal has been to develop a student-oriented BASIC text that is both logical and consistent in its presentation. I would appreciate receiving any suggestions that might improve the material.

BACKGROUND

BASIC was developed in the mid-1960s at Dartmouth College by Professors John G. Kemeny and Thomas E. Kurtz and has become one of the most popular programming languages. BASIC, short for Beginner's All-Purpose Symbolic Instruction Code, is easy to learn, can be used for a wide variety of useful tasks, and is well suited for interactive processing.

BASIC, like any language, includes rules for spelling, syntax, grammar, and punctuation. Just as the rules in English help us to understand one another, so the rules in BASIC help the computer to understand what we want it to do. In BASIC, the rules link abstract algebraic expressions with easy-to-understand English words like LET, GO TO, FOR/NEXT, INPUT, PRINT, and END.

BASIC was originally developed for use in a large, interactive computer environment; one or more BASIC users could communicate with the computer *during* processing and feel as though they had the computer all to themselves. As the demand for minicomputers and microcomputers increased, manufacturers of such computers felt pressure to develop simple but effective languages for them. Rather than create entirely new languages, most opted to offer BASIC because of its interactive capability. Many altered the original BASIC, however, to suit their equipment. The result is that, although the BASIC language has a universally accepted set of standard rules called *ANSI BASIC*, each manufacturer adds its "quirks" to this standard to make use of special features of its machines.

This supplement discusses BASIC commands common to most computer systems but highlights language variations among vendors. Most programming examples have been executed on five different computers: a DECSYSTEM 20 to represent the major time-sharing systems and the Apple, IBM Personal computer, PET/CBM, and TRS-80 to represent popular microcomputer systems. Most other microcomputers are capable of using a dialect called BASIC-80 from Microsoft Consumer Products and an operating system called CP/M produced by Digital Research. Since the IBM's BASIC and operating systems are direct derivatives of BASIC-80 and CP/M, we will group these together for convenience. The programming examples will run on the DECSYSTEM 20 computer, but important changes required to execute them on the other computers are noted. Although there are a variety of models and languages for the Apple and TRS-80 computers, this book discusses only one of each—the Apple II computer with the Applesoft language and the TRS-80 Model III computer with Model III language (essentially the same as Level II BASIC for the Model I).

AN INTRODUCTION TO COMPUTER PROGRAMMING

Computer programs are step-by-step instructions to solve a problem. Since the computer must be able to read and interpret each instruction, it must be precisely written. In order to know what instructions are required to solve a problem, the programmer follows five steps commonly called the programming process:

1. Define the problem.
2. Design a solution.
3. Write the program.
4. Submit the program to the computer.
5. Test, debug, and document the program.

In order to show how these steps are used in the programming process, let us take a sample data-processing problem: calculating our metric weight from our weight in pounds.

The first step is to define the problem. To do so, we analyze it by using the basic flow of all data processing—*input, processing, output*—but with a twist. It is often easier to determine what processing is needed by working backwards. First, analyze what output is required and then see what input is available for the program. The gap between the available input and required output will be the processing needed in the program.

Determining the output required for the problem is quite simple—we need to know our weight in kilograms. The input available is our weight in pounds. The gap is some conversion factor that translates the weight in pounds to kilograms. One kilogram equals 2.2 pounds; hence, to calculate our metric weight, we divide our weight in pounds by 2.2. We have now defined the problem.

The second step, designing a solution, requires developing a logical sequence of instructions to solve the problem. A great tool to use at this point is the flowchart. *Flowcharts* are composed of symbols that stand for program statements. For example, the symbol for a processing step is:

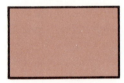

The symbol for a step that involves either input from the terminal or output to the terminal is:

The symbol that shows where the program starts or stops is:

Figure I–1 shows a flowchart depicting the steps of the programming example. Notice how the symbols are shown in logical order, top down, connected by arrows. The first symbol shows the start of the program. It may correspond to one or more remarks at the beginning of the program statements. The second symbol shows an input step—we enter our weight. The third shows the processing done by the program—conversion of weight in pounds to metric weight. After that, we want to see the result, so we output the converted weight to the terminal. Finally, another start/stop symbol signifies the end of the program. The flowchart makes it easy to see the input, processing, and output steps of the program.

If the solution has been designed carefully, the next step—coding the program—should be relatively easy. All that is required is to translate the flowchart into program statements. Figure I–2 shows this program written in BASIC. As you can see, many BASIC words, such as INPUT and PRINT, are easy to interpret. The symbol / means divide. Compare the coded BASIC statements in Figure I–2 to the flowchart in Figure I–1; the correspondence between the two is obvious.

FIGURE I–1
Flowchart Example

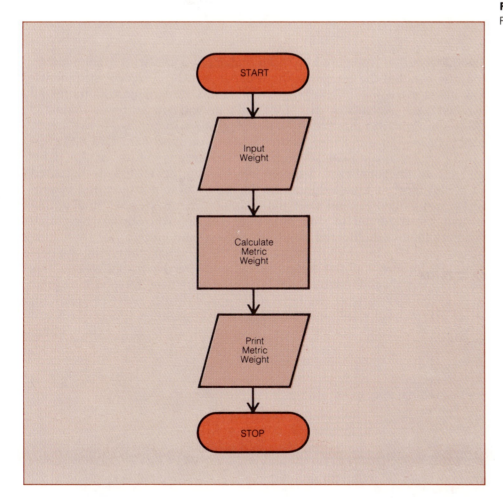

FIGURE I–2

Metric Weight Program

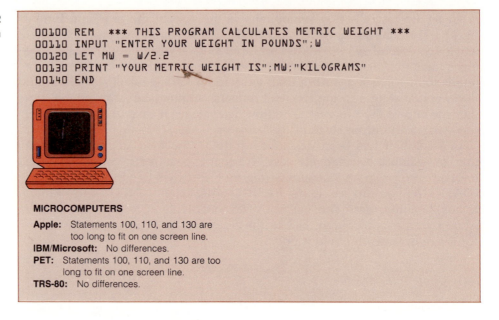

```
00100 REM  *** THIS PROGRAM CALCULATES METRIC WEIGHT ***
00110 INPUT "ENTER YOUR WEIGHT IN POUNDS";W
00120 LET MW = W/2.2
00130 PRINT "YOUR METRIC WEIGHT IS";MW;"KILOGRAMS"
00140 END
```

MICROCOMPUTERS

Apple: Statements 100, 110, and 130 are too long to fit on one screen line.

IBM/Microsoft: No differences.

PET: Statements 100, 110, and 130 are too long to fit on one screen line.

TRS-80: No differences.

In the program in Figure I–2, each statement starts with a *line number*. Line numbers tell the computer the order in which to execute statements. Line 100 is a comment describing the program. The computer ignores all such comment statements; they are for documentation purposes. Line 110 tells the computer to print out a statement (shown in quotes)—your cue to enter your weight—and then accepts it after you type it in. Line 120 is an example of an assignment statement, which assigns values on the right-hand side of the equal sign to special variables on the left (this is discussed in the next section). Line 130 instructs the computer to print out first a heading (shown in quotes) and then the computer metric weight. Finally, line 140 tells the computer to stop processing. Again, you can see how each statement follows the flow of input, processing, and output.

The fourth step involves sitting down at the terminal and typing the program, line for line, into the computer. Many interactive BASIC interpreters and compilers check for syntax errors as each statement is typed in. *Syntax* refers to the way instructions have to be written (rules must be followed, just as grammatical rules must be followed in English). A syntax check can

FIGURE I–3

Syntax Checking

```
10 PRING "I MISSPELLED PRINT"
10 PRING "I MISSPELLED PRINT"

? STATEMENT NOT RECOGNIZED
10 REM ***  EQUAL SYMBOL WILL BE IN WRONG PLACE ***
20 A + B = C
20 A + B = C

? STATEMENT NOT RECOGNIZED
```

save considerable debugging time. Figure I–3 shows an interactive session with syntax checking.

After all syntax errors have been eliminated, the program can be tested with sample data. This is the fifth step. During this stage, the logic of the program is checked for correctness; for instance, were the correct statements used to determine the metric weight? Documentation consists of all written descriptions and explanations necessary for later modification or updating of the program. Figure I–4 shows the execution of the metric weight program.

This example is relatively simple, but it shows each of the steps required to complete a program. Although other problems may be more complex, the steps involved are the same. Successful programming can only come about through diligent application of the five steps in the programming process.

FIGURE I–4
Execution of Metric Weight Program

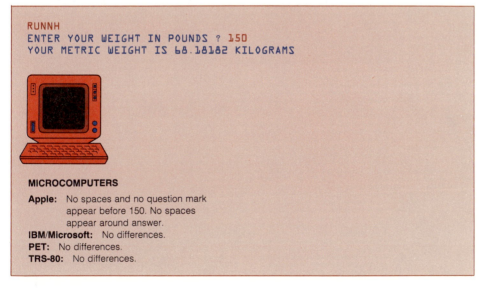

```
RUNNH
ENTER YOUR WEIGHT IN POUNDS ? 150
YOUR METRIC WEIGHT IS 68.18182 KILOGRAMS
```

MICROCOMPUTERS

Apple: No spaces and no question mark appear before 150. No spaces appear around answer.
IBM/Microsoft: No differences.
PET: No differences.
TRS-80: No differences.

SUMMARY

- BASIC (Beginner's All-Purpose Symbolic Instruction Code) was developed in the mid-1960s by Professors John G. Kemeny and Thomas E. Kurtz.
- BASIC has rules of grammar (syntax) to which programmers must adhere.
- The five steps in the programming process are: (1) define the problem; (2) plan the solution; (3) write the program; (4) enter it into the computer; and (5) test, debug, and document the program.

OVERVIEW

One of the best ways to learn any programming language is to examine sample programs. This and the remaining sections in the BASIC supplement will intersperse discussions of the language's general characteristics with program examples.

This section discusses some BASIC fundamentals: line numbers, BASIC statements, constants, character strings, and variables. All are demonstrated so that you can use them properly when you write programs.

COMPONENTS OF THE BASIC LANGUAGE

A BASIC program is a sequence of statements that tells the computer how to solve a problem. Figure II–1 is an example. (Most sections begin with a simple program example). This program calculates the area of a room with dimensions of 12½ meters by 37 meters.

Notice that each instruction contains a line number and a BASIC *statement*. Line 140 from the sample program is an example of a typical BASIC instruction. It tells the computer to multiply two values together and place the result in a location called A. A represents the area.

LINE NUMBERS

The *line number* must be an integer between 1 and 99999. The program statements are executed by the computer in the sequence in which they are num-

---

FIGURE II–1
Area of a Room Program

```
00100 REM    *** THIS PROGRAM COMPUTES THE AREA ***
00110 REM    *** OF A ROOM ***
00120 LET L = 12.5
00130 LET W = 37
00140 LET A = L*W
00150 LET H$ = "THE AREA IS"
00160 PRINT H$,A
00170 END
```

MICROCOMPUTERS

Apple: Line 100 is too long.
IBM/Microsoft: No differences.
PET: Line 100 is too long.
TRS-80: No differences.

B-9

bered, from low to high. The line numbers can also be used as labels to refer to specific statements in the program.

Line numbers do not have to be specified in increments of 1. Using increments of 10, for example, makes it easier to insert new statements between existing lines at a later time without renumbering all the old statements in the program. For example, if we wanted to insert a new statement in the sample program between statements 130 and 140, we could number the new statement 135 without disturbing the order of the existing statements and having to renumber them.

```
00100 REM    *** THIS PROGRAM COMPUTES THE AREA ***
00110 REM    *** OF A ROOM ***
00120 LET L = 12.5
00130 LET W = 37
00135 REM    *** AREA = LENGTH  X  WIDTH
00140 LET A = L*W
00150 LET H$ = "THE AREA IS"
00160 PRINT H$;A
00170 END
```

The BASIC interpreter or compiler arranges all the program statements in ascending order according to line number even though the lines may actually have been entered in some other order.

Another advantage of BASIC line numbers is that they permit changes to be made to the program as it is being entered. For example, if two lines are typed in with the same line number, the computer will accept the last one entered as the correct one. Thus, if we make a mistake in a statement, we can simply type in the same line number and the correct statement. In the example below, the computer will replace the first line 140 with the second line 140.

```
140 A = L*L  (mistake occurs here)

140 A = L*W  (corrected line)
```

BASIC STATEMENTS

BASIC *statements* are composed of special programming commands, constants, numeric or string variables, and formulas (also called *expressions*). Let us take a closer look at these elements.

Constants

Constants are values that do not change during a program's execution. There are two kinds: numeric and character string.

Numeric Constant   BASIC permits numbers to be represented in two ways: as real numbers or in exponential notation.

Real Numbers. *Real numbers* can be either integers or decimal fractions. Some examples of real numbers are:

0.67   2000   +52   −65981   5.987

There are some rules to remember about using numbers in BASIC.

1. No commas can be embedded within numbers.

2145 (valid)   2,145 (invalid)

BASIC sees the invalid example not as the number two thousand one hundred forty-five but as the number two and the number one hundred forty-five.

2. If the number is negative, it must be preceded by a minus sign.

−0.067 (valid)   0.067− (invalid)

3. If no sign is included, the number is assumed to be positive.

4906 is the same as +4906

Exponential Form, or Scientific Notation. *Scientific notation* is usually used for very large or very small numbers. Some examples are:

5.67213E+08   2.117E−04

The E represents base 10, and the signed number following the E is the power to which 10 is raised. The number preceding the E is called the *mantissa* and in most systems lies between 1.000 and 9.999. For example

Decimal	Power Equivalent	Scientific Notation
4630	4.63×10^3	4.63E+03
0.000337	3.37×10^{-4}	3.37E−04
−8841500	-8.8415×10^6	−8.8415E+06

Character String Constant   The other type of constant is the *character string*. Character strings are composed of *alphanumeric data*—a sequence of letters, numbers, and/or special characters enclosed in quotation marks. The maximum number of characters allowed in a character string varies from system to system. The following are examples of character strings:

```
"TERRY"
"349-41-6888"
"314 MARY ALICE DR."
```

There is a character string in line 150 of the sample program.

```
150 LET H$ = "THE AREA IS"
```

Variables

Any data values to be used by a program must be stored in the computer either before or during execution of the program. The computer has a great number of storage locations, which are given names by the programmer. The names, or symbols, the programmer assigns refer to data stored in the computer's memory. They are called *variable names*, because the value stored in a location can change as the program is executed. However, each variable can represent only one value at a time.

Numeric Variable   A numeric variable name represents a number that is either supplied to the computer by the programmer or internally calculated by the computer during execution of the program. A numeric variable name can be either one letter alone or one letter followed by one numeric digit. **NONSTANDARD** (Almost all BASICs permit use of two letters, and many computer systems permit more descriptive variable names—see box.) The following examples show valid and invalid numeric variable names.

Valid	Invalid and Why	
A	35	(must begin with a letter)
X5	*A	(must begin with a letter)
A2	7	(cannot be a single digit)
X4		

Note lines 120, 130, and 140 in the sample program.

```
120 LET L = 12.5
130 LET W = 37
140 LET A = L*W
```

L is a numeric variable that contains the length of the room—12.5 meters. W holds the value of the width. The length and width are multiplied in line 140 and the result is assigned to the variable A.

String Variable   A string variable name can represent the value of a character string—for example, a name, an address, or a social security number. String variables are distinguished from numeric variables by the use of the dollar

1. Microcomputers: The same rules and warnings apply to string names as to numeric names—the first two characters are all that make a name unique. For example, the computer could not distinguish NAME$ from NATION$.

2. Large Systems: More characters are available to make the name unique. On the DEC, 29 characters after the first can be used. (But $ must be at the end.) Again, the IBM and Microsoft allow 40 characters.

sign ($) following a single alphabetic character. The following are examples of valid and invalid string variables:

Valid	Invalid and Why
A$	$ 4$ (first character must be alphabetic)
R$	A Y1 (last character must be $)

Many computer systems permit use of more descriptive string variable names. However, all systems require that the first character be alphabetic and the last character to be $. See the box for examples permitted by other systems. **NONSTANDARD**

Typical examples of the proper use of string variables can be seen in lines 150 and 160 of the sample program.

```
150 LET H$ = "THE AREA IS"
160 PRINT H$, A
```

The character string "THE AREA IS" is assigned to the string variable H$. In line 160, the values of H$ and A are printed out. Figure II–2 shows the output.

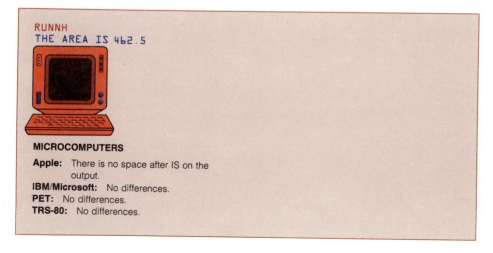

RUNNH
THE AREA IS 462.5

MICROCOMPUTERS

Apple: There is no space after IS on the output.
IBM/Microsoft: No differences.
PET: No differences.
TRS-80: No differences.

FIGURE II–2
Output from Area of a Room Program

Reserved Words

Certain words have very specific meanings in the BASIC language. These words are *reserved* and cannot be used as variable names. Look in your manuals for the reserved words on your computer system. The most common ones are (the highlighted ones are nonstandard):

ABS, AND, AT, BASE, CALL, CHR$, CLEAR, COS, DATA, DEF, DIM, END, EXP, FN, FOR, GET, GO, IF, INPUT, INT, LET, LIST, LOAD, LOG, NEW, NEXT, NOT, ON, OPTION, OR, PRINT, READ, RND, REM, RESTORE, RUN, RETURN, SAVE, SQR, SGN, STOP, SIN, STORE, TAB, TAN, TEXT, THEN, and TO

You already know what some of these words instruct the computer to do; the rest will be explained as we go along.

Reserved words can cause problems with most microcomputers. Let's say you want to use the variable name TOTAL. Since the computer recognizes only the first two characters, it will send you an error message; it thinks you are making an incorrect use of the reserved word TO!

SUMMARY

● A BASIC program is a series of instructions. Each one is composed of a line number and a BASIC statement.

● The line numbers serve (1) as labels by which statements can be referenced, and (2) as instructions to specify the order of execution of the program.

● Using line numbers in increments of 10 permits easy insertion of new statements.

● BASIC statements contain special reserved words (programming commands), numeric or character string constants, numeric or string variables, and formulas.

● Constants are values that do not change. A valid numeric constant is any real number expressed as an integer, decimal fraction, or in exponential notation. Character strings are alphanumeric data enclosed in quotation marks.

● Variables are programmer-supplied names that specify locations in storage where data values may be stored. Numeric variables represent numbers. String variables contain alphanumeric values and are distinguished from numeric variables by the symbol $.

OVERVIEW

This section describes four elementary BASIC statements—REM, LET, PRINT, and END. The LET statement is used to input, or assign, data to variables and to perform arithmetic calculations. The PRINT statement allows the programmer to see the results of processing. Processing is stopped with the END statement. The REM statement is presented here to underscore the importance of program documentation.

Let us take a look at a problem that uses these statements.

Problem Definition

Assume you see a book entitled *Solutions to BASIC Programming Problems* at a nearby bookstore for $9.87. A sign in the window says all items are on sale at 15 percent off. The problem is to calculate the sale price of the book using the original price of $9.87 and the 15 percent discount.

Solution Design

In order to find the sale price, you must first calculate how much the 15 percent discount is by multiplying the original price, $9.87, times 0.15 (the decimal equivalent of 15 percent). Once you know the discount, you subtract it from the original price to determine the sale price ($9.87 − discount).

Figure III–1 shows this solution in flowchart form. The first step in the program is to describe its purpose by using comments. These statements correspond to the START block (a). The next step is to assign the original price of the book, $9.87, to a program variable (b); the next is to take 15 percent of that price to determine the discount (c). To calculate the final sale price, we subtract the discount from the original price (d). Finally, we receive as output the sale price of the book (e) and stop the program (f). Notice the end-of-program symbol at the end. Figure III–2 shows the translation of the flowchart into program statements.

The Program

The first four lines of the program in Figure III–2 (lines 10–40) provide information to persons reading the program but do not help the computer. These REM statements document the program. Note that the REM statement in line 40 is not followed by comments; it is used to make the program more readable by separating the remarks from the body of the program.

The LET statement in line 50 enters the price of the book, 9.87, into a storage location (variable) called P. Note that no dollar sign is used in the LET statement.

The LET statement is also used to perform arithmetic calculations. Line 60 instructs the computer to multiply the price of the book (contained in P) by the discount factor 0.15. The product is then assigned to another variable called D. Line 70 subtracts the discount from the original price and places that result in a variable called SP.

FIGURE III-1

Flowchart for Book
Sale

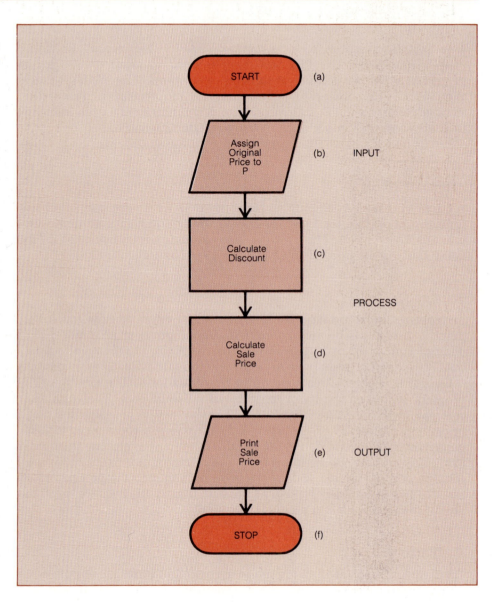

START	(a)
Assign Original Price to P	(b) INPUT
Calculate Discount	(c)
	PROCESS
Calculate Sale Price	(d)
Print Sale Price	(e) OUTPUT
STOP	(f)

FIGURE III–2

Book Sale Program

```
00010 REM  ***   THE PURPOSE OF THIS
00020 REM         PROGRAM IS TO CALCULATE
00030 REM         THE SALE PRICE OF A BOOK
00040 REM
00050 LET P = 9.87
00060 LET D = P * 0.15
00070 LET SP = P - D
00080 PRINT "THE SALE PRICE IS $"; SP
00999 END
```

At this point, the program has calculated the sale price, SP; but what is it? The computer has the result in storage, but we need to see it. To do this, we need a PRINT statement. Line 80 tells the computer to print what is enclosed in the quotation marks as well as the sale price contained in SP. The result of program execution is shown below.

```
RUNNH
THE SALE PRICE IS $ 8.3895
```

Now let us study these BASIC statements in detail.

THE REM STATEMENT

As stated earlier, the remarks (REM) statement provides information for the programmer or anyone else reading the program; it provides no information to the computer. The REM statement is used to *document* the program; the programmer generally uses it to explain program segments, to define variables used within the program, or to note any special instructions. These statements can be placed anywhere throughout the program.

The general format of the REM statement is:

line# REM comment

Some REM statements that could be used to document or explain the book sale example (Figure III–2) are:

```
00010 REM   ***   THE PURPOSE OF THIS
00020 REM         PROGRAM IS TO CALCULATE
00030 REM         THE SALE PRICE OF A BOOK
00032 REM          VARIABLES USED
00034 REM          P = ORIGINAL PRICE
00036 REM          D = DISCOUNT
00038 REM          SP = SALE PRICE
00040 REM
```

Note that each comment includes the keyword REM. Notice also that REM lines were inserted between program lines 30 and 40. No comment follows the REM in line 40; as explained earlier, the readability of the program is improved when comments are set off from executable statements.

THE LET STATEMENT

The purpose of the LET, or assignment, statement is to assign values to variables. It can be used to enter data into a program as well as to process it.

The general format of the LET statement is:

line# LET variable = expression

An example is line 50 of the sample program:

```
50 LET P = 9.87
```

The keyword LET identifies this statement to BASIC as an assignment statement. However, some compilers and interpreters do not require it. These versions accept the statement without the keyword LET as follows:

`50 P = 9.87`

The *expression* may be a constant, arithmetic formula, or variable. For example:

Statement	Expression	Type
`10 LET X = 0`	`0`	Numeric constant
`20 LET X$ = "NAME"`	`"NAME"`	Character string constant
`30 LET A = 4 * C`	`4 * C`	Arithmetic formula
`40 LET X = B`	`B`	Numeric variable
`50 LET D$ = H$`	`H$`	String variable

The LET statement can be used to assign values to numeric or string variables directly or to assign the result of a calculation to a numeric variable. In either case, the value or calculated result of an expression on the right-hand side of the equal sign is assigned to the variable on the left. It is important to note that the statement is not evaluated in the same way an algebraic expression is.

When BASIC assigns a value to a variable on the left side of the equation, it is really putting that value in a storage location in memory, labeled by that variable name. It is easy to see why only a variable can be on the left—nothing else would represent a storage location.

Some examples of LET statements are shown below.

LET Statement	Computer Execution
`10 LET X = 1`	The numeric value 1 is assigned to the location called X.
`40 LET C = A + B`	The values in A and B are added together and assigned to C.
`85 LET N$ = "JOHN HENRY"`	The character string enclosed in quotes is placed into the string variable N$ (the quotes are not).
`100 LET M = M + 1`	1 is added to the current value of M, and the result is assigned to M. This result replaces whatever was in M previously. Notice that this procedure effectively counts how many times line 100 is executed.
`200 LET A = (10 + J + 0.5)/(M * 4)`	The arithmetic expression to the right of the equal sign is evaluated and assigned to A.

Arithmetic Expressions

In BASIC, arithmetic expressions are composed of constants, numeric variables, and arithmetic operators. The arithmetic operators that can be used are shown below:

BASIC Arithmetic Operation Symbol	Operation	Arithmetic Example	BASIC Arithmetic Expression
+	Addition	$A + B$	$A + B$
−	Subtraction	$A - B$	$A - B$
*	Multiplication	$A \times B$	$A * B$
/	Division	$A \div B$	A/B
$\wedge$	Exponentiation	A^B	$A \wedge B$

Some examples of valid expressions in LET statements are:

```
10 LET L = (A1 / B) * C

20 LET J = N ^ 3

30 LET Z = X + 1.4 * Y
```

Hierarchy of Operations

When more than one operation is to be performed within an arithmetic expression, the computer follows a *hierarchy*, or priority, of operations. When parentheses are present in an expression, as in line 10 above, the operation within the parentheses is performed first. If parentheses are nested, the operation in the innermost set of parentheses is performed first. Thus, in the expression:

```
(5 * (Y + 2) / 3.12) + 10
```

the first operation to be performed is to add 2 to the value in Y.

Parentheses aside, operations are performed according to the following rules of priority:

Priority	Operation	Symbol	
First	Exponentiation	$\wedge$ or **	**NONSTANDARD**
Second	Multiplication or Division	* or /	
Third	Addition or Subtraction	+ or −	

Operations with high priority are performed before operations with lower priority (subject to our discussion on parentheses). If more than one operation is to be performed at the same level, for example:

```
4 ^ 2 ^ 3
```

the computer evaluates them from left to right. In the example above, the 4 would be raised to the second power, and then the result, 16, raised to the third power. The answer is 4096.

The following are examples of these hierarchical rules:

Expression One	**Computer Evaluation**
2 ∗ 5 + 1	
First 2 ∗ 5 = 10	Multiplication has a higher priority than addition, so it's done first.
Second 10 + 1 = 11	Then the addition is done. The result is 11.

Expression Two	
2 ∗ (5 + 1)	
First (5 + 1) = 6	In this case, the addition must be done first, because it is enclosed in parentheses.
Second 2 ∗ 6 = 12	The result is multiplied by 2. Compare this result with the result above.

Expression Three	
2 ∧ 3 / 4 − 2	
First 2 ∧ 3 = 8	The priority order tells the computer to start with exponentiation.
Second 8 / 4 = 2	Next is division.
Third 2 − 2 = 0	Last, the subtraction is done. The result is 0.

Expression Four	
4 ∗ 5 + 1 / 7 ∗ 21	
First 4 ∗ 5 = 20	There are three operations at the same level: ∗, /, and ∗. They are performed from left to right. Last, the addition is done. The result is 23.
Second 1 / 7 = 0.142857	
Third 0.142857 ∗ 21 = 3	
Fourth 20 + 3 = 23	

Another thing to be aware of is that two operators cannot be placed next to each other. For example, A ∗ −Y is invalid. Parentheses should be used to separate the operators. Thus, A ∗ (−Y) is valid.

Assigning Character Strings   The LET statement can also be used to assign a character string value to a string variable name. A character string is composed of alphanumeric data enclosed in quotes. For example:

```
10 LET H$ = "BATTING AVERAGE"

20 LET X$ = B$
```

Examples   The following examples show valid and invalid LET statements:

Valid	Invalid and Why	
`10 LET X = (2 + B)/C`	`10 LET (2 + B)/C = X`	(Only a variable can appear on the left-hand side of the equal sign.)
`20 LET N$ = "JOHN"`	`20 LET N2 = "JOHN"`	(A character string must be assigned to a string variable.)
`30 LET Z = A + R3/25`	`30 LET A = A + R$/25`	(A string variable cannot be part of an arithmetic expression.)

Figure III–3, which calculates a batting average, illustrates several uses of the LET statement. As you know, one calculates a batting average by dividing the total hits by the times at bat and then multiplying the result by 1000. The logic in this program is straightforward: first, enter the times at bat and hits; second, calculate the batting average; and third, print the result.

Line 120 is a LET statement used to enter the number of times at bat, 145, into the numeric variable TB. Line 130 assigns the number of hits, 35, to HI. The expression in line 140 calculates the batting average—that is, the number of hits divided by the times at bat, multiplied by 1000. Line 150 assigns a character string (which will later be printed out) to a string variable.

THE PRINT STATEMENT

The PRINT statement is used to print or display the results of computer processing. It also permits formatting, or arranging, of output. The general form of the PRINT statement is

line# PRINT $\left\{ \begin{array}{l} \text{variables} \\ \text{literals} \\ \text{arithmetic expressions} \\ \text{combination of above} \end{array} \right.$

PRINT statements can take several forms, depending on the output required. Let us look at some examples.

```
00100 REM  *** THIS PROGRAM CALCULATES
00110 REM       BATTING AVERAGES ***
00120 LET TB = 145
00130 LET HI = 35
00140 LET BA = HI/TB*1000
00150 LET H$ = "BATTING AVE. = "
00160 PRINT H$;BA
00170 END
RUNNH
BATTING AVE. =  241.3793
```

FIGURE III–3
Batting Averages Program

MICROCOMPUTERS

	Program	Execution
Apple:	Lines 100 and 110 are too long. Only one space before 241.3793 on output.	Answer is 241.37931
IBM/Microsoft:	No differences.	Answer is 241.379
PET	No differences.	Answer is 241.37931
TRS-80:	No differences.	Answer is 241.379

Printing the Values of Variables

We can tell the computer to print values assigned to storage locations by simply using the keyword PRINT with the variables listed after it, separated by commas:

```
160 PRINT P,I,IT
```

The comma is used to separate one variable from another; it is also used for carriage control (more on this in the next section).

Printing has no effect on the contents of storage. The PRINT statement is a simple read of the value of a variable that allows the user to see what the contents are. Normally, each time the computer encounters a PRINT statement, it begins printing output on a new line. Exceptions to this are discussed in Section IV.

Printing Literals

A *literal* is an expression consisting of alphabetic, numeric, or special characters or a combination of all three.

Character Strings   A character string literal is a group of letters, numbers, or special characters that you want printed on the output page. To have that done, you enclose the group in quotation marks (''). Whatever is inside the quotation marks is printed exactly as it is; for example:

```
30 PRINT "@#$%&SAMPLE"
```

would appear on the output page as:

```
@#$%&SAMPLE
```

To print column headings, put each heading in quotes, and separate each group by a comma:

```
40 PRINT "NAME","RANK","SERIAL NO."
```

When line 40 is executed, the character strings are printed out exactly as typed, except that the quotation marks do not appear (as shown below).

```
NAME            RANK            SERIAL NO.
```

Numeric Literals   Numeric literals do not have to be enclosed in quotation marks to be printed. For example, the statement:

```
200 PRINT 67
```

will print the following result:

```
67
```

Printing the Values of Expressions

The computer can print not only the values of literals and the values of variables but also the values of arithmetic expressions.

```
10 LET X = 4
20 LET Y = 247
30 PRINT X/Y * 100
```

First, the computer evaluates the highlighted expression according to the rules of priority. The result is printed as shown below.

```
RUNNH
 1.619433
```

If the value of the expression is extremely large or extremely small, the computer may print it in exponential notation.

Figure III–4 deals with expressions in both decimal and exponential forms.

When the PRINT statement in line 40 below is executed, the three expressions are evaluated and their values printed. Notice that the first two numbers are too large to be printed conventionally and are printed instead in exponential notation.

Printing Blank Lines

A PRINT statement with nothing typed after it will provide a blank line of output. For example:

```
100 PRINT
```

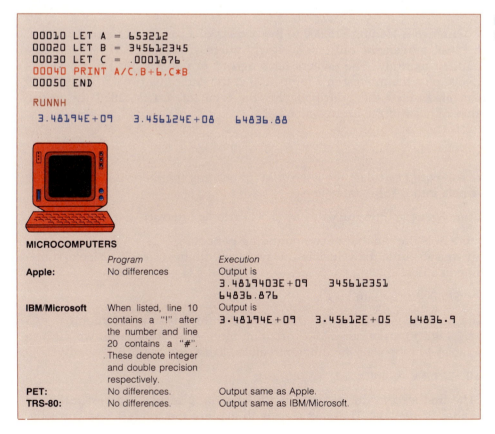

```
00010 LET A = 653212
00020 LET B = 345612345
00030 LET C = .0001876
00040 PRINT A/C,B+6,C*B
00050 END

RUNNH
 3.48194E+09    3.456124E+08    64836.88
```

MICROCOMPUTERS

	Program	Execution
Apple:	No differences	Output is
		3.4819403E+09 345612351
		64836.876
IBM/Microsoft	When listed, line 10 contains a "!" after the number and line 20 contains a "#". These denote integer and double precision respectively.	Output is
		3.48194E+09 3.45612E+05 64836.9
PET:	No differences.	Output same as Apple.
TRS-80:	No differences.	Output same as IBM/Microsoft.

FIGURE III–4
Numeric Output

To skip more than one line, simply include more than one of these PRINT statements:

```
110 PRINT
120 PRINT
```

THE END STATEMENT

The END statement indicates the end of the program and so must be assigned the highest line number in the program. The general format of the END statement is:

```
LINE# END
```

The use of an all–9s line number for the END statement is a common programming practice. This convention serves as a reminder to the programmer to include the END statement and helps to ensure that it is positioned properly. See line 999 in the book sale programs for examples of the END statement.

COMPREHENSIVE PROGRAMMING PROBLEM

Problem Definition

W. Jennings is loaning $15,000 to the owners of a bar in Luckenbach, Texas. The loan agreement calls for a yearly interest rate of 16.5 percent compounded monthly. The owners have agreed to pay Mr. Jennings back his $15,000 plus the interest in a lump sum at the end of five years. The $15,000 loan (also called the principal) plus the total interest is called the future value. What will the future value be?

Solution Design

We can easily calculate the answer by translating the following future value formula into BASIC statements:

Future Value = Present Value $\times$ (1 + Periodic Interest)^N

where N is the number of compounding periods.

If we substitute the values in this problem into the formula, it looks something like this:

? = \$15,000 * (1 + 16.5\%)^{60}

(The 60 is the result of compounding monthly, that is, 12 months $\times$ 5 years.) But to make our BASIC program more general-purpose, we can use variables to represent the different values, like this:

```
210 LET FV = PV * (1 + IM) ∧ N
```

The first step in the program is to enter the principal, interest rate, and number of periods. The next step is to express the interest rate correctly.

Now we have everything necessary to figure the future value. All that remains is to print the result.

The Program

Figure III–5 shows a listing and the output of this program. The REM statements in lines 100–150 document the meanings of the variable names. The

FIGURE III–5

Compound Interest Program

```
00100 REM    *** COMPOUND INTEREST ***
00110 REM        PV = PRESENT VALUE
00120 REM        FV = FUTURE VALUE
00130 REM        IY = YEARLY INTEREST RATE
00140 REM        IM = MONTHLY INTEREST RATE
00150 REM        N = NUMBER OF COMPOUNDING PERIODS
00160 LET PV = 15000
00170 LET IY = 16.5
00180 LET N = 60
00190 LET IM = IY / 12
00200 LET IM = IM / 100
00210 LET FV = PV * (1 + IM) ^ N
00220 PRINT
00230 PRINT
00240 PRINT "PV","INTEREST","NUMBER OF"
00250 PRINT " ","RATE","MONTHS"
00260 PRINT PV,IY,N
00270 PRINT
00280 PRINT
00290 PRINT "FUTURE VALUE =";FV
00300 END

RUNNH

PV                 INTEREST           NUMBER OF
                   RATE               MONTHS
   15000           16.5               60

FUTURE VALUE = 34036.36
```

MICROCOMPUTERS

	Program	Execution
Apple:	Lines 100, 130, 140, 150, and 240 are too long.	"NUMBER OF" is in the wrong line. There is no space between = and 34036.374.
IBM/Microsoft:	No differences.	Same, except answer is 34036.28
PET:	Line 150 is too long.	Same, except the last answer is 34036.374.
TRS-80:	In line 210, the ∧ symbol appears as the [symbol.	Same, except the last answer is 34035.8 (The reason the TRS-80 and IBM answers are different from the other three computers' is that they use a slightly less accurate method of calculating exponentiation.)

present value, or the amount to be loaned out, is assigned to the storage location PV in line 160. Line 170 assigns the interest rate of 16.5 percent to IY, and 180 assigns the number of months to N. Line 190 calculates the monthly interest rate by dividing the yearly rate by 12. This result is then divided by 100 in line 200, because interest rates are quoted as percentages (That is, 16.5 percent = 0.165). Line 210 tells the computer to evaluate the formula for compound interest and place the result in FV.

Lines 220 and 230 improve the readability of the output by having two blank lines printed before the headings of the report are printed out by the next two statements. The input values are then printed under the headings by line 260. Again the blank PRINTs are used to increase the readability of the output. Line 290 prints out the character string enclosed in quotes and the future value of the $15,000 loan.

The program concludes with the END statement.

SUMMARY

● REM statements are used to document the program; they are not executed by the computer.

● The purpose of the LET statement is to assign values to variables; LET is an optional keyword in some BASIC implementations.

● The LET statement is not evaluated as an algebraic equation. The computer first evaluates the expression on the right-hand side of the equal sign and then assigns that result to the variable on the left-hand side of the equal sign.

● Arithmetic expressions are evaluated according to a hierarchy of operations:

First—operations in parentheses.
Second—exponentiation.
Third—multiplication or division.
Fourth—addition or subtraction.

Multiple operations at the same level are evaluated left to right.

● The PRINT statement is used to print or display the results of processing.

● The END statement indicates the physical end of a program and stops execution.

OVERVIEW

Although the LET statement can be used to enter small amounts of data into programs, the two methods most commonly used are the INPUT statement and the READ/DATA statements. Printed results can be formatted by use of commas, semicolons, and the TAB function in PRINT statements.

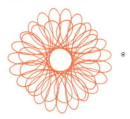

Input and Output

Problem Definition

Let us consider the following problem. You want to calculate your gas mileage on a recent trip from Kansas City to Garden City, Missouri. The distance travelled was 375 miles, and the car used 18.5 gallons of low-lead fuel. To calculate mileage, divide the distance by the gas used:

Mileage = Distance/Gas used.

The Program

Line 100 in Figure IV–1 is a REM statement commenting on the purpose of the program. The value of the distance is assigned to D in line 110. The fuel value is assigned to GS in line 120. Line 130 performs the mileage calculation. To make the output values understandable, we print headings in line 140. The character string literals are separated from one another by commas. This tells the computer to print them in the *predefined print zones* (more on these later). Finally, in line 150, the distance, gas, and calculated gas mileage for the trip are printed out—again in the predefined print zones. This section is going to discuss two other methods for entering data into a program, so keep an eye on lines 110 and 120.

THE INPUT STATEMENT

The INPUT statement is used for inquiry and response when a user application calls for a question-and-answer environment.

The last section explained how the LET statement can be used to enter

```
00100 REM  *** GAS MILEAGE ***
00110 LET D = 375
00120 LET GS = 18.5
00130 LET MI = D/GS
00140 PRINT "DISTANCE","GAS USED","MILEAGE"
00150 PRINT D,GS,MI
00160 END


RUNNH
DISTANCE        GAS USED       MILEAGE
 375              18.5          20.27027
```

FIGURE IV–1
Gas Mileage Program

data values into a program. The INPUT statement differs from the LET statement in that it allows the user to enter data at the terminal while the program is running.

The general format of the INPUT statement is:

line# INPUT variable list

INPUT statements are placed where data values are needed in a program. This is determined by the logic of the program. After the program has been keyed in, the user types the execution command RUN (see "Important keys and commands" box); the computer then starts to execute the program. Whenever the computer reaches an INPUT statement, it stops, prints a question mark at the terminal, and waits for the user to enter data. After typing in the data, the user presses the RETURN key. The computer then assigns the data value to the variable indicated in the INPUT statement and resumes processing. More than one variable can be listed in the INPUT statement; the computer keeps on printing question marks and inputting and assigning data values until all variables are used. After that, the computer resumes processing.

Let us revise the sample program by replacing lines 110 and 120. The resulting program is:

```
00100 REM  *** GAS MILEAGE = INPUT ***
00110 PRINT "ENTER DISTANCE, GAS USED"
00120 INPUT D,GS
00130 LET MI = D/GS
00140 PRINT "DISTANCE","GAS USED","MILEAGE"
00150 PRINT D,GS,MI
```

These new instructions cause the program to be executed in a question-and-answer mode. When the program is run, line 110 causes the computer to print a message at the terminal that says, "ENTER DISTANCE, GAS USED." A question mark then appears to signal the user that data values are to be entered. At this point, the user types in the requested data values, separating them with a comma, and then presses the RETURN key.

```
RUNNH
ENTER DISTANCE, GAS USED        ←Program prompt
  ?    375,18.5                 ←Computer response ( ? ) , user data entry
```

The computer then executes line 130 to calculate the mileage and prints the headings and results.

```
DISTANCE        GAS USED        MILEAGE
 375             18.5            20.27027
```

As you can see, the INPUT statement offers a great deal of flexibility; each time this program is executed, new values can be entered. Thus, the next time we take a trip, we simply run the program again and enter the new distance and gas used. We do not have to change any program statements.

```
RUNNH
ENTER DISTANCE, GAS USED
 ? 125,5
DISTANCE        GAS USED        MILEAGE
 125             5               25
```

COMPUTER	Execution Command	Carriage Control Key	Comments
APPLE	RUN	RETURN	
DEC	RUN or RUNNH	RETURN	RUNNH means "RUN No Header." With RUN alone, the computer prints out the date and a system-identifying label. Although there is no lettering on the key, we will refer to it as carriage return.
IBM/Microsoft	RUN	↵	
PET	RUN	RETURN	
TRS-80	RUN	ENTER	The ENTER key is located on the right-hand side of the keyboard. This is the location of the RETURN key on the other computers. The two keys serve the same purpose.

Prompts

Note that the INPUT instruction is preceded by a PRINT statement in line 110. This is a *prompt*. Since the INPUT statement signals the need for data with only a question mark, it is good programming practice to precede each INPUT statement with a PRINT statement that explains to the user what data is to be entered. This practice is particularly important in a BASIC program that contains numerous INPUT statements; otherwise, when the user sees only a question mark requesting data, he or she may not know what data values are to be entered and in what order.

Most computers permit the prompt to be an integral part of the INPUT statement. For example, we could substitute this line for lines 110 and 120 in the gas mileage program:

```
110 INPUT "ENTER DISTANCE, GAS USED";D,GS
```

When we run the program with this new line, the question mark appears immediately after the prompt, and no separate PRINT statement for the prompt is needed.

```
RUNNH
ENTER DISTANCE, GAS USED ? 125,5
DISTANCE        GAS USED        MILEAGE
 125              5               25
```

The variables listed in the INPUT statement may be string or numeric. Just be sure to enter the correct value to be assigned to each variable. In other words, the type of data entered must be the same as that designated by the variable.

```
250 INPUT N$,A,J$
RUNNH
?
JANICE LINDER,37,TEACHER
```

In the example above, the character string JANICE LINDER will be as-

B-29

signed to the string variable N\$. Her age will be assigned to A; and her job title, TEACHER, will be assigned to J\$. Associating a printed message with each INPUT statement can eliminate many data entry problems.

THE READ AND DATA STATEMENTS

The READ and DATA statements provide another way to enter data into a BASIC program. These two statements always work together. Values contained in the DATA statements are assigned to variables listed in the READ statements.

The general format of the READ and DATA statements is:

line# READ variable list

line# DATA constant list

This method of entering data into a program works a little differently from the INPUT statement. The READ statement tells the computer to search through the BASIC program until it finds the first DATA statement. The computer then assigns the data values consecutively to the variables in the READ statement. Each READ statement causes as many values to be taken from the data list as there are variables in the READ variable list. Figure IV–2 illustrates this process of assigning values from the data list to variables.

FIGURE IV–2
READ/DATA Example

```
00010 READ X,N$
00020 READ H,W
00030 LET P = H * W
00040 PRINT N$,P
00050 READ X,N$,H,W
00060 LET P = H * W
00070 PRINT N$,P
00080 DATA 56142,"RICHARD VOLTZ",40,5.00
00090 DATA 37298,"BARB ERNST"
00100 DATA 38,6.50
00999 END

RUNNH
RICHARD VOLTZ   200
BARB ERNST      247
```

MICROCOMPUTERS

Apple: No differences.
IBM/Microsoft: No differences.
PET: No differences.
TRS-80: No differences.

Statement 10 says to the computer: "Take the value from the top of the data list and put it in the storage location named X (throwing away any value already in X). Then take the next value from the data list and assign it to variable N$ (also throwing away any value already there)." After statement 10 has been executed, the number 56142 is in storage location X and the character string RICHARD VOLTZ is in storage location N$. This leaves the number 40 at the top of the data list.

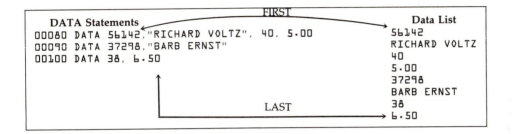

The same process occurs when the computer encounters statement 20. The data from the top of the list (40) is placed in storage location H. The number 5.00 is assigned to W.

When statement 50 is executed, the number at the top of the data list (37298) is assigned to the variable X. The number 56142, which was assigned to X by statement 10, is overlaid by the new value. In the same manner, the character string BARB ERNST is assigned to the variable N$; the number 38 is assigned to the variable H; and the number 6.50 is assigned to W. When these values are assigned, the values previously stored in the variables are also overlaid.

This process illustrates the basic concept of nondestructive read, destructive write. Once the data items are assigned to storage locations, they remain there until new data items are recorded over them. Thus, all four variables represent more than one value during execution, but never more than one at a time.

If a READ statement is attempted after the data list has been exhausted, a message is produced to indicate that the end of the data list has been reached. The message points out the line number of the READ statement in error; for example, if line 60 was such a READ statement, the computer would print:

```
LINE 60: END OF DATA
```

READ statements, like INPUT, are located wherever the logic of the program indicates the need for data. DATA statements, however, are nonexecutable and may be located anywhere in the program. The BASIC compiler simply takes all the data items in all the DATA statements and forms one combined data list, ordering the DATA statements from lowest line number to highest and then using the data from left to right. For example, the three program segments below look different, but the data lists they produce are alike.

DATA STATEMENTS	Data List

```
10 DATA 35, "JOHN",85
20 DATA "SUE",67
```

or

```
10 DATA 35,"JOHN",85,"SUE",67
```

or

```
10 DATA 35
20 DATA "JOHN"
30 DATA 85
40 DATA "SUE"
50 DATA 67
```

Data List:
```
35
JOHN
85
SUE
67
```

Note that when two or more data values occupy a line, they are separated by commas. Character strings may or may not be enclosed in quotation marks in DATA statements.

We could assign the data items above in the following manner:

```
50 READ A
60 READ N$
70 READ D
80 READ A$
90 READ G
```

or

```
20 READ A,N$,D,A$,G
```

or

```
30 READ A,N$
40 READ D,A$,G
```

It does not matter in this example how many READ or DATA statements are used. However, the order of the variables and values is important. Make sure that the arrangement of values in the DATA statements corresponds to the data required in the READ statements—that is, that character strings are assigned to string variables and numeric constants to numeric variables.

Let us return to the gas mileage program and change it to use READ/DATA.

```
00100 REM  *** GAS MILEAGE — READ  ***
00110 DATA 375,18.5
00120 READ D,GS
00130 LET MI = D/GS
00140 PRINT "DISTANCE","GAS USED","MILEAGE"
00150 PRINT D,GS,MI

RUNNH
DISTANCE        GAS USED       MILEAGE
 375              18.5          20.27027
```

Line 120 performs the same function as the INPUT statement did previously. With INPUT, the data values are assigned by the user as the program is running. With READ/DATA, on the other hand, the distance and gas values are already contained within the program in line 110, the DATA statement. The output is unchanged. If we wanted to run this program again using different data, we would change line 110, the DATA statement.

A COMPARISON OF THE THREE METHODS OF DATA ENTRY

LET, INPUT, and READ/DATA can all be used to enter data into BASIC programs. You may wonder, then, which command is best to use. That depends on the particular application. Here are some general guidelines:

1. When there is very little data to enter into a program, use the LET statement. The LET statement is often used to assign a beginning value to a variable; this is called initialization. For example:

```
10 LET X = 0
```

2. The INPUT statement is used when a question-and-answer (also called inquiry and response) environment is desired. It is also a good method to use when data values are likely to change frequently. A good application for the use of the INPUT statement might be entering data about hospital patients—a situation in which people are checked in and out every day and data about a particular patient changes frequently.
3. When many data values must be entered, then READ/DATA statements are a good option. These statements are often used to read data into arrays (to be discussed in Section VIII).

PRINTING PUNCTUATION

Section III explained that the PRINT statement lets us get the results of processing printed. When more than one item is to be printed on a line, commas and semicolons can be used to control the spacing of the output.

Print Zones and Commas

The number of characters that can be printed on a line varies with the system used. On some terminals, such as the DEC VT-100 used with the DEC-SYSTEM 20 computer, each output line consists of eighty print positions. The line is divided into five print zones, each fourteen characters wide. The beginning columns of the five print zones are shown below:

ZONE 1	ZONE 2	ZONE 3	ZONE 4	ZONE 5
COL	COL	COL	COL	COL
1	15	29	43	57

When the computer encounters the PRINT statement in the segment:

```
10 READ A,N$,B
20 PRINT A,N$,B
30 DATA 4,"JOHN",25.00
```

the value in A, which is 4, will be printed starting in the first print zone. Since 4 is a positive number, most computers will leave a blank before the number for the sign. Of course, if the value in A were negative, the minus sign would be printed starting in column 1. The comma between A and N$ tells the computer to space over to the next zone and print the value contained in N$. After JOHN is printed, the comma directs the computer to space over to the third tab zone and print the value in B. The output is as follows:

```
RUNNH
 4              JOHN            25
```

If there are more items listed in a PRINT statement than there are print zones, the computer starts printing in the first zone of the next line. For example:

```
20 READ L,E,M,O,N,T
30 PRINT L,E,M,O,N,T
40 DATA 2,4,6,8,10,12
```

```
RUNNH
 2          4          6          8          10
 12
```

If the value to be printed exceeds the width of the print zone, the computer will completely print out the value even though part of it goes into the next print zone. The comma then directs printing to start in the following print zone. Take a look at the example below and note where the value of X$ (12:00) is printed.

```
60 PRINT "THE TIME AT THE TONE IS",X$
```

Zone 1   Zone 2   Zone 3

```
RUNNH
THE TIME AT THE TONE IS    12:00
```

Table IV–1 presents the formatting differences among our four computers. The first column identifies the computer. Columns 2 and 3 give the number of columns and rows on the CRT screen. Columns 4 and 5 give the number of print zones (when commas are used as spacing control in PRINT statements) and print zone widths. Columns 6 and 7 indicate whether a space is always left in front of a number for a positive or negative sign and whether a space follows a number for ease in reading. Finally, column 8 gives the maximum number of digits output to the screen. (The DEC, IBM, and TRS-80 have provisions for double precision; however, caution must be used, be-

TABLE IV–1 Computer Display Characteristics

Computer	Screen Width (Characters)	Screen Height (lines)	Number of Print Zones	Zone Width	Space for Sign?	Space Following	Number of Digits Printed, Single Precision
Apple	40	24	2.5	16	no	no	9
DEC	80/132	24/16	5/9	14	yes	yes	7
IBM	80	24	5	14	yes	yes	7
PET	40	24	4	10	yes	yes	9
TRS-80	64/32	15	4	16	yes	yes	6

See example below

Example: With the Apple computer the statement
　　　　10 PRINT −2;−1;0;1;2
　　　　would print
　　　　−2−1012 (no spaces)

　　　　With the DEC, PET, and TRS-80 computers, the same statement would print
　　　　−2 −1 0 1 2

cause the BASIC internal functions might not be more accurate with double precision than with single precision—see your manual.)

NOTE: Now that we have explained the various screen sizes and spacing differences, we will no longer point out these differences among computers after each program.

Skipping Print Zones A print zone can be skipped by use of a technique that involves enclosing a space (the character *blank*) in quotation marks, which causes the entire zone to appear empty. Thus:

```
10 PRINT "TOTAL SCORE"," ","AVERAGE SCORE"
```

causes the literal TOTAL SCORE to be printed in the first zone beginning in column 1; the second zone to be blank; and the literal AVERAGE SCORE to be printed in the third zone beginning in column 29.

Zone 1　　　　**Zone 2**　　　　**Zone 3**

```
RUNNH
TOTAL SCORE                    AVERAGE SCORE
```

Most computers allow the user to skip by typing two consecutive commas; for example:

```
10 PRINT "TOTAL SCORE", ,"AVERAGE SCORE"
```

Ending with a Comma As mentioned earlier, output generated by a PRINT statement normally begins in the first zone of a new line. However, if the previously executed PRINT statement ends with a comma, the output of a PRINT statement starts in the next available zone. Thus, the statements

```
40 DATA 123456,6.78901E+09,4.56800E-04,33600
50 READ A,B,C,D
60 PRINT A,B,
70 PRINT C,D
```

produce the following output:

```
RUNNH
 123456          6.78901E+09    4.56800E-04      33600
```

Using Semicolons

Using a semicolon instead of a comma causes output to be packed more closely on a line. This alternative gives the programmer greater flexibility in formatting output. In the following examples, notice the difference in spacing when semicolons are used instead of commas.

Using commas:
```
10 PRINT 1,2,-3
RUNNH
 1              2              -3
```

Using semicolons:
```
10 PRINT 1;2;-3
RUNNH
 1  2 -3
```

The semicolon between the items tells the computer to skip to the next *column* to print the next item—not to the next print zone as with the comma. Generally, when the number is positive, a space is left in front of the number for the sign.

Semicolons and Character Strings   The following example shows what happens when semicolons are used with character strings.

```
60 PRINT "FIRST";"LAST"
RUNNH
FIRSTLAST
```

Since letters do not have signs, they are run together. The best way to avoid this problem is to enclose a space within the quotes.

```
60 PRINT "FIRST ";"LAST"
RUNNH
FIRST LAST
```

Ending with a Semicolon   If the semicolon is the last character of the PRINT statement, carriage control is not advanced when the printing of the statement is completed; so the output generated by the next PRINT statement continues on the same line. For example:

```
100 READ N$,S
110 PRINT N$;
120 LET A = S + 40
130 PRINT A
140 DATA JOHN,3
RUNNH
JOHN 43
```

Line 110 causes JOHN to be printed out. The semicolon after N$ keeps the printer on the same line; then, when line 130 is encountered, 43 is printed on the same line.

THE TAB FUNCTION

The comma causes the results of processing to be printed according to pre-defined print zones. The semicolon causes them to start printing in the next position on the output line. Both are easy to use, and many reports can be formatted in this fashion. But there are times when a report should be structured differently.

The TAB function allows output to be printed in any column in an output line, providing the programmer greater flexibility to format printed output.

The general format of the TAB function is:

TAB(expression)

The expression in parentheses may be a numeric constant, variable, or arithmetic expression; it tells the computer the column in which printing is to occur. The TAB function (as used in a PRINT statement) must immediately precede the variable or literal to be printed. For example, the statement

```
60 PRINT TAB(10);A$;TAB(25);B
```

causes the printer to be spaced to column 10 (indicated in parentheses) to print the value stored in A$. The printer then spaces over to column 25 as indicated in the next parentheses and prints the value in B. On many computers, such as the DEC, IBM/Microsoft, PET, and TRS-80, the value in A$ in the above example would begin in column 11 and B in column 26. In other words, instead of tabbing to the tenth column, the computer tabs to ten *spaces*.   NONSTANDARD

The program in Figure IV–3 illustrates the use of the TAB function.

Note that we have used the semicolon as the punctuation mark with the TAB function. The semicolon separates the expression from the values to be printed. If commas were used instead, the printer would default to the use of the predefined print zones and ignore the columns specified in parenthe-

FIGURE IV–3
Grades Program

```
00020 PRINT TAB(10);"GRADE REPORT"
00030 PRINT TAB(5);"NAME";TAB(20);"GRADE"
00035 PRINT
00040 READ N$,GR
00045 PRINT TAB(5);N$;TAB(21);GR
00050 READ N$,GR
00055 PRINT TAB(5);N$;TAB(21);GR
00060 READ N$,GR
00065 PRINT TAB(5);N$;TAB(21);GR
00070 DATA HARVEY,53,SANDY,85,JERRY,77
00999 END
RUNNH
          GRADE REPORT
     NAME                GRADE


     HARVEY              53
     SANDY               85
     JERRY               77
```

MICROCOMPUTERS

Apple: No differences.
IBM/Microsoft: No differences.
PET: No differences.
TRS-80: No differences.

ses. For example, if line 30 of the program in Figure IV–3 had been:

```
30 PRINT TAB(5),"NAME",TAB(20),"GRADE"
```

the output would have been:

```
RUNNH
          GRADE REPORT
               NAME                               GRADE

     HARVEY              53
     SANDY               85
     JERRY               77
```

The computer would have spaced over the five columns indicated by the first TAB function; but when it saw the comma following the parentheses, it would have skipped over to the next predefined print zone to print out "NAME". This would have happened again with "GRADE". Use semicolons rather than commas, then, in PRINT statements containing the TAB function.

Another caution: when the TAB function is used, the printer cannot be backspaced once a column has been passed. This means that if more than one TAB function is used in a PRINT statement, the column numbers in parentheses must increase from left to right. For example:

Valid:
```
00010 PRINT TAB(5);X;TAB(15);Y;TAB(25);Z
```

```
RUNNH
      0         0         2
```

Invalid:
```
00010 PRINT TAB(25);Z;TAB(15);Y;TAB(5);X
```

```
RUNNH
                        2  0  0
```

The invalid example tells the computer to print the first item starting in column 25. But because the printer does not backspace, the value in Y will simply start printing immediately after 2.

THE PRINT USING STATEMENT

Another convenient feature for controlling output is the PRINT USING statement; with it the programmer can avoid print-zone restrictions and can "dress up" the output. PRINT USING is an extension of the ANSI standards—not part of the standards. Its syntax is quite varied among different brands of computers. This section briefly describes its use on the DEC 20 computer; the principles should be similar for other computers with this feature. (Most microcomputers do not have a PRINT USING capability—the Apple and PET do not; the IBM/Microsoft and TRS-80 do; consult your manual for the proper syntax if you are using a TRS-80.) The general format of the PRINT USING statement is:

NONSTANDARD

line# PRINT USING image statement line#, expression-list

The PRINT USING statement tells which statement in the program has the print line image and what values are to be used in that print line. The expression list consists of a sequence of variables or expressions separated by commas; it is similar to the expression list in any PRINT statement. The line number of the image statement is the number of the BASIC statement that tells the computer how to print the items in the expression list.

line#: format control characters

The image statement is denoted by a colon (:) following the line number. It is a nonexecutable statement, like DATA, and can be placed anywhere in the program. The PRINT USING command, however, is placed where the logic demands. A single image statement can be referred to by several PRINT USING statements. Special format control characters are used in the image statement to describe the output image and to control spacing.

The DEC 20 format control characters are listed below. A *mask* specifies the maximum number of characters to be printed in one field.

Format Control Character	Control Image for	Example
#	Numeric data; used in a mask; one symbol for each number to be printed; pads zeroes to the left of the decimal point.	###
$	Dollar sign; printed exactly as is.	$###
.	Decimal point; printed exactly as is.	$##.##
E	Alphanumeric data; preceded by apostrophe ('); permits overflow to be printed to the right; left justifies; pads with blanks.	'E
L	Alphanumeric data; preceded by apostrophe ('); used as a mask; left justifies; pads with blanks.	'LLLLLL
R	Alphanumeric data; preceded by apostrophe ('); used as a mask; right justifies; pads with blanks.	'RRRRRR
C	Alphanumeric data; preceded by apostrophe ('); used as a mask; centers in the field; pads with blanks.	'CCCCCC

Figure IV–4 illustrates PRINT USING and the L, ., $, and # format control characters.

FIGURE IV–4
Plant Store Program

```
00003 REM *** PERSIAN POTS CO.
00005 PRINT
00006 PRINT
00007 REM *** PRINT OUT HEADINGS
00010 PRINT USING 90,
00015 PRINT USING 95,
00020 PRINT
00025 PRINT USING 120,
00030 PRINT
00035 READ N$,P
00036 IF N$ = "NO MORE" THEN 999
00040 LET R = P-(P*0.10)
00045 REM *** PRINT OUT NAME,PRICE,DISCOUNT PRICE
00050 PRINT USING 130, N$,P,R
00060 GO TO 35
00070 DATA "SWEDISH IVY", 1.50, "BOSTON FERN", 2.00
00080 DATA "POINSETTIA", 5.40
00085 DATA "JADE PLANT", 1.70, "NO MORE",0.00
00090:                    POTS AND PLANTS
00095:               PLANT DISCOUNT PRICES
00120: PLANT         REGULAR PRICE     DISCOUNT PRICE
00130:'LLLLLLLLLLL        $#.##              $#.##
00999 END
RUNNH

                    POTS AND PLANTS
                PLANT DISCOUNT PRICES

    PLANT         REGULAR PRICE     DISCOUNT PRICE

  SWEDISH IVY         $1.50              $1.35
  BOSTON FERN         $2.00              $1.80
  POINSETTIA          $5.40              $4.86
  JADE PLANT          $1.70              $1.53
```

The first three lines of the report consist solely of literal data (headings). These headings are produced by statements 5 through 30 and the corresponding image statements in the lower half of the program. Note that there are commas after the image statement line numbers in the PRINT USING statements. A comma is required even though no expression list follows.

The balance of the report prints out variables rather than literals. For example, in the sample program, line 50 tells the computer to use the image statement in line 130; print the output according to that statement's format control character layouts; and use N$, P, and R to fill in the masks in that order. The format control character L is used for the character string held in N$. The values of the variables P and R (the regular and discount prices of the plants) are printed where the two groups of # symbols are in the image statement.

Thus, the plant name is printed in the first eleven columns. The regular price is printed in the first field of #s, with two digits to the right of the decimal point. The computer will round to the last place indicated if a number with more than two decimal digits is actually stored in P. The discount price (with the 10 percent discount applied) is printed in the second field of #s, again with two digits to the right of the decimal point. The format control character $ at the beginning of these image fields tells the computer to print a dollar sign at the print position where the $ is typed.

COMPREHENSIVE PROGRAMMING PROBLEM

Problem Definition

The McHenry Farm of Edgar County, Illinois, has purchased a small computer to help in planning. The owners want to be able to make profit projections based on expected crop yield and market prices. They want to plant soybeans in field 1, which has 100 acres, and corn in field 2, which has 75 acres. The costs per acre for planting, cultivating, and harvesting the two crops are $105 for soybeans and $160 for corn.

Output is required to have the following form:

	FIELD 1	FIELD 2
CROP	XXXXXXXX	XXXXXXXX
TOTAL COST	XXXXXXXX	XXXXXXXX
TOTAL INCOME	XXXXXXXX	XXXXXXXX
PROFIT	XXXXXXXX	XXXXXXXX

The total cost per acre is calculated by multiplying the acreage by the cost per acre to plant the crops. The total income is figured by multiplying the acreage by the yield per acre and then multiplying that product by the current price of the crop planted. Profit is the total income minus the total cost.

FIGURE IV–5
Farm Profit Analysis
Program

```
00100 REM  *** FARM PROFITS ***
00110 REM      PS = CURRENT PRICE OF SOYBEANS
00120 REM      PC = CURRENT PRICE OF CORN
00130 REM      A1 = ACREAGE OF FIELD 1
00140 REM      A2 = ACREAGE OF FIELD 2
00150 REM      CS = COST PER ACRE FOR SOYBEANS
00160 REM      CC = COST PER ACRE FOR CORN
00170 REM      YS = YIELD PER ACRE OF SOYBEANS
00180 REM      YC = YIELD PER ACRE OF CORN
00200 DATA "SOYBEANS","CORN",100,75,105,160
00210 READ N1$,N2$,A1,A2,CS,CC
00220 PRINT
00230 PRINT
00240 PRINT "ENTER CURRENT PRICE,EXPECTED YIELD FOR ";N1$
00250 INPUT PS,YS
00260 PRINT
00270 PRINT "ENTER CURRENT PRICE,EXPECTED YIELD FOR ";N2$
00280 INPUT PC,YC
00400 REM BEGIN CALCULATIONS
00410 REM     TOTAL COST = ACREAGE * COST PER ACRE
00420 T1 = A1 * CS
00430 T2 = A2 * CC
00440 REM     GROSS INCOME = ACREAGE * YIELD PER ACRE * CURRENT PRICE
00450 I1 = A1 * YS * PS
00460 I2 = A2 * YC * PC
00470 REM     PROFIT = GROSS INCOME - TOTAL COST
00480 R1 = I1 - T1
00490 R2 = I2 - T2
00500 REM BEGIN OUTPUT
00505 PRINT
00506 PRINT
00510 PRINT TAB(8);"FARM PROFIT ANALYSIS"
00520 PRINT
00530 PRINT " ","FIELD 1","FIELD 2"
00540 PRINT
00550 PRINT "CROP",N1$,N2$
00560 PRINT "TOTAL COST","$";T1,"$";T2
00570 PRINT "TOTAL INCOME","$";I1,"$";I2
00580 PRINT "PROFIT","$";R1,"$";R2
00590 PRINT
00600 PRINT
00999 END
```

The Program

The program in Figure IV-5 documents the major variables used in lines 110–180. Line 200 contains some of the data for the program. The computer assigns these values to variables with the READ statement in the next line, 210. A prompt is printed by line 240. The associated INPUT statement in line 250 causes the computer to print a question mark at the terminal and wait for the user to enter the appropriate data values. When this has been done, processing continues. Lines 270 and 280 perform the same function; only this time, the user enters the price and yield for corn. Now that all the data has been entered, the computer can begin the calculations. This is doc-umented in line 400. Lines 420 and 430 compute the total costs for planting

FIGURE IV-5
Continued

```
RUNNH

ENTER CURRENT PRICE,EXPECTED YIELD FOR SOYBEANS
  ? 8.55,40

ENTER CURRENT PRICE,EXPECTED YIELD FOR CORN
  ? 3.70

  ? 59  INSUFFICIENT DATA AT LINE 00280 OF MAIN PROGRAM
  ? 110

          FARM PROFIT ANALYSIS

              FIELD 1         FIELD 2

CROP            SOYBEANS        CORN
TOTAL COST      $ 10500         $ 12000
TOTAL INCOME    $ 34200         $ 30525
PROFIT          $ 23700         $ 18525

RUNNH

ENTER CURRENT PRICE,EXPECTED YIELD FOR SOYBEANS
  ? 7.50,30

ENTER CURRENT PRICE,EXPECTED YIELD FOR CORN
  ? 3.00,75

          FARM PROFIT ANALYSIS

              FIELD 1         FIELD 2

CROP            SOYBEANS        CORN
TOTAL COST      $ 10500         $ 12000
TOTAL INCOME    $ 22500         $ 16875
PROFIT          $ 12000         $ 4875
```

APPLE: No differences.
IBM/Microsoft: No differences.
PET: No differences.
TRS-80: No differences.

soybeans and corn. After that, the gross income for each is figured in lines 450 and 460. Finally, the profit for each is calculated in lines 480 and 490.

Line 510 uses TAB to center a title on the output report. We see in line 530 that the headings have been moved over into the second and third print zones. The next four lines print out the report. Notice how the $ has been added to the output in lines 560–580.

We have illustrated two runs of this program to show how it can provide the user with predictions of the maximum and minimum profits to be made. The first run uses optimistic estimates of the market prices and yields per acre. (Notice how the computer asked for more data when we entered the price of corn but forgot to enter the yield.) The second run uses pessimistic estimates; the profit predictions are not as high.

The usefulness of this kind of program is clear. The farmer can make more and more accurate predictions about how much money can be expected as harvest time nears and has a better estimate of how weather, pests, and market prices will affect income.

SUMMARY

● The INPUT statement is used to enter data into a program in a question-and-answer mode.

● Another way of entering data into a program is to use READ and DATA statements. The READ statement causes values contained in the DATA statements to be assigned to variables.

● READ and INPUT statements are located where the logic of the program indicates. DATA statements are nonexecutable and may be located anywhere in the program.

● When more than one item is to be printed on a line of output, the spacing can be indicated by the use of commas and semicolons.

● Each line of output can be divided into a predetermined number of print zones. The comma is used to cause results to be printed in the print zones.

● Using the semicolon instead of the comma to separate printed items causes output to be packed more closely on a line.

● Using the TAB function in a PRINT statement permits results to be printed anywhere on an output line.

● The PRINT USING feature provides a flexible method of producing output. The format control characteristics in the image statement define how the output will look.

OVERVIEW

The programs described to this point contained instructions that were always executed one right after the other—from lowest line number to highest. This section will discuss ways of transferring control to program statements out of sequence by using the GOTO, IF/THEN, and ON/GOTO statements. One of the most valuable programming techniques, looping, will also be discussed. Let us see how some of these transfers work in the following problem.

Problem Definition

Fred's Fish Emporium is selling aquarium starter sets for $21.95. The super-deluxe package includes a ten-gallon tank, heater, filter, plants, and multi-colored gravel. Fred wants a program to generate an itemized bill. The input to the program should include the aquarium starter set, its price, the tropical fish purchased, and their prices.

Solution Design

The logic of this program will be more complicated than any we have written thus far, because we do not know the type or the quantity of fish a customer will purchase. Our program must be designed to accept any type and number of fish.

Since we have to itemize the bill, it would be appropriate to first have the list of items in the aquarium starter set read in from DATA statements. INPUT statements can then be used to enter the names, prices, and quantity of fish purchased. To have this done, we will set up a *loop*. Within the loop we will place a statement that accumulates the total cost of fish purchased.

To stop execution of the loop, we will test the first variable to see whether or not it has a dummy value—something Fred will enter when all fish purchased by a customer have been recorded to tell the computer to get out of the loop and calculate the grand total. After that, the report is printed out. (See Figure V–1.)

The Program

Lines 180–200 are READ and DATA statements used to enter the starter set package into the program. Line 210 is the beginning of the loop. The INPUT statement is a good choice here, since the fish purchased will be different for each customer. We use line 260, an IF/THEN statement, to test for a dummy value that is to be entered by Fred when he has finished a customer's order. As long as Fred types in names, prices, and quantities of fish, the loop (lines 210–280) will continue to be executed. Line 270 keeps a running total of the cost of the fish. Line 280 is a new command, GOTO. This statement sends the computer back up to line 210 to ask for another fish type. Note that the prompt (line 220) tells Fred (the user) how to stop the computer from continually asking for fish types. When Fred types in

B-45

FIGURE V–1
Fish Store Program
(continued on
facing page)

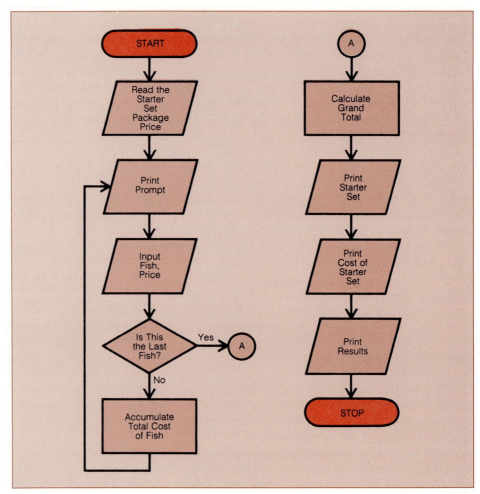

NONE, 0, 0, the computer skips down to line 290 to figure the grand total. Then the sales report is printed.

Let us take a look at these new transfer statements in greater detail.

THE GOTO STATEMENT: UNCONDITIONAL TRANSFER

All BASIC programs consist of series of statements which are normally executed in sequential order. Sometimes, however, it is desirable to perform statements in another order. It may be necessary to alter the flow of execution or bypass certain instructions. This is called *branching*, and the programmer can use the GOTO statement to do it. The general format of the GOTO statement is:

line# GOTO transfer line#

```
00100 REM  *** AQUARIUM PRICES ***
00110 REM       FS$ = FISH TYPE
00120 REM       PF = FISH PRICE
00130 REM       Q = QUANTITY
00140 REM       PA = STARTER SET PRICE
00150 REM       N1$ - N5$ = STARTER SET ITEMS
00160 REM       GRT = GRAND TOTAL
00170 REM
00180 READ N1$,N2$,N3$,N4$,N5$,PA
00190 DATA TEN GAL TANK,HEATER,FILTER
00200 DATA PLANTS,GRAVEL,21.95
00205 REM LOOP STARTS HERE
00210 PRINT "ENTER FISH TYPE, PRICE, QTY"
00220 PRINT "(TYPE NONE,0, TO QUIT)"
00230 INPUT FS$,PF,Q
00250 REM CONDITIONAL TRANSFER HERE
00260 IF FS$ = "NONE" THEN 290
00265 REM ACCUMULATING COST OF FISH
00270 FT = FT + PF * Q
00275 REM UNCONDITIONAL TRANSFER HERE
00280 GO TO 210
00285 REM GRAND TOTAL
00290 GRT = PA + FT
00300 PRINT
00310 PRINT
00320 PRINT "STARTER SET PACKAGE"
00330 PRINT ,N1$
00340 PRINT ,N2$
00350 PRINT ,N3$
00360 PRINT ,N4$
00370 PRINT ,N5$
00380 PRINT
00390 PRINT
00400 PRINT "COST OF STARTER SET = $";PA
00410 PRINT
00420 PRINT
00430 PRINT "COST OF FISH = $";FT
00440 PRINT
00450 PRINT
00460 PRINT "THE GRAND TOTAL = $";GRT
00999 END
```

```
RUNNH
ENTER FISH TYPE, PRICE, QTY
(TYPE NONE,0,0 TO QUIT)
? DANIO,1.45,1
ENTER FISH TYPE, PRICE, QTY
(TYPE NONE,0,0 TO QUIT)
? ALGAE EATER,2.15,1
ENTER FISH TYPE, PRICE, QTY
(TYPE NONE,0,0 TO QUIT)
? NEON,0.99,4
ENTER FISH TYPE, PRICE, QTY
(TYPE NONE,0,0 TO QUIT)
? NONE,0,0


STARTER SET PACKAGE
                TEN GAL TANK
                HEATER
                FILTER
                PLANTS
                GRAVEL


COST OF STARTER SET = $ 21.95


COST OF FISH = $ 7.56


THE GRAND TOTAL = $ 29.51
```

The programming command GOTO can be written as one word or as two words, GO TO.

The GOTO statement is called an *unconditional transfer* statement, because the flow of execution is altered every time the statement is encountered. It transfers control to (or causes the computer to go to) the statement indicated by the transfer line number instead of to the statement immediately after the GOTO statement.

A typical GOTO statement follows:

```
100 GOTO 60
```

This statement tells the computer that the next statement to be executed is line 60. Let us see how the GOTO statement might be used in an application

FIGURE V–2

Multiplication Program

```
00010 READ A,B
00020 LET C = A*B
00030 PRINT A;"X";B;"=";C
00040 READ A,B
00050 LET C = A*B
00060 PRINT A;"X";B;"=";C
00070 READ A,B
00080 LET C = A*B
00090 PRINT A;"X";B;"=";C
00100 DATA 2,3,8,4,7,2
00110 END

RUNNH
  2 X 3 = 6
  8 X 4 = 32
  7 X 2 = 14
```

MICROCOMPUTERS

Apple: No differences.
IBM/Microsoft: No differences.
PET: No differences.
TRS-80: No differences.

by looking at Figure V–2, which multiplies sets of numbers and prints results.

What we really have here is a single process (multiplying two numbers together) repeated three times. The programmer typed in the following three lines as many times as was necessary:

```
READ A,B
LET C = A * B
PRINT A;"X"; B;"="; C
```

Although this is not a very difficult task with a small, uncomplicated problem, imagine how time consuming and inefficient it would be to do it for a hundred sets of data!

The same result can be achieved much more simply by use of a GOTO statement. In Figure V-3 the GOTO statement in line 40 directs the computer back to statement 10. A loop is formed. In this example, the error message "End of DATA found at line 00010 of MAIN PROGRAM" was printed because an attempt was made to read data after the data list had been exhausted. The execution of the program was terminated.

Note how the loop is indicated in the flowchart. A flow line is drawn from the process step immediately preceding the GOTO statement to the process step indicated by the transfer line number.

Later, this section will show how to control the number of times a loop is repeated (eliminating the error message above).

THE IF/THEN STATEMENT: CONDITIONAL TRANSFER

The GOTO statement always transfers control. Often, however, it is necessary to transfer control only when a specified condition exists. The IF/THEN statement is used to test for such a condition. If the condition does not exist,

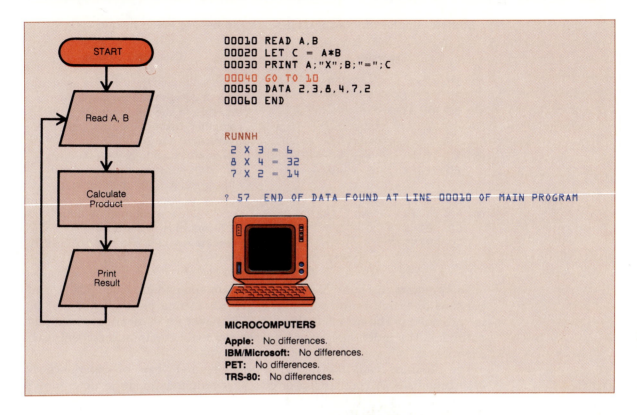

```
00010 READ A,B
00020 LET C = A*B
00030 PRINT A;"X";B;"=";C
00040 GO TO 10
00050 DATA 2,3,8,4,7,2
00060 END


RUNNH
 2 X 3 = 6
 8 X 4 = 32
 7 X 2 = 14

? 57  END OF DATA FOUND AT LINE 00010 OF MAIN PROGRAM
```

MICROCOMPUTERS

Apple: No differences.
IBM/Microsoft: No differences.
PET: No differences.
TRS-80: No differences.

FIGURE V–3
Multiplication Program
with GO TO
Statements

the next statement in the program is executed. The general format of the IF/THEN statement is:

line# IF <u>expression</u> <u>relational symbol</u> <u>expression</u> THEN line#

Conditions tested can involve either numeric or character string data. *Relational symbols* that can be used include:

BASIC Relational Symbols

SYMBOL	MEANING	EXAMPLES	
<	Less than	A < B	
<= or ≤	Less than or equal to	X < = Y	**NONSTANDARD**
>	Greater than	J > I	
>= or ≥	Greater than or equal to	A > = B	**NONSTANDARD**
=	Equal to	X = T N$ = "NONE"	
<> or ><	Not equal to	R <> Q "APPLE" <> R$	**NONSTANDARD**

Some examples of valid IF/THEN statements are given below:

	Statement	Computer Execution

(a)	`10 IF X >= 6 THEN 30`
	`20 LET A = A + X`
	`30 PRINT X`
		If the value contained in X is greater than or equal to 6, then the computer branches to line 30. If not, the computer executes the next sequential instruction, line 20.

(b)	`10 IF K <> N * 40 THEN 50` `20 LET K = N * 40`	If K is not equal to N * 40, the computer transfers to statement 50. Otherwise, it executes te next statement, line 20.

(c)	`40 IF A$ = "NO" THEN 60`
	`50 LET X = X + 1`
	`60 PRINT X`
		If the value contained in A$ is "NO", then control is passed to line 60. If A$ contains anything else, control goes to line 50.

The program in Figure V–4 uses both numeric and character string comparisons to search a firm's employee records to find an employee suitable for promotion. The firm is looking for a manager for its data-processing department. The individual must be a system analyst with at least ten years' experience.

The program reads the name, occupation, and years of experience for each candidate. A comparison of character strings is made to determine if the employee is a system analyst:

```
00110 IF O$ <> "SYSTEM ANALYST" THEN 160
```

The test is stated in such a way that only if the candidate is a system analyst will the program continue evaluating his or her credentials. Otherwise, the program transfers control to line 160.

The other job qualification requirement is ten or more years of experience. A numeric comparison is used to determine if the employee satisfies this requirement:

```
120 IF Y < 10 THEN 160
```

As above, for any candidate with less than ten years' experience, control is transferred to statement 160.

Any candidate who satisfies both conditions is acceptable. The program output indicates that only one of the candidates, Robert Johnson, should be considered for promotion to the data-processing manager position.

Note the diamond-shaped symbol in flowchart in Figure V–4. It is a *decision block*, representing the IF/THEN .test. The outcome of the test determines which flowline (path of program logic) will be followed.

THE ON/GOTO STATEMENT: CONDITIONAL TRANSFER

The ON/GOTO, or computed GOTO, statement transfers control to other statements in the program based on the evaluation of a mathematical

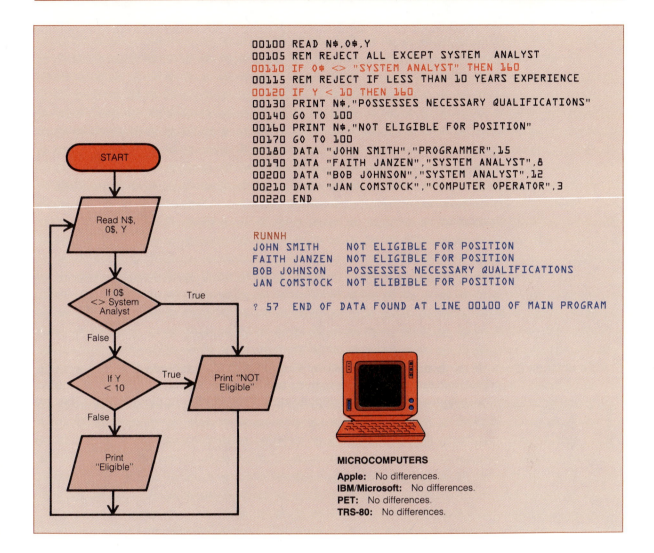

```
00100 READ N$,O$,Y
00105 REM REJECT ALL EXCEPT SYSTEM  ANALYST
00110 IF O$ <> "SYSTEM ANALYST" THEN 160
00115 REM REJECT IF LESS THAN 10 YEARS EXPERIENCE
00120 IF Y < 10 THEN 160
00130 PRINT N$,"POSSESSES NECESSARY QUALIFICATIONS"
00140 GO TO 100
00160 PRINT N$,"NOT ELIGIBLE FOR POSITION"
00170 GO TO 100
00180 DATA "JOHN SMITH","PROGRAMMER",15
00190 DATA "FAITH JANZEN","SYSTEM ANALYST",8
00200 DATA "BOB JOHNSON","SYSTEM ANALYST",12
00210 DATA "JAN COMSTOCK","COMPUTER OPERATOR",3
00220 END


RUNNH
JOHN SMITH     NOT ELIGIBLE FOR POSITION
FAITH JANZEN   NOT ELIGIBLE FOR POSITION
BOB JOHNSON    POSSESSES NECESSARY QUALIFICATIONS
JAN COMSTOCK   NOT ELIBIBLE FOR POSITION

? 57  END OF DATA FOUND AT LINE 00100 OF MAIN PROGRAM
```

MICROCOMPUTERS

Apple: No differences.
IBM/Microsoft: No differences.
PET: No differences.
TRS-80: No differences.

FIGURE V–4
Job Search Program

expression. The computed GOTO often operates as would multiple IF/THEN statements: any one of several transfers can occur, depending on the result computed for the expression. Since transfers depend on the expression, the computed GOTO is another *conditional transfer* statement. Its general format is:

line# ON expression GOTO line#1, line#2, line#3,. . ., line #n

The arithmetic expression is always evaluated to an integer, and the line numbers following GOTO must identify statements in the program.

The general execution of the ON/GOTO statement proceeds as follows:

1. If the value of the expression is 1, control is transferred to the first line number indicated.

2. If the value of the expression is 2, control is transferred to the second line number indicated.

· · ·

· · ·

· · ·

n. If the value of the expression is n, control is transferred to the nth line number indicated.

Several examples are presented below to illustrate the operation of this statement.

Statement	Computer Execution
10 ON X GO TO 50,80,100	IF X = 1, control goes to line 50. IF X = 2, control goes to line 80. IF X = 3, control goes to line 100.
30 ON N/50 GO TO 90,100	IF N/50 = 1, control goes to line 90. IF N/50 = 2, control goes to line 100.

NONSTANDARD

If the computed expression in an ON/GOTO statement does not evaluate to an integer, the value is either rounded or truncated (digits to the right of the decimal are ignored), depending on the BASIC implementation. For example:

Statement	Value of Variable	Action
40 ON N/3 GO TO 60,80	N = 7	7 ÷ 3 = 2.33. The expression is evaluated as 2.33. The remainder is truncated, and the result becomes the integer 2. Control passes to statement 80.

NONSTANDARD

If the expression evaluates to an integer less than 1 or larger than the number of statements indicated, either the program will terminate with an error message, or the ON/GOTO statement will be bypassed. For example:

Statement	Value of Variable	Action
60 ON X GO TO 100,140,170 70 LET X=X+1	X=4	The value of X exceeds the number of line numbers in the GOTO list. Control passes to statement 70.

The box, "ON/GOTO Errors" illustrates how various BASIC implementations respond to these conditions.

ON/GOTO Errors

Computer	Action if number evaluated is greater than number of line numbers	Action if number evaluated is less than 1 or greater than maximum allowed
Apple	ON/GOTO bypassed	"ILLEGAL QUANTITY" error
DEC	Execution stops/Error message displayed	"ON STMT OUT OF RANGE" error
IBM/Microsoft	ON/GOTO bypassed	"ILLEGAL FUNCTION CALL" or "OVERFLOW"
PET	ON/GOTO bypassed	"ILLEGAL QUANTITY" error
TRS-80	ON/GOTO bypassed	"?F " error

The calculator menu program (Figure V–5) illustrates a common use of the ON/GOTO statement in making a menu selection. A computer "menu" is like a menu in a restaurant. The user (diner) reads a group of possible selections on the screen (menu) and then enters a selection into the computer (describes the desired meal to the waiter or waitress).

In the following program, the user tells the computer whether to add, subtract, multiply, or divide two numbers by entering either 1, 2, 3, or 4. Line 230 transfers the program execution to the appropriate operation.

In the example, after entering the values for A and B, the user indicates that division is the desired operation by typing in the number 4, which is assigned to the variable C. Line 230, an ON/GOTO statement, causes pro-

FIGURE V–5
Calculator Menu
Program

```
00100 REM  *** CALCULATOR MENU ***          RUNNH
00110 PRINT
00120 PRINT
00130 PRINT   "ENTER A,B"                    ENTER A,B
00140 INPUT A,B                              ? 2,8
00150 PRINT
00160 PRINT
00170 PRINT "MENU SELECTION; ENTER A"        MENU SELECTION; ENTER A
00180 PRINT "     1 FOR A + B"                   1 FOR A + B
00190 PRINT "     2 FOR A - B"                   2 FOR A - B
00200 PRINT "     3 FOR A * B"                   3 FOR A * B
00210 PRINT "     4 FOR A / B"                   4 FOR A / B
00220 INPUT C
00230 ON C GO TO 240,250,260,270             ? 4
00240 T = A + B
00245 GO TO 280
00250 T = A - B
00255 GO TO 280                              THE RESULT IS 0.25
00260 T = A * B
00265 GO TO 280
00270 T = A / B
00280 PRINT
00290 PRINT
00300 PRINT "THE RESULT IS";T
00310 END
```

MICROCOMPUTERS

Apple: No differences.
IBM/Microsoft: No differences.
PET: No differences.
TRS-80: No differences.

gram execution to branch to the fourth line number, 270. The operation is then performed and the result printed.

LOOPING PROCEDURES

There are several things to consider in setting up a loop. The programmer must decide not only what instructions are to be repeated but also how many times the loop is to be executed. There are three techniques for loop control. This section covers *trailer values* and *counters*. Section VI will discuss the other method, FOR and NEXT statements.

Trailer Value

A loop controlled by a trailer value contains an IF/THEN statement that checks for the end of the data. The last data item is a dummy value that is not part of the data to be processed. (This method was used in the program at the beginning of this section.) Either numeric or alphanumeric data can be used as a trailer value. However, the programmer must always select a trailer value that will not be confused with real data.

Here is how it works. An IF/THEN statement is placed within the set of instructions to be repeated, usually at the beginning of the loop. One of the variables into which data is entered is tested. If it contains the dummy value, control is transferred out of the loop. If the variable contains valid data (does not equal the trailer value), looping continues.

Figure V–6 contains a loop pattern controlled by a trailer value. The program calculates the commission on sales made by several employees of the Rich Rugs Company.

Statement 150 tests the value in NM$ for the dummy value.

```
00150 IF NM$ = "LAST" THEN 210
```

If the condition is true, the flow of processing drops out of the loop to line 210. If the condition is false, processing continues to the next line in sequence, line 160. Note that since we used the INPUT statement to enter the data, it is necessary to tell the user how to end the looping process. This is done in line 130. The user has to enter two dummy values, LAST and 0, because the INPUT statement expects two values to be entered.

Counter

A second method of controlling a loop requires the programmer to create a *counter*—a numeric variable that is incremented each time the loop is executed. Normally, the increment is 1. A counter is effective only if the programmer notifies the computer how many times a loop should be repeated. The steps involved in setting up a counter for loop control are:

1. Initialize the counter to give it a beginning value.
2. Increment the counter each time the loop is executed.

FIGURE V–6

Sales Commissions
Program

```
00100 REM *** RICH RUGS CO. ***
00110 CO = 0.15
00115 REM BEGINNING OF LOOP
00120 PRINT "ENTER NAME,AMOUNT"
00130 PRINT "TYPE 'LAST,0' TO END"
00140 INPUT NM$,SA
00145 REM TEST FOR TRAILER VALUE
00150 IF NM$ = "LAST" THEN 210
00160 CM = SA * CO
00170 PRINT "NAME","SALES","COMMISSION"
00180 PRINT NM$,SA,CM
00190 PRINT
00200 GO TO 120
00205 REM END OF LOOP
00210 PRINT
00220 PRINT "FINISHED"
00230 END


RUNNH
ENTER NAME,AMOUNT
TYPE 'LAST,0' TO END
 ? HOWARD,2000
NAME            SALES          COMMISSION
HOWARD          2000           300

ENTER NAME,AMOUNT
TYPE 'LAST,0',TO END
 ? MOHAMMED,3570
NAME            SALES          COMMISSION
MOHAMMED        3570           535.5

ENTER NAME,AMOUNT
TYPE 'LAST,0' TO END
 ? XAVIERA,5000
NAME            SALES          COMMISSION
XAVIERA         5000           750

ENTER NAME,AMOUNT
TYPE 'LAST,0' TO END
 ? LAST,0

FINISHED
```

MICROCOMPUTERS

Apple: No differences.
IBM/Microsoft: No differences.
PET: No differences.
TRS-80: No differences.

3. Test the counter to determine if the loop has been executed the desired number of times.

The sales commission program we have been using can be modified to use a counter as shown below. Since there are three salespeople, the loop must be executed three times. The counter in this example is X. It is initialized to zero in line 115. The IF/THEN statement in line 125 tests the number of times the loop has been executed, as represented by the counter X. Line 185 causes X to be incremented each time the loop is executed. The loop instructions will be executed until X equals 3.

FIGURE V–7
Sales Commissions
Program with Counter

```
00100 REM *** RICH RUGS CO. ***
00110 CO = 0.15
00113 REM INITIALIZE COUNTER
00115 LET X = 0
00120 PRINT "NAME","SALES","COMMISSION"
00123 REM TEST COUNTER VALUE
00125 IF X = 3 THEN 230
00130 READ NM$,SA
00150 CM = SA * CO
00160 PRINT
00170 PRINT NM$,SA,CM
00185 X = X + 1
00188 REM UNCONDITIONAL TRANSFER
00190 GO TO 125
00200 PRINT
00220 DATA J.R.,10000,MOHAMMED,1500,HOWARD,560
00230 END


RUNNH
NAME            SALES            COMMISSION

J.R.            10000            1500

MOHAMMED        1500             225

HOWARD          560              84
```

MICROCOMPUTERS

Apple: No differences.
IBM/Microsoft: No differences.
PET: No differences.
TRS-80: No differences.

COMPREHENSIVE PROGRAMMING PROBLEM

Problem Definition

Jessie Smith, an instructor for Mathematics 202, needs a program that will assign letter grades to students based on their test scores. In addition, she wants to know how many students are in each grade category and how many took the test.

The grading scale is as follows:

Score	Letter Grade
90 or more	A
78–89	B
66–77	C
54–65	D
Less than 54	F

The students and their scores are:

Student	Score
Doug Wheat	96
Pat Ostrowski	89
Tom Tykodi	93
Lynn Probst	78
Kathy Brennan	77
Kathy Voss	90
T. Gregory	98
Jim Mathias	66
S. Gregory	51
W. Williams	88

The Program

The counter variables are initialized to zero by the READ and DATA statements in lines 130–140 of Figure V–8. The name and grade for each student are read in line 170. Line 180 tests for the trailer value XXX. As long as the student name does not equal "XXX", the loop is re-executed. The total number of students is accumulated in line 190. The first test to determine the grade is made in line 200. If the number grade is less than 90, it is not an A. Control is transferred to 240, where the number score is tested again to see if it is less than 78 (less than that required for a B grade). In this fashion, scores less than the lowest number required for a particular grade are passed down to the next lowest level until the correct one is found. Line 360 requires no test; any grade less than 54 is an F.

When the trailer value, XXX, is detected, control drops down to line 400, where printing of the totals occurs.

FIGURE V-8

Letter Grades Program

```
00100 REM *** ASSIGN LETTER GRADES ***
00110 PRINT
00120 PRINT
00130 DATA 0,0,0,0,0,0
00140 READ A,B,C,D,F,TOTAL
00150 PRINT "NAME"," ","SCORE","GRADE"
00160 PRINT
00165 REM LOOP BEGINS HERE
00170 READ NAME$,GRADE
00175 REM TEST FOR TRAILER VALUE
00177 REM CONDITIONAL TRANSFER
00180 IF NAME$ = "XXX" THEN 400
00190 TOTAL = TOTAL + 1
00200 IF GRADE < 90 THEN 240
00210 LETTER$ = "A"
00220 A = A + 1
00230 GO TO 380
00240 IF GRADE < 78 THEN 280
00250 LETTER$ = "B"
00260 B = B + 1
00270 GO TO 380
00280 IF GRADE < 66 THEN 320
00290 LETTER$ = "C"
00300 C = C + 1
00310 GO TO 380
00320 IF GRADE < 54 THEN 360
00330 LETTER$ = "D"
00340 D = D + 1
00350 GO TO 380
00360 LETTER$ = "F"
00370 F = F + 1
00380 PRINT NAME$," ",GRADE,LETTER$
00385 REM LOOP ENDS HERE
00387 REM UNCONDITIONAL TRANSFER
00390 GO TO 170
00400 PRINT
00410 PRINT "TOTAL # OF A'S = ";A
00420 PRINT "TOTAL # OF B'S = ";B
00430 PRINT "TOTAL # OF C'S = ";C
00440 PRINT "TOTAL # OF D'S = ";D
00450 PRINT "TOTAL # OF F'S = ";F
00460 PRINT
00470 PRINT "TOTAL # OF STUDENTS = ";TOTAL
00480 DATA DOUG WHEAT,96,PAT OSTROWSKI,89,TOM TYKODI,93
00490 DATA LYNN PROBST,78,KATHY BRENNAN,77,KATHY VOSS,90
00500 DATA T. GREGORY,98,JIM MATHIAS,66,S. GREGORY,51
00510 DATA W. WILLIAMS,88,XXX,0
00520 END
```

FIGURE V–8
Continued

```
RUNNH

NAME                     SCORE        GRADE

DOUG WHEAT                 96          A
PAT OSTROWSKI             89           B
TOM TYKODI                93           A
LYNN PROBST               78           B
KATHY BRENNAN             77           C
KATHY VOSS                90           A
T. GREGORY                98           A
JIM MATHIAS               66           C
S. GREGORY                51           F
W. WILLIAMS               88           B


TOTAL # OF A'S = 4
TOTAL # OF B'S = 3
TOTAL # OF C'S = 2
TOTAL # OF D'S = 0
TOTAL # OF F'S = 1

TOTAL # OF STUDENTS =  10
```

MICROCOMPUTERS

Apple: The variable names GRADE, TOTAL, and LETTER$ must be changed to avoid confusion with reserved words. For example, the computer thinks TOTAL is TO!
IBM/Microsoft: No differences.
PET: Same as Apple.
TRS-80: Same as Apple.

SUMMARY

• The GOTO statement is an unconditional transfer of control allowing the computer to bypass or alter the sequence in which instructions are executed.
• The GOTO statement is often used to set up loops.
• The IF/THEN statement permits control to be transferred only when a specified condition is met.
• The ON/GOTO statement instructs the computer to evaluate an expression and, based on its value, branch to one of several points in a program.
• The number of times a loop is executed can be controlled by the use of a trailer value or a counter.
• The trailer value is a dummy value entered after all data.
• A counter can be set up if the programmer knows ahead of time how many times a loop is to be executed.

SECTION VI

More About Looping

OVERVIEW

Section V discussed two methods of controlling loops—counters and trailer values. IF/THEN and GO TO statements were used to implement these methods. This section presents another method for loop control—FOR and NEXT statements. In addition, it discusses nested loops (loops within loops).

Let us review what happens when a counter is used to control a loop, since the logic of FOR and NEXT loops is very similar. First, the counter variable is set to some initial value. Statements inside the loop are executed once, and the counter incremented. The counter variable is then tested to see if the loop has been executed the required number of times. When the variable exceeds the designated terminal value, the looping process ends, and the computer proceeds to the rest of the program. For example, assume we are to write a program to compute and print the square and cube of each integer from 1 to 5. The program in Figure VI–1 does this by using a loop controlled by the counter method.

THE FOR AND NEXT STATEMENTS

FOR and NEXT statements allow concise loop definition. The general format of the FOR and NEXT loop is:

line# FOR loop variable = initial expression TO terminal expression STEP step value

.

.

.

line# NEXT loop variable

FIGURE VI–1

Looping with a Counter

```
00010 LET N = 1
00020 IF N > 5 THEN 60
00030 PRINT N, N ∧ 2, N ∧ 3
00040 LET N = N + 1
00050 GO TO 20
00060 END


RUNNH
1            1            1
2            4            8
3            9            27
4            16           64
5            25           125
```

The FOR statement tells the computer how many times to execute the loop. The loop variable (also called the index) is set to an initial value (initial expression). This value is tested against the terminal value (terminal expression) to see if the loop should be continued. These two activities required two lines (10 and 20) in Figure VI–1. The FOR statement combines these two functions into one statement.

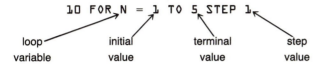

10 FOR N = 1 TO 5 STEP 1

loop variable — initial value — terminal value — step value

Lines 40 and 50 in Figure VI–1 increment the loop variable (the counter) and send control back to line 20. The functions of these two statements are combined in the NEXT statement. In Figure VI–1, after control is transferred back to line 20, the value of the loop variable is again tested against the terminal value. Once the value is exceeded, control passes to line 60. When FOR and NEXT are used, control goes to the statement immediately following the NEXT statement. Thus, the loop used in Figure VI–1 can be set up to use FOR/NEXT statements as shown in Figure VI–2.

The FOR statement in line 10 tells the computer to initialize the loop variable, N, to 1. Sandwiched between the FOR and NEXT statements is line

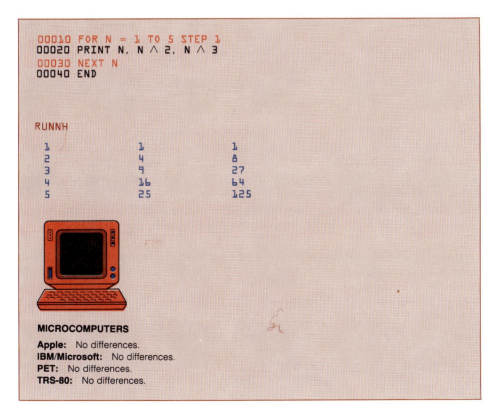

FIGURE VI–2
Looking With FOR/NEXT

20, the instruction to be repeated; it prints out N, N^2, and N^3. Line 30, the NEXT statement, increments the loop variable by the step value indicated in the FOR statement. N now equals 2. Control is then transferred back to the FOR statement. At this point, the computer tests the new value in N and decides whether to continue the loop. If N exceeds the terminal value of 5, the loop is stopped. If it does not, the loop is executed again. With N = 2, the loop is performed again. When the terminal value is exceeded—when N = 6—control is transferred to the statement immediately following the NEXT statement, line 40.

Flowcharting FOR and NEXT Loops

The following symbol can be used to flowchart the FOR and NEXT loop:

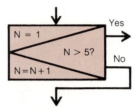

This is not a standardized flowchart symbol; but it is very convenient for representing a loop, since it shows the initial, terminal, and step values for the loop variable in one symbol.

Processing Steps of FOR and NEXT Loops

Let us review the steps followed by the computer when it encounters a FOR statement:

1. It sets the loop variable to the initial value indicated.
2. It tests to see if the value of the loop variable exceeds the indicated terminal value (this may occur the first time the FOR statement is executed).
3. If the value of the loop variable does not exceed the terminal value, the statements in the loop are executed.
4. If the value of the loop variable exceeds the terminal value, control is transferred to the statement following the NEXT statement.

When the NEXT statement at the end of a loop is encountered, the computer does the following:

1. It adds the step value (given in the FOR statement) to the value of the loop variable. If no step value is indicated in the FOR statement, the value is assumed to be +1. Thus, the following two statements are equivalent:

```
10 FOR N = 1 TO 5 STEP 1
```

or

```
10 FOR N = 1 TO 5
```

2. It transfers control back to the FOR statement.

Rules for Using FOR and NEXT Statements

Some rules to be aware of when you use FOR and NEXT statements follow:

1. There are times when it is desirable to use a negative step value. For example, to generate and print the sequence of numbers 100, 90, 80, 70, . . . , 20, 10, we can use the following code:

```
10 FOR I = 100 TO 10 STEP −10
20    PRINT I
30 NEXT I


RUNNH


 100
 90
 80
 70
 60
 50
 40
 30
 20
 10
```

The loop is terminated when the value of the loop variable, I, "exceeds" the specified terminal value, 10. In this case, though, the value of I "exceeds" in a downward sense—the loop is terminated when I is smaller than the terminal value. The initial value of the loop variable should be greater than the terminal value.

Examples of valid and invalid statements are:

Valid
```
FOR X = 100 TO 50 STEP −15
```

Invalid
```
FOR J = 50 TO 100 STEP −15
```

2. The step size in a FOR statement should never be zero. This value would cause the computer to loop endlessly. Such an error condition is known as an infinite loop.

Invalid
```
FOR J1 = 2 TO 4 STEP 0
```

3. Transfer can be made from one statement to another within a loop. For example, the program in Figure VI-3 reads five pairs of numbers and prints the sum of any pair whose value is less than 100. Control stays in the loop but bypasses statement 50 if the sum is greater than or equal to 100.

Note, however, that transfer from a statement within a loop to the FOR statement of the loop is illegal. Such a transfer would cause the loop variable

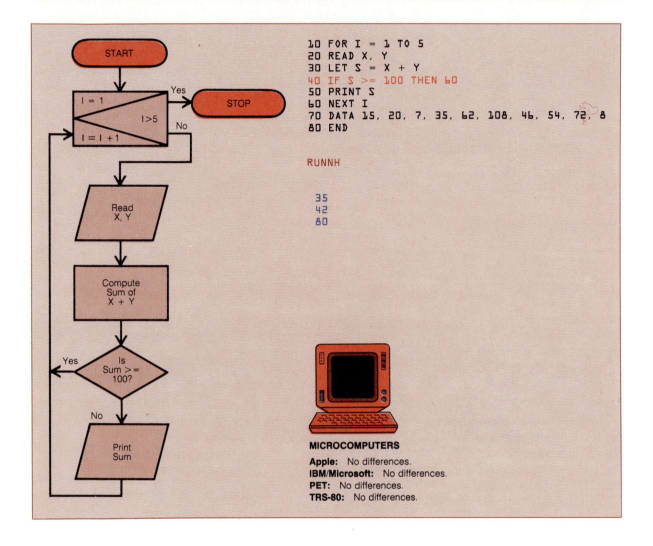

```
10 FOR I = 1 TO 5
20 READ X, Y
30 LET S = X + Y
40 IF S >= 100 THEN 60
50 PRINT S
60 NEXT I
70 DATA 15, 20, 7, 35, 62, 108, 46, 54, 72, 8
80 END


RUNNH


   35
   42
   80
```

MICROCOMPUTERS

Apple: No differences.
IBM/Microsoft: No differences.
PET: No differences.
TRS-80: No differences.

FIGURE VI–3
Exiting a Loop

to be reset (rather than simply continuing the loop process). Therefore, an infinite loop would be formed.

```
10 FOR J = 1 TO 3
20 IF J = 2 THEN 10                              Invalid Transfer
30 PRINT J + 10
40 NEXT J
```

If you want to continue the looping process but bypass some inner instructions, transfer control to the NEXT statement, as was done in Figure VI–3 (line 40).

4. The value of the loop variable should not be modified by program statements within the loop. For example, line 30 below is invalid:

```
10 FOR S = 1 TO J
20 LET A = 4 + 5
30 LET S = A                                     Invalid
40 NEXT S
```

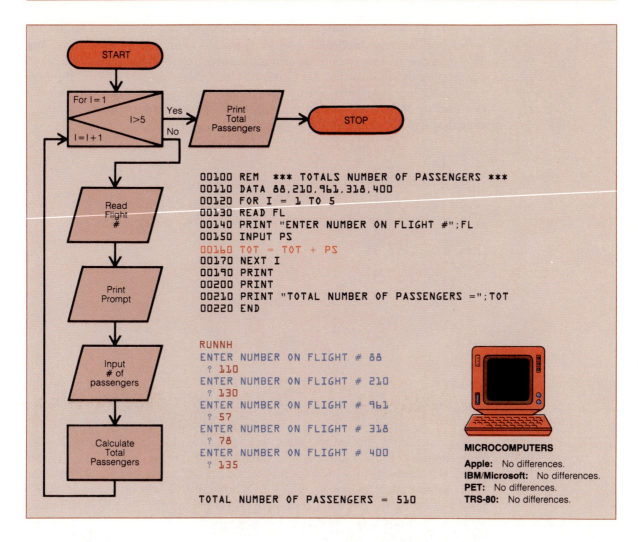

```
00100 REM  *** TOTALS NUMBER OF PASSENGERS ***
00110 DATA 88,210,961,318,400
00120 FOR I = 1 TO 5
00130 READ FL
00140 PRINT "ENTER NUMBER ON FLIGHT #";FL
00150 INPUT PS
00160 TOT = TOT + PS
00170 NEXT I
00190 PRINT
00200 PRINT
00210 PRINT "TOTAL NUMBER OF PASSENGERS =";TOT
00220 END


RUNNH
ENTER NUMBER ON FLIGHT # 88
 ? 110
ENTER NUMBER ON FLIGHT # 210
 ? 130
ENTER NUMBER ON FLIGHT # 961
 ? 57
ENTER NUMBER ON FLIGHT # 318
 ? 78
ENTER NUMBER ON FLIGHT # 400
 ? 135

TOTAL NUMBER OF PASSENGERS = 510
```

MICROCOMPUTERS

Apple: No differences.
IBM/Microsoft: No differences.
PET: No differences.
TRS-80: No differences.

FIGURE VI–4
An Adder

5. The initial, terminal, and step expressions can be composed of any valid numeric variable, constant, or mathematical formula. Both examples below are valid:

```
00005 INPUT A,B,C
00010 FOR X = A TO B STEP C
00020 PRINT "*"
00030 NEXT X


00005 READ C
00010 FOR Y = (10 - C) TO (50 + C) STEP 10
00030 LET A = A + C
00040 PRINT A
00050 NEXT Y
00060 DATA 2
```

6. Each FOR statement must be accompanied by an associated NEXT statement. In addition, the loop variable in the FOR statement must be specified in the NEXT statement.

Figure VI–4 demonstrates how FOR and NEXT statements can be used in a common looping application—adding values to an adder, or accumulator. The purpose of this particular program is to find out the total number of passengers flying daily on Air Ontario. Since there are five flights, the FOR and NEXT loop has been set up to execute five times. An accumulator has been set up in line 160 to add the number of passengers. After the loop has executed five times, the total is printed out.

NESTED FOR AND NEXT STATEMENTS

Loops can be nested; that is, all of one loop can be part of another loop or of many other loops. An example of a nested loop is shown below.

```
FOR I = 1 TO 10
  FOR J = 1 TO 10
    .
    .                    Valid
    .
  NEXT J
NEXT I
```

The inner loop is often indented to improve readability. In this case, each time the outer loop (I loop) is executed once, the inner loop (J loop) is executed ten times. When the J loop is terminated, control passes to the statement immediately below it, NEXT I. When control is transferred to FOR I (and the value of I does not exceed the terminal value, 10), the FOR J statement is soon encountered again. J is reinitialized to 1, and the J loop is again repeated ten times.

In nested FOR and NEXT statements, be careful not to mix the FOR from one loop with the NEXT of another. In other words, be sure one loop is completely inside another. The example below will not execute.

```
FOR I = 1 TO 10
FOR J = 1 TO 10
    .
    .                    Invalid
    .
  NEXT I
NEXT J
```

The following segment illustrates the mechanics of the nested loop. The outer loop will be executed two times, since N varies from 1 to 2. The inner loop will be executed three times each time the outer loop is executed once. Thus, the inner loop wil be executed a total of 2 × 3 = 6 times.

```
┌10 FOR N = 1 TO 2
 20    FOR K = 1 TO 3
 30    PRINT N, K
 40    NEXT K
└50 NEXT N
```

Outer Loop ——— **Inner Loop**

			N	K	
(a)	First time	⎧	1	1	First time through inner loop; K = 1
	through	⎨	1	2	Second time through inner loop; K = 2
	outer loop;	⎩	1	3	Third time through inner loop; K = 3
	N = 1				
(b)	Second time	⎧	2	1	Inner loop; K = 1
	through	⎨	2	2	Inner loop; K = 2
	outer loop;	⎩	2	3	Inner loop; K = 3
	N = 2				

An application of nested loops is shown in Figure VI–5, which generates three multiplication tables. The inner loop controls the printing of the columns in each row. The outer loop controls how many rows will be printed.

FIGURE VI–5
Multiplication Table

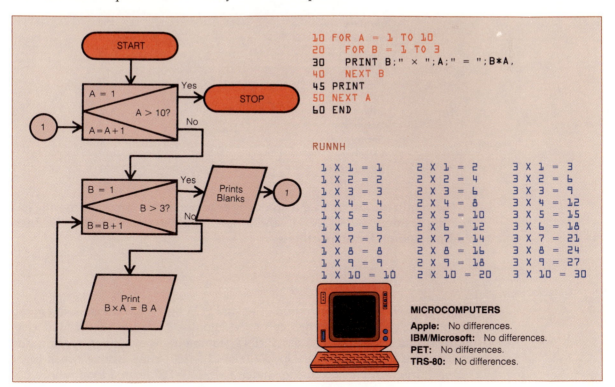

```
10 FOR A = 1 TO 10
20    FOR B = 1 TO 3
30       PRINT B;" X ";A;" = ";B*A,
40    NEXT B
45 PRINT
50 NEXT A
60 END
```

```
RUNNH

1 X 1 = 1        2 X 1 = 2        3 X 1 = 3
1 X 2 = 2        2 X 2 = 4        3 X 2 = 6
1 X 3 = 3        2 X 3 = 6        3 X 3 = 9
1 X 4 = 4        2 X 4 = 8        3 X 4 = 12
1 X 5 = 5        2 X 5 = 10       3 X 5 = 15
1 X 6 = 6        2 X 6 = 12       3 X 6 = 18
1 X 7 = 7        2 X 7 = 14       3 X 7 = 21
1 X 8 = 8        2 X 8 = 16       3 X 8 = 24
1 X 9 = 9        2 X 9 = 18       3 X 9 = 27
1 X 10 = 10      2 X 10 = 20      3 X 10 = 30
```

MICROCOMPUTERS

Apple: No differences.
IBM/Microsoft: No differences.
PET: No differences.
TRS-80: No differences.

First, A is initialized to 1. Then, execution of the inner loop begins. Line 30 tells the computer (when B = 1) to print "1 × 1 = 1." The comma at the end of that line tells the computer not to start output of the next PRINT statement on a new line but rather to continue in the next print zone. Line 40 increments B to 2 and sends control back to line 20. The variable A has not changed. The terminal value of B is not exceeded; so 2 × 1 = 2 is printed in the second print zone. The inner loop executes one more time and prints out 3 × 1 = 3. After the inner loop has executed the third time, one complete row has been printed:

```
1 X 1 = 1      2 X 1 = 2      3 X 1 = 3
```

In order to have printing start on the next line instead of in the next print zone, it is necessary to have the rest of the line printed with blanks. That is accomplished by line 45. Finally, A is incremented when line 50 is encountered. The whole process continues until A exceeds the terminal value, 10.

COMPREHENSIVE PROGRAMMING PROBLEM

Problem Definition

The Arctic Dog Snowmobile Company needs a program to display a bar chart of its monthly sales. The number of snowmobiles sold each month is given as follows:

January	39
February	37
March	28
April	26
May	12
June	10
July	5
August	3
September	4
October	12
November	21
December	33

The required output lists a three-letter abbreviation for each month in a column headed by "MONTH" and a horizontal bar chart labelled "SALES" and marked off by units of tens.

The Program

Figure VI–6 is a good illustration of nested FOR and NEXT loops. Statements 110 and 120 contain the names of the months and their associated sales figures. Lines 130–200 contain PRINT statements that adjust spacing and column headings. The outer loop (lines 210–280) runs twelve times (once for each month). Nested inside, statements 240–260 form a loop whose terminal value is the value of the variable S. The value of S is the number of

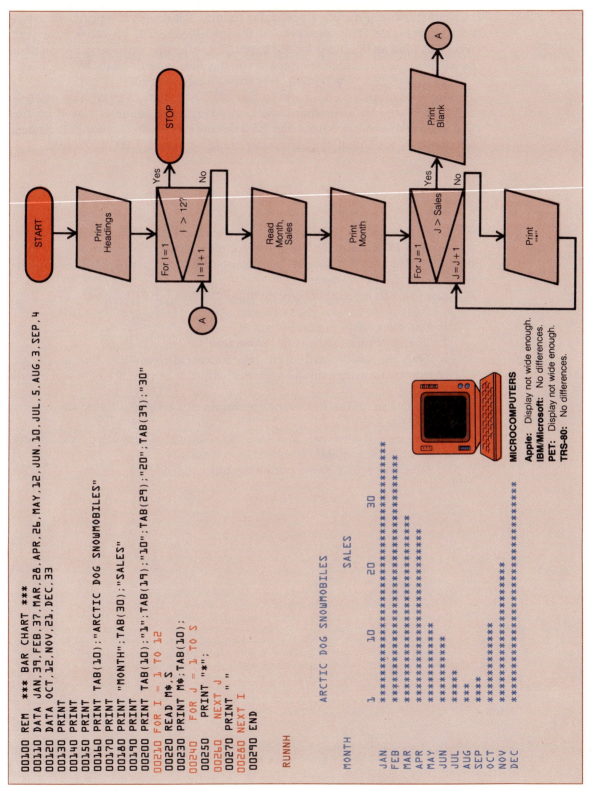

```
00100 REM *** BAR CHART ***
00110 DATA JAN,39,FEB,37,MAR,28,APR,26,MAY,12,JUN,10,JUL,5,AUG,3,SEP,4
00120 DATA OCT,12,NOV,21,DEC,33
00130 PRINT
00140 PRINT
00150 PRINT
00160 PRINT TAB(10);"ARCTIC DOG SNOWMOBILES"
00170 PRINT
00180 PRINT "MONTH";TAB(30);"SALES"
00190 PRINT
00200 PRINT TAB(10);"1";TAB(19);"10";TAB(29);"20";TAB(39);"30"
00210 FOR I = 1 TO 12
00220 READ M$,S
00230 PRINT M$;TAB(10);
00240    FOR J = 1 TO S
00250       PRINT "*";
00260    NEXT J
00270 PRINT " "
00280 NEXT I
00290 END

RUNNH

          ARCTIC DOG SNOWMOBILES

MONTH                     SALES

          1    10        20        30
JAN       *************************************
FEB       ***********************************
MAR       **************************
APR       ************************
MAY       ***********
JUN       *********
JUL       ****
AUG       ***
SEP       ****
OCT       ***********
NOV       *********************
DEC       *********************************
```

MICROCOMPUTERS

Apple: Display not wide enough.
IBM/Microsoft: No differences.
PET: Display not wide enough.
TRS-80: No differences.

FIGURE VI–6 Snowmobile Sales Chart Program

snowmobiles sold during a particular month. Statement 250 prints an asterisk for each sale. The semicolon at the end of line 250 prevents a carriage return as long as the inner loop is executing. After the inner loop is finished, however, it is necessary to prepare for the next month's line by the blank PRINT in line 270, which completes the carriage return.

Many variations can be made to the basic bar chart display. The asterisk can be replaced by any other character. Also, the limitations placed by the width of the terminal output can be overcome by using appropriate scales; for example, each displayed character could represent 1,000 units sold.

SUMMARY

● BASIC provides for concise loop definition with the FOR and NEXT statements. The FOR statement tells the computer how many times to execute the loop. The NEXT statement increments the loop variable and sends control back to the FOR statement.

● Some rules to remember when using FOR and NEXT loops are:

1. The step value can be negative.
2. The step value should never be zero.
3. Transfer can be made from one statement to another within a loop. However, transfer from a statement within a loop to the FOR statement is illegal.
4. The value of the loop variable should not be modified by statements within the loop.
5. The initial, terminal, and step expressions can be composed of any valid numeric variable, constant, or formula.
6. FOR and NEXT loops can be nested.

OVERVIEW

BASIC has several built-in functions that perform specific mathematical operations like finding the square root of a number or generating random numbers. These functions are useful to the programmer, who is spared the necessity of writing the sequence of statements otherwise needed to perform these operations. Other times, however, it may be useful for the programmer to define a function to meet the particular needs of an application. This section discusses these two tools: library functions (also called built-in or predefined functions) and user-defined functions. The following example illustrates the use of two library functions.

SECTION VII

Functions

The Problem

Father Furillo of St. Matthew's Church is in charge of the weekly turkey raffle. He needs a program that will randomly pick a winning number between 1 and N, where N is the highest-numbered ticket sold in a given week.

Solution Design

Clearly we need a random number that gives every ticket holder a fair chance of winning. However, so far we have only encountered constants, variables, and expressions that deal with specific values. Fortunately, randomly selected numbers are so useful in statistics, mathematics, science, and games that the designers of BASIC proposed a simple built-in method for producing random numbers: the randomize (RND) function.

Since the RND function returns a number between 0 and 1, we must "fix up" the result of RND to create a number between 1 and N, the number of tickets sold. We do so by multiplying the random number by N − 1 and then adding 1 to the result. One further complication is that we might end up with a fractional number, such as 256.732. Since the ticket numbers are whole numbers like 256 and 257, we must get rid of the fractional part. This can be accomplished by means of another function—the integer (INT) function.

The Program

The program in Figure VII–1 performs the necessary tasks. Line 140 asks for the number of tickets sold in the raffle. Line 150 multiplies the random number returned by RND by N − 1 and then adds 1 to the product of the multiplication. In line 160, INT returns the integer portion of the number. Lines 170–210 print the result and adjust spacing.

FIGURE VII–1
Turkey Raffle Program

```
00100 REM *** THIS PROGRAM DRAWS A RANDOM NUMBER
00110 REM *** FOR PICKING A WINNING RAFFLE TICKET
00120 PRINT
00130 PRINT
00140 INPUT "HOW MANY TICKETS WERE SOLD ";N
00150 WI = (RND * (N - 1)) + 1
00160 WI = INT(WI)
00170 PRINT
00180 PRINT
00190 PRINT "THE WINNING NUMBER IS ";WI
00200 PRINT
00210 PRINT
00220 END


RUNNH


HOW MANY TICKETS WERE SOLD  ? 352


THE WINNING NUMBER IS  69
```

LIBRARY FUNCTIONS

Table VII–1 lists the ANSI standard library functions found on most systems. The functions have been built into the BASIC language because many applications require these types of mathematical operations. The functions are included in the BASIC language library where they can be referred to easily—hence the name *library functions*.

The general format of a reference to a library function is:

function name (argument)

In the function references in Table VII–1, the variable X is used as an *argument*. In BASIC, the argument of a function can be a constant, a variable, a

TABLE VII–1
Library Functions

FUNCTION	PURPOSE
SIN(X)	Trigonometric sine function, X in radians
COS(X)	Trigonometric cosine function, X in radians
TAN(X)	Trigonometric tangent function, X in radians
ATN(X)	Trigonometric arctangent function, X in radians
LOG(X)	Natural logarithm function
EXP(X)	e raised to the X power
SQR(X)	Square root of X
INT(X)	Greatest integer less than X
SGN(X)	Sign of X
ABS(X)	Absolute value of X
RND	Random number between 0 and 1

mathematical expression, or another function. These functions are used in place of constants, variables, or expressions in BASIC statements such as PRINT, LET, and IF/THEN.

Trigonometric Functions

The first four library functions in Table VII–1—SIN(X), COS(X), TAN(X), and ATN(X)—are trigonometric functions very useful in mathematical, engineering, and scientific applications. They use radian measures of angles, since computers find them easier to understand than degrees. People, however, prefer to use degrees. The following examples show how to convert from one unit to the other:

1 radian = 57.29578 degrees

N radians = N * 57.29578 degrees

To convert 2.5 radians to degrees, multiply 2.5 by 57.29578. The product is about 143 degrees.

1 degree = 0.01745 radians

N degrees = N * 0.01745 radians

To convert 180 degrees to radians, multiply 180 by 0.01745. The result is 3.14 radians (exactly equal to pi).

Exponentiation Functions

The LOG(X), EXP(X), and SQR(X) functions deal with raising a number to a particular power.

EXP(X) The EXP(X) function makes the calculation $EXP(X) = e^X$. The constant e is equal to 2.718. We will not dwell on e, but it is useful in advanced topics in science, math, and business statistics.

LOG(X) The *natural logarithm* function is the reverse of the EXP(X) function. For example, if $X = e^Y$, then LOG(X) = Y. In other words, Y (the LOG of X) is the power e is raised to in order to find X. If we know X but need Y, we can use the following BASIC statement to find it:

```
10 Y = LOG(X)
```

SQR(X) The square root function determines the square root of an argument. In most BASIC implementations, the argument must be a positive number.

X	SQR(X)
4	2
16	4
11.56	3.4

Mathematical Functions

INT(X)   The INT function is used to compute the greatest whole number (integer) less than or equal to the value specified as the argument. The integer function does not round a number to the nearest integer. If the argument is a positive value with digits to the right of the decimal point, the digits are truncated (cut off). For example:

X	INT(X)
8	8
5.34	5
16.9	16

Be careful when the argument is a negative number. Remember the number line:

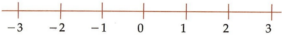

The farther left you go, the less value the number has; therefore:

X	INT(X)
−2	−2
−2.5	−3
−6.3	−7

Using INT to Round   Although the INT function does not round by itself, it can be used in an expression that rounds to the nearest integer, tenth, or hundredth or to any degree of accuracy wanted.

Figure VII–2 rounds a number to the nearest integer and the nearest tenth. Since the INT function returns the greatest integer less than or equal to the argument, it is necessary to add 0.5 to the argument to round to the

FIGURE VII–2
Rounding Program

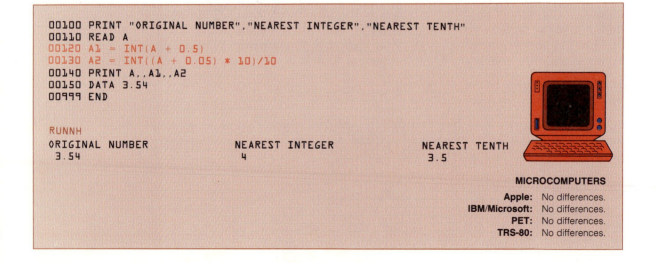

```
00100 PRINT "ORIGINAL NUMBER","NEAREST INTEGER","NEAREST TENTH"
00110 READ A
00120 A1 = INT(A + 0.5)
00130 A2 = INT((A + 0.05) * 10)/10
00140 PRINT A,,A1,,A2
00150 DATA 3.54
00999 END


RUNNH
ORIGINAL NUMBER          NEAREST INTEGER          NEAREST TENTH
3.54                     4                        3.5
```

MICROCOMPUTERS

Apple: No differences.
IBM/Microsoft: No differences.
PET: No differences.
TRS-80: No differences.

nearest integer (see line 120). Line 130 rounds the same number to the nearest tenth. We add 0.05 to A and then multiply that result by 10. The INT function is then applied, and the result is divided by 10.

SGN(X) The sign function yields one of three possible values. If X > 0, SGN(X) = +1; if X = 0, SGN(X) = 0; and if X < 0, SGN(X) = −1.

X	SGN(X)
8.34	+1
0	0
−3.5	−1
0.5	+1

This function might be used to quickly identify overdrawn accounts at a bank, as shown in Figure VII–3. After an account number and balance are read, the computer checks to see whether the balance is negative in line 20. If the balance is negative, the computer prints the "overdrawn" message; otherwise, the next account is read.

ABS(X) The absolute value function returns the absolute value of the argument. The absolute value is always positive, even if the argument is a negative value.

X	ABS(X)
−2	2
0	0
3.54	3.54
−2.68	2.68

We can use this function to identify all values that differ from a given value. For example, the IRS may want to know which individuals owe the

FIGURE VII–3
Overdrawn Accounts
Program

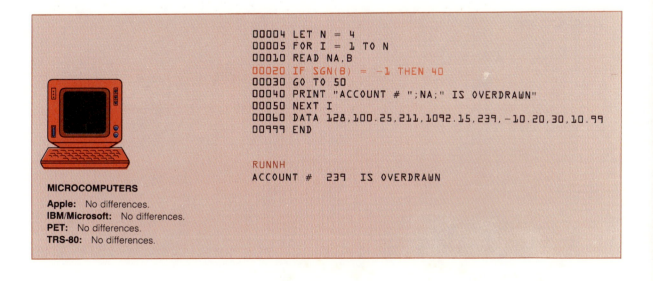

```
00004 LET N = 4
00005 FOR I = 1 TO N
00010 READ NA,B
00020 IF SGN(B) = -1 THEN 40
00030 GO TO 50
00040 PRINT "ACCOUNT # ";NA;" IS OVERDRAWN"
00050 NEXT I
00060 DATA 128,100.25,211,1092.15,239,-10.20,30,10.99
00999 END

RUNNH
ACCOUNT #  239  IS OVERDRAWN
```

MICROCOMPUTERS

Apple: No differences.
IBM/Microsoft: No differences.
PET: No differences.
TRS-80: No differences.

government a substantial sum or are owed a substantial sum by the government. Figure VII–4 shows how the absolute value function might be used to help identify these individuals. Line 20 tests for users who either owe at least $1,000 or are being refunded at least $1,000.

RND The randomize function is used to generate a random number between 0 and 1, as in the program at the beginning of this section. The term *random* means that any value between 0 and 1 is equally likely to occur. This function is especially important in applications involving statistics, computer simulations, and games. Some systems require that the RND function be used with an argument; other systems do not (see box on random numbers).

We can use the RND function to generate numbers greater than 1 by using it with other mathematical operations (see Figure VII–1). Suppose that we need a random number between 10 and 20 instead of between 0 and 1. Line 20 below computes a random number between R1, the lower limit in a selected range, and R2, the upper limit in the range.

```
20 LET R = RND * (R1 - R2) + R2
```

Sample output is shown below.

```
00010 READ R1,R2
00020 LET R = RND * (R1 - R2) + R2
00030 LET N = INT(R)
00040 PRINT "R1","R2","R","N"
00050 PRINT R1,R2,R,N
00060 DATA 10,20
```

FIGURE VII–4
Audit Search Program

```
RUNNH
R1              R2              R               N
10              20              18.05181        18
```

```
00010 READ N$,W
00020 IF ABS(W) >= 1000 THEN 40
00030 GO TO 10
00040 PRINT "WE SHOULD AUDIT ";N$
00045 GO TO 10
00050 DATA L. BUCKWELL,999,H. DONLEY,-39,S. MANDELL,-2090,R. PTAK,0.19
00060 END

RUNNH
WE SHOULD AUDIT S. MANDELL
```

MICROCOMPUTERS

Apple: No differences.
IBM/Microsoft: No differences.
PET: No differences.
TRS-80: No differences.

Random Numbers

At first thought, it might not seem hard to make up numbers whose values are arrived at only by chance. However, this task is difficult for machines with precise structure and logic (such as computers). Because it is difficult, the various computer manufacturers use different methods for obtaining random numbers. Most methods are extensions of the ANSI standard. Those that are nonstandard are shaded. You can obtain random numbers between 0 and 1 using each of our computers as follows:

DEC

Two statements are needed. The RND function needs no argument. The function used alone will give the same numbers each time a program is run; therefore, they are not truly random. Once you know that a program works the way you want it to, you should precede the statement containing RND by a RANDOMIZE statement. Now each time the program runs, RND will give a different, unpredictable number. An example is:

```
25  RANDOMIZE
    .
    .
    .
70  X = RND
```

Notice that the turkey raffle program at the beginning of this chapter was not properly randomized! Place your bets on number 69 for the next raffle! (That program was intended only to introduce the concept in the easiest possible manner.)

APPLE

Only one statement is needed. The RND function needs an argument. For example:

```
10  X = RND(3)
```

If the argument is 0 or has a negative value, an unexpected number can be generated; consult your manual.

IBM/Microsoft

Two statements are needed. The argument for RND is optional. An example is:

```
15 RANDOMIZE

20 PRINT RND
```

When the program is run, the computer prompts you with random number seed ($-32768 - +32767$)? You must enter a number within this range. Then the processing will continue.

PET

Two statements are needed. RND needs an argument. RND(0) and RND($-$N) should precede the use of RND(N). In other words, RND(0) and RND($-$N) work much as RANDOMIZE does on the DEC. An example is:

```
40  Y = RND(-RND(0))
    .
    .
    .
85  X = RND(1)
```

Now X should be a valid random number. Line 40 "seeds" the random number generator.

TRS-80

Two statements are needed. An argument is needed for RND (you should use 0 to get a number between 0 and 1). An example is:

```
30  RANDOM
    .
    .
    .
140  X = RND(0)
```

Line 10 has two numbers read into memory. In Line 20, the computer subtracts R2 from R1. The result is multiplied by a random number generated by the RND function. Finally, that product is added to R2. Line 30 finds the integer of R.

```
30 LET N = INT(R)
```

USER-DEFINED FUNCTIONS

The definition statement can be used by the programmer to define a function not already included in the BASIC language. Once the function is defined, the programmer can refer to it in a program as necessary. The DEF statement can be placed anywhere before the first reference to it. Its general format is:

line# DEF function name (argument) = expression

The function name consists of the letters FN followed by any one of the twenty-six alphabetic characters. There can be only one argument. The expression can contain any mathematical operations desired. However, a function definition cannot exceed one line of code.

When the computer encounters line 10 below, it files away into memory the defined function FNR. Line 20 initializes B to 5. When the computer comes to line 30, it remembers the definition for FNR and substitutes the value of B, 5, for X in the expression (X + 20)/2. The printed result is 12.5.

```
00010 DEF FNR(X) = (X + 20) / 2
00020 LET B = 5
00030 PRINT FNR(B)


RUNNH
12.5
```

Line 100 below defines a function to round a number to the nearest hundredth. After the values for name, wage, and hours have been read, the computer is instructed to calculate the salary and round it to the nearest hundredth. This is accomplished by substituting the result of W * HR for Y in the expression defined in line 100. The result is then printed out.

```
00100 DEF FNC(Y) = INT((Y + 0.005) * 100) / 100
00110 READ N$,W,HR
00120 LET S = FNC(W * HR)
00130 PRINT "NAME","EARNINGS"
00140 PRINT N$,"$";S
00150 DATA SALLY,5.33,40.25


RUNNH
NAME          EARNINGS
SALLY         $254.78
```

COMPREHENSIVE PROGRAMMING PROBLEM

The Problem

The ACME Sport Equipment Company manufactures leather basketballs, volleyballs, soccer balls, softballs, and so forth. The firm received orders this week for 10,000 baseballs, 5,000 volleyballs, and 250 softballs. The production manager needs to know how much leather will be needed to fill the orders.

FIGURE VII–5

Area of Leather Sport Balls Program

```
00100 REM *** THE AREA OF LEATHER SPORT BALLS ***
00110 DATA BASEBALLS,2,10000,VOLLEYBALLS,6,5000
00120 DATA SOFTBALLS,3.5,250
00130 REM **************
00140 REM DEFINE FUNCTION TO COMPUTE SURFACE AREA OF BALL
00150 REM **************
00160 DEF FNA(X) = 4 * 3.1416 * X ∧ 2
00170 PRINT
00180 PRINT
00190 PRINT "BALL TYPE","NUMBER","TOTAL AREA"
00200 PRINT ,,"(SQ. YARDS)"
00210 PRINT
00220 REM LOOP BEGINS HERE
00230 FOR I = 1 TO 3
00240 READ BL$,R,N
00250 A = FNA(R)
00260 REM TOTAL AREA = NUMBER TIMES AREA OF EACH BALL
00270 REM 1296 CONVERTS TO SQUARE YARDS
00280 TA = N * A / 1296
00290 PRINT
00300 PRINT BL$,N,TA
00310 REM LOOP ENDS HERE
00320 NEXT I
00999 END


RUNNH


BALL TYPE      NUMBER         TOTAL AREA
                              (SQ. YARDS)


BASEBALLS      10000          387.8519
VOLLEYBALLS    5000           1745.333
SOFTBALLS      250            29.69491
```

MICROCOMPUTERS

Apple: No differences.
IBM/Microsoft: No differences.
PET: No differences.
TRS-80: No differences.

Solution Design

If we know the radius of each type of ball ordered, we can figure out the total surface area to be constructed from leather. The formula for computing the surface area of a sphere is:

Surface area $= 4 \pi r^2$

We define a function in BASIC to compute this area as follows:

```
FNA(RADIUS) = 4 * 3.1416 * RADIUS ∧ 2
```

The next step is to read the type of ball, its radius, and the number of these to be made. After the surface area is computed, we know how much leather is required to make one ball. By multiplying this value by the number of this type ordered, we know how much leather is needed—in inches. We must convert this result to square yards by dividing by 1,296 (the number of square inches in a square yard).

The Program

Line 160 defines a function, FNA, to compute the surface area of a sphere. The next several lines print the headings. Line 230 initiates the FOR and NEXT loop that reads the data, calculates the surface area, converts that result to square yards, and prints the results. In line 250, the programmer refers to FNA to calculate the surface area. Line 320 marks the end of the FOR and NEXT loop.

SUMMARY

● The BASIC language includes several library functions that can make complicated mathematical operations easier to program.
● The trigonometric functions are SIN(X), COS(X), TAN(X), and ATN(X).
● The exponentiation functions are EXP(X), LOG(X), and SQR(X).
● Other mathematical functions are INT(X), SGN(X), ABS(X), and RND.
● It is also possible for the programmer to define functions by using the DEF statement.

OVERVIEW

So far, our programs have used simple variables such as A, N$, and D2 to represent single values. To store a group of values in this fashion, we must give each value a different variable name. But there is an easier way: BASIC permits us to deal with groups of related values as *arrays*. Array names are distinguished from simple variable names through the use of subscripts. The DIM statement tells the computer how much storage is necessary to hold an array. Arrays may be one-dimensional (sometimes called lists), two-dimensional (often called tables), or of higher dimensions. A method for sorting arrays is also discussed in this section.

Arrays

The Problem

The Adams Restaurant Supply Company wants a program that will keep track of the inventory of five items. These items and their starting quantities are given below:

Item	Quantity
Chef's knife	33
Food processor	9
Mixer	13
Wood chopping Block	40
Soup kettle	15

Solution Design

One way of handling this problem is to store these related items and their quantities in arrays.

A key feature of the array concept is the ability to locate (index) the elements in an array. For example, the food processor is the second element in the list of items; so we can index it by the number 2. The same number—2—is also, of course, an index to the second element in the list of quantities—the number of food processors in stock.

To use indices, we put the items into an array of strings and the quantities into a numerical array. The program will have to be able to display elements of both arrays at any time—in other words, to indicate the current inventory of the items. It will also have to provide a means of updating the inventory when a sale occurs. This will be accomplished by the program's generating a list of the items and index numbers; then the user enters the index number and quantity sold.

The Program

The program in Figure VIII-1 meets all these requirements. Lines 110–160 read the data. Notice that the variable names in line 150 have values in parentheses after them; the parentheses indicate that NM$ and AM are arrays. The first time through the FOR and NEXT loop, I has the value 1.

```
00100 REM *** INVENTORY ***
00110 DATA CHEF'S KNIFE,33,PROCESSOR,9
00120 DATA MIXER,13,WOOD BLOCK,40,KETTLE,15
00130 REM ** READ DATA
00140 FOR I = 1 TO 5
00150 READ NM$(I),AM(I)
00160 NEXT I
00170 PRINT
00180 PRINT
00190 REM ** PRINT MENU
00200 PRINT "ENTER"
00210 PRINT TAB(10);"1 FOR CURRENT INVENTORY"
00220 PRINT TAB(10);"2 FOR RECORDING NEW SALE"
00230 PRINT TAB(10);"3 TO END"
00235 REM ** ENTER CHOICE
00240 INPUT CH
00250 ON CH GO TO 270,370,999
00260 REM ** DISPLAY INVENTORY
00270 PRINT
00280 PRINT
00290 PRINT "--------------------------------"
00300 FOR I = 1 TO 5
00310    PRINT NM$(I),AM(I)
00320 NEXT I
00330 PRINT "--------------------------------"
00340 PRINT
00350 GO TO 200
00360 REM ** RECORD SALE
00370 PRINT
00380 PRINT
00390 FOR I = 1 TO 5
00400    PRINT I,NM$(I)
00410 NEXT I
00420 PRINT
00430 INPUT "ENTER INDEX # OF ITEM SOLD ";ID
00440 PRINT
00450 INPUT "HOW MANY WERE SOLD ";NU
00455 REM ** UPDATE INVENTORY
00460 AM(ID) = AM(ID) - NU
00470 GO TO 200
00999 END
```

Therefore, CHEF'S KNIFE is put into NM$ (1) and 33 is placed into AM(1). The second time through the loop, PROCESSOR is placed into NM$ (2) and 9 is placed into AM(2). Lines 190–230 display a menu selection (how appropriate for this company!). Lines 240 and 250 input the user's *CHoice* of action required and branch to the appropriate processing steps by using an ON/GOTO statement. Lines 260–340 display the current inventory. Line 350 branches back to the menu. Lines 360–460 update the inventory. Lines 390–410 print the index numbers and item names. The index number of the item sold and quantity sold are input in lines 430 and 450. The quantity of the indexed item is reduced by the number sold in line 460. Line 470 branches back to the menu. When 3 is selected, the program ends.

FIGURE VIII–1
Continued

```
RUNNH


ENTER
        1 FOR CURRENT INVENTORY
        2 FOR RECORDING NEW SALE
        3 TO END
  ? 1


------------------------------
CHEF'S KNIFE     33
PROCESSOR         9
MIXER            13
WOOD BLOCK       40
KETTLE           15
------------------------------

ENTER
        1 FOR CURRENT INVENTORY
        2 FOR RECORDING NEW SALE
        3 TO END
  ? 2

  1            CHEF'S KNIFE
  2            PROCESSOR
  3            MIXER
  4            WOOD BLOCK ·
  5            KETTLE

ENTER INDEX # OF ITEM SOLD   ? 2

HOW MANY WERE SOLD   ? 3
ENTER
        1 FOR CURRENT INVENTORY
        2 FOR RECORDING NEW SALE
        3 TO END

  ? 1


------------------------------
CHEF'S KNIFE     33
PROCESSOR         6
MIXER            13
WOOD BLOCK       40
KETTLE           15
------------------------------

ENTER
        1 FOR CURRENT INVENTORY
        2 FOR RECORDING NEW SALE
        3 TO END
  ? 3
```

SUBSCRIPTS

As stated earlier, an array is a group of storage locations in memory in which data elements can be stored. The entire array is given one name; the programmer indicates individual elements in the array by referring to their positions. The general concept is simple. Let us say there are three students in a computer science class. We would like to store the names of the students in an array called CS$. It might look like this:

Array CS$

CS$(1)	JONNY
CS$(2)	RACHEL
CS$(3)	SUE

We can gain access to an individual name within the array by telling the computer which position in the list it occupies. This is done through the use of *subscripts*. For example, Jonny is in the first position in the array—that is, CS$(1). RACHEL is in the second location, CS$(2). SUE is in CS$(3). The subscripts are enclosed in parentheses.

In BASIC, the same rules that apply to naming simple variables apply to naming arrays. Remember that only numbers can be stored in numeric variable array names, and only character strings in string variable arrays. It is good programming practice not to use the same name for both a simple variable and an array in a program.

The subscript (index) enclosed in parentheses can be any legal expression; for example, A(K), J(2), and X(B + C) are valid references to array elements.

When an array element is indicated by an expression, the computer carries out the following steps:

1. Evaluates the expression inside the parentheses.
2. Translates the result to the nearest integer.
3. Accesses the indicated element in the array.

For example, if the computer encounters A(K), it looks at the current value of K. This value indicates the position of the desired element in array A.

Array A

10
15
16
17
32

Assume that I = 2, N = 3, and K = 5. Then:

A(I) refers to A(2)—the second element in array A, or 15.
A(N) refers to A(3)—the third element in array A, or 16.
A(I + N) refers to A(5)—the fifth element in array A, or 32.
A(K) refers to A(5)—the fifth element in array A, or 32.

References to specific elements of arrays are called *subscripted variables*. In contrast, simple variables are *unsubscripted variables*. An unsubscripted variable, say P3, is used to refer to a single storage location named P3; the subscripted variable P(3), on the other hand, represents the third item in an array called P.

THE DIM STATEMENT

When a programmer uses an array, the BASIC compiler does not automatically know how many elements the array will contain. Unless told otherwise, it makes provisions for a limited number. Usually, the compiler is designed to assume that an array will have no more than ten elements. Consequently, it reserves space for ten elements in the array. The programmer cannot write a statement that refers to an array element for which space has not been reserved.

The programmer can specify the number of elements for which space must be reserved by means of a DIM (dimension) statement. The general format of the DIM statement is:

line# DIM variable1(limit1),variable2(limit2), . . .

The variables are the names of arrays. Each limit is an integer constant that represents the maximum number of storage locations required for a particular array.

Assume space is needed to store twenty-five elements in an array named X. The following statement reserves storage for twenty-five elements:

```
10 DIM X(25)
```

There is no problem if fewer than twenty-five values are actually read into array X, but it cannot contain more. Array subscripts can vary in the program from zero to the limit declared in the DIM statement, but no subscript can exceed that limit.

More than one array can be declared in a DIM statement; for example:

```
20 DIM A(30), B(20), J(100)
```

declares A, B, and J as arrays. Array A may contain up to 30 elements; B up to 20 elements; and J up to 100 elements. (If an index of 0 is used, up to 31, 21, and 101 elements can be stored.)

DIM statements must appear in a program before the first references to arrays they describe. A good programming practice is to place them at the beginning of the program. The following symbol is often used to flowchart the DIM statement:

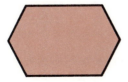

OPTION BASE

In the ANSI standard, unless the programmer declares otherwise, all array subscripts have a lower bound of zero. Therefore, a statement

```
10 DIM X(25)
```

actually reserves storage for twenty-six elements. If the programmer wants to eliminate the zero element, he or she can use the OPTION BASE statement as follows

```
5 OPTION BASE 1
```

ONE-DIMENSIONAL ARRAYS

This section has been discussing lists of related values stored under a single variable name—one-dimensional arrays. Let us look at some applications involving the use of one-dimensional arrays.

Reading Data into an Array

Using FOR and NEXT statements can be an efficient method of reading data into an array. The following program segment reads and stores a list of ten numbers in an array named J.

```
00010 FOR S = 1 TO 10
00020    READ J(S)
00030 NEXT S
00040 DATA 10,20,30,40,50,60,70,80
00050 DATA 90,100
```

The first time through this program loop, the loop variable S equals 1. When statement 20 is executed, the computer reads a number from the data lists and stores it in J(1)—the first storage location in array J. The second time through the loop, S equals 2. The next number is read into J(2)—the second location in the array. The loop processing continues until all ten numbers have been read and stored.

Printing Data in an Array

Now, assume we are to print the first eight numbers in array J in a single column. The following statements do just that.

```
60 FOR N = 1 TO 8
70    PRINT J(N)
80 NEXT N

RUNNH
   10
   20
   30
   40
   50
   60
   70
   80
```

B-86

As the loop variable varies from 1 to 8, the index changes and the computer prints elements 1 through 8 of array J.

Computations with Arrays

The following program generates a sales report that outlines the current prices of several items, the quantities sold, and the sales revenues that resulted. In addition, the program prints out the total amount of all sales.

This problem solution can be broken into the following steps:

1. Read the data into arrays.
2. Calculate the sales revenue for each item by multiplying price and quantity.
3. Calculate the total revenue by adding the sales revenues.

Three arrays are used in Figure VIII–2. Two one-dimensional arrays are read as input: a price list, stored in array P, contains a list of the prices of

FIGURE VIII–2
Sales Totals Program

```
00004 PRINT "PRICE","QUANTITY","SALES"
00005 PRINT ,"SOLD"
00006 PRINT
00010 FOR J = 1 TO 6
00020   READ P(J)
00030 NEXT J
00040 DATA 0.75,2.98,10.39,4.99,0.59,62.88
00050 FOR I = 1 TO 6
00060 READ Q(I)
00070 NEXT I
00080 DATA 11,95,6,17,89,5
00090 FOR N = 1 TO 6
00100   LET T(N) = Q(N) * P(N)
00110   PRINT P(N),Q(N),T(N)
00120 NEXT N
00121 LET T1 = 0
00122 FOR K = 1 TO 6
00123 LET T1 = T1 + T(K)
00124 NEXT K
00125 PRINT
00126 PRINT "THE TOTAL SALES IS $ ";T1
00130 END

RUNNH
```

PRICE	QUANTITY SOLD	SALES
0.75	11	8.25
2.98	95	283.1
10.39	6	62.34
4.99	17	84.83
0.59	89	52.51
62.88	5	314.4

THE TOTAL SALES IS $ 805.43

MICROCOMPUTERS

Apple: No differences.
IBM/Microsoft: No differences.
PET: No differences.
TRS-90: No differences.

six items; and a quantity list, stored in array Q, contains a list of the quantities sold of the items. In the main part of the program, a third array, T, is generated. It is a list of the gross sales of the items.

The program begins with a segment that established the price array, P. In lines 10–30, the variable J is set equal to 1, and a number is read from the data list and assigned to P(1). As the looping continues, P(2) is given a value, then P(3), and so on. When the looping is finished, array P contains the prices of the items. That is, P(1) is 0.75; P(2) is 2.98; and so on.

The next segment of the program fills array Q with values in the same manner. The values read into Q are the quantities of the six items sold. So, after execution of the loop in lines 50–70 has been completed, Q(1) is 11, Q(2) is 95, and so on.

Once the array elements have been stored, it is possible to manipulate them to obtain the desired information. For example, the main part of the program calculates the gross sales for each of the six items and stores the results in the array T. These computations are accomplished by multiplication of the elements in the price array P by the corresponding elements in the quantity array Q. All these arrays are then printed.

We are also to determine the total amount of all sales. We know that the array T contains the sales for each item. All we need to do is add all the elements in T. This is accomplished in lines 121–124.

If we wanted the total sales of only the first two items, we could simply alter the number of times the FOR and NEXT loop is executed:

```
00121 LET T1 = 0
00122 FOR K = 1 TO 2
00123    LET T1 = T1 + T(K)
00124 NEXT K
```

TWO-DIMENSIONAL ARRAYS

An array does not have to be a single list of data; it can be a table, or matrix. For example, assume that Andy's Hamburger Chain operates nine restaurants—three in each of three different cities. Andy has received the following table of data concerning the number of hamburgers sold by each of the nine stores.

| City | RESTAURANT | | |
	Main	Branch	Drive-Through
Toledo	100	50	35
Detroit	95	60	50
Columbus	110	80	100

The rows in the table refer to the cities and the columns refer to the stores. Thus, the number of hamburgers sold in Andy's main restaurant in Columbus can be found in the third row, first column.

This arrangement of data—a table consisting of rows and columns—is called a *two-dimensional array*. In this case, the two-dimensional array of data comprises three rows and three columns, a total of nine elements (3 × 3).

Two-dimensional arrays are named in the same way as other variables. If a name is used for a two dimensional array, it cannot be used for a one-dimensional array in the same program (and vice versa). An individual element in a table is indicated by a pair of subscripts in parentheses. The first number indicates the row; the second, the column. The row and column numbers are separated by a comma.

If we name the array H for Andy's Hamburger's above, then the number of numbers sold at the individual stores can be indicated by H(r,c), where r stands for the row in which a value is found and c stands for the column in which it is found:

Array H

H(1,1) 100	H(1,2) 50	H(1,3) 35
H(2,1) 95	H(2,2) 60	H(2,3) 50
H(3,1) 110	H(3,2) 80	H(3,3) 100

Thus, H(2,3) represents the number of hamburgers sold at the drive-through in Detroit, found in row 2, column 3. H(1,1) indicates the number of hamburgers sold at the Toledo main store.

Notice that it is necessary to store the cities' names in a separate array, because we cannot mix character string values with numeric values in the same array.

Array C$

C$(1) Toledo
C$(2) Detroit
C$(3) Columbus

As with one-dimensional arrays, individual elements in two-dimensional arrays may be indicated with any legal expresssion:

X(3,5)
X(I,5)
X(I,J)
X(2,I+J)

The 4 × 8 array X contains the following thirty-two elements:

Array X

10	15	20	25	30	35	40	45
50	55	60	65	70	75	80	85
90	95	100	105	110	115	120	125
130	135	140	145	150	155	160	165

Assume that I = 4 and J = 2. Then:

X(J,I)   refers to X(2,4)—the element in the second row, fourth column of array
                X, which is 65.

X(4,I)   refers to X(4,4)—the element in the fourth row, fourth column of array
                X, which is 145.

X(3,J + 4)   refers to X(3,6)—the element in the third row, sixth column of array X,
                which is 115.

X(I,5)   refers to X(4,5)—the element in the fourth row, fifth column of array
                X, which is 150.

As with one-dimensional arrays, the space needed to store a two-dimensional array must be stated if the array size exceeds a certain limit. Unless told otherwise, most BASIC compilers reserve enough space for an array with up to ten rows and up to ten columns. Therefore, for an array to exceed either the row limit or the column limit, the programmer must specify its size in a DIM statement.

```
10 DIM X(20,5)
```

reserves space for array X, which has twenty rows and 5 columns.

Reading and Printing Data in Two-Dimensional Arrays

Reading data into, and printing data from, two-dimensional arrays can be accomplished with nested FOR and NEXT statements. Thus, in Figure VIII–3 we read Andy's hamburger sales data into a two-dimensional array called H. The reading of the table follows a row-by-row sequence, from left to right across each column. The loops in lines 20–60 perform this reading process.

```
20 FOR I = 1 TO 3
30    FOR J = 1 TO3
40    READ H(I,J)
50    NEXT J
60 NEXT I
70 DATA 100,50,35,95,60,50,110,80,100
```

When the program is executed, each data value is represented by the variable H followed by a unique pair of subscripts telling its location by row, I, and column, J. As the data values are read, they fill the table, row by row (that is, after row 1 has been filled, row 2 is filled, then row 3). The outer FOR and NEXT loop controls the rows (using the variable I); the inner loop controls the columns (using the variable J). Thus, every time the outer loop is executed once, the inner loop is executed three times. While I is equal to 1, J is equal to 1, 2, and 3. The first three numbers from the data list are read into H(1,1), H(1,2), and H(1,3). Then I is incremented to 2. The inner loop is again executed three times, and the next three numbers from the data list are read into the second row, H(2,1), H(2,2), and H(2,3). I is finally incremented to 3, and the third row of the table is filled.

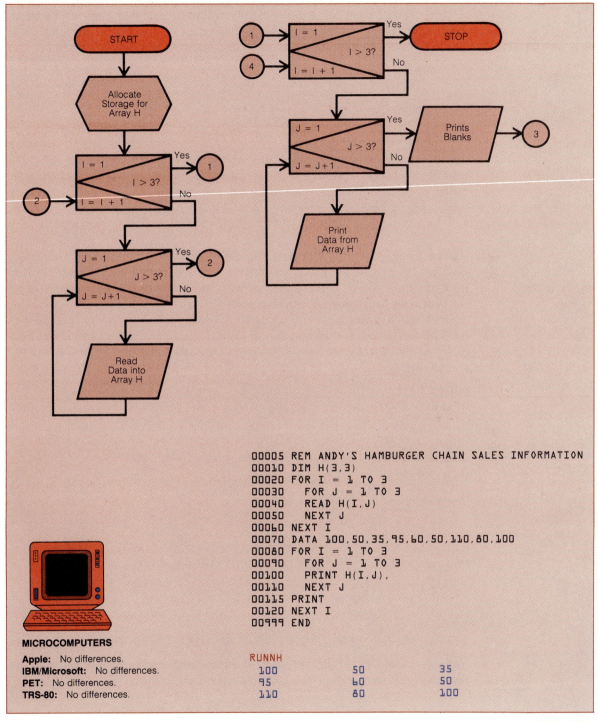

```
00005 REM ANDY'S HAMBURGER CHAIN SALES INFORMATION
00010 DIM H(3,3)
00020 FOR I = 1 TO 3
00030   FOR J = 1 TO 3
00040   READ H(I,J)
00050   NEXT J
00060 NEXT I
00070 DATA 100,50,35,95,60,50,110,80,100
00080 FOR I = 1 TO 3
00090   FOR J = 1 TO 3
00100   PRINT H(I,J),
00110   NEXT J
00115 PRINT
00120 NEXT I
00999 END
```

MICROCOMPUTERS

Apple: No differences.
IBM/Microsoft: No differences.
PET: No differences.
TRS-80: No differences.

```
RUNNH
100         50          35
95          60          50
110         80          100
```

FIGURE VIII–3
Hamburger Sales
Program

To print the entire table, a PRINT statement in a nested loop can be used. This is illustrated in lines 80–120. Let us examine the PRINT statements in this segment.

```
 80 FOR I = 1 TO 3
 90   FOR J = 1 TO 3
100   PRINT H(I,J),
110   NEXT J
115 PRINT
120 NEXT I
```

The comma in line 100 signals the computer to print the three values in predefined print zones on the same line. After the inner loop has been executed, the blank PRINT in line 115 sets the carriage return so that the next row is printed on the next line.

Adding Rows of Items   After data has been read and stored as an array, it is possible to manipulate the array elements. For example, Andy may want to find out how many hamburgers were sold in Detroit or how many hamburgers were sold at drive-throughs.

Since the data for each city is contained in a row of the array, we need to total the elements in one row of the array (the second row) to find out how many hamburgers were sold in Detroit. This can be done with the following statements:

```
00130 LET T = 0
00140 FOR J = 1 TO 3
00150   LET T = T + H(2,J)
00160 NEXT J
00170 PRINT
00180 PRINT T;"HAMBURGERS WERE SOLD IN DETROIT"
```

Notice that H(2,J) restricts the computations to the elements in row 2, while the column, J, varies from 1 to 3.

Adding Columns of Items   To find the number of hamburgers sold at drive-throughs, we want to total the elements in the third column of the array:

```
00190 LET D= 0
00200 FOR I = 1 TO 3
00210   LET D = D + H(I,3)
00220 NEXT I
00240 PRINT D;"HAMBURGERS WERE SOLD AT DRIVE THROUGHS"
```

In these statements, H(I,3) restricts the computations to the elements in the third column, while the row, I, varies from 1 to 3.

Totaling a Two-Dimensional Array   Now, suppose we need to know how many Andy's hamburger were sold altogether. This means we must add all of the elements in the array:

FIGURE VIII–4
More Hamburgers

```
00005 REM ANDY'S HAMBURGER CHAIN SALES INFORMATION
00010 DIM H(3,3)
00015 REM *** READ IN DATA
00017 REM *** OUTER LOOP CONTROLS ROWS
00020 FOR I = 1 TO 3
00025 REM *** INNER LOOP CONTROLS COLUMNS
00030   FOR J = 1 TO 3
00040   READ H(I,J)
00050   NEXT J
00060 NEXT I
00070 DATA 100,50,35,95,60,50,110,80,100
00075 REM *** PRINT ARRAY
00080 FOR I = 1 TO 3
00090   FOR J = 1 TO 3
00100   PRINT H(I,J),
00110   NEXT J
00115 PRINT
00120 NEXT I
00125 REM *** CALCULATE TOTAL OF ROW 2
00130 LET T = 0
00140 FOR J = 1 TO 3
00150 LET T = T + H(2,J)
00160 NEXT J
00170 PRINT
00180 PRINT T;"HAMBURGERS WERE SOLD IN DETROIT"
00185 REM *** CALCULATE TOTAL OF COLUMN 3
00190 LET D = 0
00200 FOR I = 1 TO 3
00210 LET D = D + H(I,3)
00220 NEXT I
00240 PRINT D;"HAMBURGERS WERE SOLD AT DRIVE THROUGHS"
00245 REM *** CALCULATE TOTAL OF ROWS & COLUMNS
00250 LET A = 0
00260 FOR I = 1 TO 3
00270   FOR J = 1 TO 3
00280   LET A = A + H(I,J)
00290   NEXT J
00300 NEXT I
00310 PRINT A;"HAMBURGERS WERE SOLD ALTOGETHER"
00999 END
```

```
RUNNH
100          50          35
95           60          50
110          80          100


205 HAMBERGERS WERE SOLD IN DETROIT
185 HAMBURGERS WERE SOLD AT DRIVE THROUGHS
680 HAMBURGERS WERE SOLD  ALTOGETHER
```

MICROCOMPUTERS

Apple: No differences.
IBM/Microsoft: No differences.
PET: No differences.
TRS-80: No differences.

```
00250 LET A = 0
00260 FOR I = 1 TO 3
00270   FOR J = 1 TO 3
00280     LET A = A + H(I,J)
00290   NEXT J
00300 NEXT I
00310 PRINT A;"HAMBURGERS WERE SOLD ALTOGETHER"
00999 END
```

A is the variable that will be used to accumulate the total. It is initialized outside the loop. To add all the elements in array H, we are going to use a nested loop. The outer loop will control the rows and the inner loop, the columns. Line 280 does the actual accumulation. The first time through the loop, both I and J equal 1; so H(1,1) is added to 0. J is then incremented, and H(1,2) is added to A to make 150. Then H(1,3), or 35, is added. At this point, I is incremented to 2 so that we can begin adding the second row values and so on until all the elements in H have been totaled.

Figure VIII–4 shows the complete program for Andy's Hamburger Chain and the resulting output.

ADVANTAGES OF ARRAYS

Although it may not be obvious at this point, arrays are useful in many applications. By using arrays we can avoid having to make up names for numerous items. Also, once data is stored in an array, the data items (elements) can be referred to over and over again without being reread. Arrays are also used extensively in file processing (discussed in Section XII).

SORTING

Many applications require that data items be sorted, or ordered, in some way. For example, names must be alphabetized, social security numbers arranged from lowest to highest, basketball players ranked from high scorer to low scorer, and the like.

Suppose that an array, BA, contains seven prices that we would like ordered from lowest to highest.

Array BA (unsorted)
2.03
4.95
1.13
3.89
2.56
3.29
4.25

It's a simple matter for us to mentally reorder this list as follows:

Array BA (sorted)

1.13
2.03
2.56
3.29
3.89
4.25
4.95

But what if there were seven hundred prices instead of seven? Then it would not be so easy for us to order the price list. However, the computer is perfectly suited for such tasks.

One method of sorting with the computer is illustrated in Figure VIII–5.

FIGURE VIII–5
Sorting Program

```
00100 REM  *** THIS PROGRAM SORTS THE STUDENTS
00110 REM        IN MIS 200 INTO ALPHABETICAL ORDER
00115 DIM ST$(15)
00120 PRINT "MIS 200 - UNSORTED"
00125 REM *** READ NAMES INTO ARRAY
00130 FOR I = 1 TO 15
00140   READ ST$(I)
00150   PRINT ST$(I)
00160 NEXT I
00165 PRINT
00166 PRINT
00170 REM *** BUBBLE SORT
00180 LET FL = 0
00190 FOR J = 1 TO 14
00200   IF ST$(J) <= ST$(J+1) THEN 250
00210   LET H$ = ST$(J)
00220   LET ST$(J) = ST$(J+1)
00230   LET ST$(J+1) = H$
00240 LET FL = 1
00250 NEXT J
00260 IF FL = 1 THEN 180
00270 PRINT "MIS 200 - SORTED "
00280 FOR I = 1 TO 15
00290   PRINT ST$(I)
00300 NEXT I
00310 DATA JANELLE,SUE,FRED,ABE,RON,KAREN
00320 DATA LES,JONNY,LYNN,RACHEL,KEN
00330 DATA BENJI,SONJA,KRIS,ELLEN
00999 END
```

```
RUNNH
MIS 200 - UNSORTED
JANELLE
SUE
FRED
ABE
RON
KAREN
LES
JONNY
LYNN
RACHEL
KEN
BENJI
SONJA
KRIS
ELLEN

MIS 200 - SORTED
ABE
BENJI
ELLEN
FRED
JANELLE
JONNY
KAREN
KEN
KRIS
LES
LYNN
RACHEL
RON
SONJA
SUE
```

MICROCOMPUTERS

Apple: No differences.
IBM/Microsoft: No differences.
PET: No differences.
TRS-80: No differences.

This *bubble sort* works by comparing two adjacent values in an array and then interchanging them according to the desired order—either ascending or descending order.

The program sorts fifteen student names into alphabetical order. To the computer, the letter A is less than the letter B, B less than C, and so on.

Lines 140—160 simply read the student names into an array called ST$ and print them out. Lines 170–260 are the bubble sort. Let us examine them carefully to see what happens.

Line 180 refers to the variable FL, short for flag. It is initialized to zero. Its value is checked later by the computer to determine if the entire array has been sorted.

Notice the terminal value of the FOR and NEXT loop that sorts the array. The terminal value is one less than the number of items to be sorted. This is because two items at a time are compared. J varies from 1 to 14. This means that the computer eventually will compare item 14 with item 14 + 1. If the terminal value were 15 (the number of names) the computer would try to compare item 15 with item 16, which does not exist in our array.

The IF/THEN statement in line 200 tells the computer whether to interchange two compared values. For example, when J = 1, the computer compares JANELLE to SUE. Since J comes before S in the alphabet, there is no need to switch these two items.

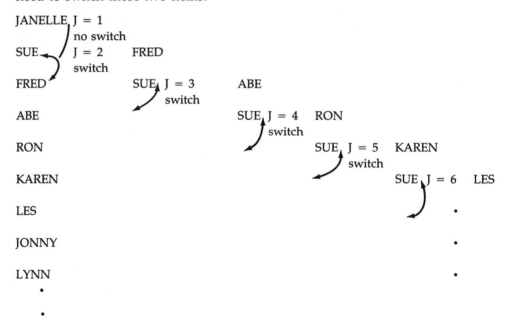

ELLEN

Then J is incremented to 2, and SUE is compared with FRED. These two names must be interchanged. This is performed by lines 210–230. Note that we have created a holding area, H$, so that the switch can be made. We move SUE to the holding area, H$, and then move FRED into SUE's previous position. Now SUE is placed in the position previously occupied by FRED. Whenever the computer interchanges two values, FL is set to 1 in line 240. This loop continues until every item in the array has been examined. After once through this entire loop, the array ST$ looks like this:

JANELLE
FRED
ABE
RON
KAREN
LES
JONNY
LYNN
RACHEL
KEN
BENJI
SONJA
KRIS
ELLEN
SUE

Although several switches have been made, the list is not sorted completely. That is why we need line 260. As long as FL equals 1, the computer knows that switches have been made and the sorting process must continue. When the computer loops through the entire array without setting FL to 1—that is, when no switches are made—the computer finds FL equal to 0 and knows that the list is ordered.

Numbers can, of course, be sorted by this same method. Two-dimensional arrays can be sorted with nested loops, too.

COMPREHENSIVE PROGRAMMING PROBLEM

The Problem

The Norm Crosby Swamp Classic Golf Tournament needs to determine quickly the tournament winner after the final round of scores are in. Five golfers have a chance to win. Their names and scores for the first three rounds are:

Tom Watson	69	69	70
Lee Trevino	65	70	72
Fuzzy Zoeller	66	71	70
Bruce Lietzke	67	72	68
Jack Nicklaus	71	66	70

FIGURE VIII–6

Sorting Golf Scores
Program

```
00100 REM *** GOLF SCORES ***
00110 DIM NM$(5),SC(5,4),TL(5)
00120 PRINT
00130 PRINT
00140 DATA TOM WATSON,69,69,70,LEE TREVINO,65,70,72
00150 DATA FUZZY ZOELLER,66,71,70,BRUCE LIETZKE,67,72,68
00160 DATA JACK NICKLAUS,71,66,70
00170 REM *************************
00180 REM READ IN DATA FOR FIRST 3 ROUNDS
00190 REM *************************
00200 FOR I = 1 TO 5
00210 READ NM$(I)
00220   FOR J = 1 TO 3
00230   READ SC(I,J)
00240   NEXT J
00250 NEXT I
00260 REM *************************
00270 REM INPUT FINAL ROUND SCORES
00280 REM *************************
00290 FOR I = 1 TO 5
00300 PRINT "ENTER FINAL ROUND SCORE FOR ";NM$(I)
00310 INPUT SC(I,4)
00320 NEXT I
00330 REM *************************
00340 REM CALCULATE TOTAL SCORES
00350 REM *************************
00360 FOR I = 1 TO 5
00370   FOR J = 1 TO 4
00380   TL(I) = TL(I) + SC(I,J)
00390   NEXT J
00400 NEXT I
00410 REM *************************
00420 REM SORT SCORES
00430 REM *************************
00440 FL = 0
00450 FOR J = 1 TO 4
00460 IF TL(J) <= TL(J+1) THEN 540
00470 H = TL(J)
00480 HH$ = NM$(J)
00490 TL(J) = TL(J+1)
00500 NM$(J) = NM$(J+1)
00510 TL(J+1) = H
00520 NM$(J+1) = HH$
00530 FL= 1
00540 NEXT J
00550 IF FL = 1 THEN 440
00560 REM *************************
00570 REM PRINT OUT PLACES
00580 REM *************************
00590 PRINT
00600 PRINT
00610 PRINT "PLACE";TAB(10);"GOLFER";TAB(30);"SCORE"
00620 PRINT
00630 FOR I = 1 TO 5
00640 PRINT I;TAB(10);NM$(I);TAB(30);TL(I)
00650 PRINT
00660 NEXT I
00670 END
```

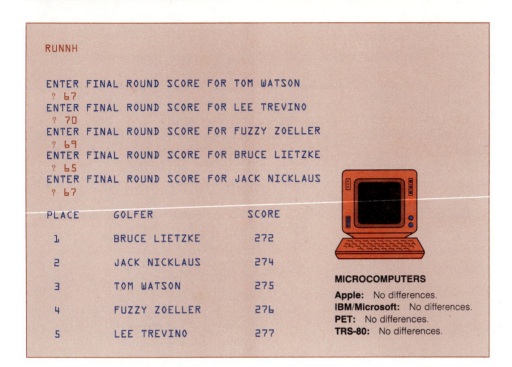

FIGURE VIII–6

Sorting Golf Scores
Program

Solution Design

Since the early round scores are known, they can be introduced to the program along with the golfers' names in READ and DATA statements. The final round scores should be entered by an INPUT statement. Next, the total scores must be calculated and then sorted from lowest to highest. A crucial point is that, as the scores are rearranged in the sorting section, the corresponding golfer's name must be carried with each score (although the name is not sorted). Finally, the results must be printed.

The Program

Figure VIII–6 shows this problem solution. Line 110 sets aside room for the variables (although this DIM statement is not strictly necessary, since the arrays have fewer than ten elements per index). Lines 200–250, a nested FOR and NEXT loop, read the data. Lines 290–320 input the final round scores. Lines 360–400 accumulate the total scores in a nested FOR and NEXT loop. The scores are sorted from lowest to highest in lines 440–550. The variable H in line 470 is the temporary storage area for scores during sorting. The variable HH$ in line 480 performs the same duty for the golfers' names. Every time the computer switches a total, TL(J), it must also switch the corresponding golfer's name. The computer performs the switches in lines 490–520. Lines 590–660 print the results.

SUMMARY

- Arrays are lists or tables of related values stored under a single variable name.
- Access to individual elements in an array can be gained through the use of subscripts.
- The DIM statement sets up storage space for arrays.
- Array manipulation is carried out through the use of FOR and NEXT loops.
- Two-dimensional arrays are also called tables, or matrices.
- Two subscript numbers identify individual items in a matrix. The first number indicates the row; the second, the column.
- The bubble sort is one method of ordering values contained in an array.

OVERVIEW

A matrix can be either a list or a table of data—essentially, the term *matrix* is just another name for a one- or two-dimensional array. Some implementations of the BASIC language have a set of matrix statements (nonstandard) that offer convenient, easy ways to carry out array operations. Unfortunately, many microcomputer systems do not include them in their basic compilers (none of ours do).

Let's take a look at a typical application of matrix, or MAT, commands.

Matrix Commands

The Problem

Al Sleet, the Channel 13 weatherman, wants a program to convert the daily high and low temperatures for five consecutive days from the Fahrenheit scale to the Celsius scale.

Solution Design

To convert a temperature from Fahrenheit to Celsius, two operations must be performed: First, 32° is subtracted from the Fahrenheit temperature. Then this result is multiplied by 0.5555.

The data for this problem fits naturally into a two-dimensional array. The high temperatures can be represented by a row of five columns; the lows by a second row of five columns. Here are the temperatures for the week of May 24:

	5/24	5/25	5/26	5/27	5/28
High temperatures	65	68	70	71	69
Low temperatures	49	50	40	47	52

It would be nice to perform the conversion calculations on all ten values with simple statements that avoid the complexity of FOR and NEXT loops. MAT commands provide this ability. We can subtract 32° from all temperatures with one command and read or print all the values with one command. Figure IX–1 illustrates the use of some of these commands.

The Program

Line 140 reads the data values (Fahrenheit temperatures) into array A according to the dimensions specified in line 110. Notice that the values in the DATA statements are in row-by-row order. Line 180 prints our array A in row order. Line 190 sets up another array, B, whose elements are initialized to constants of 1. Array B is then multiplied by 32, a scalar (a value enclosed in parentheses), in line 200, to set up array C. The values in C are subtracted from the values in A in line 210. In line 220, the new matrix, B, is multiplied by the scalar 0.5555; and the new results are placed back into C. Array C now contains the Celsius temperatures. Line 260 prints them out.

FIGURE IX–1

Fahrenheit to Celsius
Program

```
00100 REM *** CONVERT TEMPERATURES ***
00110 DIM A(2,5),B(2,5),C(2,5)
00120 DATA 65,68,70,71,69
00130 DATA 49,50,40,47,52
00140 MAT READ A
00150 PRINT
00160 PRINT
00170 PRINT "FAHRENHEIT TEMPERATURES"
00180 MAT PRINT A,
00183 REM *** INITIALIZE AN ARRAY TO 32
00190 MAT B = CON
00200 MAT C = (32) * B
00205 REM *** CALCULATE CELSIUS TEMP
00210 MAT B = A - C
00220 MAT C = (0.5555) * B
00230 PRINT
00240 PRINT
00250 PRINT "CELSIUS TEMPERATURES"
00260 MAT PRINT C,
00270 END


RUNNH


FAHRENHEIT TEMPERATURES

    65              68              70              71              69
    49              50              40              47              52

CELSIUS TEMPERATURES

    18.3315         19.998          21.109          21.6645         20.5535
    9.4435          9.999           4.444           8.3325          11.11
```

MATRIX STATEMENTS

One key word in each matrix command is the word MAT. Table IX–1 shows typical MAT commands (X, Y, and Z are all matrices).

Matrix I/O

To read data into a matrix, we can use the MAT READ statement. The general format of the MAT READ statement is:

line# MAT READ matrix name

Assume there exists a matrix X:

```
62    99    43
75    28    17
```

The following statements could be used to read the above data into array X:

```
05 DIM X(2,3)
10 MAT READ X
20 DATA 62,99,43,75,28,17
```

OPERATION	BASIC STATEMENT	FUNCTION	ARRAY MANIPULATION
Dimension	DIM X(2,2),Y(2,2),Z(2,2)	Establish matrix size	$X = 2 \times 2$; $Y = 2 \times 2$; $Z = 2 \times 2$
Input/Output	MAT READ X	Read data values into matrix X from DATA statements	X $\begin{vmatrix} 1 & 2 \\ -4 & 5 \end{vmatrix}$
	MAT INPUT Y	Enter data values into matrix Y from terminal	Y $\begin{vmatrix} 5 & 6 \\ 8 & 9 \end{vmatrix}$
	MAT PRINT X,	Print matrix X row by row	$\begin{matrix} 1 & 2 \\ -4 & 5 \end{matrix}$
Replacement	MAT Z =X	Assign matrix values on right-hand side of equal sign to matrix on left of equal sign	$Z = \begin{vmatrix} 1 & 2 \\ -4 & 5 \end{vmatrix}$
Addition	MAT Z = X + Y	Sum X and Y and place result in Z	Z $\begin{vmatrix} 6 & 8 \\ 4 & 14 \end{vmatrix}$ $= $ X $\begin{vmatrix} 1 & 2 \\ -4 & 5 \end{vmatrix}$ $+$ Y $\begin{vmatrix} 5 & 6 \\ 8 & 9 \end{vmatrix}$
Subtraction	MAT X = X − Y	Subtract corresponding elements of Y from X and place result in Z	Z $\begin{vmatrix} -4 & -4 \\ -12 & -4 \end{vmatrix}$ $=$ X $\begin{vmatrix} 1 & 2 \\ -4 & 5 \end{vmatrix}$ $-$ Y $\begin{vmatrix} 5 & 6 \\ 8 & 9 \end{vmatrix}$

The MAT READ command causes the computer to read the data in a row order according to how it was dimensioned. That is, all of the first row is read into the matrix, then all of the second row, and so on. Another point to remember is that all the positions in the array must be filled when MAT commands are used. Otherwise, an "out of data" error message will result.

The MAT READ statement is equivalent to a READ within nested FOR and NEXT statements, as shown below.

TABLE IX–1
Matrix Statements
(continued on next page)

Array Input with MAT Statement	Array Input with Nested FOR and NEXT Statements

```
10 DIM X(2,3)
20 MAT READ X
30 DATA 62,99,43,75,28,17
40 END
```

```
10 DIM X(2,3)
20 FOR I = 1 TO 2
30   FOR J = 1 TO 3
40     READ X(I,J)
50   NEXT J
60 NEXT I
70 DATA 62,99,43,75,28,17
80 END
```

OPERATION	BASIC STATEMENT	FUNCTION	ARRAY MANIPULATION		
Multiplication	`MAT Z = X * Y`	Store the products of X and Y in Z	**Z** $\begin{vmatrix} 21 & 24 \\ 20 & 21 \end{vmatrix} =$	**X** $\begin{vmatrix} 1 & 2 \\ -4 & 5 \end{vmatrix} *$	**Y** $\begin{vmatrix} 5 & 6 \\ 8 & 9 \end{vmatrix}$
Scalar Multiplication	`MAT Z = (2) * X`	Multiply each element in X by 2 and place in Z	**Z** $\begin{vmatrix} 2 & 4 \\ -8 & 10 \end{vmatrix} = 2 *$	**X** $\begin{vmatrix} 1 & 2 \\ -4 & 5 \end{vmatrix}$	
Initialization	`MAT Z = ZERO`	Initialize Z to zero	**Z** $\begin{vmatrix} 0 & 0 \\ 0 & 0 \end{vmatrix}$		
	`MAT Z = CON`	Place 1s into Z	**Z** $\begin{vmatrix} 1 & 1 \\ 1 & 1 \end{vmatrix}$		
Identity	`MAT Z = IDN`	Create the identity matrix	**Z** $\begin{vmatrix} 1 & 0 \\ 0 & 1 \end{vmatrix}$		
Transposition	`MAT Z = TRN(X)`	Enter the transpose of X into Z	**Z** $\begin{vmatrix} 1 & -4 \\ 2 & 5 \end{vmatrix}$		
Inversion	`MAT Z = INV(X)`	Enter the inverse of X into Z	**Z** $\begin{vmatrix} 0.038 & -0.15 \\ 0.031 & 0.08 \end{vmatrix}$		

TABLE IX–1
(Continued)

Similarly, we can use a MAT INPUT statement to enter data from the terminal:

```
10 DIM X(2,3)
20 MAT INPUT X
```

A MAT PRINT statement can be used to print out a matrix in row order. The MAT PRINT statement has the following general format:

line# MAT PRINT matrix name

Thus, the statement

```
10 MAT PRINT X,
```

is equivalent to the following statements:

```
10 FOR I = 1 TO 2
20    FOR J = 1 TO 3
30      PRINT X(I,J),
40    NEXT J
50    PRINT
60 NEXT I
```

The example below illustrates the use of the MAT INPUT statement to enter data into a 3 × 3 matrix and of the MAT PRINT statement to get output.

```
10 DIM B(3,3)
20 PRINT "ENTER MATRIX VALUES"
30 PRINT "SEPARATED BY COMMAS"
35 PRINT
40 MAT INPUT B
45 PRINT
50 MAT PRINT B,
```

```
RUNNH
ENTER MATRIX VALUES
SEPARATED BY COMMAS

?1,2,3,4,5,6,7,8,9
1        2        3
4        5        6
7        8        5
```

Notice that line 50 ends with a comma. If we omit the comma, the output looks like this:

```
1
2
3

4
5
6

7
8
9
```

Although the output is formatted differently, the matrix values are still printed in row order.

Matrix Math

Matrices can be added, subtracted, multiplied, and made equivalent.

Addition and Subtraction

Two matrices must have the same dimensions if they are to be added or subtracted. For example, the arrays below have the same number of rows, three, and the same number of columns, two.

```
10 DIM B(3,2),A(3,2),C(3,2)
20 MAT B = A+C
30 MAT B = B-C
```

The corresponding elements of one matrix are added to (or subtracted from) another matrix. Notice that the same matrix can be referred to on both sides of the equal sign.

$$
\overset{\textbf{B}}{\begin{vmatrix} 6 & 8 \\ 10 & 12 \\ 12.4 & 2 \end{vmatrix}} = \overset{\textbf{A}}{\begin{vmatrix} 5 & 6 \\ 7 & 8 \\ 3.4 & 2 \end{vmatrix}} + \overset{\textbf{C}}{\begin{vmatrix} 1 & 2 \\ 3 & 4 \\ 9 & 0 \end{vmatrix}}
$$

$$
\overset{\textbf{B}}{\begin{vmatrix} 5 & 6 \\ 7 & 8 \\ 3.4 & 2 \end{vmatrix}} = \overset{\textbf{B}}{\begin{vmatrix} 6 & 8 \\ 10 & 12 \\ 12.4 & 2 \end{vmatrix}} - \overset{\textbf{C}}{\begin{vmatrix} 1 & 2 \\ 3 & 4 \\ 9 & 0 \end{vmatrix}}
$$

Matrix Multiplication

For two matrices to be multiplied, the number of columns of the first matrix must equal the number of rows of the second matrix. The resulting matrix will have the same number of rows as the first matrix and the same number of columns as the second one.

```
10 DIM B(3,3), E(3,2), D(2,3)
20 MAT B = E*D
```

$$
\overset{\textbf{B}}{\underset{3 \times 3}{\begin{vmatrix} ? & ? & ? \\ ? & ? & ? \\ ? & ? & ? \end{vmatrix}}} = \overset{\textbf{E}}{\underset{3 \times 2}{\begin{vmatrix} 5 & 6 \\ 7 & 8 \\ 9 & 10 \end{vmatrix}}} * \overset{\textbf{D}}{\underset{2 \times 3}{\begin{vmatrix} 1 & 2 & 3 \\ 4 & 5 & 6 \end{vmatrix}}}
$$

The result is derived by addition of the products of the row elements of the first matrix times the column elements of the second matrix. It is:

$$
\overset{\textbf{B}}{\begin{vmatrix} 29 & 40 & 51 \\ 39 & 54 & 69 \\ 49 & 68 & 87 \end{vmatrix}} = \begin{vmatrix} (5*1)+(6*4) & (5*2)+(6*5) & (5*3)+(6*6) \\ (7*1)+(8*4) & (7*2)+(8*5) & (7*3)+(8*6) \\ (9*1)+(10*4) & (9*2)+(10*5) & (9*3)+(10*6) \end{vmatrix}
$$

When using MAT commands, you can perform only one operation at a time. The following statement is invalid:

```
20 MAT X = A*B+Y
```

Scalar Multiplication

A matrix can be multiplied by a *scalar* value (a constant, variable, or expression) enclosed in parentheses. For example:

```
10 MAT E = (2)*E
```

$$\begin{array}{c} \mathbf{E} \\ \begin{vmatrix} 10 & 12 \\ 14 & 16 \\ 18 & 20 \end{vmatrix} \end{array} = 2 * \begin{array}{c} \mathbf{E} \\ \begin{vmatrix} 5 & 6 \\ 7 & 8 \\ 9 & 10 \end{vmatrix} \end{array}$$

Replacement

Replacement takes place when whatever is on the right-hand side of the equal sign is placed into the matrix on the left-hand side of the equal sign. The matrices must have the same dimensions, of course. For example:

```
5 DIM A(2,4), B(2,4)
10 MAT A = B
```

$$\begin{array}{c} \mathbf{A} \\ \begin{vmatrix} 10 & 20 & 50 & 60 \\ 30 & 40 & 70 & 80 \end{vmatrix} \end{array} = \begin{array}{c} \mathbf{B} \\ \begin{vmatrix} 10 & 20 & 50 & 60 \\ 30 & 40 & 70 & 80 \end{vmatrix} \end{array}$$

Initialization

It is often necessary to initialize variables to specific values. The same can be done with matrices.

Initializing to Zero   The following MAT statement stores zeros in an array:

```
15 DIM B(4,2)
20 MAT B = ZER
```

$$\begin{array}{c} \mathbf{B} \\ \begin{vmatrix} 0 & 0 \\ 0 & 0 \\ 0 & 0 \\ 0 & 0 \end{vmatrix} \end{array}$$

Initializing to One   We can also use a MAT command to initialize all the elements of an array to one:

```
15 DIM J(2,4)
20 MAT J = CON
```

$$\begin{array}{c} \mathbf{J} \\ \begin{vmatrix} 1 & 1 & 1 & 1 \\ 1 & 1 & 1 & 1 \end{vmatrix} \end{array}$$

The Identity Matrix

The following statemens create an identity (IDN) matrix:

```
15 DIM Q(4,4)
20 MAT Q = IDN
```

The diagonal of an identity matrix contains ones; all the other elements are zeros.

$$
\mathbf{Q}
$$

$$
\begin{vmatrix}
1 & 0 & 0 & 0 \\
0 & 1 & 0 & 0 \\
0 & 0 & 1 & 0 \\
0 & 0 & 0 & 1
\end{vmatrix}
$$

When the IDN function is used, the number of rows in the matrix must be equal to the number of columns.

Transposition

When a matrix is transposed, the rows of the old matrix become the columns of the new matrix. For example:

```
10 MAT G = TRN(J)
```

If J looks like this:

```
1    2
3    4
5    6
7    8
```

then the transposition of J looks like this:

```
1    3    5    7
2    4    6    8
```

You must be careful that the dimensions of the matrix that will contain the transposed matrix values are the reverse of the dimensions of the matrix to be transposed. For example, J is a 4×2 matrix. Therefore, G (which is to contain the transposition of J) must be a 2×4 matrix.

Inversion

One of the most powerful matrix commands is the inverse function. It is often used to solve *simultaneous linear equations*. The inverse of A is usually written A^{-1}. The usefulness of the inverse comes from the fact that A multiplied by its inverse gives a result that is the identity matrix. (See the comprehensive program for an example of its use.)

COMPREHENSIVE PROGRAMMING PROBLEM

The Problem

We want to use MAT commands to solve two equations with two unknowns. This type of problem is very common in statistics, the sciences, engineering, and the area of business administration called operations re-search. Our method can easily be expanded for use with higher numbers of equations and unknowns.

In this example, we want to find the values X1 and X2 that simultaneously satisfy the following two equations:

$1X_1 + 2X_2 = 5$

$3X_1 + 4X_2 = 6$

Solution Design

If we look at this problem in terms of matrices, we can analyze the above equations as follows:

$$A = \begin{vmatrix} 1 & 2 \\ 3 & 4 \end{vmatrix}$$

$$X = \begin{vmatrix} X_1 \\ X_2 \end{vmatrix}$$

$$B = \begin{vmatrix} 5 \\ 6 \end{vmatrix}$$

The resulting matrix math operations are:

$$\begin{vmatrix} 1 & 2 \\ 3 & 4 \end{vmatrix} * \begin{vmatrix} X_1 \\ X_2 \end{vmatrix} = \begin{vmatrix} 5 \\ 6 \end{vmatrix}$$

In matrix notation, the two equations can be written as:

$AX = B$

We can use the inverse of matrix A to solve this problem in the following steps:

Step 1:   Multiply both sides by A^{-1} (the inverse of A):

$A^{-1}AX = A^{-1}B$

Step 2:   Notice that $A^{-1}A$ is just the identity matrix $\begin{vmatrix} 1 & 0 \\ 0 & 1 \end{vmatrix}$.

$IX = A^{-1}B$

or $X = A^{-1}B$

So all we have to do to find the matrix X is to multiply matrix B by the inverse of matrix A.

FIGURE IX–2

Linear Equations
Program

```
00100 REM *** SOLVE LINEAR EQUATIONS ***
00110 DIM A(2,2),C(2,2),D(2,2)
00120 DIM X(2,1),B(2,1)
00130 DATA 1,2,3,4
00140 DATA 5,6
00150 MAT READ A
00155 PRINT
00156 PRINT
00160 PRINT "MATRIX A"
00170 MAT PRINT A;
00180 MAT READ B
00190 MAT C = INV(A)
00200 PRINT "INVERSE OF MATRIX A"
00210 MAT PRINT C,
00220 MAT D = C * A
00230 PRINT "INVERSE OF A TIMES A -- SHOULD BE IDENTITY MATRIX"
00240 MAT PRINT D;
00250 MAT X = C * B
00260 PRINT "SOLUTION -- MATRIX X"
00270 MAT PRINT X
00280 END


RUNNH


MATRIX A

 1  2
 3  4

INVERSE OF MATRIX A

-2            1
1.5          -0.5

INVERSE OF A TIMES A -- SHOULD BE IDENTITY MATRIX

 1  0
 0  1

SOLUTION -- MATRIX X

-4

 4.5
```

The Program

Lines 110 and 120 of Figure IX–2 set the dimensions of the arrays (matrices) A, B, C, D, and X. Line 150 reads data into A. Line 180 reads data into B. Line 170 prints A. Line 190 makes C the inverse of A. C is printed by line 210. (To better illustrate how the inverse works, lines 220–240 multiply A by its own inverse and print the result—the identity matrix.) Line 250 calculates the solution (two unknowns, X_1 and X_2) by multiplying B by the inverse of A. The solution is printed in line 270.

The output of the program displays matrix A, its inverse, and these two multiplied by each other (they do produce the identity matrix). The solution shows that $X_1 = -4$ and $X_2 = 4.5$. You can check this by putting these two values in our two original equations and seeing that the numbers all work out.

SUMMARY

● Some BASIC compilers provide MAT statements to simplify array operations.

● MAT READ and MAT PRINT read data and print data in row-by-row order.

● MAT INPUT permits data to be entered into a matrix from the terminal.

● There are various MAT commands to concisely perform the math manipulations of addition, subtraction, multiplication, scalar multiplication, and replacement.

● The MAT ZER function initializes a matrix to zero; the MAT CON command initializes an array to one.

● An identity matrix can be created by use of the IDN function.

● The TRN function transposes a matrix.

● Matrix inversion is accomplished by the INV function.

SECTION X

Subroutines and String Functions

OVERVIEW

Sometimes it is necessary to have the computer execute an identical sequence of instructions at several points in a program. Rather than write the instructions over and over again, we can include them in a subroutine. Two statements are required to define a subroutine: GOSUB and RETURN; they are discussed in this section, along with the STOP statement and string functions.

The Problem

Harvey's Haberdashery is having a year-end clearance sale offering a 15 percent discount on all men's furnishings. Mr. Harvey would like a report that lists the sale price of every item, the amount of tax per item (the tax rate is 5 percent), and the total price of the item including the tax. That way, sales clerks will have a quick reference to use when serving customers.

The input is:

Item	Regular Price
Suit	$189.95
Shirt	14.99
Slacks	21.50
Socks	2.19
Underwear	6.49
Tie	9.99

Solution Design

This problem is rather straightforward, except for one little catch. The computer is far more precise than we are; so when we tell it to figure out the sale price:

```
P2 = 189.95 - (189.95 * 0.15)
```

it will give us an answer like this:

```
P2 = 161.4575
```

But we want the amount expressed in dollars and cents; so before the sale price, amount of tax, and total price of each item can be printed, we must round these values to the nearest penny.

The logic to be used is something like this:

1. Read an item and its price.
2. Calculate the discounted price.
*3. Round the discounted price.
4. Calculate the taxes.
*5. Round the taxes.
6. Calculate the total price.
7. Stop

Rather than repeat the rounding instructions in three separate sections of the program, we can use a *subroutine*; then we will only have to code one sequence of rounding instructions.

The Program

Lines 140–170 in Figure X–1 print the headings of the report. The discount rate (15 percent) and the tax rate (5 percent) are assigned to variables in lines 180–190. Once this is done, the computer can begin to figure out the sale price, tax, and total for each of the items in inventory. The loop to do this is established in line 200. After an item and its price are read, the sale price is computed in line 220. Line 230 assigns this sale price to X so that it can be rounded.

A new command, GOSUB, directs the computer out of the main line of the program to the subroutine that starts at line 390. Lines 390–400 round the value contained in X to the nearest penny. Line 410 directs the computer to the line immediately after the most recently executed GOSUB statement. In this case, processing resumes at line 250. Line 260 calculates the tax amount. This must also be rounded; so control is directed to the subroutine again. After the tax is rounded to the nearest cent, the computer starts executing the main program at line 290. Line 310 adds the tax to the sale price to get the total. Again control is sent to the subroutine to perform the rounding function. Finally, we are ready to output the item name, sale price, tax, and total. Line 370 loops back to line 200 to get another item for processing. After all the items have been processed, the program must be ended. To prevent the computer from going through the subroutine unnecessarily, we place a STOP statement at line 380—the logical end of the program.

THE GOSUB STATEMENT

The GOSUB statement is used to transfer the flow of control from the main line of a program to a subroutine. The general format of the GOSUB statement is:

line# GOSUB line#

The line number following GOSUB identifies the first statement of the subroutine.

The GOSUB statement is something like an unconditional GOTO statement. The difference is that the GOSUB command also helps the computer remember where to return after the subroutine has been executed. Statement 240 in the haberdashery program is an example of a typical GOSUB statement:

```
240 GOSUB 390
```

The computer is directed to a subroutine that rounds a number to the nearest penny.

FIGURE X–1
Clothing Discounts
Program
(Continued on facing
page)

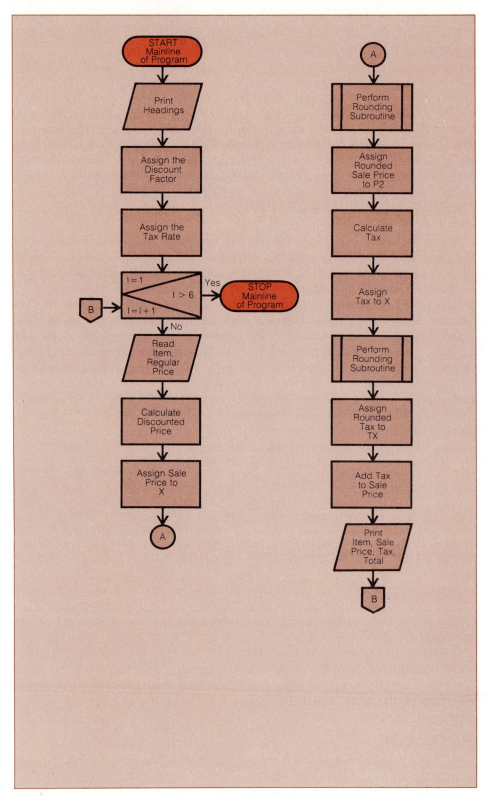

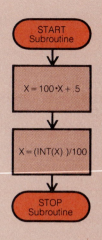

```
00100 REM *** THIS PROGRAM GIVES DISCOUNT PRICES
00110 REM      ROUNDED TO THE PENNY ***
00120 DATA SUITS,189.95,SHIRTS,14.99,SLACKS,21.50
00130 DATA SOCKS,2.19,UNDERWEAR,6.49,TIES,9.99
00140 PRINT
00150 PRINT
00160 PRINT
00170 PRINT "ITEM","SALE PRICE","TAX","TOTAL"
00175 REM DISCOUNT RATE = 15%
00180 DS = 0.15
00185 REM TAX RATE = 5%
00190 TR = 0.05
00195 REM BEGIN LOOP HERE
00200 FOR I = 1 TO 6
00210 READ N$,P1
00220 P2 = P1 - DS * P1
00225 REM NEW PRICE
00230 X = P2
00240 GOSUB 390
00250 P2 = X
00255 REM TAX
00260 TX = P2 * TR
00270 X = TX
00280 GOSUB 390
00290 TX = X
00300 REM TOTAL = NEW PRICE + TAX
00310 TT = P2 + TX
00350 PRINT
00360 PRINT N$,"$";P2,"$";TX,"$";TT
00365 REM END OF LOOP
00370 NEXT I
00374 PRINT
00376 PRINT
00380 STOP
00382 REM ***********************
00384 REM SUBROUTINE TO ROUND TO NEAREST CENT
00386 REM ***********************
00390 X = 100 * X + 0.5
00400 X = (INT(X)) / 100
00410 RETURN
00420 END
```

Flowchart boxes (left column):
- START Subroutine
- X = 100 · X + .5
- X = (INT(X))/100
- STOP Subroutine

RUNNH

ITEM	SALE PRICE	TAX	TOTAL
SUITS	$ 161.46	$ 8.07	$ 169.53
SHIRTS	$ 12.74	$ 0.64	$ 13.38
SLACKS	$ 18.28	$ 0.91	$ 19.19
SOCKS	$ 1.86	$ 0.09	$ 1.95
UNDERWEAR	$ 5.52	$ 0.28	$ 5.8
TIES	$ 8.49	$ 0.42	$ 8.91

STOP AT LINE 00380 OF MAIN PROGRAM

THE RETURN STATEMENT

After processing within a subroutine has been completed, control must be transferred back to the main line of the program. This is accomplished by the RETURN statement. The general format of the RETURN statement is:

line# RETURN

No line number need follow RETURN, because the BASIC compiler remembers to return to the statement immediately following the most recently executed GOSUB statement. In the haberdashery program, line 410 signals the end of the subroutine and tells the computer to continue executing the rest of the program.

410 RETURN

THE STOP STATEMENT

The STOP statement halts execution of a program; it is placed wherever a logical end to a program should occur. The general format of the STOP statement is:

line# STOP

The STOP statement differs from the END statement in that STOP may appear as often as necessary in a program, while the END statement may appear only once and must have the highest line number in the program.

Using STOP with Subroutines

One of the major uses of the STOP statement is with subroutines. For convenience, subroutines are generally placed near the end of a program; but the subroutine may be referred to several times in the program. A STOP statement is usually placed just before the beginning of the first subroutine to prevent unnecessary execution of the subroutine when the computer comes to the logical end of the program. For example, in the haberdashery example, the subroutine is executed three times; and then the result is printed. If there were no stop statement (line 380), the computer would execute the subroutine a fourth time before coming to the END statement in line 420.

Using STOP with Exception Handling

Many programs contain *"exception-handling"* instructions. These sequences of statements help the computer to prevent "garbage in–garbage out" errors. The STOP statement can be used to stop execution of a program after such a sequence has been executed.

Figure X–2 calculates the common logarithm of a number. Since the computer can find the logs of positive numbers only, the program includes an exception-handling instruction in line 210. If the user of the program enters

FIGURE X–2
Base 10 Logs Program

```
00100 REM  *** ABNORMAL STOP ***
00110 PRINT
00120 PRINT
00130 PRINT "THIS PROGRAM RETURNS THE BASE 10"
00140 PRINT "LOGARITHM OF A NUMBER"
00150 PRINT
00160 PRINT "ENTER THE NUMBER WHOSE LOG YOU WANT"
00170 INPUT X
00180 REM *************************
00190 REM TEST FOR NEGATIVE OR ZERO
00200 REM *************************
00210 IF X <= 0 THEN 380
00220 REM *********************
00230 REM DIVIDE NATURAL LOG OF
00240 REM THE NUMBER BY NATURAL
00250 REM LOG OF 10 TO OBTAIN
00260 REM COMMON LOG OF NUMBER
00270 REM *********************
00280 LT = LOG(X)/LOG(10)
00290 PRINT "THE COMMON LOG OF ";X;" = ";LT
00300 PRINT
00310 PRINT "DO YOU WANT TO DO THIS AGAIN? (Y OR N)"
00320 INPUT CH$
00330 IF CH$ = "Y" THEN 150
00340 STOP
00350 REM ***********************
00360 REM PRINT OUT ERROR MESSAGE
00370 REM ***********************
00380 PRINT "YOU HAVE ATTEMPTED TO TAKE THE "
00390 PRINT "LOGARITHM OF ZERO OR A NEGATIVE NUMBER"
00400 STOP
00410 END


RUNNH


THIS PROGRAM RETURNS THE BASE 10
LOGARITHM OF A NUMBER

ENTER THE NUMBER WHOSE LOG YOU WANT
 ? 25
THE COMMON LOG OF  25  =  1.39794

DO YOU WANT TO DO THIS AGAIN? (Y OR N)
 ? Y

ENTER THE NUMBER WHOSE LOG YOU WANT
 ? 10000
THE COMMON LOG OF  10000  =  4

DO YOU WANT TO DO THIS AGAIN? (Y OR N)
 ? Y

ENTER THE NUMBER WHOSE LOG YOU WANT
 ? -5
YOU HAVE ATTEMPTED TO TAKE THE
LOGARITHM OF ZERO OR A NEGATIVE NUMBER
```

MICROCOMPUTERS

Apple: No differences.
IBM/Microsoft: No differences.
PET: No differences.
TRS-80: No differences.

a number less than or equal to zero, the computer will branch to line 380 and will print an error message and stop processing. Notice that this program also contains a STOP statement in line 340; this is the logical end of the program. In lines 310–330, the user is directed to input "Y" to continue finding the logs of numbers. If the user does not wish to continue finding the logs of numbers, he or she types "N," and program execution ends. The STOP statement prevents subsequent lines from being executed (and, thus, prevents the error message from being printed unnecessarily).

STRING FUNCTIONS

Up to this point, we have manipulated numbers but have done little with strings except print them out or compare them in IF and THEN tests. Many business applications require more sophisticated manipulations of strings.

A string is simply a series of alphanumeric characters, such as #OJQ$P or HORNBLOWER, H. Usually, BASIC requires that quotes be placed around strings.

BASIC string functions allow programmers to modify, *concatenate* (add together), compare, and analyze the composition of strings. These functions are useful for sorting lists of names, finding out subject matter in text, printing mailing lists, and so forth. For example, we can help the computer to understand that John J. Simmons is the same as Simmons, John J. The most common string functions are listed in Table X–1.

TABLE X–1
String Functions

BASIC STRING FUNCTION	OPERATION	EXAMPLE
string 1$ + string 2$	Concatenation; joins two strings together	"KUNG" + "FU" is "KUNGFU"
LEN(string)	Finds the length of a string	IF H$ is "HELLO HOWARD" then LEN(H$) is 12
LEFT$ (string, expression)	Returns the leftmost characters of a string	LEFT$("ABCDE",2) is AB
RIGHT$ (string, expression)	Returns the rightmost characters of a string	RIGHT$("ABCDE",2) is BCDE
MID$ (string, expression1, expression2)	Starting with the character at expression 1, returns the number of characters specified by expression 2	MID$ ("ABCDE",3,2) is CD
ASCII (string)	Returns the ASCII code for the first character in the string	IF A$ contains "DOG" then ASCII(A$) is 68
CHR$(expression)	Returns the string representation of the ASCII code of the expression	If CHR$(F$) > "Z" then 20
VAL(expression)	Returns the numeric equivalent of the string expression	X = VAL(H$)
STR$(expression)	Converts a number to its string equivalent	STR$(123) is "123"

Concatenation

It is possible to join strings together. The segment below demonstrates what happens.

```
10 LET A$ = "GAME CALLED "
20 PRINT A$ + "ON ACCOUNT OF RAIN"
```

```
RUNNH
GAME CALLED ON ACCOUNT OF RAIN
```

LEN

This function returns the number of characters in the string.

```
10 IF LEN(H$) < 14 THEN 40
20 PRINT H$, TAB(20);A
30 STOP
40 PRINT H$,A
```

In this example, if the value in H$ is less than fourteen characters long, it can be printed within the predefined print zones. Otherwise, we might wish to use the TAB function to print out the next value.

LEFT$ and RIGHT$

The LEFT$ function returns the number of characters specified in the argument, starting from the beginning of the string. The RIGHT$ function returns a substring containing the last N characters in the argument string.

```
10 LET B$ = "HAVE A NICE DAY"
20 PRINT LEFT$(B$,6)
30 PRINT RIGHT$(B$,8)
```

```
RUNNH
HAVE A
NICE DAY
```

In this example, the computer stores a character string in B$. Line 20 tells the computer to print the first six characters in B$. Line 30 tells it to start printing at the eighth character. (With the microcomputers, this statement would print the last eight characters.) **NONSTANDARD**

The RIGHT$ function on the DEC (which is used in our examples) works differently from most other systems. This statement:

```
32 PRINT RIGHT$(B$,3)
```

would print from the third character to the end of the string. The example above was contrived to work the same on any of our systems, but see the comprehensive program for an example of the differences.

MID$

The MID$ function is more complicated. The argument is set up as follows:

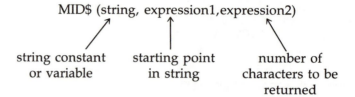

MID$ (string, expression1,expression2)

string constant
or variable

starting point
in string

number of
characters to be
returned

Sometimes expression2 is omitted, in which case all the rest of the string is returned from the starting point. In the following example, only the middle seven characters are printed.

```
20 PRINT MID$ ("LINEAR ALGEBRA",3,7)
```

```
RUNNH
NEAR AL
```

ASCII

The ASCII function returns the decimal ASCII value of the first character specified in the string argument. Some examples are shown below:

```
10 PRINT ASCII($),ASCII(DILIGENT)
```

```
RUNNH
 36                              68
```

CHR$

The CHR$ function returns the character string of the ASCII character in the expression. For example, the CHR$(72) is the letter H.

```
80 LET H$ = CHR$(72)+CHR$(69)+CHR$(76)+CHR$(76)+CHR$(79)
90 PRINT H$
```

```
RUNNH
HELLO
```

VAL

The VAL function turns a numeric string, for example, "34," into a number that can be used in arithmetic calculations.

```
10 INPUT "ENTER A NUMBER STRING";N$
20 LET A = VAL(N$)
30 PRINT "THE STRING NUMBER IS ";N$
40 PRINT "THE REAL NUMBER IS ";A
```

```
RUNNH

THE STRING NUMBER IS 5280
THE REAL NUMBER IS  5280
```

STR$

The STR$ function is just the opposite of the VAL function; it converts a real number into a string. For example:

```
10 LET HN = 123
15 READ AD$
20 DATA " E. CHURCH ST."
30 LET R$ = STR$(HN)
40 PRINT R$ + AD$
```

```
RUNNH
123 E. CHURCH ST.
```

COMPREHENSIVE PROGRAMMING PROBLEM

The Problem

The goal in this problem is to write a program that will accept a name in this form: first name—blank—last name. The program's output will be the last name followed by a comma, a space, and then the first name. For example:

```
TERRI BROWN  ————————→  BROWN, TERRI
```

Solution Design

The process can be outlined as follows:

1. Set up a loop to search each character to see if it is a blank.
2. The string to the left of the blank is the first name.
3. The string to the right of the blank is the last name.
4. Print the last name, a comma, a blank, and finally the first name.

The Program

Line 110 in Figure X–3 prompts the user to enter first and last names in response to line 120. Lines 140–200 form a FOR and NEXT loop that searches for a blank between the first and last names. The loop is set up to look at each character. The terminal value for the loop is the length of the string NM$, which contains the whole name. Line 150 picks off the leftmost I characters and places them in LS$. Line 160 picks out the rightmost character of LS$. In this example, the first three values of I produce the following:

I	LS$	RS$
1	P	P
2	PI	I
3	PIN	N

FIGURE X–3
Reversing Names
Program

```
00100 REM *** THIS PROGRAM REVERSES NAMES ***
00110 PRINT "ENTER FIRST THEN LAST NAME"
00120 INPUT NM$
00130 REM SEARCH UP TO LENGTH OF STRING
00140 FOR I = 1 TO LEN(NM$)
00150 LS$ = LEFT$(NM$,I)
00160 RS$ = RIGHT$(LS$,I)
00170 REM TEST FOR BLANK
00180 IF RS$ = CHR$(32) THEN 210
00190 REM IF NOT BLANK, THEN CONTINUE LOOP
00200 NEXT I
00210 PRINT
00220 REM PRINT OUT REVERSED NAME
00230 PRINT "LAST NAME NOW COMES FIRST"
00240 PRINT RIGHT$(NM$,I+1);", ";LEFT$(NM$,I-1)
00250 END


RUNNH
ENTER FIRST THEN LAST NAME
 ? PINCHAS ZUKERMAN

LAST NAME NOW COMES FIRST
ZUKERMAN, PINCHAS
```

MICROCOMPUTERS

Apple: Line 160 would use RIGHT$ (LS$,1)
Line 240 would use RIGHT$ (NM$,LEN(NM$) – I)
IBM/Microsoft: Same as Apple.
PET: Same as Apple.
TRS-80: Same as Apple.

Line 180 tests whether RS$ is a blank by using the CHR$ function (the ASCII code for a blank, or space, is 32). If a blank is found, line 180 sends the computer to line 210 to print the reversed name. Line 240 prints the last name (the part of the NM$ to the right of the blank), inserts a comma and blank, and then prints the first name (the part left of the blank). Since the counter I in the FOR and NEXT loop marks where the blank is, we use $I-1$ to count the number of characters in the first name and $I+1$ to begin the RIGHT$ function for the last name.

SUMMARY

- Two statements define a subroutine: GOSUB and RETURN.
- The GOSUB statement is used to transfer the flow of control from the main line of a program to the subroutine. The RETURN statement transfers control from the end of the subroutine back to the main line of the program.
- The STOP statement halts execution of a program.
- BASIC string functions permit modification, concatenation, comparison, and analysis of the composition of strings.

OVERVIEW

Since it is impractical to store large amounts of data in the computer's main memory for a long time, data is often stored on magnetic tapes or disks. This section describes some of the methods for gaining access to data files stored on these external storage devices.

The following discussion illustrates some fundamentals of file processing.

BASIC FILES

Business applications often involve large amounts of data. It is not uncommon for programs dealing with inventory, payroll, or customer balances to process hundreds, thousands, or millions of data items. Since the main memory of the computer is limited, users need some means of storing programs and data so that they do not have to retype them into the computer every time it is necessary to run the programs. Some microcomputers are so small that they cannot store internally all the data needed. In addition, it is useful to establish a single data file that several programs can use in different ways at different times. For example, personnel data can be used in applications such as handling payroll, processing medical claims, and printing mailing lists. For all these reasons, data is often stored on external storage media—usually magnetic disks and tapes.

NONSTANDARD   Unfortunately, there is no standardized method for performing operations on files stored on secondary storage devices. Many BASIC implementations include unique file manipulation commands. Fortunately, the principles on which the commands are based are similar. We look first at the fundamentals of file processing and later differentiate among implementations on the computers we've been discussing.

Access to Files

There are two main types of files: sequential and random-access. Magnetic tape and cassette tape are sequential media. Data items are stored one right after the other and must be read in sequence. For example, to recall the fifth item stored on a sequential file, you must start at the beginning of the tape and read the first four items to get to the fifth one.

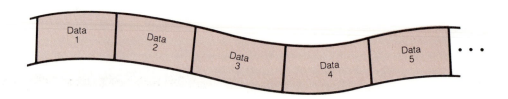

This sequential reading can be a relatively slow process when the number of items stored is large. Sequential files usually contain data items that are not likely to change much.

Alternatively, data can be stored on magnetic disk or diskette, which are direct-access media. Using this method of access is similar to playing a phonograph record. We can play any song by positioning the tone arm directly at its location; we do not have to start at the beginning of the record and play through until we get to the desired song. Similarly, the computer can locate and directly recall any item in a direct-access file, because it maintains a directory of addresses showing where the items are.

Data must be organized so that the computer can gain access to it. Each file is composed of a group of records. Each record contains a group of related data items called fields. The ASCII representations of numbers and characters comprise the fields.

**A record is composed of
several fields**

	Hover, J. Edgar	Boise, Idaho	00222
A file is a group of related records	Kee, Nyum	San Francisco, Calif.	09111
	Place, Henrietta	Waltham, Mass.	04623
	Tore, Sena	Washington, D.C.	02221

**A field is
an individual
data item**

The rest of this section will be devoted to a discussion of how the DEC, IBM, TRS-80, Apple, and PET/CBM systems handle data files. There are many enhancements to the BASICs permitted on these systems, and each of them is different. This discussion will cover how to establish a sequential file on disk, write data to the file, read data from a file, and close the file for each system. (Sequential files are easier to create than random files but are limited in flexibility and speed.) Please refer to your system manual for other enhancements.

BASIC File Processing

In general, the first step in file processing is to create the data file. The system needs some way of remembering the file; so the programmer gives the file a name. In addition, some systems also use a number to refer to the file in programs. The next step is to write data to the file. There are many ways of formatting data items; the simplest for each system are demonstrated here. (Please refer to your manual for other format instructions.) To do any file manipulation, it is necessary to read what is on the file. Often data from the file is read into arrays so that various fields can be updated. Then the entire array is written back into the file. Finally, it is necessary to close the file to protect the data from being altered or lost.

Apple

Creating or Accessing a Sequential Data File   The Apple system calls data files *text files*. To tell the system to use the disk, we need to cue the computer with CTRL-D. Since this has to be done several times in a file manipulation program, we may want to initialize a variable, D$, to CTRL-D by doing the following:

```
10 LET D$ = CHR$(4)
```

Check Section X to refresh your memory about what CHR$ does.

The general format of the command for creating or opening a text file is:

line# PRINT D$; "OPEN filename"

D$ is the CTRL-D command. The file name must begin with a letter and be less than thirty characters long. An example is:

```
10 D$ = CHR$(4)
20 PRINT D$; "OPEN SUZANNA"
```

A file called SUZANNA is now listed in our *catalog*. It is designated as a text (data) file by the letter T (the length of the file is also indicated—here by 002):

```
T 002 SUZANNA
```

The OPEN command is used in this manner whenever we want to gain access to data in a file.

Writing Data to a File   After the file has been created, we can alert the computer that we want to put some data into the file by using this command:

line# PRINT D$; "WRITE filename"

This line is followed by the command that actually does the writing to the disk:

line# PRINT expression

This PRINT command writes the expression to the disk. Since a sequential file is simply a long list of data, the computer needs to know where one data item ends and the next one begins. Pressing the RETURN button at the end of the PRINT line tells the computer this.

Closing a File   The general format of the CLOSE command is:

line# PRINT D$; "CLOSE filename"

The following program opens a file named SUZANNA, writes some data out to it, and finally closes it.

```
10 D$ = CHR$(4)
20 PRINT D$; "OPEN SUZANNA"
30 PRINT D$; "WRITE SUZANNA"
40 PRINT "OH!"
50 PRINT "DON'T"
60 PRINT "YOU"
70 PRINT "CRY"
80 PRINT D$; "CLOSE SUZANNA"
99 END
```

Line 10 initializes D$ to the disk command. The next line creates the file. Line 30 tells the computer that we are going to write some data to the disk.

In this example, the data items are different lengths—OH! is three characters long, DON'T is five characters long, and so forth. The items are separated from one another by the fact that they are on different lines. Therefore the file is a list of items, each of which ends with the ASCII character 13, the carriage return:

```
SUZANNA: OH!13DON'T13YOU13CRY13 . . .
```

Reading Data from a File   Once a file has been established, it can be read whenever the user wants to use the data. The command that alerts the computer that reading from a file on disk is to occur is:

line# PRINT D$; "READ filename"

To read the data items, we use an INPUT statement, as shown below.

```
080 D$ = CHR$(4)
090 PRINT D$; "OPEN SUZANNA"
100 PRINT D$; "READ SUZANNA"
110 FOR I = 1 TO 4
120   INPUT W$(I)
130 NEXT I
140 PRINT D$; "CLOSE SUZANNA"
```

After the file is opened, line 100 signals the computer that we are going to read data from it. The FOR and NEXT loop then reads the data into an array, W$. The file is closed by line 140.

TRS-80

Creating or Accessing a Sequential Data File on Disk   After you have turned the TRS-80 on, the computer will ask:

```
HOW MANY FILES?
```

Since we are going to deal with fewer than three files, we can simply press the ENTER button in response.

The following command permits access to a file:

line# OPEN "mode",buffer number,"filename"

The "mode" will be either I for sequential input (reading data from an existing file) or O for sequential output (writing data on the disk). After the "mode" is specified, we designate the number of the buffer where data will temporarily be held. The file name can be from one to eight characters long; the first character must be alphabetic (do not embed any blanks). An example is:

```
10 OPEN"O",1,"SUZANNA"
```

This line creates a file called SUZANNA. After the file is opened, we can use buffer 1 to write data to the file ("mode" = 0). We will see how this works later.

Writing Data to a File   After a file has been created (opened), data can be written to it. The general format of the WRITE command is:

line# PRINT #buffer number, expression

For example:

```
20 PRINT #1,"OH!"
```

prints the character string OH! as the first item in the file called SUZANNA. The 1 is the buffer number used in the OPEN statement for SUZANNA above.

Now we can write a simple program that creates a file and writes some data to it:

```
10 OPEN"O",1,"SUZANNA"
20 PRINT #1,"OH!"
30 PRINT #1,"DON'T"
40 PRINT #1,"YOU"
50 PRINT #1,"CRY"
60 CLOSE #1
```

Line 10 opens the file called SUZANNA. We use buffer 1 to write data to the file. Pressing ENTER at the end of each line separates one item from another on the disk file. Line 60 closes the file.

Closing a File   The following command closes a file:

line# CLOSE #buffer number

Make sure that the buffer number is the one specified in the OPEN statement for the file. (See lines 10 and 60 above.)

Reading Data from a File   To read data from a file, we must first gain access to it by using the OPEN statement. But the mode is now I for sequential input. The following statement should be used to gain access to data on an already existing file:

line# OPEN"I",buffer number,"filename"

The command that reads data from the file is:

line# INPUT #buffer number,variable

The program segment below reads data that has been stored in SUZANNA.

```
10 OPEN"I",1,"SUZANNA"
20 FOR I = 1 TO 4
30 INPUT #1,B$(I)
40 NEXT I
50 FOR J = 1 TO 4
60 PRINT B$(J)
70 NEXT J
80 CLOSE #1
```

Line 10 gives access to an already existing file called SUZANNA. A FOR and NEXT loop is then established to read the data into an array, B$. Data is read from the file by line 30. Note that the buffer number is the same as was designated in the OPEN statement. Lines 50–70 simply print out the file. Line 80 closes the file.

PET/CBM

Creating or Accessing a Sequential Data File   The general format of the command for creating or accessing a data file is:

line# DOPEN#file number,"filename",W

The D in the OPEN statement signals that this is a disk command. The file name is used to locate the file on disk; the file number is used to refer to the file. The W tells the computer that we are creating the file and need to write some data to it. An example is:

```
10 DOPEN#1,"SUZANNA",W
```

If the file SUZANNA already exists and we need only read what is on it, the W should be left off the statement. The example below gives us access to an existing file called SUZANNA:

```
10 DOPEN#1,"SUZANNA"
```

Writing Data to a File   After a file name has been created, we can write data to the file by using a PRINT command. The general format is:

line# PRINT#file number, expression

The file number is the one specified in the OPEN statement. The expression is the data to be written onto the disk. For example:

```
20 PRINT#1,"OH!"
```

writes OH! to file 1. Pressing RETURN at the end of the line signals the computer that this is the end of the data item.

Closing a File   The general format of the CLOSE statement is:

line# DCLOSE#filenumber

Let us put these commands together to create a file called SUZANNA, write some data to it, and close it.

```
10 DOPEN#1,"SUZANNA",W
20 PRINT#1,"OH!"
30 PRINT#1,"DON'T"
40 PRINT#1,"YOU"
50 PRINT#1,"CRY"
60 DCLOSE#1
```

Reading Data from a File   Once a file has been established, it can be read so that manipulations can be performed on the data. First, the file should be reopened.

line# DOPEN#file number,"filename"

Then we use the following command to read the data items.

line# INPUT#file number,expression

The file number must, of course, be the same as the file number in the OPEN statement. The expression is the variable that specifies where the data will be stored in internal memory.

   The example below reads data from the file called SUZANNA.

```
10 DOPEN#2,"SUZANNA"
20 FOR I = 1 TO 4
30    INPUT#2,A$(I)
40    PRINT A$(I)
50 NEXT I
60 DCLOSE#2
```

Line 10 opens file 2. Since the file has already been established, no W is specified. A FOR and NEXT loop is initiated in line 20. Line 30 reads data from file 2 into an array, A$. Line 40 is a PRINT statement. No file number is specified; it simply prints the data items on the screen of the PET. Finally, the file is closed in line 60.

DECSYSTEM 20

Creating or Accessing a Sequential (Terminal Format) File   The general format of command that creates or accesses a data file is:

line# OPEN "filename" AS FILE #number

If a file already exists with the file name specified, the computer will give us access to it. Otherwise, a new file will be created. The number can be used to refer to the file. An example is:

```
10 OPEN "SUZANNA" AS FILE #2
```

Writing Data to a File   After the file has been created, we can write data to it:

line# PRINT #number, expression

The number is the one used in the OPEN statement. The expression is the data to be written onto the disk. For example:

```
20 PRINT #2, "OH!"
```

Pressing RETURN at the end of the line tells the computer that this is the end of the data item.

Closing a File   The general format of the CLOSE command is:

line# CLOSE #number

The following program creates a file called SUZANNA as file 2 and writes some data to it.

```
10 OPEN "SUZANNA" AS FILE #2
20 FOR I = 1 TO 4
30 READ A$
40 PRINT #2,A$
50 NEXT I
60 CLOSE #2
70 DATA "OH!","DON'T","YOU","CRY"
99 END
```

Line 10 creates a file called SUZANNA. The file number at the end of the line is used later to refer to the file. Line 20 sets up a FOR and NEXT loop to read some data (in line 70) and write it to the file. Line 40 prints the values in A$ to file 2, SUZANNA. Line 60 closes the file.

Reading Data from a File   To use the data stored on a file, we read it. The general format of the INPUT command is:

line# INPUT #file number, variable list

An example is:

```
20 INPUT #1,B$
```

The following program reads data stored in a file called SUZANNA.

```
10 OPEN "SUZANNA" AS FILE #2
20 FOR I = 1 TO 4
30    INPUT #2,B$(I)
40    PRINT B$(I)
50 NEXT I
60 CLOSE #2
```

Line 10 gives access to SUZANNA as file 2. Line 20 sets up a FOR and NEXT loop that reads the items from the file, one by one, into an array, B$, and prints them out for us to see. Line 40 prints the data on the screen. Line 60 closes the file.

IBM/Microsoft

Creating or Accessing a Sequential Data File   The general format for creating or accessing a sequential data file is:

line# OPEN "filename" FOR OUTPUT AS #number
line# OPEN "filename" FOR INPUT AS #number

The filename in quotes must be less than or equal to eight characters. The number after the pound (#) sign will be used later as a shorthand reference to the file in the program. An example statement creating a file called SUZANNA is:

```
10 OPEN "SUZANNA" FOR OUTPUT AS #1
```

Writing Data to a File   Once the file has been created, we can write some data to it by using a variation of the PRINT statement. Notice, however, that the following PRINT statement looks different from that used to display the results of processing.

line# PRINT#number, expression

The "#number" distinguishes this statement from a regular PRINT command. The number should be the same one that was specified in the OPEN statement. The expression can be any valid variable, string, numeric constant, etc. Since a sequential file is simply a long list of items, the computer knows where one data item ends and the next one begins by the pressing of the carriage return at the end of the PRINT line.

Closing a File   The general format of the CLOSE command is:

line# CLOSE #number

Again, the number should be the same one that was used to open the file.
   The following program opens a file named SUZANNA, writes some data to it, and closes the file.

```
10 OPEN "SUZANNA" FOR OUTPUT AS #1
20 PRINT#1,"OH!"
30 PRINT#1,"DON'T"
40 PRINT#1,"YOU"
50 PRINT#1,"CRY"
60 CLOSE #1,
99 END
```

Line 10 creates the file as #1. That same number is used throughout the program in the file statements as a shorthand reference to SUZANNA. Lines 20 through 50 simply write four data items to the file. Line 60 closes the file.

Reading Data From a File   Once a file has been created, it can be read to access the data using the following:

line# INPUT #number, expression

The "#number" distinguishes this as a file statement. An example is:

```
20 INPUT #1, B$
```

The following program reads data stored in a file called SUZANNA:

```
10 OPEN "SUZANNA" FOR OUTPUT AS #2
20 FOR I = 1 TO 4
30    INPUT #2, B$(I)
40    PRINT B$(I)
50 NEXT I
60 CLOSE #2
99 END
```

Line 10 accesses Suzanna as file #2. Line 20 sets up a FOR/NEXT loop that reads the items from the file, one by one, into an array, B$. The items are displayed by line 40. Line 60 closes the file.

COMPREHENSIVE PROGRAMMING PROBLEM

The Problem

The departments of statistics and operations research at Western U have decided to merge into the Decisions Sciences Department. The new department chair, Dr. Janet Leland, wants a list of all faculty members in alphabetical order.

Solution Design

The fifteen faculty in the old stats department are described on a file called Stat.file. The ten faculty in operations research are described on a file called Op.file. The data in these files can be read into an array. Then the names can be alphabetized and written to a new file called Decsci.file.

The Program

Line 110 sets dimensions for the array that will hold the twenty-five names. Line 120 creates the new file that will hold the combined faculty data. The next two lines open the two existing files. Lines 190–220 put data from Stat.file into the first fifteen positions of the array N$. Line 210 simply prints them out for us to see. The next loop, in lines 280–310, does the same thing for Op.file. Note the initial and terminal values of the FOR statement in line 280. This lets us put the data from Op.file into positions 16–25 of the N$ array. Now we have a combined faculty list, but it is not alphabetized. We

FIGURE XI–1
File Processing
Program
(Continued on next
three pages)

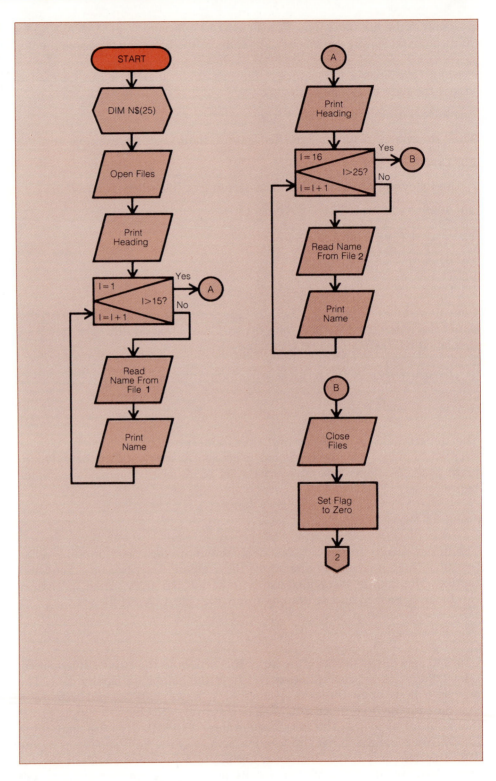

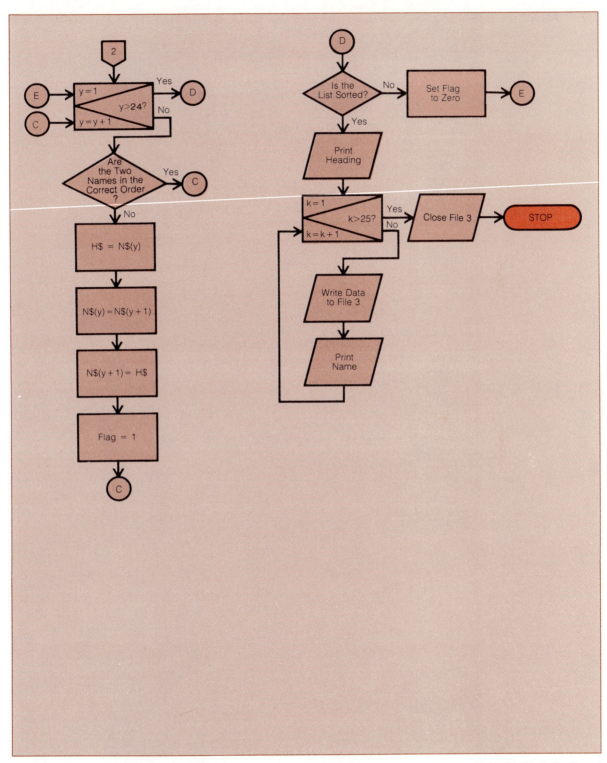

FIGURE X1–1 Continued

FIGURE X1–1

Continued

```
00100 REM *****FILE PROCESSING
00110 DIM N$(25)
00120 OPEN "DECSCI.FILE" AS FILE #3
00130 OPEN "OP.FILE" AS FILE #2
00140 OPEN "STAT.FILE" AS FILE #1
00160 REM****READ DATA INTO ARRAY & PRINT OUT
00170 PRINT "STAT.FILE"
00180 PRINT
00190 FOR I=1 TO 15
00200 INPUT #1,N$(I)
00210 PRINT N$(I)
00220 NEXT I
00230 PRINT
00250 REM****READ DATA INTO ARRAY PRINT OUT
00260 PRINT "OP.FILE"
00270 PRINT
00280 FOR I=16 TO 25
00290 INPUT #2, N$(I)
00300 PRINT N$(I)
00310 NEXT I
00320 PRINT
00330 CLOSE #1
00340 CLOSE #2
00360 REM ****SORT DATA
00370 T=0
00380 FOR Y=1 TO 24
00390    IF N$(Y)<=N$(Y+1) THEN 440
00400    H$=N$(Y)
00410    N$(Y)=N$(Y+1)
00420    N$(Y+1)=H$
00430    T=1
00440 NEXT Y
00450 IF T=1 THEN 370
00460 PRINT "DECSCI.FILE"
00480 REM****WRITE DATA TO FILE AND PRINT OUT
00490 PRINT
00500 FOR K=1 TO 25
00510    PRINT #3,N$(K)
00520    PRINT N$(K)
00530 NEXT K
00540 CLOSE #3
00550 END
```

FIGURE X1–1
Continued

```
RUNNH
STAT.FILE

HENDERSON
PECK
HICKMAN
LOCKE
LATTA
TOBIN
IRELAND
DOBISH
JOHNSON
GALBREATH
ROONEY
LEWIS
CARBER
FRARY
DYER

OP.FILE

CUMMINS
SMITH
GEORGE
FISHNAR
BERGY
MEADOWS
TRAVERS
MCLAUGHLIN
HAAS
WALTERS

DECSCI.FILE

BERGY
CARBER
CUMMINS
DOBISH
DYER
FISHNAR
FRARY
GALBREATH
GEORGE
HAAS
HENDERSON
HICKMAN
IRELAND
JOHNSON
LATTA
LEWIS
LOCKE
MCLAUGHLIN
MEADOWS
PECK
ROONEY
SMITH
TOBIN
TRAVERS
WALTERS
```

close files 1 and 2 with lines 330–340. Lines 370–450 alphabetize the faculty array. Since we will probably need these names in the future, they are stored on disk by line 510. Line 520 prints out the list for Dr. Leland.

SUMMARY

- Data is organized in the following manner: A single data item is called a field. Related fields are organized into a record. A file is composed of a group of related records.
- There are two main types of files: sequential and random-access.
- There is no standardized method for performing operations on files stored on secondary storage devices.

OVERVIEW

An important step in BASIC programming is learning to control the computer. Although this supplement cannot present the full operational details for each computer, it can discuss the principles of how to turn the computer on, make contact with BASIC, retrieve a program from external storage, display the program, alter the program, and save it for future reference.

MANIPULATING PROGRAMS

BASIC programming requires the use of different types of commands. Some of the commands, like GOTO, LET, and READ, are program language statements. They are assembled into programs to solve specific business, scientific, engineering, and mathematical problems. The BASIC Supplement describes their characteristics and how they are used.

There are also *system commands,* used by the programmer to communicate with the operating system of the computer to perform functions like saving programs for future reference and making changes to programs. Table XII–1 summarizes common system and editing commands. Some commands, like LIST, RUN, and DELETE, are almost universally used but are not covered by ANSI standards. The rest of this section will describe such commands as they relate to the four computer systems used in the programming examples in this supplement.

Apple

Hardware   The APPLE II initially contains INTEGER BASIC. Since INTEGER BASIC lacks many important features of the ANSI standard, this discussion only refers to this computer once Applesoft floating point BASIC has been loaded. The APPLE II PLUS computer automatically comes up in Applesoft.

Starting the Computer   The power switch is located in the left rear portion of the computer. Since an external monitor or CRT is required, you must remember to turn on power to this device also. If a disk drive is attached, it will whir and try to *boot* the DOS, so be sure that a diskette is placed in the disk drive before the computer is turned on. (When the disk drive "boots the DOS"—the disk operating system—it loads from a diskette the instructions that tell the computer how to manage the disk. This must be done before the computer can perform any disk-related tasks.)

The computer "comes up" with *floating-point BASIC,* as indicated by the use of the] character as a prompt.

Saving and Loading Programs   Programs are commonly accessed from either cassette tape or disk on this system.

● *Cassette:* To recall a program from a cassette tape into main memory, you must first position the tape to the beginning of the program. This means

TABLE XII–1

Common System and
Editing Commands (continues on facing page)

	DEC	APPLE	PET
POWERSWITCH LOCATION	Left rear of terminal	Left rear of terminal	Left rear terminal
SIGN-ON PROCEDURES			
User	Control-C	No response	No response
Computer response	TOPS-20 MONITOR	APPLE II	*** COMMODORE BASIC 4.0 ***
User	LOG ACCT. # PASSWORD	No response	No response
STARTING BASIC			
User	BASIC	Comes up in BASIC	Comes up in BASIC
Computer response	READY	Flashing cursor	READ (Flashing block)
User	NEW	Begin typing program	Begin typing program
Computer response	NEW FILENAME––		
User	Enter name of program; begin typing program		
SYSTEM COMMANDS			
List	LIST	LIST	LIST
Execute a program	RUN	RUN	RUN
Delete a line	DELETE line #	Type line # then RETURN	Type line # then RETURN
Store program on disk	SAVE	SAVE name	DSAVE "name"
Store program on tape	Does not apply	SAVE	SAVE "name"
Retrieve program from disk	OLD OLD FILENAME––	LOAD name or RUN name	DLOAD "name"
Retrieve program from tape	Does not apply	LOAD	LOAD "name"
SIGN-OFF			
User	GOODBYE or BYE	No response	No response
Computer response	KILLED JOB	No response	No response
User	Power off	Power off	Power off

	TRS-80	IBM	
		Cassette BASIC	Disk BASIC
POWERSWITCH LOCATION	Right front under keyboard	Right rear of computer	Same
SIGN-ON PROCEDURES			
User	No response.	No response	No response
Computer response	CASS? MEMORY SIZE? RADIO SHACK MODEL III BASIC (C) 80 TANDY	IBM Personal Computer BASIC Version C1.00 Copyright IBM Corp. 1981 61404 Bytes Free OK	Enter today's date (m-d-y): __ The IBM Personal Computer DOS Version 1.00 (c) Copyright IBM Corp. 1981 A >
User	Respond to CASS? and MEMORY SIZE? Queries	No response	Respond to Date query
STARTING BASIC			
User	Comes up in BASIC	Comes up in BASIC	Type BASIC or BASICA (For Advanced BASIC) after computer types A >.
Computer response	READY	OK	OK
User	Begin typing program	Begin typing program	Begin typing program
Computer response			
User			
SYSTEM COMMANDS			
List	LIST	LIST	LIST
Execute a program	RUN	RUN	RUN
Delete a line	DELETE line #	DELETE line #	DELETE line #
Store program on disk	SAVE "name"	————————	SAVE "name"
Store program on tape	CSAVE "name"	SAVE "name"	Does not apply
Retrieve program from disk	LOAD "name"	————————	LOAD "name"
Retrieve program from tape	CLOAD "name"	LOAD "name"	Does not apply
SIGN-OFF			
User	No response	No response	No response
Computer response	No response	No response	No response
User	Power off	Power off	Power off

Apple II
Microcomputer

that you must keep a record of where programs are located on the tape. Next, push the PLAY button and pull out the earphone plug on the recorder until you can hear the tape sounds. When you hear a constant high-pitched tone, stop the recorder and plug the earphone jack back in. Then type LOAD, push the PLAY button, and hit RETURN. The program has been loaded when you hear a beep and the cursor appears on the screen. (The *cursor* is usually a flashing character such as an underline or a block that shows where the next typed character will appear on the screen.)

To store a program, position the tape to a blank area, type SAVE, push the PLAY and RECORD buttons simultaneously, and then press RETURN. Again you will hear a beep and the cursor will return when the program has been written to the tape.

● *Disk:* The Apple has a convenient file-by-name catalog system for the DOS. To save an APPLESOFT (this is Apple's name for its floating-point BASIC) program—for example, one named TEST 3—on disk, type:

```
SAVE TEST3
```

and press RETURN. To load the same program from disk, type:

```
LOAD TEST3
```

and press RETURN. You can then run the program. Alternatively, you can type RUN TEST 3 without loading it; this causes the DOS to both load and run the program.

DEC

DECSYSTEM 20
and VT100
Terminal

Hardware   The DECSYSTEM 2050 is a large minicomputer that can have up to several million bytes of addressable internal storage for programs—as opposed to a few tens of thousands of bytes in the microcomputers discussed here. The exact form of BASIC employed here is called BASIC PLUS 2 by the manufacturer.

The detailed hardware description very much depends on what CRT terminal is used with this computer. The one used here is the standard VT-100 terminal.

Signing On   The power switch (toggle variety) is located in the lower left on the back of the terminal. If the terminal is linked directly to the computer, press the CONTROL and C keys at the same time. If the terminal is linked to the computer by telephone, dial the correct number. When you hear a constant high-pitched tone, place the phone receiver in the modem; most modems have a light that comes on when the connection is made properly. Then press CONTROL-C.

Now a header will appear, followed by the symbol @.

```
TOPS-20 MONITOR 4(3247)
@
```

This is the prompt for the TOPS-20 MONITOR—the housekeeping program that controls the computer. You must now type LOG and an account identifier followed by a password. The password should be privileged information—known only to those who need access to the programs in this particular account. For example, the programs for this manual were kept in an account called IMIS.INSTITUTE; access to the account was controlled by the password BOOK. The screen looked like this after log-in:

```
@LOG IMIS.INSTITUTE
```

The password did not appear on the screen, because the *monitor* knows that any characters following the blank after an account identifier are not to be made public.

After the RETURN key is pressed, the computer responds with a header giving the date and time. Then the monitor prompt (@) is displayed. To use the BASIC language, just type BASIC. When the computer is prepared to accept BASIC commands, it responds READY. To write a program, type NEW; and the computer asks for a name for the program.

```
READY
NEW
NEW PROGRAM NAME—LEIA

READY
```

If you hit RETURN without supplying a name, the computer will call the-program NONAME. You can now proceed to type in your program.

Saving and Loading Programs   We assume this computer uses disks for auxiliary storage. To save a program named LEIA, simply type SAVE LEIA.

```
READY
SAVE LEIA

READY
```

To load it at a later time, type OLD after the computer responds READY. The computer will ask for the old program's name. Type LEIA.

```
READY
OLD
OLD FILE NAME—LEIA

READY
```

After the computer again responds READY, you may run or list the program or perform editing operations on it.

Signing Off   When you are finished, type GOODBYE. After the computer acknowledges your message, turn the terminal off.

IBM

Hardware   The IBM personal computer contains an enhanced version of Microsoft BASIC. We will discuss the hardware configuration using disk only. Consult your documentation for cassette commands.

IBM
Personal
Computer

Starting the Computer Place the diskette into Drive A, the lefthand drive. Then turn the computer on. The power switch is located on the right rear of the machine. Don't forget to turn on the TV monitor, too. When the computer is turned on, it will try to load the *Disk Operating System*, DOS. (If no diskette has been placed into the disk drive, the computer will "come up" in Cassette BASIC.)

The IBM has three BASIC dialects—Cassette BASIC, Disk BASIC, and Advanced BASIC. For the purposes of this book, they are the same.

Once DOS has been booted, loaded, the computer asks for the date as follows:

```
ENTER TODAY'S DATE  (M-D-Y):
```

After you have typed the date and pressed the carriage return, it responds with:

```
THE IBM PERSONAL COMPUTER DOS VERSION 1.00
© COPYRIGHT IBM CORP. 1981
A>
```

The A> is the system prompt. Simply type BASIC and press the carriage return to load the disk BASIC translator. The BASIC prompt is "OK." Now you are ready to start programming.

SAVING AND LOADING PROGRAMS

Disk The IBM has a convenient file-by-name catalog system for the DOS. To save a program (for example, one named TESTS), type:

```
SAVE "TESTS"
```

The name of the program should be less than or equal to eight characters. Do not embed any spaces. To load the same program from disk, type:

```
LOAD "TESTS"
```

You can then LIST and RUN the program.

PET/CBM

Hardware The PET and CBM computers are made by the same manufacturer, Commodore Business Machines. For each number series, the two computers are nearly identical. For example, the PET 2001 and the CBM 2001 differ only as follows:

● The PET keyboard has graphics characters labelled; the CBM keyboard does not.
● The SHIFT key on a PET switches between capital letters and graphics characters; whereas the SHIFT key on a CBM switches between lower case and capital letters.

(See your manual to find out how to make the PET mimic the CBM and vice-versa with a simple POKE command.)

PET
Microcomputer

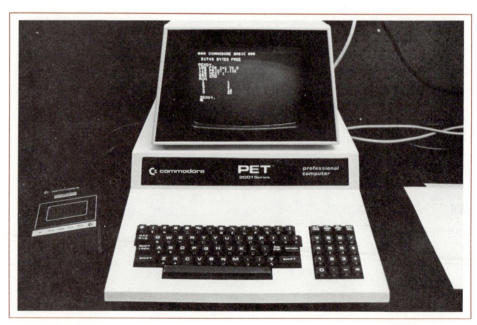

PET/CBM computers come in three basic styles. The oldest PETs have a small keyboard and a self-contained tape cassette. A later PET has a standard typewriter-style keyboard, but the tape cassette no longer fits inside the computer. Both of these styles have nine-inch diagonal CRT screens allowing twenty-five lines of forty characters each to be displayed. Recently, a larger screen allowing eighty-character rows has been introduced. All of these computers come with 8K, 16K, 24K, and 32K memories.

Starting the Computer   The power switch is in back near the left-hand corner underneath the body of the computer. When the power switch is turned on, you see something like this:

```
***COMMODORE BASIC 4.0***
31743 BYTES FREE
READY.
```

The first line tells which version of the BASIC language is available (4.0 is the most recent version).[1] The second line tells how much memory your computer has (32K in this example). The third line indicates that you can immediately begin typing in BASIC line numbers and statements.

Saving and Loading Programs   Programs are commonly accessed from either cassette tape or disk on this system.

● *Cassette:* The PET has a convenient file-by-name cataloging system. To save a program, position the tape to a blank area, and type SAVE and the program name in quotes. For example:

```
SAVE "MASTER"
```

You must also remember to press the RECORD and PLAY buttons on the cassette. If you have more than one cassette tape drive, you may have to specify the device number—otherwise, it will default to 1. For example, if you want to save MASTER on cassette tape drive 2, type

```
SAVE "MASTER",2
```

To load a stored program, you need only type LOAD and the program name (enclosed in quotes); for example:

```
LOAD "MASTER"
```

Then, when the cassette PLAY button is pressed, the computer will search for the named program. The names of other programs found during the search will be displayed on the screen. Therefore, the tape does not have to be positioned precisely for loading. The computer will tell you when it has found the desired program and when it is loading the program into main

---

[1]All programming examples in this book were run on version 4.0; but no changes should be necessary to run them on versions 2.0 and 3.0, since the main differences are in disk commands that are beyond the scope of this book.

memory. An example—loading a program named GODOT, the third one on a tape—is shown below.

```
LOAD "GODOT"

PRESS PLAY ON TAPE #1
OK

SEARCHING FOR GODOT
FOUND METRIC
FOUND DCLOCK
FOUND GODOT
LOADING
READY.
```

● *Disk:* The PET floppy disk system has two drives housed in one cabinet and a file-by-name catalog. To save a program named MASTER on drive 0, you type:

```
DSAVE "MASTER"
```

To specify drive 1, type:

```
DSAVE "MASTER",D1
```

If you alter a program that was read in from a disk and you want to replace the existing version on the disk, use @ as follows:

```
DSAVE "@MASTER",D1
```

To load a program from disk, you need only type:

```
DLOAD "MASTER"
```

or

```
DLOAD "MASTER",D1
```

The first example loads from drive 0, since that is the default unit.

TRS-80

Hardware   These programs have all been tested on the TRS-80 Model III with the Model III BASIC language. An older computer, the Model I with Level II BASIC, is very similar to the Model III. The comments about BASIC programs here generally apply to either computer but do not deal with the Level I BASIC language.

Starting Model III   The power is turned on by use of a rocker switch beneath the keyboard on the right side nearest the programmer. When the switch is turned on (consult your manual about proper sequence if you use peripherals), the computer responds:

```
CASS?
```

Radio Shack's
TRS-80
Microcomputer

The computer is asking whether you want to use low speed (63 characters per second) or high speed (190 characters per second) for cassette tape communication. Respond by typing L and pressing the ENTER key, typing H and pressing the ENTER key, or simply pressing the ENTER key. The L and H indicate low speed and high speed, and the default is high speed.

Next, the computer displays:

```
MEMORY SIZE?
```

Simply pressing the RETURN key is the standard response unless you want to save some space in memory for machine-language programs. Next, the computer displays:

```
RADIO SHACK MODEL III BASIC
(C) 80 TANDY
READY
>
```

You can now begin using BASIC commands.

Saving and Loading Programs   Programs are commonly accessed from either cassette tape or disk on this system.

● *Cassette:* The TRS-80 has a convenient file-by-name cataloging system. To save a program:

1. Position the tape to a blank area.
2. Type SAVE "program-name"; for example, SAVE "PROGRAM1".
3. Press the RECORD and PLAY buttons on the cassette.

To load a stored program, you need only type:

CLOAD "program-name"

When the cassette PLAY button is pressed, the computer will search for the program. The names of the programs found during the search will be displayed on the screen. After the computer has found the desired program, it will load it into main memory.

● *Disk:* To save a program (for example, PROGRAM1) just type:

SAVE "PROGRAM1"

and hit the ENTER button. To load the same program from disk, type

LOAD "PROGRAM1"

BASIC SYSTEM AND EDITING COMMANDS

The system and editing commands are *immediate-mode commands;* that is, they are executed as soon as the carriage control key (RETURN, ENTER) is pressed. They differ from BASIC language commands, which are not executed until the program is run. The most commonly used system commands are discussed below.

System Commands

New   This command tells the computer to erase any program currently in active memory. After typing this command, you can start entering a new program.

List   After typing in a long program, you may want to admire the finished product. Type LIST to see the program displayed at the terminal. If you have a very short program, LIST can display the whole program on the screen. However, if the program has more lines than the screen does, only the last part of the program will remain on the screen. Some screens permit only twenty-four lines to be displayed. You can display portions of programs by specifying the lines to be listed—LIST 250–400, for example. Most computers also allow you to suppress scrolling—that is, to freeze the listing temporarily (see controlling the scroll later in this section).

Save After you have typed many program lines, you will want to avoid losing them when the computer is turned off. To do this, you have to move the program from internal memory to an external storage medium such as cassette tape or disk. This move is accomplished by the SAVE command. There are generally several options to this command; for example, you may supply a name that distinguishes this particular program from all others. The discussions of each computer earlier in this section summarized the most elementry forms of SAVE.

Controlling the Scroll If your program's output consists of forty lines of information but your screen only has a twenty-four line capacity, how will you see all of your output? The forty lines will be displayed so quickly that you will not be able to read them until the listing is finished. But by then the first sixteen lines will be gone—scrolled off the top of the screen.

Most computers have a means of controlling the scroll of the screen. The programmer can simply push one or two keys to freeze the display, and then he or she can press the same keys to resume listing when desired. This method can also be used to freeze the output listing of a program during execution.

The box on the following page summarizes the method of scroll freezing and also the type of editor used on each of the four computers.

Editing Commands

Everybody makes typing mistakes. You should quickly learn how to correct yours. You may find a mistake before you press the RETURN key, or you may find it at some later time. These two conditions call for different methods of correction.

1. *Before RETURN is pressed.* Suppose you type LOST when you wish to LIST a program. If you noticed the error before pressing RETURN, you can move the computer's cursor back to the 0 in LOST by pressing the "DELETE" key (on the DEC) or the "←" key (on the Apple, IBM, PET, and TRS-80). Then you can retype LIST correctly.
2. *After RETURN has been pressed.* If you notice an error after RETURN has been pressed, the simplest correction in principle is to retype the whole line.

```
10 PRINT "I GOOFED"
```

This may get tiresome for long lines, however—especially if you need to change only one character. Each computer has a means of correcting mistakes within a given line. There is not enough space here for a full explanation of these methods, but there are two general kinds.

To use the screen editor, list the portion of the program containing the error. Then move the cursor to the position of the error—typically, by pressing four keys with arrows that move the cursor up, down, left, or right. The incorrect characters can then be typed over or deleted or new characters can be inserted between existing characters.

Type of Editor and Scroll Control

	Screen Editor?	Line Editor?	Scroll Stop/Start
Apple	x		CTRL-S
DEC	x	x	NO SCROLL
IBM	x		CTRL-NUMLOCK
PET	x		Software
TRS-80		x	SHIFT-@

Notes:
1. CTRL-S means hold down the CONTROL key and the S key at the same time.
2. NO SCROLL is a separate, single key.
3. CTRL-NUMLOCK means hold down the control key and the NUMLOCK key at the same time.
4. On the PET, you must write programs so that they pause long enough for you to view necessary information before continuing with more output.
5. SHIFT-@ means hold down the SHIFT key and the @ key at the same time.

The second type of editor works on individual lines. The user specifies the line containing the error and uses commands such as REPLACE, INSERT, and DELETE instead of moving the cursor to the error.

SUMMARY

● System commands are used by the programmer to communicate with the operating system of the computer. Some commonly used ones are NEW, LIST, and SAVE.
● There are also editing commands to help you correct mistakes.
● Table XII–1 summarizes start-up procedures and common system and editing commands.

**BASIC Language
Commands**

STATEMENT	EXPLANATION	EXAMPLE
DEF	Defines a function	10 DEF FNR (X) = 4 * 3 1416 * X∧2
DIM	Sets dimensions for arrays	20 DIM A(25)
END	Last statement in a program	999 END
FOR/NEXT	Sets up a loop	30 FOR I = 1 TO 5
		.
		.
		.
		70 NEXT I
GOSUB/RETURN	Branches to a subroutine; then returns to main line of program	100 GOSUB 350
		.
		.
		.
		400 RETURN
GOTO	Unconditional transfer of control	15 GOTO 60
IF/THEN	Conditional transfer of control	200 IF N$ = "LAST" THEN 400
INPUT	Allows data to be entered at terminal	40 INPUT J$, A
		or
		40 INPUT "NAME, AGE"; J$, 4
LET	Assignment statement	90 LET B = B + A
MAT	Command for various matrix operations	400 MAT PRINT A
ON/GOTO	Conditional transfer of control	10 ON J GOTO 40, 50, 60
PRINT	Displays or prints output	60 PRINT "TOM"
PRINT USING	Permits flexibility in formatting output; used with image	40 PRINT USING 90, B
		.
		.
		90: ###.#
READ/DATA	Reads data into variables from data list	30 READ A, B, C
		40 DATA 40, 50, 60
REM	Provides documentation	10 REM LOOP BEGINS
STOP	Stops execution of a program	75 STOP
TAB	Used in PRINT statement to format output	80 PRINT TAB(5); N

BASIC Arithmetic Functions

FUNCTION	PURPOSE
SIN(X)	Trigonometric sine function, X in radians
COS(X)	Trigonometric cosine function, X in radians
TAN(X)	Trigonometric tangent function, X in radians
ATN(X)	Trigonometric arctangent function, X in radians
LOG(X)	Natural logarithm function
EXP(X)	e raised to the X power
SQR(X)	The square root of X
INT(X)	The greatest integer less than X
SGN(X)	The sign of X
ABS(X)	The absolute value of X
RND	A random number between 0 and 1

BASIC String Functions

BASIC STRING FUNCTION	OPERATION	EXAMPLE
string 1$ + string 2$	Concatenation; joins two strings together	"KUNG" + "FU" is "KUNGFU"
LEN(string)	Finds the length of a string	IF H$ is "HELLO HOWARD" then LEN(H$) is 12
LEFT$ (string, expression)	Returns the leftmost characters of a string	LEFT$("ABCDE",2) is AB
RIGHT$ (string, expression)	Returns the rightmost characters of a string	RIGHT$("ABCDE",2) is DE
MID$ (string, expression1, expression2)	Starting with the character at expression 1, returns the number of characters specified by expression 2	MID$ ("ABCDE",3,2) is CD
ASCII (string)	Returns the ASCII code for the first character in the string	IF A$ contains "DOG" then ASCII(A$) is 68
CHR$(expression)	Returns the string representation of the ASCII code of the expression	If CHR$(F$) > "Z" then 20
VAL(expression)	Returns the numeric equivalent of the string expression	X = VAL(H$)
STR$(expression)	Converts a number to its string equivalent	STR$(123) is "123"

Alphanumeric data   A sequence of letters, numbers, and/or special characters. As opposed to numerical data which contains only numbers.

ANSI BASIC   A programming language that has a universally accepted set of standard rules. Basic is short for *Beginners All-purpose Symbolic Instruction Code.*

Argument   The quantity to be evaluated by a function. It can be a constant, a variable, a mathematical expression, or another function and is enclosed in parentheses.

Blank   An empty space.

Boot   A term used to describe the process in which the disk drive loads the instructions that tell the computer how to manage the disk.

Branching   A method of transferring control from one part of the program to another by skipping past some statements in the program.

Bubble sort   A method of sorting that works by comparing two adjacent values in an array and then interchanging them according to the desired order.

Catalog   The contents of a disk.

Character string literals   A group of letters, numbers, or special characters assigned when a program is written (i.e., not calculated by a program) that are to be printed exactly as is on the output page.

Column   Vertical segregations on the print line.

Concatenate   Add together.

Conditional transfer   A transfer of control to other statements in the program based on the evaluation of a mathematical expression.

Constants   The numeric or character string data referred to by a variable name.

Cursor   Usually a flashing character such as an underline or a block that shows where the next type character will appear on the screen.

Decision block   A diamond-shaped symbol used in flowcharting to represent an IF/THEN test.

Exception-handling   A sequence of statements that help the program to gracefully handle problems that would otherwise lead to a premature stop.

Expression   A valid literal, variable, or mathematical formula.

Floating-point BASIC   A version of the language that allows use of decimal fractions. See Integer BASIC.

Hierarchy   The priority path a computer follows when performing more than one operation.

Immediate-mode commands   System and editing commands that are executed as soon as the carriage control key (RETURN, ENTER) is pressed.

Integer BASIC   A version of the language that does not use decimal fractions, e.g., 1 divided by 3 would yeild an answer of 0 not 0.3333. See Floating-point BASIC.

Library functions   Functions which have been built into the BASIC language because many applications require these types of mathematical operations. These functions are included in the BASIC language library.

Line number   The number that preceeds each statement. Line numbers tell the computer the order in which the statements are to be executed.

Mantissa   The number preceding the "E" which in most systems lies between 1.000 and 9.999.

Matrix   Another name for a one- or two-dimensional array.

Monitor   A housekeeping program that controls the computer.

Natural logarithm   A function that is the reverse of the EXP(x) function.

Numeric constant   A constant that is represented by a real number.

Numeric literals   A real number assigned when a program is written (i.e., not calculated) that is to be printed exactly as is on the output page.

Numeric variable   Represents a number that is either supplied to the computer by the programmer or internally calculated by the computer during execution of the program.

Prompt   A message printed out to explain to the user what data is to be entered in an INPUT statement.

Real numbers   Composed of either integers or decimal fractions.

Relational symbols   Symbols that can be used for condition testing. For example, the < symbol means "less than."

Scalar   A numeric constant that a matrix can be multiplied by.

Scientific notation   Commonly used for very large or very small numbers. The "E" represents base 10, and the signed number following the "E" is the power to which 10 is raised.

Skipping print zones   A technique that involves enclosing a space (the character blank) in quotation marks.

Statement   The fundamental building-block of a computer program.

String variable   Represents the value of a character string—for example, a name, an address, or a social security number.

Subroutine   A sequence of statements not within the main line of the program. This saves the programmer time by not having to write the same instructions over again in different parts of the program. It must end with a RETURN statement.

Subscripted variables   Elements of an array. The subscript is the integer enclosed within parentheses that allows reference to a specific element—e.g. $X(6)$.

Syntax   Refers to the way rules must be followed while coding instructions, just as grammatical rules must be followed in English.

System commands   Commands used by the programmer to communicate with the operating system of the computer.

Text files   What the Apple system calls data files.

Two-dimensional array   The arrangement of data in a table consisting of rows and columns.

Unconditional transfer   Another name for a GOTO statement. The flow is altered every time the statement is encountered.

Unsubscripted variables   Simple variables.

Variable names   The names, or symbols, the programmer assigns to data stored in the computer's memory whose values can change as the program is executed.

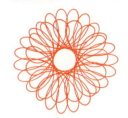

GLOSSARY

Access   To locate a particular record.

Access mechanism   The physical device that positions the read/write head of a direct-access storage device over a particular track.

Accounting machine   Forerunner of the computer; could mechanically read data from punched cards, perform calculations, rearrange data, and print results in varied formats.

Accumulator   A register that accumulates results of computations.

Accuracy   The constancy of computer-generated results.

Action entry   One of four sections of a decision logic table; specifies what actions should be taken.

Action stub   One of four sections of a decision logic table; describes possible actions applicable to the problem to be solved.

Address register   A register that holds the address of a location containing a data item called for by an instruction.

Alphanumeric   A character set that contains letters, digits, and special characters such as punctuation marks.

Alphanumeric data   A sequence of letters, numbers, and/or special characters. As opposed to numerical data which contains only numbers.

American Standard Code for Information Interchange (ASCII)   A seven-bit standard code used for information interchange among data-processing systems, communication systems, and associated equipment.

Amount field   The field where a clerk manually inserts the amount of the check, used in the processing of bank checks.

Analog computer   A computer that measures continuous electrical or physical magnitudes rather than operating on digits; contrast with digital computer.

Analog transmission   Transmission of data over communication channels in a continuous wave form.

Analytical engine   A machine conceived by Charles Babbage, capable of addition, subtraction, multiplication, division, and storage of intermediate results in a memory unit; too advanced for its time, the analytical engine was forgotten for nearly one hundred years.

ANSI BASIC   A programming language that has a universally accepted set of standard rules. Basic is short for *Beginners All-purpose Symbolic Instruction Code.*

APL   *A Programming Language;* a terminal-oriented, symbolic programming language especially suitable for interactive problem-solving.

Application programming   The programmer in business data processing must apply the capabilities of the computer to problems such as customer billing.

Applications program   A sequence of instructions written to solve a specific problem facing organizational management.

Architecture   Another name for the internal design of a computer.

Argument   The quantity to be evaluated by a function. It can be a constant, a variable, a mathematical expression, or another function and is enclosed in parentheses.

Arithmetic/logic unit (ALU)   The section of the CPU that handles arithmetic computations and logical operations.

Array   An ordered set of data items; also called a table or matrix.

Array variable   A symbol that can be used to represent groups of similar data items.

Artificial intelligence   A field of inquiry developing techniques whereby computers can be used to solve problems that appear to require imagination, intuition, or intelligence.

ASCII-8   An eight-bit version of the ASCII.

Assembler program   The translator program for an assembly language; produces a machine-language program.

Assembly language   A symbolic programming language that uses convenient abbreviations rather than groupings of 0s and 1s; intermediate-level language in terms of user orientation.

Attributes   A field containing information; a descriptive property associated with a name to describe a characteristic of items that the name may represent.

Audio input systems   (see Voice recognition modules)   Data entered into a computer system and responses received through human-voice audio transmissions.

Audio output   The computer is given a vocabulary of half-second records of voice sounds allowing the computer to "speak" to the user.

Audio   (or voice) response units   See Audio output.

Automated office   The combination of office electronics and data processing.

Automatic data processing (ADP)   The collection, manipulation, and dissemination of data by electromechanical machines to attain specified objectives.

Automation   Machine-directed processes.

Auxiliary storage   Also known as external storage or secondary storage; supplements primary storage but operates at slower speeds.

B

Back-end processor   A small CPU serving as an interface between a large CPU and a large data base stored on direct-access storage device.

Background partition   In a multiprogramming system, a partition holding a lower-priority program that is executed only when high-priority programs are not using the system.

Background program   In a multiprogramming system, a program that can be executed whenever the facilities of the system are not needed by a high-priority program.

Backup   Alternate procedures, equipment, or systems used in case of destruction or failure of the original.

Bandwidth   The range, or width, of the frequencies available for transmission on a given channel.

Bar-code reader   A device used to read a barcode by means of reflected light, such as a scanner that reads the Universal Product Code on supermarket products.

BASIC   *Beginners' All*-Purpose *Symbolic Instruction Code*; a programming language commonly used for interactive problem solving by users who may not be professional programmers.

Batch/sequential processing   A method of processing data in which data items are collected and forwarded to the computer in a group; normally uses punched cards or magnetic tape for generating periodic output, e.g., payroll.

Binary number system   The numeric system used in computer operations that uses the digits 0 and 1 and has a base of 2.

Binary representation   Uses a two-state, or binary, system to represent data; as in setting and re-setting the states of a magnetic core.

Binary system   A form of data representation in which two possible states exist.

Bit (short for *BI*nary digi*T*)   A binary digit; the smallest unit of information that can be represented in binary notation.

Bit cells   The name for storage locations in semiconductors.

Blank   An empty space.

Block   In block-structured programming languages, a section of program coding treated as a unit.

Block diagram   See Flowchart.

Blocked records   Records grouped on magnetic tape or magnetic disk to reduce the number of interrecord gaps and more fully utilize the storage medium.

Boot   A term used to describe the process in which the disk drive loads the instructions that tell the computer how to manage the disk.

Branch   A statement used to bypass or alter the normal flow of execution.

Branching A method of transferring control from one part of the program to another by skipping past some statements in the program, leaving them unexecuted.

Broad-band channels Communication channels that can transmit data at rates of up to 120,000 bits per second; e.g., laser beams and microwaves.

Bubble The magnetic domain of a bubble memory.

Bubble memory A recently developed memory device in which data is represented by magnetized spots (magnetic domains) that rest on a thin film of semiconductor material.

Bubble sort A method of sorting that works by comparing two adjacent values in an array and then interchanging them according to the desired order.

Buffer Storage used to compensate for a difference in rate of flow of data, or time of occurrence of events, when transmitting data from one device to another.

Built-in function A common or often-used procedure that is permanently stored in the computer; examples include square root, absolute value, and logarithms.

Bundled Opposite of unbundled; the practice whereby the cost of a computer system may include not only the CPU but also an operating system, peripheral devices, maintenance agreements, etc.; has largely been dropped as a result of litigation.

Business data processing The application of the computer and related techniques to solving problems encountered in business; e.g., payroll, inventory, personnel files, etc.

Byte Some number of bits; a unit of storage.

C

Calculate The arithmetic and/or logical manipulation of data.

Card punch (also keypunch) See Keypunch.

Catalog The contents of a disk.

Cathode-ray tube (CRT) A visual-display device that receives electrical impulses and translates them into a picture on a television-like screen.

Central processing unit (CPU) Also known as the "main frame," or heart of the computer; composed of three sections—primary storage unit, arithmetic/logic unit (ALU), and control unit.

Certificate in Computer Programming (CCP) This certification indicates experience and professional competence at the senior programmer level.

Certificate in Data Processing (CDP) A certificate awarded by the ICCP to qualified candidates who have successfully passed an examination consisting of five sections—data-processing equipment, computer programming and software, principles of management, quantitative methods, and system analysis and design.

Chain printer An output device that has the character set engraved in type and assembled in a chain that revolves horizontally past all print positions; prints when a print hammer (one for each column on the paper) presses the paper against an inked ribbon that presses against the characters on the print chain.

Channel   A limited-capacity computer that takes over the tasks of input and output in order to free the CPU to handle internal processing operations.

Character-at-a-time printers   Prints just one character of information at a time.

Character string literals   A group of letters, numbers, or special characters assigned when a program is written (i.e., not calculated by a program) that are to be printed exactly as is on the output page.

Chief programmer team (CPT)   A method of organization used in the management of system projects where a chief programmer supervises the programming and testing of system modules; programmer productivity and system reliability are increased.

Classify   To categorize data according to certain characteristics so that it is meaningful to the user.

Clustered-key-to-tape device   Several keyboards are tied to one or two magnetic-tape units.

COBOL   *CO*mmon *B*usiness-*O*riented *L*anguage; a high-level programming language generally used for accounting and business data processing.

CODASYL   *CO*nference on *DA*ta *SY*stems *L*anguages; a committee formed by the Department of Defense to examine the feasibility of establishing a common business programming language.

Code   To express a problem solution in a programming language; a set of rules for data conversion and representation.

Collect   To gather data from various sources and assemble it at one location.

Column   Vertical segregations on the print line.

Comments   Statements inserted at key points in the program as documentation; notes, that have no effect on the program execution.

Communicate   A step in the output phase of data flow; to transfer information in intelligible form to a user.

Communication channel   A medium for carrying data from one location to another.

Comparison   A statement that allows two items to be compared.

Compiler program   The translator program for a high-level language such as FORTRAN or COBOL; translates source-program statements into machine-executable code.

Computations   Instructions that perform arithmetic operations such as addition, subtraction, multiplication, division, and exponentiation.

Computer   A general-purpose machine with applications limited only by the creativity of the humans who use it; its power is derived from its speed, accuracy, and memory.

Computer operator   Data-processing operations personnel whose duties include setting up the processor and related equipment, starting the program run, checking to insure proper operation, and unloading equipment at the end of a run.

Computer output microfilm (COM)   Miniature photographic images of output. Computer output is placed on magnetic tape which serves as the input to a microfilm processor.

Computer store Retail store that sells computers and is structured to appeal to the small business person or personal user.

Computer-assisted instruction (CAI) Direct interaction between a computer and a student in which the computer serves as an instructor.

Concatenate Add together.

Concentrator A device that systematically allocates communication channels among several terminals.

Concurrently Over the same period of time; in multiprogramming, processing of operations rotates between different programs, giving the illusion of simultaneous processing.

Condition entry One of four sections of a decision logic table; answers all questions in the condition stub.

Condition stub One of four sections of a decision logic table; describes all factors (options) to be considered in determining a course of action.

Conditional transfer A transfer of control to other statements in the program based on the evaluation of a mathematical expression.

Constants The numeric or character string data referred to by a variable name.

Continuous form A data-entry form, such as cash register tape, utilized by OCR devices.

Contract programmers Programmers who are not employees of the organization using their services.

Control program A routine, usually part of an operating system, that aids in controlling the operations and management of a computer system.

Control unit (I/O) An electronic device, intermediate between a computer and an I/O device, that performs functions such as buffering and code conversion.

Control unit (of CPU) The section of the CPU that directs the sequence of operations by electrical signals and governs the actions of the various units which make up the computer.

Convert To translate information into a humanly readable form.

Cost/benefit analysis A quantitative form of evaluation in which benefits are assessed and costs associated with achieving the benefits are determined.

Counters A method of controlling a loop in which a specific value is entered into the program and that value is tested each time the loop is executed; when the proper value is reached, the loop can be terminated.

CPM Critical Path Method; see PERT.

Crash conversion A method of system implementation in which the old system is abandoned and the new one implemented at once; also known as direct conversion.

Cursor Usually a flashing character such as an underline or a block that shows where the next typed character will appear on the screen.

Cut form Data-entry form such as phone or utility bill, used by the OCR devices.

Cylinder All tracks on a magnetic disk that are accessible by the read/write heads with one movement, or positioning, of the access mechanism.

D

Daisy-wheel printer An output device resembling an office typewriter; it employs a flat disk with petal-like projections with characters on the surfaces; printing occurs one character at a time.

Data A fact; the raw material of information.

Data base The cornerstone of a management information system; basic data is commonly defined and consistently organized to fit the information needs of a wide variety of users in an organization.

Data buffering Reading data into a separate storage unit normally contained in the control unit of the input/output subsystem.

Data communication The electronic transmission of data from one site to another, usually over communication channels such as telephone/telegraph lines or microwaves.

Data processing A systematic set of techniques for collecting, manipulating, and disseminating data to achieve specified objectives.

Data representation The manner in which data is depicted within the computer; e.g., binary or hexadecimal notation.

Data set A grouping of related records; also called a file.

Data-base administrator (DBA) The individual responsible for the orderly development of a data base project.

Data-base analyst A key person in the analysis, design, and implementation of data structures in a data base environment.

Data-base management system (DBMS) A set of programs that serves as an interface between the data base and three principal users—the programmer, the operating system, and the manager (or other information user); provides a method of arranging data to limit duplication, an ability to make changes easily, and a capability to handle direct inquiries.

Data-base packages See data-base management system.

Data-entry operator Data-processing operations personnel whose job includes transcribing data into a form suitable for computer processing; e.g., by keypunching.

Decimal number system A number system based on powers of 10.

Decision block A diamond-shaped symbol used in flowcharting to represent an IF/THEN test.

Decision logic table (DLT) A standardized table that organizes relevant facts in a clear and concise manner to aid in the decision-making process.

Decision support system (DSS) Information obtained from this system is used as a supportive tool for semistructured tasks in managerial decision making.

Declarations Statements that define items used in the program such as files or records.

Decrypted Data that is translated back into regular text after being encrypted for security reasons.

Default   A course of action chosen by the compiler when several alternatives exist but none has been stated explicitly by the programmer.

Definition mode   When APL is used in this mode, a series of instructions is entered into memory, and the entire program is executed on command from the programmer.

Demodulation   The process of retrieving data from a modulated carrier wave.

Density   The number of characters that can be stored in one inch of tape. The storage capacity of the tape depends in part on its density.

Desk-checking   A method used in both system and program debugging in which the sequence of operations is mentally traced to verify the correctness of the processing logic.

Desk-debugging   See Desk-checking.

Detail diagram   Used in HIPO to describe the specific function performed or data items used in a module.

Detail flowchart   Depicts the processing steps required within a particular program.

Difference engine   A machine developed by Charles Babbage in 1822; used to compute mathematical tables with results up to five significant digits in length.

Digit rows   The lower ten rows, numbers 0 through 9, that are found on an 80-column punched card.

Digital computer   The type of computer commonly used in business applications; operates on distinct data (e.g., digits) by performing arithmetic and logic processes on specific data units.

Digital transmission   The transmission of data as distinct "on"/"off" pulses.

Direct access   Same as random-access processing; a method of processing in which data is submitted to the computer as it occurs; individual records can be located and updated without reading all preceding records on a file.

Direct conversion   See Crash conversion.

Direct-access storage   A method of storing data whereby it can be retrieved in any order, at random.

Directory   Consists of two columns, the first containing the key of the record and the second containing the address of the record with that key.

Disk drive   The mechanical device used to rotate a disk pack during data transmission; common speeds range between 40 and 1,000 revolutions per second.

Disk pack   A stack of magnetic disks.

Diskette   See Flexible diskette.

Drum printer   An output device consisting of a metal cylinder that contains rows of characters engraved across its surface; one line of print produced with each rotation of the drum.

Dummy modules   A temporary program module of coding that is inserted at a lower level to facilitate testing of the higher-level modules; used in top-down design to enable higher-level program modules to be coded prior to completion of lower-level modules.

Dump Hard-copy printout of the contents of computer memory; valuable in debugging programs.

Dump program A printout that lists the contents of registers and main-storage locations.

E

EDSAC *E*lectronic *D*elay *S*torage *A*utomatic *C*omputer; the first "stored-program computer."

Eighty-column punched card See Hollerith card.

Electronic data processing (EDP) Data processing performed largely by electronic equipment such as computers rather than by manual or mechanical methods.

Electronic funds transfer (EFT) A cashless method of paying for services or goods; the accounts of the two parties involved in the transaction are adjusted by electronic communication between computers.

Electronic mail The transmission of messages at high speeds over telecommunication facilities.

Electrostatic printer A nonimpact printer in which electromagnetic impulses and heat are used to affix characters to paper.

Electrothermal printer A nonimpact printer that uses a special type of paper which is heat sensitive and forms characters on the paper using heat.

Encrypted A term describing data that is translated into a secret code for security reasons.

ENIAC *E*lectronic *N*umerical *I*ntegrator *A*nd *C*alculator; the first "electronic digital calculator."

Erasable programmable read-only memory (EPROM) This memory unit can be erased and reprogrammed, but only by being submitted to a special process.

Even parity A method of coding in which an even number of 1 bits represents each character; enhance detection of errors.

Exception-handling A sequence of statements that help the program to gracefully handle a problem that would otherwise lead to a premature stop.

Execution mode When APL is used in this mode, the terminal can be used much like a desk calculator.

Expression A valid literal, variable, or mathematical formula.

Extended Binary Coded Decimal Interchange Code (EBCDIC) An 8-bit code for character representation.

External storage (also auxiliary storage) Storage not directly controlled by the CPU; supplements main storage.

F

Facsimile system Produce a picture of a page by scanning it.

Feedback A check on the system to see whether or not predetermined standards are being met.

Field   A meaningful item of data, such as a social security number.

File   A grouping of related records; sometimes referred to as a data set.

First-generation computers   Used vacuum tubes; developed in the 1950s; much faster than earlier mechanical devices, but very slow in comparison to today's computers.

Flexibility   The degree to which a computer system can be adapted or tailored to the changing requirements of the user.

Flexible disk   See Flexible diskette.

Flexible diskette   Also called a flexible disk or floppy disk; a low-cost, random-access form of data storage made of plastic and having a storage capacity equivalent to that of 3,000 punched cards.

Floating-point BASIC   A version of the language that allows use of decimal fractions. See Integer BASIC.

Floppy disk   See Flexible diskette.

Flow lines   The lines that connect flowchart symbols.

Flowchart   Of two kinds: the program flowchart which is a graphic representation of the types and sequences of operations in a program, and the system flowchart which shows the flow of data through an entire system.

Foreground partition   Also called foreground area; in a multiprogramming system, a partition containing a high-priority applications program.

Foreground program   In a multiprogramming system, a program that has high priority.

Formal design review   An evaluation of the documentation of a system by a group of managers, analysts, and programmers to determine completeness, accuracy, and quality of design; also called structured walk-through.

FORTRAN   *FOR*mula *TRAN*slator; a programming language used primarily in performing mathematical or scientific operations.

Four-bit binary coded decimal (BCD)   A four binary digit computer code that uses the unique combinations of zone bits and numeric bits to represent specific characters.

Fourth-generation computers   Use large scale integration and offer significant price and performance improvements over earlier computers.

Front-end processor   A small CPU serving as an interface between a large CPU and peripheral devices.

Full-duplex   A type of communication channel capable of the most versatile mode of data transmission; can transmit data in both directions simultaneously.

G

Garbage in-garbage out   A phrase used to exemplify the fact that the meaningfulness of data-processing results relies on the accuracy or relevancy of the data fed to the processor.

General-purpose registers Registers that can be used for both arithmetic and addressing functions.

Grade The range, or width, of the frequencies available for transmission on a given channel.

Graphic display device A visual-display device that projects output in the form of graphs and line drawings and accepts input from a keyboard or light pen.

H

Half-duplex A type of communication channel through which communication can occur in only one direction at a time, but that direction can change.

Hard copy Printed output.

Hard-wired Memory instructions that cannot be changed or deleted by other stored-program instructions.

Hashing See Randomize.

Heuristics Rules of operation that may or may not work every time; they have to be tested to see if they have value; used to solve complex problems and in situations that do not yield to conventional mathematics.

Hexadecimal number system A base 16 number system commonly used when printing the contents of main memory to aid programmers in detecting errors.

Hexadecimal representation A notation in which a group of four binary digits is represented by one digit of the hexadecimal (base 16) number system.

Hierarchical A design alternative in which each level within an organization is provided with necessary computer power; responsibility for control and coordination goes to the top level.

Hierarchical network A design approach in which an organization's needs are divided into multiple levels which receive different levels of support.

Hierarchy The priority path a computer follows when performing more than one operation.

High volatility A high frequency of changes to a file during a certain time period.

High-level languages English-like coding schemes that are procedure-, problem-, and user-oriented.

HIPO *Hierarchy plus Input-Process-Output;* a documentation technique used to describe the inputs, processing, and outputs of program modules.

Hollerith card An 80-column punched card.

Hollerith code A method of data representation named for the man who invented it; represents numbers, letters, and special characters by the placement of holes in 80-column punched cards.

I

I/O control unit A device that performs code conversion and is located between one or more I/O devices and the CPU; is used only to facilitate I/O operations.

Immediate-mode commands   System and editing commands that are executed as soon as the carriage control key (RETURN, ENTER) is pressed.

Impact printer   A printer that forms characters by physically striking a ribbon against paper.

In-house   An organization's use of its own personnel or resources to develop programs or other problem-solving systems.

Index   An ordered reference list of the contents of a file, or the keys for identification or location of the contents.

Indexed-sequential   A file organization technique in which records are placed on a file in sequence and a multiple-level index is maintained, thus allowing both sequential and direct-access processing.

Industrial robots   Industrial machines that are controlled by computers usually to do simple, repetitive tasks.

Informal design review   An evaluation of system-designed documentation by selected management, analysts, and programmers prior to the actual coding of program modules to determine necessary additions, deletions, and modifications to the system design.

Information   Data that has been organized and processed so that it is meaningful.

Information Revolution   The name given to the present era because of the impact of computer technology on society.

Inhibit wire   A wire through a magnetic core that keeps the contents of the core from being destroyed when read.

Ink-jet printer   A nonimpact printer that uses a stream of charged ink to form dot-matrix characters.

Input   Data that is submitted to the computer for processing.

Input/output management system   A subsystem of the operating system that controls and coordinates the CPU while receiving input from channels, executing instructions of programs in storage, and regulating output.

Input/output statements   Used to bring data into main storage for use by the program and to transfer data from the main storage to output media such as printouts.

Input/output-bound   A situation in which the CPU is slowed down because of I/O operations, which are extremely slow in comparison to CPU internal processing operations.

Instruction register   A register where each instruction is decoded by the control unit.

Instruction set   The fundamental logical and arithmetic procedures that the computer can perform such as addition, subtraction, and comparison.

Integer BASIC   A version of the language that does not use decimal fractions, e.g., 1 divided by 3 would yield an answer of 0 not 0.3333; see Floating-point BASIC.

Integrated circuit   A small chip less than 1/8-inch square containing hundreds of electronic components permitting much faster processing than with transistors and at a greatly reduced price.

Intelligent terminal   A terminal with an internal processor that can be programmed to perform specified functions, such as data editing, data conversion, and control of other terminals.

Interblock gap   A space on magnetic tape that facilitates processing; records are grouped and separated by interblock gaps.

Internal storage (or main storage)   Another name for the primary storage unit of the CPU.

Interrecord gap   A space that separates records stored on magnetic tape; allows the tape drive to regain speed during processing.

Interrupt   A control signal from a sensor-band input or output unit that requests the extension of the control unit of the CPU from the current operation.

Inverted structure   A file structure that permits fast, spontaneous searching for previously unspecified information; independent lists are maintained in record keys which are accessible according to the values of specified fields.

J

Job   A unit of work to be processed by the CPU.

Job-control language (JCL)   A language that serves as the communication link between the programmer and the operating system.

Job-control program   A control program that translates the job-control statements written by a programmer into machine-language instructions that can be executed by the computer.

K

K   A symbol used to denote 1024 (2^{10}) storage units when referring to a computer's primary storage capacity.

Key   A unique identifier for a record; used to sort records for processing or to locate a particular record within a file.

Keypunch   A keyboard device that punches holes in a card to represent data.

Keypunch operator   A person who uses a keypunch machine to transfer data from source documents to punched cards.

Key-to-disk   Hardware designed to transfer data entered via a keyboard to magnetic disk or diskette.

Key-to-diskette   A floppy disk is used instead of the conventional (hard) disk.

Key-to-tape   Hardware designed to transfer data entered via a keyboard to magnetic tape.

L

Label   A name written beside an instruction that acts as a key or identifier for it.

Language-translator program   Software that translates the English-like programs written by programmers into machine-executable code.

Large-scale integrated (LSI) circuits Circuits containing thousands of transistors densely packed in a single silicon chip.

Laser printer A type of nonimpact printer that combines laser beams and electro-photographic technology to form images on paper.

Laser storage system A secondary storage device using laser technology to encode data onto a metallic surface; usually used for mass storage.

Librarian Data-processing personnel responsible for the control and maintenance of files, programs, and catalogs of same for subsequent processing or historical record-keeping.

Librarian program Software that manages the storage and use of library programs by maintaining a directory of programs in the system library and appropriate procedures for additions and deletions.

Library functions Functions that have been built into the BASIC language because many applications require these types of mathematical operations. These functions are included in the BASIC language library.

Library programs User-written or manufacturer-supplied programs and subroutines that are frequently used in other programs; they are written and stored on secondary media and called into main storage when needed.

Light pen A pen-shaped object with a photoelectric cell at its end; used to draw lines on a visual-display screen.

Line-at-a-time printer Prints an entire line of information at a time.

Line number The number that precedes each statement. Line numbers tell the computer the order in which the statements are to be executed.

Linear structure A sequential arrangement of data records.

Linkage editor A subprogram of the operating system that links the object program from the system residence device to main storage.

List A sequential arrangement of data records.

Local system Peripherals connected directly to the CPU.

Logic diagram See Flowchart.

Logical Logical data structure/design is a view of the data that is meaningful to an individual user or program unrelated to physical storage.

Loop A series of instructions that is executed repeatedly as long as specified conditions remain constant.

Low activity When a small proportion of the total records are processed during an updating run.

M

Machine language The only set of instructions that a computer can execute directly; a code that designates the proper electrical states in the computer as combinations of 0s and 1s.

Machine-oriented language Examples are machine language and assembly language.

Macro flowchart   See Modular program flowchart.

Magnetic core   An iron-alloy doughnut-shaped ring about the size of a pinhead of which memory is commonly composed; an individual core can store one binary digit (its state is determined by the direction of an electrical current).

Magnetic disk   A storage medium consisting of a metal platter coated on both sides with a magnetic recording material upon which data is stored in the form of magnetized spots; suitable for direct-access processing.

Magnetic domain   A magnetized spot representing data in bubble memory.

Magnetic drum   A cylinder with a magnetic outer surface on which data can be stored by magnetizing specific portions of the surface.

Magnetic tape   A storage medium consisting of a narrow strip upon which spots of iron-oxide are magnetized to represent data; a sequential storage medium.

Magnetic-ink character reader (MICR)   A device that reads characters composed of magnetized particles; often used to sort checks for subsequent processing.

Main control module   The highest level in the module hierarchy; controls other modules below it.

Main frame   The central processing unit (CPU) of a full-scale computer.

Main storage   See Primary storage unit.

Maintenance programming   The responsibility of the programmer to change and improve existing programs.

Management information system (MIS)   A formal network that extends computer use beyond routine reporting and into the area of management decision-making; its goal is to get the correct information to the appropriate manager at the right time.

Management information system (MIS) manager   The person responsible for planning and tying together the entire information resources of the firm.

Mantissa   The number preceding the "E" which in most systems lies between 1.000 and 9.999.

Mark I   The first automatic calculator.

Master file   A file that contains relatively permanent data; updated by records in a transaction file.

Matrix   Another name for a one- or two-dimensional array.

Memory   See Storage.

Memory management   In a multiprogramming environment, the process of keeping the programs in main memory separate.

Memory protection   See Memory management.

Message-switching   A communications processor with the principal task of receiving messages and routing them to appropriate destinations.

Microcomputer   A very small computer; often a special-purpose or single-function computer on a single chip.

Microprocessor   The CPU of a microcomputer.

Microprogram A sequence of instructions wired in read-only memory; used to tailor a system to meet the user's processing requirements.

Microprogramming The process of building a sequence of instructions into read-only memory to carry out functions that would otherwise be stored program instructions at a much slower speed.

Minicomputer A computer with the components of a full-sized system but having a smaller memory.

Mnemonics A symbolic name (memory aid); used in symbolic languages (e.g., assembly language) and high-level programming languages.

Modem Also called data set; a device that modulates and demodulates signals transmitted over communication facilities.

Modular approach Simplifying a project by breaking it into segments or subunits.

Modular program flowchart Also called macro flowchart; a diagram that represents the general flow and major processing steps (modules) of a program.

Modulation A technique used in modems (data sets) to make business-machine signals compatible with communication facilities.

Module A part of a whole; a program segment; a subsystem.

Monitor A housekeeping program that controls the computer.

Multiplexer A device that permits more than one terminal to transmit data over the same communication channel.

Multiplexor channel A limited-capacity computer that can handle more than one I/O device at a time; normally controls slow-speed devices such as card readers, printers, or terminals.

Multiprocessing A multiple CPU configuration in which jobs are processed simultaneously.

Multiprogramming A technique whereby several programs are placed in primary storage at the same time, giving the illusion that they are being executed simultaneously; results in increased CPU active time.

N

Narrow bandwidth channels Communication channels that can only transmit data at a rate of forty-five to ninety bits per second; e.g., telegraph channels.

Natural logarithm A function that is the reverse of the EXP(x) function.

Network The linking together of several CPUs.

Next-sequential-instruction feature The ability of a computer to execute program steps in the order in which they are stored in memory unless branching takes place.

Nondestructive read/destructive write The feature of computer memory that permits data to be read and retained in its original state allowing it to be referenced repeatedly during processing.

Nonimpact printers The use of heat, laser technology, or photographic techniques to print output.

Numeric bits The four rightmost bit positions of 6-bit BCD used to encode numeric data.

Numeric constant A constant that is represented by a real number.

Numeric literal A real number assigned when a program is written (i.e., not calculated) that is to be printed exactly as is on the output page.

Numeric variable Represents a number that is either supplied to the computer by the programmer or internally calculated by the computer during execution of the program.

O

Object program A sequence of machine-executable instructions derived from source-program statements by a language translator program.

Octal number system Each position represents a power of eight.

Odd parity A method of coding in which an odd number of 1 bits is used to represent each character; facilitates error checking.

Office information system Can include a variety of word processors, data-entry terminals, graphics terminals, information distributors, and printers.

"On us" field The section of a check that contains the customer's checking account number.

Online In direct communication with the computer.

Op code Operation code; the part of an instruction that tells what operation is to be performed.

Operand A part of an instruction that tells where to find the data or equipment to be operated on.

Operating system A collection of programs designed to permit a computer system to manage itself and to avoid idle CPU time while increasing utilization of computer facilities.

Operation code See Op code.

Optical characters Special types of characters that can be read by optical-character readers.

Optical-character recognition (OCR) A capability of devices with electronic scanners that read numbers, letters, and other characters, and convert the optical images into appropriate electrical signals.

Optical-mark page reader A device that senses marks on an OMR document as the document passes under a light source.

Optical-mark recognition (OMR) Also mark sensing; a capability of devices with electronic scanners that read marks on a page and convert the optical images into appropriate electrical signals.

Output Information that comes from the computer as a result of processing.

Overlapped processing A method of processing where the computer works on several programs instead of one.

Overview diagram Used in HIPO to describe, in greater detail, a module shown in the visual table of contents.

P

Page frame In a virtual storage environment, one of the fixed-size physical areas into which primary storage is divided.

Pages In a virtual-storage environment, portions of programs which are kept in secondary storage and loaded into real storage only when needed during processing.

Paging A methods of implementing virtual storage; data and programs are broken into fixed-size blocks, or pages, and loaded into real storage when needed during processing.

Parallel conversion A system implementation approach in which the new system is operated side-by-side with the old one until all differences are reconciled.

Parity bit (also check bit) A means of detecting erroneous transmission of data; internal self-checking to determine if the number of 1 bits in a bit pattern is either odd or even; also called check bit.

Partition In multiprogramming, the primary storage area reserved for one program; may be fixed or variable in size; see also Region.

Pascal Named after French mathematician Blaise Pascal, an example of a language developed for educational purposes, to teach programming concepts to students.

Peripherals Also referred to as peripheral devices; I/O devices, secondary storage devices, and other auxiliary computer equipment.

PERT (*Program Evaluation and Review Technique*) Network model used to plan, schedule, and control complex projects; identifies all activities to be performed, their sequence, the time necessary to complete each activity, and the time required to complete the total project.

Phased conversion A method of system implementation in which the old system is gradually replaced by the new one; the new system is segmented and gradually applied.

Physical design Refers to how the data is kept on storage devices and how it is accessed.

Pilot conversion The implementation of a new system into the organization on a piecemeal basis; also known as modular conversion.

PL/1 Programming Language One; a general-purpose programming language used for both business and scientific functions.

Plotter An output device that converts data emitted from the CPU into graphic form; produces hard-copy output.

Point-of-sale (POS) terminal A terminal that serves the same purpose as a cash register, but is also capable of relaying sales and inventory data to a central computer for immediate updating of records.

Primary storage unit Also known as internal storage, memory, or main storage; the section of the CPU that holds instructions, data, and intermediate and final results during processing.

Print area   The upper part of the 96-column punched card.

Print-wheel printer   An output device consisting of 120 print wheels, each containing 48 characters. The print wheels rotate until an entire line is in the appropriate print position, then a hammer presses the paper against the print wheel.

Printer   A device used to produce permanent (hard-copy) computer output; impact printers are designed to work mechanically; nonimpact printers use electronic technology.

Privacy   An individual's right regarding the collection, processing, storage, dissemination, and use of data about his or her personal attributes and activities.

Problem-oriented language   RPG is an example of this type of language.

Procedure-oriented language   Examples consist of COBOL, FORTRAN, and PL/1.

Process   To transform raw data into useful information.

Process-bound   A condition that occurs when a program monopolizes the processing facilities of the computer making it impossible for other programs to be executed.

Processing program   A routine, usually part of the operating system, that is used to simplify program preparation and execution.

Program   A series of step-by-step instructions that provides a problem solution and tells the computer exactly what to do; of two types—application and system.

Programmable communications processor   A device that relieves the CPU of the task of monitoring data transmissions.

Programmable read-only memory (PROM)   Read-only memory that can be programmed by the manufacturer or can be programmed by the user for special functions to meet the unique needs of the user.

Programmer   The person who writes step-by-step instructions for the computer to execute.

Programmer/analyst   This person is responsible for system analysis and programming and is usually found in small organizations.

Prompt   A message printed out to explain to the user what data is to be entered in an INPUT statement.

Proper program   A program using the structured approach and top-down design and having only one entrance and one exit.

Pseudocode   An informal design language used to represent the control structures of structured programming.

Pulse form   A pulse of current used to store data in computers.

Punch area   The lower part of the 96-column punched card.

Punched card   A commonly used, sequential-storage medium in which data is represented by the presence or absence of strategically placed holes.

R

RAM (Random-access memory)   Refers to the random-access capability of semiconductors.

Random access   See Direct access.

Randomize   To compute relative record numbers from actual keys through any of a number of mathematical techniques.

Read-only memory (ROM)   The part of computer hardware containing items that cannot be deleted or changed by stored-program instructions because they are wired into the computer.

Read/write head   An electromagnet used as a component of a tape or disk drive; in reading, it detects magnetized areas and translates them into electrical pulses; in writing, it magnetizes appropriate areas, thereby erasing data stored previously.

Real numbers   Composed of either integers or decimal fractions.

Real storage   See Primary storage unit; contrast with virtual storage.

Real time   Refers to the capability of a system or device to receive data, process it, and provide output fast enough to control an activity being performed.

Record   A collection of data items, or fields, that relate to a single unit.

Region   In multiprogramming with a variable number of tasks, a term often used to mean the internal storage space allocated; a variable-size partition.

Register   An internal computer component used for temporary storage of an instruction or data; capable of accepting, holding, and transferring that instruction or data very rapidly.

Relational symbols   Symbols that can be used for condition testing. For example, the < symbol means "less than".

Remote input   Input that must be sent to a central computer for processing.

Remote system   A system where terminals are connected to the central computer by a communication channel.

Remote terminal operator   A person who uses a remote terminal to enter data to a computer.

Remote terminal   A terminal that is placed at a location distant from the central computer.

Reprographics   A technique of producing output whereby the computer is connected to a typesetting machine and the output is film "repro" paper.

Resident routines   The most frequently used components of the supervisor which are initially loaded into main storage.

Retrieve   The accessing of previously stored information by the computer so that it can be referenced by the user.

Ring configuration   A type of distributed system in which a number of computers are connected by a single transmission line in a ring arrangement.

RPG   *Report Program Generator;* an example of a problem-oriented language originally designed to produce business reports.

Run book   Sometimes known as operator's manual; program documentation designed to aid the computer operator in running the program.

S

Scalar   A numeric constant that a matrix can be multiplied by.

Scientific applications   Tasks that are traditionally numerically oriented and require advanced mathematical capabilities.

Scientific notation   Commonly used for very large or very small numbers. The "E" represents base 10, and the signed number following the "E" is the power to which 10 is raised.

Second-generation computers   Used transistors; smaller, faster, and had larger storage capacity than first-generation computers.

Secondary storage   See Auxiliary storage.

Segment   A variable-size block or portion of a program used in a virtual storage system.

Segmentation   A method of implementing virtual storage; involves dividing a program into variable-size blocks called segments, depending upon the program logic.

Selection   Program logic that includes a test; depending on the results of the test, one of two paths is taken.

Selector   A channel that can accept input from only one device at a time.

Semiconductor memory   Circuitry on silicon chips which are smaller than magnetic cores and allow for faster processing; more expensive than core memory and requires a constant source of power.

Sense wire   A wire through a magnetic core that determines whether the core contains a 0 bit or a 1 bit.

Sequential file   Data (records) stored in a specific order, one right after the other.

Sequential processing   See Batch/sequential processing.

Sequential-access storage   Auxiliary storage from which records must be read, one after another, in a fixed sequence, until the needed data is located; e.g., magnetic tape.

Serial processing   A method of processing where programs are executed one at a time, usually found in simple operating systems such as the earliest computer systems.

Silicon chip   Solid-logic circuitry used in the primary storage of third-generation computers.

Simple sequence   Program logic where one statement after another is executed in order, as stored.

Simplex   A type of communication channel that provides for unidirectional, or one-way, transmission of data.

Six-bit BCD   A six-bit digit computer code that uses unique combinations of zone bits and numeric bits to represent specific characters.

Skipping print zones   A technique that involves enclosing a space (the character blank) in quotation marks.

Soft-copy Data displayed on a CRT screen; not a permanent record; contrast with hard-copy.

Software compatibility Refers to the ability to use programs written for one system on another system with little or no change.

Software package A set of standardized computer programs, procedures, and related documentation designed to solve problems of a specific application; often acquired from an external supplier.

Sort To arrange data elements into a predetermined sequence to facilitate processing.

Sort/merge programs A part of the operating-system utility programs; used to sort records to facilitate updating and subsequent combining of files to form a single, updated file.

Source program A sequence of instructions written in either assembly language or high-level language.

Source-data automation The use of special equipment to collect data at its source.

Spider configuration A type of distributed system in which a central computer is used to monitor the activities of several network computers.

Stand-alone key-to-tape device A self-contained unit that takes the place of a keypunch device.

Statement The fundamental building-block of a computer program.

Storage The part of a computer that provides the ability to recall information; memory.

Storage register A register that holds information being sent to or taken from the primary storage unit.

Store To retain processed data for future reference.

Stored program Instructions stored in the computer's memory in electronic form; can be executed repeatedly during processing.

Stored-program computer A computer that stores instructions for operations to be performed in electronic form, in main memory.

String variable Represents the value of a character string; for example, a name, an address, or a social security number.

Structure chart A graphic representation of top-down programming; displaying modules of the problem solution and relationships between modules; of two types—system and process.

Structured programming A top-down modular approach to programming that emphasizes dividing a program into logical sections in order to reduce testing time, increase programmer productivity, and bring clarity to programming.

Structured walkthrough See Formal design review.

Subroutine A sequence of statements not within the main line of the program. This saves the programmer time by not having to write the same instructions over again in different parts of the program. It must end with a RETURN statement.

Subscripted variables   The subscript is the integer enclosed within parentheses that allows reference to a specific element—e.g., X(6).

Summarize   To reduce large amounts of data to a more concise and usable form.

Supervisor   Also called a monitor or an executive; the major component of the operating system; coordinates the activities of all other parts of the operating system.

Swapping   In a virtual-storage environment, the process of transferring a program section from virtual storage to real storage, and vice versa.

Symbolic language   Also called assembly language; uses mnemonic symbols to represent instructions; must be translated to machine language before it can be executed by the computer.

Syntax   Refers to the way rules must be followed while coding instructions, just as grammatical rules must be followed in English.

System   A group of related elements that work together toward a common goal.

System analysis   A detailed, step-by-step investigation of an organization for the purpose of determining what must be done and the best way to do it.

System analysis report   A report given to top management after the system analysis phase has been completed to report the findings of the system study; includes a statement of objectives, constraints, and possible alternatives.

System analyst   The communication link or interface between users and technical persons (such as computer programmers and operators); responsible for system analysis, design, and implementation of computer-based information systems.

System commands   Commands used by the programmer to communicate with the operating system of the computer.

System design   Alternative solutions to problems uncovered in the system analysis phase are designed, the cost effectiveness of the alternatives is determined, and final recommendations are made.

System flowchart   The group of symbols to represent the general information flow; focuses on inputs and outputs rather than on internal computer operations.

System implementation   The final phase in the development of a new or revised system; the goal of implementation is to insure that the system is completely debugged and operational and is accepted by the users.

System library   A collection of data sets in which various parts of an operating system are stored.

System packages   Sets of programs that make it possible to operate computers more conveniently and efficiently.

System program   A sequence of instructions written to coordinate the operation of all computer circuitry and to help the computer run quickly and efficiently.

System programming   Creating and maintaining system software.

System residence device   An auxiliary storage device (disk, tape, or drum) on which operating-system programs are stored and from which they are loaded into main storage.

T

Tape cartridge   See tape cassette.

Tape cassette   A sequential-access storage medium (similar to cassettes used in audio recording) used in small computer systems for high-density digital recording.

Tape drive   A device that moves tape past a read/write head.

Telecommuting   Computer hookups between offices and homes, thereby allowing employees to work at home.

Telecopier system   See Facsimile system.

Teleprocessing   The combined use of communication facilities, such as the telephone system and data-processing equipment.

Teletypewriter system   Transmits messages as strings of characters.

Terminal   A device through which data can exit from or be entered into a computer.

Text files   What the Apple system calls data files.

Third-generation computers   Characterized by the use of integrated circuits, reduced size, lower costs, and increased speed and reliability.

Thrashing   Programs in which little actual processing occurs in comparison to the amount of swapping.

Tiers   Three equal, 32-column, horizontal sections into which the punch area of a card has been divided.

Time-sharing   An arrangement in which two or more users can access the same central computer resources and receive what seem to be simultaneous results.

Time-slicing   A technique used in a time-sharing system that restricts each user to a small portion of processing time.

Top-down design   A method of defining a solution in terms of major functions to be performed, and further breaking down the major functions into subfunctions; the further the breakdown, the greater the detail.

Touch-tone device   A terminal used with ordinary telephone lines to transmit data.

Trace   Hard-copy list of the steps followed during program execution in the order they occurred.

Trace program   A program that is used for a trace.

Track   A horizontal row stretching the length of a magnetic tape on which data can be recorded; one of a series of concentric circles on the surface of a disk; one of a series of circular bands on a drum.

Trailer values   A method of controlling a loop in which a unique item signals the computer to stop performing the loop.

Transaction file   A file that contains new records or modifications to existing records; used to update a master file.

Transfers of control   A type of instruction that allows the sequence of instruction execution to be altered by transferring control.

Transient routines Supervisor routines that remain in auxiliary storage with the remainder of the operating system.

Transistor A type of circuitry characteristic of second-generation computers; smaller, faster, and more reliable than vacuum tubes but inferior to third-generation, large-scale integration.

Transit field The section of a check, preprinted with magnetic ink, that includes the bank number.

Two-dimensional array The arangement of data in a table consisting of rows and columns.

U

Unbundled The practice of establishing a separate price for each segment of a computer system.

Unconditional transfer Another name for a GOTO statement. The flow is altered every time the statement is encountered.

Unit record One set of information; the amount of data on one punched card.

UNIVAC I *UNIVersal Automatic Computer*; the first commercial electronic computer; became available in 1951.

Universal Product Code (UPC) A code consisting of ten pairs of vertical bars that represent the manufacturer's identity and the identity code of the item; commonly used on most grocery items.

Unsubscripted variables Simple variables.

Utility program A subsystem of the operating system that is capable of performing specialized, repeatedly used functions such as sorting, merging, and transferring data from one I/O device to another.

V

Variables Meaningful names assigned by the programmer to storage locations.

Verify To check the accuracy and completeness of data.

Very-large-scale integration (VLSI) Use large scale integration and offer significant price and performance improvements over earlier computers.

Virtual memory See Virtual storage.

Virtual storage Also called virtual memory; an extension of multiprogramming in which portions of programs not being used are kept in secondary storage until needed, giving the impression that primary storage is unlimited; contrast with real storage.

Visual display terminal A terminal capable of receiving output on a cathode-ray tube (CRT) and, with special provisions, of transmitting data through a keyboard.

Visual table of contents Similar to a structure chart; each block is given an identification number that is used as a reference in other HIPO diagrams.

Voice message system (VMS)   The sender activates a special "message" key on the telephone, dials the receiver's number, and speaks the message. A button lights on the receiver's phone, and when it is convenient, the receiver can activate the phone and listen to the message.

Voice recognition modules (VRM)   A system that allows close to a natural language, with an accuracy of 99 percent word recognition.

Voice-grade channels   Communication channels that have a wider frequency range and can transmit data at a rate of forty-five to ninety bits per second, e.g., telegraph channels.

W

Wand reader   A device used in reading source data represented in optical bar-code form.

Wire-matrix printer   Also dot-matrix printer; a type of impact printer that creates characters through the use of dot-matrix patterns.

Word processing   The manipulation of text data to achieve a desired output.

Word processor   An electronic device that performs text-editing functions, primarily used by secretaries.

X

Xerographic printer   A type of nonimpact printer that uses printing methods similar to those used in common xerographic copying machines.

Z

Zone bits   Used in different combinations with numeric bits to represent numbers, letters, and special characters.

Zone rows   The upper three rows, numbered 12, 11, and 0, that are found on an 80-column punched card.

INDEX